CHALLENGE TO MARS:
ESSAYS ON PACIFISM FROM 1918 TO 1945

Käthe Kollwitz, *Nie Wieder Krieg* (Never Again War), 1924

Challenge to Mars: Essays on Pacifism from 1918 to 1945

EDITED BY
PETER BROCK AND
THOMAS P. SOCKNAT

UNIVERSITY OF TORONTO PRESS
Toronto Buffalo London

© University of Toronto Press Incorporated 1999
Toronto Buffalo London
Printed in Canada

ISBN 0-8020-4371-2

Printed on acid-free paper

Canadian Cataloguing in Publication Data

Main entry under title:

Challenge to Mars : Pacifism from 1918 to 1945

Includes index.
ISBN 0-8020-4371-2

1. Pacifism – History – 20th century.   I. Brock, Peter, 1920–   .
II. Socknat, Thomas Paul.

JZ5560.C42 1998   303.6′6   C98-931057-4

University of Toronto Press acknowledges the financial assistance to its publishing
program of the Canada Council for the Arts and the Ontario Arts Council.

Contents

Part Two The Second World War

Part Three Pacifist Outreach: Japan and India

Preface

The modern pacifist movement emerged in 1918 as a result of the experiences of both combatants and war resisters during the First World War. It rapidly expanded in the interwar years, embracing humanist as well as religious pacifists, and soon became organized on a transnational basis. But in the course of the 1930s, with the rise of Hitlerism and the spread of other forms of totalitarianism, a crisis occurred among those who hitherto regarded themselves as pacifists, so that by 1939–41 pacifism had redefined itself as more a faith or ethos than a practical policy. As such, it succeeded in weathering the storm of the Second World War, though it emerged from the conflict with depleted energy. Only slowly during the Cold War years did it regain strength and adapt to the exigencies of the nuclear era. The twenty-eight essays in this volume illustrate the changes and tribulations experienced by the pacifist movement between 1918 and 1945.

For working purposes we define 'pacifism' in the sense generally accepted in English-speaking areas – an unconditional rejection of all forms of warfare. We are aware, however, that the line dividing this kind of pacifism from the antiwar position often defined as internationalism or pacif*ic*ism is tenuous; we try not to act here in a doctrinaire spirit. Our contributors, who are drawn from eleven countries, include both pacifists and non-pacifists; we regard peace history as a historical subdiscipline, in which only scholarly considerations should prevail.

The geographical range of our volume is, we believe, unique in the literature, ranging through eastern and western Europe, North America, and Japan and India. While there are general histories of pacifism in Britain, Canada, and the United States for the whole of our period, and in France for the interwar years, there is nothing equivalent to these works, at any rate in English, for any other country. For some countries indeed it is difficult to discover materials of value available on interwar and Second World War pacifism. On many detailed topics there exists, of course, a growing literature – especially in English – in the form of monographs, articles, and biographies of leading peace activists as well as memoirs written by conscientious objectors of the Second World War.

Our volume does not attempt to cover comprehensively the various manifestations of pacifism during the period. While not neglecting the mainstream, we have tried to bring into prominence aspects of pacifism and areas of pacifist activity for which few, if any, sources of information are otherwise readily available.

On 11 November 1918 the Great War had at last ended, and two decades of relative peace ensued – the subject of our first fourteen essays, in which contributors look at pacifism in eastern Europe, western Europe, and Britain and North America. From 1918, however, armed conflict continued for several more years in the territories of the former Russian Empire, now being transformed through revolution and civil war into the Union of Soviet Socialist Republics (USSR). The first two chapters of our volume deal with the large-scale religious pacifist movement that flourished during the early years after the Russian Revolutions of 1917, largely under the inspiration of Tolstoy's leading disciple, Vladimir Chertkov. Lawrence Klippenstein (chapter 1) and Paul Steeves (chapter 2) discuss the changing attitudes to the military question of its two leading components – the Mennonites, whose military exemption dated back to tsarist times, and the Baptists, a sizeable denomination whose group pacifism emerged only after 1917. In independent Finland, once part of the Russian Empire, conscientious objectors – and pacifists generally – had to struggle hard to maintain their anti-war principles. Thomas Hackman and Katja Huumo (chapter 3) describe their vicissitudes in face of a usually hostile government and often hostile public opinion. The situation for the spread of pacifism was even less favourable in recently liberated and reunited Poland than in Finland, as Peter Brock shows in his brief account of a 'lost' pacifist leader from that country's Belarusan minority (chapter 4).

In Germany, in contrast, radical war resistance enjoyed during the Weimar era a brief period of expansion. Guido Grünewald's essay (chapter 5) traces its history down to 1933, when the Nazis took power and destroyed the peace movement in all its forms. Adherents of pacifism may have been fewer in interwar Holland than in Weimar Germany – or, for that matter, in Britain or the United States. But the Netherlands then produced one of the most remarkable pacifist theoreticians of our century – Bart de Ligt, whose anarchopacifism is the subject of Herman Noordegraaf's chapter. Two chapters deal with interwar France, where the tradition of *la gloire* has often tended to make even pacifists fervently patriotic. Peter Farrugia (chapter 7) has taken the tiny, but resolute, minority of absolute pacifists among French Protestants as his theme, while Norman Ingram (chapter 8) looks in detail at the debates that raged during the 1930s within the Ligue des droits de l'homme between defenders of the duty of armed resistance to aggression and the 'integral' pacifists, who called for unilateral disarmament as the only way to permanent peace.

On the European continent, pacifism remained a tender plant even before the Second World War saw almost the whole continent submerged under indigenous totalitarianism or foreign occupation and pacifism suppressed, along with other democratic ideologies. It was Great Britain and North America therefore that provided the most fertile soil for the growth of pacifism during the interwar years. Martin Ceadel (chapter 9) demonstrates how by this time the British peace movement, including its pacifist variant, had become 'legitimate' in the eyes of both government and public opinion. Women were now beginning to play an important role in various peace organizations in Britain. In her essay Josephine Eglin (chapter 10) reviews the different positions on war taken by these women during the interwar period and then examines the links between feminism and pacifism in the thinking of three outstanding women who rejected war of every kind. Andrew Rigby (chapter 11) throws further light on Ceadel's thesis by examining the role of the Peace Pledge Union (PPU) from its emergence in 1936 down to the end of the Second World War. Kenneth McNaught (chapter 12) gives us another example of the legitimization of pacifism in the person of James Shaver Woodsworth, the respected leader of Canada's democratic socialist party and a principled opponent of war.

For the pacifism of the interwar United States we have selected two themes in this much-studied subject that are, we believe, significant but have not so far received the scholarly attention they undoubtedly deserve. Anne Marie Pois (chapter 13) examines, on the basis of archival sources, the debate between 'practical' and 'absolute' pacifists, which took place during the 1920s within the American section of the Women's International League for Peace and Freedom (WILPF). The fight against war by the historic peace churches constitutes one of the major topics in American peace history, but historians of U.S. pacifism of the 1920s and 1930s have generally concentrated instead on the mainstream pacifist movement, whether secular or non-denominationally religious. Donald Durnbaugh's study of attitudes to war (chapter 14) among interwar American Quakers, Mennonites, and Brethren, which follows Pois's chapter, should help to fill this gap.

Chapter 15–26 deal with pacifism from 1939 to 1945 (though several of the earlier chapters stretch to 1945 as well), as it responded to war in Britain and the Commonwealth, the United States, and Nazi-occupied Europe. The second global conflict broke out in September 1939, involving from the outset Great Britain and the Empire/Commonwealth. Lyn Smith (chapter 15), writing on the British Friends Ambulance Unit (FAU), outlines its remarkable achievement in balancing the call of conscience and members' desire to aid the victims of war alongside the army on the battle-field. Whereas in the First World War not all members of the earlier unit had been conscientious objectors, in the Second World War almost all of its 'Quakers in uniform' had had first to appear before a government-appointed tribunal to establish their pacifist credentials as con-scientious objectors (COs).

Commonwealth countries that followed Great Britain by introducing wartime conscription included Canada, Australia, and New Zealand. The fate of COs in these three dominions is told – for Canada, by Thomas Socknat (chapter 16), for Australia, by Peter Brock, with the assistance of Malcolm Saunders (chapter 17), and for New Zealand, by John Cookson (chapter 18).

In the United States, which entered the war in 1941, most of that country's comparatively large CO community spent the war years in Civilian Public Ser-vice (CPS) projects. The dilemmas of conscience that some of these pacifist civilian servicemen experienced, and the efforts made by a still-free society to accommodate such dissidents, despite the pressures of war, are the subject of Mitchell Robinson's essay (chapter 19). Rachel Waltner Goossen (chapter 20) examines the response of women pacifists in the professions to the same kind of pressures towards conformity – a topic largely neglected till now in the fairly abundant literature on American COs of the Second World War. Next, Larry Gara (chapter 21) – historian and pacifist activist – gives us a personal account of his experiences in prison and reflects on the stand of the minority of Ameri-can COs who rejected CPS (or non-combatant service in the armed forces) for jail. Finally, Jennifer Frost (chapter 22) looks at the response of wartime public opinion in the case of Lew Ayres, when a popular Hollywood star chose to become a weaponless CO in the Army Medical Corps rather than serve his country under arms.

The position of European pacifists under German occupation has been largely ignored in the historiography of the resistance movement, except per-haps in the case of the heroic non-violence of the Protestant pastor André Trocmé and his wife, Magda, at Le Chambon in Vichy France. We have pre-sented three studies on this subject here, preceded by an overview by Peter Brock (chapter 23) of the fate of those courageous Germans who refused to fight for Hitler. In Denmark only passive resistance was offered to the Nazis after they had taken over the country; Peter Kragh Hansen (chapter 24) analyses the response to occupation of the small, but active pacifist movement against the background of the general situation in the land. In Norway, violence-oriented resistance developed quickly. Pacifists, few in number and sharing, as Danish pacifists did, the abhorrence of fascism felt by most of their fellow citizens, faced a serious dilemma. Was it really possible to participate actively in resistance while remaining loyal to non-violence? Torleiv Austad (chapter 25) tells us how Norwegian pacifists resolved this sometimes-agonizing question. The position of pacifism in the Netherlands differed from that in Scandinavia (or even France) in that Dutch pacifists between the wars had possessed a widely respected Christian pacifist organization, which enjoyed something of the legitimacy that Ceadel has assigned to the British pacifist movement. Drawing on their monograph on this body – *Kerk en Vrede* (Church and Peace) – which is available only in Dutch, Henk van den Berg and Ton Coppes (chapter 26) have shown how its members carried on in extremely difficult circumstances the pacifist mission that they had undertaken in peacetime.

The chapters described above deal with Europe, North America, or Australia. The two last studies of this volume venture outside this area. In the first, Cyril H. Powles (chapter 27) looks at the fate of Christian pacifism in Japan; his chapter is necessarily brief, since the Japanese environment remained extremely unpropitious for its development. The opposite, however, was true of India, where Mohandas Karamchand Gandhi was practising *satyagraha* (non-violent soul force) in his campaigns to achieve national liberation and social justice, while at the same time preaching *ahimsa* (non-injury) as the best way to establish world peace. Of course, Gandhi had a strong influence on Western pacifists through the 1920s and 1930s – a theme that has been studied by a number of scholars. Though not rejecting the role of Western influences (the New Testament, Tolstoy, Thoreau, and so on) in shaping Gandhi's philosophy of non-violence, Antony Kozhuvanal (chapter 28) shows the powerful impact of India's past on the Mahatma's thinking and practice.

We believe that the topics raised in this volume can help to shed light on at least some of the ethical and practical problems surrounding the issues of war, peace, and conflict resolution in today's world. These chapters should also contribute to a better understanding of a critical stage in the history of pacifist theory and organization.

We hope, in addition, that readers may find that the essays stimulate them to explore further the history of pacifist thought and action. Topics are raised here that cannot be exhausted within the limited framework necessarily imposed on our authors. We may point, for instance, to the widely differing treatment of COs in various conscriptionist countries, ranging from the liberal attitude of the

British government during the Second World War (or of the Soviet government immediately after the First World War) to the harsh policy of interwar France (or the even more brutal treatment of COs in Nazi Germany). There are, too, the numerous sources of tension between pacifism and the less absolute varieties of internationalism that arose most notably in the British and French peace movements or within an organization such as the WILPF. The contribution of women to pacifist history, inside women's organizations such as the WILPF and the British Women's Co-operative Guild, has only recently begun to emerge and calls for continued study on a comparative basis. Again, the role of traditionally pacifist sects such as the Quakers, Mennonites, and Brethren contrasts strikingly with the almost complete absence, in the twentieth century at any rate, of sectarian pacifism on the European continent outside Russia. The fact that pacifism generally has been much weaker there than in Britain, Canada, and the United States can be explained only by reference to the past history of these countries, as Ceadel's chapter shows.

PETER BROCK
THOMAS P. SOCKNAT

Acknowledgments

We would like to thank Dr D. Ben Rees, editor of *Reconciliation Quarterly*, for permission to publish a revised version of chapter 23, which originally appeared in that journal. We would also like to thank Dr Ron G. Schoeffel, editor-in-chief, and Anne Forte, managing editor, of the University of Toronto Press, for their continued support of our project, as well as John Parry, for his able and sensitive copy-editing of the final manuscript. Other persons who at one time or another have helped us in our task include Diana K. Ayres, John Brownlee, Peter van den Dungen, Anne C. Kjelling, Arthur Robinson, Gordon White, Solomon E. Yoder, and the staff of E.J. Pratt Library, Victoria University, Toronto. We are indeed grateful to them as well as to all of those, listed on page 455, who have given permission for the use of illustrations.

Contributors

Torleiv Austad, Professor of Systematic Theology and Academic Dean, Norwegian Lutheran Seminary, Oslo

Henk van den Berg, Dutch historian

Peter Brock, Professor Emeritus of History, University of Toronto

Martin Ceadel, Fellow of New College and Lecturer in Politics, University of Oxford

John E. Cookson, Reader in History, University of Canterbury, Christchurch, New Zealand

Ton Coppes, Dutch historian

Donald F. Durnbaugh, Professor Emeritus of Church History, Bethany Theological Seminary, Oak Brook, Illinois, and Archivist, Juniata College, Pennsylvania

Josephine Eglin, Teacher of sociology and politics in an English sixth-form college

Peter Farrugia, Lecturer in History, Wilfrid Laurier University, Waterloo, Ontario

Jennifer Frost, Assistant Professor of History, University of Northern Colorado

Larry Gara, Professor Emeritus of History, Wilmington College, Ohio

Rachel Waltner Goossen, Assistant Professor of History, Goshen College, Indiana

Guido Grünewald, PhD (history), financial consultant, Cologne, Germany

Thomas Hackman, MSc, astronomer at the Observatory of the University of Helsinki, and Council Member of the War Resisters' International

Peter Kragh Hansen, Graduate of University of Odense, Denmark

Katja Huumo, Student of history, University of Helsinki, Finland

Norman Ingram, Associate Professor of History, Concordia University, Montreal

Lawrence Klippenstein, Historian-Archivist, Mennonite Heritage Centre, Winnipeg

Antony Kozhuvanal, DTheol (Toronto), priest at Pro-Cathedral Church, Thiruvampady, Kerala, India

†**Kenneth McNaught**, Late Professor Emeritus of History, University of Toronto

Herman Noordegraaf, Sociologist, theologian, and biographer of Bart de Ligt

Anne Marie Pois, Instructor, Women's Studies Program and Department of History, University of Colorado at Boulder

Cyril H. Powles, Professor Emeritus of Church History, Trinity College, University of Toronto

Andrew Rigby, Reader in Peace Studies, University of Bradford, England

Mitchell L. Robinson, PhD (Cornell), U.S. Navy contract negotiator at the Fleet and Industrial Supply Center Detachment, Philadelphia

Malcolm Saunders, Lecturer in History, Central Queensland University, Australia

Lyn Smith, Interviewer for Sound Archives of Imperial War Museum, London, England, and Lecturer in International Politics, Open University, England, and Webster University, United States

Thomas P. Socknat, Co-ordinator of Canadian Studies, Woodsworth College, University of Toronto

Paul D. Steeves, Professor of History, Stetson University, Florida

PART ONE
FROM PEACE TO WAR

1

Mennonites and Military Service in the Soviet Union to 1939

LAWRENCE KLIPPENSTEIN

In 1917, the year of the October Revolution, Mennonites in Russia were looking back on 130 years of residence in the country.[1] The years just prior to the First World War have been termed their 'golden age,' though dark clouds had already begun to gather. Nationalist journalists had been aiming hostile broadsides at non-Russian minorities such as the Germans for over twenty years, and land-expropriation legislation also directed quite obviously at Germans had been passed in 1912. During the First World War Mennonites had to deal with heightened anti-German feelings generated by the conflict, as well as the issue of military service, which emerged with new dimensions the day that actual hostilities began.[2] This essay examines Mennonites and military service under the tsars, under Lenin, and under Stalin.

The Mennonite State Service Tradition under the Tsars

To understand the context for the Mennonite dilemma regarding military service in the Soviet era one needs to recall the terms of the original colonization charter (*Privilegium*) under which the Mennonites from the Prussian Vistula basin had come to the southern province of New Russia in 1789 and the years following. Their representatives had asked for exemption from military service, which was in fact offered to all potential foreign colonists at that time. They asked as well for exemption from what was termed 'ordinary public services' – the billeting of soldiers when military detachments marched through their colonies – and from *podwod* services, meaning transportation of provisions for military personnnel.[3] Vice-Regent Grigorii A. Potemkin, governor of New Russia, granted Mennonites exemption from military service 'for all time,' without any apparent qualifications. He also promised exemption from other designated state services, except during times of war, when active troop movements might occur.[4]

Five Russian wars of the nineteenth and the early twentieth centuries were to put this crucial contract to the test. In Nicholas I's reign, Mennonites had received confirmation in writing of their original charter. And later they sent assurances several times that the tsar could count on non-military support from Mennonites in times of war as well as peace. At one point they presented 130 horses to the tsar to illustrate the point.[5]

There is little evidence to suggest that the Crimean War of 1853–6 rekindled the earlier lively debates on the issue of war support by Mennonite communities. However, it did show their readiness to support the war effort in non-combatant ways. The *podwod* wagon convoys taking supplies to the front lines – dozens, perhaps hundreds of them – formed a central feature of their assistance, along with the care of wounded soldiers in Mennonite hospitals and the contribution of very considerable sums of money, as well as many wagons and horses, which were being asked for to meet the military needs of the country.[6]

A crisis arose for the Mennonites in the 1870s. At that time the 'Great Reforms' of Alexander II had included a revision of military service regulations. Universal military conscription, imposed in 1874, signalled the end of the total exemption from military service which Mennonites had enjoyed. The search for a solution to the crisis finally split the community almost down the middle. One result of this debate was that about one-third of the Mennonite population of Russia (about seventeen thousand persons) emigrated to North America in the belief that the solution eventually reached represented an unjustified compromise of the Mennonite peace principle, as traditionally understood.[7]

The government permitted young Mennonite men who were liable to the draft to perform a non-military type of service in the form of labour in forestry camps. Those persons would be required to serve a period equivalent to that demanded of regular military recruits and would work in special camps staffed and funded largely by the Mennonites themselves. The first camp, established near Azov, somewhat north of Mariupol, near the Mennonite settlement of Bergthal, opened its doors to the first recruits in 1881, and the last of the eleven camps (if one counts some auxiliary locations) was erected on the Transsiberian Railroad at Issyl Kul in 1913.[8]

Meanwhile, Mennonites had rendered non-military services during the Balkan War of 1877–8, and once again their efforts had received the government's recognition. A number of volunteers from Mennonite communities joined the medical corps of the Russian army in the war with Japan in 1904 and 1905. They were the forerunners of thousands of others who during the Great War performed essential medical duties at the front under non-military auspices.[9]

The work of these men, and of all those who had joined an expanded forestry camp network during the war, ceased with the collapse of the provisional government in October–November 1917. The Bolsheviks' accession to power under Lenin soon brought the war to an end. All the property of the original Mennonite camps was then disposed of, and by the end of 1918 these premises appear to have been vacated completely.[10]

State Service under the Soviets: The First Phase

The disturbing question of state service, military or otherwise, came up again almost immediately after Lenin's new government had seized power. At first there were signs of hope for pacifists. All Mennonite conscientious objectors (COs) had been released from their alternative service duties when the Soviets took control, and a large number of other religious objectors, who had been jailed, also gained their freedom at this time.[11] The possible clash of religious convictions and the requirements of state service could, however, be detected early, in emerging legislation.

A decree of 2 February 1918 stated categorically that 'no one may evade his civic responsibility on account of his religious views.'[12] Lenin may have considered making exceptions to this decree almost from the outset. In the margins of an original draft the possibility was noted that certain forms of alternative service might be declared acceptable by a people's court.[13] It would be only a few months, however, before the idea of granting privileges on the basis of religious convictions would be reviewed by the authorities, and their conclusions built into legislation.

The issue of military service loomed larger for non-resistants, Mennonite or others, when the chairman of the Central Executive Committee, Yakov Sverdlov, announced early in June 1918 that voluntary enlistment in the Red Army would be changed to compulsory mobilization for several categories of recruits.[14] During that year the size of the army was to increase from about 50,000 to 500,000 men as the new regime placed itself more solidly on a war footing in order to repel attacking counter-revolutionary forces.

Quite possibly more aware of these developments than most Russian Mennonites, a group of three dozen ex-medical corpsmen living in Moscow took it on themselves on 24 September 1918 to submit a petition for exemption from military service to the Commissariat of War. The spokesmen of this group appear to have been Peter Froese and Cornelius F. Klassen, both soon to become leaders in the Russian Mennonite community. It is not clear whether at this point they officially represented any other Mennonites besides those in their small Moscow group.[15]

Some non-Mennonite denominations in the city, such as the Evangelical Christians and Baptists, had begun to apply for exemptions also. As early as

June 1918 delegations of evangelicals had begun to raise publicly the issue of imprisoned Russian (non-Mennonite) pacifists. The first official decree to follow this request seems to have been Order No. 30, issued by Trotsky on 22 October 1918.[16] It granted permission to apply to a court of inquiry for exemption from military service on religious grounds. If the court approved such a request, alternative forms of service could be granted in military hospitals, or even in various kinds of civilian work.

A large number of COs among the Moscow evangelicals found these arrangements unacceptable or inadequate and took steps to obtain still-greater concessions. A special conference was called in November 1918 to plan such action. Klassen and Froese from the Moscow Mennonite group were apparently also present and were invited to become members of a proposed inter-faith council – the United Council of Religious Societies and Groups for the Defence of Conscientious Objectors.[17]

A clarification of procedures for obtaining exemptions came with a decree worded by Lenin himself and issued on 4 January 1919.[18] Like the order of 22 October, this decree too permitted any person who wished to claim military-service exemption for religious reasons to appear before a people's tribunal to plead his case. It also enlarged the role of the United Council in assessing the credentials brought forward by applicants seeking exemption and alternative service. By this time the spread of violence in the country had begun to cloud the whole issue, especially for Mennonites in Ukraine. The Treaty of Brest-Litovsk with Germany, signed in March 1918, had opened the door for the advance of the German army into Ukraine, allowing it to occupy the Mennonite area till the autumn of the same year.[19]

During this relatively short period, large numbers of Ukrainian peasants had rallied to the cause of property expropriation, led by a young anarchist activist, Nestor Makhno, who had recently returned from a term of imprisonment in Moscow.[20] Roving through the countryside, these loosely organized units called for resistance to the German invasion, and to the Red Army's advance, and with their own resources attempted direct redistribution of land and property, which the revolution appeared to make possible.

Makhno's struggle with the foreign occupying forces became a direct threat for the Mennonites when the invading German–Austrian army departed as the war in western Europe drew to a close. A number of villages in the Mennonite colonies of southern Ukraine now had to face the direct onslaught of Makhno's men. Several villages were completely destroyed and virtually all the residents put to death. Much property was destroyed throughout the area, countless women were molested, and a general sense of terror fell on the region.[21]

On 30 June 1918 Mennonite representatives had met to discuss various matters, including a directive from the German authorities in Berdiansk that a self-defence militia be organized in the Mennonite colonies. After vigorous discussion of the principles of non-violence and non-resistant peace theology, they agreed that a decision about whether or not to use weapons for self-defence should be left solely to individuals' consciences. That seemed to leave the field open to those who were convinced that a self-defence body must be created in order to protect villagers from the Makhno attackers, and a Selbstschutz (as that body was commonly known) soon came into existence.[22] Some delegates even saw joining the White Army as an option.

However, a number of individuals, and some entire congregations, such as the one at Rudnerweide in the Molotschna settlement, continued to oppose the use of arms even for self-defence.[23] They contended that even that constituted a forthright denial of a cardinal tenet of Christian faith – that is, the call to live a peaceful life as Christ himself had done. Moreover, they argued, there was a strong likelihood that self-defence would backfire, resulting in more deaths and greater destruction than would otherwise have been the case.

The Mennonite self-defence militia set up in November 1918 included a three-hundred-man cavalry and twenty companies of infantry, of perhaps two thousand men altogether. It repulsed the early attacks by Makhno and his followers, while a victorious pitched battle in the Russian village of Chernigovka added lustre to its name. However, attempts by White Army officers to integrate it into their own forces created problems for the Mennonite corpsmen. Then came a defeat at Blumental in March 1919. A large number of militiamen decided to flee to the Crimea, and then, as the Red Army moved into the area, the struggle of the Selbstschutz came to an end.[24]

When the Red Army in 1921 finally overcame the White counter-revolutionary forces led by Denikin and Wrangel, and the Makhno bands too had been dispersed, a semblance of order returned to the Mennonite colonies and surrounding regions. With considerable difficulty, Mennonite leaders were able to persuade the Red military leaders that Mennonite Selbstchutz militia units had never intended to resist the Red Army but had been formed only for self-defence against Makhno. They were told, however, that any person found guilty of having fought in the White Army would be executed if apprehended.[25]

Several meetings were then called in Mennonite communities to reaffirm the tenet of non-resistance and to plan a strategy for reclaiming the privilege of military-service exemption from the Red Army. In some communities large numbers of men had already been able to take advantage of the decree of 4 January 1919, and the availability of such recourse for COs was further publicized.[26] Mennonite court 'experts' such as a certain Peters from the Ufa settlement, Johann Bueckert from Arkadak, and Aron Toews from the Old Colony

(Chortitza) helped conscripts deal successfully with the court interrogations that they nearly always had to face when seeking exemption.

But some local Soviet officials seemed to be unaware of the decree of 4 January or else simply refused to grant any of its exemptions.[27] In such cases it became necessary for conscripts to travel to Moscow to get a proper hearing. In Siberia a local Mennonite businessman from Omsk, Jacob J. Hildebrand, was able to work out with the authorities a kind of regional charter for exemptions, which served the people of his area for some time.[28]

When late in 1920 the United Council seemed to be losing legal status and influence, Mennonite representatives sought to appeal directly to Joseph Stalin, who was commissar of nationalities.[29] However, efforts by C.F. Klassen and Peter Froese to have the Mennonites reclassified as a distinctive minority – i.e., neither German nor Dutch – did not succeed. The two were simply informed that a German section existed in the commissariat and that it would deal satisfactorily with the concerns of all Germans, Mennonites included.[30]

Still there were fears that this rather shaky setup would break down. Local authorities often seemed exceedingly haphazard, indeed vindictive, in their judgments, and sometimes appeals got no hearing at all. In January 1921, Mennonites had submitted two petitions in this connection, one to the Commissariat of Agriculture and the other to the Commissariat of Justice. Intense negotiations followed, as a result of which the Commissariat of Agriculture agreed to both of the requests that it had received – abolition of the court system of exemption appeals and the acceptance of agricultural work as an alternative to military service. But the Commissariat of Justice saw things differently. It wanted to have the courts retained, formally at least, and it had no sympathy with agricultural work as an alternative form of service. A mixed commission set up by the People's Council of Commissars felt that this question should be dealt with comprehensively, so as to cover all non-resistant groups, not the Mennonites alone. The matter was then pursued along that line.[31]

New Efforts to Organize

Some months before this decision on 19 February 1921 the Molotschna and Chortitza Mennonites had sought to reorganize their efforts to deal with military exemption and other pressing issues.[32] Information about the United Council was brought to this meeting. During the ensuing discussion Benjamin B. Janz, a retired schoolteacher from Tiege, Molotschna, called for an explicit and open review of the principles involved in obtaining exemption for draft-age young men. He wondered if the assembly could really make its appeal for better treatment of objectors with a clear conscience, given the serious compromises that he felt had been made in supporting the Selbstschutz initiative two years earlier.

Immediate action was now needed, however. The Mennonites had been informed that they must immediately draw up a list of persons who would be seeking exemption in the immediate future. The United Council was requesting this information in order to represent these men before the Soviet authorities. The Mennonite assembly now set out to create a new organization to deal with all aspects of obtaining exemption from military service. Janz was asked to chair the new body. Several people were then authorized to travel to Moscow in this connection. Janz insisted, however, that the convention must publicly reaffirm its commitment to peaceful service and non-resistance. The resulting proposal, though passed, did not fully satisfy Janz, but he agreed to accept the new position.

The name chosen for the new body, Verband der Mennoniten Südrusslands (Association of the Mennonites of South Russia), was later changed to Verband der Bürger holländischer Herkunft (Association of Citizens of Dutch Extraction).[33] Its work in seeking military-service exemptions would not be easy. For one thing, the authorities could not totally repress their suspicions that the Mennonites had collaborated with the German army during the invasion and occupation of 1918 and that they had supported the White Army forces during the Civil War. Quartering of Red Army soldiers in Mennonite homes did not end till 1922, as the search for weapons in their villages continued. Thirteen people were shot as hostages, and young people were beaten to obtain information, as more and more weapons came to light.[34]

Janz felt that he could perceive a divine purpose in all this suffering. As he put it in one of his many reports, 'This is how Mennonites were made non-resistant again. The confession of conscientious objection by the Molotschna Mennonites was now difficult in the extreme.'[35] In the autumn of 1921 a number of applications for exemption from military service did succeed, but they cost eleven thousand rubles each to submit. Five Rempel brothers seeking exemptions were tortured in prison at Melitopol and again at Ekaterinoslav. Five others, also objectors, were executed in Halbstadt at the end of the year.[36]

It was not easy to regularize application procedures. Many Mennonite men were left to their own resources in securing exemptions. They were sometimes quite unaware of the existence of the Verband, hence unable to take advantage of any influence that Janz himself might have had. Janz reported at the end of 1922 that a member of the Revolutionary Committee of the Republic (referred to by Janz as 'chief of the conscription section of military affairs'), Comrade Spector, had promised to approach Trotsky's substitute with the idea of a special medical-service alternative to be put under the health section, with men serving in groups. The chief had also promised to recommend agricultural service as an alternative.[37] Janz then noted that another alternative to combatant service – i.e., medical service – had been promised but would be placed under military jurisdiction. He was particularly concerned about a large number of men who had been consigned to active military duty in the Caucasus, and others who were still in prison for refusing to serve in the army.[38]

Meanwhile Klassen and Froese continued to press for a solution to their problems in Moscow. When the War Commissariat prepared a new proposal for circulation in the new year,[39] a memo from them noted pressure from Mennonites being exerted by means of a proposed emigration that would be undertaken if more acceptable forms of alternative service were not legalized soon. Mennonite leaders now were called in to explain the connection between emigration and military exemption in their home communities. Janz and the Moscow Mennonite representatives had already been very busy trying to obtain permission for several thousand Mennonites to leave the country.[40]

In the spring of 1923 Mennonites were informed that their service problems now would be dealt with in the context of a revision of all existing military regulations.[41] The conclusions reached by the several commissariats working on this issue would not receive legislative status, for the time being at least. The Mennonites meanwhile had formed yet another new organization, the All-Russian Mennonite Agricultural Union, within which they were also discussing military exemption.[42] At the union's first delegate meeting in October, some representatives, seemingly always on the lookout for better service options, urged creation of more interesting types of work, so that 'depressing and unproductive kinds of labour such as forestry work' would not again need to be resorted to as alternatives to military service.[43]

Thus Mennonites continued their search for a special service status. Their reports from this period noted that while they had been recognized as a non-resistant group again, this was not the case for Baptists and Evangelical Christians or certain other Russian sectarians.[44] Under severe pressure, congresses of the Baptists and Evangelicals in 1923 formally accepted military service for their members, and there is little doubt that this is exactly what the Soviet government hoped would happen at the All-Mennonite Union congress held in Moscow in January 1925.[45] Surprisingly, delegates actually gave relatively little attention to the military question. A report on ongoing negotiations was submitted, and delegates did endorse an eight-point statement on basic requirements for sustaining their denomination as a religious group. The latter document also included calls for exemption from the military oath and for the right to some form of military-service alternative. The results of issuing this statement were not too encouraging; many men were in fact not getting exemption. Some Mennonite servicemen who returned from active duty in the Red Army actually denounced the pressure to obtain exemption as 'totally inappropriate.'[46]

What one person now called 'the general shallowness of consciousness about the significance of non-resistance' led the Mennonites of Ukraine to call a series of local conferences, where the matter was to be discussed more thoroughly. Among other things, it was agreed at these meetings that those who had actually entered military service should be excommunicated by their congregations; they would be received back into full fellowship only if they indicated a change of views on the issue of service.[47]

New Military Legislation

The passage of a new military law on 18 September 1925 did not improve the situation as much as Mennonites had hoped. It was now apparent, however, that their concerns would receive more attention from the government.[48] All those who before 1917 had belonged to religious groups forbidding military service would now be eligible for exemption from service by the district courts. Those wishing to obtain this status would need to apply to the court six months before recruitment or else be subject to conscription without further consideration. The courts alone would decide whether applications for exemption would be approved. The law did not mention a specific alternative-service project for Mennonites, though it did refer to possible assignments to work fighting epidemics, timber fires, and other services of general national significance.[49]

From a Mennonite perspective, little had been gained by these alterations. Leaving almost all decision-making power in the hands of local courts did not promise much help in dealing with anti-pacifist biases, misjudgments, and so on. Legal protection against compulsory involvement in the military remained quite weak. Mennonites could conclude only that all the negotiations of the past eight years had accomplished very little. An attempt to convene another general Mennonite conference in 1926 exposed the sect's precarious position even more dramatically. The men who travelled to Moscow to obtain permission to hold the conference were informed bluntly that there would be no gathering if the Kommission für kirchliche Angelegenheiten (Church Concerns Commission) would not bring in a resolution pledging full loyalty to the state, and that meant explicitly endorsing military service. The representatives replied, after some deliberation, that since no such declaration would be forthcoming, they would not hold the proposed conference.[50] Nevertheless, developments in other areas looked less discouraging. Several periodicals had been launched, notably *Unser Blatt* (Our Paper) and *Praktischer Landwirt* (The Practical Farmer).[51] In addition, emigration was proceeding at a fast pace.[52] Agricultural redevelopment seemed well under way. And in October, an All-Mennonite conference did in fact convene in Melitopol, Ukraine.[53]

Under the new military law, from late 1925 on large numbers of Mennonite men began the more strictly enforced two years of alternative service, in accordance with the specifications laid down by the courts in their case. Over the next few years the authorities indicated railway and forestry work as the most appropriate types of service.[54]

Increased Pressures under Stalin

Ideological demands and stepped-up propaganda under Stalin heralded a new phase of church–state relations with the launching of the first Five-Year Plan in 1928.[55] This initiative, and the harsh conditions of the alternative-service camps, no doubt explain in part the increased enlistment of Mennonite men for active Red Army service. In the Crimea one such group gained considerable publicity for its alleged vigorous rejection of the Mennonite peace stance, adding to its challenge a patriotic call to serve the motherland under the new regime.[56]

More restrictive religious legislation in 1929[57] created further problems for Mennonite communities, as it did for other religious groups. Added attention came to be focused now on reducing the influence of ministers and their associates, who were seen as delaying acceptance of the new social and economic changes being introduced by the government. Several ministers were imprisoned specifically for assisting persons who had applied for exemption from military service.

Meanwhile some Mennonites, having become supporters of the new regime (such as a certain David Penner, who published his views under the pseudonym Reinmarus), had begun to add their voices to the chorus of criticisms directed at pacifists in the Mennonite community. Reinmarus claimed, without offering any supporting evidence, that in 1929 several Mennonite ministers had conceded that service in the Red Army need not necessarily violate the conscience of 'Menno's sons.'[58]

Quite a few young Mennonites in the call-up group of men born in the years 1903–6 found themselves en route before long to work in the forests around Novosibirsk in Siberia. Others were making their last, desperate move to leave the Soviet Union in the 'rush to Moscow,' which led to the total termination of the emigration in 1930.[59] All negotiations with the government had ceased, as local communities reeled under the impact of draconian taxation, which in turn led to the imprisoning of countless numbers who could not meet these demands.

Surprisingly, the exemption provisions of 1925 remained in force and continued to influence alternative-service assignments for the next half-dozen years. Even the revised military law of 13 August 1930 still retained certain privileges for COs. Those who were fit for alternative service had to remain on the recruiting list until the age of forty and in peacetime would be allowed to participate in projects such as working in forestry, extracting peat, battling epidemics, and fighting forest fires for the same length of time as was required for military training – i.e., two years. In wartime, special labour units would be created to work behind the lines or on the front.[60]

Alternatives to Military Service Abolished

It may have been the 1930 legislation that made the next year seem to be what one recruit called the 'still before the storm.' Many COs were now placed at the disposal of heavy industry to assist in constructing dams for bridges to cross the Dnieper River near the island of Khortitza. Work there continued year-round. The food seemed to have improved, and political education was kept to a minimum. However, some men were getting three-year assignments because they were being seen as 'tylovoye opoltschenyiy' ('TOs') – that is, part of the 'hinterland reserves.' This meant that they were being dealt with as persons from former kulak families and given the same harsh treatment as others in that category.[61] COs were actually brought under military jurisdiction in 1931. This left them under the discipline of military commanders, who were always accompanied by the dreaded 'political instructors.'

All these new recruits were now in effect not COs but 'TOs,' and to uphold any form of legal alternative service would become an even greater struggle than before.[62] That explains why 1932 through 1935 has been designated the 'worst years' of service, when the government was concerned not so much with offering alternative-service opportunities as with making those who refused to perform combatant service pay the bitter price of their 'disloyalty.'

Only a few personal memoirs and letters of COs who experienced those years are extant.[63] One group reported on its labours in a stone quarry, where members were locked up for a period because they refused to work on Sundays. Large numbers were still sent in 1932–4 to work in the coal mines of Artemovsk in the Far East or to build railway ties at Khabarovsk. Sometimes these men had their terms extended because they were alleged to be sons of kulaks. Others applied to become 'good citizens' and gave up the struggle to remain COs.

Little or no evidence has been found to indicate that Soviet courts continued to accept CO applications after 1935. At least one source suggests that the last of the COs to complete their terms were released in 1937 and that the category of 'TOs' also continued to exist till then.[64] Such labour units would form the basis of the so-called Trudarmiia (labour forces), which came into their own during the war years and persisted as late as the early 1950s.

The Soviet constitution of 1936 ('the Stalin Constitution') placed all power in the leader's hands. Article 132 stated unequivocally that military service in the armed forces 'is an honourable duty for citizens.' Another article said that 'treason to the Motherland – violation of the oath of allegiance, desertion to the enemy, impairing the military power of the state, espionage – is punishable with all the severity of the law as the most heinous of all crimes.'[65] In this context, all special legal provisions for objectors, or any form of exemption on religious and other grounds had completely vanished. The charge of 'treason to the motherland' could become the label for any type of protest or dissent and be punished accordingly.

Germany's signing of the Non-Aggression Pact with the Soviet Union coincided almost exactly to the day with the Universal Military Law, passed in the USSR in August 1939. In an early commentary on this new legislation, Marshal K.Y. Voroshilov, people's commissar of defence, sought to explain the unique and otherwise specially noteworthy features of these laws.[66] He also declared (did he have chiefly the Mennonites in mind?) that the new law did not contain a section on exemption from military service for reasons of religious conviction because not a single request for such an exemption had been received during the 1937 and 1938 military drafts; therefore it was clear there was no longer any need to include such a section in the new law.[67]

Conclusion

Had the Mennonites in effect now changed their position on military service completely, as the Baptists and Evangelical Christians had done officially a decade earlier? One could assume, I think, even in the absence of documents, that a principle for which these people had risked or sacrificed their lives, and which they had upheld (albeit with lapses in the Selbstschutz period) at least until 1937, would not have been surrendered voluntarily overnight. One might well have asked the people's commissar of defence whether his department had not ignored or silenced in some way the voices that would normally have requested the continued right to military exemption and whether the channels through which such Mennonite leaders could have otherwise communicated had not disappeared altogether.

That the Soviet authorities countenanced two decades of Mennonite negotiations and insistence of their right to be granted civilian alternatives to military service is perhaps a surprising feature of the early post-revolution period. The

Mennonites had continued to present their view on military service to the authorities and obtain at least partial – albeit often grudging – recognition of this claim. And they did this for ten years after some of the other pacifist groups had given way on this issue.

How can this difference be explained, and how significant was the relatively successful Mennonite initiative in the long run? Perhaps the Mennonites could persevere longer because they were not viewed as being really Russian, or perhaps because the relatively faster-spreading influence of other evangelical groups made the Mennonite pacifist 'threat' appear less dangerous to the Soviet state. Speculations of this kind are of course not at present subject to documentary proof. The decisions taken by the two major evangelical groups in the early 1920s did not eliminate pacifist thought in Russian evangelical circles altogether. After 1945 it would surface again in such communities.[68] The pacifist stance of the Mennonites had become a symbol of their self-identity and community maintenance during the early years of the Soviet period. To surrender that tenet of faith still seemed to many of them to mean giving up the faith altogether. This in the past they had never been willing to do under any circumstances, and so long as they continued to exist as a community, they would surely not do in the present.[69]

It was not until community and church appeared to collapse entirely under collectivization, together with the pressures of the Second World War and the early postwar years, that the situation changed significantly. Deprived of their strong institutional base, Mennonites decided to abandon a group approach to the issue and instead to leave decisions about military service up to the individual.[70] The Mennonite view on military service had deep roots in the history of the church's centuries-long experience and its self-understanding as a nonresistant and separated community. When the Communists became overtly hostile and sought to remove all dissenting elements in their midst, the Mennonites had to choose between violently resisting this move, which was scarcely feasible, or finding another non-violent way. In deciding on the latter, they could avoid confrontation – and somehow survive. But only the future could reveal whether, despite the cost, their bare survival would vindicate the decision in the end.

NOTES

1 For the first century of Mennonite life in Russia, see James Urry, *None But Saints: The Transformation of Mennonite Life in Russia, 1789–1889* (Winnipeg 1989). See also John Friesen, ed., *Mennonites in Russia, 1788–1988: Essays in Honour of Gerhard Lohrenz* (Winnipeg 1989).

2 See Lawrence Klippenstein, 'Mennonite Pacifism and State Service in Russia: A Case Study in Church–State Relations, 1789–1936,' PhD dissertation, University of Minnesota, 1984, 159–64.

3 David G. Rempel, 'Mennonite Migration to New Russia (1789–1870),' *Mennonite Quarterly Review* (Goshen, Ind.) 9 (April 1935), 71–91 (July 1935), 109–28.

4 Klippenstein, 'Mennonite Pacifism,' 12, 13.

5 Franz Isaac, *Die Molotschnaer Mennoniten: Ein Beitrag zur Geschichte derselben* (Halbstadt 1908), 23–5.

6 James Urry and Lawrence Klippenstein, 'Mennonites and the Crimean War, 1854–1856,' *Journal of Mennonite Studies* (Winnipeg), 7 (1989), 9–32.

7 Gustav E. Reimer and G.R. Gaeddert, *Exiled by the Czar: Cornelius Jansen and the Great Mennonite Migration, 1874* (Newton, Kan., 1956), 193ff.

8 A list of pre–First World War camps is given in Peter M. Friesen, *Die Altevangelische Mennonitische Brüderschaft in Russland (1789–1910)* (Halbstadt 1911), 512; see also Klippenstein, 'Mennonite Pacifism,' 85ff, and 147ff.

9 See Jacob Hoemsen, 'Als Sanitäter im russisch–japanischen Kriege,' *Der Bote* (Saskatoon), 8 (Feb. 1972), 11, and Klippenstein, 'Mennonite Pacifism,' 131ff. A collection of memoirs from men who served in the forestry camps and First World War medical-service units, and so on, is in Waldemar Guenther, David P. Heidebrecht, and Gerhard I. Peters, eds., *'Our Guys': Alternative Service for Mennonites in Russia under the Romanows*, trans. and ed. Peter H. Friesen (Keewatin, Ont., n.d.). One story has been added to the original German version published in 1966; see 267ff.

10 'Der heurige mennonitische Kongress in Orloff,' *Friedensstimme* (Halbstadt), 7 (Sept. 1918), 6.

11 M.S. Timasheff, *Religion in Soviet Russia* (New York 1942), 16–17, and Bruno Coppieters, 'Die pazifistischen Sekten, die Bolschewiki und das Recht auf Wehrdienstverweigerung,' in Reiner Steinweg, ed., *Lehren aus der Geschichte? Historische Friedensforschung* (Frankfurt am Main 1990), 308ff. In tsarist Russia only Mennonites were granted exemption from military service for all their draft-age men.

12 The original text is in P.V. Gidulianov, ed., *Otdelenie tserkvi ot gosudarstva v SSSR* (Moscow 1926), 615ff.

13 A.I. Klibanov, *Religioznoe sektanstvo i sovremenost* (Moscow 1969), 188.

14 James H. Meisel and Edward S. Kozera, eds., *Materials for the Study of the Soviet System, State and Party Constitutions, Laws, Decrees, Decisions and Official Statements of the Leaders in Translation* (Ann Arbor, Mich., 1950), 73.

15 C.F. Klassen, 'Die Lage der russischen Gemeinden seit 1920,' in D. Christian Neff, ed., *Bericht über die Mennonitische Welt- Hilfs- Konferenz vom 31. August bis 3. September, 1930 in Danzig* (Karlsruhe n.d.), 49–64.

16 The full text of Order 130 is not available. On its introduction, see Klibanov, *Sektanstvo*, 190, where the contents of the order is summarized.

17 Ibid., 191ff. See also Andrew Blaine, 'The Relations between the Russian Protestant
   Sects and the State, 1900–1921,' PhD dissertation, Duke University, 1964, 221ff.
   For the United Council, see chapter 2, below.
18 See below chapter 2, note 17.
19 On the occupation of Ukraine by the Germans, see Oleh S. Fedyshyn, *Germany's
   Drive to the East and the Ukrainian Revolution, 1917–1918* (New Brunswick, NJ,
   1971), 60ff.
20 Michael Palij, *The Anarchism of Nestor Makhno, 1918–1921: An Aspect of the
   Ukrainian Revolution* (Seattle and London 1976), 67–74. See also Victor Peters,
   Nestor Makhno: The Life of an Anarchist (Winnipeg 1970), 32ff.
21 Many observers have written about these events. See, for example, Diedrich Neu-
   feld, *A Russian Dance of Death: Revolution and Civil War in the Ukraine*, trans. and
   ed. Al Reimer (Winnipeg 1977).
22 John B. Toews, 'The Origins and the Activities of the Mennonite *Selbstschutz* in
   Ukraine (1918–1919),' *Mennonite Quarterly Review* 46 (Jan. 1972), 5–40; Klippenstein, 'Mennonite Pacifism,' 235–7.
23 H. Goossen, 'Unsere grosse Vaterlandsliebe,' manuscript in B.B. Janz Papers, Centre
   for Mennonite Brethren Studies, Winnipeg.
24 Al Reimer, '*Sanitaetsdienst* and *Selbstschutz*: Russian-Mennonite Nonresistance in
   World War I and Its Aftermath,' *Journal of Mennonite Studies*, 11 (1993), 135–48.
25 John B. Toews, trans. and ed., 'The Mennonite *Selbstschutz* in the Ukraine,' *Mennonite Life* (North Newton, Kan.), 26 (July 1971), 138–42.
26 On early Mennonite efforts to secure military exemption in the Soviet period, see
   Peter F. Froese, 'Wie entstand der Allrussische Mennonitische Landwirtschaftlicher
   Verein?' *Mennonitische Rundschau* (Winnipeg), 76 (29 April 1953), 2.
27 These experiences were recorded by Diedrich Wiebe of Winnipeg in an unpublished
   manuscript, 'Forsteidienst 1920–1922 bei den Sowyets,' dated February 1976; in the
   author's files.
28 J.J. Hildebrand, *Siberien* (Winnipeg 1949), 80ff; Klippenstein, 'Mennonite Pacifism,' 280, 281.
29 Klippenstein, 'Mennonite Pacifism,' 282, 283.
30 Froese, 'Wie entstand?' 3.
31 Benjamin H. Unruh, 'Der Kampf der russischen Gemeinden um die Wehrlosigkeit,'
   Mennonitische Jugendwarte (Ibersheim), 5 (June 1925), 56.
32 For information on this conference, see B.B. Janz, 'The Founding of the Union in
   Alexanderwohl,' in John B. Toews, ed., *The Mennonites in Russia from 1917–1930:
   Selected Documents* (Winnipeg 1975), 89–93.
33 See also B.B. Janz, 'Verband der Bürger holländischer Herkunft (Association of Citizens of Dutch Extraction),' *The Mennonite Encyclopedia* 4 vols. (Scottdale, Pa.,
   1955–9), 4:809. The original records of this organization have recently been located

in a Moscow archive by Dr Walter Sawatsky of Elkhart, Indiana. Related reports, minutes of meetings, and so on appear in translation in Toews, ed., *Selected Documents*, 89–193.

34 B.B. Janz, 'The Constitution Again,' in Toews, ed., *Selected Documents*, 105.

35 Ibid.

36 See diary entries for 12 October and 26 December 1921, in John P. Dyck, ed., *Troubles and Triumphs, 1914–1924: Excerpts from the Diary of Peter. J. Dyck Ladekopp, Molotschna Colony, Ukraine* (Springstein, Man., 1981), 156, 163.

37 The best analysis of Janz's role in these negotiations is still the illuminating, if somewhat one-sided portrayal by John B. Toews in 'The Russian Mennonites and the Military Question, 1921–1927,' *Mennonite Quarterly Review*, 43 (April 1969), 153–68.

38 See a letter of B.B. Janz to A.A. Friesen and B.H. Unruh, dated 26 November 1922, in the A.A. Friesen Papers, Mennonite Library and Archives, North Newton, Kan., file 55, and related items at the same location.

39 See the broader discussion of these details in Klippenstein, 'Mennonite Pacifism,' 293.

40 On the Russian Mennonite emigration plans of this period, see John B. Toews, *Lost Fatherland: The Story of the Mennonite Emigration from Soviet Russia, 1921–1927* (Scottdale, Pa., 1967).

41 Unruh, 'Der Kampf,' 60.

42 See 'Minutes of the Alexandertal Congress of Oct. 10–16, 1923,' in Toews, ed., *Selected Documents*, 255–6.

43 Klippenstein, 'Mennonite Pacifism,' 299–303.

44 See Froese's report in A.A. Friesen Papers, file 30 (General Correspondence, Ont.–Dec., 1923).

45 'Moscow Conference, January 13–18, 1925,' in Toews, ed., *Selected Documents*, 428ff.

46 [B.H. Unruh], 'Ein weiterer Beitrag zum Kampf der Mennonitengemeinden Russlands um die Wehrlosigkeit,' *Mennonitische Jugendwarte*, 5 (Dec. 1925), 134–5.

47 Klippenstein, 'Mennonite Pacifism,' 306–9.

48 Mennonites were probably introduced to these new laws through a quotation from the exemption section published in *Unser Blatt* (Melitopol), 1 (Dec. 1925), 52. It was drawn from the complete text of the new law, which had appeared in the 25 September 1925 supplement to *Izvestiia*, no. 217.

49 For a brief discussion of this legislation, see Michael Garder, *A History of the Soviet Army* (New York 1966), 6–7.

50 From a report of C.F. Klassen to B.H. Unruh and A.J. Fast, dated 29 May 1926, in Canadian Mennonite Board of Colonization Records, Mennonite Heritage Centre Archives, Winnipeg, vol. 1317, file 900.

51 *Unser Blatt* (1925–8) was published by the *Kommission für Kirchenangelegenheiten*

(KfK), and *Praktischer Landwirt* (1925–6) by the central Mennonite office in Moscow.

52   The total number of persons who emigrated in 1923 – the first year of this move – was 2,759. The largest emigration, in 1926, numbered 5,940. See Toews, *Lost Fatherland*, 136ff., and Frank H. Epp, *Mennonite Exodus: The Rescue and Resettlement of the Russian Mennonites since the Communist Revolution* (Saskatoon 1962), 228–9.

53   See 'Protokoll der Allukrainischen Konferenz der Vertreter der Mennonitengemeinden in der USSR in Melitopol vom 5.–9. Oktober 1926,' *Unser Blatt*, 2 (Nov. 1926), 47–51.

54   Numerous reports from men serving during these years were published in Hans Rempel and George K. Epp, eds., *Waffen der Wehrlosen: Ersatzdienst der Mennoniten in der UdSSR* (Winnipeg 1980), 45ff.

55   See one analysis of these events in Roy A. Medvedev, *Let History Judge: The Origins and Consequences of Stalinism* (New York 1973), 71ff.

56   See J.K., 'Die mennonitische Jugend in Russland bekennt sich zur Roten Armee,' *Mennonitische Rundschau*, 51, 18 Nov. 1928, 3.

57   For a comprehensive collection of the 1929 Soviet religious legislation, see *Zakon o religioznykh obedineniiakh RSFSR i deistvuiushchie zakony, instruktsii, s otdelnymi kommentariiami* (Moscow 1930).

58   See A. Reinmarus (David Penner) and G. Frizen (Heinrich Friesen), *Mennonity* (Moscow 1930), and A. Reinmarus, *Anti-Menno: Beiträge zur Geschichte der Mennoniten in Russland* (Moscow 1930), 153–4.

59   A scholarly treatment of the 'flight to Moscow' and the context for it is in Harvey L. Dyck, 'Collectivization, Depression, and Immigration, 1929–1930: A Chance Interplay,' in H.L. Dyck and H. Peter Krosby, eds., *Empire and Nations: Essays in Honour of Frederic H. Soward* (Vancouver and Toronto 1969), 144ff.

60   Devi Prasad and Tony Smythe, eds., *Conscription: A World Survey. Compulsory Military Service and Resistance to It* (London 1968), 135.

61   Klippenstein, 'Mennonite Pacifism,' 322–27.

62   See Rempel and Epp, eds., *Waffen der Wehrlosen*, 102ff.

63   See, for example, Diedrich Hildebrand, 'Erlebnisse im waffenlosen Dienst in Russland,' *Der Bote*, 52, 1 April 1975, 9.

64   According to one oral source, all COs were released from service in 1937. See Peter H. Rempel, 'Mennonites and State Service in the USSR, 1917–1939,' unpublished paper, Conrad Grebel College, Waterloo, Ont., 1975, 12.

65   For an English translation, see Meisel and Kozera, eds., *Materials*, 242–67. The text of the constitution was first published in *Izvestiia* on 6 December 1936.

66   See K.Y. Voroshilov, 'O proekta zakona o vceobshchei voinskoi povinnosti,' *Voenniia Mysl* (Moscow) no. 9 (Sept. 1939), 5–11.

67   Ibid., cited in Prasad and Smythe, eds., *Conscription*, 135.

68 Conscientious objection in the Soviet Union and other areas of eastern Europe after
   1945 is discussed by Klippenstein, 'Conscientious Objectors in Eastern Europe: The
   Quest for Free Choice and Alternative Service,' in Sabrina Petra Ramet, ed., *Protes-*
   tantism and Politics in Eastern Europe and Russia: The Communist and Postcom-
   munist Eras (Durham and London 1992), 276–309.
69 One story of a Mennonite congregation's struggle in this regard is told in Heinrich
   Woelk and Gerhard Woelk, *A Wilderness Journey: Glimpses of the Mennonite Breth-*
   ren Church in Russia, 1925–1980, trans. Victor G. Doerksen (Fresno, Calif., 1982).
70 How Mennonites managed to reorganize and establish a semblance of community
   life after being liberated from Soviet special security regulations in 1955 is described
   in Walter Sawatsky, 'Mennonite Congregations in the Soviet Union Today,' *Menno-*
   nite Life, 33 (March 1978), 5–20. See also his essay, 'From Russian to Soviet Mennonites, 1941–1988,' in Friesen, ed., *Mennonites in Russia*, 299–338.

2

Russian Baptists and the Military Question, 1918–1929

PAUL D. STEEVES

For a short time in the first half of the 1920s people who promoted principles of non-violence dominated the leadership of the central administration of the Russian Baptist Union. The ascendancy of these men, most of them second-generation Baptists, became possible largely because of the success of Lenin's political revolution and the Bolsheviks' victory in the civil war following their seizure of state power in October 1917. The decline of pacifist influence over the administrative and creedal development of Russian Baptists coincided with the emergence of Stalin's domination of the Soviet Communist party.

The period when religious pacifism dominated the Russian Baptist Union proved to be an anomaly of a little more than five years in the history of the organization dating back to the 1880s. But its brevity does not mean that the pacifist interlude lacked significance. Baptist non-resistance of the 1920s signified the important role that ideas of non-violence played in the experience of sectarianism in Russia in the nineteenth and twentieth centuries. Furthermore, the memory of Russian evangelicals such as Karev, Levindanto, Orlov, Pavlov, and Zhidkov, associated with active objection to military service, endured into the second half of the twentieth century, when the All-Union Council of Evangelical Christians-Baptists served as successor to the Russian Baptist Union and the kindred-spirited Union of Evangelical Christians.[1]

The Russian Baptist Union arose in the 1880s to coordinate the activities of evangelical sectarian congregations in the south of Russia that went by various names, including Baptists, Shtundists, and Shtundo-Baptists. Before 1905 the union existed clandestinely, and so its structure was not well developed. Better organization became possible following the imperial grant of religious toleration in 1905. Annual congresses of representatives of Baptist congregations met, and there emerged an executive structure that oversaw the missionary activity that expanded the network of Baptist groups and that published the monthly journal *Baptist*. For a short time the Baptist movement enjoyed vigorous growth, and the Baptist Union extended its administrative reach into the northern cities of St Petersburg and Moscow. But after 1911 its work was devastated, first by reactionary repression of sectarian activity, then by world war, and finally by revolution and the subsequent disintegration of the empire as a result of civil war and foreign intervention.

After Lenin's government settled in Moscow in 1918, the acting minister of the local Baptist congregation undertook to reconstruct the Russian Baptist Union throughout territory that was coming under Bolshevik control. Pavel Vasil'evich Pavlov (1883–1935) was the son of one of the most effective agents of the spread of the Baptist movement throughout the Russian empire, V.G. Pavlov.[2] Assisted by Mikhail Danilovich Timoshenko (1884–1935?), Pavel Pavlov began to publish a Baptist magazine, *Slovo istiny* (Word of Truth), and to prepare for a congress of the union, which convened on 27 May 1920. That gathering, comprising fewer than three dozen representatives of Baptist congregations, elected Pavlov president of the executive board.[3]

The Pacifist Interlude

The ten-day congress in the spring of 1920 formally signalled the beginning of the pacifist interlude in the Russian Baptist Union. It reconstituted the union and defined its program for the new conditions in Russia, declaring that Baptists rejected military service. Specifically, the participants resolved that 'whereas ... the participation of Evangelical Christian Baptists in the shedding of human blood under every state system is a crime against conscience and the explicit teaching and spirit of Holy Scripture, and whereas for Evangelical Christian Baptists bearing of arms, or making of such for military purposes of any kind, as well as training in military affairs, would be equivalent to the actual shedding of blood ... [we] consider our sacred obligation to be to refuse military service in all of its forms.'[4]

That this attitude was shared by Baptists elsewhere was confirmed by a resolution adopted at the Kuban regional congress at the end of December 1920: 'To declare to all existing authorities and to all mankind that we, Evangelical Christian Baptists, on the basis of our evangelical convictions (Matt. 5.44), cannot participate in war and in any activity connected with it.' The Kuban meeting asserted that it based its position solely on scriptural teaching and that no other premises or sources underlay it.[5] By that caveat the Baptists apparently intended to distance themselves from both the politics of bolshevism and the ideologies of any other movement, such as Tolstoyism, that did not focus exclusively on the religious authority of Christian scriptures, as the Baptists claimed to do.

But adherence to principles of non-resistance and non-violence was not common to all Russian Baptist leaders. Some of the most influential figures from the pre-revolutionary years did not participate in the Moscow congress of 1920 and quickly rejected its action. The union's preceding congress had met in April 1917 in the southern Russian city of Vladikavkaz. It elected an executive council of ten men and appointed Dei Ivanovich Mazaev (d. 1922) president. Mazaev, a wealthy landowner, had been president of the union most of the years since its organization and imprinted his personality on it during its formative years, especially before legalization in 1905.[6] Mazaev and seven other council members were not in Moscow in 1920 because most of them were located on territory not controlled by Bolsheviks. Three of those eight absentees circulated an open letter among Baptist congregations following the Moscow congress alleging that it was not valid because it had been called by only two members of the council and without the approval of the president and other members of the administration.[7]

Two developments may explain the emergence of pacifism to a position of control in the Baptists' central administration. First, the ideas of pacifism held by those who exercised leadership from Moscow represented one of several influences that spurred the rise of the Baptist movement in Russia. Second, the steps by which the new leaders took power were facilitated by specific favourable policies of the Bolshevik government towards sectarian religious groups.

The confessional position of the Baptist Union before the Great War had stated: 'We consider ourselves obliged to perform military service when the government demands it of us.'[8] Not far below the surface of the official position, however, ran a strong pacifist current. This propensity reflected the influence of the Mennonites and Molokans on Baptists in the south. Since the Mennonites had given aid to the Shtundist movement in Ukraine, and because the original Baptists of the Caucasus came out of Molokan communities, there were natural conduits through which pacifist sentiments could flow into Baptist ranks. Baptists maintained close relations with both Mennonites and Molokans throughout the history of the Baptist Union. Pacifist tendencies were strengthened by Tolstoyan ideas at the end of the nineteenth century. Some editions of the Baptist Confession of Faith, reflecting the presence of pacifists within the denomination, even inserted a qualification on the official affirmation of military service, noting that Baptists 'can sincerely unite with those who do not share our convictions regarding ... military service.'[9] A secret report from a police commander in Tambov, dated 31 December 1913, stated that pacifism was found among Baptists.[10] During the First World War a list compiled by the Ministry of Internal Affairs named 114 Baptists who refused to enter the imperial army for religious reasons between 1914 and 1917.[11]

The number of Baptist conscientious objectors (COs) on the government's list represented only a tiny percentage of all potential Baptist inductees. But if the majority of Baptists were willing to serve in the army in the first years of the war, following the position of leaders of the union and particularly of the president, Mazaev, by the last days of the war pacifist sentiment was bubbling to the surface. In 1918 *Slovo istiny* ran a series of articles addressing the question: should a believer participate in military service?

The negative response dominated the discussion. One writer named Khromov argued that a believer deciding whether to participate in the shedding of blood should first understand the divine perspective on war. While he acknowledged that the Bible contained no clear prohibition of war, Khromov argued that wars in biblical times of which God approved 'always had a divine plan and their purpose was the glorification of the Lord.' Since modern wars were waged not 'for the glory of God, but only for the sake of earthly goals,' under such circumstances 'Christians cannot participate in any kind of shedding of blood, but they should always be at peace with everyone.' Another writer declared, 'War is murder and plunder. In no way can this evil be justified, for force remains force.'[12]

OSROG

Control of the Baptist periodical was in the hands of Pavel Pavlov, and the discussion mirrored his predilection. At the same time Pavlov played a major role in an organization that united the efforts of pacifist sectarians of various denominations, including Adventists, Evangelical Christians, Mennonites, and Tolstoyans, and he received favourable attention from the highest levels of the Bolshevik government. The Ob"edinenyi sovet religioznykh obshchestv i grupp, or OSROG (United Council of Religious Societies and Groups) was formed in 1918 by Leo Tolstoy's secretary Vladimir G. Chertkov (1854–1936), who was president. Pavlov served as vice-president, and Timoshenko also joined the council.[13]

In the Autumn of 1918 OSROG petitioned the government for a decree specifying the right of COs to be exempted from military service and assigned to perform some alternative form of service. Some young sectarians had been excused from military service by appealing to the decree of February 1918 separating church from state. While that decree declared that religious views could not be used to justify refusal to perform civic obligations, it provided for 'exceptions in individual cases by decision of a people's court.' But other conscripts had been imprisoned, and some even executed, when they tried to assert their right to be freed from violating their consciences by participation in combat.[14]

In October an order of the Bolshevik Revolutionary War Council signed by Leon Trotsky directed local officials to permit persons who could prove that their religious convictions prohibited military service to substitute medical service for combat duty.[15] But such advice apparently was not sufficient. When five Evangelical Christians were sentenced to death in Vladimir for their refusal to enter the Red Army, the government's supervisor of affairs, Vladimir D. Bonch-Bruevich, interceded for them directly with Lenin. As a result, Lenin ordered that a law providing for exemption from combat service be drafted for adoption by the Council of People's Commissars (Sovnarkom). Lenin appointed Chertkov a member of the drafting committee.[16]

The law, adopted by Sovnarkom on 4 January 1919, established for persons 'unable to participate in military service because of their religious convictions the right to substitute medical service for such service ... on the basis of a decision of a people's court.'[17] Of particular significance for the promotion of pacifist influence within the Russian Baptist Union, the law specified OSROG as official agent to certify for the courts the eligibility of COs for alternative service or even, in special cases, for 'complete exemption from military service without any substitution of another civic duty.' OSROG had received this assignment as a result of Chertkov's direct appeal to both Lenin and Trotsky.[18] It indeed did much to advance OSROG's prestige on territory controlled by the Red Army for the remainder of the civil war, especially within congregations of pacifist sectarians. Because Baptists played a prominent role in OSROG's fulfilment of its task, Baptist pacifists parlayed OSROG's prestige into control of the Baptist Union.[19]

Through a network of member councils throughout the territory held by the Red Army, OSROG obtained court rulings exempting thousands of young sectarians from military service. One estimate set the number at forty thousand from all sects, though this figure probably is exaggerated.[20] Agents of the Moscow OSROG were appointed to major cities to serve the surrounding provinces by providing information and support for men of draft age. Most of the 117 agents were Baptists, because the geographical distribution of Baptists was considerably greater than that of others sects represented in OSROG.[21] In many cases, the simple fact of a draftee's membership in a Baptist congregation was sufficient for OSROG to secure a favourable decision on a request for exemption, especially in the larger cities.[22] Ordained Baptist clergymen generally were exempted without any requirement of alternative service, on the basis of a declaration from their congregations that their services were irreplaceable and that 'believers would be deprived of the possibility of collectively satisfying their religious needs' if their pastors were sent off to the army.[23]

From the start, difficulties in implementing the provision for legal exemption from combat service boded ill for the pacifists. The indulgence towards sectarian pacifism that Lenin and Trotsky displayed was not shared by other Bolshevik leaders, especially not by provincial officials.[24] By the end of the summer of 1920, OSROG had compiled a list of sixty-six sectarians who had been executed by local authorities when they refused to serve in the Red Army, including a group of thirty-four Baptists in a village of Voronezh province in August 1920.[25] A Baptist from the village of Kalach named Yakovlev reported the repression in a letter to Pavlov. Pavlov took the information to Bonch-Bruevich, who wrote to the Commissariat of Justice on 26 October directing that body to investigate this 'completely obvious violation of the decree' on exemption.[26]

The commissariat did nothing to correct the injustice. Indeed, its personnel had from the start been among the most active opponents of the legal provision for alternative service.[27] Lenin had argued vigorously to coerce a reluctant faction of Sovnarkom to accept the exemption law. Even after its acceptance, opponents delayed the law's publication for almost five months while they did much to frustrate its implementation.[28] When, for example, in June 1919 a court in Petrograd reassigned three Baptists, K.Kh. Dunkur, P.F. Freimut, and P.I. Tugov, to non-combatant service away from the front, the commissariat demanded a judicial review of the decision. P.A. Krasikov, head of the division responsible for matters pertaining to religion, argued that the court had misapplied the decree because it based its decision merely on OSROG's testimony that the men were members of a Baptist congregation. Krasikov asserted that the decree required OSROG to certify the sincerity of objectors individually.[29]

The effectiveness of OSROG did not long survive the end of the civil war. In particular, its functioning ebbed in parallel with the decline of Lenin's health after 1921. A decree of 14 December 1920 rescinded its exclusive right to provide expert judgment for the courts regarding the sincerity of the religious convictions of those seeking exemption from military service. Joseph Stalin used his position as head of the party's Orgburo to cripple OSROG by means of a criminal trial of Chertkov's closest associate, Konstantin S. Shokhor-Trotskii (1892–1937).[30] The Orgburo instructed the Cheka to initiate prosecution of Shokhor-Trotskii on the charge that he acted illegally in the way he presented certification of the sincerity of objectors' convictions. The trial was held 14–18 March 1921.[31] Though the court concluded that the defendant had violated the law, he was not sentenced to prison. The trial demonstrated to OSROG that the pacifist council no longer enjoyed protection from Sovnarkom.

Baptist participation in OSROG lost most of its practical meaning when on 30 August 1921 the Commissariat of Justice issued a circular stating that courts could not grant exemption to men who became Baptists after 1919.[32] This prohibition was based on the suspicion that potential draftees used the Baptist congregations in order to evade conscription. The congress of the Baptist union in December 1921 decided that future cooperation with OSROG was not in the interest of Baptists.[33] A later directive from the justice commissariat in November 1923 sorely undermined the position of pacifists within the Baptist Union. It took the form of instructions for implementing the exemption law, but its effect was to nullify the Leninist provision of alternative service. The commissariat told courts that exemption could be granted only to members of sects that had included refusal of military service among their obligatory dogmas prior to the revolution and whose members had been convicted and punished for that refusal by the tsarist government. Such sects included Doukhobors, Mennonites, Molokans, and some Old Believers, but not Baptists.[34] The next month the Baptist Union officially changed its stated position on military service. That action culminated about two years of complex interplay between the Baptist Union and the Communists, who pressed the Baptists to reject pacifism, which the party portrayed as a matter of displaying political reliability.

Communist Pressure

The official pressure on the Baptists to give up their pacifism was expressed as early as 1921 by a significant voice. Bonch-Bruevich charged that the Baptists' unwillingness to serve in the military could not be a matter of sincere belief; so it must signify, he claimed, their hostility to the Soviet state. Since he had been the one who advocated the pacifists' cause in the inner circle of the government, his criticism of Baptist pacifism was especially ominous. The greatest vulnerability of the Baptist pacifists lay in their own confession of faith. Quoting the confession, Bonch-Bruevich argued that it was 'completely clear ... that an antimilitarist, nonresistance attitude is entirely unrelated to the essence of their belief.' He stated that either they should change their confession of faith or 'Baptists should fulfil their military obligation now.' Assuming that they would not revise their belief system, he charged that their supposed pacifism veiled their true political views, which were anti-Bolshevik because of the essentially bourgeois nature of the Baptist religion.[35]

In order to defend themselves against this kind of argument, the Baptists turned for support to the Baptist World Alliance (BWA). Their strategy was to send twenty-four delegates to the BWA's congress in Stockholm in July 1923 with a mandate to convince it to adopt a resolution that would 'defend the position, held by Russian Baptists,' by declaring 'the refusal by Baptists of all the world to participate in military service in any way.'[36]

BWA, however, rejected the proposal. The most that the Russians could salvage was a resolution expressing the 'sense of the horror and wickedness of war' that members of BWA felt, but leaving the choice between military service or pacifism to the individual's conscience. The resolution stated the gratitude of the congress 'that the Russian Soviet government accepts alternative service from those who on conscientious and religious grounds are unable to serve in the army.'[37]

When Pavel Pavlov had reported to the congress in Stockholm about the situation of the Baptists in Russia, he had evidently attempted to answer the Communists' charges. He began with the observation that Russia was terra incognita to most foreigners and that many absurd ideas about conditions there were circulating. Much of what he had heard, he said, in no way corresponded to reality and represented only 'tendentious fabrications.' He did not, however, specify the contents of such rumours, claiming that he did not have the time to refute them. He went on to recall the aid that Baptists of the world had sent to Russia during the recent famine, in response to the appeal from Russian Baptists, despite the attempts of many 'enemies of Soviet Russia' to prevent it. The aid had saved many from starvation, and, because of it, the name of the Baptists was appreciated and remembered with respect by the Russian people. Pavlov thus implied an answer to the Communist charge that the Baptists were hostile to the regime. They actually had resisted those who were hostile and had thereby served the interests of the Bolsheviks.

Pavlov then went to the heart of the charge that the Baptists were bourgeois and therefore servants of capitalist enemies of the Communist government. The Russian Baptist movement, he declared, was indigenous and self-sustaining. It grew up out of the 'depths of Russian sectarianism.' It was not some 'exotic growth, transplanted ... from abroad to Russian soil, but an original Russian phenomenon ... appearing as a protest against political and religious oppression.' This was the argument that Bonch-Bruevich himself had used years earlier to demonstrate that the sectarians were sympathetic to socialism.[38] Pavlov concluded that the Baptists should not be accused of serving foreign interests. Nor should they be charged with being essentially bourgeois and therefore inevitably hostile to socialism. 'The founders of Russian Baptism came out of this environment [i.e., of Russian sectarianism] that was ninety-five percent peasant in social composition.' The present economic condition of Baptist preachers showed that they still were part of the poor, labouring class who 'know all the needs and grief of their brothers.'

Stating that 'under Soviet rule full religious freedom has been declared,' Pavlov took special note of the decree concerning exemption from military service. It was, he said, 'an act overwhelming in its significance in the area of religious freedom.'[39] Pavlov seems here to have been challenging the Communists to continue to demonstrate their profession of guaranteeing liberty of conscience.

It was a commendable performance under the circumstances. By presenting an unqualifiedly favourable view of the Soviet government as regards freedom of conscience and a picture of the Russian Baptists as natural supporters of that state, Pavlov acted boldly in his attempt to retain for Baptists their right to remain pacifists and to continue to conduct religious activity freely. But if he dared to entertain the hope that the Communists would relent in their attempt to force the Baptists to abandon pacifism and declare unconditional submission to the regime, he was soon relieved of his illusions.

The Congress of 1923

For a full two years, since October 1921, the government had refused to grant Baptists permission to hold a congress of their union. Though the Baptist system envisioned annual congresses, the Baptists had not been permitted to convene one in 1922. The Baptist Union rescinded its call for a congress on 8 July 1923, just before its delegation departed for Stockholm.[40] The reason that the authorities withheld approval for a congress was suggested in September, when the chief anti-religious writer announced the price that the Communists assessed for a congress. In an article titled 'What Will the Baptists Say?' Emil'ian Yaroslavskii declared: 'The first task of a congress of Baptists will be to express itself on the question of their attitude towards the Soviet state and its protector, the Red Army. All evasions on this question are inappropriate.'[41] It seems that the Baptists could not meet in congress until the Communists were assured that the union would abandon its pacifism.

The congress convened in December 1923. Delegates debated the military question with intensity. The resolution finally adopted was an evident compromise that abandoned the firm pacifist stance of the 1920 congress but did not return fully to the Baptists' earlier recognition of military service: 'With respect to attitude towards military obligation and the means of its fulfilment, unity of views among Baptists has not been achieved. Recognizing war as the greatest evil and greeting the peaceful policy of the Soviet state and its call to the peoples of the world for universal disarmament, the congress leaves the determination of his own attitude towards the means of fulfilling his military obligation to the individual conscience of each Baptist. In line with this decision, the congress established 'that Baptists may fulfil their military obligation (1) by substituting public work, (2) by medical service in the army, and (3) by performance in the army of duties compatible with the convictions of each Baptist.' The congress also condemned the conduct of any 'antimilitarist propaganda with the goal of weakening the Red Army' and stipulated that any person who was guilty of doing such 'thereby excludes himself from membership in the Baptist brotherhood and stands alone before the law.' The resolution concluded with the assertion that Baptists had no intention of causing 'any kind of harm to the Soviet state and the Red Army.'[42]

This action ended the period of official pacifism in the Baptist Union. It apparently reflected the leaders' calculation that the change was a practical necessity for the good of the Baptist Union, undertaken to win from the Communist rulers permission to practise religion openly. Some of the delegates still refused to compromise their pacifism. Twelve of them were arrested by the secret police, the GPU.[43]

Continuing Disagreement

The compromise reached by the congress and administrative pressures did not eliminate disagreement within the Baptist Union on the subject. For a few more months pacifists continued to occupy influential positions in the union, and two factions became clearly identifiable – 'New Baptists' and 'Old Baptists.'[44] Both sides accepted the union's official statement of support for the Soviet state: 'The congress affirms the unfailingly loyal attitude of Baptists to the Soviet government ... and, recognizing that it really strives sincerely to protect the interests of the working people, considers it inadmissible for Baptists to participate in unions and organizations which pursue the overthrow of existing authority.'[45] The New Baptists, headed by Pavlov and Timoshenko, continued to argue that believers should not participate in combat and that individual Baptists should take advantage of the law providing exemption. The Old Baptist, headed by Pavel Ivanov-Klyshnikov (1886–1941), maintained that Baptist doctrine always had correctly required believers to serve in the army when called. These three men made up the executive board of the union elected by the 1923 congress.[46]

In February 1924 the council of the union issued a circular letter to Baptists of the Soviet Union. The careful wording showed that the New Baptists still held a slight edge in the union's leadership. The letter acknowledged that Christians were instructed by the Word of God 'to fulfil their obligations with respect to the state, including military service.' But since 'Baptists are sons of freedom,' no Baptist organization had the authority to determine how individual believers might fulfil those obligations. Consequently the union should not declare that Baptists will serve in the army, nor should it adopt a pacifist position, especially since the latter created serious problems for Baptists in their relations with the surrounding society. Therefore the council acknowledged that the state acted correctly when it examined closely every person who called himself a Baptist when he applied for alternative service.[47]

This letter, like the congress, showed signs of compromise between the two factions. Some of the Old Baptists on the council, from the south of Russia, where this faction appears to have been the strongest, registered their dissent from the text when they signed the letter. A regional congress of Baptists held in Tsaritsyn in February emphatically rejected 'that indefinite line' adopted by the leadership and 'advocated full performance of military service by Baptists of the USSR.'[48]

The state apparently continued to intervene in the dispute, weakening further the position of the New Baptists. Throughout 1924 the Baptists failed to receive from the government permission either to publish a journal or to convene a congress, two things that they very much desired to do. At the end of the year the plenum of the council met in Moscow and carried out what Sergei Belousov called a 'revolution.' It abolished the executive board appointed by the congress a year earlier, thus removing Pavlov from the presidency. In place of the board the council appointed a president. In the resolution carrying out this change, adopted by a vote of twenty-eight to five, the plenum stated: 'In view of the changed conditions and for greater fruitfulness in our spiritual work, the plenum considers it necessary, and itself competent, to return to the former system of administration in the form of a president with two assistants.'[49]

As president of the union the council selected Il'ia Andreevich Goliaev (1859–1942), who had held that office in 1910. Pavlov and Nikolai V. Odintsov (1870–1935) were named his assistants. At the same time three of Pavlov's colleagues, Levindanto, Shilov, and Timoshenko, were arrested by the government and sentenced to a year in exile.[50]

The change in leadership made the influence of the two factions nearly equal at the centre. Odintsov was an Old Baptist. Goliaev, who was the oldest member of the council at sixty-five, appears to have been a compromise choice. It is not difficult to identify evidence of state's pressure behind the action of the council. Immediately after Goliaev had been appointed president, permission to begin publishing a Baptist magazine arrived, while the council was still meeting.

During 1925 the New Baptists made several attempts to argue their case against the Old Baptists and defend themselves before the state. The Baptist journal printed a long memorandum, written during the war by a governor of Astrakhan and marked 'top secret,' instructing the police to observe Baptists closely. The writer alleged that Baptists were the sect that was 'most harmful for the political and religious life of the country' because they rejected military service. He quoted the Russian Baptist journal as saying in 1911: 'War for us is a crime.'[51] This memo's publication in 1925 served the New Baptists' cause by demonstrating that pacifism was not a novel, post-revolutionary phenomenon among Baptists, implying that those who were pacifists were not counter-revolutionary. In fact, the political and economic views of New Baptists were more sympathetic to socialism and hostile to capitalism than were those of the Old Baptists. In June, at a conference of the Siberian section of the Baptist Union, the president, A.S. Anan'in, reflected the New Baptists' position when he said that Baptists must obey all the laws including 'the substitution of socially useful work for the military obligation, in accordance with existing laws on this subject.'[52]

To support the position of the New Baptists, Pavlov participated in the release of a document composed by a Tolstoyan writer named Tregubov, which argued that sectarians who opposed military service were not enemies of the Communists, but 'some of the best coworkers in soviet-communist construction.' Echoing the Baptist circular letter, the article welcomed careful review of each claim for exemption to ascertain the sincerity of the objector. The loyalty to the Soviet regime of those sincere sectarians who requested exemption was demonstrated, the document affirmed, by their rejection of private property and 'readiness to be builders of the new soviet-communist life.'[53]

The New Baptists sought to demonstrate that Baptists who were pacifists for religious reasons should not be suspected of oppositionist attitudes towards the Soviet government. They willingly submitted to its laws, including that which gave them the right to be exempted from combat duty.

But the government apparently did not want to have advocates of pacifism in the leadership of the Baptist Union. No permission for a congress was forthcoming in 1925. At the end of the year Pavlov was forced from office. At the plenum of the council in December he resigned 'for reasons of health.' A year later Odintsov acknowledged that health was not the real reason for the change. Nor, he added, did Pavlov have disagreements in principle with President Goliaev.[54]

Goliaev himself seems to have displeased the authorities. The council decided to convoke a congress in October 1926, but permission was not obtained. The state eventually approved a gathering for December only after Goliaev had been removed from office. At the September 1926 session of the council, he was relieved of his responsibilities 'on account of disability' and succeeded by Odintsov. In this case as well, Odintsov later reported, disability was not the reason. Goliaev was removed because of 'a situation that did not correspond to the needs of our work.'[55] It seems probable that this 'situation' was that he did not give the state assurances that when the Baptist Union met in congress it would issue an unqualified rejection of pacifism.

The 1926 Congress

With Goliaev removed, the union met in December 1926 for what proved to be its last congress. (Of course, the Baptists did not know at the time that no more congresses would be permitted and that the state would crush their union in the 1930s.) The military question occupied the minds of participants. Pavel Datsko wrote that wherever a group of them gathered, the conversation focused on this 'burning issue.' All delegates, he said, had a desire 'to settle this tormenting question somehow, in order never again to return to it.'[56]

In his presidential address on the second day, Odintsov went straight to the heart of the matter. Recalling the decision of the 1923 congress that stated the loyalty of the union to the Soviet state and rejecting anti-militarist propaganda, he declared that if any delegate comported himself in such a way as to contradict either 'the spirit or letter' of that decision, he would be considered a provocateur, intent on disrupting the work of God in Russia and 'the unity of the people of God.'[57]

In contrast to 1923, Old Baptists clearly dominated the congress. Ivanov-Klyshnikov made the principal presentation on military service. He observed that disagreement on this matter had become so acute that many 'brothers and sisters' could not bear even to hear the phrase. Some considered those who became soldiers 'traitors and apostates.' This was strange, he said, since as recently as ten years previously Baptists had entered the army and engaged in battle. Ivanov-Klyshnikov traced the steps by which pacifism rose to the dominant position in the Baptist Union, treating it as an aberration in Baptist history produced by revulsion against the horrors of the civil war and the political decision of Lenin's government to accommodate pacifist inclinations among sectarians. But pacifism, he said, was not a Baptist principle in that it comported neither with the 'Word of God nor the views and past practice of the brotherhood of Baptists.'

As long as the Baptists presented themselves as a pacifist sect, Ivanov-Klyshnikov asserted, they were 'in a completely impossible position with respect to society and the government.' In the interest of retaining for the Baptist Union its freedom of activity it was necessary for the congress to reject pacifism forthrightly. Ivanov-Klyshnikov then delivered an exposition of his view of biblical teaching concerning war, arguing that since God had commanded people to fight wars it could not be a sin to be a soldier. 'I call all of you,' he concluded, 'returning under the old and tested banner of Baptism, to stand on ... the firm and stable foundation of the Word of God.'

Yakov Vins (1874–1944) delivered a major address supporting the Old Baptist position. Then general discussion followed. Twenty delegates reserved time to speak to the issue, forcing the discussion into a second day. Debate was vigorous. One delegate reported that the body divided into two almost equal parts. It often seemed that the question would not be settled. 'At such a time the heart was terror struck and it feared for the general work which in such moments seemed to be concentrated on this one ill-fated question.' Datsko told of one

Baptist, V.V. Skaldin, seated throughout the congress in a 'modest place at the entrance,' who walked to the front of the hall during the controversy and declared, 'Brothers, we must bury this military question here.'[58]

The breakthrough came when one delegate asked for the relevant article of the Baptist confession to be read. Someone then suggested that the congress merely reaffirm the article as it stood. This suggestion was accepted almost immediately. A resolution was drawn up:

Having discussed the question concerning the relationship to the state and to military service, and taking into consideration (1) that the resolutions of the congress of Baptists in recent years (beginning from 1920) brought to this question unclarity and indefiniteness and a direction alien to the views of Baptists, which has led to the fact that anarchistic elements have appeared within the ranks of Baptists; (2) that the Soviet government has implemented in its legislation full freedom of belief, guaranteeing the free fulfillment of the requirements of our Christian faith, which obligates us to have a precise and clear definition of our attitude towards this power and towards the fulfillment of all civic duties; and (3) that among these duties Baptists always have recognized, and now recognize, the performance of military service on an equal basis with all citizens, which is expressed in the thirteenth article of our Confession of Faith, published in 1906; therefore the 26th All-Union Congress of Baptists of the USSR resolves: In abrogation of the resolutions of the all-Russian congresses of Baptists in 1920 and 1923, and all explanations apropos the attitude of Baptists towards the government and military obligation made before this time, to adopt the Thirteenth Article of the Confession of Faith of Baptists, published in 1906.[59]

The resolution then quoted the entire article. When the vote was taken, only nine of the 230 votes cast were negative. Datsko later reported that most Baptists were satisfied with the outcome because the issue had been decided 'not by any new interpretation but, on the contrary, by a rejection of all new resolutions on this question and a return to the former Baptist understanding.'[60] The 'new resolutions' included the position that the Old Baptists proposed.[61] Most members of both factions could agree on the formulation of their predecessors that was sanctified in their memories by the sufferings they had endured together under the tsarist autocracy. Still, some rejected the change and withdrew from the union, creating a separate pacifist Baptist sect of 'Red Gate Groups,' so named because it was in the Red Gate section of Moscow that they organized.[62]

Decline and Fall

The 1926 congress made a substantial change in the structure of the Baptist

Union, replacing a centralized administration with a federated structure. The new constitution provided for creation of 'independent and equal' local unions of Baptists, united voluntarily in the Federated Union of Baptists of the USSR. Initially the federation comprised eight regional unions.[63] The new federated union never held a congress in the nine years up to the time the state destroyed it in 1935.

Congresses of regional unions, as they met throughout 1927 to reorganize under the new structure, confirmed the position on military service taken by the 1926 congress.[64] New Baptists, led by Pavlov, tried to organize a regional union centred on Moscow, but they had problems doing so.[65] To lay the foundation of the 'Union of Baptist Congregations of the Central Provinces of Russia,' a temporary committee of the region convened a conference in June 1927. Pavlov, Dovgoliuk, Skaldin, and Timoshenko presented reports dealing with a complex of political and social questions. The result was adoption of a 'Declaration Concerning the Establishment and Defence of a Just Social Order.' In order to acquit themselves of the charge that Baptist pacifists were motivated by hostility to the Soviet system when they refused to bear arms, the declaration used strong words to advocate socialism as 'that form of human society that most corresponds to evangelical ideals.' It called the Soviet government 'the most honest and steadfast champion' of the socialist order and said that Baptists should support it. Even more, they should defend it by all means consistent with the dictates of conscience against 'the anti-God beast arising out of the abyss, called Capitalism in our era, which is armed with a warmaking machine, called Militarism.'[66]

The conference designated Timoshenko president of the regional union. But the council of the Federated Union of Baptists, meeting in August 1927, declined permission for him to participate as a voting member of the council. While the council conceded that the position taken by the New Baptists on military service did not differ significantly from that of the 1926 congress, it said that the rationale for the declaration 'expressed views alien and contradictory to the Word of God and the doctrine of Baptists of all countries.'[67]

Though the New Baptists were more forthright than the Old Baptists in their advocacy of socialism, they were the first to suffer when the storm of repression of religion instigated by Stalin broke out. In early 1928 the newspaper *Trud* (Labour) charged that Pavlov was a Menshevik and Timoshenko an anarchist.[68] Soon afterward Pavlov was arrested and exiled. His family was deprived of its apartment in Moscow. In 1936 he was killed in exile.[69] Timoshenko also was arrested. He was released to work briefly with Odintsov in the Moscow office of the union in 1930 but soon was sent into exile, and he never returned.[70]

Conclusion

The distinct period when pacifist views dominated the administration of the Russian Baptist Union coincided with a time of extraordinary numerical growth in participation in the Baptist movement. From fewer than 100,000 adherents in 1917, membership increased to about a quarter-million in 1922 and approximately a half-million by 1926.[71] It is impossible to establish a causal relationship between Baptist pacifism and the movement's expansion. But it is understandable that the Baptists' success in attracting a remarkable number of the ordinary people of Soviet Russia would impel the government, concerned about its military requirements, to ensure that the network of Baptist congregations would not serve as a haven for a growing number of young men avoiding service in the Red Army. As a result, the young Baptist leaders who advocated both pacifism and socialism and to whom events gave temporary control of the Baptist Union surrendered their positions in the union and quickly lost their personal freedom.

Lenin and Trotsky allowed the evangelical sectarians to practise their pacifist convictions, calculating that thereby they could win sectarian support for the Bolshevik cause when it was under threat from the White Armies in the civil war. In this calculation they seemed justified. But when the terms of the contest changed, and the Baptists' success in mobilizing the masses challenged the totalitarian pretensions of the Bolsheviks who exercised power after Lenin and Trotsky, the pacifists were doomed to oblivion. The pacifist domination of the Baptist Union proved to be little more than a revolutionary interlude.

NOTES

Much of the research for this essay was made possible by support from the (U.S.) National Endowment for the Humanities Summer Seminar for College Teachers.

1 In 1971 the principal Soviet anti-religious journal published an article specifically responding to contemporary appeals among Baptists to the precedents of conscientious objection to military service from the early 1920s. Z. Kalinicheva, 'Baptizm i voennaia sluzhba,' *Nauka i religiia*, no. 2 (1971), 18–20. Walter Sawatsky, *Soviet Evangelicals since World War II* (Scottdale, Pa., 1981), 120, gives information about COs among Baptists in the 1970s.

2 'P.V. Pavlov,' *Bratskii vestnik* (Moscow), no. 5 (1983), 54.

3 The other four members of the board were Timoshenko, Pavlov's father, I.N. Shilov, and P. Melis. *Slovo istiny* (Moscow), no. 5–6 (1920), 43; no. 1–2 (1921); 'Zapis' zasedaniia kollegii soveta baptistov RSFSR,' 18 March 1922; Southern Baptist His-

torical Commission (SBHC), 'Historical Papers of Mrs. Neprash on Religion in Russia' (microfilm); *Bratskii vestnik*, no. 1 (1945), 25.

4 'Otchet vserossiiskogo s"ezda evangel'skikh khristian-baptistov' 24, quoted in Z. Kalinicheva, *Sotsial'naia sushchnost' baptizma* (Leningrad 1972), 56.

5 *Slovo istiny*, nos. 1–2 (1921), 12.

6 N.A. Levindanto, 'Pamiati Deia Ivanovicha Mazaeva' *Bratskii vestnik*, nos. 2–3 (1953), 95.

7 'Kratkii otchet o vserossiiskom s"ezde baptistov' *Slovo istiny*, nos. 5–6 (1921), 38; *Pervyi svobodnyi s"ezd russkikh baptistov vsei Rossii* (Baku 1917), 3.

8 Confession of Faith, Article XIII, *Baptist* (Rostov-on-Don), no. 8 (1908), 1–2.

9 Quoted in *Entsiklopedicheskii slovar'*, (Moscow 1911), 4: col. 610.

10 A.I. Klibanov, 'Sovremennoe sektantstvo v tambovskoi oblasti,' *Voprosy istorii religii i ateizma* (Moscow), 8 (1960), 81, citing Tambovskii oblastnoi istoricheskii arkhiv.

11 F.M. Putintsev, *Politicheskaia rol' i taktika sekt* (Moscow 1935), 97.

12 S. Khromov, 'Khristianstvo i voennaia sluzhba' *Slovo istiny*, nos. 9–12 (1918), 88–9; V. Mamontov, 'Otnoshenie khristian k voine,' ibid., no. 14 (1918), 102.

13 Otdel rukopisei Rossisskoi gosudarstvennoi biblioteki (ORRGB), Moscow, f. 435 k. 61 ed. 10; Chertkov's mother was a patron of the Baptists in St Petersburg. *Fond* 435 contains the extensive Chertkov Papers.

14 V.M. Martsinkovskii, *Zapiski veruiushchego* (Prague 1929), 92; Waldemar Gutsche, *Religion und Evangelium in Sowjetrussland* (Kassel 1959), 26.

15 Gosudarstvennyi arkhiv Rossiiskoi Federatsii (GARF), f. 130, op. 3, ed. 765, 1. 10.

16 V.D. Bonch-Bruevich, 'O tom, kak sozdalsia dekret ob osvobozhdenii ot voinskoi povinovesti po religioznam ubezhdeniam' 4 May 1933, ORRGB, f. 369, k. 37, d. 2, 1. 32–4; *Leninskii sbornik* (Moscow 1933), 24: 187; V.G. Chertkov, 'Zapiska o neobkhodimosti otmeny tsirkuliara narkomiusta ot 5 noia. 1923, "O poriadke razbora dlia osvobozhdenii ot voennoi sluzhby po rel. ubezh,"' 9 June 1924, ORRGB, f. 435, k. 78, ed. 50.

17 *Sobranie uzakonenii i rasporiazhenii raboche-krestianskogo pravitel'stva*, 1919 (Petrograd 1920), 109; English translation of the law is in 'Conscientious Objection, Leninist Decree Providing for,' in Paul D. Steeves, ed., *Modern Encyclopedia of Religions in Russia and the Soviet Union* (Gulf Breeze, Fla., 1993), 5: 223–6.

18 Tsentralnyi gosudarstvenyi arkhiv (TsGA), f. 353, op. 3, ed. 780, 1. 25.

19 P. Ivanov-Klyshnikov, 'Ob otnoshenii k gosudarstvu i voennoi sluzhbe' *26-oi vsesoiuznyi s"ezd baptistov SSSR* (Moscow 1927), 103–4; I.V. Dovgoliuk, 'Baptisty i sotsial'noe neravenstvo,' 3, in Southern Baptist Historical Commission, 'Historical Papers of Mrs. Neprash.'

20 Klibanov, *Sektantstvo i sovremennost'* (Moscow 1969), 203; cf. R.M. Iliukhina, *Rossiiskii patsifizm vchera i segodnia* (Moscow 1992), 33; A.B. Roginskii,

ed., *Vospominaniia kresti'ian-tolstovtsev, 1910–1930-e gody* (Moscow 1989), 465–7.

21 The Baptists who worked as OSROG agents included the following: in Petrograd, Ivan Shilov; in Novgorod, Karl Bravinsky and Yakov Dubel'zar; in Kazan', Fedor Belousov; in Astrakhan, Mikhail Shishkin; in Tsaritsyn, Timofei Reztsov (he worked with Yakov Zhidkov, who was to become the first president of the postwar Union of Evangelical Christians-Baptists); in Samara, Nikolai Levindanto; in Pskov, Karl Grigorovich and Nikolai Morgunov; in Tula, Nikolai Odintsov; in Tambov, Pavel Malin; in Penza, Klausnits; in Saratov, Grigory Morokov; in Orenburg, Waldemar Gutsche; in Orsk district, Ivan Dovgoliuk; in Novokhopersk district, Vasily Stepanov; in Voronezh, Ivan Shishkin; in Gomel, Mina Kravchenko; in Kiev, Dementy Pravoverov; in Ekaterinoslav, Vasily Skaldin; in Omsk, Grigory Ostapets; in Piatigorsk, Vasily Martynov. ORRGB, f. 435 k. 61, ed. 13.

22 'Protokoly s"ezda 6–8 iunia 1920,' ORRGB, f. 435, k. 62, ed. 6, 1. 3; P.V. Gidulianov, ed., *Otdelenie tserkvi ot gosudarstva v SSSR* (Moscow 1926), 383; Z.V. Kalinicheva, *Sotsial'naia sushchnost'*, 54.

23 *Slovo istiny*, nos. 5–6 (1921), 45.

24 P. Pavlov, 'Svoboda sovesti na mestakh,' *Slovo istiny*, nos. 5–6 (1920), 41.

25 TsGA, f. 353, op. 3, ed. 780, 1. 29–44.

26 Ibid., 1. 11, 79.

27 Chertkov, 'Zapiska ... ,' 1. 12.

28 'Protokoly malogo soveta narodnykh komissarov i material k nym' GARF, f. 130, op. 3, ed. 765; Bonch-Bruevich, 'Kak sozdalsia,' 38–40; 'Ob otnoshenii V.I. Lenina k sektantskomu dvizheniiu,' ORRGB, f. 435, k. 67, ed. 28, 1. 1; Mark Popovskii, *Russkie muzhiki rasskazyvaiut: Posledovateli L.N. Tolstogo v Sovetskom Soiuze 1918–1977* (London 1983), 71.

29 TsGA, f. 353, op. 3, ed. 783, 1. 30.

30 Ibid., op. ed. 414, 1. 13.

31 'Materialy sudebnogo razbiratel'stva po delu K.S. Shokhor-Trotskogo,' protokol no. 31, ORRGB, f. 435, k. 89, ed. 11, 1. 1–15.

32 ORRGB, f. 435, k. 78, ed. 20, 1. 8.

33 *Slovo istiny*, nos. 5–6 (1921), 45.

34 Circular of NKIu, no. 237, 5 November 1923, ORRGB, f. 435, k. 78, ed. 20, 1. 11; Gidulianov, *Otdelenie tserkvi*, 387. The commissariat's action effectively terminated the activity of OSROG; letter of Chertkov to Institute of V.I. Lenin, ORRGB, f. 369, k. 363, ed. 17, 1. 28; Chertkov, 'Zapiska ... ,' 17.

35 Bonch-Bruevich, 'Krivoe zerkalo sektantstva,' *Izbrannye ateisticheskie proizvedeniia* (Moscow 1973), 293.

36 'Zapis' zasedaniia kollegii soveta baptistov RSFSR', no. 45, 14 Sept. 1922; no. 73, 16 May 1923.

37 W.T. Whitley, ed., *Third Baptist World Congress* (London, 1923), xxx–xxxi.

38 Bonch-Bruevich, 'Raskol i sektantstvo v Rossii,' *Izbrannye sochineniia* (Moscow 1959), 174–5, 185–8.

39 'Doklad Pavlova,' *Baptist* (Moscow), no. 3 (1925), 7.

40 'Zapis' zasedaniia kollegii soveta baptistov RSFSR,' no. 73 (16 May 1923), no. 74 (13 June 1923). A congress planned for September 1922 was also cancelled; 'Zapis' zasedaniia kollegii soveta baptistov RSFSR,' no. 27 (22 March 1922), no. 42 (14 Sept. 1922).

41 E. Iaroslavskii, 'Chto skazhut baptisty?' *O religii* (Moscow 1957), 44–5.

42 *Izvestiia* (Moscow), 9 Dec. 1923, 4.

43 Gutsche, *Religion und Evangelium*, 46, 116.

44 Dovgoliuk, 'Baptisty,' 3.

45 *Pravda* (Moscow), 9 Dec. 1923, 3.

46 'Sendschreiben des allrussischen Baptistenbundes,' in Gutsche, *Religion und Evangelium*, 124; Dovgoliuk, 'Baptisty,' 3.

47 'Sendschrieben ... ,' 123.

48 *Pravda*, 10 Feb. 1924, 4.

49 *26-oi vsesoiuznyi s"ezd*, 29.

50 'Protokol zasedaniia plenuma soveta soiuza baptistov SSSR, 5 Dekabria 1925 goda v Moskve,' Southern Baptist Historical Commission, 'Historical Papers of Waldemar Gutsche on Religion in Russia and Poland' (microfilm).

51 'Iz proshlogo,' *Baptist*, nos. 4–5 (1925), 56–7.

52 S.V. Belousov, 'Pervyi nazidatel'nyi s"ezd baptistov v Omske,' *Baptist*, nos. 6–7, 1925, 39.

53 *Bezbozhnik* (6 Dec. 1925), 2, quoted in Putintsev, 358–9.

54 'Protokol ... 5 Dekabria 1925,' 1–3; N.V. Odintsov, 'Otchet pravleniia soiuza baptistov SSSR,' *26-oi vsesoiuznyi s"ezd*, 29.

55 Odintsov, 'Otchet,' 29.

56 P.Ia. Datsko, '26-i vsesoiuznyi s"ezd baptistov v Moskve,' *Baptist Ukrainy*, no. 2 (1927), 47.

57 Odintsov, 'Otchet,' 28–30.

58 Datsko, '26-i vsesoiuznyi s"ezd,' 49.

59 *26-oi vsesoiuznyi s"ezd*, 13–5.

60 Datsko, '26-i vsesoiuznyi s"ezd,' 49.

61 Dovgoliuk, 'Baptisty,' 3.

62 Putintsev, 'Politicheskaia rol,' 355.

63 *26-oi vsesoiuznyi s"ezd*, 93–7.

64 *Baptist*, no. 8 (1927), 27; no. 9 (1927), 21, 25.

65 'Zapis' zasedanii soveta federativnogo soiuza baptistov SSSR,' *Baptist*, no. 8 (1927), 24.

66 'Deklaratsiia ob ustanovlenii i zashchite spravedlivogo obshchestvennogo stroia,' in Southern Baptist Historical Commission, 'Historical Papers of Mrs. Neprash.'

67 'Zapis' zasedaniia kollegii soveta baptistov SSSR,' no. 14 (10–12 Aug. 1927).

68 Reprinted in *Maiak* (Moscow), no. 5 (1928), 6–7; German translation in Gutsche, *Religion und Evangelium*, 125–8.

69 'V.V. Pavlova,' *Bratskii vestnik*, no. 3 (1991), 76.

70 W. Gutsche, 'Aufzeichnungen über meine Reise nach der Union der soz. Sowjet Republiken,' 9, Historical Papers of Waldemar Gutsche; Gutsche, *Religion und Evangelium*, 27, 89.

71 'Zapis' zasedaniia kollegii soveta baptistov RSFSR, no. 19, 24 February 1922'; *Baptist*, nos. 1–2 (1926), 11; no. 1 (1927), 21; A.A. Rudenko, 'Evangel'skie khristiane-baptisty i perestroika v SSSR,' D.E. Furman and Mark Smirnov, eds., *Na puti k svobode sovesti* (Moscow 1989), 345.

3

Pacifism and Conscientious Objection in Finland, 1918–1945

THOMAS HACKMAN AND KATJA HUUMO

The Roots of Finnish Pacifism

The Grand Duchy of Finland was under Russian rule from 1809 to 1917, and the organized peace movement established itself there rather late. By the end of the nineteenth century pacifist ideas, especially those of Leo Tolstoy, had begun to spread to Finland. In addition, sectarian pacifism of Western origin appeared for the first time, including the pacifism of Baptists and Seventh-day Adventists.[1] In 1898, Suomen Rauhanyhdistys (Finnish Peace Association) was formed on the initiative of Jean Boldt, but there are no traces of its actually functioning.[2] The first proper peace organization, the so-called first Suomen Rauhanliitto (Finnish Peace Union) was established in 1907, but it was banned in 1913 by Governor-General Seyn.

Conscription had been introduced in Finland in 1881 by the law of 1878, but there is very little documentation on conscientious objection before 1900. From discussions in the Finnish Diet, there seem at that time to have been very few conscientious objectors (COs), and these were all members of certain religious sects. It is probable that the army dealt with them in a way that did not lead to prison sentences. For, though conscientious objection was not recognized by law, the army could assign conscripts to non-combatant duties. In any case, conscription was selective, with only about 7 per cent of the male population actually having to serve in the army.[3]

In 1901, as part of a russification campaign, the Finnish army was incorporated into the Russian army. This led to a strong campaign against conscription, involving massive civil disobedience. In 1902, 58 per cent of the young men failed to register for conscription. The campaign was successful, and conscription was abolished in 1905.[4] This result, of course, was not due only to the campaign but reflected the political crisis of the regime.

Though most of the people involved in the campaign against conscription were far from being pacifists, a few of them, mainly Tolstoyans, opposed military service for pacifist reasons. The Tolstoyans thus formed the first group in Finland to advocate conscientious objection as a step towards ending war.

By the time of independence in 1917, pacifism had spread within the workers' movement and among liberal intellectuals, as well as in the women's movement, the churches, and a range of religious and youth organizations. And it included among its adherents members of both the Finnish-speaking majority and the Swedish-speaking minority. But the pacifists naturally formed a very small minority within these groups. Nevertheless, the fact that Finland had got rid of conscription provided a favourable background for conscientious objection. In this essay we look at pacifism between the wars, conscientious objection in the same period, and COs and pacifists during the Second World War.

Pacifism, 1918–1939

Pacifists and the Civil War, 1918

Finland became independent in December 1917 but faced a civil war in the spring of 1918. Before and during this war, the so-called Vaasa senate (the 'white' side) organized call-ups (referring to the law of 1878), but at least 8,000, possibly as many as 25,000, of the men summoned to arms failed to report for service.[5]

Since both sides in the civil war in practice introduced some sort of conscription in the areas they controlled, there were cases of conscientious objection with regard to both the 'white' and the 'red' armies. Punishment could be very severe, and certainly at least some deserters were shot. Cases of conscientious objection are, however, very poorly documented. In the literature usually only the case of two Tolstoyans, the brothers Akseli and Eelo Isohiisi who were shot on the red side, is mentioned.[6]

The civil war, lasting from the end of January to mid-May 1918, involved atrocities on both sides. All in all, at least 17,000 people were killed during or just after the war, while another 12,500 died of disease and starvation in the prison camps after the victory of the white side. The cruelty of the war also inspired some pacifist action. On the red side there were instances when the socialists were not keen on using arms. Perhaps the best-known case took place in Oulu, where the railway worker and trade union leader Yrjö Kallinen (1886–1976) managed to minimize the violence after the red side had taken over the city. Kallinen also succeeded in making an agreement to surrender without fighting when the militarily superior white army approached. But the white army then broke the agreement, insisting on using arms. Paradoxically, Kallinen was sentenced to death (later changed to a prison sentence, which he served in the horrible conditions of the post–civil war prison camps) for allegedly being part of the 'red uprising.' After being released from jail Kallinen more or less withdrew from political activities but still remained an important figure for the peace movement.

There were others too who worked on the basis of reconciliation, such as Mathilda Wrede (1864–1928). Wrede, an aristocrat by birth and a Christian pacifist by conviction, became a leading figure in the Fellowship of Reconciliation (FOR) in Finland; she symbolized this work by having a red and a white flower in one vase on a table in her room.[8] The civil war had the same effect on Finnish peace activism as did the First World War on a European scale. Many pacifist activists of the 1920s had committed themselves to non-violence as a result of their recent experiences of war.

The Pacifist Movement of the Early Republic

Religious Groups Favouring Conscientious Objection
Though the Tolstoyans were never organized in a movement of their own and were never very numerous, they had great influence, especially on Finnish religious pacifism. The most famous Finnish Tolstoyan was the novelist Arvid Järnefelt (1861–1932), who in 1917 stirred a lot of attention with his radical pacifist speeches in churches. Later, when conscription was reintroduced, Järnefelt publicly called on young men to refuse army service. Other well-known Tolstoyans were two army officers, Georg Fraser (1849–1937) and Oscar von Schoultz (1872–1947),[9] who had both left the imperial army when they became pacifists. Though Tolstoyism was no longer very visible by the twenties and thirties, its indirect influence continued on practically all social movements, sections of the state churches, and some religious sects. In particular, its advocacy of conscientious objection shaped the evolution of religious pacifism in Finland.[10]

While sectarian pacifism had appeared in Finland at the end of the nineteenth century, it was not until independence that a confrontation with the state arose for COs over conscription. The people first to take an initiative in the matter were the Skutnabbists, who in 1917 began to protest against plans for reintroducing conscription. Named after Akeseli Skutnabb (1875–1929), they formed a rather unorganized movement, which had developed from the Darbyite Free Church (offshoot of the Plymouth Brethren). The Skutnabbists were particularly active in demanding the right to conscientious objection during the years

1918–20.[11] Although many COs in the period were Skutnabbists, the group as such ceased fairly soon to be actively involved in this matter. Kristillinen työväenliitto (Christian Workers' Union) was also a strong supporter of conscientious objection. Some of its local sections demanded a pledge from their members not to participate in any armed forces.

There have never been any Mennonites in Finland, but a small group of Quakers appeared during the interwar years; however, in 1939 there were only nine Quakers in Finland.[12] Still, some of them, such as Deryck Sivén, exercised a great influence in the peace movement. The Quakers also had an indirect influence in Finland through their general impact on Western pacifism.

The other pacifistically oriented churches were silent concerning conscription. The Free Church made some proposals concerning the right to conscientious objection but kept its official position neutral towards military service.[13] The Adventists, Baptists, Methodists, and Pentecostals – and even the Jehovah's Witnesses (or Russelites) – were more or less silent, even though a majority of the COs belonged to these bodies.[14] Nevertheless, in September 1918 a group of Adventists, Christian Workers, Methodists, Pentecostals, and Skutnabbists, and people from the Free Church held a public meeting in Tampere demanding the right for COs to perform civilian, in place of military, service.[15] A 'Christian-social cooperation' delegation was formed, and more meetings were held in other parts of the country. In September 1919 a public meeting organized by this delegation demanded both civilian service and gradual abolition of compulsory military service.

The Pacifist Wing of the Peace Movement

In October 1919 Mathilda Wrede and Felix Iversen (1887–1973) had participated in the conference of Christian pacifists at Bilthoven, in the Netherlands; this gathering was to give birth to the International FOR. At the beginning of 1920 a Finnish FOR (Sovinnonliitto) was founded in Helsinki. At its inaugural meeting not only the right of conscientious objection was demanded, but also the right not to pay war tax.[16] These demands went further than previous demands from the 'Christian–social cooperation' delegation. Later, in 1920, the Helsinki and Tampere groups organized a joint meeting in Tampere calling for the right to civilian service for COs. Some of the Helsinki group refrained from signing its petition, apparently because they did not accept any kind of substitute service. This petition, however, did probably influence the law of 1922, which introduced non-combatant service.

Though the Fellowship of Reconciliation gathered some outstanding personalities such as Mathilda Wrede, rural dean Uno Wegelius (1867–1925), and Felix Iversen, it never became a large movement. It acted rather as a loose tie between religious pacifists.[17] Most FOR activists participated in the work of other Finnish peace groups, especially in the Peace Union of Finland, founded in May 1920 on the initiative of the writer Selma Anttila. The Peace Union became the largest peace organization in the 1920s and 1930s, numbering about two thousand members at its peak and acting as a rallying point for the movement. Practically all peace activists in the other peace groups became members. This diversity led to some disputes between moderate *pacificists* and radical pacifists. Arvi Grotenfelt, the first chair, resigned in 1925, seemingly because the union protested against the civil guard (i.e., the militia) and the building of a navy. The fact too that it supported COs contributed to the dispute.[18] After Grotenfelt, Uno Wegelius became chair for a short period, followed by Felix Iversen, who remained chair until 1968. The Peace Union continued to play a leading role in the peace movement. Many of its activists were pacifists, which was reflected in its magazine *Rauhaa Kohti* (Towards Peace). None the less the group pursued a fairly moderate policy.

In 1923 a group of radical pacifists formed the organization known as Suomen ehdottomat rauhanystävät/Finlands obetingade fredsvänner (Finland's Unconditional Friends of Peace). Later, in 1923 Suomen antimilitaristinen liitto (Anti-militarist League of Finland)[19] was set up. Both of these bodies joined the War Resisters' International (WRI). The main difference between them was that the Anti-militarists were inclined more to political pacifism (leftist and anarchist), and the Unconditional Friends of Peace, towards religious and liberal pacifism. Thus the Anti-militarist League also joined the radical International Anti-militarist Bureau (IAMB). The Unconditional Friends had about ninety members, many of whom also belong to the Peace Union, FOR, or Anti-militarist League. The Unconditional Friends remained rather inactive and later merged with the Anti-militarist League.[20] In the 1930s Sodanvastustajain liitto (Union of War Resisters)[21] appeared. It apparently represented a not-very-successful attempt to gain broader participation for the work of the Anti-militarist League.[22] The Anti-militarist League and the Union of War Resisters shared the same chair (Arndt Pekurinen) and secretary (Aarne Selinheimo).

The Anti-militarist League required every member to sign the declaration of the WRI.[23] The league opposed any kind of war, including a 'war of defence,' and in addition to the WRI's statement it also used the slogan: 'Not one man, not one penny, not any kind of work for militarism.' The league advocated complete and universal disarmament, believing that disputes between states could be decided by international courts of arbitration, and it demanded total abolition of conscription as well as complete freedom for COs to act according to their conscience. It strove against nationalism, capitalism, and imperialism as being causes of war. It wanted particularly to raise awareness of, and resistance to, war among the workers.[24] In this way it differed from the more liberal approach of the Peace Union.

The Anti-militarist League organized mass meetings and petitions against conscription and for unilateral disarmament, but it was known mostly for its work for COs. The league was fairly active despite its small numbers: just over one hundred members, with an inner circle consisting of five or six activists. The work of the league was mainly propagandist: organizing public meetings, distributing leaflets, writing to the newspapers, and so on. It received plenty of publicity when its chair, Arndt Pekurinen (1905–41) was sentenced to prison for being a CO. The Anti-militarist League had its own newspaper, called *Sodanvastustaja* (The War Resister). The activists also wrote in other papers whenever this was possible. In the 1930s the activities of the league became more and more dependent on its indefatigable secretary, Aarne Selinheimo, but he died of consumption in 1939. Since Pekurinen was imprisoned again at the beginning of the Winter War, there was thereafter no one to keep the Anti-militarists going.

Pacifists were also active in the youth organizations and women's and workers' movements. Lucina Hagman and Maikki Friberg, for example, were both engaged in the peace movement as well as in the women's movement. The Finnish section of the Women's International League for Peace and Freedom (founded in 1926) functioned as a natural link between these two groups. In the workers' movement the civil war had meant a serious defeat for pacifist socialists, but some continued to have influence in the Social Democratic (SD) party; the war resisters even had three SD MPs among their adherents. The results could be seen in Social Democrats' support for COs and their unwillingness to vote for armaments. Pacifists were also supported in various ways by some liberal MPs, especially in the Swedish People's party.

Political Pressure on Pacifists

Especially before the Conscience Act of 1931, the peace organizations, particularly the Anti-militarist League, were active in trying to improve the situation of the COs. The league strove to make it possible for the latter to serve without helping the military machine to function. Because of its propaganda against the army, the state police suspected pacifists of having secret links with the Communists and followed them intensively, trying to find among them persons dangerous to the government and the legal order. Their reports concerning peace activists had a disparaging tone, and the police tried to label pacifists as simpleminded and gullible people. The league itself denied having any connections with the Communists, arguing that Communists wanted to make a revolution, a violent one if necessary, and therefore wished to have nothing to do with pacifists. Though no links between the pacifists and the Communists could be discovered, the reports made by the police got more virulent with the passage of time, and Selinheimo especially was repeatedly taken in for questioning.[25]

Despite the suspicions of the authorities, very few of the COs wished to do anything that would harm the Finnish state. On the contrary, they respected the state and wanted to serve it in some way; they simply had an aversion to learning how to kill another human being. For most of them, the question was a matter not of politics but of religion or ethics. The authorities, in contrast, usually regarded a pacifist as a representative of some hostile political group and therefore as a threat to the legal order.[26]

In the late 1920s and early 1930s the ultra-right, especially the Lapua movement, harassed peace activists. Arndt Pekurinen was assaulted and humiliated by the Lapua movement in 1930. Right-wing activists also campaigned against pacifists within the church and university. The Lapua movement, for instance, tried to get the county vicar Edvin Stenwall (1899–1976) removed from office because of his pacifism but failed because of the local support that Stenwall received.[27]

In addition, Finland's friendly relations with Germany during the 1930s led to problems for pacifists. In 1935, for instance, Felix Iversen was fined for criticizing Hitler, while the Peace Union temporarily lost its government funding because of its chair's indiscretion vis-à-vis the Nazi regime in Germany.[28]

Conscientious Objection, 1919–1939

Non-combatant Service in the 1920s

General conscription was reintroduced with the Military Service Act of 1919. Though it did not grant a right to conscientious objection, it allowed for the possibility of assigning to non-combatant duties any conscript deemed sincere in his refusal to bear arms.[29] A new act in 1922 clarified the situation; it permitted COs to do either non-combatant army or labour service, but the period of such service was six months longer than that of the ordinary conscript. The alternative forms of labour service, moreover, had to be in the interest of the military. Non-combatant or labour service was granted mainly on religious grounds and only in especially 'delicate cases' on other grounds of conscience. Between 1922 and 1931, just under two hundred COs, the vast majority of them religious (mostly Adventists, Baptists, members of the Free Church, Jehovah's Witnesses, and Pentecostals) performed non-combatant or labour service.

Unconditional objectors unwilling to accept the alternatives offered by the state were invariably sentenced to prison; non-religious objectors, even if not unconditionalists, were also liable to imprisonment. Even though the number of unconditional objectors (about twenty during the period 1919–31[30]) was quite small, they received publicity through the efforts of peace activists on their behalf. The outlook for those sentenced to prison was bleak. It was indeed possible to sentence a person repeatedly, for the time spent in prison was not regarded as part of the period of service, and after each sentence the objector was called up again. Thus Tauno Tapanainen (1909–1995) spent a total of four years and three months in prison.[31] This 'cat-and-mouse' treatment and the absence of legal relief caused great hardship and even tragedy: some objectors fled the country, a few even committed suicide,[32] and at least one ended up in a mental hospital.[33]

Publicity and the 'Pekurinen Case'

In the late 1920s the Anti-militarist League, with the help of the Peace Union, succeeded in attracting the public's attention through the cases of Arndt Pekurinen, Karl Nickul (1900–1971), and Tauno Tapanainen. Pekurinen had not answered his call-up in 1924. Soon afterwards he got involved in the Anti-militarist League and became its chair in 1928, when its first leader, Aarne Selinheimo, became its secretary. Pekurinen attended public meetings, made speeches, and spread information about the conditions of the COs, despite his ambiguous position vis-à-vis the army. But in 1929 he was arrested and forcibly dragged off to military service, which he refused. He was first stripped of his civilian clothes, then examined by an army doctor, and finally sent to the Uusimaa regiment. Because of further refusal of military orders, including wearing an army uniform, he was placed in custody, sent to a military hospital, and there made to undergo a mental examination. When Pekurinen was found sane he was returned to the army, this time to a penal battalion, where he was forcibly put into military uniform. But then Pekurinen started a hunger strike, which he continued until he was at last permitted to wear his civilian clothes.[34]

The peace organizations (mainly through Selinheimo) tried to get Pekurinen released by sending reports of his treatment abroad. This led some internationally known figures, such as Henri Barbusse, Albert Einstein, and H.G. Wells, to sign a letter to Finland's minister of defence, Juho Niukkanen, in which they called for Pekurinen's release. A number of British MPs also supported this appeal. Niukkanen wrote to Einstein claiming incorrectly that it was possible for every Finnish CO to do his service as a civilian; Einstein replied by expressing his satisfaction that the situation of COs was well taken care of in Finland. The peace organizations, however, strongly criticized Niukkanen's falsehood and made this exchange of letters public. As a result, Einstein wrote another letter to Niukkanen, in which he withdrew his words of approval.[35]

As an incidental result of this episode, Pekurinen became widely known to the public and the COs got some much-needed publicity. Nevertheless the repeated sentencing of Pekurinen continued. He was in the headlines again in 1930, when some members of the fascist Lapua movement kidnapped him while he was on his way from the Ilmajoki prison to Helsinki. The kidnappers fired shots, intentionally missing his head by a few centimetres, put him into military dress, then assaulted him and forced him to sign a document in which he promised to do his military service in the armed forces and expressed regret for 'having been misled' into becoming chair of the Anti-militarist League. His hands were tied in a horizontal position with a wooden stick, and two libelous signs were hung around his neck. He was dumped in that position near the railway station at Seinäjoki.[36] Pekurinen was sentenced twice more before being released in 1931. By that time the new 'Conscience Act' was in force. According to the law he had now 'completed his military service' and was therefore placed on the reserve list of the army.

The cases of Tauno Tapanainen and Karl Nickul also received attention abroad. Nickul (secretary of the Peace Union from 1931 to 1966) was imprisoned for only three months for refusing reservist training, but Tapanainen spent more than four years in jail.

The publicity arising from these cases most certainly helped to bring about the new legislation of 1931 and the introduction of civilian service for COs. It has been said that this new law was largely a result Pekurinen's struggle against the old legislation. But without Selinheimo's contacts and hard work, the campaign would not have been possible. Of course, there were also other forces that worked in the same direction: repeated petitions to parliament since independence for an extension of COs' rights, a more positive attitude towards peace work on the part of the Social Democratic party, newspaper articles dealing with the matter, and the fact of equivalent legislation in the other Scandinavian countries.[37]

The 'Conscience Act' of 1931

The situation of COs changed in 1931, with the so-called Conscience Act. This new law made it possible for them to perform alternative service that did not have to benefit the military. But it was to be eight months longer than compulsory military service, which lasted twelve months. Conscience alone was now sufficient for receiving CO status. The new law, however, was not valid in wartime,[38] and COs were not able to declare their decision to be COs until after being placed in a military unit. Thus they had to first receive the status of a soldier – even if only temporarily – before gaining recognition as COs.

If a conscript wished to obtain alternative civilian service, he had to explain his reasons for this choice to a board of inquiry, consisting of an officer, a military chaplain, and another clergyman. The decision whether or not to grant civilian service was then made by the Ministry of Defence.

Most of the COs (over 90 per cent) still applied on religious grounds. It was certainly easier to refer to the Bible than to state other reasons for conscientiously objecting to bear arms. If his objection was 'only' ethical, a man could be suspected of having links to the Communists. A majority of those who based their objection on religious grounds belonged to one of the sects, and almost half of these were Pentecostals. Many other objectors were Seventh-Day Adventists or Jehovah's Witnesses.[39] It was common for the court of inquiry to try to persuade a person to do full military service, but in only a few cases did they succeed.[40] There are no figures available on how many COs were refused civilian service.

When a man's convictions proved unshakeable, he had still to remain in his military unit waiting for the ministry's decision. However, if suspected of having 'a bad effect' on other conscripts, he was temporarily discharged from the unit. Those assigned non-combatant service usually performed it in the same military unit as they had been sent to at call-up. Civilian labour service was performed either in a hospital or at a farm run by the state.

After the change in military legislation in 1931 only one CO, Tauno Tapanainen, was sent to prison for refusing alternative service.[41] All the others agreed to do non-combatant army or civilian labour service. Tapanainen's unconditional objection was not supported by most of the peace movement, but the Anti-militarist League continued campaigning for him. Finally, in 1935 he was freed from conscription for 'reasons of health.'

During the period from 1932 to 1938, 259 men performed non-combatant service in the army, while sixty-nine took advantage of the opportunity to do civilian labour service. Between 1918 and 1938 about six hundred men did their service in some alternative form that did not entail the bearing of arms.[42]

The sources indicate in general a fairly neutral attitude towards COs on the part of both public and authorities once they were performing labour service. After all, most COs belonged to religious groups, which were very strict in following the law and observing Christian morality. Certainly becoming a CO was a tough decision for many, and the small number of COs reflects the harsh social climate of that time. But once CO status had been granted, most COs seem to have been satisfied with their treatment. However, the situation changed drastically with the coming of war, for then freedom of conscience and religion was not permitted to interfere with the interests of the military.

COs and Pacifists in the Second World War

The Winter War

For Finland, the Second World War began when the Soviet Union attacked the country on 30 November 1939. Though the 'Winter War' came as a surprise to some, it should not have been so for the peace movement, which, especially in the late 1930s, had criticized Finnish militarism and fascism and warned about the government's foreign policy – hostile towards the Soviet Union and friendly with Germany.[43] Still, the Winter War was seen, even by the majority of the peace movement, as a war of self-defence against an overwhelmingly strong aggressor. Most people of the left, hitherto critical of the Finnish military, now supported the struggle. Particularly, Stalin's decision to set up a Communist puppet government was interpreted as a prelude to annexing Finland. The political opposition thus consisted mainly of a small number of Communist sympathizers. About two hundred people were taken into preventive detention, and another 120 were made prisoners of state because of their political sympathies or activities.[44]

The radical war resisters, including the Anti-militarist League, had in practice ceased to exist as a movement after the death of Aarne Selinheimo. The pacifists within the Peace Union saw the war as part of a general failure of the international community, especially the League of Nations, and did not publicly blame Finland for using military means to defend itself. Neither did the Peace Union in any way advocate conscientious objection or even support COs publicly (even though some COs were active union members). Instead the Peace Union concentrated on humanitarian work, and Felix Iversen, though himself a pacifist, even travelled abroad to gain sympathy for the 'cause of Finland.'[45]

The number of COs during the Winter War was quite small. Probably fewer than two hundred men applied for registration as COs, most of them on religious grounds. The law of 1931 did not provide for conscientious objection during wartime. It was therefore up to each military unit to decide whether a CO could perform non-combatant duties instead. Often permission to do so was not granted, even though most COs would have been willing to work as, for example, army nurses.

COs repeatedly refusing to bear arms were sentenced to prison or placed in special labour units of the army together with criminals. The special labour company of Turku was well-known for its chief, Captain Kartano, who took a special interest in mistreating COs, especially Adventists refusing to work on Saturdays and Jehovah's Witnesses refusing to wear uniforms. The harsh conditions and acts of cruelty in Turku have been documented by several of the COs serving there.[46] As for Arndt Pekurinen, he was sentenced to two years and two months in prison and spent most of the Winter War and the Interim Peace in the prison at Sukeva,[47] where he was not permitted visits from his family.

The number of deserters during the Winter War was quite low. During the special general military training in the autumn of 1939 there were only 160 court cases for failing to report, out of an army of 340,000. During the Winter War about seven hundred men were sentenced for desertion or absence without leave, and 120 for 'cowardice.'[48] When the Winter War ended with an armistice in March 1940, the authorities saw no need to carry through all the prison sentences imposed on deserters, and many were pardoned. The COs, however, usually remained in prison or in punitive labour camps.

The Interim Peace, 1940–1941

After the Winter War was over, the political climate gradually hardened, as Finland began gliding towards military alignment with Germany. The Peace Union tried to work against the glorifying of the Winter War and rising revanchism over the recently lost territories. Its papers, *Rauhaa Kohti* and *Frid på jorden* (Peace on Earth) in Swedish, were frequently censored, and *Rauhaa Kohti* was banned just before the 'Continuing War' began. However, the authorities allowed the Swedish journal to be published throughout the war.

The left opposition organized itself in the Suomen-Neuvostoliiton rauhan ja ystävyyden seura (Finland–Soviet Union Peace and Friendship Society). This organization and Työläisrintamaliitto (Workers' Frontier Union) arranged mass meetings, printed propaganda, and spread leaflets against war preparations and also encouraged potential conscripts not to heed the call-up in case of a new war against the Soviet Union. These organizations were, however, far from pacifist. The Peace and Friendship Society, with more than 35,000 members, was banned as pro-Communist after only a few months of functioning.

The COs were in most cases kept in prison or labour camps during the whole interim peace. Their conditions in Turku had deteriorated still further when the Winter War ended. A former member of the state police engaged in trying to force COs to bear arms. His methods included threats, false executions, cold dark cells, and systematic ill-treatment. The terror ended when the military headquarters started to investigate conditions in Turku, and the unit was then moved to Helsinki. The discipline was loosened there, and short periods of leave were granted for some interned COs.

The Continuing War

When Germany attacked the Soviet Union in the summer of 1941, Finland quickly joined the war against the Soviet Union. It is understandable that public opinion reacted differently to this war than to the Winter War. Even though the Soviet Union had been far from pacific in its attitude towards Finland during the interim peace, this time Finland played the role of aggressor. Quite soon Finnish forces reached the old border, but the offensive continued eastwards, almost reaching the railway to Murmansk. Protests arose, especially because of the alliance with Germany and the awakening of ultra-nationalist dreams of a Great Finland uniting all the areas with a Finno-Ugrian population in northeastern Europe. The left opposition against the war was much stronger than during the Winter War. The number of political prisoners quickly rose; just a few weeks after the outbreak of the war in 1941, it reached about seven hundred, including even some Social Democrat MPs.

The peace movement was not able to function properly during this period, though the Peace Union did arrange some meetings. Censorship prevented it from publishing material critical of Finland's war policy. The existing anti-war movement consisted mainly of socialists and Communists working underground. Some of them were influenced by pacifism, but their advocacy of conscientious objection and refusal of military orders was politically oriented and directed against the Finnish government.

Dissatisfaction with the war can also be seen in the large number of deserters and of soldiers refusing to obey orders, especially after the old border had been crossed. About fifteen hundred men were taken to court for failing to obey their call-up during mobilization in the summer of 1941. During the 1941 offensive about thirty-seven hundred cases of desertion or 'cowardice' were brought into court.[49] The number of desertions peaked again during the Soviet offensive in 1944. Deserters or draft evaders usually went into hiding in the countryside or forests. (They are therefore often called the 'forest guard.') Some joined the Soviet side (mainly in 1941),[50] while about fifteen hundred men fled to Sweden[51] (mainly in 1944). The total number of cases of military evasion during the Continuing War is estimated to be around 37,000 to 38,000, or roughly 5 per cent of all conscripts.[52] Most deserters received only prison sentences, but they were sent back to the front immediately to prevent conscripts from deliberately getting sentences to avoid the fighting. The death penalty was used in some cases, though it is not clear how many men were shot for deserting or refusing orders. In battle, execution could be carried out without trial, and it is therefore by no means certain if all cases have been reported. Some estimates are below one hundred[53] and others are around five hundred;[54] in addition, there are claims of graves of deserters in eastern Finland.[55] Executions occurred especially during the Soviet offensive in the summer of 1944, when, according to official documents, about sixty soldiers were shot for desertion or disobeying orders.[56]

It is not clear how many of the deserters were COs. One would expect that at least the religious objectors would normally have already made their position clear when called up, since becoming a deserter was certainly a more hazardous undertaking than seeking status as a CO. However, politically oriented pacifists, especially socialists, might have had reasons to conceal their ideas and choose instead to become draft evaders or deserters. Also, one may well question whether in the circumstances it really makes sense to distinguish between COs and others. Many of the deserters were young men, who might not yet have given questions of peace and war much thought. It is, however, clear that desertion and draft evasion tended in 1941 to be conscious gestures, whereas in 1944 they were more likely simply to indicate war weariness or psychological problems experienced at the front.

The COs[57] remained either in prison or in punitive labour camps. During the Continuing War, labour units were moved to the front, where some COs were used as nurses while others were employed as non-armed personnel or on fortification work. Even though earlier many COs would not have agreed to work at the front on any duties that served the war, most of them now proved willing to compromise rather than become 'peace martyrs.' In order to provoke them to disobey, COs were often deliberately given orders that went against their conscience, and some military personnel were very eager to get an opportunity to punish the COs. In some units, however, COs were treated in a correct manner and assigned to duties that they could in good conscience perform. Thus the main problem for COs during the war was that their destiny remained completely dependent on the attitude of the military personnel to whose orders they were subject. They had no support in law, and there was no organization monitoring their treatment.

Just as in the Winter War, Adventists and Jehovah's Witnesses in particular usually had a tough time in following their conscience. According to estimates,[58] about half the total number of COs were sentenced to prison, their sentences ranging from a few months to several years. The sentences were usually served in the jails where political prisoners were kept. Conditions there were often terrible, ill-treatment and starvation were part of daily life.

Cases also occurred of COs being shot during the war, of which only the case of Pekurinen has been investigated. Immediately after being released from prison in October 1941, Pekurinen was forced into military service, which he once more refused. A couple of weeks later he was taken to the front. There he refused to wear an army uniform or carry a rifle; they would, he said, have to carry him to the front-line, since he would not go voluntarily. Pekurinen was shot on 5 November 1941.[59] Even though this took place allegedly in accordance with the army's penal code, it is obvious that his execution was illegal.

His relatives were not informed of his execution; when they made inquiries the military even claimed that he had been killed in battle and had his body placed in a soldier's grave. His wife, however, threatened to press charges of desecration of her husband's body and, three months after his death, finally got his mutilated body buried in an ordinary grave in Helsinki.[60]

Kalevi Kalemaa has summed up Pekurinen's role in the development of Finnish pacifism: 'Pekurinen was not an inspiring speaker nor an impressive writer. His main contribution to the cause of peace was his brave and consistent refusal to perform military service and, thereby, heightening public awareness of the plight of conscientious objectors. By his life and concrete activity, he committed himself to the cause of peace.'[61]

With Germany's defeat at Stalingrad, attitudes towards the war started to change. In August 1943, thirty-three prominent citizens appealed to President Ryti for a speedy start of peace negotiations. A new kind of peace opposition, one including liberal politicians, emerged. Finland remained in the war – on Germany's side – until the armistice in September 1944. The dissolution of the alliance between Finland and Germany resulted in the so-called Lapland war, in which German troops withdrawing from Finland burned practically every building in the northern towns and villages. By the end of 1944, in accordance with the armistice, imprisoned COs, as well as deserters claiming political, religious, or ethical reasons for their action, were released from jail.

After the armistice in 1944 relations between the state and the peace movement began to normalize. Pacifists gained a new kind of influence in politics. The most remarkable instance was the appointment of Yrjö Kallinen as minister of defence, an office that he held from 1946 to 1948.[62] In addition, a few pacifists were elected to the first postwar parliament. The authorities initiated investigations into atrocities within the army and prison units. Of the CO cases, only the murder of Pekurinen was investigated, but in the end nobody was charged.

The Peace Union had already become active again in 1944 after the conclusion of the armistice. One of its postwar projects was collecting information about Finnish COs during the Second World War. A problem, however, arose from the fact that only a few of the COs were active in the peace movement, and information was not easily obtainable from the sects that had provided the overwhelming majority of COs. (Of these, the largest groups had been the Jehovah's Witnesses, Pentecostals, and Seventh-day Adventists.)

Conclusion

Around the turn of the century Finland had engaged in what would become a classic example of non-military struggle against outside encroachment on the country's autonomy. But this contest, though mostly non-violent, did not result from any pacifist sentiment on the part of Finnish nationalists. Thus, after Finland became independent, the country was torn apart by a devastating civil war. There was little understanding of pacifism or the position of the CO in the new state. Only very inadequate provision for the latter existed.

The pacifist and anti-militarist peace activists tried to challenge Finnish militarism, and conscription in particular. In the 1920s some cases of imprisoned COs got a lot of publicity. The results of the campaign were limited to improvements in the legislation on conscientious objection in 1931, enabling COs to do civilian instead of military service. Still, this was felt to be an important achievement, considering the political climate. The situation of COs worsened, however, during the Second World War, when civilian service was not permitted.

Most objectors based their refusal to bear arms on religion and belonged to sects that were usually not active in the peace movement. Thus, even though the anti-militarist peace activists strongly supported conscientious objection, they had very little contact with the majority of the objectors. But this situation finally changed in the 1960s, when 'secular' conscientious objection became part of the radical youth culture.

NOTES

The authors thank Göran von Bonsdorff, Peter Brock, Ulla Holmberg, Harri Markkula, Deryck Sivén, and Ilkka Taipale for assistance with materials for this essay.

1 Jyrki Järnefelt, *Omantunnonarat ja Suomen asevelvollinen armeija vuoteen 1939* [Conscientious Objectors and the Finnish Conscript Army to 1939] (Mikkeli 1958), 71.

2 The Baptists as a whole were not pacifists, but in neighbouring Sweden a smaller splinter group, known as Free Baptists, adopted pacifism as a tenet of their faith.

3 Martin Scheinin, *Aseistakieltäytymisoikeus* [The Right to Conscientious Objection] (Helsinki 1988), 110.

4 A thorough account of this campaign is given in Steven Duncan Huxley, *Constitutionalist Insurgency in Finland: Finnish 'Passive Resistance' against Russification as a Case of Nonmilitary Struggle in the European Resistance Tradition* (Helsinki 1990).

5 Jukka Kulomaa, *Käpykaartiin? 1941–1944: Sotilaskarkuruus Suomen armeijassa jatkosodan aikana* [To the 'Forest Guard'? 1941–1944: Desertion in the Finnish Army during the Continuing War] (Helsinki 1995), 28.

6 Järnefelt, *Omantunnonarat*, 199.

7 Adolf Turakainen, 'Kansalaissodan pyörteissä' [In the Whirl of Civil War], interview with Yrjö Kallinen on Finnish national radio, 1965.

8 Vera Brittain, *The Rebel Passion: A Short History of Some Pioneer Peace-makers*
   (London 1964), 176.

9 Fraser resigned from the Russian army in 1887, and von Schoultz in 1898. However,
   von Schoultz was called up again during the First World War and sentenced to two
   and a half years' imprisonment.

10 See Armo Nokkala, *Tolstoilaisuus Suomessa* [Tolstoyism in Finland] (Helsinki
    1958), for a detailed account of the impact of Tolstoy's literary and sociopolitical
    ideas, including non-resistance. Also see Alexander Fodor, 'Leo Tolstoy and
    Arvid Järnefelt,' *Slavic and East-European Studies* (Quebec), 18 (1973 [1974]),
    112–16.

11 Järnefelt, *Omantunnonarat*, 139, 140.

12 *Friends in Europe: Handbook of the Society of Friends (Quakers) in Europe* (Lon-
    don 1946), 14.

13 Järnefelt, *Omantunnonarat*, 147–9.

14 Ibid., 150.

15 Ibid., 164–7.

16 Ibid., 171, 172.

17 Kalevi Kalemaa, *Suomalaisen rauhanliikkeen juuria* [Roots of the Finnish Peace
    Movement] (Vaasa 1981), 33.

18 Göran von Bonsdorff, *Med freden som rättesnöre: Finlands Fredsförbund 1920–
    1979* [With Peace as the Guideline: The Peace Union of Finland 1920–1979]
    (Jyräskylä 1991), 20–1.

19 Anti-militaristic Union is also used as a translation.

20 Kalemaa, *Suomalaisen rauhanliikkeen*, 39.

21 Sometimes also called in translation the League of War Resisters.

22 Cf. *Sodanvastustaja* [The War Resister] (Helsinki), no. 1 (1936).

23 'War is a crime against humanity. I am therefore determined not to support any kind
    of war and strive for the removal of all causes of war' (Constitution of WRI).

24 See, for instance, the program leaflet of the Anti-militarist League published in Hel-
    sinki in 1924.

25 See the Records of the Finnish State Police in the National Archives, Helsinki.

26 This attitude is reflected in documents dealing with CO applications in the Ministry
    of Defense records deposited in the Military Archives, Helsinki.

27 Edvin Stenwall, *Frid på jorden* [Peace on Earth] (Närpiö 1976), 118–27.

28 Bonsdorff, *Med freden*, 100, 101.

29 Such duties were conceived as a kind of punishment for refusal to serve with weap-
    ons.

30 Järnefelt, *Omantunnonarat*, 210.

31 Olavi Antila, 'Puolustuslaitoksen ulkopuolella palvelleiden asseettomien suhtau-

58   Thomas Hackman and Katja Huumo

tuminen asevelvollisuuteen 1930-luvulla' [The Relation to Conscription of Those Who Served Unarmed Outside the Military during the 1930s], MA thesis, University of Turku, 1977, 24–34.

32 *The War Resister* (Enfield, Middlesex), no. 14 (Dec. 1926), 8, and no. 26 (spring 1930), 8.

33 Järnefelt, *Omantunnonarat*, 202.

34 Juha Tuomikoski, *Aseistakieltäytyjän maailma* [The World of the Conscientious Objector] (Helsinki 1989), 86.

35 Ibid., 86, 87.

36 Ibid., 88, 89. See also *Rauhaa Kohti* [Towards Peace] (Helsinki), 18 (1930), 144–6, and *War Resister*, no. 27 (winter 1930–1), 7.

37 Järnefelt, *Omantunnonarat*, 252.

38 See the Statute Book of Finland for 1922 and 1931.

39 Antila, 'Puolustuslaitokssen,' 55.

40 During the period from 1932 to 1938 eleven men were persuaded to accept armed service. See Järnefelt, *Omantunnonarat*, 198.

41 Antila, 'Puolustuslaitoksen,' 45, 240.

42 Ibid., 51, 52.

43 These friendly relations with Germany obviously did not help Finland in its plight because of the pact then existing between Germany and the Soviet Union.

44 Jussi Nuorteva, *Vangit-vankilat-sota: Suomen vankeinhoitolaitos toisen maailman-sodan aikana* [Prisoners-Prisons-War. The Finnish Prison System during the Second World War] (Helsinki 1987), 303.

45 Bonsdorff, *Med freden*, 106. The British, Quaker-run Friends Ambulance Unit sent fifty-six men, all COs, with twenty ambulances to Finland during the Winter War to assist with the wounded. They remained for four months; see chapter 15 below, by Lyn Smith.

46 Deryck Sivén, 'Brytningstid' [Critical Period], in M. Andersén, E. Andrén, and H. Fågelbärj, eds., *Ur tystnaden* [From the Silence] (Vaasa 1989), 105–7; Alwar Sundell, *I fredens tjänst* [In the Service of Peace] (Vaasa 1991), 43–74; and Bengt Lillas, *Aseeton taistelija* [Nonarmed Warrior] (Helsinki 1963), 27ff.

47 Jukka Linstedt, 'Valtio näyttää voimansa: Arndt Pekurisen viimeiset päivät syksyllä 1941' [The State Shows Its Power: The Last Days of Arndt Pekurinen in the Autumn of 1941], *Lakimies* [The Lawyer] (Helsinki), 6 (1995), 1045–65.

48 Kulomaa, *Käpykaartiin?*, 32.

49 Ibid., 502.

50 Ibid., 218.

51 Matts Andersén, *Flykten västerut* [Escape to the West] (Vaasa 1987), 150.

52 Kulomaa, *Käpykaartiin?*, 501.

53 Ibid., passim.

54 A total of 468 executions during the two wars, according to Erik Andrén, *Var är din Broder?* [Where Is Your Brother?] (Vaasa 1983), 11.

55 Most scholars do not take the rumours about mass graves of deserters seriously.

56 Kulomaa, *Käpykaartiin?*, 509.

57 The term 'COs' here refers only to those who were regarded as COs by the authorities and does not apply to 'deserters.'

58 Hikka and Teuvo Rasku, *En voi omantunnon tähden* [I Cannot Because of My Conscience] (Helsinki 1958), 106.

59 The record of the investigation of Pekurinen's case (20 June 1945) is deposited in the Military Archives, Helsinki.

60 Lindstedt, 'Valtio.'

61 From entry on Pekurinen by Kalemaa in Harold Josephson, ed., *Biographical Dictionary of Modern Peace Leaders* (Westport, Conn., 1985), 739. Pekurinen's formal education did not go beyond elementary school; at first he had earned his living as a truck driver. His pacifism derived from his ethical principles, not from religious belief; this accounts, at any rate in part, for the continued persecution that he endured as a CO, ending with his brutal murder by the army in the battle zone where he had steadfastly refused to carry a gun.

62 Kallinen was (reluctantly) persuaded to become minister of defence as a sign that Finland was really sincere in its postwar peace policy. See above, 42, 43.

4

In Search of a 'Lost' Belarusan Pacifist Leader

PETER BROCK

Pacifism attracted few adherents in interwar Poland. The country had regained its independence in 1918 as a result of war. Before that date, in partitioned Poland a tradition of insurrectionary nationalism possessed deep roots stretching back to Kościuszko's unsuccessful uprising against the occupying Russian forces in 1794, just before the old Commonwealth (Rzeczpospolita) finally succumbed to its three neighbours' aggressive designs. In the 1920s and 1930s the Polish army became a symbol of the nation's will to live again; all able-bodied male citizens were required to undergo military training. The penalties for refusing to bear arms, when required to do so, were severe; and no legal provision existed for conscientious objection, even if this was based on religious conviction. Thus objectors to military service suffered long – and repeated – terms of imprisonment. The army eventually allowed members of certain specified pacifist sects to serve without weapons if they were ready to undertake non-combatant duties. But many were unwilling to accept such conditions, regarding them as an impermissible compromise of their pacifist witness.

Almost all ethnic Poles belonged, at least nominally, to the Roman Catholic church, which did not recognize pacifism as an acceptable position. Young Poles refusing military service were drawn therefore from small religious groups such as the Baptists and Jehovah's Witnesses; with few exceptions they shared a working-class or peasant background. From 1927 a section of the War Resisters' International (WRI) existed in Warsaw – the centre of the efforts of a small group of middle-class pacifists who, on account either of age or of gender, were not liable to conscription. These urban war resisters, in some cases of Jewish extraction, usually based their pacifism on ethical or humanist grounds, in contrast to the objectors themselves, who were all religious sectarians of one kind or another.

The new Poland, in the eyes of its successive governments and the over-whelming majority of its Polish-speaking citizens, appeared as a nation-state, the *patria* of the Poles. In fact it formed a multinational state, with Belarusans, Germans, Jews, Lithuanians, and Ukrainians constituting together almost a third of the total population.[1]

The majority of interwar Poland's conscientious objectors (COs), we must note, were Belarusans and not ethnic Poles (or members of the other nationali-ties). The reason for this – at first sight perhaps surprising – fact lay in the past of the Belarusan-inhabited territories of the new state. This area, situated in the northeast, had been under Russian rule since the first partition of Poland in 1772. Most Belarusans belonged to the Orthodox church; but not only was there a Roman Catholic minority, there were also numerous peasant sectaries, who shared their faith with coreligionists in eastern Belarus, just across the Polish–Soviet borders. And some of the sectarians, such as the Mal-evantsy and the Tolstoyans, were staunch pacifists, who, before the collapse of tsardom, had endured imprisonment for their refusal to serve in the Rus-sian army.

I have argued elsewhere[2] that with these people conscientious objection, even though the outcome of an apolitical religious pacifism, represented at the same time an aspect of emergent Belarusan national consciousness. Sons of the Belarusan village, the objectors – and their families – regarded the Polish army as a symbol of the alien rule of the Polish landowning gentry, who continued to dominate western Belarus politically, as well as socially and culturally, in the fashion of past centuries.

Though the sectaries did not participate in the still-weak political agitation of the Belarusan nationalists, in this period often closely allied – and sometimes actually identical – with the Communists, they remained close in spirit to the aspirations of their politically oriented brethren. Thus, while refusal to bear arms by interwar Belarusan village lads arose from their sect's Bible-centred non-resistance, and was a religious act, their war resistance was tinged, even if only lightly, with a cultural-nationalist colouring. For, by refusing to serve in the Polish army they were giving expression, in however veiled a form, to their deep attachment to a Belarusan national identity.

The WRI section in Warsaw did its best to bring all these cases to the atten-tion of pacifists abroad who would, it was hoped, exert pressure on the Polish government to ameliorate the often-harsh treatment meted out to objectors, whether of Belarusan or of other ethnic origin. Who, we may ask, acted as link between the urban humanist pacifists in the capital and the Belarusan peasant war resisters? Here indeed two cultural worlds met; contact might not be always easy. Since sources for interwar Polish pacifism are extremely exiguous, it is difficult to give an answer to the question just posed.[3]

But a brief obituary appearing in 1938 in the WRI's organ, published in England, points to its subject, Iosif Vigdorchyk (Józef Wigdorczyk) as the one who provided this liaison; he also seems to have supplied leadership to the hard-pressed peasant war resisters of interwar Poland whether Belarusans or from another nationality.[4]

The obituary is not sparing in its praises, going so far as to describe Vigdorchyk as 'a great man.' The most striking trait of his character is said to have been 'indomitability.' 'In spite of an infirmity that entailed constant suffering, he became the friend and protector of countless war resisters who endured long years of imprisonment ... He visited them in prison, faced authorities with demands for their release, toured over Poland and became the centre of a great movement.' In addition, 'Josef's work was not limited to Poland'; he translated – 'and neatly duplicated' – WRI literature into Russian, thus becoming 'our instrument for much of our contact with the Russian people.'

Vigdorchyk, 'Brother Josef as we called him,' died in the town of Białystok in northeastern Poland on 4 March 1938. Though the obituary just cited describes him as 'of Russian origin,' it seems almost certain that ethnically he was in fact a Belarusan. Białystok, his place of residence, was situated in a Belarusan area; his name is not infrequently found among Belarusans. That an educated Belarusan should know the Russian language as well as Vigdorchyk obviously did was not surprising, since he must have received his education in a Russian school. Moreover, the *War Resister*, in its reports on Poland, sometimes confuses 'Russian' with 'White Russian,' i.e., Belarusan. It was not easy at that date for the English to get these subtle ethnic distinctions straight. But even were Vigdorchyk of Great Russian origin (which I think is very unlikely), surely he may be regarded as a Belarusan by adoption as a result both of his habitat and of his leadership role among Belarusan war resisters?

But, we may also ask, has Vigdorchyk not left some further trace of his existence in the surviving record? Is a thirteen-line obituary in a rather inaccessible journal the only notice we have of this man, who after all played a significant part in a vigorous, if small, movement of war resistance and gained the respect and admiration of its adherents, even to the point of adulation?[5] Unfortunately my quest for Vigdorchyk, unlike A.J.A. Symons's famous quest for 'Baron' Corvo, has proved entirely fruitless, despite the assistance of kind friends in Poland.[6]

To begin with the Archiwum Akt Nowych (Warsaw). This public record office covering the more recent history of Poland does indeed hold a number of files dealing with the province of Białystok during the interwar years (Zespół urząd wojewódzki białostocki). While these files include materials relating to the interwar Communist movement in that area, there is nothing there on Vigdorchyk – or indeed on any pacifist activity in the province. The local Belarusan and Polish press seems also to have remained silent on the occasion of our 'great man's' death, so far at any rate as one may judge by copies that have survived the wartime destruction of newspaper depositories. Of course somewhere in present-day Poland, Belarus, or even Lithuania a document or the file of some interwar newspaper or journal may be resting quietly on the shelves with just the information about Vigdorchyk that we have been seeking in vain. But if so, I failed, alas, to discover any clues to the whereabouts of such materials. And without preliminary clues of some sort, any research effort must in this instance resemble the proverbial search for a needle in a haystack!

What indeed adds a note of irony is that, first as a relief worker in postwar Poland and then as a graduate student and postgraduate researcher in Polish history, I had been personally acquainted with Amelia Kurlandzka, who was described in Vigdorchyk's obituary as his close associate in aiding COs. After his death she was his successor in the leadership of the small Polish war resistance movement, until the outbreak of hostilities put an end to it in the following year. A question from me would undoubtedly have sufficed to elicit comprehensive answers from Kurlandzka to all the questions I have been asking here. But at that date I was ignorant of Vigdorchyk's existence; anyhow, my interests were focused on matters remote from the life of the elusive Belarusan.[7]

All we are left with then, apart from the scraps of information supplied in Vigdorchyk's obituary, is the photograph reproduced on page 64 showing 'Father Josef' surrounded by some of his war-resisting followers, mostly – and perhaps all – of Belarusan nationality. We may see him there in his 'home circle,' as it were, and can feel, if only remotely, something of the charisma that he radiated among these simple and devout peasant sectaries. But even now a certain ambiguity remains. The *War Resister*'s reproduction of the photograph is of poor quality. Vigdorchyk is perhaps the frail and rather sad-looking man seated in the middle of the picture, for this person seems to be marked with an 'x.' But one cannot be quite sure of this, and thus Vigdorchyk's identity even on the photograph remains unclear. But perhaps that too is symbolic: the obscure, but charismatic leader and his humble followers are blended here in one design – to overthrow the incubus of militarism in a land whose peoples had suffered from repeated wars throughout the centuries.

Iosef Vigdorczyk and other Polish war resisters in interwar Poland

NOTES

1 'In 1921 69.2 per cent of the population gave their nationality as Polish, while in 1931 69.8 gave Polish as their mother tongue.' See Antony Polonsky in R.F. Leslie, ed., *The History of Poland since 1863* (Cambridge 1980), 144–6. Naturally there is controversy concerning the exact numbers of Poles and non-Poles at any given date in the history of interwar Poland.

2 See my article, 'Belarusan National Identity as an Aspect of Conscientious Objection in Interwar Poland,' *East European Quarterly* (Boulder, Col.), 29 no. 3 (Sept. 1995), 285–92; also 'The Small-Sect Antimilitarists of Interwar East Central Europe,' *Reconciliation Quarterly* (London), (autumn 1995), 6–16, where alas the printers made complete havoc of my page 12.

3 The records of the WRI's Polish section, deposited for safekeeping in Warsaw Public Library, were destroyed during the uprising of 1944. The WRI headquarters archives, after spending some time in crates in the general secretary's garage in south London, are now happily located in the library of the Institute of Social History in Amsterdam. They contain very little, however, on interwar Poland. (What little there is was very kindly sent me in xerox by that library's information officer, Ms Mieke Ijzermaans.) The WRI's organ the *War Resister* therefore, at any rate from 1927 on, remains the most informative source for conscientious objection in Poland. In view of the enormous losses in archival and library resources suffered during the last war by Poland and Belarus, it is not surprising that a fragile group such as the war resisters also underwent devastating losses.

4 *War Resister* (Enfield, Middlesex), no. 44 (summer 1938), 2, 3. The obituary was unsigned; it was based probably on information sent to WRI headquarters by Amelia Kurlandzka, a librarian of Jewish extraction who was active in WRI work until the outbreak of war. Kurlandzka, at that time a humanitarian pacifist who had translated some of Bertrand Russell's books into Polish, survived the war and later joined the Society of Friends (Quakers) as an overseas members of London Yearly Meeting.

5 An anonymous article in the *War Resister*, no. 33 (n.d. [1933]), 13–17, entitled 'Until the End' may contain references to Vigdorchyk, though it does not mention him by name. The article includes an account of a trip made by a middle-aged pacifist to see two imprisoned COs, one a Belorusan peasant lad and the other a working-class boy of Lithuanian nationality, both of whom were then on hunger strike in the hospital of a military jail in Vilnius (Wilno). 'I was one with them in thought,' the anonymous prison visitor stated; 'to me the two sentenced men were almost like sons.' Describing himself 'as a friend of the nearest friend of Tolstoi,' the visitor went on to explain that, living 'at a long distance,' he could make only 'very rare' visits to the two jailed COs.

 If we accept that in those days Białystok might have seemed a long way from Wilno, especially if the traveller were in a poor state of health, the person in question could well have been Vigdorchyk himself. I suspect indeed that the latter was by religious affiliation a Tolstoyan. And 'the nearest friend of Tolstoi,' mentioned here as being a personal friend of the prison visitor, can be only Vladimir Chertkov, who led the anti-militarist movement in the Soviet Union from 1918 until his death in 1936. As the Chertkov Papers in the Russian State Library in Moscow (*fond* 435) become accessible to scholars, we may find materials there on Vigdorchyk, provided of course that my tentative identification of Vigdorchyk as the anonymous prison visitor is correct.

6 I would like to thank Professor Krzysztof Dunin-Wąsowicz, Dr Antoni Mironowicz, and Tadeusz A. Olszański for their investigations on my behalf in Warsaw and Białystok. They were not able, however, to uncover in archives and libraries there anything that would throw further light on Vigdorchyk either as man or as pacifist activist.

7 If indeed he really was a Belarusan ...

5

War Resisters in Weimar Germany

GUIDO GRÜNEWALD

The Peace Movement to 1918

Conscientious objection was a concept foreign to the peace movements of nine-teenth-century continental Europe. With their principles derived from the intel-lectual legacy of the Enlightenment, and their roots in liberal middle-class, or *bürgerlich* identity, they saw themselves as part of a more encompassing reform movement; they had pursued five fundamental goals: 'arbitration, arbitration treaties and clauses in treaties, an International Authority or Tribunal or Con-gress, and [simultaneous and proportional] disarmament.'[1] That conscientious objection was discussed at all at world peace congresses before 1914 can be attributed chiefly to the influence of nonconformist Protestant denominations in the Anglo-Saxon peace movement, and most notably the Quakers, who advo-cated unconditional non-violence.[2]

The international socialist labour movement also saw itself as anti-militaristic. Holding militarism to be an expression of the capitalist system, it believed that destroying that system would be necessary for world peace.[3] The Dutch anti-mil-itarist – and later anarchist – Domela Nieuwenhuis's resolutions for a general strike against war and against military service received, however, a negative response at congresses of the Second International in Brussels in 1891 and Zürich in 1893, as did the French socialist Gustav Hervé's call in 1907 in Stuttgart for a military strike and Eduard Vaillant's and Keir Hardie's, in 1910 in Copenhagen, for a general strike against war.[4] The German delegation, more than any other, spoke out against these resolutions. In fact, the Sozialdemokratische Partei Deut-schlands, or SPD (German Social Democratic party), sought to restrict the role of the military to national defence by the device of a 'People's Army.'[5]

Translated from the German by Philip W. Giltner

The Deutsche Friedensgesellschaft, or DFG (German Peace Society) which, after several unsuccessful attempts in this matter, finally gave the German peace movement organizational expression in 1892, was completely within the internationalist tradition.[6] Up to the First World War, under the influence of Alfred Hermann Fried, the DFG accepted national self-defence as a sine qua non. The German pacificists saw themselves as patriots in the best sense of the word. Accordingly, they decisively rejected unilateral disarmament and conscientious objection. Fried called anti-militarism the 'pacifism of cretins,'[7] while Otto Umfrid, vice-chairman of the DFG and publisher of its *Friedensblätter* (Peace Papers) regarded Tolstoyan non-resistance as 'inapplicable' to the international state system.[8]

In Germany there were only a few hundred conscientious objectors (COs) during the First World War: a small group of Seventh-day Adventists and some Mennonites, as well as middle-class intellectuals and left-socialists, who acted in any event as isolated individuals.[9] Opposition to the war was more striking among the German anarchosyndicalists, though their protest was in the form not so much of conscientious objection as of open anti-war propaganda and desertion.[10] After the war, large sections of the German anarchosyndicalists, especially the Berlin Working Commission of the Freie Arbeiter Union Deutschlands, or FAUD (German Free Workers' Union), viewed non-violent 'direct action' as the most effective anarchosyndicalist tool in the fight against war.[11] The German anarchosyndicalists consequently adopted anti-militarism, categorically rejecting not only military service but also the production of armaments.[12]

The First World War had considerable consequences for the German peace movement. Established in 1914, the Bund Neues Vaterland (New Fatherland League) – from 1922 the Deutsche Liga für Menschenrechte (German League for Human Rights) – represented a peace organization whose explicit purpose was the pursuit of domestic and international peace as well as domestic reform in the form of democratization and social and legal equality.[13] Towards the end of the war, the DFG began to realize that peace had to be accompanied by domestic political and social reforms. At this time some German advocates of peace began to discover the significance of conscientious objection. Disillusioned by the collapse of the organized peace movement, they recognized now that mass murder had been made possible by general conscription.[14] Those of them who had been taken prisoner of war by the British were impressed by what they then learned of the experiences of British COs, and this information too played a role in spreading the idea of conscientious objection in postwar Germany.[15]

Conscription and Conscientious Objection

After the war was over the German peace movement became more diversified in ideological and organizational terms. At the end of 1921 the German Peace Cartel had emerged as a loose association to coordinate pacifist activities; in 1928 it reached its peak with twenty-two member peace and cultural-political organizations representing up to 100,000 members.[16] The German peace movement, including the cartel, clearly shifted leftward during the 1920s. Alongside the internationalist-oriented, liberal middle-class pacifism of the pre-war era, a radical and often aggressive pacifism now found adherents among intellectuals, petty bourgeois, and sections of the social-democratic labour movement. Followers of this new trend could be classified mainly as supporters of the SPD and left-socialists; they strove to build a vaguely defined socialist society through democratic means.

Conscription and conscientious objection, taboo subjects in the pre-war era, had clearly gained new legitimacy. The Weimar-era peace movement – with a few exceptions, including members of the liberal minority of the German Peace Society (such as Ludwig Quidde and Count Harry Kessler[17]) as well as the semiofficial Liga für Völkerverbund (German League of Nations Union) and the Verband für international Verständigung (Association for International Understanding) – rejected universal military service. Despite the disarmament clauses of the Versailles Treaty (forbidding conscription in Germany and limiting that country to an army of 100,000 long-term professional solders), this was not a purely theoretical discussion, as the right-wing parties called for the restoration of conscription, while sections of the SPD held on to the idea of a 'people's army' and the liberals wanted to replace the standing army with a militia.

Yet in the Weimar peace movement conscientious objection was a more controversial issue than conscription. The non-party Bund der Kriegsdienstgegner, or BdK (War Resisters' League) advocated non-violence; members pledged themselves to refuse to perform any sort of war service. Established in 1919, the BdK was one of the founding members of the War Resisters' International (WRI) in 1921.[18] Another member of the WRI,[19] the Großdeutsche Volksgemeinschaft or GVG (Catholic Greater German Peoples' Community) and the German branch of the International Fellowship of Reconciliation (IFOR), with a mainly Protestant membership, drew its non-violent principles from religious sources.[20] Most of this essay deals with these three organizations – the BdK, the GVG, and the German FOR.

At its 1924 Washington congress, the Women's International League for International Peace and Freedom (WILPF) similarly rejected any form of war or preparations for war.[21] During the brief Soviet regime in Bavaria in the spring of 1919, and during the Kapp Putsch of March 1920, women from the German branch of the WILPF had some success in bringing the conflicting parties in the civil war into contact so as to hinder the outbreak of violent conflict.[22] After the 1919 founding congress of the WILPF in Zürich, the German branch established a conscientious-objection section whose activity apparently remained only peripheral.[23]

Principled adherence to conscientious objection was supported by the Deutsche Pazifistischer Studentenbund (German Pacifists Students' Union) at its fifth congress at Frankfurt-am-Main in 1926[24] and by the Vereinigung der Freunde von Religion und Völkerfrieden (Association of the Friends of Religion and Peace among the Peoples), whose activities, however, were confined mainly to the Berlin area:[25] both organizations had only limited capacity for action.

In the Weimar peace movement, not only principled pacifists saw conscientious objection and the general strike against war as the only proper response to war. Both methods, as well as abolition of the army altogether, were also advocated by the Friedensbund der Kriegsteilnehmer (Veterans League for Peace), which for a few years after the war had initiated a series of powerful 'no more war' demonstrations.[26] After 1918, the DFG – which was also the largest and most active German peace organization in the Weimar period – proposed recognition of the 'moral right' of conscientious objection.[27] The aggressive pacifism of Fritz Küster's journal *Das Andere Deutschland* (The Other Germany) came to be the dominant ideology of the DFG from the mid-1920s.[28] Most of the aggressive pacifists calling for large-scale conscientious objection and for a general strike against war as well as the end of all armaments production did so for purely practical reasons,[29] and their attitude was not fundamentally non-violent.[30] Likewise, the more conservative Friedensbund Deutscher Katholiken (Peace League of German Catholics) recognized defensive war as deriving from the principle of just war and therefore rejected absolute non-violence.[31] But there were radical Catholic pacifists from the GVG and the Grossdeutsche Jugend (Greater German Youth) with its leader, Nikolaus Ehlens, as well as people such as Father Ohlmeier who agitated within the Peace League of German Catholics in favour of unconditional conscientious objection, while the 1929 congress of the Peace League, held in Frankfurt-am-Main, called for alternatives to a just (i.e., defensive) war and for the 'organization of other and better defensive methods,' such as 'a general strike against foreign tyranny, passive resistance,' and the practice of conscientious objection 'as an act of self-defence of the governed.'[32]

An original view of pacifism was expressed by Kurt Hiller's Gruppe Revolutionärer Pazifisten (Revolutionary Pacifist Group). Established in 1926, it reached at its peak a membership of some 160 left-wing intellectuals, located mainly in Berlin.[33] A member of Berlin's literary expressionist circles since about 1910, Hiller had urged a Nietzschean vitalistic life philosophy and developed an elitist concept of 'logocracy' (political leadership by intellectuals). After the First World War he became one of the leading advocates of radical pacifism within the peace movement. He rejected every form of war and saw the basis of pacifism in 'the sacredness of human life and its absolute inviolability';[34] the duty of the peace movement was 'to prepare conscientious objection carefully and to organize on the widest possible scale – nationally as well as internationally – for an emergency.'[35] From the mid-1920s, Hiller's perspective moved from an ethical-psychological focus on unconditional pacifism to concentrate on questions of power politics and techniques of domination. He now believed that only completion of the social revolution and victory over capitalism could finally serve peace. Under capitalism, the Revolutionary Pacifists indeed rejected defensive war – even as an enforcement action under the League of Nations – and offensive war;[36] Hiller, however, now stressed the right of the individual to renounce the right to life for the sake of self-chosen ideals such as socialism.[37] While Hiller's theory of revolutionary pacifism bolstered conscientious objection and non-violence, he favoured the use of violence in a 'Red civil war' as well as a defensive war in the event of a socialist state being attacked by the capitalists.[38]

Bund der Kriegsdienstgegner

The BdK, whose members were required to sign the pledge of the WRI,[39] categorically rejected limits on pacifism in the name of these kinds of goals. The war resisters simply would not accept a separation of ends and means. Their basic principle was 'recognition of the sanctity of human life,' which they aspired to make the 'fundamental law of human society.'[40] Hence the BdK rejected not only every kind of defensive war or military sanctions under the League of Nations, but also a 'war to defend and liberate the oppressed proletariat.' Yet this stance did not mean that it accepted the social status quo. In accordance with the WRI pledge, which was marked by a confusing mixture of anarchistic and liberal thought,[41] the BdK vowed to fight all the causes of war, including racial and ideological differences, class distinctions, nationalism in league with economic imperialism, and the false notion that the individual should be subservient to the state.

While war resisters criticized the League of Nations as ineffective and undemocratic and reproached its most powerful members for being dilatory about disarmament and turning the league into a de facto alliance against the Soviet Union,[42] they did believe in the need for an international organization. War resisters did not place 'the axiom of preserving human life' above 'justice itself,' wrote Martha Steinitz, a BdK member and WRI secretary, in a discussion over creating a League of Nations executive to defend peace.[43] In contrast to Tolstoy, most war resisters acknowledged the right of individual self-defence.[44] But a League of Nations war involving military sanctions against a transgression of international law would – given the nature of modern war – destroy the innocent as well as the guilty and bring with it 'new [and] ruthless injustices' along with the injustices for which the guilty were responsible.[45] Therefore the goal of pacifism must be 'to find a life-affirming humanitarian (menschenbeglückende) method of protecting life, law, and justice.'

The BdK saw itself as clearly non-partisan. Within the German Peace Cartel, however, it was part of the left wing; and its most active members were clearly anti-capitalist and sympathized with socialist or anarchosyndicalist ideas.[46] Against this background emerged repeated discussion within its ranks whether the principle of non-violence could also be justified in a revolutionary civil war. Arnold Kalisch, BdK delegate to the German Peace Cartel and later editor of the BdK's paper *Die Friedensfront* (Peace Front), clearly affirmed non-violence also in such situations; the revolutionary forces, he asserted, did not fire just 'bunches of roses.'[47] Robert Pohl, a cofounder of the BdK, rejected violence in 1923, even in defence against a putsch of the extreme right.[48] Above all, Helene Stöcker, one of the dominant personalities of the German peace movement after the First World War and the BdK's chief theorist,[49] repeatedly stressed the painful discrepancy between 'our ethical desires and reality.'[50] Stöcker, who was also a member of the Revolutionary Pacifist Group – she promoted the interpretation of its 'work for social revolution' along the lines of Friedrich Lassalle's peaceful evolution (Umwälzung)[51] – had argued cogently that it was 'an insolubly tragic characteristic' of this world that made all equally guilty, since also the libertarian struggle that she thought necessary 'would almost certainly require death and destruction as part of the solution.'[52] Though she warned against the dangers of being hypocritical vis-à-vis the class struggle, and therefore even pleaded for the sacrifice of internal peace if that would hinder a new world war,[53] she was nevertheless one of the few pacifists who would maintain their ideals of non-violence against the Nazis.[54]

To secure the peace, the BdK advocated general disarmament (i.e., disbanding of armies), illegalization of war for any reason,[55] and – in case any government should break the peace – massive conscientious objection. The military would anyhow be unable to prevent an invasion physically, argued Arnald Kalisch, 'it could only execute a counterattack.' As real defence existed 'now only in renouncing aggression i.e., in voluntary disarmament,'[56] Germany should consider the disarmament called for at Versailles as a sort of liberation and make itself an example to the world.[57] The war resisters saw conscientious objection as more than just refusing to perform military service; they viewed it in the wider sense of refusing to produce or transport war materiel or weapons, lend money for warmaking, or perform alternative duties that would make others available for military service. This last point was, however, disputed; while some members supported legal alternative service for COs,[58] the majority, supporting voluntary service, warned against any kind of compulsory service as 'contrary to the interests of society, in particular if it were a substitute for military service in time of war.'[59] The BdK energetically resisted the introduction of conscription and the obligatory service demanded by the nationalists as an equivalent to military service.[60] The International Manifesto against Conscription of 1925, promoted by the WRI and signed by some famous personalities, was a BdK initiative.[61] When the creation of a militia system through international negotiation crystallized as a policy goal of the republican parties in 1927, it was the BdK again that had publicly, as well as inside the German Peace Cartel, warned against militias as a force for the militarization of society.[62] The BdK joined with syndicalist youth and other groups against proposals for a national labour service on the grounds that this would be a serious constraint on personal freedom, as well as an attack on the rights of the working man and his pay levels, and would lead to militarization, thereby increasing the risk of war.[63]

Even if a prominent pacifist such as the ethical reformer Magnus Schwantje had hoped in the 1920s that massive conscientious objection would inhibit war,[64] the leading members of the BdK were aware of the limited effect of conscientious objection, no matter what their fairly radical rhetoric might have held. Conscientious objection could 'not [be] a method to stop a war that had already broken out,' argued Johann Orthmann; it constituted rather 'a spiritual attitude' and a 'symbol of a personal contribution in the fight for the peace of nations.'[65] Max Barth saw conscientious objection as a method of controlling the state by the citizen, 'a pressure tactic of the governed,' and 'a moral demonstration.'[66] The BdK regarded it as a way to get the individual to enter the struggle against war directly. In opposition to the segments of the peace movement that uncritically accepted some military experts' visions of future wars of aerial bombardment and poison gas attacks that would be led by small elite groups,[67] the BdK maintained its belief in the role of mass armies and hence also the importance of conscientious objection.[68] Albert Einstein's declaration that conscientious objection of only 2 per cent of those called up would stop a war also raised hopes.[69] Yet when war resisters thought about how a future war could be hindered by strikes,[70] the trade unions' bland declarations of their intention to call a general strike in the event of a war, alongside the SPD's dismissive attitude, failed to convince them that, when things got serious, the workers could really be counted on.[71] Conversely, while war resisters could look proudly to Gandhi's example of non-violent resistance, they were unable in fact to envisage non-violent defence against a potential aggressor.

The BdK saw itself above all as a 'community of conscience' and saw its task as 'getting other organizations to discuss and implement' conscientious objection.[72] Accordingly, it was active in the districts of Zwickau as well as in the Rhineland and Westphalia in the war-resistance plebiscite, initiated in 1927 on an international scale by the British Labour politician and pacifist Arthur Ponsonby. Some 224,000 people in these districts signed the pledge to 'deny military service or labour to any government that resorts to arms.'[73] Yet as the BdK mostly worked together with other peace organizations, its small membership – at its peak in 1930, it had barely 3,000 members, of which only about one hundred were active – usually meant that its influence was small. High unemployment among members following the onset of the world economic crisis further limited its activities.[74] Its increasing marginalization, together with the growth of National Socialism at the beginning of the 1930s, led to a fundamental examination of strategy. War propaganda by the Nazis and the nationalist right was so effective because it drew on 'youthful lust for adventure,' argued Arnold Kalisch. The pacifist's task was therefore 'to create the peace adventure.'[75] As the kind of task that would encourage dedication, personal self-sacrifice,' and a 'feeling of personal involvement,' the war resisters valued the work of the International Voluntary Service for Peace (IVSP), founded in 1920 by the Swiss Quaker Pierre Ceresole.[76] With the IVSP, the BdK adopted the WRI's notion of a 'peaceful heroism' and transformed the self-sacrifice ideal of the warrior hero in the service of his fatherland to a life-affirming heroism.[77] In November 1932 the BdK organized a conference on the practical implications of pacifism that called for a civilian alternative service for COs – clearly a reflection of Ceresole's thought. In connection with the conference, a German branch of the IVSP was established, which, as it turned out, was unable to achieve anything before the establishment of the Nazi regime.

Grossdeutsche Volksgemeinschaft (GVG)

GVG was a loosely organized group centring around the newspaper *Vom Frohen Leben* (From the Happy Life), established in October 1921 by the Catholic priest and author Ernst Thrasolt.[78] Followers of the group – it had no formal membership, dues, or rules – had come mostly from the Greater German Youth and other Catholic youth associations.[79] The GVG saw itself as a part of the

New Life Movement and viewed its mission as comprehensive Christian renewal of the people. The goal of its work of 'creating a German life and nation' was the 'essential man,' freed from such 'limits of this existence' as 'alcohol, nicotine, fashion, the city,' pursuing a life of 'natural simplicity, in spirituality and in brotherhood.'[80] The prescribed turn towards 'healthy, happy poverty and its riches of true happiness' revealed a blood-and-soil mythology that, however, was not rooted in a racial ideology but motivated by the quest for the primordial and the natural.[81] For the GVG, politics was 'a continuation of the individual's humanity into the realm of public life,' with the goal of building the 'kingdom of God on earth.'[82] As the GVG recognized the proletariat and 'his struggle for human justice and human dignity,' it rejected 'immoral capitalism' and the social model of 'Mammonism.'[83] In spite of several realistic social demands,[84] its alternative model – promoted above all by Ernst Thrasolt – of rural settlement was not really a suitable solution for social problems.[85] Its motto, 'back to nature,' hinted at hostility to industry and civilization;[86] it compared the complexities of industrial society unfavourably to the transfigured ideal of a society of rural peasant settlements.[87]

The GVG saw itself not merely as a community of opinion, but above all as a society of deeds.[88] Readers of *Vom Frohen Leben* were constantly encouraged to give generously to charity and to participate freely in a spirit of 'Christian love' in welfare work – for example, in organizing children's groups and summer camps, the care of convicts (prison visits, support after release), and volunteering to help build houses for the needy.[89] Such works of charity, which the GVG could perform with its slim organizational resources and small memberships,[90] formed a concrete part of its peace work, the central element of which was the idea of conscientious objection. The GVG conceded both the individual and the state the right to self-defence, believing, however, that the true followers of Christ completely rejected violence.[91] In modern war, which would guarantee 'complete ruin' and was 'immoral and unchristian beyond all measure,' conscientious objection was not only a right but a duty.[92] Like the BdK, the GVG also held that conscientious objection excluded any direct or indirect support of the war effort; it could include refusal to work and the general strike.[93] Similarly, it rejected all forms of war, including civil war and military sanctions.[94] However, the GVG admitted the need for a police force for the League of Nations – which it sharply criticized as a necessary but flawed institution.[95] If there should ever be a foreign occupation, the GVG saw complete 'rejection of violence' and passive resistance as the only effective way to shake it off.[96]

After some initial ambivalence, the GVG rejected conscription of labour.[97] Instead, it advocated voluntary labour, and it also encouraged Ceresole's IVSP, without taking an explicit position on the question of a legal alternative service for COs.[98] The GVG saw conscientious objection as being rooted in the Christian tradition (for example, the Sermon on the Mount, the church of martyrs, Francis of Assisi). Conscientious objection therefore was by no means contradictory to the teaching of the church, even if the church universal had still to grow into 'a perfect successor of Jesus Christ.'[99] In the final analysis, war was for the GVG a moral and religious problem; only through 'the spirit of Christ and the Sermon on the Mount' could it be overcome.[100] The GVG saw work for radical pacifism as 'core storm troops' inside Catholicism as its mission. Its followers represented the radical wing of the Peace League of German Catholics. In 1926, with the BdK and other groups, the GVG formed the Union of Radical Pacifist Groups of Germany; little resulted from this cooperation, however.[101] The GVG, which joined the WRI in 1928, had been calling on its members to register themselves as potential COs since the summer of 1925.[102] But this call evoked little response; up to the summer of 1930, the organization had attracted only 706 registrations, of whom 118 were from women.[103]

The GVG saw radical pacifism as an embodiment of a 'new heroism.'[104] As with the BdK, this aspect also came to the foreground for the GVG as militarism grew in the late 1920s.[105] In any event, neither the BdK nor the GVG disavowed patriotism; they pointed out that refusal to serve in a modern war was 'not treason to the fatherland, but an effort to rescue the fatherland.'[106] Within the GVG one could even detect a kind of idealistic Enlightenment nationalism, for Germany was attributed a 'world historic' peace mission.[107] The GVG had an equally rosy picture of democracy, which was its pronounced goal. While the BdK supported the republican parties and underestimated the dynamic strength of National Socialism,[108] the GVG denigrated the Weimar republic as 'a monstrosity,' as 'a mix of dopiness, stupidity, weakness, cowardice, half-measures, and dishonour.'[109] The GVG supported the radical pacifist Christlich-Soziale Reichspartei (Christian Social People's party) in the 1928 Reichstag elections, only to back off as the Christian Socialists moved closer to the Communist party after 1930.[110] The GVG advocated a transitional dictatorship as a cure for Germany's ills, until a true democracy emerged, with free personalities who would represent the nation in place of parties.[111] Its call for a 'true dictatorship' and the fight against Weimar's party democracy was motivated by disappointment with the failure of the republic to address the rebuilding of society, but it ended by contributing to the general weakening of democracy. When the National Socialists had taken power, the GVG still bravely held to it democratic ideal.[112]

As in the case of the larger organizations of the Weimar peace movement, the radical pacifists also engaged in international reconciliation.[113] The BdK was not able to make any lasting contact with Polish peace advocates,[114] but in its journal it attempted to counter anti-Polish hate propaganda and to transmit fairly the Polish point of view.[115] In its journal the GVG too fought hate propaganda against the Poles and attempted, by giving balanced information, to create a basis for understanding.[116] Members of the Greater German Youth, and Father Ernst Thrasolt as well, took part in various German–Polish meetings organized by the Quakers and the Veterans' League for Peace.[117] The BdK favoured a solution of the border problem within a European union, which would retain the existing frontiers while making them invisible and thereby impossible to oppose.[118] Thrasolt, in contrast, was ready to recognize Germany's eastern border, but at the same time he did not refrain from criticizing cases of Polish misconduct.[119] The BdK and GVG both defended the cultural autonomy of national minorities, the GVG under the condition that the interests of nationalities were protected.[120]

German Fellowship of Reconciliation (FOR)

In addition to social work, mainly within the framework of the Soziale Arbeitsgemeinschaft Berlin-Ost and of Christian settlements such as those at Sannerz and Sonnefeld, work for international understanding was the chief sphere of activity for the German branch of the International Fellowship of Reconciliation (IFOR). It seems that the German FOR had fewer than two hundred members during the Weimar period and only a very rudimentary organization.[121] Based on Christian-inspired non-violence, the IFOR left it up to each member to decide his/her precise stand on conscientious objection.[122] The German branch, which tended to think in national terms because of the influence of the eminent Protestant churchman Friedrich Siegmund-Schultze – a co-founded of the IFOR and president of the German fellowship – was indeed split on this issue.[123] At that time, Siegmund-Schultze saw conscientious objection as a prophetic act of individuals, of men specially chosen; he therefore refrained from any sort of open encouragement of conscientious objection.[124] On the other side of this issue stood Hermann Stöhr, who was executed in 1940 as a CO; he wished to give conscientious objection a more prominent role in FOR policy.[125]

In spite of sharp criticism of the Versailles Treaty and French armaments, the German FOR strove above all to build understanding with France. This effort was especially strong in 1923–5, when the IFOR helped sponsor a great many Franco–German meetings, visits, and speaking tours, as well as a number of Franco–German hiking expeditions.[126] The overriding goal of these efforts at reconciliation was to create a solid mutual basis of information; the IFOR was indeed well aware that, as a small group, its influence was limited. In connection with the Disarmament Conference the Franco–German question returned to the foreground yet again in 1932.[127] While the predominantly Protestant German FOR found an active partner for its reconciliation work in the French branch of the IFOR, in Poland it had no such contact (since the IFOR did not possess a branch there). The FOR's efforts to build understanding with Poland in the second half of the 1920s was the result mostly of the efforts of the scholarly Catholic priest Hermann Hoffmann, assigned by the IFOR to work for reconciliation with Catholic countries.[128] On occasion with the IFOR's secretary, the Austrian Kaspar Mayr,[129] Hoffmann established contacts with Catholic peace organizations in Poland during numerous speaking tours there. These efforts helped make possible the Catholic German–Polish conferences, organized in collaboration with the IFOR in Berlin in 1929 and in Cologne in 1931. Hoffmann and Mayr were also among the leading speakers at the international youth camp organized by the IFOR in August 1930 at Sromowce in Poland's Tatra Mountains, where participants were chiefly German and Polish young people.[130] And in 1932 Hoffmann and Mayr made one last peace trip to Poland.

Conclusion

At the end of the Weimar era the war resisters found themselves in an unenviable position. It had fallen to them to introduce conscientious objection as a matter for open debate in a German political culture where this was regarded as an alien concept, as well as to spread the idea of conscientious objection among the various sections of the traditional German peace movement. In fact radical pacifists were marginalized at this time. The economic crisis had hit working-class and petty-bourgeois supporters of the radical pacifist organizations especially hard and reduced their sphere of influence to a minimum. The war resisters found it difficult to defend themselves openly against the defamatory onslaught of the Ministry of War and the attacks of the National Socialists.[131] After sober reflection, they were forced to agree with Heinrich Ströbel's assessment that conscientious objection was not going to secure world peace.[132] Ironically, the idea of conscientious objection, through its radical character, was also responsible, by revealing the fragility of the republican concept of defence, for the break within the republican parties and organizations between the pacifistic elements and the elements ready to fight. Nevertheless, the war resisters cannot be held responsible for the resulting further weakening of the republic's defence against National Socialism.

NOTES

A German version of this essay appeared under the title 'Kriegsdienstverweigerung in der Weimarer Republik,' in A. Gestrich et al., eds., *Gewaltfreiheit: Pazifistische Konzepte im 19 und 20 Jahrhundert (Jahrbuch für Historische Friedensforschung 5)* (Münster 1996), 80–102. I would like to thank Helmut Donat (Bremen) and Hans Gressel (Minden) for their valuable advice and the loan of materials.

1 A.C.F. Beales, *The History of Peace: A Short Account of the Organised Movements for International Peace* (London 1931), 8.

2 On radical pacifism before 1914, see Peter Brock, *Freedom from War: Nonsectarian Pacifism, 1814–1914* (Toronto 1991). For a discussion of conscientious objection at the international peace congresses, see Hans Wehberg, 'Das Problem der Kriegsdienstverweigerung auf den Weltfriedenskongressen der Vorkriegszeit,' *Friedens-Warte* (cited below as *FW*) (Berlin, etc.), 24 (1924), 290–92.

3 See, for example, the concise statement in the resolution passed at the Third Congress of the Second International at Zürich in 1893: 'The fall of capitalism means world peace (*der Sturz des Kapitalismus ist der Weltfriede*).' Cited by Christoph Butterwegge and Heinz-Gerd Hofschen, *Sozialdemokratie, Krieg und Frieden: Die Stellung der SPD zur Friedensfrage von den Anfängen bis zur Gegenwart. Eine kommentierte Dokumentation* (Heidelberg 1984), 46.

4 For Nieuwenhuis's resolutions and proposals, see Gernot Jochheim, *Antimilitaristische Aktionstheorie, Soziale Revolution und Soziale Verteidigung: Zur Entwicklung der Gewaltfreiheitstheorie in der europäischen antimilitaristischen und sozialistischen Bewegung 1890–1940, unter besonderer Berücksichtigung der Niederlande* (Assen and Amsterdam 1977), 90–2. Resolutions by Hervé as well as by Hardie and Vaillant are printed in Butterwegge and Hofschen, *Sozialdemokratie, Krieg und Frieden*, 70, 82. Ian McLean, *Keir Hardie* (New York 1975), 142, is unfortunately not very informative on this issue. Hardie was then chairman of the Independent Labour party.

5 See Karl-Heinz Rambke, 'Diesem System keinen Mann und keinen Groschen? Sozialdemokratische Wehrpolitik 1907–1914,' PhD dissertation, University of Würzburg, 1983; Wolfram Wette, 'Die deutsche Sozialdemokratie zur Krieg und Frieden: Ein Überlick,' in his *Militarismus und Pazifismus: Auseinandersetzung mit den deutschen Kriegen* (Bremen 1991), 11–25.

6 For the DFG, see Friedrich Karl Scheer, *Die Deutsche Friedensgesellschaft (1892–1933): Organisation, Ideologie, politische Ziele. Ein Beitrag zur Geschichte des Pazifismus in Deutschland* (Frankfurt am Main 1981); Guido Grünewald, ed., *Nieder Die Waffen! Hundert Jahre Deutsche Friedensgesellschaft (1892–1992)* (Bremen 1992).

7 Remark made at the sixteenth International Peace Congress at Munich in 1907; in Wehberg, 'Das Problem,' 291.

8 Otto Umfrid, 'Warum wir keine Antimilitaristen sind,' *Friedens Blätter* (Esslingen) 10 (1909), 38.

9 See Marceline Hecquet and Martha Steinitz, 'Kriegsdienstverweigerung während des Weltkrieges,' in Franz Kobler, ed., *Gewalt und Gewaltlosigkeit: Handbuch des aktiven Pazifismus* (Zürich and Leipzig 1928), 259.

10 Ibid., 257. See also Ulrich Klan and Dieter Nelles, 'Es lebt noch eine kleine Flamme,' in *Reinische Anarcho-Syndikalisten/-innen in der Weimar Republik und im Faschismus* (Grafenau-Döffingen 1990), 19.

11 Klan and Nelles, 'Es lebt noch eine kleine Flamme,' 34, 35. However, the anarcho-syndicalists of Berg and the Rhineland approved – and practised – the use of armed force under certain circumstances: for example, resistance to the Kapp Putsch in the ranks of the 'Red Army of the Ruhr.'

12 See the speech of Rudolf Rocker at the general conference (*Reichskonferenz*) of workers in the armaments industry held at Erfurt in March 1919 – *Der Syndikalist* (Berlin), 1 (1919) nos. 17 and 18 – as well as the resolution passed in 1921 by the Metalworkers Federation of the FAUD – *Der Syndikalist*, 3 (1921), 4.

13 For the history of this organization, see Otto Lehmann-Rußbüldt, *Der Kampf der Deutschen Liga für Menschenrechte, vormals Bund Neues Vaterland für den Weltfrieden 1914–1927* (Berlin 1927); also Ernst Gülzow, 'Der Bund "Neues Vaterland": Probleme der bürgerlich-pazifistischen Demokratie im Ersten Weltkrieg (1914–1918),' PhD dissertation, University of Berlin/GDR, 1969.

14 See, for example, Siegmund Münz, 'Gegen die allgemeine Wehrpflicht,' *FW*, 21 (1919), 14, 15.

15 For example, Robert Pohl, who was among the founders of the War Resisters' League; *FW*, 28 (1928), 358.

16 For the cartel, see Reinhold Lütgemeier-Davin, *Pazifismus zwischen Kooperation und Konfrontation: Das Deutsche Friedenskartell in der Weimarer Republik* (Cologne 1982).

17 For the controversy in the DFG over conscription, see Scheer, *Die Deutsche Friedensgesellschaft*, 473–8.

18 For the BdK, see Grünewald, 'Friedenssicherung durch radikale Kriegsdienstgegnerschaft: Der Bund der Kriegsdienstgegner (BdK) 1919–1933,' in Karl Holl and Wolfram Wette, eds., *Pazifismus in der Weimarer Republik* (Paderborn 1981), 77–90.

19 Unfortunately so far no history of the GVG exists. Useful information about it can be found in Dieter Riesenberger, *Die katholische Friedensbewegung in der Weimarer Republik* (Düsseldorf 1976), 77–80, 95–7, 158–81, and 244–6, and Franz Henrich, *Die Bünde katholischer Jugendbewegung: Ihre Bedeutung für die liturgische und eucharistische Erneuerung* (Munich 1968), 23–55.

20 Likewise no history of the German FOR is available, but see Lilian Stevenson, *Towards a Christian International: The Story of the International Fellowship of Reconciliation*, 3rd ed. (London 1941); Vera Brittain, *The Rebel Passion: A Short History of Some Pioneer Peace Makers* (London 1964); Hans Gressel, *Der Internationale Versöhnungsbund: Ein Modell des christlichen Pazifismus* (Uetersen 1993).

21 According to the organization's principles approved at the Washington congress; *FW*, 25 (1925), 217. The question of revolutionary violence had before been debated only at the Zürich congress in 1919. See Gertrude Bussey and Margaret Tims, *Pioneers for Peace: Women's International League for Peace and Freedom, 1915–1965* (London 1980), 39; also chapter 13 below by A.M. Pois.

22 *Völkerversöhnende Frauenarbeit*, part 2 (Nov. 1918–Dec. 1920) (Stuttgart 1921), 14–17.

23 This commission, which was dissolved in the mid-1920s, gathered signatures for a declaration that it circulated among women renouncing all support of a future war and, in case war did break out, promising to participate in an international general strike of women. Clearly not many signatures were obtained. *Völkerversöhnende Frauenarbeit*, part 2, 27, 28.

24 According to its new program; *FW*, 27 (1927), 90.

25 See Siegfried Heimann, 'Die Vereinigung der Freunde von Religion und Völkerfrieden (August Bleier, 1892–1958),' in *Internationale Wissenschaftliche Korrespondenz zur Geschichte der Arbeiterbewegung*, 28 (Berlin 1992), 52–62. The German League for Human Rights, however, did not support conscientious objection, as incorrectly stated by Riesenberger,' Die Friedensbewegung in der Weimarer Republik,' in Thomas M. Ruprecht and Christian Jenssen, eds., *Äskulap oder Mars? Ärzte gegen den Krieg* (Bremen 1991), 208.

26 See Lütgemeier-Davin, 'Basismobilisierung gegen den Krieg: Die Nie-Wieder-Krieg-Bewegung in der Weimarer Republik,' in Karl Holl and Wolfram Wette, eds., *Pazifismus in der Weimarer Republik* (Paderborn 1981), 47–76. From 1922 the Veterans' League for Peace declined rapidly. The 1935 Nobel Peace Prize winner and Nazi concentration camp victim Carl von Ossietzky was a member of the Veterans' League and edited its journal, *Nie Wieder Krieg* (No More War). From 1927 on he was editor-in-chief of the radical anti-militarist paper *Die Weltbühne*. He died in 1938.

27 See its 1919 program in *FW*, 26 (1926), 330, and its 1929 program, in *FW*, 29 (1929), 380.

28 See Helmut Donat, 'Die radikalpazifistische Richtung in der Deutschen Friedensgesellschaft (1918–1933),' in Karl Holl and Wolfram Wette, eds., *Pazifismus in der Weimarer Republik* (Paderborn 1981), 27–45; Donat and Lothar Wieland, eds., *Das Andere Deutschland: Unabhängige Zeitung für entschiedene republikanische Poli-*

tik. Eine Auswahl (1925–1933), (Königstein 1980), xxxi–lxviii (from editor's introduction).

29 See, for example, Hein Herbers, 'Der Kriegsdienstverweigerungsbazillus,' *Das Andere Deutschland* (cited below as *AD*) (Hagen-Berlin) 7 (1927), no. 24.

30 'We will defend ourselves with all available means against reaction if it ever uses violence against us'; (Heinz Kraschutzki, 'Gegen den Kleinkaliber-Unfug,' *AD*, 6 (1926) nos. 51–2. Later, however, the usefulness of violence in domestic political conflicts came to be viewed with increasing scepticism; see 'Wie ists mit dem Bürgerkrieg?' *AD*, 11 (1931), no. 32. Leading associates of the *AD* such as the SPD Reichstag deputy Heinrich Ströbel advocated a strong executive for the League of Nations.

31 See *FW*, 24 (1924), 347, and 31 (1931), 188. Because of the destructiveness of modern war, however, the Peace League of German Catholics considered the conditions for a just war to be scarcely realizable in practice. For the Peace League, see Riesenberger, *Die katholische Friedensbewegung;* Beate Höfling, *Katholische Friedensbewegung zwischen zwei Kriegen: Der 'Friedensbund Deutscher Katholiken' 1917–1933* (Waldkirch 1979); Konrad Breitenborn, *Der Friedensbund Deutscher Katholiken 1918/19–1951* (Berlin, GDR, 1981).

32 From the guidelines passed at Frankfurt am Main; Höfling, *Katholische Friedensbewegung*, 139, 140.

33 See Rolf von Bockel, *Kurt Hiller und die Gruppe Revolutionärer Pazifisten (1926–1933): Ein Beitrag zur Geschichte der Friedensbewegung und der Szene linker Intellektueller in der Weimarer Republik* (Hamburg 1990).

34 Kurt Hiller, 'Linkspazifismus' (Speech at the general meeting of the DFG, Braunschweig, 30 Sept. 1920), in the collection of his speeches, *Radioaktiv: Reden 1914–1964. Ein Buch der Rechenschaft* (Wiesbaden 1966), 28.

35 Ibid., 42.

36 See the 1926 program of the Group of Revolutionary Pacifists, in *FW*, 26 (1926), 288, and its 1929 program, in *FW*, 31 (1931), 314.

37 'Revolutionary pacifism ... is not based on the "sacredness of human life" but on the inviolability of the right to life. There is a great difference here. The "sacredness of human life" is unconditional whereas the "right" to life can be surrendered or alienated.' Letter from Kurt Hiller to Hans Wehberg, dated 5 May 1927; cited in von Bockel, *Kurt Hiller*, 93.

38 See Hiller, 'Militanter Pazifismus,' in the collection of his speeches, *Sprung ins Helle: Reden, offene Briefe, Zwiegespräche, Essays, Thesen, Pamphlete gegen Krieg, Klerus, und Kapitalismus* (Leipzig 1932), 19. At the general conference of the BdK, held in Berlin 28–30 March 1929, Hiller declared, 'The goal of revolutionary pacifism is nonviolence but one cannot reach this goal without a minimum of violence. The absolute rejection of violence is a counter pacifist principle'; *FW*, 29

(1929), 184. The Communist faction left the Group of Revolutionary Pacifists in 1929 when its proposal to embody revolutionary use of violence in the new program was not accepted.

39 This ran as follows: 'War is a crime against humanity. We therefore are determined not to support any kind of war and to strive for the removal of all the causes of war.' Cf. the program of the BdK in *FW*, 31 (1931), 313.

40 Ibid.

41 This point has been made by Wolfram Beyer. See his 'Die War Resisters' International,' in *Widerstand gegen den Krieg: Beiträge zur Geschichte der War Resisters' International* (Kassel 1989), 17.

42 See Helene Stöcker, 'Bringt Locarno den Frieden,' *Neue Generation* (Berlin), 22 (1926), 1–7, and the article 'Genf' in her *Verkünder und Verwirklicher: Beiträge zum Gewaltproblem* (Berlin-Nikolassee 1928), 28–33.

43 Steinitz, 'Zur Frage der Ablehnung jeder militärischen Gewaltanwendung,' *FW*, 25 (1925), 138. For a positive view, see, for example, Hellmut von Gerlach, 'Eine Völkerbundexekution und die Sicherheit Frankreichs,' *FW*, 23 (1923), 76–8.

44 See the systematic treatment of the problem by Magnus Schwantje, *Das Recht zur Gewaltanwendung* (Berlin 1922). Schwantje was one of the founders of the BdK.

45 Stöcker, 'Völkerbundexekutive, Frankreich und Sicherheit,' *FW*, 24 (1924), 320.

46 See, for example, Hermann Greid, 'Pazifismus – Sozialimus – Kapitalismus,' *Die Friedensfront* (cited below as *Ff*) (Heide [Holstein]), 2 (1930), no. 12.

47 Arnold Kalisch, 'Bürgerkrieg und Dienstverweigerung,' *FW*, 26 (1926), 143.

48 Wehberg, 'Grundsätzliche Erörterungen zur Politik der deutschen Friedensbewegung,' *FW*, 27 (1927), 164.

49 For Stöcker, see Rolf von Bockel, *Philosophin einer 'neuen Ethik' Helene Stöcker (1869–1943)* (Hamburg 1991); also Christl Wickert, *Helene Stöcker (1869–1943): Frauenrechtlerin, Sexualreformerin und Pazifistin. Eine Biographie* (Bonn 1991).

50 Stöcker, 'Klassenkampf und Gewaltlosigkeit. Ein Gespräch,' in Franz Kobler, ed., *Gewalt und Gewaltlosigkeit: Handbuch des Aktiven Pazifismus* (Zürich and Leipzig 1928), 145.

51 Stöcker, 'Vom Kampf gegen die Gewalt,' *Neue Generation*, 22 (1926), 247, 248.

52 Stöcker, 'Klassenkampf und Gewaltlosigkeit,' 145.

53 See Stöcker, 'Zum vierten Mal in Rußland,' in her *Verkünder und Verwirklicher*, 78, 79.

54 Von Bockel, *Philosophin*, 84, 86; Wickert, *Stöcker*, 153.

55 See the resolution at the BdK's general conference in Berlin on 3 April 1926 in WRI, *Bulletin No. XII: Der Kriegsdienstgegner* (Enfield, Middlesex) (May–June 1926), 12.

56 Kalisch, 'Die Kriegsdienstgegner: das internationale Volk,' *Ff*, 3 (1931), no. 15.

57 Kalisch, 'Abrüstung als Beispiel oder als Forderung,' *Ff*, 2 (1930), 19, and his 'Kriegsdienstverweigerung und Abrüstung,' *Ft*, 4 (1932), 6.

58 WRI, *Bulletin*, no. 2 (Nov. 1923), 3, 4.

59 Resolution of the BdK general conference in Berlin on 29–30 Dec. 1923, *Neue Generation*, 19 (1923), 234.

60 See Henning Köhler, *Arbeitsdienst in Deutschland: Pläne und Verwirklichungsformen bis zur Einführung der Arbeitsdienstpflicht im Jahre 1935* (Berlin 1967).

61 International Action against Conscription, Archives of the League of Nations, Quidde Papers, D II 3 d.

62 Lütgemeier-Davin, *Pazifismus*, 162, 163.

63 See the resolution of a meeting in Berlin in the autumn of 1924, *Neue Generation*, 20 (1924), 328, and an article 'Arbeitsdienstpflicht und Arbeitslosigkeit,' *Ft* (1931), 4.

64 Schwantje, *Das Recht zur Gewaltanwendung*, 12.

65 Johann Orthmann, *Die Kriegsdienstgegner-Bewegung: Von schlichtem Heldentum* (Heide 1932), 26. Orthmann was a member of the national committee (*Reichausschuß*) of the BdK and editor of the *Deutsche Zukunft*, in which *Die Friedensfront* appeared as a supplement from October 1929 on. See Donat, 'Johann Orthmann (1898–1978),' *Grenzfriedenshefte* (Flensburg 1983) no. 2, 90–102.

66 Max Barth, 'Kriegsdienstverweigerung?' *Neue Generation*, 22 (1926), 335. Barth was one of the editors of the democratic leftist *Sonntagszeitung*. See Manfred Bosch, ed., *Mit der Setzmaschine in Opposition. Auswahl aus Erich Schairers Sonntagszeitung 1920–1933* (Moos and Baden-Baden 1989).

67 See Riesenberger, 'Der Kampf gegen den Gaskrieg,' in *Lehren aus der Geschichte? Historische Friedensforschung* (*Friedensanalysen* 23) (Frankfurt am Main 1990), 267.

68 The military specialist Ernst Buchfinke wrote: 'The decision to engage in war will certainly be answered by a protest movement of pacifists and conscientious objectors. Every movement of that sort will be put down ruthlessly.' From his book *Der Krieg von Gestern und Morgen* (Langensalza 1930), 35; cited in Riesenberger, 'Der Kampf gegen den Gaskrieg,' 268.

69 Speech on 14 December 1930 at the Ritz-Carlton Hotel, New York, printed in Otto Nathan and Heinz Norden, eds., *Einstein on Peace* (New York 1960), 116–18.

70 See, for example, Kalisch, 'Die Kriegsdienstgegner und der nächste Krieg,' *Ff*, 1 (1929), no. 1, and Heinz Kraschutzki, 'Generalstreik oder Dienstverweigerung?' *FW*, 30 (1930), 207, 208.

71 The closest approach between trade unions and the peace movement came at the international peace congress organized by the former at the Hague on 10–15 December 1922. In her comments on the practical results of the congress, Helene Stöcker expressed great disappointment; 'Der Haager Weltfriedenkongreß der Gewerkschaftsinternationale,' *FW*, 23 (1923), 39–42. Armin T. Wegner for the BdK, with other

members of the German peace movement, issued a protest against the resolution of the congress peace commission, which had failed to bring up the subject of conscientious objection; Hiller, 'Haager Friedenskongreß,' in his *Verwirklichung des Geistes im Staat: Beiträge zu einem System des logokratischen Aktivismus* (Leipzig 1925), 242.

72 Alfred Oehmke, 'Zur Reichskonferenz des Bundes der Kriegsdienstgegner,' *FW*, 29 (1929), 212.

73 See Lütgemeier-Davin, *Pazifismus*, 240–9.

74 According to its 1930 annual report, only six local groups of the BdK were still active then, while only two groups were represented at its 1931 general conference. There was no money to sponsor a visitation of local groups for reactivating contacts. See *Ff*, 3 (1931), no. 21.

75 Else Hartmann, 'Arbeitstagung für werktätigen Pazifismus,' *Ff*, 4 (1932), no. 23. See also Kalisch, 'Das Schöne an Krieg und Frieden,' *Ff*, 4 (1932), no. 10, and Alfred Seligmann, 'Friedensbegeisterung!' *Ft*, 4 (1932), no. 13.

76 See Daniel Anet, *Pierre Ceresole, la passion de la paix* (Neuchâtel 1969); Hélène Monastier and Alice Brügger, *Paix, Pelle et Pioche: Histoire du Service civil international de 1919 à 1965* (N.p. 1966). The first international work camp (Hilfsdienst) in Germany was held in October 1930 at the Bruderhof near Fulda; twenty-five persons took part. As yet there was no direct contact with Ceresole's organization. See *Die Eiche* (Munich, etc.) (1931), 118.

77 See Beyer, *Widerstand gegen den Krieg*, 23ff. It is probably not a coincidence that the pacifists' idea of peace heroism surfaced when the remilitarization of German public opinion began in 1929.

78 For Ernst Thrasolt, the adopted name of Josef Matthias Tressel, see Walther Ottendorff-Simrock, *Es geht die Zeit zur Ewigkeit: Eine Begegnung mit Ernst Thrasolt* (Ratingen 1959).

79 For an introduction to the Greater German Youth, see Henrich, *Die Bünde*, 23–55.

80 Christian Imboden (E. Thrasolt), 'Untergang oder Ausstieg?' *Vom frohe Leben* (cited below as *VfL*) (Berlin-Würzburg), 2 (1922–3), 4.

81 Christian Imboden, 'Ein dreifacher deutscher Mythos: Scholle, Blut und Nation!' *VfL*, 11 (1931–2), 256ff.

82 Gottschalk (E. Thrasolt), 'Reichgottes-Politik,' *FfL*, 3 (1923–4), 143.

83 'Bekenntnis zum Proletariat! Revolution!' *FfL*, 9 (1929–30), 492.

84 See, for example, Gottschalk, 'Reichgottes-Politik,' 145.

85 Antaeus (E. Thrasolt), 'Rettung der Wirtschaft? Das Reich siedelt!,' *VfL*, 11 (1931–2), 349ff.

86 'Mörderin Zivilisation,' *VfL*, 7 (1927–8), 154. Thrasolt saw, above all, in the large modern cities a reflection of moral decay.

87 See, for example, Imboden, 'Ein dreifacher deutscher Mythos,' 258; Antaeus, 'Wesentliches Leben? Baurnleben!' *VfL*, 11 (1931–2), 366.

88 'Großdeutsche Volksgemeinschaft und "Vom Frohen Leben,"' *VfL*, 9 (1929–30), 258.

89 See 'Veränderungen beim "Fohen Leben,"' *VfL*, 7 (1927–8), 475; 'Grossdeutsche Volksgemeinschafts-Arbeiten. Helft Mit!,' *VfL*, 10 (1930–1), 39–40.

90 In 1931 *Vom frohen Leben* had around 3,500 regular subscribers (a thousand of whom received, however, complimentary copies); *VfL*, 11 (1931–2), 126. But only a few of its readers participated regularly in the activities of the Greater German People's Community (GVG).

91 'Conscientious objection is true faith (*Kriegsdienstverweigerung ist wahrer Glaube*).' Gottschalk, 'Vom Wesen und Sinn der Kriegsdienstverweigerung,' *VfL*, 8 (1928–9), 465; also his 'Gewalt oder Gewaltlosigkeit?', *VfL*, 8 (1928–9), 23.

92 Gottschalk, 'Der Sieg des Pazifismus,' *VfL*, 2 (1922–3), 154–61; also his 'Grund und Leitsätze eines christlich entschiedenen Pazifismus,' *VfL*, 8 (1928–9), 463.

93 See the text of the declaration members of the GVG were required to sign, printed in *Der Kriegsdienstgegner*, Bulletin no. 21 (Sept.–Oct. 1928), 21.

94 See Gottschalk, 'Gewalt oder Gewaltlosigkeit?' 23.

95 See Gottschalk, 'Die Wege vom Krieg zum Frieden,' *VfL*, 10 (1930–1), 409, also 'Völkerbund?' *VfL*, 12 (1932–3), 216.

96 See Gottschalk, 'Vom Wesen und Sinn der Kriegsdienstverweigerung,' 465, and the outline of non-violent methods of resistance in 'Passiver Widerstand?' *VfL*, 2 (1922–3), 134, 135.

97 See Damian Wiroth, 'Gegen die Arbeitsdienstpflicht, '*VfL*, 3 (1923–4), 264ff.; also 'Freiwilliger Arbeitsdienst?' *VfL*, 11 (1931–2), 169.

98 'Taten des Friedens! Ruf an junge Menschen!' *VfL*, 9 (1929–30), 379.

99 Gottschalk, 'Der Sieg des Pazifismus,' 161.

100 Gottschalk, 'Sieghafter Pazifismus,' *VfL*, 9 (1929–30), 82.

101 The leading figures in the union were Kurt Hiller, Helene Stöcker, and Ernst Thrasolt. Its program was printed in *Neue Generation*, 22 (1926), 246, 247.

102 'Einschreibung der Kriegsdienstverweigerer,' *VfL*, 4 (1924–5), 202.

103 'Kriegsdienstverweigerer aus Gewissen,' *VfL*, 9 (1929–30), 482. In the spring of 1931, 944 Catholics signed a new pledge of conscientious objection; *Der Kriegsdienstgegner*, Bulletin no. 28 (spring 1931), 7.

104 See Gottschalk, 'Der Sieg des Pazifismus,' 161.

105 Alfons Erb, 'Vom neuen Heldentum,' *VfL*, 11 (1931–2), 142ff.; also his 'Erziehung zum Frieden durch positive Zielsetzung,' *VfL*, 12 (1932–3), 131ff.

106 Gottschalk, 'Grund und Leitsätze eines christlich entschiedenen Pazifismus,' 461.

107 See Hans Konrad, 'Die Probe auf den Pazifismus oder Großdeutschlands Geburtsstunde,' *VfL*, 2 (1922–3), 136; also Imboden, 'Ein dreifacher deutscher Mythos,' 259.

108 Kalisch, 'Vom Anschluß Deutschland. Eine Wahlbetrachtung,' *Ff*, 4 (1932), no. 21.

109 'Diktatur?' *VfL*, 5 (1925–6) 150.

110 For the CSRP, see the entry *in Lexikon zur Parteiengeschichte: Die bürgerlichen und kleinbürgerlichen Parteinen und Verbände in Deutschland (1789–1945)* (Leipzig 1983), 1: 455–63.

111 See 'Kardinal Faulhaber und Faschismus? Diktatur,' *VfL,* 8 (1928–9), 328; also 'Diktatur oder Demokratie?' *VfL,* 8 (1928–9), 328, 329.

112 See, for instance, 'Demokratie?' *VfL,* 12 (1932–3), 334.

113 For work by the German peace movement on behalf of German–Polish reconciliation, see Höfling, *Katholische Friedensbewegung,* 202–31; Lütgemeier-Davin, *Pazifismus,* 211–14; Riesenberger, 'The German Peace Movement and Its Attitude towards Poland in the 1920s and Early 1930s,' in Grünewald and Peter van den Dungen, eds., *Twentieth-Century Peace Movements: Successes and Failures* (Lewiston/Queenston/Lampeter 1955), 57–79.

114 'Tätigkeitsbericht 1930/31,' *Ff,* 3 (1931), no. 9.

115 See, for instance, Carl Mertens, 'Schluß mit der Korridorhetze,' *Ff,* 2 (1930), no. 13; also Alfred Falk, 'Gerechtigkeit gegenüber Polen,' *Ff,* 2 (1930), no. 18.

116 See for instance, 'Oberschlesienabstimmung und Teilung,' *VfL,* 8 (1928–9), 398, 399; also 'Die antipolnische Greuelpropaganda. Wie sie lügen und hetzen,' *VfL,* 10 (1930–1), 224–7.

117 For instance, in February 1926 and Easter week 1927 in Warsaw and in May 1929 in Berlin, when the first Catholic German–Polish conference took place.

118 Georg Risse, 'Ost-Locarno,' *Ff,* 2 (1930), no. 13.

119 'Garantie-Verträge,' *VfL,* 8 (1928–9), 517, 518; 'Der deutsch-polnische Komplex: Kriegs-Höchstgefahrenzone,' 10 (1930–1), 389, 390; 'Piaristen-Manöver in Polen,' 12 (1932–3), 116, 117.

120 See Kalisch, 'Pazifisten und nationale Minderheit,' *Ff,* 1 (1929), no. 3; 'Völkische Minderheiten?' *VfL,* 8 (1928–9), 521. Assignment of disputed territory should take place according to 'the viewpoint of the majority of the people.' 'Nationale Mehrheiten und Minderheiten,' *VfL,* 8 (1928–9), 329.

121 Lütgemeier-Davin, *Pazifismus,* 51; Eberhard Röhm, *Sterben für den Frieden. Spurensicherung: Hermann Stöhr (1898–1940) und die ökumenische Friedensbewegung* (Stuttgart 1985), 36.

122 Stevenson, *Towards a Christian International,* 29.

123 For Siegmund-Schultze, see Gressel, 'Für eine solidarische Kirche der Zukunft. Friedrich Siegmund-Schultze, Mitbegünder der Ökumene und Pionier der Friedensbewegung,' offprint from *Junge Kirche* (Bremen), 8/9 and 10 (1985); Friedrich Siegmund-Schultze, *Friedenskirche, Kaffeeklappe und die ökumenische Vision: Texte 1910–1969* (Munich 1990); Stefan Grotefeld, *Friedrich Siegmund-Schultze, Ein deutscher ökumeniker und christlicher Pazifist* (Gütersloh 1995).

124 See Grotefeld, *Siegmund-Schultze,* 83, 84. 'For fairness,' Siegmund-Schultze proposed a non-military type of alternative service that would last longer than the nor-

mal term of service for conscripts and would involve danger – for example, at a
hospital for epidemic diseases or where there was a risk of lethal explosions. Siegmund-Schultze, 'Zivildienst,' *Die Eiche*, 13 (1925), 35. After 1945, Siegmund-
Schultze aggressively campaigned for conscientious objection.

125 For Stöhr, who from 1923 to 1925 was assistant secretary of the German FOR, see
Röhm, *Sterben für den Frieden.*

126 See the reports in *Die Eiche*, 11 (1923)–14 (1926).

127 Report on the annual meeting of the German FOR held at Falkenburg (bei Herre-
nalb) in *Die Eiche* 20 (1932), 374, 375.

128 See Hermann Hoffmann, *Im Dienste des Friedens: Lebenserinnerungen eines
katholischen Europäers* (Stuttgart and Aalen 1970), 188–241. In his book, *Die
Kirche und der Friede: Von der Friedenskirche zur Friedenswelt* (Vienna and
Leipzig 1933), 120, Hoffmann called conscientious objection a necessary consequence of realizing that 'today a just war is no longer possible.'

129 In 1931, the International FOR distributed a booklet written by Kaspar Mayr entitled *Ist eine Verständigung zwischen Polen und Deutschland möglich?* (Is an
Understanding between Poland and Germany Possible?). From February 1931 to
May 1933 Mayr published under the FOR's imprint a *Polnisch-Deutsche Korrespondenz*, which then continued for a few numbers under the name *Die Brücke.*

130 Report in *Die Eiche*, 19 (1931), 114, 115.

131 In a publication of the Ministry of War (*Reichswehrministerium*) during the winter
of 1931 it was stated: 'The conscientious objector, like the traitor, deserves the
enmity and contempt of every German.' 'Das Reichswehrministerium beschimpft
Kriegsdienstverweigerer und Pazifisten,' *VfL*, 11 (1931–2), 209. Members of the
Catholic peace movement protested – anonymously, to avoid reprisals – against this
statement. See 'Katholischer Protest gegen das deutsche Reichswehrministerium,'
VfL, 12 (1932–3), 16. In 1931 the National Socialist party (NSDAP) presented a
bill in the Reichstag, according to which (at a future date) conscientious objection
to military service would be punished by death; 'Blut- und Zuchthaus-Kodex Hitler!' *VfL*, 11 (1931–2), 248.

132 Ströbel had written in answer to an inquiry from Arnold Kalisch: 'On the outbreak
of war a war psychosis will be spread by means of the radio and cinema so effectively that the conscientious objectors will remain an insignificant minority, particularly in the most warlike states.' 'Die Schwere unserer Aufgabe,' *Ff*, 3 (1931), no.
10. For Ströbel's socialist pacifism, see Wieland, 'Heinrich Ströbel (1869–1944).
Entwurf einer deutschen Friedenspolitik in der Zwischenkriegszeit,' in Christiane
Rajewski and D. Riesenberger, eds., *Wider den Krieg: Große Pazifisten von Kant
bis Böll* (Munich 1987), 139–46.

6

The Anarchopacifism of Bart de Ligt

HERMAN NOORDEGRAAF

The Dutchman Bart de Ligt (1883–1938) ranks among the most influential anti-militarists of the interwar period. His activities up to 1919 – his Christian-socialist period – were largely confined to his own country. Thereafter, when he was to link his anti-militarism to a free-religious anarchism, he became active in international networks of antimilitarists. An intellectual with a wide and deep erudition, he was not only an organizer but also an important theoretician who made original contributions to the debate on non-violent means of struggle. Following a concise biographical sketch, I present de Ligt's main ideas and conclude with an overview of his final years, when fascism and National Socialism were growing stronger and a new war appeared on the horizon.

Career[1]

Bartholomeus de Ligt was born 17 July 1883 in Schalkwijk (near Utrecht). His father was a clergyman in the Netherlands Reformed Church (the largest of the country's Protestant churches); he belonged to its orthodox wing, which regarded the classical Calvinistic truths as unassailable. The development of de Ligt as an adolescent can be seen as a breaking out of a milieu that he increasingly experienced as a straightjacket. While at secondary school he became acquainted with the social writings of Tolstoy, Ruskin, and others. This evolution continued during his theological studies at the university in Utrecht where, largely outside the official syllabus, he was affected by influences that led him to liberal systems of belief. As a result of the Hegel renaissance in the Netherlands, German idealists – Kant, Fichte, Schelling, and especially Hegel – made an impression on him, and his thought in later years reveals this impact.

Translated from the Dutch by Peter van den Dungen

In 1910 he was appointed preacher in Nuenen, a small municipality in the predominantly Roman Catholic south of the country. Soon he also became involved in various political activities as a member of the Union of Christian Socialists. This combination of Christianity and socialism was unusual and was regarded as very controversial by both sides. The union was therefore very small and initially operated independently of the Sociaal-Democratische Arbeiders Partij, or SDAP (Social Democratic Workers' party), by far the largest socialist party in the Netherlands. Officially this party's basis was Marxism, but it evolved in a reformist and revisionist direction. De Ligt, who soon became one of the Union's principal theoreticians, argued for its independence from the SDAP because of their fundamental differences: it was the Christian-ethical principle of love, not the idea of the class struggle, that made the Christian Socialists decide in favour of socialism (while at the same time not denying the reality of the class struggle).

During the First World War, the Netherlands remained neutral, though the army was mobilized. Whereas the SDAP supported mobilization, under de Ligt's leadership the Union of Christian Socialists adopted a principled opposition to the war, which the union condemned as imperialist, at odds with socialist internationalism, and a violation of the Christian love ethic. De Ligt became one of the most important influences on and organisers of the war resisters' movement, which brought him into sharp conflict with both the church and the SDAP. In 1915 he was banned from the southern provinces, after delivering a fiery antimilitarist sermon. The following year he was imprisoned for fifteen days for his role in the formulation of the *Dienstweigeringsmanifest* (War Resistance Manifesto) of September 1915. No longer able to fulfil his duties as a clergyman, he used the opportunity to devote himself fully to the revolutionary and antimilitarist propaganda campaign.

His clashes with church and state, his study of anarchism and of the writings of free thinkers, and his growing contacts with left-revolutionary groups all contributed to his decision in 1919 to leave the Union of Christian Socialists, since he no longer regarded himself as a Christian. The International Anti-Militarist Union (Dutch: IAMV), founded in 1904 by the leader of Dutch anarchism, Ferdinand Domela Nieuwenhuis (1846–1919), now became the focus of his activities. De Ligt was centrally involved, initially as chairman, in efforts to expand and internationalize the work of the IAMV through establishment of the International Anti-Militarist Bureau (IAMB). His close involvement with the Dutch war resistance movement brought him another prison sentence (twenty-six days) in 1921.

The strain of his campaigns, public lectures, and writings resulted in exhaustion and a temporary (eventually permanent) move to Switzerland. De Ligt was less directly involved in campaigning but published even more prolifically. He visited the Netherlands several times a year to give lectures and maintained his contacts with antimilitarists throughout the world through correspondence and at international congresses in Geneva and elsewhere. In 1929 he joined the international council of the War Resisters' International (WRI). Having overburdened his frail constitution, de Ligt died on 3 September 1938.

De Ligt's Ideas

The Human Being as a Person: Fate and Action

Both during and following his Christian socialist period, de Ligt always regarded resistance to war as part of a wider cultural-philosophical task. A central concept of his thought was the human being as a person, as a being that expresses its rational and moral faculties and on this basis helps to shape itself and the surrounding environment. This view has been advocated throughout history by minority groups, albeit frequently in mythical and religious language and images. Scientific and technological progress has made possible what in the past had been impossible – the possibility now exists to bring about a community of free persons. De Ligt argued that humanity was on the threshold of a 'new history,' but backsliding remained a constant danger. The human being is precariously balanced between the sub-animal and (viewed from the present perspective) the superhuman. War is a striking example of the sub-bestial. The point is to become ever more human so as to bring about further historical progress. De Ligt believed in progress, and he showed here the influence of Hegel especially – history as the unfolding of freedom. However, he was no adherent of a naïve belief in progress: progress had always to be conquered by the conscious and deliberate efforts of those who refused to accept certain circumstances as their fate and who, through action, raised themselves above that fate.

De Ligt regarded the war resisters of his day as belonging to those minorities who were the harbingers of a higher culture: 'At the same moment when we refuse to put our person in the service of the capitalist-militarist regime, we, for our part, render capitalism impossible. Not circumstances (which are incidental) achieve this, nothing external, ... but the internal self, the spiritual-mental: that is, the human personality which creates its own freedom through, and despite, circumstances and which can demonstrate its freedom-creating power even in the face of superior, annihilating circumstances – by remaining faithful to itself while on the point of collapse externally, economically, physically.'[2]

De Ligt argued for a 'two-fold revolution' (also the title of a pamphlet that he wrote in 1917), of society and of the individual. His main goal, however, was the internal, individual revolution: changing the external circumstances (as Marxism correctly demanded) was not sufficient. De Ligt emphasized the human person and the key concepts of responsibility and solidarity: 'What is new in the world, and relatively still uncommon, is a person, man or woman, who quite consciously and responsibly has decided to work for a future worthy of human beings and, from this standpoint, as much as possible to determine his or her attitude toward the present.'[3]

The basis for such a position is human solidarity, or even more, solidarity with all living things. (De Ligt was a convinced vegetarian.) In this sense his anarchism was indeed religious, even though he had abandoned Christianity and belief in a personal God.

Spiritual-mental Resistance and Direct Action

De Ligt's opting for anarchism (instead, for instance, of revolutionary Marxism) can be explained by the strong role that he assigned to the human being as a creative and responsible actor in the historical process. Anarchism puts individual freedom and responsibility in the centre, implying grassroots and direct action. This can and, one hopes, will result in mass action without a surrender of the notion of personal, individual decision-making. It is a characteristic feature of the anarchist position that responsibility cannot be transferred to the state and that the individual act remains central. De Ligt elaborated the methods of direct action with respect to the antimilitarist struggle. Though the refusal of military service continued to play a vital role in it, already during the First World War he started to pay attention to other forms of non-cooperation. He increasingly focused on the idea of 'responsible production' and hence on the idea of industrial – and, more broadly conceived, social – resistance. He borrowed this notion from the English writer and social reformer John Ruskin (1819–1900), who, though not a pacifist, had during the Franco-Prussian War urged British workers not to engage in munition-making.

De Ligt's increasing insistence on this kind of refusal was intimately connected to his analysis of modern war: not only the front was important, but also the hinterland, where the tools of war were manufactured. Total war required total mobilization, and the connection between front and hinterland had become crucial. The most vulnerable links in this chain were the industrial resources and the means of transportation. Thus responsibility for war and preparation for war was widely shared. Like the German anarchist Rudolf Rocker, de Ligt argued that not only the guns but also the hammers had to be downed, and with his Austrian friend, Franz Kobler, he pleaded: 'War resisters! Conquer the factories.' The old slogan of the IAMV, 'Neither man nor money for the army,' he rephrased as 'Neither man nor money nor labour for militarism.'

With these ideas de Ligt also followed in the steps of Domela Nieuwenhuis, who had pleaded unsuccessfully at the congresses of the Socialist International in Brussels (1891) and Zürich (1893) for adoption of the general strike as a tool to prevent war. This emphasis on direct action was a reflection of the belief that the key problem consists not in the fact that there are leaders and a ruling class but in the fact that there are people willing to obey their orders. De Ligt made a distinction between an active and passive militarism, the latter making possible the former: 'Ultimately, the millions of non-revolutionary workers are the greatest force for conservatism. A people in uniform is its own tyrant. The real foundation of the imperial pyramid is formed by a contra-, anti-, and non-revolutionary proletariat.'[4]

This position explains de Ligt's admiration for Étienne de la Boétie's slim essay *Discours de la servitude volontaire*, which also influenced Thoreau, Tolstoy, and Gandhi. De la Boétie (1530–1563) argued that the will to freedom is inherent in the human being, who is oppressed and exploited as a result of voluntary bondage. As soon as this fact was realized all slavery would vanish, as if by magic. De Ligt ensured that the essay was also available in a Dutch translation (1933), for which he wrote an extensive introduction.

De Ligt concentrated his efforts on the theoretical and practical elaboration of direct action, based on non-violent means of struggle. The key concept in this respect was 'spiritual-mental resistance,' an expression that he coined at the end of the First World War. Without his realizing so at the time, it partly embodied the same idea as Gandhi had expressed in the concept of 'ahimsa.' Non-violence can be the result of weakness or of cowardice, allowing injustice and war to take place. Violent resistance and action are preferable to this kind of non-violence. However, there exist non-violent means of struggle: based on love, they represent a force that surpasses that of violent means. These means presuppose an inner moral force that constantly makes an appeal to the humanity of the other; thus one aims not to conquer others but to convince them, partly by showing willingness to suffer oneself.

De Ligt argued that not only on moral but also on pragmatic grounds non-violent means of struggle were preferable; this perspective was gaining in strength on account of developments in weapons technology, which rendered the consequences of war increasingly gruesome and wide-ranging. Hence the urgency from a practical point of view of applying non-violent means of struggle. This principled yet utilitarian reasoning is characteristic of de Ligt's ethics.[5] The development and use of non-violent means of struggle were seriously hampered by the prevalent faith in violence. De Ligt observed: 'Even more disquieting than the actual practice of violence is the confidence people repose in it.'[6] This view was reinforced by nationalism, which led people to believe that their own country was superior to others.

De Ligt therefore assigned a pivotal role to education, in order to achieve a process of mental detoxification. Together with his wife, Ina de Ligt-van Rossem, who was deeply interested in educational issues, he followed closely experiments and developments in pedagogy. These were, he believed, essentially anarchistic, since the general principles underlying them were those of self-realization through freedom, freedom in society, and active and free discipline. Together the de Ligts visited new schools in Hamburg and Vienna and reported on them in their book *Nieuwe scholen in Hamburg en Weenen* (1930).

In his main work, *Vrede als Daad* (2 vols., 1931 and 1933), de Ligt showed that the idea of spiritual-mental resistance, and of nonviolent method of struggle based on it, could be found throughout history in many cultures: it belonged to all humanity.[7] It was true, of course, that ceratin groups – because of their oppression – at times showed greater receptivity to change in the direction of an all-encompassing humanity; and here he referred to the proletariat, women (De Ligt was a strong advocate of women's emancipation, to break the one-sidedly male domination of society), and the 'coloured peoples.' Their way of struggle, if conducted non-violently, would serve as an example, and he therefore attached great importance to Gandhi's position. In his correspondence with Gandhi, however, he requested clarification of the latter's willingness to compromise during the Boer War and the First World War and wondered what his position would be if a new war threatened.[8]

For de Ligt it was essential to appeal in the first instance not to humans' class interest, to other similar interests, or to their social position, but to their being human. The appeal to interests could be justified but could also result in the exclusion of many people and in this way prevent application of nonviolent methods of struggle. De Ligt asserted: 'In the critical moments of history, it is not a question of appealing to what is "plebeian" in the masses; what is needed, is to awaken in them a human personality ... It is [precisely] because they are men [sic] that they have to free themselves one and all from their state of being "proletarians" and "plebeians." '[9]

His insistence on direct action as well as his anarchist ideas generally made de Ligt an opponent of the League of Nations: 'The nearer to Geneva, the further from a league of nations and peace.' He characterized faith in the league as 'a false belief in the Messiah,' and those who trusted in it were 'confessing to the devil.'[10] De Ligt saw in the league an attempt to regularise the imperialist system, since lack of order constituted a threat to the system. The League of Nations gave priority not to universal human needs, but to those of the ruling classes in the national states. It did not touch the imperial system – the source of continuing conflict. Negotiations about disarmament could have only limited success; they helped to obfuscate the hidden mechanisms of imperialism. De Ligt concluded: 'The "real league of nations" has to be created by revolutionaries outside, and against, the bourgeois governments.'[11]

Revolution and Violence

De Ligt made strenuous efforts to undermine the belief in violence prevalent in revolutionary circles, as his comments on the Russian Revolution clearly show. Shortly after the assumption of power by the Bolsheviks, de Ligt wrote a critical article, 'This Is Not the Way' (in *Opwaarts*, organ of the Union of Christian Socialists, 16 November 1917). In it, he welcomed the revolution as an advance in the history of humanity. However, the acceptance of military means for the defence of the revolution was tantamount to an attack on, and a diminution of, the essence of the revolution. Violence must be combated, and could only be conquered, by means that in their essence went beyond militarism. His position can be characterized as one of critical solidarity: sharing the goals of the revolution, he defends it against those who reject socialism, but he is critical of the violence and terror used.

The relationship between ends and means was for de Ligt, on both principled and pragmatic grounds, crucial. He regarded the view that the means used were neutral for the achievement of ends as fundamentally flawed: violence inextricably created, organizationally as well as spiritually and mentally, new forms of oppression. De Ligt rejected the Marxist-Leninist notions that a free society would eventually emerge from revolution but that in the meantime this required a dictatorship. For him, a revolution could grow only from the bottom upward; with Lukács he posits that freedom is not the result but the engine of revolution.

A social dictatorship, together with a hardened bureaucracy and a systematic militarization of the masses, fatally undermines the subjective conditions necessary for the success of a truly social and spiritual-mental revolution. For historical materialism, methods are not seen as problematical on account of that theory's moral and psychological deficiencies. It is precisely belief in violence, de Ligt argues, that promotes use of violence also in the revolution and which blocks development of nonviolent methods of struggle. In this way, an irrational fatalism obscures the view of the human being as a creative factor in the historical process. For de Ligt, it was the task of radical antimilitarists to promote a *revolutie van de revolutie* (revolution of the revolution)[12] by making use of nonviolent means of struggle also in revolutionary situations. Though de Ligt always insisted on the significance of the Russian Revolution for world history, he became increasingly critical of it because of its reliance on terror and dictatorship. He took fellow-travellers such as Romain Rolland and André Gide to task for their uncritical attitude. Following Lenin's death he still referred to his 'world historical significance,' though he regarded Lenin primarily as a tyrant and an opportunistic and exceedingly cunning politician. He wrote: 'We anarchists do not play this game ... We do not want any dogmatism, no inner militarism, no intellectual uniform which renders our mind inaccessible for the rich diversity of life. We strive for a free, new philosophy of life and are also eager to understand our adversaries, appreciate them as much as possible. Isn't this the purest and most efficient way of combating them?'[13]

Mobilization against War: The 1930s

With Fascism and National Socialism growing increasingly stronger, the radical peace movement saw itself confronted more explicitly with the question whether non-violence offered an effective answer to those super-violent movements. This issue was all the more acute for de Ligt because he continued resolutely to reject the arms policies of the parliamentary democracies. For him, imperialism remained the framework for interpreting world history. Though he recognized the existence of a qualitative difference between the totalitarian regimes and the parliamentary democracies, he refused to identify himself with the latter, because of their imperialistic-capitalistic nature. In his view the 1930s were characterized by a war psychosis and fever that gripped even some of his antimilitarist comrades (such as Einstein for instance).[14] Carefully studying the publications issued by the military on rearmament and strategy, de Ligt concluded that a total war was on the horizon unless there were forceful antimilitarist countervailing actions. The new war would require the total mobilization, in mind and deed, of the entire population. Against this total mobilization, which was already under way, a no-less comprehensive mobilization against war and preparation for war had to be mounted, this one aimed at total peace.

That task occupied de Ligt intensely from the early 1930s on; gripped almost obsessively by the successive threats of war (the stakes were enormous!), he worked feverishly on the alternatives. For instance, during the WRI congress in Lyon in 1931 he proposed the distribution, in millions of copies and as soon as practicable, of a 'Manual of War Resistance.' Again, at the congress in Grenoble in 1932 of the Women's International League for Peace and Freedom he pointed out the need for a permanent counter-mobilization. He presented a first, fairly elaborate outline of this proposal at a 'Student Peace Action' conference in the Netherlands on 16 February 1933. He entitled it *War against War* (the lecture subsequently appeared as a pamphlet).

De Ligt went further at the WRI congress that took place in Welwyn, England, from 26 to 30 July 1934. There, in a '100-minute speech,' he explained in detail his plan of action: *Mobilization against war!* In it he put forward suggestions for direct action to prevent war before it broke out and, if this was unsuccessful, to oppose mobilization and then the actual waging of war. He distinguished between individual and collective direct action; such action was based on the ideas of conscientious objection to military service as well as resistance in the workplace. In all of this de Ligt paid full attention to the mental-spiritual component: the need to bring about a universal mentality that replaces belief in violence with respect for and love of others.

The International Council of the WRI immediately adopted the plan for further study and for this purpose forwarded it to all WRI branches, supporting organizations, and sympathetic trade unions. This *Plan of Campaign against All War and All Preparation for War* was translated into several languages and was widely studied and discussed.[15] In England a committee of study was established especially to examine de Ligt's scheme. In the Netherlands, study centred in the Jongeren Vredes Actie, or JVA (Young People's Peace Action) and resulted in the concept of a 'pacifist people's defence.' Discussion also took place in the Christian antimilitarist society Kerk en Vrede (Church and Peace), though there it eventually proved impossible to find a majority willing to support the plan.

An outgrowth of these efforts for a 'mobilization against war' was that de Ligt became totally committed to persuading the antimilitarist organizations from various countries to unite their efforts. He was the driving force behind the Rassemblement International contre la Guerre et le Militarisme (RIGM), which held its inaugural conference in Paris from 1 to 5 August 1937. The RIGM aimed at uniting all individuals and organizations that strove for general, immediate and unilateral disarmament. Its minimum program consisted of the refusal to engage in any kind of war preparation (military, industrial, and social), including military service; the demand for political, economic, and social justice as an essential condition for the achievement of a comprehensive peace; and the demand for the freeing of the five hundred conscientious objectors then in prison in a number of countries.

The extent to which the advance of Fascism confronted the antimilitarist movement with the question of whether or not to use violence was clearly revealed in the discussions on the Spanish Civil War (1936–9). They provoked a crisis, for instance, in the IAMB: those who rejected, in a principled manner, any form of violence were confronted by those who admitted violence as a last resort against an oppressive regime. Though this divergence of views had always existed in the IAMV and the IAMB, it had so far remained a theoretical question, but now, under the pressure of events, it had come out into the open and was forcing members to decide one way or the other. De Ligt's position was in a way an intermediate one: he refused to condemn those who accepted violence (in accordance with his view that violent resistance was preferable to resignation or submission); yet he believed that the IAMB should come to the support only of those who advocated nonviolent resistance.[16] The ensuing clash of opinions meant that, practically speaking, the IAMB ceased to function.

De Ligt continued during these years to devote himself intensely to research; on the occasion of the four-hundredth anniversary of Erasmus's death in 1936, he published his important biography. De Ligt was a great admirer of this Christian humanist and prominent educator, who had made strenuous efforts to mobilize all the intellectual, moral, religious, and social forces of his day in the cause of peace. The central element in Erasmus's philosophia christiana was that of peace as an inner reality and as a creative, life-renewing force: 'peace as deed.' In de Ligt's view, Erasmus was primarily a humanist; as a precursor of freedom of thought he was indeed 'driven by rational conviction.' He had 'equipped himself as a warrior so as to persuade his contemporaries of the abnormality, criminality, and stupidity of war, and [he] attempted to steer all their actions in the direction of the normal: that all-encompassing peace, which amounted to global solidarity and universal justice, and through which the whole world would be humanised.' The intensity that characterised de Ligt's life and work was now seriously undermining his constitution, which was never strong. He was frequently ill and once commented, 'Erasmus nearly killed me!'

In his last years de Ligt and Aldous Huxley became close friends.[17] As a delegate of the Peace Pledge Union, Huxley met de Ligt at the Universal Peace Congress held in Brussels in September 1936. Afterward, Huxley visited de Ligt in Switzerland for intensive discussions on the use of non-violent means of struggle in the pursuit of a socialist society. These discussions influenced Huxley's *Ends and Means*, while his recommendation contributed to the publication in English of de Ligt's *Conquest of Violence*. (Both books appeared in 1937.) At the start of 1938 de Ligt involved Huxley, together with Maria Montessori and others, in the establishment of a Peace Academy. Its task was the development of a 'science of peace'. As de Ligt explained it: 'The science of peace should ... elaborate a whole system of non-violent fighting and prepare a new system of education for individuals and the masses. In a word, whereas the science of war, having reached its culminating point, can only aim at [total] war, the science of peace can only aim at [total] peace. This means that all the moral and intellectual forces of [people], in all professions and all branches of science and art, must be mobilized in the service of peace and its natural complement: social justice.'[18]

Thus de Ligt insisted on the responsibility of intellectuals for the development of this science of peace. The first summer school of the Peace Academy was held in August 1938 in Jouy-en-Josas (near Paris). It took place, however, without its founder, who had suffered a sharp decline in health over the summer. He attempted to regain his strength in Brittany in the company of his wife, but at Nantes on 3 September 1938, on the return journey home, he suffered a fatal heart attack. He was aged fifty-five. In the words of his wife: 'His life was like a flame which burnt out too quickly.'[19]

NOTES

1 For the life of de Ligt, the commemorative volume published shortly after his death remains an invaluable source: *Bart de Ligt, 1883–1938* (Arnhem 1939). I deal extensively with his life up to 1919 in a book based on my doctoral thesis: *Niet met de wapenen der barbaren: Het christen-socialisme van Bart de Ligt* (Baarn 1994).

2 Cf. his pamphlet *Socialisme en dienstweigering* (1916), which was reprinted in a collection of articles by de Ligt: *Kerk, cultuur en maatschappij* (Arnhem 1925), 115.

3 Introduction by de Ligt in J. Giesen, *Nieuwe Geschiedenis: Het anti-militarisme van de daad in Nederland* (Rotterdam 1923), xxvi.

4 De Ligt, *De antimilitaristen en hun strijdwijzen* (The Hague 1921), 15.

5 Cf. the characteristic title of chapter 6 of de Ligt, *The Conquest of Violence*, first pub. 1937 (reprinted London 1989): 'The Effectiveness of the Non-violent Struggle.'

6 De Ligt, *The Conquest of Violence*, 3.

7 For a retrospective appreciation of this work (in its French, and partial, translation), see Peter Brock, *Bart de Ligt (1883–1938): Reflections on Rereading 'La Paix Créatrice' after Fifty-one Years* (Zwolle 1995).

8 The correspondence was published in *Een wereldomvattend vraagstuk: Gandhi en de oorlog* (Utrecht 1930). De Ligt and Gandhi met in 1931 in Geneva following Gandhi's participation in the Round Table Conference.

9 De Ligt, *The Conquest of Violence*, 187.

10 Quotations taken from de Ligt's work, *The Conquest of Violence*, 57; *Nieuwe vormen van oorlog en hoe die te bestrijden* (Lochem 1927), 11; and *De Wapens Neder* (The Hague, Jan. 1927), respectively.

11 De Ligt, *De antimilitaristen en hun strijdwijzen* (The Hague 1921), 20. For de Ligt's analysis of the League of Nations see, for example, *The Conquest of Violence*, chap. 11.

12 Cf. his lecture at the anarchist congress in Berlin, 25–31 December 1921; an extended version was published as *Anarchisme en Revolutie* (Baarn 1922).

13 De Ligt, 'Bij de dood van Lenin,' in *De Vrije samenleving: Orgaan van het Socialis-tisch-Anarchisten Verbond* (Amsterdam), 2 Feb. 1924.

14 Cf. de Ligt's article 'Het geval Einstein in wijder verband,' in *Bevrijding* (Utrecht) (Oct. 1933). He talks of the shock that the 'world-wide antimilitarist movement' experienced following Einstein's announcement that he no longer supported the war resistance movement. See also his *The Conquest of Violence*, 21, 82.

15 The plan also appeared as an appendix in de Ligt, *The Conquest of Violence.*

16 For de Ligt's view of the Spanish Civil War, see, for example, ibid., 191ff.

17 Cf. Peter van de Dungen, 'Bart de Ligt, Aldous Huxley and "The Conquest of Vio-lence,"' in *Bart de Ligt (1883–1938): Peace Activist and Peace Researcher* (Zwolle 1990).

18 De Ligt, *Introduction to the Science of Peace* (London 1939), 31.

19 *Bart de Ligt, 1883–1938*, 226.

7

The Conviction of Things Not Seen: Christian Pacifism in France, 1919–1945

PETER FARRUGIA

Surveying the years between 1919 and 1945, we can see that French religious pacifism underwent an evolution that can be broken down into four major stages. The years 1919–25 represented a wilderness experience, when Christian pacifists were among the very small minority crying out for reconciliation between France and Germany. The second phase, between 1925 and 1932, saw a transfiguration, when French religious pacifists basked in the new-found respectability that the achievements of Aristide Briand gave to all forms of opposition to war.[1] Following Briand's death in 1932 there began a Gethsemane experience that endured until the outbreak of the Second World War. The deterioration of the international situation led to some new initiatives aimed at revitalizing pacifism and to much soul-searching on the question of war and peace. Finally, the war years can be viewed as a time when religious pacifism was on the cross. Following the defeat of 1940, French religious pacifists faced the difficult questions of whether they were called to resistance and, if so, how best to register their opposition while remaining true to their rejection of violence.

Historians of peace movements tend to relegate French antiwar activism to the second rank, which is understandable. French pacifist organizations never attained the numbers or cohesiveness of their cousins elsewhere in Europe. For instance, there was no organization in France comparable in size to the Peace Pledge Union in Britain.[2] Indeed, conditions in France were anything but conducive to the development of strong organizations dedicated to the eradication of war.[3] One of the most striking features of French religious pacifism – and one of the reasons frequently advanced for its inability to exert greater influence – was its domination by a small minority of activists drawn almost exclusively from the Reformed Protestant churches.[4] Another thing that has damaged the reputation of French pacifism has been its equation with sympathy to fascism. The view that pacifism was tantamount to philofascism gained classic expression from George Orwell in July 1942, when he wrote: 'Pacifism is objectively pro-Fascist. This is elementary common sense. If you hamper the war effort on one side you automatically help that of the other ... In so far as it takes effect at all, pacifist propaganda can only be effective against those countries where a certain amount of freedom of speech is still permitted; in other words it is helpful to totalitarianism.'[5] The tenacity of this view has been all the more evident in France, where the experience of Vichy created deep wounds that have yet to heal.[6]

From Wilderness Experience to Transfiguration, 1919–1932

In October 1919, in the Dutch town of Bilthoven, fifty Christians from ten nations gathered to create the International Fellowship of Reconciliation (IFOR).[7] They included the English Quaker Henry Hodgkin, the well-known German pacifist Friedrich Siegmund-Schültze, and a young French Protestant theology student named Henri Roser.[8] Roser would become the leader of the French section of the fellowship – the Mouvement international de la réconciliation (MIR).

The basis of this group's pacifism was apparent in one of its earliest leaflets. Its creators maintained that, beyond the apparent differences of class, religion, and national interest, there was an underlying human unity that compelled everyone to work for peace. Humanity was called to build a new world order 'in which mutual trust, justice and fraternal cooperation serve to untangle the most daunting political and economic conflicts.' Such a transformation in human affairs 'cannot be accomplished by the game of words and programmes, nor by a humanitarian sentimentality. Everything must begin with the transformation of individuals.'[9] Here is the emphasis on individual spiritual renovation that would mark much of French religious pacifism between 1919 and 1945. It has been characterized as both its greatest strength and its foremost weakness.

The MIR's creed emphasized that war was diametrically opposed to the law of love preached by Jesus Christ. Its adherents were convinced that 'there is such an antagonism between war and the Gospel that it has become impossible for them even to prepare for it ... That is why they oppose military service and military training, support efforts towards the complete and simultaneous disarmament of all states and call for the use of international institutions in the peaceful settling of all conflicts.'[10] The MIR therefore rejected not only the practice of war but also all military preparations, in particular compulsory military service. This stance would lead the group into direct conflict with the state, especially when French leaders attempted to increase military readiness in response to the rise of fascism in the 1930s.

The MIR's early years were ones of struggle both for the fledgling group and for its inexperienced leader. The one constant was a refusal to compromise, which came directly from Henri Roser himself. Constancy was much valued in the Roser family. Roser's father had been forced to move his family from Alsace to France after refusing to swear allegiance to the German emperor in 1871. Initially at least, Henri pursued a conventional path. After graduating from the Sorbonne in 1918, he started his three years of military service. In March 1921, he began theological studies at the Paris Missionary College. However, in the wake of the Ruhr invasion, he returned his military papers to the authorities and made it clear that he now refused to bear arms. As a result, the Missionary Society declined to offer him any appointment. Years later he was still prevented from receiving ordination on account of the conscription law.[11]

Initially, the MIR's fortunes mirrored Roser's. The group struggled to gain cohesion and to expand. Gradually, the situation improved. A growing number of young theology students sharing the same principles of unconditional renunciation of war began to coalesce around Roser. In the mid-1920s the MIR undertook numerous initiatives, including a tour of Germany by thirty youths. One of the participants was a young man named Jacques Martin. He was to help ensure that the movement was on more solid ground, thanks to his work for the MIR organ, the *Cahiers de la réconciliation*.[12]

Public estimation of pacifism had also changed markedly in the interim. The international situation had been transformed by the Treaty of Locarno. To paraphrase Léon Daudet of the Action Française: 'Versailles had fallen into Lake Locarno.' This accord among Britain, France, and Germany ushered in a new era of hope in European politics.[13] In France, Foreign Minister Aristide Briand was hailed as a visionary. Of course his opposition to war was always conditional and predicated on a shrewd calculation of France's interests. Still, the advent of warmer relations among the former combatants encouraged peace advocates of all shades of opinion. Religious pacifists were no exception.

The increased interest in anti-war philosophies was symbolized by the Bierville conference of 1926. Bierville was the brain-child of the Catholic peace activist Marc Sangnier and was part of a plan for an entire 'International Month.' This month also featured a pilgrimage from First World War battlefields to Paris and a series of lectures on international relations. Despite some opposition, Bierville proved a great success. A declaration in support of the conference was signed by 117 prominent politicians, including Paul Painlevé, minister of war, and Edouard Herriot, minister of public instruction.[14] The Catholic church also gave its imprimatur. The bishops of Arras, Châlons, Monaco, and Versailles all took part in the proceedings.[15]

Unfortunately, Bierville represented the apex of popular interest in the ideals espoused by religious pacifists and 'eirenicists.'[16] As attempts at Franco–German reconciliation stumbled, a more intransigent view of how best to combat war gained attention. It was the view espoused by men such as Henri Roser, who went so far as to advocate conscientious objection to military service. Conscientious objection was not sanctioned in France by either the Catholic or Protestant churches. However, Roser had always eschewed a collaborative approach, which accepted the possibility of alliance with eirenicists, whose opposition to war was conditional.[17] Roser resisted compromise because he believed conscientious objection was a natural outgrowth of a clear reading of the scriptures. He maintained that in matters of theology it was best to 'stick to the Gospel. And the Gospel ... seems to suggest that the motor of history is sacrifice. I conceived conscientious objection as a living testimony, allowing that which could not be understood on an intellectual level to be felt.'[18] Roser's attachment to conscientious objection was in large part emulation of the sacrifice of his Lord. It was also a rejection of the imposition of certain obligations by the state. Roser called compulsory military service 'an absolute right that the State assumes over the lives of human beings and their consciences. For a Christian, there is nobody except God who has absolute rights on consciences, and we are not free to choose between the State and God.'[19] This libertarian streak meant that Roser was not averse to supporting anarchist conscientious objectors (COs).[20]

The core of Roser's protest, however, remained his faith. In 1929 he laid out his peace theology in a letter to a friend. He saw two conceptions of pacifism constantly offered, in contrast to each other. The first was 'an activist or so called Anglo-Saxon conception, which, in placing the accent on human cooperation, limits the part of God ... to a secondary or even dubious role.' Roser opposed this view, maintaining that 'the initiative, the inspiration, the direction of the Kingdom of God belongs to God alone.' Still, for His plan to succeed He needed 'souls completely delivered, lives in which all is submitted ... to His will.'[21] Roser envisioned pacifism not so much as a movement that would convince people of its effectiveness but rather as a natural consequence of faith.

Pacifism in the Garden of Gethsemane, 1932–1939

On 7 March 1932 Aristide Briand died. Even before his passing, the spirit of Locarno had appeared moribund. As the optimism of the Locarno era faded away, religious pacifism in France was put to the test. The temporary cachet that opposition to war had enjoyed when hope was running high in Europe had led some religious pacifists to adopt a more collaborative stance in their efforts to avert war. Now, as the international situation grew darker, the majority of religious pacifists retreated from the political realm entirely.

Withdrawal from the wider world was the approach chosen by the MIR. Increasingly the MIR stressed the need to maintain purity of conscience without regard to consequences in the temporal world. This was shown in the group's approach to military service. Roser spoke for his colleagues when he said that 'the instant that it is a matter of a truth expressed in the Gospel, one must follow it immediately and not tomorrow when the law will permit it, when the State will have sanctioned the truth, when it will no longer cost anything.'[22] The legality of their actions did not concern the COs.

This resolve to place God's law before that of the state was put to the test when conscientious objection emerged into national prominence in France. A number of factors combined to thrust the issue into the limelight. The reputation of Mahatma Gandhi, who had been leading Indian civil disobedience against Britain since 1919, was growing rapidly. His appearance at the London Round Table conference in 1931 stimulated much interest.[23] In addition, on all sides there was mounting frustration at the increasing tension in international relations. Pacifists were greatly discouraged by the endless debates at the Disarmament Conference in Geneva, which seemed destined to fail. The French government was determined to take a more truculent stand in the face of rising nationalism in Germany, introducing legislation that increased the penalties for resistance to military service; all this served to arouse passions regarding conscientious objection.

The focal point of debate was a series of well-publicized trials beginning in 1932; many of the defendants were MIR militants.[24] Jacques Martin, who at first 'for family reasons' had performed his military service, now refused. His trial took place in Paris in October, and he was given a one-year sentence for refusing to bear arms. After seven months, thanks to the work of the Ligue des Droits de l'Homme, he was set free. However, he was called up again in 1934 and again refused to serve, receiving a further year in jail in 1935. As a result of his stand, he was rejected when he presented himself for ordination. Philippe Vernier, then in training for the pastorate and also, like Martin, active in the MIR, refused military service in 1933 and in 1934, when he was sentenced to one- and two-year prison terms, respectively.[25] Vernier's case in particular attracted foreign attention. In November 1934, the French Foreign Ministry received a petition signed by a number of prominent British MPs. Two months later came an appeal from the No More War Movement signed by Aneurin Bevan, Julian Huxley, Bertrand Russell, and Dick Sheppard, among others.[26] The following July, the French ambassador in London reported receiving a delegation of Quakers who urged that, at the very least, Vernier and his comrades be allowed to undertake alternative service.[27] Their concern was that 'everything suggests that his decision is irrevocable and that he will therefore go from condemnation to condemnation if his liberation is accompanied each time by a new refusal to serve.'[28]

The Protestant community in France had been thrown into turmoil by the controversy surrounding conscientious objection. The Lutherans ruled against allowing pastors to practise conscientious objection; the Methodists saw no incompatibility between this stance and the fulfilment of pastoral duties; the Baptists called for mandatory civil service for COs; the Reformed Evangelical Church stressed that ministers should not place themselves in controversial and potentially divisive positions; and the Reformed church delayed a decision until the findings of an interdenominational commission established in the summer of 1934 were made public.[29] Finally, on 9 April 1935 the commission, chaired by Marc Boegner, president of the Fédération Protestante, issued a report which, though not openly critical, implied that COs were wrong. It claimed that the church could and should speak out on important issues, but it found no explicit condemnation of war in the scriptures. It therefore asserted that the fulfilment of military obligations represented an exemplary form of submission to authority which ought indeed to be encouraged.[30] The COs could no longer doubt that they were on their own.

The stand of the COs also elicited a response from the government. In January 1933 the minister of the interior, Camille Chautemps, had addressed a circular to the various prefects in which he spoke of a 'campaign presently being conducted in France in favour of conscientious objection ... *for apparently moral motives.*'[31] In the next few months the spread of conscientious objection was the subject of numerous government reports. But why the concern? The government's obsession with a small group of anarchists and religious pacifists may seem odd. However, the authorities were motivated by fear not so much of them as of those who might profit from their example. In the hands of anarchists and Communists 'the idea of simple non-resistance, which is that of the pure objectors, is being replaced by that of rebellion ... For the objectors rebellion is the individual gesture, for these others it is the mass movement.'[32] The government was terrified at the prospect of the left appropriating the nascent conscientious objection movement.[33] Fortunately, the notoriety of the Chautemps Circular, and that of the COs, were short-lived. The Interior Ministry would soon become preoccupied with the threat of fascism, both domestic and foreign.

The path chosen by the COs suggested one response to the deteriorating international situation – individual action. Underpinning this position was the conviction that political action was either irrelevant or impossible. Tempting though these conclusions were in the early 1930s, there remained a number of religious pacifists who sought a large pacific coalition that could educate the people and exert pressure on political elites. The most successful attempt at such an alliance was the Rassemblement universel pour la Paix (RUP), launched in 1936.[34] Always an uneasy alliance, it was eventually wrecked on the rocks of the Spanish Civil War. In Spain, the RUP faced a situation in which use of force appeared unavoidable. Those religious pacifists who had been attracted to the RUP by its potential continued to oppose military measures, and consensus broke down. The RUP's failure was a bitter pill to swallow for French anti-war activists. However, absolutists such as Roser and the MIR were never attracted by the vision of a mass movement. What sectarian and collaborative pacifists did share was a dilemma, for debate on the issue of war and peace was becoming increasingly polarized between advocates of appeasement and the partisans of collective security. Roser and his colleagues remained sceptical of both options. The only escape was to counsel individual action that testified to the sanctity of human life.

The opportunity to pursue a via media between the options of appeasement and violence still existed, however, during the civil war in Spain. Roser, for example, was sympathetic to the plight of the Republicans but asked: 'Are we going to accept the deliberate renunciation for the sake of an ideology – even if it is a just one – of the profoundly held views ... we have professed as to the illegitimate character of war, even when it is clearly defensive?'[35] Roser's support for non-intervention left him open to the charge of being unpatriotic. Yet in reality he was fully conscious of the threat posed by Nazi Germany. He was disgusted by its preoccupation with race and spoke out against its belligerent foreign policy. He went so far as to state: 'Fascism is war. Dictatorship is war ... The struggle against fascism, against Hitlerism is, then, a part of the struggle against war. And no pacifist has the right to shirk this struggle.' Clearly, Roser was not a man to wring his hands in impotence at the sight of evil.[36]

Nevertheless, as the international situation grew worse, Roser seemed caught on the horns of a dilemma. Either he opposed war and was thus willing to let facism triumph, or he was determined to fight fascism and was thereby diluting his opposition to war. Roser refused to accept this false dichotomy. That was clear in his negative response to the Munich Agreement of 1938. He contended that 'egotistical, spineless and blind fear' had prompted Britain and France to 'mine the ground beneath the foot of their friend and ally [Czechoslovakia], to deny [that country] use of arguments of law, to disarm [it] morally.'[37] The arrangement was an act of cowardly self-preservation; only one founded on a principled repudiation of all violence had value in preserving peace in the long term.

Pacifism on the Cross, 1939–1945

The outbreak of the Second World War represented the failure of all that pacifists of every kind had been working so hard to achieve. Religious pacifists in France lived through an experience during the war that was similar to that of their Lord. They were, it appeared, beaten. The situation was further complicated by defeat and the suggestion that pacifists had prepared the way for this disaster by preaching against war in the first place. For those who did carry on, their pacifism could be only a faith – a conviction of things hoped for but not seen.

Much has been made of the fact that Vichy did not face a great deal of opposition in the first two years of the occupation. Certainly, for Catholics in particular there were reasons for the delay in resistance. Marshal Pétain was a good Catholic and a beloved war hero, and the National Revolution seemed a breath of fresh air to many Catholics after the anti-clerical Third Republic. However, a significant number of Catholics felt increasingly uncomfortable under Vichy. Marc Sangnier and the generation of young Catholics that he influenced chose the path of resistance. Sangnier himself was active in the resistance movement. His greatest contribution was the donation of his printing facilities to publish clandestine material. In October 1942 the first issue of the journal *Résistance* was published in the shop on the boulevard Raspail in Paris. Thereafter the 'groupe de la rue de Lille,' as it became known, published some two thousand resistance leaflets.[38]

French Protestants tended to respond more quickly to the occupation than Catholics, aided by a number of factors. For instance, the doctrine of the priesthood of all believers meant that the church structure was more decentralized than in Catholicism. As a result, the individual had greater latitude in making up his or her own mind on such issues as what attitude to assume with regard to a government that was yielding to, and participating in, evil acts.[39]

Most COs had remained faithful to their rejection of military service after the outbreak of war. Henri Roser again declined to serve in the French army, even though he was told he would be required to do nothing more violent than serve in the army bakeries at St Denis. He had refused this concession on the grounds that his work would free another man to assume a combatant role. As a result he received a prison term of four years. In jail he was visited by Marc Boegner of the Fédération Protestante. Boegner was able to get assurances from the authorities that COs would be used as stretcher bearers, but Roser held out for a complete unit of ambulancemen comprised of objectors; no deal was ever reached. The rush of events soon made negotiations irrelevant. In the face of the German advance of June 1940, Roser and his fellow prisoners were released by their captors.[40]

COs were thus able to keep their faith, even if their gestures remained of necessity an individual witness. But there were ways in which opposition to violence could be coupled with resistance to the German occupiers and the Vichy regime. One highly effective organization was the Comité Inter-Mouvements auprès des Évacués (CIMADE), though its inspiration was not, strictly speaking, pacifist. CIMADE had been formed in 1939 by various scout and guide troops and the Fédération des Associations chrétiennes d'Étudiants. It was originally intended to assist those evacuated from the Alsace-Lorraine region of France.[41] However, with the creation of the internment camps under German occupation, CIMADE turned its attention to those incarcerated, trying to improve conditions within the camps. Initially it did so from outside, but eventually its volunteers were permitted to reside in the camps themselves, so as better to meet the needs of the prisoners, both Jews and non-Jews. As the conditions deteriorated, however, the position of the volunteers became untenable. As Madelaine Barot, one of the most active workers, put it: 'Compiling dossiers, interviewing, pleading for exceptions, it was like accepting, being a party to what was happening'[42]

A significant initiative undertaken by French religious pacifists took place at Le Chambon-sur-Lignon, where Protestantism was deeply rooted. Some twenty-five hundred refugees found shelter there during the course of the occupation. A large number of these were eventually smuggled to freedom with assistance from CIMADE or other organizations, such as Témoignage chrétien.[43] The man behind Le Chambon was Pastor André Trocmé, yet another associate of the MIR. Trocmé and his wife, Magda, went to Le Chambon in September 1934, and four years later they, along with Pastor Édouard Theis and his wife, founded the Collège Cévenol, an independent Protestant school.[44]

Trocmé's first act of resistance against Vichy was largely symbolic. An early government decree stipulated that the people of France raise the flag daily and offer the fascist salute. Trocmé opposed this ceremony, seeing it as a first step in the complete abdication of conscience. With the assistance of the head of the adjacent public school for boys, he managed to avoid compliance. The school would raise the flag, and any students or teachers wishing to comply with Vichy regulations could attend the ceremony.[45] In the aftermath of this incident, Trocmé received word of a forthcoming official visit to the town by Georges Lamirand, Vichy's secretary general for youth. He received a cool reception, which culminated in the presentation of a text outlining the refusal of the Chambonnais to take part in the persecution of the Jews. It read:

We have learned of the frightening scenes that took place three weeks ago in Paris, where the French police, on orders of the occupying power, arrested in their homes all the Jewish families to hold them in the Vel d'Hiv ... Knowing by experience that the decrees of the occupying power are, with brief delay, imposed on Unoccupied France, where they are presented as spontaneous decisions of the head of the French government, we are afraid that the measures of deportation of the Jews will soon be applied in the Southern Zone.

We feel obliged to tell you that there are among us a certain number of Jews. But we make no distinction between Jews and non-Jews. It is contrary to the gospel teaching.

If our comrades, whose only fault is to be born in another religion, received the order to let themselves be deported, or even examined, they would disobey the orders received, and we would try to hide them as best we could.[46]

The most striking feature of this declaration is its directness. Trocmé and his colleagues never attempted to hide their disobedience and worked right under the noses of officials.

Virtually the entire town of Le Chambon was in revolt. When refugees arrived, they obtained temporary shelter in the presbytery. Next, they received false identification.[47] Finally, they would be billeted, either with a family in the town or, more commonly, in one of the school residences on the outskirts. These residences were ideally situated for quick escape in the event of raids, as they backed onto thick forests. The funding for these safe havens came from numerous sources, including American Congregationalists, British and American Quakers, Catholics, and even national governments, such as those of Sweden and Switzerland. All of this was in addition to the funding provided by groups such as CIMADE.[48]

Clearly, an effort such as the one launched at Le Chambon required a leader with a strong commitment to non-violent resistance. Trocmé was such a person, yet the evil of Nazism had moved even him to contemplate other forms of resistance. In 1939, he wondered: 'Should I not make use of my knowledge of German to slip into Hitler's entourage and assassinate him before it is too late, before he plunges the world into a catastrophe without limits? It is because I feared separating myself from Jesus Christ, who refused to use arms to prevent the crime that was being prepared for him, and because of a kind of stubborn perseverance in the growing darkness that I stayed in place.'[49] Non-violence was in no way a sign of acquiescence for André Trocmé. He was – as his good friend Édouard Theis noted – *un violent vaincu par Dieu*. It was the desire to be like Jesus Christ that fired his rejection of force.

This zeal to be like Christ freed Trocmé from anxiety concerning the efficacy of his actions. He argued that 'the majority is right in so far as non-violence cannot be made into an article of law apart from faith. Non-violence can overcome evil on earth only if it is the act of God's power on earth acting through men.'[50] Beyond any question of success or failure was the simple necessity of complying with the will of God. Trocmé and the Chambonnais found in the Bible an unconditional view of life as sacred, and they made this their own.

Prevention of suffering was seen as a corporate responsibility. The Chambonnais modelled their town on the Cities of Refuge given in the Bible by God to the Jews: 'So innocent blood will not be shed in the midst of your land which the Lord your God has given you as an inheritance.'[51] The people of Le Chambon believed that, were they to acquiesce in the doing of evil, they too would be guilty of the deaths of those who perished in the camps. The cooperation necessary to the success of the work at Le Chambon was revealed in the words of the participant who noted: 'When the gendarmes from Tence received the order to make arrests, they developed the habit of travelling very openly along the road, stopping at a café before arriving in town and stating very loudly that they were going to arrest some of those dirty Jews.'[52]

And so the work continued. After Lamnirand's visit it was impossible for Vichy to turn a blind eye to the activities going on in Le Chambon. There were many raids, but they met with little success. Invariably, on the day of the operation, the presbytery would receive a telephone call and a terse warning. The refugees would immediately scatter into the surrounding countryside, leaving the frustrated authorities to hunt in vain for 'undesirables.'

The people of Le Chambon were aided in their work by the respect in which they were held by members of the Resistance. Léon Eyraud, or 'Père Noël' as he was widely known, was a key figure in its paramilitary structure of the region. The British Broadcasting Corporation was in constant touch with him regarding supply drops, and the Maquis leaders often passed through his home. Probably because his wife ran one of the most central and therefore most exposed of the *pensions* in the village, Eyraud knew of the valuable work going on in Le Chambon and discouraged violent resistance. Thus reprisals were never required, and the work of saving lives could continue unabated.[53] In the end, only a handful of refugees was ever apprehended by the Germans, and very few villagers were punished for their part in this most open of acts of disobedience.

Conclusion

The period 1919–45 was undeniably one of momentous change for French pacifism. During these years proponents of peace – of all shades of opinion – had to deal with changes in public attitudes, from hostility in the aftermath of the Great War, through greater acceptance in the late 1920s, to antagonism once again as the possibility of a second war loomed and then became reality. Since then, peace activists in France have endured the double criticism that their movement was too weak to prevent the outbreak of the Second World War but sufficiently strong to undermine French morale and allow the triumph of Fascism. While the former approach may be well-founded, the latter is certainly unjustified.

French religious pacifism of the interwar years was indeed confined to a very small minority. Having accepted this fact, what can be concluded from an examination of the period 1919–45? First, while religious pacifists clung tenaciously to their repudiation of violence, they were not, as some have suggested, the unwitting advance guard of fascism. The resistance activities of a significant group among French Christians who rejected violence prove that interwar pacifism did not necessarily lead to wartime collaboration. Second, French religious pacifists operated while giving little consideration to the long-term effect of their actions; what counted for them, above all, was purity of conscience. This individualism was in fact perfectly suited to the role they were called on to play during the occupation. The decision to resist is, by its very nature, intensely personal.

The ability of many religious opponents of war to remain true to their renunciation of violence while opposing the Vichy regime and Nazi Germany earned them the respect of their countrymen. Though the Mouvement républicain populaire (MRP) was a Catholic confessional party, its postwar influence throughout the life of the Fourth Republic underlines the enhanced prestige that religion enjoyed as a result of the various types of Christian resistance during the Vichy years. While they themselves would have characterized their actions as simply following the dictates of conscience, the religious pacifists who agonized as their faith was put on the cross during the Second World War helped ensure its postwar resurrection as well as that of nonviolent resistance as a way of life in a world struggling to come to terms with the possibility of nuclear holocaust.

NOTES

1 Herein lies one of the major problems facing the student of French religious pacifism. Briand's efforts in favour of peace did not represent pacifism in the Anglo-Saxon sense of the word – that is, unconditional rejection of war. However, Briand's immense popularity lent a great deal of prestige to interwar French *pacifisme* – an amalgam of movements, with different inspirations and with varying attitudes to violence as a last resort.

2 Membership in this organization – which admittedly included opponents of war with very different reasons for their repudiation of violence – reached a peak of 136,000

in April 1940; see Martin Ceadel, *Pacifism in Britain, 1919–1945: The Defining of a Faith* (Oxford 1980), 318.

3 See Peter Farrugia, 'French Religious Opposition to War, 1919–1939: The Contribution of Henri Roser and Marc Sangnier,' in *French History* (Oxford) 6, no. 3 (1992).

4 It is something of a truism to say that French Protestantism lacked the unity of Catholicism. Of the three main groups in France, the largest consisted of the Reformed churches (the orthodox Reformed Evangelical church and the more liberal Reformed church). The second was the Lutheran church. Finally, a number of smaller denominations included Baptists, Mennonites, Methodists, Quakers, and the Salvation Army. Beginning in 1905 with the Law of Separation of Church and State, these groups were gathered together in the Fédération Protestante. For a detailed description of the Protestant sects, see André Encrevé, *Les Protestants en France de 1800 à nos jours: Histoire d'une réintégration* (Paris 1985), 29–33.

5 Sonia Orwell and Ian Angus, eds., *The Collected Essays, Journalism and Letters of George Orwell*, 4 vols. (London 1970), 2:261.

6 Witness the recent discussion surrounding French President Chirac's admission of French guilt in the persecution of Jews under Vichy.

7 This organization was an outgrowth of the British Fellowship of Reconciliation, which was heavily influenced by the nonconformist churches and, in particular, by the Quakers; see Ceadel, *Pacifism in Britain*, 35.

8 *Cahiers de la réconciliation* (Jan. 1990), 9. See also the recent biography of Roser by Pierre Kneubühler, *Henri Roser, l'enjeu d'une terre nouvelle* (Paris 1992).

9 *Mouvement international de la réconciliation* (Paris n.d.), 1.

10 Ibid., 3.

11 Claire Roser, *Henri Roser* (London 1939), 3, 5. Roser was not ordained until 1949; see *Cahiers de la réconciliation* (1990), 9.

12 *Cahiers* (1990), 10. Jacques Martin, like a significant number of his colleagues in the MIR, was an adherent of the French Socialist movement. He was also the Paris secretary of the Federation of Christian Students. The influence of the *Cahiers* was more widespread than circulation figures might suggest. Pastor Roger Chaptal has claimed that the publication was avidly read by theological students at Montpellier and that there was 'a mystique' surrounding it; see Jean Baubérot, *Le retour des Huguenots: La vitalité protestante XIXe–Xxe siècles* (Paris 1985) 228n.

13 Cited in Jean-Claude Delbreil, *Les Catholiques français et les tentatives de rapprochement franco–allemand (1920–1933)* (Metz 1972), 139.

14 'La Paix par la Jeunesse: VIe congrès Democratique International pour la Paix,' 2–3, in Archives Nationales (AN), Paris, F7/13962; Madelaine Barthélemy-Madaule, *Marc Sangnier (1873–1950)* (Paris 1973), 255. The delicious irony of Painlevé providing tents for the guests from the stores of the Ministry of War was not lost on those in attendance.

15 'La Pàix par la Jeunesse,' 6–7; Delbreil, *Les Catholiques français*, 86.

16 At the next congress of the Democratic International in Würzburg, only ninety French youths attended, and proceedings were dominated by acrimonious debate on eastern Europe, evacuation of the Rhine, and German disarmament; see Marc Sangnier, *La Paix par la jeunesse* (Paris, n.d.), 91–2.

17 I prefer the term 'eirenicist' to the more commonly used 'pacificist,' which is too easily confused with 'pacifist.' For an excellent discussion of the various orientations among pacifists, see Martin Ceadel, 'Christian Pacifism in the Era of the Two World Wars,' in *Studies in Church History* (Oxford 1983), 20:393.

18 'Interview with Henri Roser,' cited in Majagira Bulangalira, 'Le Mouvement international de la réconciliation et le problème du pacifisme dans le protestantisme français de 'entre-deux-guerres (aperçu jusqu'à 1960),' diploma thesis for the École pratique des hautes études, 2 vols., 1988), 2 annexe A, 6.

19 *Controverse: Cahiers libres d'études sociales*, no. 6 (April–June 1933), 380.

20 Ibid., 379.

21 Henri Roser, 'Lettres ouvertes à mes deux amis,' *Cahiers de la réconciliation* (Dec. 1983), 4.

22 Cited in *Controverse*, no. 6 (April–June 1933), 379.

23 Bulangalira, 'Le Mouvement international de la réconciliation,' 109; *Cahiers de la réconciliation* (1990), 11.

24 Conscientious objection was by no means a relgious preserve. The best work on the subject is Michel Auvray, *Objecteurs, insoumis et déserteurs* (Paris 1983). Nicolas Faucier, *Pacifisme et antimilitarisme dans l'entre-deux-guerres* (Paris 1983) is also useful, especially 55–7 and 196–206, on the libertarian current among objectors.

25 *Cahiers de la réconciliation* (1990), 11 (Jan. 1983), 5–6. See also Remi Fabre, 'Les pacifismes protestants français de l'entre-deux guerres,' in Maurice Vaïsse, ed., *Le pacifisme en Europe des années 1920 aux années 1950* (Brussels 1993), 245, and Vera Brittain, *The Rebel Passion: A Short History of Some Pioneer Peace-makers* (London 1964), 156–9, 162, 163.

26 These various petitions can be found in Archives des Affaires Étrangères (AE), Paris, série Y, Internationale 1918–1940, vol. 392.

27 In 1920 Pierre Ceresole resigned from the secretaryship of the IFOR to create Service Civil International (SCI), which advocated alternative humanitarian service for objectors. In the 1920s the SCI was involved in reconstruction projects throughout Europe; see Pierre Ceresole, *Peace and Truth*, trans. John Harvey and Christina Yates (London 1954), and also *Cahiers de la réconciliation* (Jan. 1990), 5–7.

28 'L'Ambassadeur de Royaume-Uni au Ministère des Affaires Étrangères, 16 juillet 1935,' 3, in AE, série Y, Internationale, vol. 392; under French law, the time a CO spent in prison was not counted towards fulfilment of his military obligations. Thus he was still liable on release to be called up to complete the original tour of duty.

29 Baubérot, *Le retour des Huguenots*, 229.

30 Ibid., 229–230n. The commission's members were Boegner, Auguste Lecerf and Pierre Maury from the Reformed church; André Arnal, Jean Cadier, and Henri Monnier from the Reformed Evangelical church; André Jundt and Adolphe Lods from the Lutheran church; Théophile Roux representing the Methodists; Georges Rousseau, the Baptists; and André Aeschimann and Jean Grosjean, from the Free Churches.

31 'Le Ministère de l'Intérieur à Monsieur le Président du Conseil, 9 janvier, 1933,' in AN, F7/13352; see also 'Note: la propagande pacifiste et le mouvement en faveur de l'objection de conscience, 19 avril 1933,' 1, in AE, série Y, Internationale 1918–1940, vol. 392; emphasis added.

32 Cited in Norman Ingram, *The Politics of Dissent: Pacifism in France, 1919–1939* (Oxford 1991), 303–4.

33 Many of the witnesses who testified on behalf of the objectors were drawn from the left; see Fabre, 'Les pacifismes protestants,' 248–9.

34 The RUP was a vast coalition supporting the League of Nations and as a last resort the application of military measures. It enjoyed temporary success, but it was never fully able to shake the perception, especially strong in religious circles, that it was a Communist front organization. Henry van Etten, a French Quaker who attended the first congress of the RUP, later wrote: 'The communist influence was preponderant; all the major leaders were there. Everything was a pretext for propaganda.' For a complete account of his views, see Henry van Etten, *Journal d'un Quaker de notre temps (1893–1962)* (Paris 1962), 131.

35 Henri Roser, 'Devant le drame espagnol,' in *Cahiers de la réconciliation* (Jan. 1984), 16–7.

36 Henri Roser, 'Notre pacifisme et Hitler,' in ibid. (Jan. 1984), 18–9.

37 Henri Roser, 'Notre pacifisme et la Tcéchoslovaquie,' in ibid. (Jan. 1984), 24. There are many in France who can barely conceal their frustration with advocates of this position, which they feel fails to offer any real solutions to the problem of aggression; see Bulangalira, 'Le Mouvement international de la réconciliation,' 300).

38 Henri Noguères, *Histoire de la Résistance en France de 1940 à 1945*, 2 vols. (Paris 1969), 2:667 and 433–4.

39 Stuart R. Schram, *Protestantism and Politics in France* (Alençon 1954), 41–2. The best study of French Catholics and Protestants during the occupation remains Xavier Montclos, ed., *Églises et Chrétiens dans le IIe Guerre mondiale*, Actes du colloque national tenu à Lyon du 27 au 30 janvier 1978 (Lyon 1982).

40 The story of Roser's incarceration can be found in 'Mon Commandant,' in *Cahiers de la réconciliation* (Feb. 1983), 19–22. Philippe Vernier and his younger brother, Pierre, were also among those sentenced for refusing to join the army.

41 Jeanne Merle d'Aubigne et al., *Les clandestins de Dieu: CIMADE 1939–1945* (Paris

1968), 29; Madelaine Barot, 'Le CIMADE et les camps d'internement de la zone sud, 1940–1944,' in Xavier Montclos, ed., *Eglises et Chrétiens dans le IIe Guerre mondiale*, Actes du colloque national tenu à Lyon du 27 au 30 janvier 1978 (Lyon 1982), 293–4.

42   Barot, 'Le CIMADE,' 297, 302.

43   For the work of Témoignage chrétien, see Renée Bédarida, *Pierre Chaillet: Témoin de la résistance spirituelle* (Paris 1988).

44   *Cahier de la réconciliation* (1990), 12.

45   Philip Hallie, *Lest Innocent Blood Be Shed* (New York 1979), 90–1.

46   Text delivered to Georges Lamirand on the occasion of his official visit, cited in ibid., 102.

47   The blanks essential to create these papers would appear unannounced whenever they were needed. The people of Le Chambon had many theories as to who the anonymous supplier was, but the benefactor's identity was never discovered; see ibid., 199–200.

48   Barot, 'Le CIMADE,' 300; Hallie, *Lest Innocent Blood*, 176.

49   These figures come from notes written by Trocmé and cited by Hallie in *Lest Innocent Blood*, 265. Trocmé's dilemma was not dissimilar to that of Dietrich Bonhoeffer in Germany. One of Trocmé's postwar associates, Jean Laserre, had been a close friend of Bonhoeffer's when the two were studying at the Union Theological Seminary in New York in the early 1930s. See F. Burton Nelson, 'The Relationship of Jean Laserre to Dietrich Bonhoeffer's Peace Concerns in the Struggle of Church and Culture,' *Union Seminary Quarterly Review* (New York), 40 nos. 1–2 (1985), 71–84.

50   André Trocmé, *Jesus and the Nonviolent Revolution*, trans. Michacl H. Shank and Marlin E. Miller (Scottsdale, Pa., 1973), 159.

51   Deut. 19:9–10.

52   Cited in d'Aubigne, *Les clandestins de Dieu*, 34.

53   Hallie, *Lest Innocent Blood*, 185. Another striking example of the respect displayed for non-violent *résistants* by their fighting brethren was the unusual deal struck by the local Maquis on behalf of Jacques Martin following his arrest by the Gestapo. Shortly before he was to be executed, a group of farmers exchanged a thousand sheep for the prisoner; see Brittain, *The Rebel Passion*, 163.

8

Defending the Rights of Man: The Ligue des droits de l'homme and the Problem of Peace

NORMAN INGRAM

Historians have only recently begun to examine the history of French pacifism in the interwar period.[1] Despite claims by some[2] that pacifism in France was strongly influenced by religious culture, it seems clear that for the most part it was far more political than religious in inspiration. This holds true both for what I have called *pacifisme ancien style*, which had a liberal, internationalist, and juridical epicentre as opposed to a primarily religious one, and also for the *pacifisme nouveau style* that emerged from it in the late 1920s. The latter form was integral or absolute and arose from a dissenting, essentially anti-political stance vis-à-vis the rest of French political society, which was expressed paradoxically in uniquely political ways. This is not to deny the existence of major voices preaching various forms of pacifism from a Christian *point de départ*, but merely to argue that most French pacifists, be they of the old or the new style, expressed their pacifism in consistently political terms.

The debate on French pacifism is really part of a larger one that attempts to isolate, define, and describe the essence of non–Anglo-American pacifism. It is one that most French historians seem loath to enter. The contours of the larger debate have been set very much by Martin Ceadel, in two immensely thought-provoking books.[3] Nevertheless, there remains much to be said about the nature of French, and indeed of other, pacifisms in the twentieth century. Ceadel seems to take as given, first, the idea that France did not experience the same level of pacifist sentiment and engagement as did the United Kingdom; and second, that the indigenous peace movement was much more 'legitimate' in the eyes of the British public than was the case in France or elsewhere.[4] Both assertions are questionable. While France did not have the equivalent in numerical terms either of the Peace Pledge Union or the League of Nations Union, there was nevertheless a numerically significant, albeit thoroughly balkanized, French peace movement, especially in the early 1930s. One must also deal carefully with differences in political culture between the two countries. At the risk of a gross generalization, we might say that the French are much less prone to joining mass organizations for whatever cause. But one has only to compare the participation rates in trade unions in Britain and France during the interwar period to see the truth of that proposition.

It is the question of 'legitimacy,' however, that calls for further comment. The question of 'peace,' of 'the Peace,' and indeed of pacifism itself was central to French political debate throughout the interwar era. It was perhaps the single most consistently discussed question of the period. Indeed, as this essay argues, the problem of peace and of pacifism is essential to any explanation of interwar French politics. Antoine Prost has shown that a certain sort of pacifist sentiment – what he calls 'patriotic pacifism' – was an integral part of the political discourse and historical vision of the war veterans in interwar France.[5] Other historians have demonstrated that pacifism was an important issue in various other segments of French life. What has been lacking, however, is any analysis of how ideas and debates moved from the peace movement itself into more mainstream society. What were the means of this transmission? Which ideas were accepted, and which rejected? What types of organization proved to be the best *fil conducteur*?

It is my purpose here precisely to track such a transmission, to demonstrate the linkage, the *trait d'union*, between the ideas of the peace movement per se and the more diluted expression of the same within the broader society. In essence this essay seeks to examine the fulcrum on which the pacifist–non-pacifist debate rested in interwar France. That fulcrum, in the political context at least, was the Ligue des droits de l'homme et du citoyen (LDH). The centrality of the pacifist debate within the LDH, and hence within French republican political society, makes it possible to affirm that the peace movement enjoyed a similar level of legitimacy to that experienced by its counterpart in Britain.

This thesis will not lack opponents. It challenges the implicit Ceadelian notion that pacifism, and indeed peace sentiment, are somehow *more* Anglo-American than anything else. And it challenges too a certain prevailing attitude within both French public opinion and mainstream French historiography which holds that pacifism is, for a variety of reasons, a subject better left untouched.[6] But as Pierre Nora and Robert Gildea most notably have argued, there exist various 'lieux de mémoire' in France, and several 'pasts' in French history.[7]

The pacifist past is central to an understanding of French history between the wars. This essay demonstrates the extent of the penetration of the pacifist idea during this period first by establishing the degree to which the LDH was one of the *terrains de combat* on which the pacifist debates occurred and, second, by examining the nature of the pacifist–anti-pacifist debate within the Ligue, with particular reference to the pivotal 1937 congress in Tours, which had as its theme 'How to defend both democracy and peace.'[8] All of this serves to demonstrate the extent to which the LDH was a transmitter for pacifist ideas into the broader society.

The LDH as Battleground for the Pacifist Debate

There can be little doubt that the LDH was a meeting place for the representatives of the two opposing strands of pacifism in France. Looking at the fifty-four candidates for the twenty-four positions to be filled on the Ligue's Comité central (CC) in 1937, one finds the names of at least eleven representatives of the new-style dissenting pacifism of the thirties,[9] opposed by four persons representative of old-style pacifism.[10] In other words, about 28 per cent of the candidates had direct links with either new- or old-style pacifism.

When one considers the members of the CC actually elected in 1937, the impression gained is similar. Out of twenty-four elected members, six were active in the peace movement, and five out of the six were active in new-style pacifist groups.[11] There were of course other pacifists on the CC who were not subject to re-election in 1937. One such was Jules Prudhommeaux, the secretary-general of the Association de la Paix par le droit (APD). Of the fifty-five members of the executive committee and of the CC as a whole, nine had direct links with pacifism.[12] In a sense, however, this was but the tip of the iceberg. A large part of the CC had tangential links with pacifism,[13] and among its honorary members one also finds a strong pacifist presence.[14] This list of the pacifist members does not include the seven who resigned in the wake of the 1937 Tours congress.[15] The CC was not only a gathering place for representatives of the different tendencies within French pacifism, but also a focal point for the pacifist–non-pacifist debate in France.

Also of interest are the themes for the yearly LDH congresses. Throughout the interwar years, the LDH debated the question of peace, or perhaps more specifically, of *the* peace. This did not always occur as a function of the pacifist debate, but questions relating to the peace of Europe were always at the centre of the Ligue's preoccupations, and because of the pacifist presence these debates carried a certain pacifist flavour.

Given the above, should the historian consider the LDH a significant forum for the pacifist–non-pacifist debate and, if so, a transmitter of pacifist ideas? There is little doubt about the LDH's role in terms of the size of its membership. Albert Bayet, one of its vice-presidents, noted after the 1937 congress that the LDH had more than 150,000 members within France (to say nothing of those in the colonies), most of whom were socialists or radicals. The outcome of the debate on how to defend democracy and peace was thus particularly instructive and revealing because the LDH 'represents, in its totality, the average opinion of French republicans.' Bayet viewed the vote as 'a precious indicator of the state of mind of French republicans.'[16] He was undoubtedly correct that the LDH debate can be considered a vote in favour of a firm stance against fascist aggregation, but the dissent within this quintessentially French republican institution is a measure of how much the pacifist debate continued to play a major and unsettling role in French politics. In other words, the evidence shows that Bayet was both right and wrong: right in the general sense of his conclusions, but wrong to discount the latent power of the pacifist message in French political society.

The 1937 Congress and Its Impact on the Peace and War Debate within the LDH

The LDH's crucial 1937 congress was held from 17 to 19 July in the city of Tours in the Loire valley. The theme of 'How to defend both democracy and peace' was one that encompassed a variety of distinct issues – most important, of course, the Ligue's position on the Spanish Civil War, but also the weakening of the League of Nations and the position that the democracies should take vis-à-vis the dictators.

Albert Bayet, professor at the École des Hautes Études, and a vice-president of the LDH, presented the main report, which launched the debate.[17] He examined in turn three possible methods to defend democracy and peace in Spain and more generally in Europe – the 'great philosophical solution,' namely conscientious objection or non-resistance, the option of neutrality between aggressor and victim, and mediation.[18]

Bayet said that he profoundly respected the position of real objectors. He and the LDH had always therefore favoured some sort of law regulating the position of COs. It was not the Ligue's fault that the latest amnesty in France had not included COs. But Bayet further stated: 'In admitting that each one of us has the duty to practise nonresistance when it concerns only his own life, I say that one is obliged to protect his wife, his children, and in a general way any weaker person of whom he is the natural protector, as well as freedom which is the property of all. One has the right to sacrifice oneself; one never has the right to sacrifice others.'[19]

The second alternative was that of localizing a conflict so that war would not spread. His claim that in France Pierre Laval was to be thanked for this idea provoked vehement protests from Georges Pioch and Madame Léon Emery, who insisted that the idea had a preeminent socialist heritage, having first been enunciated by Jaurès in 1914. Bayet countered by saying that the League of Nations had done its duty in proclaiming sanctions in the Ethiopian war but that Laval was to be blamed for not having applied them, for Laval's 'localization' of the conflict really meant letting the Ethiopian people be massacred by Mussolini. Thus, according to Bayet, 'one does not localize a war. One kills it or it kills you. As soon as it appears in one part of the world, it breaks out fatally somewhere else too.'[20] Thus, non-intervention, or the practice of localizing conflicts, was a 'dupery,' in Spain as much as in Ethiopia. To those who would respond, 'What then, war?,' Bayet replied that if France had spoken loudly and clearly the language of law and the Ligue, there would have been no danger of war, but that if this language were not spoken, the risks of war would become 'formidable,' and he predicted presciently that if Spain were abandoned, then Czechoslovakia would be next on Hitler's list of nations to attack and conquer.[21]

The third option was that of mediation, and it disgusted Bayet the most. He asked rhetorically how one could hope to negotiate in Spain with a band of 'traitors, vendus, and felonious generals.' Furthermore, who would mediate such a dispute – the Nazis, the Italian Fascists, the Western democracies? If it were the former two, then the executioners would have become the judges. Mediation would be impossible because neither the republican government nor the insurgents wanted any part of it. In Bayet's view, the whole notion of mediation was a 'knife in the back of the Spanish republic.'[22]

Bayet proposed a two-fold solution. The failure of the League of Nations was mostly to blame for the terrible situation in Spain, and he ascribed it to the 'hesitant attitude' of the democracies. The CC therefore believed that the League of Nations needed to regain a sense of its mission, to reinstill respect for the law in international affairs, and thereby to render a verdict on whether Hitler and Mussolini had in fact attacked the Spanish republic. Once a verdict against them had been reached, France would apply the sentence of Geneva and start to resupply republican Spain.[23]

Bayet recognized that even before the crisis in Spain occurred, the seeds of other conflicts had existed in Europe. The festering Franco–German problem was at the root of the trouble, and it was so serious that it might very well provoke another general conflagration. The only way to stop the European infection from spreading was through treaty revision, 'even though it is sad and bitter for us ... to think that we might give to Hitlerian Germany that which we criminally and foolishly refused to give to republican Germany.'[24]

Bayet's prescription came with strings attached, however. Germany and Italy would have to agree to two conditions: first, the cessation of hostilities against republican Spain, and the immediate and supervised withdrawal of the two expeditionary corps there, and second, a first-step disarmament agreement. The Spanish question must not be disengaged from the general European one.[25]

Bayet's report, sanctioned by the CC, drew a variety of responses, most notably from Camille Planche, deputy for the Allier and president of the Ligue des anciens combattants pacifistes, Léon Emery, a professor at the École normale supérieure in Lyon; and Félicien Challaye, a *professeur agrégé* at the Lycée Condorcet and sometime president of the Ligue internationale des combattants de la paix.

Planche charged that Bayet had undertaken a facile and yet tendentious proceeding ('un procès trop facile de tendance') against the members of the LDH minority. He emphasized that the minority was just as committed to the republican cause in Spain as the majority; it wanted the republicans supplied with goods, and credits if possible, and this 'by all possible means.' But he denied that there was any other course open to France back in August 1936 than the one it had followed. He agreed that Laval had dealt the League of Nations a heavy blow but maintained that it was impossible for France to divorce itself from the actions of the other democracies, especially Britain. Further, French public opinion was divided on Spain, and so was the Popular Front. Thus, according to Planche, if the French government had taken any other position, not only would it have found itself isolated from the rest of the democracies, but the Popular Front would probably have disintegrated as well – a singular way of defending the Spanish Popular Front, he commented drily. And at the outset of the conflict, it appeared as if all involved were prepared to accept the principle of non-intervention; even the leaders of the Spanish socialist party, which was not yet in power, published articles in its newspapers approving this policy. Thus France had done the only thing it could have done; there was nothing to be gained by playing the 'lonesome cowboy' ('jouer les cavaliers seuls').[26]

Planche cited a passage from a speech made by the great feminist pacifist journalist Séverine (Caroline Rémy) to the 1916 congress of the LDH about the need for negotiation and mediation at a time when the Great War was being fought on French soil. Séverine was greatly loved and respected in the Ligue, and Planche applied her reasoning of 1916 to the Spanish situation and argued that mediation did not necessarily put aggressor and victim on the same moral footing. Wars generally do not end with the complete annihilation of one side or the other – they eventually and usually end in negotiation of one sort or another. And so it would be in Spain: the time would come when it would be necessary to sit down and negotiate. As he put it, 'It will be necessary to decide that the war will end with peace.'[27] Planche concluded by denying emphatically that mediation or negotiation spelled the annihilation of republican Spain. In his mind, 'mediation is a plebiscite, controlled by the League of Nations, or by an assembly of the powers.'[28]

Léon Emery's speech continued the attack on the CC's motion. He disputed the idea that the League of Nations could simply demand withdrawal of the volunteers in Spain. If the League wanted to see this demand through to reality, it would have to be prepared to go as far as military sanctions.[29] And who in the world, he asked, was prepared to go that far? 'Of course I remain a partisan of collective security, such as it was defined at the Dijon congress [of the LDH]; of course I remain a partisan of a regenerated League of Nations, such as we tried to define it at Dijon. But do not forget that according to the resolution voted at Dijon this regenerated League of Nations was one in which Germany could again be a member. You all defined it as such. So we were not talking simply about a League of Nations put together as an anti-German coalition, and yet that is how the question is posed at the present moment.'[30] He concluded by asking which policy would best protect France from the immediate danger: one that attached itself 'in almost mystical fashion' to the idea of an international community in which France would be more or less alone or one that clung desperately but determinedly to the idea of accords, compromises, and progressive solutions that could limit and contain the danger? Emery said that this latter path would save not only the peace, but also the Spanish people, and the Spanish revolution.[31]

Félicien Challaye offered the most cogent attack on the CC's position. He charged that Bayet had made a caricature of integral pacifism by presenting a 'very imprecise exposé of the idea of the localization of conflicts.'[32] He defined integral pacifism as the condemnation of all wars and of all kinds of war whatever their pretext, whether they be international, national, or ideological. But integral pacifism did not necessarily mean absolute non-violence or the refusal of all individual resistance. 'We believe that the integral pacifist can very well defend himself and defend his own,' said Challaye.[33] Localization, which he said was a natural corollary of integral pacifism, had been badly presented by Bayet. It was not at all a question of indifference to these conflicts, or of putting aggressor and victim on the same moral footing. But, according to Challaye, 'given that war is both crime and folly, it is essential not to extend this crime and this folly'; it was necessary to ensure that a 'partial war' not develop into a 'general war.'[34]

Taking Jaurès as a historical example, Challaye examined his position on the Russo–Japanese war of 1904. Jaurès had done all in his power to ensure that Britain and France did not enter the conflict on opposing sides. In 1914 Jaurès took the same position vis-à-vis Austria-Hungary and Serbia: 'When war broke out between Austria–Hungary and Serbia, the principal task of Jaurès was not at all to put these two powers on the same footing; in any case he freely criticized Austrian imperialism while at the same time not accepting the excesses of Serbian militarism. But above all, he wanted this conflict to remain localized, for the other nations not to get involved.'[35] If he had succeeded, according to Challaye, not only the French, but also the Russians, the Germans, and the Serbs would have been saved; if Austrian troops had occupied Belgrade the Serbian people would have suffered less than they did in the war.

Challaye concluded with some reflections on the impact of war on civilian society, which he thought ought to be of some interest to the LDH: 'I want to underline in conclusion that there is a question which in my opinion ought to be have been dissociated from the others more clearly in any debate over how to defend both democracy and peace. One ought to have disengaged more the idea that war, in order to be successfully prosecuted, demands a military dictatorship which is the complete opposite of democracy. War is the antithesis *par excellence* of democracy. This was the idea of the great Robespierre ... Today we shall transpose this idea in saying that war is fascism. It realizes, through the intermediary of an inevitable military dictatorship, the suppression of all freedoms.'[36]

Léon Emery intervened in the debate once again to present a new and revised countermotion. He and the minority had been amazed to hear the ideas ascribed to them, so they had decided to submit a long resolution, which would in great detail outline the minority's position.[37] The minority counter-resolution declared that the LDH was 'fraternally united' with the Spanish Republicans and affirmed its commitment, above all else, to helping the Spanish in their fight against fascism. It outlined two fundamental principles that guided the LDH in its day-to-day policy on Spain. First, the LDH considered that foreign intervention in the conflict could only hinder the Spanish people in its quest to choose its destiny freely. Furthermore, this intervention could only increase the danger of its becoming a generalized European one. Hence, the LDH remained firmly attached to the idea of non-intervention. Second, the LDH believed that non-intervention must be general and, in order to be general, must be supervised (*contrôlé*). At no time would the LDH admit a policy that would maintain non-intervention at the expense of the republican government by tolerating policies to the profit of the Junta of Salamanca.

Bayet responded to Emery's speech, and indeed to all the critiques of the CC's position, by declaring that he clung to the League of Nations as the solution. Betraying his innate sympathy for the theses of the old-style pacifism in France, he asked what other solution had ever been proposed to the problem of war: 'If you want war to disappear forever from the world, then all the nations must unite and make it understood this time that whoever the aggressor might be, the fifty others will take him by the collar.'[38] He asked rhetorically on what basis France could proceed by itself to mediate in Spain, given that it had signed pacts that required mediation through the League. And in fact, fortuitously for Bayet, Miguel Azaña had stated emphatically in that morning's newspapers that the Spanish government wanted nothing to do with talks between aggressor and victim.[39]

Victor Basch, president of the Ligue, intervened at the end of the debate to say that for him and for the CC the question at issue reduced itself simply to one of choosing between two different paths: 'Us – the League of Nations. You – mediation.'[40]

Thus ended the tumultuous and pivotal debate within the LDH on how to defend both democracy and peace. Two opposing conceptions of international affairs, domestic politics, and pacifism had finally come face to face in the Ligue. When the issue was put to the vote, the CC's motion garnered 1,244 votes against 161 opposed and twenty-two abstentions. The minority position thus reflected a little over 11 per cent of the votes cast. Is this an insignificant number? It is certainly nowhere near a majority; still, it is significant that in mid-1937, on an issue as important as the Spanish Civil War, 11 per cent of the Ligue's membership, through its mandated representatives, could vote against the traditional foreign policy not just of any French government, but essentially of a Popular Front government. Together with the debate on the Moscow purge trials, which had shown an even greater level of dissent from the path followed by the CC (18.4 per cent of votes being cast for Challaye's motion, which accused the Ligue effectively of suppressing the truth about the Moscow trials, against that of the CC), the debate on the Spanish Civil War and how to defend the precarious peace of Europe seems to indicate the disintegration of the left-wing consensus within the LDH.

After Tours

The fall-out from the congress in Tours began at the gathering itself when Berg-ery, Challaye, Emery, and Michon announced their resignations from the CC, to which they had all just been re-elected.[41] As Emery said in announcing their decision, 'We have the feeling that the Ligue has, in these past few days, renounced its own originality, its constitutive and in a sense statutory mission, in order to take refuge in a political opportunism.'[42] He and his colleagues emphasized that they would continue to work within the Ligue but could no longer accept what he called 'the community of responsibilities' with the CC.[43]

Resignations did not end at Tours. Subsequently Magdeleine Paz, Georges Pioch, and Elie Reynier also stepped down from the CC. Their reasons were similar – a mixture of factors relating to the Ligue's position on the Moscow trials combined with disagreement over the position taken on the problem of peace.[44]

The seven *démissionnaires* declined to go quietly either. A collective letter of resignation, sent to the CC at the end of August, was not officially discussed until the first meeting of this body after the summer break, on 14 October. It was published a fortnight later in the *Cahiers*.[45] But in the meantime, Léon Emery had put out a number of articles in the *Feuilles libres de la quinzaine*, all of them critical of the LDH's position on the issues discussed at Tours.[46] Bergery printed a critical account of the Tours congress in *La Flèche* shortly after the congress.[47] And Challaye published a severely critical account of the Ligue's congress in *La Patrie humaine* on 15 October.[48]

All of this led in early November to a lengthy rebuttal by Victor Basch.[49] Reading Basch's article, one is struck by the heaviness of heart that accompanied this fulfilment of his presidential duties. He wrote that in 'beginning this article, which must be a rectification, my heart failed me ... At this tragic hour to have to go through the quarrels of the congress, to have to refute accusations that I can only consider miserable, I truly feel a sense of humiliation.'[50] Basch outlined the attacks made on the CC, which alleged that it had white-washed the Moscow purge trials, that it had not protested as it ought against false reports in the press which had led to panic in the population, and that there had not been genuine and open discussion of the problem of peace and no serious documentation on the situation in Spain. 'In summary, the Ligue's leaders who, in the past, had enrolled the Ligue blindly in the *union sacrée*, had now brought it to the worst moral lapse.'[51]

Basch rejected these accusations categorically. The central issue was the problem of peace. Basch declared that it was a complete lie to say that this had not been discussed fully and freely at Tours. He wrote that the debate had never been stifled and that accusations to the contrary were 'derisory.'[52] In fact, Basch said, the great resolution passed on peace had been in large part composed by Bergery, one of the *démissionnaires*. 'Is it our fault,' he asked, 'if today this resolution appears feeble and inefficacious to its author?'[53] As to Spain, Basch argued that it was incontrovertible that there were no Soviet military corps present in the peninsula, only some pilots and technicians – this in contradistinction to the presence of German and Italian ground troops.[54]

With regard to the Moscow trials, which had provided the political counterpoint to the debate on Spain and pacifism at the congress, Basch wrote how filled he was with doubts about the whole affair, but he defended the CC's actions by saying that the commission set up to investigate the trials had done the very best it could, given the lack of information available, the little time at the disposal of its members, and the other crises that were occurring at the same time. On the last point, Basch said that 'we have consecrated the best of ourselves to the fraternal and moral support being given to republican Spain ... We have reckoned that this was a work of such importance (*une œuvre de vie*) that it took precedence over all other tasks ... I have given my all to the Ligue, to the Popular Front, to the Spanish cause. I cannot give more.'[55] This had not prevented him from studying closely the reports on the Moscow trials, and he admitted to being still puzzled and doubtful about the outcome.

But he also believed that the motives of the minority at Tours were not pure, that it was also the politics of the French Communist party that the minority condemned.[56] This the LDH refused to do. The Ligue was concerned about the Moscow trials, not about the internal politics of French Communism. And he went on to contrast the ferocious attitude of the minority vis-à-vis Stalin and the excesses of his regime with the indulgence shown in the immediate postwar period for the Leninist revolution and regime in the Soviet Union.[57]

In conclusion, Basch examined why it was that the Ligue had not voted for the minority position, and he had several answers. First, the average Ligue member could not understand why, in the face of the Spanish tragedy, the minority had not shuddered with the same horror. The Ligue has as its raison d'être the fight against tyranny and 'what the Ligue condemned the minority for was that it did not have the same reaction, that instead it had excuses for Hitler, that it treated him like a saint, that it exalted his word as an ex-serviceman, that it made of him, despite his aggressive policies, an apostle of peace, that it contested the volume of aid being supplied to Franco by Italy and Germany, that it always had excuses for the provokers of wars, and that it always made of France, the pacifism of which it would be wrong to deny, the only party responsible for the European situation.'[58]

Second, the Ligue remained 'obstinately' attached to the Popular Front, in contradistinction to what Basch called the minority's 'disabused distrust' and Challaye's 'outright hostility.'[59] And finally, the LDH was sick to death of the 'intestinal quarrels' that divided it; it wanted 'all members of the Comité central, instead of fighting one another, to dedicate their efforts to fighting the common enemy: fascism and war.'[60] In this sense, Basch prefigured the coming struggle over appeasement. He described the minority's position as one of 'giving in, giving in some more, always giving in,' and, he wrote, sooner or later the fatal moment would come for the democracies when they would be able to give no more. The path of Emery et al., he claimed, was the path of resignation, of utter fatigue, of lying down in the dust and crying, 'Brothers, we are going to die!' The majority, in contrast, cried: 'Brothers, we must live, we must act, we must vanquish! It will be long, it will be hard, the struggle will be bitter, but we believe we have Reason on our side, and we believe with all our heart that it will carry the day.'[61]

Challaye responded to Basch's article in his essay on *La Crise de la Ligue des droits de l'homme* (November 1937).[62] For the historian of French pacifism, and of the pacifist–non-pacifist debate within the LDH, Challaye's essay demonstrates the extremely deep roots of the crisis of 1937. Challaye takes the reader all the way back to 1914 and the decision by the Ligue to support the *union sacrée.* He then examines the way in which the LDH dealt thereafter with the question of peace, not merely pacifism. In 1916 at the Ligue's first wartime congress, a debate between Basch and Georges Demartial began over the origins of the war.[63] At this same conclave, a resolution put forward by Séverine, Michel Alexandre, Oscar Bloch, Louis Guétant, Alphonse Merrheim, and Mathias Morhardt in favour of a plan for immediate arbitration received only thirty votes. According to Challaye, 'on that day the minority of the LDH was born.'[64]

The 1920s had seen little progress towards acceptance of the theses of the minority; Challaye criticized the early alliance with the Bund Neues Vaterland in Germany, which believed uncritically in Germany's unilateral responsibility for the outbreak of the Great War. By the turn of the decade the fortunes of the minority had begun to change, however. At the 1929 Rennes congress, for example, a motion submitted by Alexandre, Challaye, and Pioch received 513 votes, against 1,200 for the motion of the majority; and in 1932 the Paris congress passed a motion submitted by Challaye, Paul Langevin, and Planche against use of military sanctions and plans for an international army. In 1934, at Nancy, a motion by Alexandre was passed that condemned Édouard Herriot, mayor of Lyon, for having fired or demoted twenty-two municipal employees of the city slaughter-house because they had refused to participate in so-called passive defence measures. Challaye claimed that it was at this point that the Ligue's executive committee began to become seriously concerned at the increasing success of what was still supposed to be the 'minority,' and therefore began a campaign of attacks, at times subtle and at times forthright, against it.[65]

Challaye charged that the CC was faithful only to a view of saving the peace through the League of Nations; the minority, too, was loyal to the idea of what he called a 'Society of Peoples.' But it believed that the League had lost all its force, vitality, and authority and that it was hopeless to count on it to save the peace. Regarding military sanctions, Challaye wrote that the minority agreed on the need for collective security, but that, in conformity with the resolution passed at the Ligue's 1932 congress, this must be done without recourse to military sanctions. The French government had never undertaken a sincere policy of rapprochement with Germany coupled with disarmament, and that was why the situation had reached such a terrible impasse. The majority had always refused to admit that Germany and its allies were not the only nations responsible for the Great War and consequently had done nothing to create a feeling of rapprochement between their two countries.

The Nazi seizure of power had only served to increase the hostility towards Germany within the LDH. Challaye was careful to emphasize that the minority condemned the 'stupid racism' of the Nazis and their persecution of communists, socialists, pacifists, and Jews, as much as did the majority. But he took the position that opposition to an internal regime must not serve as pretext for creating a war psychosis, and he charged that that was precisely what the CC was doing.

Conclusion

What can be concluded from the above? It should be clear that the LDH was intimately bound up in the peace and war debate. This debate was conducted through the 1920s and 1930s and, like the support for pacifism itself, seems to have peaked in the early to mid-1930s. It came to a head at the Tours congress of the LDH in 1937. There two conceptions of peace came face to face. The majority saw peace as an essentially internationalist and juridical phenomenon that had to be constructed laboriously over time and with all due respect to international agreements and law. Supporters clung to a notion of peace that was closely allied to *pacifisme ancien style* and the success of the League of Nations. Facing it was the minority view, which placed peace above all other values in the socio-political equation. It was a view of European politics that had had much to commend it in the 1920s and early 1930s before the Nazis' seizure of power but which increasingly left its proponents isolated on their own small island of despair as the 1930s progressed. It was a view of peace that sought to be political but which ended up appearing as an unconscious and somewhat twisted ethical view of the world. It seemed unable to appreciate that 1933 had changed so many things, the peace-and-war debate above all.

But did it all matter? Was the LDH immune from what could be called the 'pacifist temptation'? It is clear that by 1937 at least the LDH no longer contemplated the theses of *pacifisme nouveau style* with the level of acceptance one could argue was present in the late 1920s and early 1930s. However, one would do well not to denigrate too much the influence of the peace-and-war debate within the LDH even as late as 1937. The fact that over 11 per cent of the Ligue's sections voted for the minority resolution indicates a groundswell of firm opposition to the majority position. The fact, too, that Emery topped the list of non-resident members elected to the CC must signify some support for the man and his ideas within the Ligue. As I have tried to show, the LDH – or, at the very least, its Comité central – was full of men and women active in either old-style or new-style pacifism. By 1937 a wide gulf separated the two sorts of French pacifism. But one cannot deny the centrality and 'legitimacy' of the pacifist debate within France's most important cross-party republican institution, and hence the penetration of the pacifist idea in interwar France.

NOTES

An earlier version of this essay was read to the Second International Conference of Peace Historians at Stadtschlaining, Austria, in September 1991. The editors would like to note that the author uses the term 'pacifism' in a broader sense than it is used in most of the other essays in this volume.

1 Until recently French historians seemed almost allergic to the discussion of pacifism in the historical context, though this situation is now changing. The tendency in French historiography has been to examine pacifism, if at all, as a function of debates within political parties or within larger interest groups for which pacifism was merely one issue among many that preoccupied them. See Norman Ingram, *The Politics of Dissent: Pacifism in France, 1919–1939* (Oxford 1991), 1–16, for a general introduction to the historiography of pacifism. For recent French contributions to the literature, see Nicolas Offenstadt and Philippe Olivera, 'Pour une histoire de l'engagement pacifiste en France 1919–1939: sources et bibliographie,' *Bulletin de l'Institut d'Histoire du Temps présent* (Paris), no. 51 (March 1993), 11–109.
2 Notably Peter Farrugia, 'French Religious Opposition to War, 1919–1939: The Contribution of Henri Roser and Marc Sangnier,' *French History* (Oxford), 6 no. 3 (Sept. 1992), 279–302.
3 See Martin Ceadel, *Pacifism in Britain, 1914–1945: The Defining of a Faith* (Oxford 1980), and his *Thinking about Peace and War* (Oxford and New York 1987).
4 On 'legitimacy,' see Ceadel, chapter 9, below.
5 See Antoine Prost, *Les Anciens Combattants et la société française*, 3 vols. (Paris 1977), especially, vol. 3, *Mentalités et idéologies*, 77–119.
6 For example, in a conversation with the author on 19 June 1991, Professor Madeleine Rebérioux, the first woman president of the Ligue des droits de l'homme (LDH) and an important historian of nineteenth- and twentieth-century France, categorically denied that the LDH could in any way be considered a transmitter for pacifist ideas into broader French political society. In her view, the LDH was in no sense

'pacifist' during the interwar years; it was rather, '100% patriotic.' The language and simplistic dichotomy (pacifist/non-pacifist; patriotic/unpatriotic) indicate the extent to which French political (and academic) society since the Second World War has been unable to incorporate notions of pacifist dissent.

7 See Pierre Nora, *Les Lieux de mémoire* (Paris 1984–92), and Robert Gildea, *The Past in French History* (New Haven, Conn., 1994).

8 Of particular significance therefore are the stenographic minutes of the congress. See Ligue des Droits de l'Homme. *Le Congrès National de 1937. Compte rendu sténographique* (*LDH 1937 Congress*), Tours, 17–19 July 1937 (Paris 1937).

9 Notably Michel Alexandre, Gaston Bergery, Lucien Cancouet, Armand Charpentier, Fernand Corcos, Léon Emery, René Gerin, M. Goldschild, Robert Morel, Camille Planche, and Maurice Weber.

10 Notably, Henri Guernut, Jacques Hadamard, Jean Lahargue, and M. Milhaud.

11 *LDH 1937 Congress*, 356–7. The new-style pacifists elected were Gaston Bergery, Fernand Corcos, Léon Emery, René Gerin, and Camille Planche. The one representative of what I have called old-style pacifism elected in 1937 was Jacques Hadamard, a professor at the Collège de France.

12 Most notably, Fernand Corcos, Francis Delaisi, René Gerin, Jacques Hadamard, Paul Langevin, André Philip, Camille Planche, Jules Prudhommeaux, and Théodore Ruyssen.

13 Notably, Victor Basch, Léon Brunschvicg, J.-M. Caillaud, Marc Casati, René Château, Henri Guernut, Léon Jouhaux, Jacques Kayser, and Dr. Sicard de Plauzoles.

14 Including most notably, Emile Borel, Célestin Bouglé, Justin Godard, and Mme Avril de Sainte-Croix (all representatives of the old-style pacifism) and Mathias Morhardt (a precursor of the new style).

15 Namely, Gaston Bergery, Félicien Challaye, Léon Emery, Georges Michon, Magdeleine Paz, Georges Pioch, and Elie Reynier. See Félicien Challaye, *La Crise de la Ligue des droits de l'homme* Extrait de la *Grande Revue* (Paris, Nov. 1937), 1.

16 Albert Bayet, 'Après le Congrès de Tours,' *Cahiers des Droits de l'Homme* (Paris) (cited hereafter as *Cahiers*), 37 no. 18, 15 Sept. 1937, 612.

17 Ibid. 256–72. For the printed text of Bayet's report, see Albert Bayet, 'Comment défendre ensemble la démocratie et la paix?', in *Cahiers*, 37 no. 9, 1 May 1937, 259–66. This differs in places from the version that he presented at the congress.

18 *LDH 1937 Congress*, 256.

19 Ibid., 257.

20 Ibid., 259.

21 Ibid., 262–3.

22 Ibid., 264–5.

23 Ibid., 265–6.

24 Ibid., 267–8.

25 Ibid., 269–70. Even René Gerin apparently had been convinced to support this idea. For Gerin's integral pacifist response to the problem posed by the civil war in Spain, see René Gerin, *Pacifisme 'intégral' et guerre civile* (Paris. 1937).

26 *LDH 1937 Congress*, discours de M. Camille Planche, 275–8.

27 Ibid., 280.

28 Ibid.

29 Ibid., discours de M. Emery, 281–3.

30 Ibid., 283.

31 Ibid., 285.

32 Ibid., discours de M. Challaye, 308.

33 Ibid., 308–9.

34 Ibid., 310.

35 Ibid.

36 Ibid., 311.

37 Ibid., intervention de M. Emery, 333–7. The resolution is long, covering 334–7.

38 Ibid., réponse de M. Albert Bayet, 339. Bayet's response is long, covering 338–46.

39 Ibid., 340.

40 Ibid., intervention de M. Victor Basch, 348.

41 Ibid., déclaration de M. Emery, 389–91.

42 Ibid., 390.

43 Ibid., 391.

44 See Challaye, *Crise*.

45 'Déclaration des démissionnaires,' *Cahiers*, 37 no. 21, 1 Nov. 1937, 692–3. The declaration was in fact signed by only six of the minority: Gaston Bergery, Félicien Challaye, L. Emery, Georges Michon (all of whom had resigned on 19 July at the congress itself), Magdeleine Paz, and Elie Reynier. Georges Pioch sent a separate letter of resignation to Victor Basch, also published in the *Cahiers*. See 'Lettre de M. Georges Pioch,' ibid., 693–4.

46 See especially L. Emery, 'Une Expérience démocratique,' *Feuilles libres de la quinzaine*, no. 42, 25 Sept. 1937, 212–14.

47 See Gaston Bergery, 'Feue la Ligue des Droits de l'Homme: le Congrès des bouches cousues,' *La Flèche*, 24 July 1937, cited in Challaye, *Crise*, 1–2.

48 This was reproduced in the *Cahiers*. See 'Un article de M. Challaye,' *Cahiers*, 37 no. 21, 1 Nov. 1937, 694–5.

49 Victor Basch, 'Mise au point,' *Cahiers*, 37 no. 21, 1 Nov. 1937, 683–91.

50 Ibid., 683.

51 Ibid., 683–4.

52 Ibid.

53 Ibid., 686.

54 Ibid.

55 Ibid., 687–8.
56 Ibid., 688.
57 Ibid., 688–90.
58 Ibid., 690.
59 Ibid.
60 Ibid.
61 Ibid., 691.
62 See Challaye, *Crise*.
63 On the role of Demartial in the origins of what I have called the new-style pacifism in France, see my *Politics of Dissent*, 122–5.
64 Challaye, *Crise*, 3.
65 Ibid., 3–4.

9

A Legitimate Peace Movement:
The Case of Britain, 1918–1945

MARTIN CEADEL

The British peace movement was not only the most influential of any major country's during the period covered by this volume but also the most legitimate in the sense of being accepted even by its opponents as idealistic and public-spirited rather than subversive or selfish.[1] In this essay I try to explain why this was the case by examining the deep roots that the movement had put down; the connections that it made with the mainstream of politics; its interwar strength, resulting in part from the integrity and prudence of its leadership; the demeanour of the peace movement and conscientious objectors during the Second World War; and the favourable political culture and strategic situation within which it operated.

First, however, I must make it clear how I define 'peace movement.' I do not understand it simply as an organized campaign against war: so loose a definition would have the effect of treating isolationists, defeatists, and appeasers as peace activists. If they were to be included, the strongest peace movements would have been those of the United States, where the executive was severely constrained in its foreign policy by a powerful isolationist lobby, and of France, where defeatist sentiment contributed to the creation of the Vichy regime; and the dominant element in the British peace movement would have been the Conservative supporters of the pro-appeasement prime minister, Neville Chamberlain.

Here the 'peace movement' is defined as an organized campaign not only against war but also against the view, held by virtually every government, that the best way of preventing war is simply to maintain strong defences – a stance often called 'realism' by international-relations scholars but which I prefer to call 'defencism.'[2] Defencists assume that international society is inevitably anarchical:[3] they believe that the risk of war is ever present.

People who form peace movements, however, believe in the attainability of a higher and more permanent condition of peace than the armed truce among states for which defencists settle: they believe that war can be abolished. This can be achieved through either pacifism (the absolute renunciation of military force) or pacif*i*cism (the reform of international or domestic politics so as to remove the structural causes of war but without the renunciation of such defensive force as may be needed to protect such a reform). Pacifism is to international relations what anarchism is to domestic politics. Pacificism is the application to the international sphere of reformist ideologies: those applying liberal assumptions argue that nationalism or the cult of state sovereignty causes war; those inspired by radicalism blame the blinkered perspectives of elites or vested interests; socialists indict capitalism; feminists blame patriarchy or gender; and so on.[4]

This strict definition limits the peace movement to pacifists and pacif*i*cists. It treats isolationists, defeatists, and appeasers as fellow travellers of the peace movement rather than members. This is because, though their calculations of their own or the national interest cause them to oppose the policies (rearmament, alliances, deterrence) normally favoured by defencists, they do so only in particular circumstances and on prudential grounds, not because of a principled objection to defencism itself.

When we compare peace movements, shorn of their fellow travellers, it becomes clear that Britain's was the most influential in the world. Uniquely, it was a factor to be reckoned with, even if only marginally, in national politics. For example, by the late 1920s Conservative politicians felt obliged by pressure from the League of Nations Union (LNU), a peace association that collected more than 400,000 annual subscriptions in 1931, to conceal their private doubts about the efficacy of the League of Nations or the prospects of the World Disarmament Conference (1932–3) in Geneva in order to avoid being accused of war-mongering. As well, the Peace Ballot, a nationwide private referendum organized by the LNU during 1934–5, which involved an astonishing 38 per cent of the adult population and for the most part elicited the answers sought by the organizers, influenced the government's political strategy.[5] After the outbreak of war moreover the peace movement was even blamed for preventing the British government from standing up to Hitler: indeed, it was still trying to rebut this charge years later.[6]

History

Yet, though its critics insisted that it hindered the government and encouraged the country's enemies, they did not normally accuse it of doing so deliberately. One reason for this was that the movement had too long and respectable a history to be explained in terms of disloyalty or treachery. Pacifism in Britain could be traced back in an unbroken line to the proclamation by the Quakers of their peace testimony in 1661; and pacifism grew out of the rational Christianity and political radicalism that became significant influences in the late eighteenth century.[7]

The Quakers differed significantly from the previous pacifist sects which, as Peter Brock in particular has shown,[8] appeared intermittently in Europe from the 1170s onward. Their thinking had a modern character, which, for example, that of the Mennonites lacked. Because of their origins and the circumstances in which they had committed themselves to pacifism, Quakers did not reject either political action or political authority. They had emerged in the 1650s as a popular movement working for a politico-religious revolution in an environment in which such an eventuality seemed practical politics. When the Cromwellian era ended and the monarchy was restored, they accepted its legitimacy and in 1661 renounced all violence. And, though retreating for a time into sectarianism, their self-discipline, clannish mutual help, and reputation for honesty brought them prosperity through trade, commerce, and industry, which gradually drew them back into society.

By the late eighteenth century they were prominent in philanthropic movements alongside other evangelical Protestants. Yet their peace testimony was unwavering and highly principled: they stuck to their declaration of 1661 and refused under any circumstances to serve in the militia and also – unlike the Mennonites – to hire substitutes or pay fines, thereby making it clear that their pacifism was more than a plea for the exemption of an esoteric minority. In time their principles began to spread outside their own ranks: the pacifism that, albeit on a very small scale, surfaced in the Church of England and some dissenting Protestant denominations soon after the outbreak of the French wars of 1793–1815 owed much to Quakerism.

So too did the formation of Britain's first pacifist society – the Society for the Promotion of Permanent and Universal Peace, generally known as the Peace Society – which was formed on 14 June 1816 in the troubled aftermath of those wars and was to remain fairly active for almost exactly a century. Only an association of unimpeachably evangelical rather than political intent could have survived the difficult climate of its first decade and a half; and, though thereafter affected by the decline of evangelicalism and the rise of economic and political liberalism, the Peace Society always had a majority of Quakers among its members (though to avoid seeming a mere front organization for the Society of Friends, it was careful to avoid a Quaker majority on its committee) and thus retained a predominantly religious rather than partisan identity. British pacifism thus established itself before the appearance of adventist sects, which rejected military service for idiosyncratic reasons.

To sum up: the socially engaged, respectable, and non-political character that British pacifism owed to its Quaker roots made it more difficult than in other countries to accuse its adherents of either closet oppositionism or sectarian peculiarity.

Pacif*i*cism had almost as long a history as pacifism and had put down even deeper roots in British politics. It emerged first in the late eighteenth century as a combined product of rational Christianity and political radicalism. Rational Christianity, which later developed into Unitarianism, was the most extreme expression of British Protestantism's willingness to accommodate Enlightenment thinking. Having adopted the Enlightenment view that war was an irrational and inhumane means of resolving international disputes, rational Christianity was to play a leading role in the first-ever peace campaign – that against the French wars of 1793–1815.[9] Radicalism, which benefited from Britain's comparative political tolerance, was a protest against the power of the aristocracy and other vested interests, which it accused of, among other selfish actions, fomenting wars from which they alone benefited. In the course of the nineteenth century moreover liberalism developed an even more influential strand of pacificism, and socialism produced yet another one, albeit of minority appeal.

However, pacificism was surprisingly slow to generate a successful peace association. The Society for Abolishing War, launched three months before the Peace Society, and the Peace of Nations Society, founded in 1849, both flopped: indeed, their very existence was discovered only recently.[10] Because its early operations were subsidized by the Peace Society, the Workmen's Peace Association, set up in 1870, only gradually made it clear that it was not a pacifist body, doing so only after restyling itself the International Arbitration League in 1888. The first overtly pacificist society was the International Arbitration and Peace Association, formed in 1880. Pacificism's real asset was its political connections: it had significant support within the Liberal party as well as within the nascent labour movement.

Mainstream Connections

The respectability that Britain's long-established peace movement had achieved by the early twentieth century was symbolized in 1908, when London hosted the Universal Peace Congress: the delegates were given a reception by the king at Buckingham Palace and a dinner by the government, at which Prime Minister Asquith proposed a toast to 'the International Peace Movement.'[11] Four years later, a wealthy industrialist and a Conservative former prime minister were among the backers of a campaign to promote the 'New Pacifism' of Norman Angell.[12]

Admittedly, the First World War temporarily damaged the climate of acceptability and tolerance that the peace movement had been enjoying. All existing peace associations went into sharp decline. And the new generation of organizations that replaced them during 1914–15 – the radical-pacificist Union of Democratic Control (UDC), the socialist-pacifist No-Conscription Fellowship, the Christian-pacifist Fellowship of Reconciliation, and the liberal-pacificist League of Nations Society[13] – behaved at first with considerable circumspection in the face of public hostility to pacifism or anything that remotely resembled it. By far the boldest initiative came from the women who launched the feminist-pacificist Women's International League in an international congress at the Hague in April 1915:[14] not being eligible for military service, they were harder to accuse of shirking their patriotic duty.

None the less, peace activism never wholly lost its legitimacy. When conscription was introduced in Britain for the first time in 1916 (compulsory militia service not having been required since 1831), statutory provision was made for conscientious objectors (CO's) that was far more generous than that of even those very few other countries that recognized them. In 1917 the political climate began to improve from the peace movement's point of view, and two of its sections re-established contact with the political mainstream. U.S. entry into the war under Woodrow Wilson ensured that the League of Nations, an idea formerly dismissed as pacifist, would be implemented in some form.

Supporters of the British government (a coalition since 1915) tried to persuade the League of Nations Society to advocate creation of a League that at least at first would exclude Germany and its allies, and when they failed, they set up a separate League of Free Nations Association. In October 1918, with the war about to end, the two League societies merged as the League of Nations Union (LNU). The new body was thus from the outset more broadly based than most peace associations, being endorsed by well-connected supporters of the war such as the Liberal academic Gilbert Murray and the Conservative statesman who was shortly to play a major role in establishing the League of Nations, Lord Robert Cecil.

Also in 1917, as a result of war-weariness at home and revolution in Russia, the Labour party qualified its previous support for the war: worried by the social risks involved in holding out for a crushing victory, it left the coalition government and took up the UDC's call for a postwar settlement without annexations and indemnities. This was of considerable political significance: what was about to become the main opposition party had aligned itself with an only recently disparaged peace association.

Interwar Strength

Though the armistice of November 1918 and the next month's general election generated a revival of the patriotic intolerance that had marked the early years of the war, the peace movement entered the postwar era in an underlyingly strong position, having for the first time created strong pacificist associations – the UDC and the LNU. As disillusionment with the fruits of victory set in, opposition to the recent war began to lose its stigma: in 1921 a former CO was elected to Parliament, and members of the No-Conscription Fellowship, which had wound itself up when conscription ended, formed a new socialist-pacifist association, the No More War Movement. The following year, the Labour party restored Ramsay MacDonald, who had opposed the war and helped to found the UDC, to its leadership, and in 1924 the first Labour government included no fewer than fifteen UDC members, nine in the cabinet and six as junior ministers.[15]

The UDC's rather negative ideas did not prove useful in office, however, and it went into rapid decline. With the League of Nations gaining in popularity even within the Labour movement,[16] the LNU stepped into its shoes as the best-connected peace association. The leaders of all the political parties agreed to be its honorary presidents (except for MacDonald, who had an obscure personal grievance against the League movement dating from the First World War); and in 1925, when it was already collecting more than a quarter-million annual subscriptions, it even obtained a royal charter. In 1927 Lord Robert Cecil, who by then had been translated to the House of Lords as Viscount Cecil of Chelwood, resigned from Stanley Baldwin's Conservative government in protest at its reluctance to pursue disarmament and thereafter devoted himself almost full-time to the LNU.

Never before or since has a peace association enjoyed such support and status and – with a literary reaction against the 1914–18 war in full swing from 1928 onwards – such a capacity to embarrass the government. In the early 1930s Sir Austen Chamberlain, the former Conservative leader who had served as foreign secretary from 1924 to 1929, sat uncomfortably on the LNU's executive committee in an effort to mute its criticisms of the Conservative-dominated National Government, though his attempt to obstruct the Peace Ballot proved counterproductive.

What had above all irritated Chamberlain and other defencists was the LNU's unstated implication that the League of Nations could normally expect to ensure peace and justice merely through disarmament, moral pressure, or economic sanctions. But after the three-fold crisis of 1935–6 in which Mussolini attacked Abyssinia, Hitler remilitarized the Rhineland, and Franco launched the Spanish

Civil War, it became apparent that aggression of this kind could be prevented only by willingness to use military force. The LNU split on the issue: its leaders remained loyal to collective security even though they now came to accept that this required rearmament and military alliances; but many of its rank and file either called for 'peaceful change' – in other words, revision of the Versailles Treaty in Germany's favour – or joined a new pacifist association founded in May 1936, the Peace Pledge Union (PPU).

However, defencists were themselves divided as to whether the national interest was better served by the containment or the appeasement of Germany. They could not therefore form a common front against the peace movement. The appeasement policies of Neville Chamberlain, who became prime minister in 1937, received considerable support from advocates of peaceful change and from pacifists. And pro-containment defencists received support from the collective-security wing of the peace movement. Winston Churchill, who realized that his campaign for more vigorous rearmament would attract more support if it was justified in terms of the enforcement of international law rather than the maintenance of the balance of power, was elected to the LNU's executive committee but decided instead to accept the presidency of the New Commonwealth Society, a small offshoot of the LNU that campaigned for an international police force.[17]

The same reasoning had led the National Government's astute prime minister, Stanley Baldwin, to make a sensitive defence-policy speech during the campaign for the November 1935 general election to a meeting organized by the Peace Society. The latter's name helped to forestall accusations of war-mongering, and the fact that the society was by then virtually moribund made it possible for him to address it without incurring the critical attention that an LNU meeting would undoubtedly have provided. Because both strands within defencism had admirers or supporters in the peace movement, they found it hard to dismiss the latter as wholly misguided.

The PPU's respectability also protected British pacifism from much of the obloquy that might have followed its call for a policy of defencelessness while the fascist states were embarking on policies of militarism. This was true even in late 1936, when, having already received 118,000 pledges, it seemed to be growing quickly enough to have an outside chance of becoming a mass movement. The PPU was the creation of the Revd H.R.L. (Dick) Sheppard, a wealthy and well-connected Anglican clergyman, who had achieved national fame as the first parson to have his church services broadcast by the British Broadcasting Corporation (BBC).

Sheppard's extraordinary charm, his high social standing (he was the son of a minor canon in the royal chapel at Windsor), and his conservatism on issues other than foreign policy (he had voted for the National Government in the 1931 election) made it hard for opponents to accuse the PPU of subversive intent. (Its appeal to those who did not take a left-wing position in domestic politics helps to explain why the PPU did so much better than the No More War Movement, which never claimed more than three thousand members and, weakened by defections caused by the Spanish Civil War, merged with the PPU in 1937.[18]) The intellectual distinction and independence of mind of the 'Sponsors' whom Sheppard assembled as the governing body of the PPU – they included Vera Brittain, Aldous Huxley, John Middleton Murry, Canon Charles Raven, and Bertrand Russell – discouraged charges of simple-mindedness.

By the time of Sheppard's death in October 1937 it was apparent that the PPU's period of rapid growth had ended and that there was therefore no chance of Britain's being converted to a policy of non-violence. Some pacifists threw their weight behind the pacificist campaign for 'peaceful change' until Hitler's occupation of Prague in March 1939 made it clear that his demands went beyond anything that he could be offered in the name of international justice. A few went on trying to placate Germany even after Prague: for example, Stuart Morris, the PPU's leading organizer after Sheppard's death, joined The Link, an organization sympathetic to Nazi Germany; and George Orwell accused the PPU of 'a moral collapse' after Sheppard's death, on the grounds that some members even joined the British Union of Fascists.[19]

Had this been its dominant tone, pacifism might have lost legitimacy. An increasing number of pacifists, however, ceased to assert that they had a practical policy to offer and claimed merely that theirs was a faith to which they were personally committed irrespective of its consequences. This had always been the view of most members of the Fellowship of Reconciliation, which trebled in size from 3,300 to 9,800 members in the late 1930s. The growing quietism of the majority of the pacifist movement facilitated a tacit agreement between most pacifists and most defencists and pacificists: the pacifists did not dispute that in terms of practical politics these other groups were in the right; and they in turn agreed to recognize the legitimacy of the pacifists, if only as an easy way of demonstrating Britain's moral superiority over its totalitarian foes.

The pacificist idealism that had pinned its hopes successively on disarmament, collective security, and peaceful change found a final outlet in Federal Union – an association set up late in 1938 to campaign for replacement of the discredited League of Nations with a federation of the democracies. Publication in March 1939 of *Union Now: A Proposal for a Federal Union of the Democracies of the North Atlantic*, a best-seller by the American journalist Clarence K. Streit,[20] greatly boosted the supporters of Federal Union. Since federalism proved to be a popular war aim for progressives, just like the League of Nations a quarter-century earlier, Federal Union was helped rather than damaged by the outbreak of the Second World War, with its emphasis shifting from Atlantic to European federation. Despite its ambitious goals – Viscount Cecil, still loyal to the LNU, thought it guilty of 'fantastic utopianism'[21] – it attracted distinguished supporters. Its leading figure was William (later Lord) Beveridge, soon to design Britain's welfare state; it was endorsed by Clement Attlee and Ernest Bevin, who after the war were to be labour prime minister and foreign secretary, respectively; Harold Wilson, another future Labour prime minister, attended some of its meetings; and its economic committee was graced by such talented intellectuals as Evan Durbin, F.A. Hayek, James Meade, Lionel Robbins, and Barbara Wootton. It was a peace association of impeccable respectability.

Wartime Demeanour

The good reputation of the peace movement was finally assured by the generally self-effacing wartime behaviour of both the PPU, whose membership peaked at 136,000 in April 1940 and thereafter slowly declined, and the conscientious objectors (COs) of 1939–45. Despite the opposition of a Forward Movement of young activists keen to resist the war effort, the PPU behaved with circumspection. Sixty thousand British men successfully claimed a conscientious objection during the Second World War (1.2 per cent of those called up) – almost four times as many as in the First World War, when there had been sixteen thousand COs (0.125 per cent of those either volunteering before 1916 or called up thereafter) – and nearly twice as many had their claims rejected outright.[22]

Yet the COs of 1939–45 made much less impact on the public mind than those of 1916–18, as shown by the obscurity of the bodies that catered for them by comparison with the No-Conscription Fellowship. And COs accepted rejections more willingly, particularly as the tribunal gained a reputation for fairness and flexibility. Particularly after the May 1940 fall of France, which provoked a number of recantations of pacifism and started a progressive fall in the proportion of COs (which had been 2.2 per cent for the first cohort called up during the war and was to be only 0.2 per cent for the last), many pacifists felt some unease and even guilt about their stand.

The obscure discomfort they suffered, often at the hands not of the state but of their fellow citizens, who refused to employ them or work alongside them, was more demoralizing than the harsh prison sentences experienced during the First World War. The PPU's journal *Peace News* was never banned, for example, but suffered a boycott by wholesale newsagents from May 1940 onward. And, whereas in that earlier war acceptance of alternative service was widely held to be a less admirable stance by a CO refused unconditional exemption than going to prison as an absolutist, this time most pacifists were keen to do work of national importance.

The sentiments expressed privately by an elderly pacifist early in 1940 were common among British pacifists throughout the war: 'Had I been of military age I should probably have joined [the Friends Ambulance Unit] too. The Government, on the whole, is treating pacifists very fairly, and it is hard to follow the logical *non possumus* attitude: and it is idle to maintain that one is indifferent to the result: a win for Germany would imprison freedom of person, of thought, and conscience for a generation.'[23] One of the minority of intransigent pacifists even complained that the British state was practising what would later be called repressive tolerance, noting: 'There is a feeling that somehow we have been diddled.'[24]

A Favourable Context

That Britain was able to practise such tolerance during the period under study was, as I have argued elsewhere,[25] a consequence in large part of its moderately secure strategic position and its moderately liberal political culture. By 'strategic position' I mean the extent to which geography, military strength, and diplomatic situation made a country secure. The more vulnerable a country, the more pessimistic its view of the prospects of abolishing war and the more it will regard its peace movement not as an idealistic attempt to construct a better world but as a treacherous attempt to weaken the country's prospects of survival. Moderate insecurity encourages an averagely strong nation to adopt defencism, since it can perceive a threat to its security but not feel a defensive effort to be futile. Extreme insecurity increases the temptation for a strong country such as Nazi Germany to espouse militarism; it also predisposes a weak one such as Vichy France to embrace defeatism.

Security, in contrast, encourages an optimistic view of international relations. A country as invulnerable from attack as the United States, particularly before the invention of the intercontinental ballistic missile, was assured of a reasonably significant peace movement. Yet because it was so well protected from the direct effects of war, haters of war there could simply opt out of conflict rather than work to prevent it, and this fact weakened the country's peace movement. If, as in the American case, the secure country was also strong, it was sometimes tempted to divert its moralism into a crusade for justice and ultimate peace, since it did not fully understand the horrific side effects that make aggressive war an inappropriate instrument for the promotion of such goals.

For this reason peace movements do best in conditions of moderate security. In such circumstances, the level of security is sufficient to foster some belief in the achievability of true or positive peace and to allow critics of defencism to be viewed as at worst utopians rather than as traitors. But it is insufficient for simple escapism: if war breaks out, the country risks becoming embroiled and so must work to prevent it. And a state that is only moderately secure has sufficient experience of warfare not to share the crusader's confidence that it can make things better. Its hopeful and moralistic feelings about international relations are thus channelled exclusively into peace activity.

Interwar Britain was a clear example of a moderately secure country. As an island it felt safe enough for its peace associations generally to escape accusations of sympathy with the nation's foes, as I noted above. But it was too close to continental Europe for escapism to be possible. Admittedly, the UDC had isolationist instincts, which reflected its origins in the ill-fated neutralist movement of July–August 1914; but these stopped it from developing a constructive policy for solving the European problems of the mid-1920s and contributed to its rapid decline. Similarly, in response to the Franco–German quarrel that paralysed the World Disarmament Conference in 1933–4, some on the right, notably Canadian-born newspaper magnate Lord Beaverbrook, and on the left, such as the dissident Labour politician Sir Stafford Cripps, argued for repudiation of Britain's obligations under Locarno and the League of Nations Covenant. But the general consensus was that in the era of air power this was no longer practicable. The popularity of the League of Nations in Britain until its failure in the Abyssinian crisis of 1935–6 reflected a belief that Britain had to be engaged in the attempt to resolve Europe's problems.

The other factor affecting the strength of a peace movement is a country's political culture – the historically created attitudes and values that shape its politics. Every strand within a political culture affects the peace-or-war debate to some extent; but for the sake of simplicity, my theory singles out one ideology as crucial. This is liberalism, defined here as the belief that people's interests are essentially compatible and human individuality can be allowed almost free expression. To an extent greater than other ideologies, liberalism recognizes the legitimacy of viewpoints other than its own: it is tolerant and pluralistic, encouraging creation of competing political parties, pressure groups and religious associations.

Illiberal cultures – those that show positive hostility to liberalism – have the most negligible and persecuted peace movements and the strongest militarist traditions. Japan in the 1930s was a case in point. Non-liberal cultures – those in which liberalism is relatively weak but not regarded as subversive – have a small peace movement and are most staunchly defencist. France, famous for the comparative weakness of its peace movement, is a good example. Despite its contribution to the Enlightenment, it is traditionally Roman Catholic and was slow to industrialize; it therefore lacked the moralizing Protestantism and free-enterprise enthusiasm from which Anglo-American liberalism, as we see below, has drawn its strength. Its political left has been characterized instead by the Jacobin tradition of republican defence and Marxism.

A degree of liberalism is thus necessary for peace activity: it provides a climate in which pacifist sects, peace associations, and war-prevention ideas of all kinds can flourish, and it generates liberal pacifism, which has been historically the most influential single strand of thinking within the peace movement. But if liberalism is too influential within a political culture, it can give rise to a moral intensity that encourages crusading; and the existence of an overwhelmingly dominant ideology, however well-intentioned, inevitably restricts pluralism.

The United States is the best example of a culture dominated by liberalism. It lacks an indigenous feudal elite, and so both conservatism and (as a reaction against inequality) socialism have been weaker than in Europe. Its liberal constitution and its early transition to democracy have somewhat muted the sort of scepticism towards governmental decisions to go to war that in Britain produced a conspicuous tradition of 'trouble making,' as A.J.P. Taylor has called it.[26] Compared with Britain again, its moralistic liberalism, rooted in Protestantism and free enterprise, has not been counterbalanced to the same extent by either realist scepticism or competing forms of idealism; and its egalitarianism has produced a conformist culture, in which COs have been less well treated.

A moderately liberal culture such as Britain's is thus ideal for peace movements. It has been sufficiently liberal to develop a vigorous tradition of free speech, party competition, and pressure-group activism. Its transition to representative government and democracy took place without major violence after the seventeenth century: this evolution encouraged its progressives to take a pacificist view of international relations rather than the crusading one preached by some of their continental counterparts, such as Mazzini, who assumed that force was necessary to liberate or unite their nations and so create the basis for a just and peaceful international order.

British Protestantism, as shaped in particular by the dissenting denominations and summed up neatly in the phrase 'nonconformist conscience,' has combined harmoniously with secular reformism to produce a moralistic but moderate progressivism not found in Roman Catholic, Lutheran, or Calvinist countries. This progressivism helped to nourish the Liberal party in the nineteenth century and the Labour party in the twentieth: these parties proved more helpful to the peace movement than the more revolutionary or anti-clerical parties of the European left have been.

Britain's liberalism has been offset by two major factors. First, a moderate but tenacious conservatism, whose influence on foreign and defence policy in particular has encouraged scepticism towards the state, has helped both the peace movement and conscientious objection. Second, rival idealisms such as socialism have further helped to prevent liberal moralism from becoming a crusading force. In addition, the self-confident complexity of Britain's mature social structure has permitted greater eccentricity and individualism than is possible in settler societies.[27] Britain has thus allowed peace movements to oppose even those wars that the great majority of progressives believe to have been justified.

Conclusion

In conclusion, what is remarkable about interwar Britain is not that in the autumn of 1935 George Lansbury and Lord Ponsonby felt unable to continue as the Labour party's leaders in the Commons and Lords, respectively, but the fact that two such outspoken and uncompromising pacificists had been acceptable in these positions during the four previous years. Likewise, it is less surprising that pacifists disappeared from BBC broadcasts at the end of the 'phoney war' in the spring of 1940 than that so many of them had appeared in front of the microphone before then.[28]

This remarkable toleration of peace activism in Britain from 1918 to 1945 is the result of four main factors. First, by 1918 both pacifism and pacificism had long and respectable histories. Second, despite the adverse circumstances of the First World War, the LNU and the UDC had established connections in governing circles which linked the peace movement to the political mainstream. Third, during the interwar period and the Second World War leading peace associations attracted distinguished supporters and avoided unnecessarily provocative behaviour: the fact that the PPU was created by a much loved high-society figure contributed considerably to its respectability. And fourth, the degrees of security and liberalism that Britain has enjoyed helped to make the peace movement acceptable.

NOTES

1 I first became interested in the question of the legitimacy of peace movements after being invited by Professor Karl Holl of the University of Bremen to address a con-

ference on 'The Acceptance of Peace Movements in National Societies during the Inter-war Period 1919–1939; A Comparative Study,' held at Stadtschlaining, Austria, 25–29 Sept. 1991. This essay is based on that paper.

2 I give my reasons for doing so in Martin Ceadel, *Thinking about Peace and War* (Oxford 1987), chap. 5.

3 A label made famous by Hedley Bull, *The Anarchical Society: A Study of Order in World Politics* (London 1977).

4 See Ceadel, *Thinking about Peace and War*, chaps. 6–7.

5 See Ceadel, 'The Peace Movement between the Wars: Problem of Definition,' in Richard Taylor and Nigel Young, eds., *Campaigns for Peace: British Peace Movements in the Twentieth Century* (Manchester 1987), 73–99, and 'The First British Referendum: The "Peace Ballot", 1934–5,' *English Historical Review* (London), 95 (1980), 810–39.

6 See, for example, the pamphlet by the University Group on Defence Policy, *The Role of the Peace Movements in the 1930s* (London 1957).

7 The early history of the British peace movement is told in Ceadel, *The Origins of War Prevention: The British Peace Movement and International Relations 1730–1854* (Oxford 1996).

8 Most recently in *Freedom from Violence: Sectarian Nonresistance from the Middle Ages to the Great War* (Toronto 1991).

9 See J.E. Cookson, *The Friends of Peace: Anti-War Liberalism in Britain, 1792–1815* (Cambridge 1982).

10 By the remarkable Dutch scholar W.H. van der Linden, *The International Peace Movement, 1815–1874* (Amsterdam 1987), 1–3, 203–5.

11 *Herald of Peace* (London) (Sept. 1908), 164, 173–4.

12 J.D.B. Miller, *Norman Angell and the Futility of War* (London 1986), 6–7.

13 For these associations, see respectively Marvin Swartz, *The Union of Democratic Control in British Politics during the First World War* (Oxford 1971); Thomas Kennedy, *The Hound of Conscience: A History of the No-Conscription Fellowship, 1914–1919* (Fayetteville, Ark., 1981); Henry Winkler, *The League of Nations Movement in Great Britain, 1914–1919* (New Brunswick, NJ, 1952); and Jill Wallis, *Valiant for Peace: A History of the Fellowship of Reconciliation, 1914 to 1989* (London 1991). For an overview, see Keith Robbins, *The Abolition of War: The 'Peace Movement' in Britain, 1914–1919* (Cardiff 1976).

14 See Anne Wiltsher, *Most Dangerous Women: Feminist Peace Campaigners of the Great War* (London 1985).

15 Swartz, *The Union of Democratic Control*, 221.

16 See Henry Winkler, *Paths Not Taken: British Labour and International Policy in the 1920s* (Chapel Hill, NC, 1994).

17 See Ceadel, 'A Pro-War Peace Movement? The British Movement for Collective

Security, 1936–1939,' in Maurice Vaïsse ed., *Le Pacifisme en Europe des années 1920 aux années 1950* (Brussels 1993), 167–92.

18 For the Peace Pledge Union and No More War Movement, see Ceadel, *Pacifism in Britain, 1914–1945: The Defining of a Faith* (Oxford 1980).

19 Ibid., 282–5. Sonia Orwell and Ian Angus, eds., *The Collected Essays, Journalism and Letters of George Orwell*, 4 vols. (Harmondsworth 1970), 2:69.

20 See Andrea Bosco, 'Lothian, Curtis, Kimber and the Federal Union Movement (1938–40),' *Journal of Contemporary History* 23 (1988), 465–502; and Richard Mayne and John Pinder with John C. de V. Roberts, *Federal Union: The Pioneers: A History of Federal Union* (London 1991), chaps. 1–3.

21 Donald S. Birn, *The League of Nations Union, 1918–1945* (Oxford 1981), 205.

22 Rachel Barker, *Conscience, Government and War: Conscientious Objection in Great Britain, 1939–45* (London 1982), 121. Ceadel, *Pacifism in Britain*, 302.

23 E. Whitaker to Mrs Cadoux, 26 Feb. 1940, Cecil John Cadoux Papers (General Correspondence 1940), Bodleian Library, Oxford.

24 *Peace News* (London) 5 April 1940.

25 Ceadel, *Thinking about Peace and War*, chap. 8.

26 See A.J.P. Taylor, *The Trouble Makers: Dissent over Foreign Policy, 1792–1939* (London 1957).

27 This point is made in Mulford Q. Sibley and Philip E. Jacob, *Conscription of Conscience: The American State and the Conscientious Objector, 1940–47* (Ithaca, NY, 1952), 6–7, 16–17, 480; and David Grant, *Out in the Cold: Pacifists and Conscientious Objectors in New Zealand during World War II* (Auckland 1986), 11, 32.

28 For statements of pacifism, see the following issues of the *Listener* (London): 14 Nov. 1934, 799–800; 21 Nov. 1934, 872; 22 Jan. 1936, 145–6, 178; 28 April 1937, 818; 16 Feb. 1938, 343; 2 March 1938, 445–6, 477–9; 3 Nov. 1938, 954; 1 Dec. 1938, 1188; and 2 March 1939, 460. In addition, both Canon Charles Raven and John Middleton Murry gave religious broadcasts in the period from December 1939 to May 1940, though these did not mention pacifism. It is a pity that Asa Briggs did not discuss the BBC's policy towards pacifists in *The Golden Age of Wireless*, which covers the period 1927–39 and is the second of his four volumes on *The History of Broadcasting in Britain* (London 1961–79), though his third volume, *The War of Words*, states that they were 'more or less excluded' during wartime.

10

Women Pacifists in Interwar Britain

JOSEPHINE EGLIN

In the late 1920s, writes a leading British peace historian, pacifism was frequently linked with vegetarianism: 'The unwillingness to take life explains this connection; less logical but almost as strong was pacifism's affinity for ... feminism.'[1] The intention of this essay is to investigate this affinity by looking specifically at women pacifists in interwar Britain. In the first part I look at three members of each of three groups of women holding anti-war views – socialist anti-militarists, pacifi*c*ists, and pacifists. In the second part I describe the three types of links that three particular pacifists – Vera Brittain, Helena Swanwick, and Virginia Woolf – believed to exist between feminism and pacifism. I conclude with a critical look at these theoretical connections.

The 1920s and 1930s provided a sympathetic background for pacifism; 'peace was regarded as the natural rule.'[2] Anti-war views, held by a minority in the early 1920s, revived and flourished in the late 1920s and 1930s: 'For a little while they were the accepted orthodox opinion of the decade.'[3] Consciousness of the horrors and human losses of the First World War and a historical awareness that cleared Germany of exclusive responsibility for it both contributed to a 'Never Again' attitude.[4] This was reinforced by a proliferation of anti-war novels, poetry, and films between 1928 and 1930.[5] In 1933 the Oxford Union passed a resolution: 'This House will not fight for King and Country,' and a second wave of anti-war literature appeared.[6] Peace societies flourished. First came the Fellowship of Reconciliation (FOR) and the Union of Democratic Control (UDC), both established in 1914. The Women's International League (WIL), founded in 1915, was the British section of the International Committee of Women for Permanent Peace (ICWPP), organized at the Women's International Congress at The Hague the same year. Later there emerged the League of Nations Union (LNU) in 1918, the No More War Movement (NMWM) and War Resisters' International (WRI) in 1921, the British Movement against War and Fascism in 1932, and the Peace Pledge Union (PPU) in 1936. In addition, the Independent Labour Party (ILP) and the Women's Cooperative Guild (WCG) both had a strong commitment to peace during the interwar period. 'Pacifism was all the rage. It really did seem like that – a craze.'[7] In response to Italy's invasion of Ethiopia in October 1935, Hitler's taking of the Rhineland in March 1936, and the Spanish Civil War of the same year, 'most English people displayed little concern. They wanted peace.'[8] Right up to 1939 they shared Neville Chamberlain's desire for appeasement.[9]

The desire for peace was not, however, synonymous with pacifism, though in the enthusiasm for avoiding war the term 'pacifism' tended to be used indiscriminately. In this essay 'pacifism' refers only to a total rejection of war and violent revolution of any kind, a moral belief that war is always wrong and should never be resorted to whatever the consequences, and personal refusal to take part in any war. Thus I distinguish women pacifists of the period from women pacificists. The latter believed that war is an irrational and inhumane way of settling disputes and that its prevention should always be a priority. They were committed to working to maintain peace but were prepared to support the use of force in 'peace keeping' operations and accepted that in the last resort war might be justified. There were also socialist anti-militarists, who opposed capitalist wars but were ready to support a war to speed the downfall of capitalism.[10]

These are not easy distinctions to make,[11] and many women belonged to a range of organizations,[12] which they variously joined, left, and rejoined, or disagreed with their policies but none the less remained members. Others operated mainly outside any organized societies at all. Accordingly I look at individual women, chosen because of their leading roles in interwar politics,[13] and attempt through them to illustrate the three strands of the interwar peace movement.

Three Types

Socialist Anti-militarists

In the 1920s socialist anti-militarists, who opposed war on socialist rather than pacifist grounds, were still allied with pacifists. There had been a rift between the two groups at the time of the Bolshevik Revolution, but this had not been critical. In the case of some socialists, such as Sylvia Pankhurst, it was to be the invasion of Ethiopia that proved critical. For many socialists, however, such as Ellen Wilkinson and Ethel Mannin, the Spanish Civil War proved a turning point, because they interpreted it as a 'people's war' and therefore justified.

Sylvia Pankhurst had been a committed pacifist between 1914 and 1916. She had been on the executive of the WIL, opposed conscription, helped conscientious objectors (COs), and organized demonstrations for peace in London's East End.[14] In 1917, however, full of enthusiasm for the Russian Revolution, she had joined with others to foment a similar uprising in Britain through her speeches and her newspaper the *Workers' Dreadnought*, subtitled 'the organ of the Communist Party.' Though her criticism of the party was to lead to her expulsion from it, she remained a Marxist all her life. In the early 1920s, however, she still considered herself a pacifist, but gradually she came to believe that fascism was itself such a threat to world peace that it could be defeated only by resort to arms. Mussolini's attack on Ethiopia confirmed this belief and led her to crusade on behalf of that country for the rest of her life. She opposed appeasement, and the Second World War had her full support.[15]

Similarly Ellen Wilkinson, MP for Jarrow, had been a pacifist and a member of the WIL during the First World War, even though, like Pankhurst, she had sympathized with the Russian Revolution. In the 1920s she continued to work for the WIL on the basis that all war was caused by imperialism and fascism. At the same time, however, she was a founder member of the British Communist party in 1920, and, though she resigned again in 1924, she always retained her belief in class war.[16] In the 1930s the contradictions inherent in these beliefs became apparent, and, again like Pankhurst, her antifascism proved stronger than her pacifism. She had become a sponsor of the PPU in 1936 but always had doubts about it and resigned in 1937. Similarly, early in 1937 she had denounced rearmament, but she changed her mind six months later. Her visit to Spain in 1937 convinced her, like many other erstwhile pacifists, that the civil war there was part of the international struggle against fascism. She asked rhetorically, 'Do you really expect us to go to Spain and return impartial? No longer is it a civil war, it is a fight between right and wrong.'[17] From then on she opposed appeasement; as a member of the wartime coalition government she was committed to winning the war.

For Ethel Mannin, too, Spain was a turning point. She had considered herself strongly pacifist in 1935[18] and had spoken on public platforms against war in 1936 but found herself at the end of that year in complete sympathy with the anarchosyndicalists in Spain. Alongside Emma Goldman she wrote, spoke, appealed for money, and supported the lifting of the arms embargo on Spain.[19] In *Women and the Revolution*, published in 1938, she wrote that it was necessary to distinguish between wars to preserve capitalism and wars to defend the workers' state: 'Sentimental pacifism, mere hatred of war, is not enough. The peace movement which does not attack the causes of war is futile. It cannot be too strongly emphasised or too often reiterated that war is the inevitable outcome of capitalism and imperialism.'[20] She reminded her female readers that fascism was antifeminist, seeking to return women to the home, closing careers to them, bribing them into marriage and maternity, and making child-bearing a duty to the state. Women should therefore fight alongside men to overthrow fascism.[21] Later, however, along with her husband, Reginald Reynolds, she adhered once again to absolute pacifism.

Pacificists

If the Spanish Civil War polarized opinion between socialist anti-militarists and pacifists, pacificists first began to realize the incompatibility of the collective security they favoured and pacifism in 1933. Until that time collective security was still being interpreted as a rival policy to rearmament, and there was a tendency to believe that peace could be maintained by economic blockade.[22] In 1933 Hitler came to power and Germany withdrew from the League of Nations; many of its supporters acknowledged that this meant the failure of disarmament and that collective security to the point of military sanctions might be justified to preserve democracy. The polarization of opinion between pacifists and pacificists became more marked following the Italian attack on Ethiopia and the remilitarization of the Rhineland in 1935, after which the LNU officially supported rearmament as part of collective security. All three pacificists looked at here – Mary Agnes Hamilton, Storm Jameson, and Mary Sheepshanks – found their idea changing substantially during the mid-1930s.

A classic example of a woman's following this path towards compromise with militarism was Mary Agnes Hamilton. A Labour MP from 1929 to 1931, when she refused to join the National Government, Hamilton had been a pacifist and member of the UDC during the First World War. She described the period of 1918–31 as one of relative optimism and commitment to 'No More War,'[23] but later she gradually ceased to consider herself a pacifist, and, following the invasion of Ethiopia, she became convinced that it was necessary to put military force behind the League of Nations in order to halt Italian aggression. She became critical of the notion that 'belief in peace would *ipso facto* secure it,'[24] and she retrospectively felt that she and others had been oversentimental about Germany, unwilling to apportion any of the blame for the First World War to its government, and overly critical of the Versailles Treaty.[25] At the same time she felt that too much confidence had been placed in the League. She clearly articulated her position as a pacificist, rejecting absolute pacifism in favour of collective security, rejecting appeasement in the 1930s as 'peace at any price, paid by anybody,'[26] and declaring that after Munich the only alternative to war 'was to be eaten alive.'[27]

Storm Jameson, too, had been sympathetic towards the FOR and the WIL during the First World War and became more actively involved in the anti-war movement in the 1920s and 1930s through her speaking and writing activities.[28] In 1933 her autobiography, *No Time Like the Present*, offered a strong plea for pacifism. Considering herself a pacifist, she was at the same time a supporter of the LNU and collective security, though she did acknowledge the irrationality of this position.[29] In 1937 she became a sponsor of the PPU, declaring herself an absolute pacifist, but in the same year she supported the Spanish Republicans. As president of the PEN she witnessed at first hand the effects of Nazi persecution while helping to rescue Jewish writers from countries under German domination. As a result she came to loathe Nazism as much as war and faced a dilemma that she was later to describe as follows: 'The price of surrendering to the Nazi barbarism is Auschwitz, the camp guards pushing the living bodies of children into the gas chamber, the killing of prisoners for pleasure ... The price of war is a million, ten million, broken tortured bodies.'[30] Ultimately she concluded that the concentration camps were a worse evil than bombed cities: 'I knew that war bred as much evil as it destroyed, perhaps more. Yet I could not, with the pacifists, cry: Submit, submit. The price was too high; the smell from the concentration camps, from cells where men tortured men, from trains crammed to suffocation with human cattle, choked the words back in my throat.'[31]

Even more reluctant was Mary Sheepshanks's eventual renunciation of pacifism. She had been an early member of the UDC and of the WIL and during the First World War had used her editorship of *Ius Suffragi*[32] to publish proposals for a permanent peace. After the war was over, she, as an ardent internationalist, had criticized the punitive Treaty of Versailles, worked for famine relief, protested against the enormous reparation payments demanded of Germany, and laboured for the admission of Germany to the League of Nations. From 1925 to 1929 she worked in Geneva as the international secretary of the Women's International League for Peace and Freedom (WILPF). She organized conferences, published pamphlets, travelled, and spoke in favour of total disarmament. Though herself anti-fascist, she was instrumental in opposing some of the French and German members of the WILPF who were committed to the overthrow of capitalism by force. During the Spanish Civil War she organized relief for child victims and housed refugees in her own home but opposed intervention. At the same time she tried to increase the influence of the WIL at the League. It was not until 1939 that this long-term pacifist, like many of her colleagues in the WIL, reluctantly acknowledged the inherent contradiction between pacifism and collective security and gave her support to the war against fascism.[33]

Pacifists

There remains the third group: women who committed themselves uncompromisingly to pacifism throughout the 1920s and 1930s. These women, despite their sympathy for the Spanish Republicans, made no distinction between capitalist war and revolutionary war and, despite their horror of Nazism, believed that attempting to combat violence with violence – albeit under the cosy title of collective security – was not only unworkable but morally unacceptable.

Helena Swanwick (1864–1939) is perhaps the best example of a woman consistently holding these views. She had participated in anti-war demonstrations prior to the First World War, and in 1914 her commitment to peace had become her chief concern. She was a founding member of the UDC, established by anti-militarists who believed that war destroyed democracy and 'Prussianized' nations that resorted to it. The UDC sought to keep democratic principles alive in wartime, to promote negotiation, and to combat prowar propaganda. Swanwick explained that this was a movement not to 'Stop the War' but to 'Plan the Peace.'[34] In autumn 1915 she had also become the first chairman of the WIL, a position that she held for seven years, and on its behalf she produced a number of peace pamphlets,[35] attended conferences, and went on speaking tours all over Britain.[36] During the war years attempts were made in Parliament and the press to discredit her as 'a German Woman,'[37] and her meetings were broken up by soldiers convinced that she was in the pay of the Germans.

   When the war ended, Swanwick continued to work for peace through the WIL, the UDC, and her journalism. With other members of the UDC she sought a democratic peace treaty, and Versailles was a bitter disappointment to her: 'The war destroyed Security; the peace trampled on Security's corpse.'[38] She described the blockade as 'a modern massacre of the innocents'[39] and was dismayed by the reparations, the army of occupation in the Rhineland, and the victors' garnering of the fruits of secret treaties. This conquerors' peace, she believed, could lead only to more war.

   Swanwick joined the newly formed LNU but soon left, appalled by the League's exclusion of 'enemy' nations. She rejoined in 1924 when she was the first British woman delegate to attend an assembly of the League. Despite her reservations about it – 'the League was half aborted at birth'[40] – she became a regular speaker for the LNU. She continued, however, to criticize the League for its failure to be an international body,[41] for its failure to promote disarmament among the allies, for its members' forming other alliances and secret treaties, and above all for its sanctions, 'which brought us back to the old international anarchy, but with the additional slime of hypocrisy'[42] and effectively provided for a League war.

Swanwick remained consistently opposed to collective security based on sanctions and devoted much of her writing to illustrating the moral inadequacy and certain failure of such a policy,[43] which 'imposed on sovereign states combining to keep the peace, an obligation to make war.'[44] 'When is war not war?' she asked rhetorically, and she replied: 'When it accords with an Article of the Treaty of Versailles.'[45] Moreover, she reasoned, if people were prepared to break their pledge not to go to war, they would also forget their promise to punish an aggressor if it were an ally or dangerously formidable, or if their own domestic situation were precarious, or their armaments inadequate.[46] Thus the French invasion of the Ruhr elicited no response from the League; the Japanese invasion of Manchuria in 1931 went unchecked; and Haile Selassie's appeal for help against the Italian invasion went unanswered. Nothing, Swanwick concluded, could come from the threat of war by a body like the League of Nations. It had no central authority, being ultimately an alliance of powers concerned with their own sovereignty: 'governments kept their diplomatic and their League duties in watertight compartments,'[47] and therefore sanctions were unworkable. It would be even more disastrous were the League to succeed in imposing sanctions: 'a League war however lofty its motives would be no different from any other modern war.'[48]

Swanwick also categorically opposed a revolutionary war. This not infrequently brought her into disagreement with some of the French, German, Austrian, and Irish members of the WILPF, many of whom supported intervention in Spain; and she described them as 'opportunists who drop their principles when it inconveniences them' in favour of 'catastrophic revolution.'[49]

In place of any sanctions, any military alliances, Swanwick sought to promote a long-term program of education for peace. In 1914 she had attributed much of the jingoism to the way in which history was taught in schools and to the influence of officer training corps there. When she was attacked at WIL public meetings during the war she attributed this to 'propaganda [taking] the place of truth. This is the very essence of war and always will be.'[50] She wanted the WIL to educate its members: 'I feared that nothing much could come out of a pacifism that refused hard political thought and relied on emotion.'[51] She herself was involved in research and the dissemination of information about conditions in Ireland and Germany on behalf of the WIL. Similarly, as editor of the UDC organ *Foreign Affairs* from 1925 to 1928, she sought to provide people with informed knowledge of current affairs, to get past propaganda to the truth. She argued that trust and confidence leading to international cooperation could be engendered in the young only by making peace education direct and implicit in all education – by the honest teaching of history, psychology, politics, and citizenship.[52]

In the late 1930s, Swanwick, old, ill, and in theory retired from political life, continued to write about the need for discussion of the objects and causes of war. She still advocated disarmament, beginning with the air force, which constituted a new and terrible threat to civilians. In the event of war she proposed collective neutrality and the withdrawal of all neutrals from warring countries, suggesting that the ordinary Spanish people would have suffered less in 1936 if volunteers had kept out of the war; continuous mediation via the League; and passive resistance by the civilians of the warring countries.[53] Helena Swanwick died in November 1939.

Unlike the women discussed above, Vera Brittain (1893–1970) was not a pacifist during the First World War, and paradoxically it was not until 1936, when many others felt that they could no longer subscribe to pacifism, that she committed herself irrevocably to it. Brittain's diary entries immediately before and during the early months of the First World War express a naïve jingoism,[54] and, though her sense of war as an adventure gave way to a certain bitterness as she counted friends, acquaintances, and ultimately her fiancé and brother among its victims, still she did not question its necessity. While she was nursing in France, however, the horror of war became increasingly apparent to her,[55] and Gorham suggests that the seeds of her pacifism were sown in 1917, when she was nursing German soldiers.[56]

In the immediate postwar period Brittain was still uncertain and confused: 'My mind groped in a dark, foggy confusion, uncertain of what had happened to it or what was going to happen.'[57] She knew little of the existing pacifist organizations. Returning to her interrupted studies at Oxford, she determined to read history instead of English in order to understand how wars happened and how they might be prevented, and on graduating she offered herself to the newly formed LNU, for which she was active as a speaker and writer (advocating collective security) throughout the 1920s.

In 1933 Brittain's *Testament of Youth*, recounting her war experiences, appeared among the second wave of anti-war books. In the same year she began to question the LNU's policy of collective security reinforced by military sanctions. She started to wonder if war should be even a last resort. Visiting the war graves at the Somme she thought: 'What a cheating and a camouflage it all is, this combined effort of man and nature to give one the impression that war is noble and glorious,'[58] and she wrote in the visitors' book at Étapes: 'No More War.'[59] Though remaining a member of the LNU, she also joined the UDC and the WIL.

Finally in 1936, as many former pacifists supported military sanctions against fascism, Brittain reasoned: 'I fear war more than Fascism; anyhow I am sure you can't use Satan to cast out Satan.'[60] In June 1936 she attended a peace rally, prepared to speak on behalf of collective security, but after hearing the pacifist speeches of Lansbury, Sheppard, and Soper, she changed her speech and with it her life, committing herself to Christian pacifism.[61] In 1937 she joined the PPU and became one of its regular speakers. The following year she finally resigned from the LNU, disappointed that its leaders had turned out to be 'sorry apologists for militarism.'[62]

From 1937 on, Brittain wrote and lectured extensively on the theme that war was morally wrong in all circumstances. In December 1937 she observed, 'As an uncompromising pacifist, I hold war to be a crime ... whoever fights it and against whomever it is fought ... I detest fascism and all that it stands for, but I do not believe that we shall destroy it by fighting it.'[63] She reasoned that 'any kind of peace is better than any variety of war,'[64] and 'the mercilessness of others does not release us from the obligation to control ourselves.'[65]

During the Second World War Brittain worked for the PPU's 'Stop the War Campaign' and produced a regular 'Letter to Peace Lovers' discussing the principles and problems of pacifism. After the war she continued to the end of her life to work for peace and disarmament.

By comparison with Swanwick and Britain, Virginia Woolf (1882–1941) had little active interest in politics, but she was always a pacifist by conviction. Most of her male friends had been COs in 1916, many of them working on Philip Morrell's farm at Garsington. 'All of them reacted against the chauvinism and hysteria of the home front.'[66] Woolf was herself a regular visitor to Garsington in 1917–18, and her diary entries during that period indicate her eagerness to see the end of war.[67]

In the 1920s and 1930s Woolf's absolute pacifism was apparent: she made no compromise with either collective security or socialist anti-militarism. In October 1935 she and her husband, Leonard Woolf, were attending the Labour Party Conference (he was active in the ILP) and were horrified by the debate in which Ernest Bevin, arguing for collective security, harshly demolished Lansbury upholding pacifism.[68] Nor, though she did not underestimate the horrors of fascism and attended anti-fascist gatherings, could Woolf sympathize with the decision of her nephew Julian to go to Spain in 1935: 'Though I understand that this is a "cause," can be called the cause of liberty and so on, still my natural instinct is to fight it intellectually.'[69] When Julian was killed in action after only a month, she wrote about the grief of her sister, Vanessa Bell: 'Only to see what she has to suffer makes one doubt if anything in the world is worth it.'[70]

Woolf hated both violence and fascism, but she did so not on the basis of political or economic analysis – the machinery of politics exasperated her'[71] – but as an instinctive moral response. 'To her ... the true answer to all this horror and violence lay in an improvement of one's own moral state; somehow one had to banish anger and the unreason that is bred of anger. Thus she tended, unlike Leonard, to be an out-and-out pacifist.'[72] In June 1940 she was even critical of Leonard's joining the Local Defence Volunteers, though she was fully aware that there would be no pity for a Jewish socialist and his wife if the war were lost. She and Leonard had discussed the option of suicide in this event and had a lethal dose of morphia ready.[73] Virginia Woolf drowned herself in 1941, fearing the recurrence of her earlier insanity.

Feminism and Pacifism

These three women – Swanwick, Brittain, and Woolf – though very different in many ways, shared a common commitment to pacifism in the interwar years. All three were also equal-rights feminists, campaigning for equal education and job opportunities, equal pay, and the admission of women to the trade unions and the professions.[74] Unlike many of their colleagues in the WIL and the WCG, they did not envisage the women's peace movement as a predominantly maternalistic affair, based on mothers' love of their children and their traditional nurturing roles.[75] Rather they perceived their feminism as an integral part of their pacifism, and vice versa. There are three aspects of this relationship apparent in their works – political activity, women as 'outsiders,' and the role of the glorification of war in subordinating women.

First, they all believed that women had a responsibility, born of equal rights and their recent enfranchisement, to be politically active. They all appealed to women to shake off their apathy and to speak their minds on public questions. Brittain railed against women who hid behind wifehood and maternity, claiming that these responsibilities left them no time for others;[76] Swanwick chided women who prefaced their remarks with 'my husband says,' were parasitic on men, and echoed their views, refusing to think for themselves.[77] In particular both women felt that emancipated women had an obligation to overcome docile acceptance of war, to shake off their conviction that war was not their business, and to protest against it. Swanwick wrote, 'I marvel at the torpor of the mass of women in this matter,'[78] and in similar vein Brittain criticized 'the terrible inert mass of lethargic womanhood who need to be roused from apathy to work for peace.'[79] She suggested, 'If women are indifferent – if they remain politically non-conscious – if – in brief – they choose not to choose – then they are indirectly but nonetheless certainly assisting those forces which are pushing civilisation towards chaos.'[80] Similarly, Woolf urged women to express their views through literature: 'The private printing press is ... not beyond the reach of a moderate income. Use it, typewriters, duplicators ... express views independently of boards, policies, editors.'[81]

Second, these women reasoned from a practical standpoint that women, being still largely excluded from the political and military status quo, might view it more critically than men and make deliberate use of their prescriptive female role to promote pacifism. This possibility is most famously associated with Woolf's suggestion that women, as 'outsiders,' had less to gain than men from war and bellicose patriotism; excluded still from most positions of authority, women were therefore free of the unreal loyalties and interested motives that led men to crave the excitement of war and made them easily manipulated patriots. She wrote: ' "Our country" throughout the greater part of its history has treated me as a slave; it has denied me education or any share of its possessions. "Our country" still ceases to be mine if I marry a foreigner. "Our country" denies me the means of protecting myself, forces me to pay others a very large sum annually to protect me ... Therefore if you insist upon fighting to protect me or "Our country" let it be understood soberly and rationally between us, that you are fighting to gratify a sex instinct which I cannot share ... but not to gratify my instincts or to protect either myself or my country. For ... as a woman I have no country. As a woman I want no country, as a woman my country is the whole world.'[82]

Similarly, Swanwick suggested that men got an exhilaration from war that could be harnessed by politicians, whereas women had less to gain and suffered more from war: 'The losses of women who see their children maimed or killed or slowly starved have a quality of lonely desolation unmatched even by the sufferings of men in battle.'[83] Like Woolf, she warned that 'women who are carried away by the notion that they are protected *by* men' would do well to remember that in wartime 'it is also *from* men that they are being protected (or not, when they are victims of invasion).'[84] So too Brittain: 'Because women produce children, life and the means of living matter to them in a way that these things can never matter to men.'[85]

Though there is a tendency for both Swanwick and Brittain to lapse into the rhetoric of an earlier generation in overly romanticizing motherhood and women's virtues, they both made it clear that men would not have been able to make war had women 'not been admiringly, even adoringly, with them.'[86] Something atavistic in women leads them to idealize the hero in battle,[87] so that women too are liable to be carried away by wartime emotion.[88] Woolf put it more strongly, accusing women of conniving with men to perpetuate war by admiring their deeds: 'Women have served all these centuries as a looking glass ... reflecting the figure of man at twice its natural size. Without that power ... the glories of all our wars would be unknown ... Mirrors are essential to all violent and heroic action.'[89]

It is the responsibility of women, all three writers agreed, to overcome this tendency and to use their positions not to support but to counteract men's attraction to war. Thus Swanwick, 'Since for the most part it is the young men who fight in war, so for the most part it is the young women who must fight war.'[90] Similarly, Brittain reasoned that practically speaking women were in the stronger position to protest against war and to organize civil disobedience in the form of a general strike against it.[91] And Woolf advocated the formation of an 'Outsiders Society,' without hierarchy, committees, secretaries, meetings, or conferences, whose members would refuse to nurse the wounded, make munitions, or incite their sons or brothers to fight.[92]

The third and probably most vital connection that these women made between feminism and pacifism was that both the subordination of women and the glorification of war were based on force. Swanwick reasoned that militarism is the enthronement of physical force as an arbiter between nations and that women cannot compete with men in terms of force. Therefore so long as force continues to dominate the world, men will continue to dominate women. The domination of weak nations by strong is analogous with the domination of the female by the male. Only when moral laws are accepted between nations will there be freedom and security for women. Thus pacifism and women's claim to freedom are based on the same principle: the control of physical by moral force.[93]

In a series of articles in the 1930s Brittain argued in almost identical terms that 'a civilisation in which military values prevail is always hostile to women's interests,' because 'militarism and the oppression of women are both based on force,'[94] whereas the women's movement, like pacifism, is based on the assumption that reason is superior to force. 'The women's movement began when ... [an] enlightened minority perceived that the operation of reason was superior to force as a factor in human affairs. That is why the struggle against war, which is the final and most vicious expression of force, is fundamentally inseparable from feminism.'[95]

Finally Woolf suggested that patriarchy, war, and fascism were all closely allied, being all based on the will to dominate. The desire to make war, she suggested, derived from men's notions of manliness as dominance and their desire to prove themselves. Feminists were the advance guard of the pacifists struggling against the tyranny of the patriarchal state, in the same way that pacifists were struggling against the fascist state.[96]

A Critique

It would be difficult to dispute the feminist-pacifists' first argument – that women seeking equal rights had a duty to take an active, responsible role in politics. The assumption that this action should take the form of peace activism, however, reflects only their own subjective values. Other feminists might have sought to express their political commitment by supporting wars – as indeed Emmeline and Cristabel Pankhurst had done – or even by participation in the armed forces.

Their second argument – that women, as outsiders with no vested interest in the status quo, might use their structurally different position to promote change – rests on a number of assumptions. Certainly in the 1920s and 1930s, though women had the vote (but not on equal terms until 1928), they lacked equal educational and employment opportunities and their experiences were still confined mainly to the private sphere. It is, however, questionable whether women would necessarily have experienced contradictions between their own values and the dominant political and military ones. Arguably many women did not regard themselves as 'outsiders' at all but identified with the power held by husbands, brothers, and fathers. The assumption that men had a vested interest in fighting to maintain their position and power, whereas women were free from this condition, and that indeed their conditioning made them more caring, is not borne out by the behaviour of the majority of women who (like the majority of men) did not question militarism or experience any sense of duty to be peacemakers. It may be that in so far as women did regard themselves as 'outsiders' they tried especially hard to conform rather than to question the status quo: equal-rights feminists of the 1920s and 1930s were fighting to obtain precisely the same education and precisely the same career opportunities as men, not questioning whether these systems and structures were necessarily the best ones. There was therefore no reason to expect that these feminists would necessarily question war and militarism either.

Even allowing that pacifist women might choose to express their pacifism as 'outsiders,' and that they might choose to use their own non-hierarchical methods of organization, as advocated by Woolf, it remains questionable how effective these methods would have been. The attempt to combat power from outside the power structure may leave the real centre of power untouched. The emphasis on personal experience rather than politics may, even if it produces a protest, result in one that is politically invisible and easily ignored.

It is possible as well that a movement of outsiders might prove counterproductive, both for feminism and for pacifism. If it is assumed that women are different, even if only because of conditioning and stereotyping, this assumption could become a justification for limiting their role, perpetuating their exclusion from power, and confining them to the home on a permanent basis. For pacifism, becoming a movement of outsiders could be divisive. Woolf advocated a separate peace society for women: 'Since we are different our help must be different ... We can best help you prevent war not by repeating your words and following your methods but by finding new words and creating new methods.'[97] At worst such separatism could produce a split in the pacifist movement, with women claiming a monopoly on the compassionate virtues and alienating men.

It is quite clear, however, that none of the three women discussed wanted women to monopolize compassion. Swanwick argued that ultimately there is no such thing as men's questions and women's questions and that war will be ended not by men or women but by 'Man – the bisexual human creature.'[98] Similarly, Brittain stated categorically that 'it will only be by men and women working together that war will be finally brought to an end.'[99] The only justification for a separate women's association so far as Swanwick and Brittain were concerned was that since men dominated bodies such as the LNU a separate women's society might be a temporary necessity for women to learn self-direction and assertion,[100] so that they could then work more effectively on mixed bodies, 'where the struggle for peace and freedom is best continued.'[101]

Even in their own day they felt that this need for a separate organization was already in decline: Swanwick opposed the UDC's attempts to sideline women into a separate branch, arguing that politically advanced men and women should work together,[102] and Brittain refuse to participate in the PPU's Women's Peace Campaign, regarding it as a piece of unnecessary duplication, reactionary and out of date.[103] Woolf too sought to end ultimately the rigid designation between so-called masculine and feminine values. In *Three Guineas*, though she gave her first two guineas to help educate and establish employment for women, intending this to encourage them to speak out as 'outsiders,' the third went to a mixed peace society, and she declared herself in sympathy with its aims.[104] She too envisaged the 'outsiders' as only a temporary society, born of particular circumstances, and she believed that ultimately 'the great mind is androgynous.'[105]

There remains the third, tripartite argument of the pacifist feminists – that patriarchy and militarism are both based on force, that women and small nations are kept in subordinate positions by violence and the threat and fear of violence, and that feminism and pacifism require that reason and morality should reign instead. This connection cannot be lightly dismissed: as Roszak has pointed out, fascination with the atrocities of war often goes hand in hand with contempt for women and an attempt to thwart their desire for equality. This is particularly apparent under Nazism and fascism, when women are faced with the paradox of contempt and the celebration of the 'feminine virtues' at the same time.[106] This essay ends with the suggestion that for feminist pacifists today, as for those of the interwar period, 'Peace isn't just about removing a few pieces of war furniture, or bringing about an international ceasefire; it is about the condition of our lives. Peace is the absence of greed and domination by a few over the rest of us.'[107]

NOTES

1 Martin Ceadel, *Pacifism in Britain, 1914–1945: The Defining of a Faith* (Oxford 1980), 84.
2 A.J.P. Taylor, *English History, 1914–1945* (Oxford 1965), 289.
3 Ibid., 361.
4 Joyce Avrech Berkman, 'Pacifism in England: 1914–1939', PhD dissertation, Yale University, 1967, 118.
5 Peter Brock, *Twentieth-Century Pacifism* (New York 1970), 128. In addition to the books mentioned there by Brock, see also Helen Zenna Smith *Not So Quiet*, first pub. 1930 (London 1988).
6 Berkman, 'Pacifism in England,' 158–84.
7 Ethel Mannin, *Young in the Twenties* (London 1971) 165.
8 Taylor, *English History*, 398.
9 Ibid., 420.
10 Ceadel, *Pacifism in Britain*, 47, argues that 'all socialists were by definition *pacificists*,' because, though they accepted the use of military force to defend the socialist state or to overthrow capitalism, the withering away of war was one of the ultimate benefits expected in international socialism. Geoffrey Ostergaard, *Resisting the Nation State: The Pacifist and Anarchist Traditions* (London 1982), 1, 2, argues, with some justification, that socialist militarists are a third distinct group.
11 Some organizations such as FOR, NMWM, PPU, and WRI may be identified as pacifist, and others, such as the LNU and the UDC, as pacificist. The Women's Labour League ultimately committed itself to a pacificist position, supporting the League of Nations and collective security. Women against War and Fascism (WAWF) was clearly a socialist anti-militarist organization, with a strong Communist party membership. Less easy to categorize are bodies such as the WIL and the WCG.
    Some authorities have described the WIL as pacificist but with a strong pacifist element; Ceadel, *Pacifism in Britain*, 319. Others have labelled it as pacifist, though containing some members who could not accept pacifism; Brock, *Twentieth-Century Pacifism*, 110–11. Jill Liddington, *The Long Road to Greenham: Feminism and Anti-militarism in Britain since 1820* (London 1989), 144, suggests that the WIL's absolute pacifism grew stronger in the 1930s. Certainly while its members supported the League of Nations they maintained reservations about the imposition of military sanctions in the name of collective security. See Gertrude Bussey and Margaret Tims, *Pioneers for Peace: WILPF, 1915–1965* (London 1980), 148. The

WIL's pedigree is further complicated by the fact that in 1919 it became a section of the Women's International League for Peace and Freedom (WILPF, the successor body from 1919 to the ICWPP), whose French and German branches increasingly sought links with socialist anti-militarist groups such as the Women's World Committee against War and Fascism. See Bussey and Tims, *Pioneers for Peace*, 120–5, 146. Throughout my essay I refer to the British organization simply as WIL.

Similarly, the WCG steered an uncertain course among socialist anti-militarism, pacificism, and pacifism. It supported the League of Nations without committing itself to collective security and economic sanctions: this was, however, a close-run issue in 1938, when collective security was outvoted by only 897 to 623; see Bussey and Tims, *Pioneers for Peace*, 115. It condemned Fascism without supporting armed conflict against it, but this stance drove some members away; see Liddington, *The Long Road*, 152–71.

Official policy of both the WIL and the WCG remained pacifist in 1939, but they faced many resignations, despite members' being free to act according to their convictions.

12 In the socialist anti-militarist group, Sylvia Pankhurst, for example, belonged to both WAWF and WIL; Ellen Wilkinson, to the PPU, WAWF, and WIL; and Ethel Mannin, to the PPU and the Women's Labour League. Storm Jameson adhered to the PPU, WAWF, and WIL. Among the pacifists, Helena Swanwick belonged to the LNU, WIL, and the Women's Labour League, and Vera Brittain to the LNU, PPU, WAWF, WIL, and the Women's Labour League.

13 'Political involvement' is interpreted broadly to include all public activities promoting pacifism. Many of the women pacifists of this period were writers and intellectuals.

14 E. Sylvia Pankhurst, *The Home Front: A Mirror to Life in England during the World War* (London 1932), 16, 18, 66, 67, 91, 124.

15 Richard Pankhurst, introduction to E.S. Pankhurst, *The Home Front* (London 1987).

16 Betty D. Vernon, *Ellen Wilkinson, 1891–1947* (London 1982), 64.

17 Ibid., 165.

18 Mannin, *Young in the 1920s*, 131.

19 Ethel Mannin, *Brief Voices: A Writer's Story* (London 1959), 13.

20 Ethel Mannin, *Women and the Revolution* (London 1938), 282–3.

21 Ibid., 283–4.

22 Taylor, *English History*, 369.

23 Mary Agnes Hamilton, *Remembering My Good Friends* (London 1944), 98–100.

24 Ibid., 294.

25 Ibid., 101–3, 294.

26 Ibid., 304.

27 Ibid., 304.

28 Storm Jameson, *Journey from the North*, 2 vols. (London 1969–70), 1:291–5, 306–7, 341–4.

29 Ibid., 326–8.

30 Ibid., 2:313.

31 Ibid. Jameson resigned from the PPU in May 1940. See Ceadel, *Pacifism in Britain*, 297.

32 *Ius Suffragi* was the official publication of the International Women's Suffrage Association.

33 Sybil Oldfield, *Spinsters of This Parish: The Life and Times of F.M. Mayor and Mary Sheepshanks* (London 1984), 285.

34 Helena Swanwick, *I Have Been Young* (London 1935), 254.

35 These pamphlets included *Women and War* (1915) and *War in Its Effect upon Women* (1916), reprinted in the Garland Library of War and Peace (New York 1971).

36 A vivid description of her travels can be found in Swanwick, *I Have Been Young*, 293–301.

37 Ibid., 286–7. Swanwick's father was actually Danish, but the first four years of her life were spent in Germany, following the Prussian conquest of parts of Denmark.

38 Ibid., 271.

39 Ibid., 317.

40 Ibid., 266.

41 Germany was not admitted to the League until 1926.

42 Swanwick, *I Have Been Young*, 407, 408.

43 See especially Helena Swanwick, *Collective Insecurity* (London 1937) and *The Roots of Peace* (London 1938).

44 Swanwick, *Collective Insecurity*, 16.

45 Ibid., 98.

46 Ibid., 50.

47 Swanwick, *I Have Been Young*, 458.

48 Swanwick, *Collective Insecurity*, 19.

49 Swanwick, *I Have Been Young*, 451.

50 Ibid., 288.

51 Ibid., 343.

52 Swanwick, *Roots of Peace*, 149–53.

53 Swanwick, *Collective Insecurity*, 284. Earlier in her career she had expressed reservations about unilateral disarmament and non-violence. However, her opposition to sanctions, based on 'a strong ethical faith,' became, as Ceadel writes (*Pacifism in Britain*, 157) 'indistinguishable ... from pacifism.'

54 Alan Bishop, ed., *Chronicle of Youth: Vera Brittain's War Diary* (London 1981), 84, 89, 101, 104–6, 113.

55 Vera Brittain, *Testament of Youth*, first pub. 1933 (London, 1979), 395.

56 Deborah Gorham, 'Vera Brittain and the Great War,' in Ruth Roach Pierson, ed., *Women and Peace* (London 1987) 141.

57 Brittain, *Testament of Youth*, 470, 471.

58 Alan Bishop, ed., *Chronicle of Friendship: Vera Brittain's Diary of the Thirties, 1932–1939* (London 1986), 135. See also Brittain, 'Illusion on the Somme,' *New Clarion*, 30 Sept. 1933, in Paul Berry and Alan Bishop, eds., *Testament of a Generation: The Journalism of Vera Brittain and Winifred Holtby* (London 1985), 213–16.

59 Bishop, ed., *Chronicle of Friendship*, 143.

60 Ibid., 256.

61 Brittain, *Testament of Experience* (London 1979), 165. Brittain was an Anglican, whereas the pacifism of Swanwick and Woolf was based on a humanist ethic.

62 Brittain, 'No Compromise with War,' *World Review of Books* (May 1937), in Paul Berry and Alan Bishop, eds., *Testament of a Generation: The Journalism of Vera Brittain and Winifred Holtby* (London 1985), 222–8. For the PPU at this time, see chapter 11 below, by Andrew Rigby.

63 Vera Brittain in *Authors Take Sides on the Spanish Civil War*, a Left Review Pamphlet (Dec. 1937), in Paul Berry and Alan Bishop, eds., *Testament of a Generation: The Journal of Vera Brittain and Winifred Holtby* (London 1985), 228.

64 Vera Brittain, 'Pacifism after Munich,' *Friendship* (Nov. 1938), in Paul Berry and Alan Bishop, eds., *Testament of a Generation: The Journalism of Vera Brittain and Winifred Holtby* (London 1985), 231. Cf. Maude Royden's renunciation of Christian pacifism in 1940.

65 Ibid., 237.

66 Quentin Bell, *Virginia Woolf: A Biography*, 2 vols. (London 1972) 2:30.

67 Ibid., 62.

68 Ibid., 187.

69 Virginia Woolf, 'Memoir of Julian Bell,' in Quentin Bell, *Virginia Woolf*, 2 vols. (London 1972), 2:258.

70 Bell, *Virginia Woolf*, 2:202.

71 Ibid., 188.

72 Ibid., 187.

73 Ibid., 216.

74 Swanwick had been a member of the National Union of Women's Suffrage Societies and editor of the *Common Cause*. Brittain lectured and wrote in *Time and Tide* on behalf of the Six Point Group, which sought equal education and employment for women. Woolf expressed her feminism through her writing. In *A Room of One's Own* (1938) she rails against the inferior education that women receive.

75 For a discussion of the women in the WCG and the WIL who did think this way, see Liddington, *The Long Road*, 143.

76 Deborah Gorham, *Vera Brittain: A Feminist Life* (London, 1996), 183.

77 Swanwick, *Roots of Peace*, 186–8, 191.

78 Swanwick, *I Have Been Young*, 243.

79 Gorham, *Vera Brittain*, 183.

80 Yvonne [Aleksandra] Bennett, 'Vera Brittain and the Peace Pledge Union,' in Ruth Roach Pierson, ed., *Women and Peace* (London 1987), 192.

81 Virginia Woolf, *Three Guineas* (London 1977), 112. This was of course precisely what Woolf herself was doing, expressing her pacifism through her novels and publishing her works with the Hogarth Press, which she and Leonard had set up in 1917.

82 Woolf, *Three Guineas*, 125.

83 Swanwick, *Roots of Peace*, 185.

84 Ibid., 187.

85 Brittain, 'Can the Women of the World Stop War?' (1934), in Paul Berry and Alan Bishop, eds., *Testament of a Generation: The Journalism of Vera Brittain and Winifred Holtby* (London 1985), 216.

86 Swanwick, *Roots of Peace*, 187.

87 Ibid., 189.

88 Gorham, *Vera Brittain*, 183.

89 Virginia Woolf, *A Room of One's Own*, first pub. 1938 (London 1978) 35, 36.

90 Swanwick, *Roots of Peace*, 192.

91 Bennett, 'Vera Brittain,' 195.

92 Woolf, *Three Guineas*, 164.

93 Swanwick, *Woman and War*, 2–6.

94 Brittain, 'Can the Women of the World Stop War?' 216–20.

95 Brittain, 'Women and Pacifism,' *Peace News*, 15 Aug. 1941, in Yvonne [Aleksandra] Bennett, *Vera Brittain: Women and Peace* (London 1987), 8.

96 Woolf, *Three Guineas*, 118.

97 Ibid., 164.

98 Swanwick, *War in Its Effects*, 29.

99 Brittain, 'Letters to Peace Lovers,' in Yvonne [Aleksandra] Bennett, *Vera Brittain: Women and Peace* (London 1987), 26.

100 Swanwick, *Women and War*, 14.

101 Vera Brittain, *Lady into Woman: A History of Women from Victoria to Elizabeth II* (London 1953), 206.

102 Helena Swanwick, *Builders of Peace: Being Ten Years' History of the Union of Democratic Control* (London 1924), 60.

103 Bennett, 'Vera Brittain,' 201.

104 Woolf, *Three Guineas*, 164.

105 Woolf, *A Room of One's Own*, 94.

106 Theodore Roszak, 'The Hard and the Soft: The Force of Feminism in Modern Time,' in Betty Roszak and Theodore Roszak, eds., *Masculine/Feminine: Readings in Sexual Mythology* (New York 1969), 87–104.

107 Barbara Harford and Sarah Hopkins, eds., *Greenham Common: Woman at the Wire* (London, 1984), 3.

11

The Peace Pledge Union: From Peace to War, 1936–1945

ANDREW RIGBY

In 1937 H.R.L. ('Dick') Sheppard, founder and moving spirit behind the Peace Pledge Union (PPU), defeated Winston Churchill in an electron for the rectorship of Glasgow University. Unfortunately, Sheppard died of a heart attack a few days after his victory, on 31 October 1937, at the age of fifty-seven. At the time of his death the organization that he had launched was at its peak. It had a membership in excess of 118,000, a network of over 440 local groups, and a newspaper, *Peace News*, with weekly sales approaching 15,000; and there was reason to hope that his vision of a pacifist movement large enough to force the governments of the world to take notice might be fulfilled.

As the months passed, however, the dream faded. In March 1938 Germany annexed Austria. In September 1938 the dismemberment of Czechoslovakia was agreed to at Munich. Just over a month later, on 9–10 November 1938, there was the Kristallnacht, a night of unprecedented violence against the Jewish population and its property in Germany. In March 1939 Germany annexed the non-German remainder of Czechoslovakia and proceeded to make demands on Poland. Few in Britain could doubt that there was going to be a war. In the same week that the British prime minister, Neville Chamberlain, announced that Britain was prepared to stand by the Polish government in the face of any German threat to its independence, Andrew Stewart was writing in *Peace News*: 'If there is another war in our time the Peace Pledge Union will have failed ... Another war will indicate that, however hard we have worked we haven't worked hard enough. We shall have failed collectively because we failed individually.'[1] On 1 September 1939 Germany invaded Poland, and on 3 September Britain and France declared war.

The aim of this essay is to explore how the pacifists of the PPU coped with their collective and individual 'failure' as the late 1930s saw approaching war and how they attempted to reconstruct a role for themselves as pacifists during the course of the 'phoney war,' the war itself, and the peace that eventually followed.

Saying 'No' to War, 1936–1939

The origins of the PPU dated back to October 1934, when Dick Sheppard, an extremely popular Anglican clergyman, had published his Peace Letter, inviting people to join with him in pledging to renounce war and never support or sanction another one. He based his appeal on the utter barbarism of war and determination to avoid a repetition of the horror and slaughter of the First World War. He directed his appeal initially to men only and evoked a tremendous response. By December 1935 some 100,000 postcards had been received, and new pledges were being returned at a rate of about four hundred a day.

The desire to settle international disputes without recourse to war was virtually universal throughout Britain in the 1920s and 1930s, and Sheppard's appeal tapped this concern. As a result, the PPU attracted a wide range of anti-militarists: religious pacifists, socialists, anarchists and, in the words of Derek Savage, 'an amorphous mass of ordinary well-meaning but fluffy peacelovers.'[2] From June 1936 women could join, but membership remained overwhelmingly male.

Throughout this early period control of the burgeoning organization was firmly in the hands of Sheppard. He was advised by a group of sponsors who, according to Martin Ceadel, 'comprised perhaps the most intellectually distinguished committee ever assembled by a controversial British pressure group.'[3] They shared his view that the PPU should steer clear of sectional, oppositional movements and campaigns that might cause internal division and threaten public support. The aim was to attract as many people as possible. All one had to do to join was to sign the pledge; nothing more was required. If enough people in Britain and around the world pledged their refusal to participate in war, then governments would have to take notice and be forced to choose the conference table rather than the battle-field for sorting out their differences. The PPU was to be a 'broad church,' within which pacifists of all persuasions and degrees of commitment might cooperate. Sheppard did not intend it to be a vehicle for organizing collective war resistance – a view that was shared by the leading sponsors after his death.

None the less, pressure grew from the grass roots and from the full-time staff at headquarters for clearer policy guidelines. In part this demand reflected the impulse introduced by the socialist pacifists of the No More War Movement (NMWM), which had merged with the PPU in February 1937, after Sheppard had promised to introduce a more democratic decision-making structure within the union and agreed to the NMWM's nominating two sponsors.

Thus it was that in March 1938 the 'grandfather' of British pacifism and prominent Labourite, George Lansbury, launched the PPU's first manifesto. The main theme of the accompanying campaign was that a war to defend democracy was a contradiction; in a period of total war, democracy would be submerged beneath totalitarianism. To avoid war a new foreign policy was required, based on economic redistribution and reconciliation between the 'have' nations of Britain and France and the 'have-nots' such as Germany, Italy, and Japan.

In emphasizing its belief that the roots of the current crisis lay in the treatment meted out to Germany at Versailles, in seeking to 'humanize' the German people and distinguish between them and the Nazi regime, the PPU laid itself open to charges of being 'soft on fascism.' That such accusations were made is understandable. In arguing that Germany had some legitimate grievances, in daring to suggest that it was rather hypocritical for Britain to condemn Germany in the light of Britain's acts of conquest and repression in India and elsewhere, correspondents and writers in *Peace News* sometimes revealed an apparently callous disregard for the fate of people and countries threatened by Nazi Germany.

But the pacifists of the PPU were driven by the desire to avoid war. They were thus prepared to advocate all kinds of concessions and sacrifices in order to appease the fascists and, in the process, save Europe from what they believed would be total destruction. At the heart of this position lay the conviction, expressed by former Labour MP James Hudson in *Peace News*, at the time of the Anschluss: 'We must have truck with dictators, either on the battlefield or round the conference table – and I choose the conference table.'[4] But in that same issue a correspondent warned: 'There is no surer way of ruining our cause than by giving the appearance of being pro-fascist. We are determined not to go to war with fascist countries, but that does not alter the fact that fascism is the greatest enemy in the world today of everything we stand for.'[5]

The most balanced assessment of this aspect of the PPU's history has been made by David Lukowitz. He concludes that, while it would be nonsense to charge the PPU with pro-Nazi sympathies, 'it is hard to escape the conclusion that there was too much sympathy for the German position, often the product of ignorance and superficial thinking. There was also a complete failure to grasp the nature of the Hitlerian system; Germany's policies with regard to colonies, Austria, Czechoslovakia, and Poland could not be disassociated from the whole ruthless spirit and philosophy of the Nazi state.'[6]

Given the 'broad church' nature of the PPU and the reluctance of its leading figures to lay down a 'party line,' it is not surprising that a whole range of opinions were expressed in the columns of *Peace News* and elsewhere within the movement. As war drew closer, its failure to organize a campaign of active war resistance, as well as the leadership's refusal to contemplate any form of civil disobedience, highlighted the divisions within the union. Thus for many members it was imperative to oppose the government's attempt to introduce civil-defence measures such as air-raid drills, in so far as they were seen to be an integral part of war preparation, fostered a 'war mentality,' and represented one more step towards totalitarianism.

A further step along this path came in May 1939 with the introduction of limited conscription – for youths aged twenty and twenty-one. The PPU failed to mobilize its members around these issues. John Middleton Murry, who was to become the dominant intellectual force within the PPU during the war years, confessed that 'an anti-conscription campaign seems to me obsolete and irrelevant,' while his friend Max Plowman proclaimed that 'pacifists stand for peace, not anti-conscription.'[7] The No-Conscription League, formed in January 1939, attempted to fill the vacuum left by the PPU's immobility, but its campaign collapsed with the introduction of conscription, as more and more people became resigned to the inevitability of war.

With the benefit of hindsight, it is clear that even a mass campaign of active war resistance, as advocated by many of the PPU's members, would have been something of a vain effort. The PPU never approached the one million members that Sheppard thought necessary to block any governmental attempt to declare war. The Labour party had forsaken its war-resistance stance in the mid-1930s in favour of collective security, and without the active support of organized labour there was no way in which a peace movement such as the PPU, with its predominantly white-collar membership, could organize and mobilize sufficient support to frustrate the government's war preparations.

But even if the realists in the PPU felt that there was little they could do to halt the drift to war, many in the rank and file still believed that it was worth trying and that it was necessary at least to attempt to avoid the catastrophe of total war. Up and down the country local PPU groups increased their activity as the international situation worsened. There were discussion meetings and study circles, with *Peace News* suggesting topics and questions. For example, the topic proposed for April 1937 was: 'Can one practise pacifism in one's daily life?' Was it right to participate in air-raid drill? Should one continue to pay income tax or that part of it that went towards war preparations? Was it right to support economic sanctions?[8]

At the time of the Munich crisis, the PPU sponsors offered to send five thousand pacifists to the Sudetenland as a non-violent presence. In the event, war was avoided without the intercession of the pacifists. But Stuart Morris, the PPU's general secretary, spoke for many members when he observed that the sacrifices demanded of the Czechs and Slovaks could be justified only 'and the ultimate peace won insofar as we, and others, are prepared to make sacrifices similar to those which we have demanded.'[9] Munich was a reprieve, a final opportunity to avert war, which must not be wasted. An upsurge in new members ensued, and a drive was launched to 'activate' new (and old) sympathizers. Lists of those who had signed the pledge were sent out from head office to the local groups, who took it on themselves to visit the signatories in the hope that they might be persuaded to participate in local activities. This was not always a rewarding experience, as these extracts from the diary of Harold Ford, a PPU activist in Liverpool, reveal:[10]

Monday, 3 October: In the evening I went to the post, and then to the PPU group meeting ... Discussed various matters – we are hoping to start 2 or 3 new groups soon, as some members have done very successful visiting of signatories. Got back about 11 pm.
Tuesday, 4 October: After tea I went out visiting PPU signatories ... being out from 6 till 10 pm. Made a good many calls, and again found that several people had moved. Saw 3 of the signatories and had interesting talks, but none of them seemed to be 100% pacifist.
Wednesday, 5 October: ... went out to do some more PPU visiting. It was most disappointing, as I only saw one man. The others has mostly gone away, and one had joined the Air Force.[11]

Supporters also sold (and read) *Peace News*, wrote letters to the local press, distributed petitions for a world conference, organized public meetings, stuck up posters, handed out leaflets, and raised funds, among a range of activities. One particular initiative of the PPU was an attempt at citizen-to-citizen diplomacy. It involved members' sending letters to addresses in Germany. Thus, on Friday, 28 October 1938, Harold Ford recorded in his diary that he was preparing a letter that he planned to post to an address in Munich. 'We are hoping to send many thousands of the letter altogether – it tells of the existence and aims of the PPU, which we want to make known in Germany.' A few months later, in February 1939, PPU members were urged to send a second letter – this time to addresses in Berlin. However naïve and pointless such an exercise might seem to us, it represented a genuine effort to communicate with the German people, as distinct from their regime, in order to impress on them that there were people in Britain who sought peace and who refused to 'demonize' them.

A more practical form of peace work involved helping refugees escape Nazi oppression. The War Resisters' International, based in London, had initiated a scheme for sponsoring refugees which satisfied the requirements of the British Home Office.[12] Another plan was organized by the Quakers. The issue of refugees took on an added urgency after the pogrom of November 1938, and *Peace News* appealed for readers to sponsor Jewish refugees during their period of residence in Britain. Local PPU groups responded, raising money and providing accommodation, support, and assistance to those who had been resettled in their neighbourhood. Thus Harold Ford recorded in his diary for Thursday, 11 May 1939: 'Herr and Frau Landau, the Austrian refugees came to supper ... They are happy in Liverpool, and think the English are wonderful people – judging us by the Quakers!'

When on 3 September 1939 Britain and France declared war on Germany, all the efforts of the pacifists to avert war seemed to have been in vain. They now faced a new challenge – constructing a pacifist role for themselves in wartime.

Pacifism in the 'Phoney War,' 1939–1940

For most people in Britain, the declaration of war brought little change. There was no sign of the expected bombing raids and gas attacks. For the PPU, the outbreak of war brought with it an influx of new members, just as the heightened war fears at the time of the dismemberment of Czechoslovakia had resulted in a surge of new signatories. During the first eight or so months of the war – the period of the 'phoney war' – there seemed to many pacifists to be a chance now that the war might be stopped and a negotiated peace achieved.

As part of the emergent 'Stop the War' campaign there were demonstrations held throughout the country, including a women's march in Liverpool with the theme 'For the sake of children everywhere, we appeal to men to stop this war.' PPU activists stood as 'Stop the War' candidates in parliamentary by-elections, including Andrew Stewart, a full-time worker with the PPU and on the staff of *Peace News*, who stood at Clackmannan in central Scotland, and Stanley Seamark, who stood at Northampton. The Northampton PPU group was among the most active. A week after the war began it held its first communal breakfast with a guest speaker, a practice that it continued throughout the war, with attendances ranging from forty to one hundred. Members were also out on the streets selling *Peace News*, with sales increasing from thirty, just prior to the outbreak of war, to one hundred a week in October 1939.[13]

But the Northampton group was by no means alone in its level of campaigning. For instance, the Eastleigh PPU group in Hampshire was very active in its stop-the-war activities. One of its members, Ronald Mallone, recalled later how he was kept busy organizing public meetings, attending the weekly meetings of his local PPU and Fellowship of Reconciliation (FOR) branches, writing letters to the press, distributing 'Stop the War' leaflets outside a local armaments factory, and preaching Christian pacifist sermons each Sunday.[14] Another activist,

Cyril Wright, was also determined to keep the peace banner flying in his home town of New Malden, Surrey. He continued to wear his PPU badge and display PPU posters in his front garden. Eventually, however, his neighbours began to take exception, and he took down the poster, feeling that 'it was perhaps wrong to give this sort of aggravation to people who were obviously sincere in their beliefs.'[15] One PPU poster, however, caused particular offence and resulted in the prosecution of six leading members of the PPU for alleged breaches of the Defence Regulations. The poster read: 'War will cease when men refuse to fight. What are YOU going to do about it?' The PPU reluctantly decided to withdraw it, and the six were bound over for twelve months.[16]

A major worry of the PPU during this period was that if its 'hot bloods' campaigned too vigorously, they would bring down on the organization the wrath of the state, and the PPU would lose what space it had enjoyed hitherto to propagate the cause of pacifism. Thus Harold Ford recorded in his diary that on 3 February 1940 there was a Merseyside meeting of the PPU to discuss policy: 'There was some division of opinion as to whether we should go "all out" in an effort to stop the war, or whether we should regard this as impossible, and rely on slower methods, and influencing the public towards a just peace.'

Such concerns were occasioned in part by the practice of picketing outside local employment exchanges, where young men were required to register for military service. In February 1940 a Conservative member of Parliament complained to the home secretary that the pacifists were 'endeavouring to induce men to join their organisation and avoid military service by claiming to be conscientious objectors, for which purpose special instructional classes have been arranged.'[17] At the subsequent PPU annual general meeting in May 1940 a message from the president, George Lansbury, appealed 'most earnestly to all members of the PPU to give up picketing the Employment Exchanges when men are registering for service.'[18]

Local PPU groups were advising and supporting conscientious objectors (COs) to conscription. As the war continued, the age range of men (and eventually women) liable to be called up was steadily extended. If a man required to register for military service objected on the grounds of conscience, he could apply to be placed on a register of COs. His case would then be considered by a local tribunal. If a CO was unhappy with its decision, he could take his case to an appellate tribunal.

A tribunal could arrive at four possible judgments. First, it could reject the application and direct the applicant to combatant duties in the armed services. Second, it might direct the CO to non-combatant duties with the Royal Army Medical Corps or, after April 1940, with the new Non-Combatant Corps. Third, it could exempt him from military service, on condition that he perform civilian work deemed to be of national importance, as directed by the tribunal. Fourth, it might grant him unconditional exemption.

The tribunals were inundated during the first months of the war, and objectors were having to wait up to six or seven months before having their application heard. According to Fenner Brockway, in 1939 'the need was not an organisation *of* conscientious objectors but an organisation *for* conscientious objectors.'[19] As a result the Central Board for Conscientious Objectors (CBCO) was formed. Seventeen organizations were affiliated to it – most notably, the PPU, in whose London premises in Endsleigh Street the CBCO was housed. Its main work lay in helping COs, publishing information sheets and advisory pamphlets (including the weekly *COs Hansard*), and representing COs' interests. Much of the personal support for COs came from local representatives of the CBCO, who were invariably members of local peace groups such as the PPU. They would help prepare an objector for his tribunal appearance and even hold 'mock tribunals' to rehearse the kind of presentation necessary to satisfy the tribunal members, who sat in judgment on his conscience.

The records would seem to indicate that during the 'phoney war' the tribunals reflected the general public tolerance of objectors, with 14 per cent of all objectors granted unconditional exemption in 1939.[20] This proportion dropped to 5 per cent for 1940 and to 2 per cent by 1941, reflecting the transformation in the British experience of the war during the spring and early summer of 1940.

In April 1940 the Germans invaded Norway and Denmark, the next month Holland and Belgium were overrun, and British forces retreated towards Dunkirk. Following the fall of France in June 1940, it was clear that Britain was to be the next target of German expansionism. Churchill, who had replaced Chamberlain as prime minister, appealed to the British people to stand firm in the face of the imminent invasion, determined to resist the fascist threat to the last.

In such circumstances, many pacifists reconsidered their position and felt that they could no longer hold to their pledge of personal renunciation of war, while public attitudes towards pacifists and COs hardened. The PPU had to review its stance. In the words of Sybil Morrison, 'It was no longer possible to expect or to try to achieve support for a negotiated peace ... It was only possible to hold together ... awaiting the moment when an attempt could be made to break into the vicious circle of violence and disaster.'[21]

For individual pacifists the problem of creating an appropriate role for themselves in wartime was sharpened: how were they to reconcile the promptings of their conscience with their concern for their fellow citizens and neighbours, who now faced the prospect of a war to the finish against what appeared to be overwhelming odds?

Pacifism in Total War

Throughout the summer of 1940, while the 'Battle of Britain' was being fought in the skies above southern England, the civilian population in major target zones such as London and Liverpool was enduring nightly bombing raids. As Frances Partridge, the wife of a CO, recorded in her diary on 26 August 1940: 'The news is entirely concerned with air-raids. Inside every head in England the same questions are revolving: "How many killed? How many injured? How is everyone 'standing up' to the raids?" Oh, the sordid horror of the news; now it is just one long description of destruction, smashing, mashing and killing.'[22]

That same month, in Liverpool, Harold Ford and his wife, exhausted by lack of sleep as a consequence of the nightly air raids, moved out of the city to Southport, a few miles up the coast. Within a few weeks, Harold was attending a meeting of pacifists drawn from the PPU and FOR, where discussion 'soon got on to the question of what practical things we could do. It was suggested and agreed that we could run some sort of a place where people from Liverpool could come for a few night's sleep.'[23] Over the next few months they worked with agencies and groups such as the Pacifist Service Unit in Liverpool and various committees of the local Quakers. Eventually they established a rest centre where evacuees from Liverpool could sleep. The running of the centre was taken over by the Friends Ambulance Unit, with the voluntary assistance of the local pacifists. Later in the war Harold Ford joined with a group of local pacifists in a study circle to learn German, in the hope that they would be able to meet with German prisoners of war and begin to sow the seeds of reconciliation.

Just prior to his involvement with the rest centre project, Ford had worked with other pacifists on Merseyside in cultivating a vegetable allotment and distributing the produce to local families in need. He was also active with local pacifists in supporting the refugees whom they had 'sponsored' prior to the outbreak of war. Under wartime regulations, many of the men had been interned as 'enemy aliens,' which left their families in a difficult situation. Local pacifists and PPU groups looked after them.

In directing his energies into all these forms of relief work, Ford was typical of those pacifists who felt the need to bear witness to their belief in the fellowship of humanity through practical action, particularly by assisting the victims of war. The Pacifist Service Units, the Friends War Victims Relief Committee (renamed the Friends Relief Service in 1943), the Friends Ambulance Unit, and many other such groups channelled this kind of humanitarian impulse.[24] It was a similar urge that led other pacifists to participate as 'guinea pigs' in medical research, involving experiments to discover how scabies was contracted, the effects of a calcium-deficient diet, and the length of time one could live on a 'ship-wreck diet.'[25]

There was lively discussion in the columns of *Peace News* from time to time as to whether relief work was a pacifist response to war or a general humanitarian one, which any decent person would do.[26] One distinctive feature of some pacifists' relief work was their eagerness to volunteer services to the wider community and their reluctance to do so under compulsion. This sensibility became particularly apparent in relation to civil-defence duties such as fire-watching. In March 1941, a bill was introduced in Parliament to make civil-defence duties compulsory, and also render those COs granted conditional exemption from military service liable to full-time civil-defence work. As Harold Ford confided to his diary in August 1941: 'Firewatching and other ARP [air-raid precautions] duties are to be compulsory for all. We have done voluntary firewatching at the church and volunteered for the street – but a state scheme of compulsory organisation for carrying on the war is different.'[27] Many pacifists shared this concern about compulsory participation in war-related activities, and a total of 475 COs were prosecuted for offences related to fire-watching during the war, including some women.[28] Nora Page was sentenced to fourteen days in prison for her stand. 'If you were fighting conscription, you had to refuse direction. My attitude was that I am not going to do anything in war-time that you would not have asked me to do in peace-time ... I was in a fire-watch team in our road and I took my turn stopping up all night ... We were directed to register for fire-watching. Now, I did not just not register like thousands of others did. I wrote and told them I had not registered because I did not believe in conscription ... I got 14 days.'[29]

Of 1,074 women who registered as COs up to 31 December 1948, 64.1 per cent were granted objector status on condition that they undertake civilian work, 6.4 per cent were registered unconditionally, 3.5 per cent were directed to non-combatant duties in the military, and 26 per cent had their application rejected. Of the 61,227 men who applied for registration as COs, 29.7 per cent had their application rejected, 28.1 per cent were directed to non-combatant duties, only 4.7 per cent were registered unconditionally, and 37.5 per cent had their registration accepted on condition that they undertake civilian work.[30]

The majority of the men granted conditional exemption were directed to agricultural work, while a smaller number later in the war agreed to work down the coal mines. The bulk of the COs were drawn from white-collar groups, with little or no experience of land work. During the early years of the war, when public disapproval of 'conchies' was at its height, there was some reluctance among farmers to employ inexperienced 'trouble-makers.' To help cope with this problem, Henry Carter, a Methodist minister, established the Christian Pacifist Forestry and Land Units. Percy Patten joined one of these units, where he witnessed the contrariness of some of his fellow objectors. One of their number always wore gloves at work. When it was suggested to him that he would get on a lot better if he took them off, he replied, 'When I agreed to do land work, I swore I would never get my hands dirty for this government!'[31]

While each pacifist and war resister, whether member of the PPU or not, was waging his or her own individual struggle, weighing moral principles against pragmatic expediency, coping with the sense of exclusion and relative isolation that came from being part of a 'deviant' minority, the ideologues and the senior figures within the PPU were seeking to establish some kind of 'party line' for the organization and its members during war.

The terms of this debate were set primarily by the members of the Forethought Committee, a group of ex-sponsors including Canon Charles Raven, Middleton Murry, Max Plowman, and Wilfred Wellock. In 1940 they issued a document containing four Peace Affirmations as an expression of the 'corporate mind' of the PPU. They stressed there the supreme value of the individual. The full development of the individual depended on the establishment of right relationships with others; the possibility of achieving such a qualitative change in our way of life was threatened by totalitarian tendencies within society. Hence 'our task is always to take the most creative and constructive action in the face of existing circumstances. The way of justice and love, to many expressed as "the way of Christ" is the straight way to the redemption of the individual and of society.'[32]

Basically, they were advocating a return to the traditional role of pacifists as a redemptive minority. If pacifists had no immediately practicable proposals as to how the war might be stopped, then they should extend their time scale to address the challenge of how to re-create civilization after the barbarism of war had ended. Pacifists could play a prophetic role as witnesses to an alternative set of values and way of life and thereby sow the seeds of a new society.[33]

While not denying the role that pacifists could play as witnesses of peace, some members of the PPU believed that they could still be active instruments of peace in various ways. Thus, at the fourth general meeting of the PPU in April 1941, Roy Walker criticized the orientation of the Forethought Committee; he bemoaned the fact that the Union's policy had been nothing but a series of 'strategic withdrawals' in the face of the demands of a country at war. 'In place of action we have been given moral uplift,' he asserted, and he urged a campaign for a negotiated peace. Any battle would be better than 'another twelve months of retreat.'[34]

Bill Grindlay, of the socialist Peace Commentary Group, also opposed the

Forethought Committee's approach. In his view the PPU was a political organization, and it should express its pacifism as a political program rather than as a religious faith. Pacifists 'must speak politically. In the relative sphere of human politics, we have, now as always, to choose the lesser of two evils, and honourably to support the bad against the worst. We cannot avoid the most obvious implication of the pledge; we cannot philosophise out of the obligation to demand the lesser evil of peace negotiation rather than the greater evil of war.'[35]

Another approach was expressed by those associated with the Forward Group of anarchistic, libertarian pacifists such as Frederick Lohr and David Spreckley. They dreamed of converting the PPU into a revolutionary, non-violent movement for the total transformation of society. At the 1940 general meeting Spreckley proclaimed: 'If this is total war, the propaganda we have been putting forward against war is useless; we have got to fight against the system.' The PPU's slogan should be not so much 'Peace by negotiation' as 'Peace by revolution.' If it took such a stance, then he believed thousands would join.[36] In the event, David Spreckley resigned the following year, disgusted at the 'deadweight majority of the PPU who just signed their postcards and then sat on them.'[37]

Despite such opposition, the dominant 'corporate theme' within the PPU during the war years was that represented by the Forethought Committee, with Middleton Murry playing a dominant role. He had been appointed editor of *Peace News* in July 1940, and under his influence more and more space was devoted to coverage of community ventures being launched by pacifists. In his history of conscientious objection during the war, Denis Hayes identified three types of motivation for people who joined these agricultural colonies: definite calling, a desire for an escape, or the need for a job to fulfil the conditions of their exemption from military service. The majority of the predominantly young and single males who gravitated towards them would appear to have belonged to the second and third categories.[38]

Cyril Wright, however, was one with a genuine vocation. He helped to establish a community at Charney Bassett in Oxfordshire. In his words: 'The idea was we should put all our available capital in a pool and purchase a farm ... This would not only be a source of livelihood and subsistence for a number of people, but would also illustrate to the world, we hoped, ways in which people could live together without fighting one another – a very small example of a peaceful world. And we would put into practice our ideas on tolerance, nonviolence and love towards one another at a time when other people were engaged in smashing themselves to bits.'[39] The communal life at Charney Bassett lasted just over two years. Cyril Wright attributed its eventual collapse to interpersonal difficulties among strong individualists.

Despite the relative failure of such communities, those who were involved could at least justify their position by reference to a larger purpose of social reconstruction. Those who were, in contrast, sceptical of the significance of such efforts to build the 'New Jerusalem in England's green and pleasant land' still needed a positive role beyond that of bearing witness as COs. In 1941 one pacifist observed in *Peace News*: 'I have found it rather difficult to adjust myself to a pacifism with no poster-parades, no street-corner meetings, no mass demonstrations; for these strivings were an essential part of our movement ... Mere doctrinaire discussion, with a dash of social service, as we know it, is not enough to weld together the mass of pacifists and like-minded people, who must feel they are taking part in a crusade.'[40]

The 'Stop the War' campaign had proved ineffectual, as had the campaign for a negotiated peace by mid-1941. However, PPU members did get involved in a number of pressure-group efforts concerned with mitigating the effects of war. In a letter to *The Times* in April 1941 the (non-pacifist) bishop of Chichester had proposed a cessation of night-bombing by Britain if the Germans would give a similar assurance. Though the PPU, as a pacifist organization opposed to all war, did not participate formally, many of its members did get involved in the resulting campaign – most notably, the novelist Vera Brittain; Arthur, Lord Ponsonby; and the well-known actress Sybil Thorndike.

Then, in the summer of 1941, reports started to emerge of famine among the civilian population in occupied Belgium due to the total blockade imposed by the Allies. This was followed by news of the many civilians dying from starvation in occupied Greece. In response, the PPU launched its Food Relief Campaign in 1941, led by Roy Walker, with Vera Brittain as its chair. Local groups began to write letters to the press, hold public meetings, and petition their MPs for a relaxation of the blockades to allow food supplies to the starving. The bishop of Chichester took up the cause and succeeded in gaining some concessions from the government. Brittain then suggested to the bishop that he should form a group of public figures to protest against British policy, which would carry more weight than the pacifists could muster.[41] As a result the national Famine Relief Committee was established in May 1942. A network of local committees developed, including one at Oxford. It was out of the Oxford Famine Relief Committee that the charity Oxfam was to emerge.[42] The PPU's Food Relief Campaign continued with its own activities for the duration of the war.

For many COs, scattered around the countryside working on the land, the main source of information about such activities came through the columns of *Peace News*, their lifeline to the rest of the pacifist community. For so many of them, as for their fellow citizens, the war seemed to drag on and on. They did not suffer danger so much as tendium and depression. Harold Ford spent the bulk of the war working on the land, away from his home in Southport, and he expressed some of these feelings in his diary. Thus on 28 September 1943 he recorded, 'Another day much the same, there is little to distinguish one day from another here ... It gets tedious, and one longs for the end of the war and a return to some kind of normal life.'

In June of the following year the Normandy landings took place, and it was clear that the tide of war had turned in favour of the Allies. On 5 September 1944 Ford was recording that in the light of the Allied advances 'everyone thinks the end is near.' It was during this period that the PPU's campaign for a negotiated settlement revived, as its supporters sought to mobilize pressure against Churchill's insistence on 'unconditional surrender' and initiate debate on what would constitute a constructive peace. But the PPU exercised no observable influence on government policy concerning conduct of the war, which was pursued to its bitter end.

What the PPU did achieve during the war was to provide advice, support, and fellowship to all those pacifists who experienced the isolation and doubts of being a minority of moral dissidents within a society engaged in total war. Few suffered persecution comparable to that experienced by their First World War forebears. But many lost their jobs and suffered discrimination, ostracism, and disapproval. In such a situation, the support and reassurance provided to the individual pacifist by the PPU were very encouraging. As Cyril Wright expressed it, 'I was conscious that I was out on a limb, when you are one and you have hundreds around you taking exactly the opposite view. You felt more and more out on a limb, on your own, until you got together with your fellow pacifists. And one of the great things was the fellowship of the PPU. It enabled people of like mind to get together, and you felt you were not alone.'[43]

The PPU and the Impact of Peace

Pacifists, like their fellow citizens, felt relief at the end of the war – the tyranny of Hitler had been overcome, and they could begin to pick up the threads of their old life. But pacifists felt ambivalent over the national celebrations that accompanied victory. After all, they had not 'fought' for the victory. There can have been few pacifists who had not experienced periods of doubt about their stance, some degree of shame that they were avoiding the pain and discomfort that others in the services were facing, some concern that maybe they had no non-violent answer to the Nazi aggression other than 'peace at any price.' Such heart-searching did not end with the cessation of hostilities.[44]

This doubt was felt at the very heart of the PPU. The full disclosure of the horrors of the concentration camps had a powerful impact on Middleton Murry. He came to believe that there was no non-violent answer to totalitarianism and that the only possibility of obtaining world peace was by collective security through a new world authority armed with the atomic bomb. He even went so far as to urge the Western powers to use their monopoly of the bomb to force the Soviet Union into accepting the sovereignty of such a world authority.

His change of heart had a profoundly debilitating effect on the PPU. Here was the dominant personality within the union, the editor of its newspaper, advocating an international police force equipped with atomic weapons. Roy Walker led the attack on Murry, dismissing his position as inimical to pacifism and calling for an 'internationalism from below' that would deprive 'all national governments of the mandate, the power and the means to threaten, pre-pare or wage war.' 'Unless,' he continued, 'we can imagine such a world we shall never achieve it, if we can imagine it we can support no present policy that denies it, if we cannot imagine it we have passed judgement on our civilization and may be sure that its final destruction is not far distant.'[45]

But to many within the PPU in 1945 Walker's call for an assertive pacifism was unreal. The negative effect of Murry's espousal of 'heretical' views was compounded by the decline in the general pacifist movement throughout the country. The end of the war brought with it not just relief but a weakening of rank-and-file commitment to the PPU. Throughout the war members had needed each other for mutual support. Now they were beginning to pick up the threads of their interrupted careers and lives, merging once again with the wider public, and they did not need their fellow pacifists or the PPU as they once had done.

Lily Butcher, a stalwart of the Northampton PPU contingent, expressed something of the disappointment felt by activists as she reviewed the relative decline of the PPU after the war:

It is inevitable that in 1946 we should look back to the halcyon days of big group meet-ings in the early years of the war, and regard with sorrow the lack of interest and support which has been apparent since its end. We must face the fact, however, that in those days we became an isolated fellowship, firstly for common defence against the mechanisms of conscription, and secondly, for maintaining our morale and strengthening our faith as an unpopular minority in a hostile community. This drew us closer together and gave us a sense of solidarity and common purpose, if only a negative one. Moreover, it cannot be denied that many adhered to the pacifist movement during the war from motives which were not always devoid of expediency and self-interest; it was inevitable that those who had not grown to an awareness of their social responsibilities as pacifists should forego their opinions when the war is over.[46]

NOTES

1 'Pacifism and the Peace Pledge Union,' *Peace News* (London), 24 March 1939, 3.
2 D.S. Savage, 'Testament of a Conscientious Objector,' in Clifford Simmons, ed., *The Objectors: The Personal Story of Five Conscientious Objectors* (Douglas, Isle of Man, and London 1965), 95.
3 Martin Ceadel, *Pacifism in Britain, 1914–45: The Defining of a Faith* (Oxford 1980), 223.
4 *Peace News*, 26 March 1938, 1.
5 Ibid., 13.
6 David C. Lukowitz, 'British Pacifists and Appeasement: The Peace Pledge Union,' *Journal of Contemporary History* (London), 9 no 1 (Jan. 1974), 126. See also his series of articles on the early history of the PPU in *The Pacifist*, 10 nos. 8–9 (June–July 1971), no. 11 (Sept. 1971), and 11 no. 4 (Feb. 1972).
7 *Peace News*, 3 Feb. 1939, 6.
8 Ibid., 3 April 1937, 9.
9 Ibid., 8 Oct. 1938, 1.
10 Harold Ford, diary, entry for 3–5 Oct. 1938. I am grateful to Diana Francis for the loan of her father's diaries.
11 Many people signed the pledge as an expression of their desire for peace, rather than as a firm commitment to pacifism. See, for example, Mark Holloway, 'Offender-at-large,' in Clifford Simmons, ed., *The Objectors: The Personal Story of Five Conscientious Objectors* (Douglas and London 1965), 126.
12 See H. Runham Brown, *The War Resisters' International in War-time* (London 1941), 8–9.
13 See *The Story of Pacifism in Northampton: Through War to Peace, 1939–1946* (Northampton 1946).
14 Interview with Ronald Mallone, Imperial War Museum Oral History Recordings (IWM), ref. no. 4581/5, reel 4.
15 Cyril Wright, IWM, 4789/8, reel 4.
16 Sybil Morrison, *I Renounce War: The Story of the Peace Pledge Union* (London 1962), 45–9.
17 Sir William Davison, quoted in Rachel Barker, *Conscience, Government and War: Conscientious Objection in Great Britain, 1939–45* (London 1982), 99.
18 Quoted in *Peace News*, 3 May 1940, 4.
19 Denis Hayes, *Challenge of Conscience: The Story of the Conscientious Objectors of 1939–1945* (London 1949), vii.
20 Barker, *Conscience, Government and War*, 22.
21 Morrison, *I Renounce War*, 45.
22 Frances Partridge, *A Pacifist's War* (London 1983), 56–7. Her husband, the writer

Ralph Partridge, was a First World War veteran who became a pacifist as a consequence of his war experience.

23 Harold Ford, diary, 9 Oct. 1940.

24 See Hayes, *Challenge of Conscience*, 222–41.

25 Ibid., 219–22.

26 See, for example, Alex Thompson, *Peace News*, 22 Nov. 1940, 3.

27 Harold Ford, diary, 6 Aug. 1941.

28 Barker, *Conscience, Government and War*, 108.

29 Nora Page, IWM, 4659/7, reel 4.

30 These figures are taken from Barker, *Conscience, Government and War*, 145. Male conscription for military service began in May 1939, whereas the military conscription of women commenced only in December 1941.

31 Percy Patten, IWM, 4665/7, reel 4. For an interesting account of one pacifist's time as a land worker during the war, see Edward Blishen, *A Cack-handed War* (London 1972).

32 Quoted in Morrison, *I Renounce War*, 101–2.

33 They were criticized by Ronald Mallone, among others, for failing to refer to the need to end the war. See *Peace News*, 3 May 1940, 4.

34 Ibid., 25 April 1941, 4.

35 Ibid., 30 May 1941, 3.

36 Ibid., 3 May 1940, 4.

37 Ibid., 11 July 1941, 4.

38 See Hayes, *Challenge of Conscience*, 217. For a fuller examination, see Andrew Rigby, 'Pacifist Communities in Britain in the Second World War,' *Peace and Change* (Newbury Park, Calif.), 15 no. 2 (April 1990), 107–22.

39 Cyril Wright, IWM, 4789/8, reel 3.

40 Quoted in Ceadel, *Pacifism in Britain*, 309.

41 A rather different interpretation from mine can be found in Y. Aleksandra Bennett, 'A Question of Respectability and Tactics: Vera Brittain and Food Relief for Occupied Europe, 1941–1944, in Harvey L. Dyck, ed., *The Pacifist Impulse in Historical Perspective* (Toronto 1996), 388–90.

42 See Maggie Black, *A Cause for Our Times: Oxfam, the First Fifty Years* (Oxford 1992).

43 Cyril Wright, IWM, 4789/8, reel 4.

44 See Blishen, *A Cack-handed War*, 196, for an honest 'confession.'

45 *Peace News*, 31 Aug. 1945, 3.

46 *Pacifism in Northampton*, 17.

12

J.S. Woodsworth and War

KENNETH McNAUGHT

On 8 September 1939, James Shaver Woodsworth, Canada's leading democratic socialist, rose at his desk in the House of Commons. The Speaker had called for a vote on the country's first independent declaration of war. In the preceding debate several French Canadians had opposed the commitment, observing that the conflict was yet another product of imperialism, Britain's war. When the vote was called, however – a voice vote – only Woodsworth asked that his negative be recorded. Members had muttered disapproval as he gave his reasons during the debate. Far more striking than this momentary disapproval was the respect accorded the lone dissenter amid the heady enthusiasm pervading Parliament in the first week of the Second World War.

Prime Minister William Lyon Mackenzie King, at the end of his long opening speech, made clear the reason for the startling calm in which Woodsworth would deliver his passionate argument for Canadian neutrality. 'There are few men in this Parliament,' said King, 'for whom, in some particulars, I have greater respect than the leader of the Co-operative Commonwealth Federation. I admire him in my heart because time and again he has had the courage to say what lay on his conscience regardless of what the world might think of him. A man of that calibre is an ornament to any Parliament.'[1] What was there in Woodsworth's convictions, character, career, that had set the stage for his remarkable final witnessing?

Woodsworth's pacifism, eventually so strong, so forthright, grew out of his essentially Canadian experience. One of his most notable admirers, Frank H. Underhill, called Woodsworth an 'untypical Canadian.' By this, Underhill meant that 'J.S.' was not instinctively a compromiser. In all other respects, however, Woodsworth was typical of the evolutionary process that has made Canada multicultural without destroying its British legal-parliamentary continuities, emphatic in its commitment both to law and order and to peacekeeping.

Like Canada's own complex evolution, Woodsworth's pacifism sprang from no sudden revelation; it was as inseparable from his socialism as it was from his Methodist roots. He was concerned more with the evil causes and results of war even than with the actual killing that revolts the 'pure' pacifist.

Woodsworth was born into an Ontario farm home in 1874. His maternal fore-bears had come from 'High Germany' to Pennsylvania in the 1760s and moved on to Canada after the War of Independence. His paternal grandfather had come to Canada in 1830 from Yorkshire. The mix of Pennsylvania Dutch and north-ern British Methodism gave to Woodsworth's home a strong sense of order, of discipline. Its puritanism was, however, tempered by belief in service and a cooperative spirit – at least as strong as the individualism that allegedly charac-terized the North American frontier.

Certainly Woodsworth could claim to be a son of the Canadian frontier. His father, Dr James Woodsworth, after ordination by a visiting British preacher, served in a series of mission circuits in northern Ontario. Shortly after moving to Manitoba he was appointed first superintendent of Methodist missions for the Canadian North-West. The younger Woodsworth often accompanied his father by buckboard, canoe, and stern-wheeler on tours across the prairies. But it was not on these rigorous journeys that he encountered even an inkling of pacifism. His father remarked of the 1885 Riel rebellion: 'Many lives were lost in this unfortunate disturbance. On the other hand, much good resulted. Disaffected half-breeds and rebellious Indians were taught a salutary lesson; they learned something of the strength of British rule and likewise experienced something of its clemency and righteousness.'[2]

Though committed by his parents to the Methodist ministry – from birth – J.S. questioned orthodoxy from the outset. Graduated from Wesley College in Winnipeg in 1896, he rode a mission circuit in southern Manitoba for two years, striving in vain for the 'personal conversion' expected of Methodists. Instead he began to question the church's too-specific creed; and beyond the credal ques-tion lay a deeper concern. The Methodist church had become an institution pre-dominantly of the middle class. To its comfortable congregations it preached a gospel of personal salvation. Uneasy about the church's apparent indifference to social inequity in the here and now, Woodsworth felt no weakening of his innate need to serve. During a year at Toronto's Victoria College (1898–9), followed by a year at Oxford, his questioning persisted. At Victoria he encountered the 'social gospel' and the Fred Victor city mission. While in England he spent con-siderable time at Mansfield House in London's slums. There he heard much criticism of the South African War.

If one searches, however, for the primary source of Woodsworth's pacifism, one will find it in his desperate need to rectify social injustice. Militarism, imperialism, war, and social violence he came to abhor primarily as causes of the human degradation he saw in the cities of Canada and Britain. Nor would he ever lose his Methodistical attachment to order and efficiency. During a side trip to Germany in 1900 he recorded: 'There does not seem to be that degraded element which is everywhere in evidence in the great cities in England ... Today at Duisberg I saw a fine company of German soldiers ... The presence of large numbers of soldiers gives a lively appearance to a crowd.' At Heidelberg he enjoyed the hospitality of some students who had invited him to watch a duel. 'I confess,' he wrote, 'that I shall always have a kindlier feeling towards those organizations which English students call "Duelling Societies" and "Beer Drinking Clubs."'[3]

Woodsworth himself maintained that he became a pacifist after visiting London's Army and Navy Museum in 1906. Viewing the bloodied relics of imperial wars he recalled a chilling account he had recently heard of the methods of governing dependent colonies. Yet even in his own later recollection, his revulsion seems to have sprung from observing the results of social violence and war. Nowhere, down to his last noble stand against war, can one find an unambiguous assertion that to kill is in any circumstances a sin. Perhaps the closest he came to enunciating his always-evolving position was in a short article that he wrote at Christmas 1914: 'We plead that no one demand of us absolute consistency – and yet we must bear witness to the truth as it comes to us. To overcome militarism by physical force seems like attempting to cast out Beelzebub by the power of Beelzebub. To secure his own victory, Jesus refused to call out even the legions of angels that awaited his bidding. He, true to his teaching, could save his life only by losing it. Is the disciple above his Lord?'[4]

In 1904 Woodsworth had married Lucy Staples, a woman of commanding charm and intelligence. In a later day I think Lucy Woodsworth's role in the story of Canadian pacifism might well have been more widely recognized than it is. In 1921 she organized and became first president of Vancouver's branch of the Women's International League for Peace and Freedom. In 1924 she accompanied Agnes Macphail, Canada's first woman member of Parliament, in a large delegation to the WIL's international congress in Washington, DC. Throughout the 1920s, 1930s, and 1940s she worked closely with Beatrice Brigden, Laura Jamieson, Alice Loeb, Violet McNaughton, Agnes Macphail, and other Canadian women active in the cause of peace, organizing the educational initiatives of the WIL. Like Macphail, she was particularly concerned with replacing cadet training and the celebration of military virtues with development of peace activities that might induce young people to find 'making peace as interesting as war.'[5]

Like J.S., however, Lucy was a child of her times. She accepted a primary role as wife and mother (of six children) in a home centred entirely on her husband. Nor did she see this as entailing undue sacrifice. Their partnership, their joint commitment to the linked goals of social justice and peace, was complete. In a letter of 1919 she wrote, while her husband was under threat of prison for his part in the Winnipeg strike of that year: 'With James, I have entirely ceased to wish for luxury, ease, comfort or advantage for us, yes, or for our children, while countless thousands never do and never will, under our present system, get a chance for ordinary decent living.'[6]

Woodsworth was ordained in 1900. From then until 1918 he moved steadily to the 'left' – in the church and in his political-social thinking. As assistant minister in a prosperous Winnipeg church he gave sermons that shook the elders: 'Jesus said very little about saving souls – He spoke often about the establishment of the Kingdom ... Need constitutes a claim – this is Christian Socialism, Christian charity, Christian love. This is the great principle that must be applied to our social problems.'[7] While he continued to reject a literal meaning for most of the creed, he hoped that a new Protestantism could capture the church and make it the principal instrument of social concern, of noncompetitive compassion. He read most of the contemporary social gospel writing and, of more enduring influence, the works of British Christian socialists and Fabians.

By 1907 Woodsworth and the upright burghers of Grace Church had to part company. Having drifted far from orthodoxy he felt obliged to resign from the ministry. The Manitoba Methodist Conference persuaded him to withdraw the resignation; it then appointed him superintendent of its inner-city mission. From 1907 to 1913 he ran All Peoples' Mission as an 'institutional church,' providing every possible facility from language education to recreation for the ever-growing number of immigrants who occupied fetid tenements owned by respected church members. Disillusioned finally by the inadequacy of church charity, he helped organize the Canadian Welfare League in 1913 and shortly afterward became head of a provincial Bureau of Social Research.[8]

In the midst of his social activism and analysis, Woodsworth firmed up the convictions that would lead him finally out of the church and into a clear political commitment. His friends now included the principal social gospellers and pacifists, many of whom were already democratic socialists. People such as Francis Marion Benyon, Salem Bland, F.J. Dixon, William Ivens, Nellie McClung, and A.V. Thomas agreed that neither social injustice nor war could be ended without substantive alteration or complete replacement of the capitalist system, which relied on state violence at home and abroad to sustain itself.

At the end of 1916, with horrendous Canadian casualties in France and recruiting at a near standstill, the dominion government announced a program to register all men between the ages of sixteen and sixty-five. Woodsworth, in a letter to the *Winnipeg Free Press*, denounced the scheme: 'This registration is no mere census. It seems to look in the direction of a measure of conscription. As some of us cannot conscientiously engage in military service, we are bound to resist what, if the war continues, will inevitably lead to forced service.' Underlining the linkage of war and social injustice, he noted that 'conscription of material possessions should in all justice precede an attempt to force men to risk their lives and the welfare of their families.'[9] The provincial government immediately fired him from the Bureau of Social Research.

At the suggestion of friends in British Columbia the Woodsworths moved to a small coastal community just north of Vancouver. As supply minister in the mission church J.S. steered straight into his decisive confrontation with Methodism. Having actively supported a cooperative store operated by Finnish socialists in Gibson's Landing, he incurred the wrath of the town's leading merchant and Methodist layman. When Woodsworth refused to place recruiting posters in the church, a small local group induced the B.C. Methodist Conference to terminate his appointment. In June 1918 he penned a long letter of resignation to the Manitoba Conference.

Once again the issues of social justice and pacifism ran in tandem. After reviewing his social service work he wrote: 'I began to see that the organized church has become a great institution with institution aims and ambitions ... Anything like a radical program of social reform became in practice almost impossible ... Nor, through the war, do I see any way out of our difficulties. The devil of militarism cannot be driven out by the power of militarism without the successful nations themselves becoming militarized ... For me, the teachings of Jesus are absolutely irreconcilable with the advocacy of war ... The position of the church seems to be summed up in the words of a General Conference officer – "We must win the war, nothing else matters ..." Apparently the church feels that I do not belong and reluctantly I have been forced to the same conclusion.'[10]

Cast out by the middle class, Woodsworth became a longshoreman on the Vancouver docks. Of twelve hundred union workers he alone refused to load munitions on the ships of the expeditionary force sent against the new Russian government. This frail man, with his trim vandyke beard, quickly earned the respect of his fellow workers. All the while he lectured and wrote articles in support of the B.C. Federated Labour party. Now committed to the politics of democratic socialism and labour's right to collective bargaining, he undertook a speaking tour of the western provinces in the spring of 1919. The events of that spring blew away any lingering mists of doubt about the course that he must follow.

Woodsworth arrived in Winnipeg half-way through a general strike that closed down the city's economic life for six tumultuous weeks. He immediately plunged into active support of the strikers. Their cause – union recognition and higher wages to help assuage war-induced high costs of living – he fully endorsed. He, as well as the strike leaders, saw clearly the potential for violence. With virtually every worker in the city idle, all services either limited or shut down, and daily mass meetings being held in the city's parks, tension rose steadily. The strike leaders warned strongly against *agents provocateurs* and in their *Strike Bulletin* proclaimed: 'There is great cause for congratulations during this struggle, in that until the present moment the participants are more orderly than a crowd of spectators at a baseball game ... There has evolved a weapon of great power – orderliness.'[11]

It wasn't to last. Through a Citizens' Committee, Winnipeg's employers and professional people conjured up the full power of the state. Rejecting entirely the strikers' demands, they charged that the leaders were Bolsheviks intent on overthrowing constituted government. Though all of the strike leaders were either Canadian or British born, the Citizens' Committee played on middle-class fear of the city's numerous immigrants, charging tirelessly that the strike was an alien conspiracy. City, provincial, and dominion governments rallied quickly to the flag. City council fired its unionized police force, replacing it with untrained 'specials'; the province fired any employee who refused to foreswear sympathetic striking. In the strike's fifth week, Ottawa swung into action. Mounted police arrested the leaders on charges of sedition and bundled them off to Stony Mountain penitentiary.

Among those arrested was William Ivens, who had been editing the *Western Labour News*, the only non-establishment source of news. Woodsworth and his close friend F.J. Dixon at once took over the paper and continued to urge 'peaceful idleness' in face of the repressive state action. The method of non-violence had, however, reached its limit – of near success. When pro-strike war veterans organized a large 'silent parade' to protest the leaders' arrests, the mayor read the Riot Act, conveniently making the parade illegal. At once a large contingent of Mounties rode through the crowds, while heavily armed militiamen occupied the centre of the city. Under the heading 'Bloody Saturday,' Woodsworth and Dixon editorialized in the *Western Labour News*: 'Whether the radical changes that are inevitable may be brought about peaceably largely depends upon the good sense of the Canadian businessmen who now control both the industry and the government of the country. We confess the prospects are not very bright.'[12] Charging that Kaiserism had come to Canada, Woodsworth quoted Isaiah: 'Woe unto them that decree unrighteous decrees ... and take away the right from the poor of my people, that widows may be their prey, and that they may rob the fatherless' (Isa. 10: 1–2).

Woodsworth was immediately arrested on a charge of seditious libel. A few days later Dixon was also seized. From a neighbouring cell he told Woodsworth that the strike was ended. After Dixon had defended himself brilliantly against the charge of seditious libel, the crown dropped the similar charge against Woodsworth. Seven of the strike leaders received prison sentences ranging from six months to two years.

During the following two years Woodsworth worked with the creedless Labour Church, which Ivens had begun after he was expelled by the Methodists for preaching pacifism and socialism. Struggling to put the events of the strike into perspective, Woodsworth wrote of the Labour Church: 'We believe that physical force settles nothing ... What is won by physical force must be maintained by physical force ... Moral ends can be attained only by moral means ... Education, then, not the sword is to be the instrument of our emancipation.'[13] But how to control the sword of state, which had been used so effectively to crush the strike? Woodsworth's answer was political action. The time was right. Winnipeg's workers had been radicalized by the strike. In the 1920 provincial election three strike leaders, still in jail, won seats in the legislature, and Dixon had headed the polls. Together with other democratic socialists, including Dixon and Ivens, Woodsworth organized the Manitoba Independent Labour party (ILP) specifically to gain a voice in Ottawa.

Woodsworth wrote most of the ILP manifesto, modelling it closely on the program of the British Labour party. In addition to its call for socialist reconstruction of Canada, the manifesto stressed the need for worker representation to prevent future police repression and denial of free speech; it included a strong statement against Canadian participation in any future war. Woodsworth and his friends took care also to dissociate the ILP from Canada's new Communist party. The ILP's rejection of force in the struggle for socialism was oft-repeated. On election night, 12 December 1921, a plurality of voters made Woodsworth the first MP to be elected by a socialist party.

Allen Mills, in his analysis of Woodsworth's political thought, writes that 'for him, the act of witnessing to the truth of pacifism did not so much carry individuals into alliance with others as lift them into a sort of ethereal space of individual protest and self-sacrifice outside history.'[14] True, I suppose, if one judges only from his final stand in 1939. However, the road to the Second World War saw Woodsworth almost furiously pursuing alliance with others. He mastered the rules of the House of Commons and the techniques of parliamentary debate; by the end of his first session few members tangled with him without qualms. He used the Commons as a public platform for constant reiteration of the need for socialism. He used Parliament also as a weapon in the always-inseparable causes of pacifism and free speech.

Seizing the opportunity offered by a minority government in 1926, he secured the initiation of an old-age pension law. His successful denunciation of the coordinated use of force, the courts, and repressive legislation during the Winnipeg strike (and later) achieved two significant purposes. They made crystal clear the availability of state force in support of social-economic privilege and eventually led to modification of the ludicrously broad criminal-code clauses on sedition and the equally capacious deportation provisions of the Immigration Act. Soon dubbed 'the conscience of the country,' Woodsworth made close political alliance with a baker's dozen of the sixty-five Progressive MPs who had been elected in 1921. This 'ginger group' gave vigorous support to his crusade against militarism, war, and militia 'aid to the civil power.'

During the 1920s a series of desperate strikes in the coal-steel towns of Nova Scotia revealed the helplessness of workers faced with militia-police intervention and, again, harsh application of the criminal code. Woodsworth unveiled the human misery week after week in the House. Pilloried as a 'red,' he became the champion of Canada's working classes. In the eyes of most MPs, however, he was equally dangerous when he linked social injustice, militarism, and war. Throughout the 1920s and 1930s almost single-handedly, Woodsworth forced the Commons to debate Canada's military and foreign policies. Without his goading, military estimates and treaty and other commitments would have received only their usual, perfunctory attention. To these debates, frequently initiated by Woodworth's deft use of advance-notice questions and private members' bills, he brought an irritating range of informed analysis. He read widely in British studies of the war, the peace treaties, and the future of socialism – including the writings of H.N. Brailsford, J.A. Hobson, J.M. Keyness and E.D. Morel. He had also met and corresponded with George Lansbury and kept abreast of Fabian and Labour publications.

Though J.S. found himself regularly subjected in the House and in the press to charges of disloyalty, communism, and cowardice, he also discovered much support across the land. Each year he delivered hundreds of speeches coast to coast and managed also a stream of articles dealing, more often than not, with the interconnectedness of socialism and non-violence. It is difficult to convey the luminous rectitude of the man. His prophetic aura and impeccable credentials won an ever-widening response from the common people. He regularly 'tithed' himself to support the ILP (and later the CCF). On country-wide train journeys he eschewed the sleeping-car, sitting instead in a day-coach with his reading material and food in paper parcels. At speaking stops he needed no hotel; hospitable friends were eager to accommodate him.

Woodsworth's long assault on the military estimates, funds for cadet training, war memorials, the RCMP, and militia owed much to his understanding of Hobson's analyses of imperialism and capitalism.[15] This is quite evident in his speech supporting a neutrality motion put by Henri Bourassa of Quebec in 1935:

First, I believe that military force is stupid; that it settles nothing and that it creates serious trouble. This conviction may be the result of Christian idealism, but it is confirmed by a reading of history.

Second, I believe that among the many causes of war the economic are the most fundamental, especially in modern times. Capitalism, social injustice, imperialistic expansion and war are inseparable. In my judgment, war will not end until we destroy capitalism, with its social injustice and imperialism.

Third, as a born individualist and an inheritor of the pioneer tradition, I have an instinctive desire to keep myself and my country out of the troubles of other people. In this I think that I am fairly Canadian.

Fourth, as a student of our complex industrial and social structure I realize that no individual can live to himself, or that no nation can live to itself. Self-sufficiency, independence, sovereignty and isolationism belong to the past ... I would emphasize that the mere declaration of neutrality is not sufficient ... Military defence does not seem to me to be an adequate defence. However, I do not think that mere disarmament will settle our problems.

Fifth, in practice, political power, with its military force, is still largely in the hands of the predatory classes,[16] hence national and international policies are dominated by anything but idealistic motives.

Sixth, as an individualist I refuse to participate or to assist in war, yet I am a citizen of a country which still relies upon force and as a public representative I must vote on alternative military policies.

Though Woodsworth rejected the literal meaning of original sin, he recognized well its pervasive reality – and the concomitant need to choose, often between two evils rather than between good and evil. Thus he added a codicil to his 1935 remarks: 'In the actual world of affairs, one must try to hold to his own convictions and keep the ultimate objective in view, yet advocate measures that are recognized as merely ameliorative. One must accept the half loaf and even support procedures which, though repugnant to his principles, represent a real advance in public welfare and public morality ... In a decently organized society we would not need a police force, but in our present semi-barbarous civilization I prefer a police force to bandits and vigilantes. So in international relations, until war is actually and wholeheartedly repudiated as an instrument of national policy, an international police force under proper control, if possible, might be preferable to anarchy.'[17]

This formulation of his beliefs explains many agonizing decisions. While it led to apparent inconsistencies, especially on such matters as League of Nations sanctions and his apparent willingness to rely on American power to safeguard Canadian neutrality, it did not impede vigorous condemnation of specific policies and attitudes. In 1923 he electrified the House of Commons when he said that the British and Canadian people had been 'tricked into the war in 1914' and also into the punitive terms of the Versailles Treaty. Worse, he moved that 'in the opinion of this House it is in the interest of world peace that Canada should withdraw all claims on Germany for reparation.'[18]

Quoting from Keynes, Hobson, and others, Woodsworth argued that the Carthaginian character of the 1919 peace settlement pointed directly to another war, probably more horrible than the first. Observing that the war-guilt clause simply ignored the complex imperialist-capitalist causes of the 1914 war – the alliances, the arms race, the secret treaties, colonial rivalries, and revenge – he demanded revision of the treaty. Economic strangulation of Germany should be stopped, all nations should be allowed to join the League of Nations, and all should be equally committed to disarmament. A tempest of rage greeted his speech. To the grotesquely ahistorical statement of the Conservative leader, Arthur Meighen, that 'if Germany had been made to pay for her crime in 1870 there would not have been a war in 1914,' Woodsworth replied, 'We may demand our pound of flesh, but all through the world's history there has run another strain of teaching – that mercy is greater than justice.'

Throughout the 1930s Woodsworth pressed for reform and opening up of the League and for unilateral Canadian disarmament – *pour encourager les autres.* In both these areas he was open to the charge of inconsistency; an inconsistency, however, resulting from his position as a representative required to choose between the lesser of two evils. As an individual he had no doubts. Thus he urged Canadian disarmament and neutrality on the grounds that 'those who rely on military force may rest assured that the United States would resist outside aggression. Some may feel that we should not be under obligation of this kind. On the other hand, why should we not take advantage of our advantageous position'[19]

With respect to the League, Woodsworth was frequently ambivalent; it was, after all, a league of victors. He urged Canada to accept jurisdiction of the Permanent Court of International Justice, and he argued that economic sanctions should have been applied against Japan's aggression in Manchuria in 1931. By 1935, however, as Italy signalled its impending invasion of Ethiopia, he hedged his support of sanctions, arguing that Canada should support them only if the government undertook serious investigation of the causes of war and accepted a policy of disarmament. He had been confronted by the inescapable conundrum: economic sanctions could themselves provoke war.

In 1933 Woodsworth's close association with the small group of Progressives who had resisted the blandishments of Mackenzie King's Liberal party, as well as with labour leaders, university Fabians, and a number of tiny provincial socialist parties, had matured in the establishment of Canada's first country-wide socialist party, the Co-operative Commonwealth Federation (CCF). The CCF's Regina Manifesto of 1933 spelled out a full democratic-socialist program. Its clause on foreign policy was precise: 'We believe that genuine international cooperation is incompatible with the capitalist regime which is in force in most countries, and that strenuous efforts are needed to rescue the League from its present position of being mainly a league of capitalist Great Powers. We stand resolutely against participation in imperialist wars ... Canada must refuse to be entangled in any more wars fought to make the world safe for capitalism.'

As the CCF's national president, Woodsworth dissociated the party completely from the Communist campaign for a 'united front,' on the grounds that Communists accepted the inevitability of violence in the overthrow of capitalism. He was less successful, however, in combatting erosion of support for unqualified neutrality within the CCF itself. Though a great many Canadians, including not a few in government, favoured isolationism in the late 1930s, support for neutrality dwindled in the face of German threats and growing evidence about the nature of Nazism. Among the seven CCF MPs and in the party at large, uneasiness spread inexorably. Woodsworth's eldest daughter, Grace, and her husband, Angus MacInnis, returned from a 1936 European trip persuaded that Hitler might have to be opposed by force if all else failed. Other party leaders such as David Lewis and M.J. Coldwell argued that neither socialism nor unionism would be safe in a world dominated by the Nazis.

When Britain finally declared war on Germany on 3 September 1939, Prime Minister King summed Parliament to decide Canada's position. The outcome, as Woodsworth had with mounting gloom foretold, was no surprise; arrangements for complete military cooperation with Britain had already been made, and the Commons debate would be perfunctory – despite French-Canadian reluctance. Less perfunctory, if equally predictable, was discussion in the CCF's national-council emergency meeting. In that conclave Woodsworth moved: 'That this Council refuse to discuss any measure that will put Canada into the war.'[20] After heart-rending rehearsal of all the arguments, his resolution was lost.

For Woodsworth the time of choosing the lesser of two evils had passed. Resigning his leadership, he decided to speak for himself (and for the many CCFers across the country who would be shaken by the council's reversal of policy) in the special session of Parliament that would authorize George VI to declare war on behalf of Canada. Preparing the House for Woodsworth's lonely testament, the prime minister had defended the impending war declaration: 'You can persuade men; you can convert them, but there are times – and history is there to record them – when if force had not been opposed by force there would have been no Christianity left to defend.'[21]

When Woodsworth rose to speak in a House that was nearly silent, if largely hostile, he reviewed his past warnings about refusing to take the League seriously, about condoning violation of covenants, about creating the conditions favorable to the rise of a Hitler, and about permitting the profitable flow of war materials to Germany and Japan. 'I submit,' he said, 'that if any shooting is to be done the first people who should face the firing squad are those who have made money out of a potential enemy.' Then, with palpable tension, he gave his ultimate testimony:

I left the ministry of the church during the last war because of my ideas on war. Today I do not belong to any church organization. I am afraid that my creed is pretty vague. But even in this assembly I venture to say that I still believe in some of the principles underlying the teachings of Jesus and the other great world teachers throughout the centuries ... War is an absolute negation of anything Christian. The Prime Minister, as a great many do, trotted out the 'mad dog' idea; said that in the last analysis there must be a resort to force. It requires a great deal of courage to trust to moral force. But there was a time when people thought that there were other and higher types of force than brute force ... Yes, I have boys of my own and I hope that they are not cowards, but if any of those boys, not from cowardice but really through belief, is willing to take his stand on this matter and, if necessary, to face a concentration camp or a firing squad, I shall be more proud of that boy than if he enlisted for the war.

At this point came the single interjection – a cry of 'shame' from an outraged patriot. It prompted Woodsworth to conclude his statement thus: 'Now you can hammer me as much as you like. I must thank the House for the great courtesy it has shown me. I rejoice that it is possible to say these things in a Canadian Parliament under British institutions. It would not be possible in Germany, I recognize that ... and I want to maintain the very essence of our British institutions of real liberty. I believe that the only way to do it is by an appeal to the moral forces still resident among our people, and not by another resort to brute force.'

In his long struggle for peace, social justice, freedom of speech, and democratic socialism, Woodsworth had shown remarkable realism as he worked within the constraints of an increasingly political life. He rejected slavish acceptance of dogma; he saw his own inconsistencies. But on the futile wickedness of war he gave not an inch. Like all prophets he was greatest as critic. As such he lived essentially in isolation – an isolation the more complete because of his moral courage.

In the snap wartime election of 1940 Woodsworth retained his Winnipeg constituency with a much-reduced majority. He had, however, suffered two strokes and died in 1942.

NOTES

1 Canada, *Debates* of the House of Commons, Special Session, 1939, 19ff.
2 Kenneth McNaught, *A Prophet in Politics: A Biography of J.S. Woodsworth* (Toronto 1959), 4.
3 Ibid., 18.
4 Ibid., 87.
5 Thomas P. Socknat, *Witness against War: Pacifism in Canada, 1900–1945* (Toronto 1987).
6 McNaught, *A Prophet*, 131.
7 Ibid., 26.
8 In these years Woodsworth wrote two thoroughly researched books on immigration and urban social problems: *Strangers within Our Gates*, first pub. 1909 (Toronto 1972), and *My Neighbour*, first pub. 1911 (Toronto 1972).
9 McNaught, *A Prophet*, 76.
10 Ibid., 82ff.
11 *Western Labour News Strike Bulletin*, 17 May 1919.
12 Ibid., 21 June 1919.
13 J.S. Woodsworth, *The First Story of the Labour Church* (Winnipeg 1920), 13.
14 Allen Mills, *Fool for Christ: The Political Thought of J.S. Woodsworth* (Toronto 1991), 195.
15 Especially *Imperialism*; but also *The Economics of Unemployment* and *The Evolution of Modern Capitalism*.
16 Woodsworth had read Thorstein Veblen's *Theory of the Leisure Class*.
17 Canada, *Debates* of the House of Commons, 1935, 2292.
18 Ibid., 1923ff.
19 *Manitoba Commonwealth*, 25 Dec. 1936.
20 McNaught, *A Prophet*, 305.
21 Canada, *Debates* of the House of Commons, Special Session, 1939, 42, 43.

13

'Practical' and Absolute Pacifism in the Early Years of the U.S. Women's International League for Peace and Freedom

ANNE MARIE POIS

The Women's International League for Peace and Freedom (WILPF) confronted challenges to define its pacifist identity and to establish a women's peace and justice community in the years immediately following the First World War. As full citizens who had withstood the surge of wartime nationalism and opposed the war, the women of WILPF committed themselves to building a peaceful world but faced a number of choices about how best to work for their goals. During 1919–21 WILPF, and in particular its US section (WILPF US), debated the use of pledges as a means of giving concrete and explicit expression to members' pacifism. More militant pacifist women promoted two types of pledges as requirements for membership in WILPF US and the international body. One was a pledge of non-resistance, which upheld the inviolability of all human life under all circumstances, while the other required a vow of non-participation in any future wars. Pledges gained support among many because they offered women a public means of repudiating war, of adopting the stance of war resistance. The ensuing controversy surrounding pacifist pledges and its resolution shaped the group's organizational basis and political approach, while revealing the contours of community in this first international women's peace group.

The issue of pledges within WILPF reflected concerns of postwar pacifists everywhere who felt impelled to search for ways to prevent such a devastating war from ever occurring again. Aside from using a pledge to establish a group's pacifist identity, activists employed the strategy of circulating pacifist pledges widely among the general population. Pacifists believed that if masses of people publicly committed themselves to refuse to participate in any future war, governments would not attempt to pursue war and be forced to follow peaceful methods. Such war resistance had backing in Germany and Austria in the 1920s, but during the interwar period pledges proved to have the most support in Great Britain and the United States.[1] Albert Einstein's 1928 commentary on pledges reveals the thinking of such pacifists: 'I am convinced that the international movement to refuse participation in any kind of war service is one of the most encouraging developments of our time. Every thoughtful, well-meaning and conscientious human being should assume, in time of peace, the solemn and unconditional obligation not to participate in any war, for any reason.'[2] While pledges became popular among some pacifists as a means of building war resistance, WILPF ultimately repudiated them.

In this essay I argue that WILPF US[3] rejected pacifist pledges mainly because of its support for the interrelated goals of developing a pluralistic women's peace community and an efficacious and diverse political program. Rejecting pledges did not imply that these women did not adhere to pacifist principles. Indeed, by 1920 the group's program included opposition to all wars, support for universal disarmament, and promotion of non-violent solutions to conflicts. Its pacifism, however, was informed by its belief in social justice and in transnational and feminist ideals. Bringing these elements together into a harmonious synthesis and translating them into consistent political practice was an important experiment for the group throughout the interwar years.

Zürich and After

Integral to this complex organizational identity were the feminist ideas and gendered view of politics to which the founders of WILPF adhered. When they first organized in 1915, social reformers and suffragists comprised the leadership and main constituency of the US Woman's Peace Party (WPP) and the International Committee of Women for Permanent Peace (ICWPP), established after the International Congress of Women at The Hague in 1915. From these two groups the international WILPF and WILPF US, respectively, emerged as a result of a congress in Zürich in 1919. Many members embraced women's equal citizenship and a female politics of moral and humanitarian reform of industrialized society. They had worked for years gradually to expand their public and political roles in an effort to make women's concerns for fostering human life part of male-dominated political life. The outbreak of the Great War only served to highlight the second-class status of these privileged, white, middle-class women when it came to crucial political, foreign-policy, and military decision-making. They accepted their share of culpability for the war and resolved to assume their responsibility for creating peace and freedom in the postwar world. Thus these reformers and suffragists, combining the reform impulse for social justice and the demand for women's equality with the now-urgent need for peace, became feminist peace activists.

In the formative years, the organization's commitment to transnationalism provided another crucial factor in shaping WILPF's identity. Its members viewed the world's peoples as interconnected, sharing many of the same human needs and aspirations. The world for them was a web of communities, where communal values of respect for diversity and mutual responsibility for the quality of life would someday emerge. As the organization took shape, key leaders, such as Jane Addams and Emily Greene Balch, first international secretary, sought to translate such principles into organizational practice and culture. This impetus also emerged from a strong belief that women in particular could transcend nationalism and cooperate to work for a nonviolent and just world. They wished to form a pluralistic organization that was inclusive and practised respect for diversity. They desired to create a women's peace community, as well as an activist reform group. Such pluralism meant in practice that members viewed certain components of the WILPF credo as more significant than others; for some, resisting injustice might take precedence over adherence to strict pacifist principles. Most important, however, leaders desired to maintain diversity and find ways to translate their principles into a political program. Soon after the war the debate over pacifist pledges provided the first major challenge to the development of a pluralistic community that upheld and acted on pacifist ideals.

In the autumn of 1919 prospects for revitalizing a US women's peace movement were uncertain. Even after the Zürich congress gave birth to the WILPF in the spring – an act that motivated American women to return home to build a new organization on the foundations of the WPP, the immediate work proved daunting indeed. The WPP since 1917 had dwindled to a small, committed core of women opposed to American participation in the First World War – a group that was mostly inactive, except for the New York branch. Thus when the WPP met and re-formed as the US section of WILPF (WILPF US) in the autumn, the women needed to address basic questions about the nature of its future organization, membership, and program. In addition, the intense nationalism generating during the war continued, creating a climate of hatred for groups and individuals deemed un-American. For instance, Jane Addams, who was targeted for 'smearing' as a 'Red' by super-patriots, thought the times inauspicious for active organizing in the United States. She chose to focus on building the international WILPF and providing famine relief for the millions of malnourished central and eastern Europeans.[4] As the decade began, WILPF US was in flux, as the women essentially started a new group in a nation at peace, but hardly congenial towards peace reform.

Anna Garlin Spencer, newly elected president of WILPF US, surveyed the group's outlook and decided, in contrast to Addams, that it should quickly move to build a national membership that would engage actively in peace work in the

United States and thus support the international platform set up at Zürich. In a letter to Addams, she wrote, 'I am eager for the development of an earnest and widespread movement in the United States.' Emily Balch, from her vantage point as international secretary in Geneva, encouraged Spencer to support their European WILPF sisters by gaining new members in order to build WILPF into a strong international group composed of vital national sections.[5] As Spencer made plans in the spring of 1920 to publicize and expand WILPF US, the issue of pacifist pledges first emerged from the Women's Peace Society (WPS), another newly organized women's peace group.

WPS members were no strangers to WILPF women. Its leaders, including Caroline Lexow Babcock, Elinor Byrns, and Fanny Garrison Valliard, had all been members of the activist New York branch of the WPP. By 1917, anti-war work absorbed most of their attention; they resigned their positions in suffrage organizations after these groups adopted a pro-war position. They then left the NY WPP in September 1918 because they rejected its broad social-justice approach. Instead they wished to work solely on non-resistance and peace issues, such as anti-militarism. The WPS thus formed in early 1919 as a women's non-resistant pacifist group.[6]

While a relative latecomer to the suffrage movement, Fanny Garrison Villard, president of the WPS, had responded immediately to the outbreak of the Great War by organizing a women's protest march against the war in August 1914. She combined the belief that women as mothers and as the moral caretakers of society had a special duty to protest war with the philosophy of non-resistance developed by her father, William Lloyd Garrison. The Garrisonian idea of non-resistance required absolute commitment to non-violence, opposition to war, and recognition that human life is sacred. The WPS thus required all members to pledge: 'Believing that under no circumstances is it right to take human life, I hereby apply for membership in the Women's Peace Society and pledge myself to further its high aims by every means in my power.'[7] The group quickly established itself, and by late 1920 it had one thousand members.

Even as they expanded their membership, leaders of the WPS challenged both US and international WILPF in a number of ways that caused WILPF's leadership to reflect more deeply on the nature of its pacifism and organization. The WPS began to send its literature to European members of WILPF, appealing for women to join a truly pacifist group, one to which Jane Addams belonged. At the same time, WILPF members in New York heard that Villard made claims that the WPS was a part of WILPF – at times asserting that it was the US section of WILPF! Eleanor Karsten, secretary of WILPF US, wrote to Balch to clarify whether both the WPS and her group could affiliate as US national sections with the international WILPF.[8]

Further, WILPF members in New York, where the national office located in 1920, feared the possibility of confusion and competition between themselves and the WPS at home and in Europe.[9] Writing to Addams, Spencer voiced concern that rivalry from the WPS and its assertions of orthodox pacifism would lead to a split in the international WILPF. The militant pacifism of the WPS matched that of the German and Austrian members, who might be persuaded to join Villard's group 'under the mistaken belief that hers alone is "true blue."' In speaking to a visiting English member of WILPF, Spencer found her fearful of a schism in essence because members of her group would not take a pledge of non-resistance. For Spencer, the really tragic aspect of such a schism would be the fragmentation of the only truly international group of women. She noted that in contrast even the International Council of Women excluded German and Austrian women from meetings.[10]

While Spencer tried anxiously to arrange for a US member to go to the international executive meeting, her fears of an imminent 'take-over' by WPS proved premature. Leaders of both groups started a dialogue about their differences. Elinor Byrns of the WPS told Marion Cothren, the new WILPF US secretary, that her group was unwilling to join as a branch of WILPF US but did indeed wish admission as a separate section to the international WILPF. She felt that the WPS would be a small group and basically engage in educational efforts by circulating literature, while WILPF would undertake wider peace activism. Cothren even agreed to send out WPS literature as long as it made no appeals for membership.[11] Cothren may have been reassured by Byrns's letter to WPS members, which mentioned that their representative to various European meetings 'will make it clear that our society was organized, not because of any friction with the WIL, but merely because it has not endorsed the principle of non-resistance.'

In September, Byrns joined WILPF US, stating that women should affiliate with both groups because they stood for the same thing – except that the WPS also championed non-resistance.[12] While Byrns and Cothren endeavoured to develop a spirit of cooperation between the groups, the WPS insisted on maintaining its stance of unequivocal pacifism, expressed in its pledge, arguing that this constituted a key difference separating the two groups. The emerging issues seemed to be which group best represented a commitment to peace and how WILPF US could best define its pacifism.

During this same period in Geneva, Balch, as international secretary of WILPF and as an American concerned with the US section, grappled with the challenges and issues raised by the WPS. After her initiation as a pacifist activist during the Great War, Balch's commitment to peace work flowered after the war's conclusion. Fired from Wellesley College for participation in anti-war activities, she began a second career working for WILPF. Balch considered herself a pacifist and believed that WILPF stood for unequivocal pacifist principles.

Indeed, at the Zürich congress of 1919, members showed a passionate commitment to ending war and violence. One memorable incident occurred when Lida Heymann of Germany greeted the late-arriving French delegates with flowers and warm embraces. Jeanne Melin encouraged women of the world to develop their power as citizens in order to work for peace by ending nationalist hatreds and militarism. The friendship that French and German women displayed there stood in stark contrast to the continuing nationalist rancor and to the despair of those mourning the dead millions. Deeply moved, Balch asked the congress delegates to stand and vow 'to do everything in their power towards the ending of war and the coming of permanent peace.'[13] The assembly rose and pledged together. This collective act came to haunt Balch when the pledge debate heated up, because various women interpreted this dramatic action as a formal pledge that committed WILPF to absolute pacifism.

The Zürich congress also passed a resolution reiterating the group's opposition to war as a means of settling disputes and another urging the national sections 'to work for an international agreement between women to refuse their support of war in money, work or propaganda.'[14] German and Austrian delegates presented the 'war strike' resolution, and subsequently their sections gathered signatures supporting a pledge. Given these recent events, Balch was puzzled by news of the WPS's invitation to European WILPF members to join together in a women's international peace society, which stood 'uncompromisingly for non-resistance under all circumstances.'[15]

In 1920, Balch wrote two letters to Villard in order to convey her reasoned opposition to Villard's appeals for forming another international women's peace group. She wrote one in April and one in September, both of which she circulated among WILPF US leaders. Balch confessed that she had written many drafts of the letter, since she feared doing more harm than good' with regard to resolving the two groups' differences.[16] Since it is unclear whether Balch ever sent the letters to Villard, their importance lies in Balch's defence of WILPF's pacifism and her approach to organizing.

In the first letter Balch listed resolutions passed at Zürich and noted the spontaneous and informal vow by members there to prevent war, all of which meant that the international group 'as a whole has chosen the uncompromising path of out and out pacifism.' She insisted that both groups shared the same goal: 'the most far-reaching peace action possible.' WILPF had not yet achieved a popularity that threatened to dilute principles – it was still in its 'Christians-in-the-Catacombs period.'[17]

In her second letter, Balch qualified more carefully her assertions of WILPF's pacifism in the light of the growing pressure to require pledges as part of membership. She claimed that the group at Zürich had not pledged 'never again to support future wars' or to organize an international strike against war by women. She felt that the majority of members opposed efforts to secure signatures to a pledge to refuse to support any war because it was not 'a fruitful line of effort in most countries.' At the same time she did appreciate efforts by WILPF's German women and others to get pledges.[18]

By this time, as the popularity of pledges grew among more militant pacifists, Balch realized that pledges had become the defining proof of pacifism. She found herself interpreting recent developments at Zürich not as evidence of WILPF's pacifism but as proof that WILPF had no pledge requirements and that obtaining them was not a priority on its agenda. In short, as Balch saw it, WILPF was in reality a pacifist group that did not require pledges or collect them.

For Balch, pacifist principles did not exist in a vacuum of abstraction but were instead the foundation for peace work carried on by diverse women. Thus in defending and then qualifying the WILPF's pacifism in these letters, she also related peace thinking to group organizing. In both letters Balch endorsed the idea of 'many rather homogeneous peace groups, acting freely and not hampering one another.' She believed in 'different groups speaking in a little different accent or approaching the subject from a little different angle or led by persons that appeal to different determinations.'[19] In a place such as New York City, Balch envisioned six women's peace groups using their own methods to exert political pressure for their particular programs more effectively than one large group. Cooperation and coalitions could be fostered by annual conferences meeting under the auspices of WILPF US, which she imagined might coordinate a women's peace movement. While this was an invitation to the WPS to cooperate with WILPF, Balch's musings reveal her commitment to pluralism. There was room for diversity, and autonomy, even as women worked together for peace under WILPF's umbrella.[20]

Balch did acknowledge the difficulties that diversity caused within WILPF US. According to her, the US section differed from European ones, since it included from its beginnings a conservative group of women of the 'Hague-and-League-of-Nations' variety. While its timidity hindered 'their common action at times,' Balch thought that 'on the whole we did well to keep in fellowship.'[21]

Conflicting Visions

By the autumn of 1920, the future of such fellowship seemed dubious, as Balch found that pledges to demonstrate pacifist purity had become threats to a working community of peace activists. In writing to a militant member of the WILPF US executive committee who decried the lack of pacifist conviction among her colleagues, Balch provided her view of the importance of preserving community values in WILPF. She wrote: 'I am one of those terrible moderate half and half people who always want to include everybody. I am terribly afraid of all sorts of tests, creeds and dogmas. I believe that every attempt to find an exact common formula for a belief creates schisms and separation and that what unites people is a common purpose. If people will unite with me in trying to make war for ever impossible, to educate people away from the spirit that breeds wars and to correct the injustices that make wars possible, I am most happy to cooperate with them whether or not they would say that a group of Armenian men trapped in a valley by Curds [sic] ought not to attempt to defend their women by arms. That sort of question leads to endless casuistry.'[22]

Thus, in Balch's eyes, pledges distracted women from the real work of translating principles into a peace program and went against respect for diversity – a value that cemented this mosaic of peace groups. At the same time Balch recognized the dilemma of maintaining the group's inclusiveness and unity, given differences between radicals and conservatives.

Balch herself helped to deepen divisions within the US section by requesting the international executive committee, which met in Geneva in June 1920, to consider a new objective for WILPF. At the Zürich congress of 1919, WILPF delegates chose a fairly nondescript 'object,' which stated that the organization stood for the resolutions passed by the congress. Balch may have felt the need for a more explicit definition of WILPF's peace work because of questions raised by the WPS, but her expressed reason was simply that the 'object' was too 'clumsy.' A committee wrote drafts of an objective; Balch then edited the final version. It began with the statement: 'The WILPF aims at binding together women in every country who will give no support, direct or indirect to any war.'[23]

This opening phrase caused great consternation among members of the WILPF US executive board. While admitting that many members agreed with this introductory clause, the board protested that this aim of non-participation in war in effect made the Zürich congress's resolution number 37 – which urged national sections to work for a women's war-strike pledge – a test of membership for WILPF.[24] Marion Cothren thought that the new 'object' had changed the original basis of membership too fundamentally; now WILPF appeared to require members to be non-resisters.[25] This pacifist approach was 'the exact line of demarcation between Mrs. Villard's Society and ours.'[26]

Addams, in writing to Balch, concurred with Cothren's opinion and questioned whether the international executive committee could make such a drastic revision, especially since no WILPF US representative had attended. Addams

BART DE LIGT

THE CONQUEST OF VIOLENCE

AN ESSAY ON WAR AND REVOLUTION

INTRODUCTION BY ALDOUS HUXLEY

NEW INTRODUCTION BY PETER VAN DEN DUNGEN

Libertarian Critique

Bart de Ligt: Painting by Ingrid van Peski–de Ligt

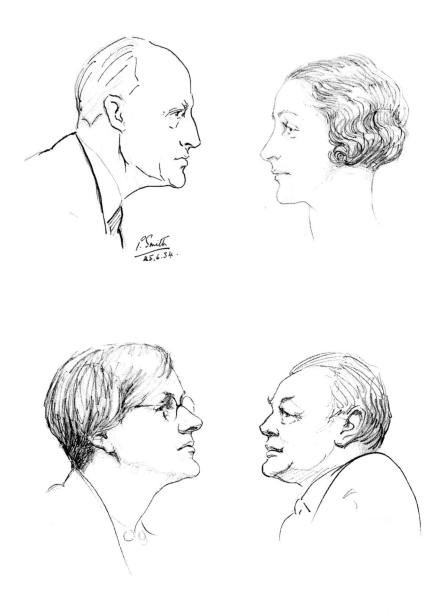

Drawings of leading British pacifists of the interwar period by Peggy Smith: Lord Ponsonby, Vera Brittain, Maude Royden, H.R.L. ('Dick') Sheppard

James Shaver Woodsworth

Volunteer from Friends Ambulance Unit addressing Chinese villagers during the Second World War

Canadian conscientious objectors in alternative service work camp. Jasper National Park, Alberta

Civilian Public Service kitchen crew at Luray, Virginia

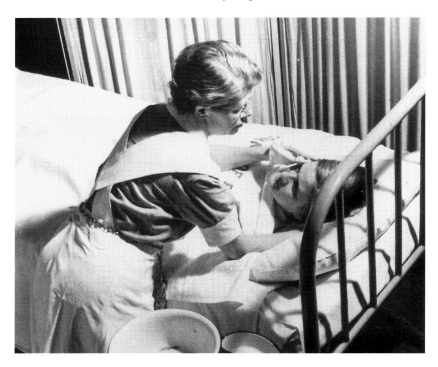

Pacifist woman giving bed bath to patient in Philadelphia State Hospital, 1944

Lobby poster of Lew Ayres, *All Quiet on the Western Front,* 1930

Lew Ayres as Paul Baumer in *All Quiet on the Western Front*

Peggy Smith 1931

Mohandas Karamchand Gandhi: drawing by Peggy Smith, 1931

added, 'Of course it is impossible not to give indirect support to war in war time and that is the pity of it all.'[27] From her perspective, strict pacifist principles always gave way to humanitarian ones of helping those in need, as evidenced by her work with food conservation and famine relief.

Balch regretted the revision on hearing of the reaction of WILPF US. She did not agree with the US leaders that the new 'object' was a test of membership, but if they understood it to be one, they could change it at the next congress. Opposing any sort of test for membership, Balch asserted, 'What I feel strongly is that it is too stupid to let any division arise through differences of opinion on this point when there is so much to be done to prevent a war cloud upon the horizon from developing.'[28] While Balch wished the American section to refocus on political work, the issue of pledges and defining the pacifist identity of WILPF US continued to occupy the group.

The divisions between radicals and conservatives grew that autumn of 1920, as more leaders supporting absolute pacifism and 'pledges' took an activist role in WILPF US. Some supported joining the WPS and adopting absolute pacifism. Yella Hertzka, a visiting Austrian member of WILPF and early promoter of the war-strike pledge, criticized WILPF US as dominated by 'timid old women' and thought the WPS 'more worthwhile, younger, more active and courageous.'[29]

Even the chair of the US section, Mabel Hyde Kittredge, lamented what she saw as a weak-spirited group that had no unified message, purpose, or program to rally women to the cause of peace. Thinking that the WPS offered an uncompromising stance more in harmony with European WILPF members and the Zürich congress resolutions, she wrote to Jane Addams: 'I think that Mrs. Villard takes a stronger stand than ours, more real and gripping. They are absolutely non-resistant and not afraid.' Further, she recommended that 'those who are not absolute non-resistants should not belong to the W.I.L.' Once WILPF US became an absolute-pacifist group, those disagreeing could cooperate loosely, and in time, she asserted, they would rejoin. Kittredge insisted that she would not desert Addams but added, 'I am not able to make a dead thing live and I cannot find the life.' In a telegraphed reply, Addams advised Kittredge to make no drastic changes at the time, but they could consider 'possible amalgamation' at their annual meeting. She closed with: 'In despair if [you] do not stick.'[30]

In retrospect, WILPF US appeared to be weak and paralysed, but it was going through a period of development, which entailed a necessary formulation of its peace principles, organizational basis, and political program. As 1921 approached, pacifist pledges clearly remained a significant and divisive issue. WILPF US faced a number of choices. It could adopt a pledge of non-resistance and/or a war-strike pledge. If it did, WILPF US could join with the WPS but in so doing would lose many members just as it was experiencing slow, but steady growth. The leadership could also hold wider and more open discussions and let the members decide for themselves. WILPF US embarked on this latter course, which entailed discussions that took place during the next year and a half.

A few new leaders in WILPF US – Ellen Winsor, her sister Mary Winsor, who was closely affiliated with the WPS, and Harriet Connor Brown – promoted militant pacifism. They supported a women's pledge of non-support or non-participation in any future wars as key aspects of membership and a program for WILPF US. For militants who defined themselves as war resisters, the WPS's pledge of non-resistance was too vague and thus assumed less importance as an objective. The war-strike pledge of course was similar to the one adopted by the German and Austrian sections of WILPF and which, though phrased variously, proved popular among pacifists in the 1920s and 1930s.

Within the WPS itself, disagreement over its pledge arose early in 1921 between Fanny Villard and the younger leaders, such as Caroline Lexow Babcock and Elinor Byrns. Byrns wished to rephrase the pledge so that all members refused any activities that sanctioned wars, including relief work. Villard, who confessed to having bought Liberty Bonds during the war, favoured the original, which was more flexible and had broader membership appeal. Desiring to combine the philosophy of non-resistance with an active political program, Byrns stated, 'I would gladly reduce our membership to fifty if only fifty are ready to be practical as well as theoretical non-resistants.'[31] By the summer of 1921, Byrns and other militants split off from the WPS and formed the Women's Peace Union of the Western Hemisphere, which required the more definitive pledge of war resistance. On this basis, they defined a political program for the interwar years.

At the same time as the WPS was experiencing controversy, WILPF US moved boldly to offer a war-strike pledge to its members. The militants in particular backed a plan of Harriet Connor Brown to experiment with an optional membership pledge. Those attending the executive committee's meeting claimed that they could take this action without prior approval by the whole committee because 'adherence to the pledge was not a prerequisite to membership of the League.' The national office subsequently sent members the pledge, which stated: 'Believing that true Peace can be secured only through reconciliation and good will and that no cause justifies the organized destruction of Human Life, I urge immediate disarmament and promise never to aid in any way in the prosecution of War.'[32] Those willing to take it sent in their names.

Brown, who represented WILPF at hearings of the U.S. Congress to oppose military appropriations, wrote a pamphlet titled *America Menaced by Milita-*

rism: An Appeal to Women, which the national office also sent to members. Brown urged women to exercise their newly acquired political power to defeat the militarists' bloated and wasteful spending program, which if passed would leave no resources for women's reform and social justice and realization of dreams 'of a glorified earth without sickness or poverty or ignorance or crime.'[33] After analysing the military and civilian budgets, Brown proposed a list of actions against militarism. These included organizing in every congressional district, demanding that newly elected President Harding call a disarmament conference, and joining WILPF US, which would connect women internationally. Most important, women needed to sign a pledge of resistance to war. According to Brown, this method of war resistance, as yet untried, would put men on notice that when they declared war, 'they would go without women.' Resisting with 'tongue and pen, with brain and ballot, with moral and spiritual forces,' women must adopt 'this passive strike against war and preparation for war'; they must 'try this means of stopping the mad suicide of the race.'[34] Brown then presented an ambitious program that linked a war-strike pledge to a political program of disarmament and anti-militarism.

WILPF US supported a program of disarmament and opposition to military spending, as witnessed by its involvement with peace groups at the Washington Disarmament Congress of 1921. During the annual meeting, members praised Brown for her work at the hearings, but they offered little support for the pledge that Brown had recommended as a significant part of their program. Jane Addams reported that Illinois members opposed this 'credal method.' Delegates at the annual meeting voted that 'individual members might feel free to sign or not as their judgment dictated.'[35] Their action did not, however, put to rest the pledge controversy. Showing a desire to air the issue internationally, the annual meeting voted to extend an invitation to Fanny Villard to attend the upcoming Vienna congress of the international WILPF in order to speak about the WPS's pledge of non-resistance.

The Vienna Congress, 1921

The Vienna congress proved a turning point in the debate over pacifist pledges. In contrast to the Zürich congress, where pacifist resolutions caused less debate, the main obstacles by 1921 were requiring pledges for membership and determining how these pledges related to political work. In keeping with its practice of open discussion, the congress heard from all sides on the question.

The Austrian and German delegates gave impassioned speeches in support of a women's war-strike pledge as a true affirmation of WILPF ideals. It was a matter of principle for them, as well as a political program that would lead to a mass movement of war resistance. Olga Misar (Austria), backing a newly worded pledge, asserted that the WILPF should not focus on the League of Nations or revision of the peace treaties, which some delegates recommended for the focus of their work. According to Misar, the real end to war would come when the masses of people refused any form of war service. The incredible power of the people would prevent the diplomats from going to war. If peace leaders believed in the pledge, they must have faith in the people and act in solidarity with them. For her, the will of the people was stronger than cannons. German delegates insisted that they had discussed and shown great support for this pledge at Zürich and that the time was ripe for women to make it an oath for members.[36]

Opposition to a membership pledge was strong as well. As her call for a pledge at the Zürich congress continued to haunt her, Balch reminded the women of the German 'misunderstanding' of the spontaneous pledge taken at Zürich; they had not taken an oath to refuse war service, they had promised to oppose all war. Ethel Williams (Great Britain) raised a point of order: a pledge would change the basis of membership in the league, something that could be done only in consultation with the national sections. Gabrielle Duchene (France) agreed with Williams and added that each section should decide how these principles ought to be applied.

Some delegates asked for a delay on the vote on the pledge resolution. Because of the divisions among the delegates, the committee reconsidered it through intense discussion and finally devised a resolution based on all opinions. This statement simply reiterated the resolution passed at Zürich, urging national sections to work for an international agreement among women to refuse support of war, but it made two additions. It expressed the unity of all sections 'as to the necessity of individual opposition against war' and stated that 'every section is however free to work for the attainment of this aim by any means which appear to it the most suitable.' The assembly voted for it – WILPF as an international group would not require members to take a pledge, though the resolution expressed support for the idea of such war resistance. Jane Addams interpreted this compromise as the result of 'practical' pacifism.[37] Indeed, she expressed her support for this decision, which respected the autonomy of individuals and national sections, as the best path for a women's peace community as diverse and inclusive as WILPF. The compromise based on 'practical' pacifism, however, gave little satisfaction to the passionate proponents of the initial resolution.

After this vote, Villard gave a speech promoting the pledge of nonresistance. In light of the previously heated discussion, it was anticlimactic, since the women had agreed that pledges were at most optional. She explained that non-resistance was 'not a state of passivity. On the contrary it is a state of activity, ever fighting the fight of faith, ever foremost to assail unjust power, ever struggling for liberty, equality, fraternity, in no national sense, but in a world-wide spirit. It is passive only in this sense, that it will not return evil for evil, not give blow for blow, nor resort to murderous weapons for protection or defense.'[38] Further, she linked nonresistance to the WPS program of universal and total disarmament and free trade. She, along with Mary Winsor, now offered a resolution that stated: 'Whereas we believe that wars will never cease until human life is held sacred and inviolable, be it hereby resolved that we adopt the principle and practice of Non-resistance under all circumstances.' There was no discussion, and before delegates voted, Addams made it clear that the vote expressed individual support only, and did not apply to the national sections. The majority voted in favour.[39]

Thus the conflict between absolute and 'practical' pacifism for the international WILPF was resolved through long discussions aimed at finding a common ground. Certainly some women desired a more concrete and militant definition of pacifism during this formative stage. Earlier congresses had established WILPF as an inclusive and diverse group of pacifists, based on a shared sense of women's transnationalism, as well as rejection of war. As a diverse group of pacifists, some of the pragmatic members would not let the group tie itself to a fixed response to future events. Instead, their urge for political activism led them to endorse a variety of paths, some of them perilous, for a 'true' pacifist to follow.

Proponents of pledges did not make it entirely clear how WILPF would translate pledges into an immediate and varied reformist program. Endorsing militant pacifism, however, might have been a first step in defining women's war resistance – a prospect far too radical for a majority of the sections, which desired political efficacy even as they envisioned a just and peaceful world. Significantly, this conflict did not lead to resignations or splits. WILPF still provided a community for women peace activists who, despite differences, could count on an open forum for their ideas – one that hardly existed for women in male- and military-centred national governmental institutions.

Annual Meeting, 1922

While the Vienna congress ended the debate on pledges of nonresistance and nonparticipation in war, US militants pressed for further debate. The Winsor sisters and others desired a definitive organizational commitment to absolute pacifism. In December 1921, Ellen Winsor offered a resolution to the executive committee that asked for a special convention of WILPF US to consider both pledges and also the causes of war and future methods of work. Expressing opposition, the committee recommended instead that the annual meeting in April should discuss it.[40]

WILPF US's annual meeting of 1922 was the last forum for formal debate on pledges. Ellen Winsor offered a resolution written by Lola Maverick Lloyd, which outlined the types of activities that women should refuse to do during war. She also moved that a pledge of such refusal be made a test of membership, which would in effect amend the body's constitution. The pledge stated: 'In case our country is at war, I will not join nor work for the Red Cross, nor make hospital supplies; I will not urge food conservation; I will not buy Liberty Bonds or any other similar war loans; I will not make munitions nor take a man's place in order to enable him to go to war.'[41] While Winsor prefaced her speech by saying that she did not wish to criticize anybody, by essentially attacking women's war work during the First World War she indirectly attacked women such as Jane Addams, who had participated in food-conservation programs. Her comments sharply delineated the 'true' pacifist from the 'practical,' humanitarian pacifist.

She began by denouncing all women's wartime activities as essentially hypocritical, in that they provided the sinews of war or promoted military victory. Since women were essential to winning wars, they had to take a stance against women's participation in war-related work and adopt a new way of thinking in preparation for future conflicts. She said: 'We cannot be militarists and pacifists. Some people say: "I am a pacifist, but I cannot take the pledge because I don't know what I would do if my country were attacked." I say, if I reserve to myself the right to shed blood when I think the occasion demands it, where do I differ from militarists who think the same?'[42]

Winsor thought that pacifists were 'discredited' because they insisted that war was the greatest crime and then went on to support their government's war effort. The time had come for women to abide by their convictions and form an organization of women who would not participate in war. They could lead the movement against war. She asserted that 'women must join with the working classes of the world and resist what the governing classes of men want, and to uphold the moral idea of peace, security and dignity instead of blindly following on as women have done through the ages, by doing this or doing that, and staying at home when they wanted us to do it.'[43] Thus Winsor's speech suggested that women's acknowledged peacetime passive resistance to war through a pledge could have real political ramifications. The meeting received this speech with great applause.

Following Winsor's remarks, Villard spoke in favour of a pledge of passive resistance by once again underscoring her absolutist belief in the sacredness of human life. She criticized the lack of inspiration shown by the Vienna congress and once again reminded her audience of the 'pledge' of nonresistance that Emily Balch had invited the participants at Zürich to take. Villard insisted that women stand for principle, because, as her father used to say, 'moderation in theory is perpetuity in practice.' Indeed, this pledge could give people strength to make a real commitment against war. WILPF US could lead the way, for not only were the women of Europe waiting to follow its example, but men would support this opportunity to 'save mankind.' In response, Addams rebutted Villard's version of the Zürich 'pledge' and interjected some background information about the debate over pledges at Vienna. She pointed out that a number of national sections could not accept this pledge. One implication was that it would damage the internationalism of the WILPF.[44]

The ensuing debate revealed a number of viewpoints, mostly in opposition to pledges. Some felt that it would hurt organizational work to require the pledge as a prerequisite, and delegates from Chicago and Boston stated that their branches would not support a pledge. Yet another pointed out that, since Quakers did not make pledges (in fact she was confusing pledges with oaths), commitment to any pledge would cause a serious organizational dilemma. Others addressed the question of relating pledges to a political program of peace reform. Mrs Mathes, a leading member from Chicago, believed that pledges proved meaningless in the long run and insisted that in order to accomplish their purpose women should organize politically and help elect anti-war congressmen who would vote for US entrance into the World Court. Still others advocated working with other groups to attain the outlawry of war as the means to prevent war. At the end of the discussion, the women voted overwhelmingly against the pledge, and the controversy over this issue formally ended within the organization.[45]

Members of WILPF US by a clear majority rejected pacifist pledges for two related reasons: to preserve the inclusive and diverse nature of the organization and to pursue a reformist and pragmatic political strategy. Emily Balch best addressed the former in her international report to the annual meeting of 1922. Her report can be viewed as an attempt to foster unity among members as they faced this divisive issue by reminding them of their organizational process and basis. She wrote of the varied membership of WILPF, composed as it was of women of diverse nationalities, races, religions, and political affiliations as well as varying temperaments and approaches to peace work. Within sections they used a number of methods and cooperated with different groups. But she reminded the US women that they had a common aim. She wrote: 'What unites us is something more than the utter repudiation of all war ... It is a belief that it is possible, by positive methods free from violence and coercion, to lessen injustice and to actively create right conditions.' Balch pointed out that while the majority did not support pledges, its uncompromising attitude would in fact attract only those who 'turn their backs on war and oppose it and all its works.' Finally, she spoke of the spirit in which members approached their work and, by extension, their dealings with one another as one of conciliation, tolerance, and collaboration. Their respect for diversity meant 'a vivid pleasure in the element of unlikeness and variety.'[46] Repudiating pledges for Balch thus meant rejecting dogma or a formulaic approach that would run counter to the diversity of groups and stifle their attempts to actualize their values within an inclusive community.

Second, these women rejected pledges because they, as organized citizens, hoped to effect change through influencing the political process. The delegates' opposition represented an expression of support for political methods that would allow for a broad and diverse political program. By endorsing a strict and, for many, radical membership requirement, they would keep potential supporters away and perhaps exclude gradualist approaches to reform. The American women of WILPF, by virtue of their commitment to active political reform, supported a flexible definition of pacifism, of 'practical' pacifism, which in turn promoted an inclusive organization.

Epilogue

While the debate over pacifist pledges ended in 1922, other controversies within WILPF during the interwar years revealed the continuing tensions about members' identity as pacifists. In contrast to WILPF US, the women of the Women's Peace Union, by requiring adherence to absolute pacifism, created a more cohesive group, which, however, did not survive. WILPF US had members who located themselves all along the spectrum of opinion opposed to war. Adherents included many absolute pacifists – most notably, US Quaker women, whose politics at base were shaped by a pacifist 'faith.' During the 1930s, when the world faced fascist and other militarist onslaughts, WILPF experienced increasing dissent as peace and justice issues divided into choices for peace or justice. And during the Second World War, absolute pacifists sustained WILPF US, when many 'practical' pacifists left the organization. Women such as Emily Balch, facing the dilemma that confronted all those committed to a non-violent and just world, chose not to oppose the war but still remained within the WILPF community. WILPF survived the war to continue working for peace and justice, bringing together once again practical and absolute pacifists. That it could revitalize itself was a legacy of the commitment by the early women of WILPF to the values of their women's peace community.[47]

NOTES

1 Peter Brock, *Twentieth-Century Pacifism* (New York 1970), 110–11.

2 Quoted in Ibid., 130–1.

3 Carrie A. Foster deals in a more general way with pledges and the early WILPF US in *The Women and the Warriors: The U.S. Section of the Women's International League for Peace and Freedom, 1915–1946* (Syracuse, NY, 1995), 38–45.

4 Jane Addams to Anna Garlin Spencer, 2 Dec. 1919, Eleanor Barr, ed., *Records of the WILPF U.S. Section, 1919–1959*, microfilm edition (Wilmington, DC: Scholarly Resources, 1988), reel 38. These papers are located at Swarthmore College Peace Collection, Swarthmore, Pa.

5 Anna Garlin Spencer to Jane Addams, 23 Feb. 1920, *Records of WILPF*, 38.

6 Harriet Hyman Alonso, *The Women's Peace Union and the Outlawry of War, 1921–1942* (Knoxville, Ky., 1989), 9, 10.

7 Ibid., 14. Foster quotes not the original WPS pledge of 1919 but a later pledge, which Eleanor Byrns suggested in 1921 and which was adopted by the Women's Peace Union. See Foster, *The Women and the Warriors*, 39.

8 Eleanor Karsten to Emily Balch, 23 March 1920, and Karsten to Balch, 22 April 1920, Women's International League for Peace and Freedom Papers (WILPF Papers), Archives, University of Colorado at Boulder Libraries, series III, box 31, fldrs. 7 and 8. In fact, the structure of WILPF allowed for only one national section, composed in turn of local groups.

9 Karsten to Addams, 3 April 1920, *Records of WILPF*, reel 38.

10 Spencer to Addams, 2 May 1920, ibid.

11 Marion Cothren to Addams, 10, July 1920, ibid., reel 13.

12 Elinor Byrns to member, 30 June 1920, and Byrns to Cothren, 14 Sept. 1920, ibid., reel 42.

13 Women's International League for Peace and Freedom, *The Report of the International Congress of Women, Zürich, May 12th to 17th 1919* (Geneva 1920), 156, WILPF Papers, series V, box 5.

14 Ibid., 156–61, 261.

15 Fanny Garrison Villard and Elinor Byrns to the Women of Europe, undated, c. 1919, WILPF Papers, series II, box 4, fldr. 3.

16 Balch to Mrs Leach, 29 Sept. 1920, Mary Lynn McCree, ed., *Jane Addams Papers* (Ann Arbor, Mich., University Microfilms, 1985), reel 13, SCPC.

17 Balch to Villard, 1 April 1920, WILPF Papers, series II, box 4, fldr. 3.

18 Balch to Villard, 28 Sept. 1920, WILPF Papers, series II, box 4, fldr. 3.

19 Ibid.

20 Balch to Villard, 1 April 1920, WILPF Papers, series II, box 4, fldr. 3.

21 Ibid.

22 Balch to Ellen Winsor, 18 Oct. 1920, and see also Winsor to Balch, 30 Sept. 1920, WILPF Papers, series I, box 1, fldr. 14.

23 Minutes of the WILPF Executive Committee Meeting, Geneva, 1–4 June 1920, 8–9, WILPF Papers, series I, box 6 fldr. 8. In addition, the 'object' stated that the WILPF promoted 'the creation of international relations of mutual cooperation and good-will in which all wars shall be impossible, the establishment of political, social and moral equality between men and women and the introduction of these principles into all systems of education.'

24 Summary of Minutes, US WILPF, 28 Sept. 1920, *Records of WILPF*, reel 5.

25 The 1920 'object' of WILPF US stated that the group would promote 'methods for the attainment of that peace between nations which is based on justice and good will and to cooperate with women from other countries who are working for the same ends.' This statement was more moderate and far less specific than the international 'object.' See WILPF flier, 1920, *Records of WILPF*, reel 33.

26 Cothren to Balch, 5 Oct. 1920, WILPF Papers, series III, box 31, fldr. 8.

27 Addams to Balch, 26. Oct. 1920, *Jane Addams Papers*, reel 13.

28 Balch to Cothren, 19 Oct. 1920, WILPF Papers, series III, box 31, fldr. 8.

29 Alice Hamilton to Balch, 15 Oct. 1920, *Jane Addams Papers*, Reel 13, SCPC.

30 Kittredge to Addams, 31 Oct. 1920, and Addams to Kittredge, 2 Nov. 1920, *Records of WILPF*, 38.

31 Alonso, *Women's Peace Union*, 14–15.

32 Minutes of the Executive Committee Meeting, 6 January 1921, *Records of WILPF*, reel 5.

33 Harriet Connor Brown, 'America Menaced by Militarism: An Appeal to Women,' reprint (Washington, DC, 1921), 3, 4, *Records of WILPF*, reel 33.

34 Ibid., 24–6; see also 19–23, 27–31.

35 Minutes of the Annual Meeting, 11 April 1921, *Records of WILPF*, reel 5.

36 WILPF, *Report of the Third International Congress of Women, Vienna, July 10–17, 1921* (Vienna 1921), 103–6, WILPF Papers, series V, box 5.

37 Ibid., 107–9.

38 Ibid., 147.

39 Ibid., 148–50.

40 Minutes of the Executive Committee, 10 Dec. 1921, *Records of WILPF*, reel 5.

41 Minutes of the Annual Meeting, 28–30 April 1922, 4, *Records of WILPF*, reel 5.

42 Ibid., 6.

43 Ibid., 9.

44 Ibid., 9–13.

45 Ibid., 13–16.

46 'Report of Miss Balch to the Annual Meeting,' 28–30 April 1922, *Records of WILPF*, reel 5.

47 This essay was written in 1995 before the publication of Linda K. Schott, *Reconstructing Women's Thoughts: The Women's International League for Peace and Freedom before World War II* (Stanford, Calif., 1997). Schott's valuable intellectual history of the WILPF US analyzes the ideas of Jane Addams and Emily Greene Balch on peace and social justice.

14

The Fight against War of the Historic Peace Churches, 1919–1941

DONALD F. DURNBAUGH

In April 1922 Wilbur K. Thomas sent an appeal to a number of persons associated with North American religious bodies affirming 'both in creed and in practice that enduring Peace among peoples and Nations can only be secured by an earnest adherence to the teachings of Jesus.' Thomas was the executive of the recently founded and Philadelphia-based American Friends Service Committee (AFSC). He had taken up his duties in Pennsylvania after directing relief work in France and Belgium during the First World War, as well as in Germany, Austria, and Russia in the immediate postwar period. In reflecting about the past six years, Thomas concluded that the peace-oriented bodies had 'been sadly misunderstood,' and had 'suffered more or less of persecution.' Moreover 'the thought of their inability to prevent war or even utter an effective protest against it was so overwhelming that they either compromised or suffered in isolated silence.'

To break the sense of frustrated isolation, Thomas and a committee of invitation – largely from eastern Pennsylvania and comprised of members of the Society of Friends (Quakers) and the Brethren, Mennonite, and Schwenckfelder churches – announced a conference to be held at Bluffton College in Bluffton, Ohio, in early August 1922. Planners hoped to bring together those 'who profess discipleship of Jesus Christ and who hold that war has no place among Christians,' to discuss ways of furthering these convictions among other Christians.[1]

From 1919 to 1935

The mood of discouragement identified by the callers of the Bluffton conference accurately depicted the state of mind after 1918 of members of what came in the United States to be called the 'Historic Peace Churches.' Both elder statesmen and younger members among the Brethren, Friends, and Mennonites came out of the war with the conviction that their denominations had not been well prepared for the onslaught. A sobering number of their young men had abandoned long-standing peace principles and teachings of their church bodies to accept non-combatant and even full military service.

This declension had several causes. Members of the peace churches felt increasingly at home in the broader society, no longer living in isolated rural enclaves and following a plain way of life. This shift was more visible among the Brethren and Mennonites, whose German origins, Anabaptist foundations, and sectarian posture of withdrawal had kept them much farther from the mainstream than the Religious Society of Friends, with its Anglo-Saxon orientation, reforming posture, and positive understanding of human nature.

With this greater sense of being at home in the world, marked by more extensive employment in the professions and widescale abandonment of prescribed patterns of dress, it became much more difficult for Brethren and Mennonites, as well as Friends, to withstand the pressures and expectations of government in time of war. They were not immune from the effective and all-pervasive government propaganda that in 1917–18 swept the United States along in a war crusade. Appeals to contribute to a war that promised to make the world safe for democracy and to end all wars by defeating the 'bloodthirsty Hun' were hard to resist by those who wished to be understood as loyal citizens.[2]

Noted leaders among the Brethren advised their young members that the perquisites of citizenship also brought with them responsibilities of loyalty; they recommended acceptance of the non-combatant service called for in the conscription act passed by the US Congress in May 1917, soon after the US declaration of war in the previous month. The language of the bill permitted members of 'any well recognized religious sect,' the creed or principles of which 'forbid its members to participate in war in any form,' to avoid carrying weapons. They had, however, to perform non-combatant military duties in assignments to be spelled out later by the government.[3]

A combination of clever tactics on the part of the War Department and brutal treatment of conscientious objectors (COs) in the army camps to which they had been sent produced in large measure the desired result; of the perhaps 25,000 men who identified themselves as COs in 1917, only four thousand persisted to the end in refusing to take the non-combatant or full military options.[4]

Many of the young COs came out of their gruelling wartime experiences determined to throw their lives into programs of peace education and training so that another time of testing for their churches would find members better prepared to withstand its pressures. Virtually all of those who led the peace churches in the interwar period came from these ranks – Ray Newton, Clarence E. Pickett, and E. Raymond Wilson among the Friends; Harold S. Bender, Henry Fast, Guy F. Hershberger, and Orie O. Miller from the Mennonites; and Rufus D. Bowman, C. Ray Keim, Dan West, and M.R. Zigler, among the Brethren.

They were keenly aware of the mistreatment suffered in the army camps by many of their pacifist brethren. Thoughtful writers such as Guy F. Hershberger, C. Henry Smith, and Dan West prophesied that in another war even more stringent demands could be made. They were alert to the new developments of total war; nations with democratic political systems, ironically, were now even more insistent on complete participation by their citizens than autocratic regimes had been in the past. The excesses of the war just past raised in sensitive spirits auguries of worse yet to come.[5]

In a sense, the discouragement and disappointment felt by these young leaders mirrored the larger society after 1918. The fervour, superpatriotism, and crusade mentally of the war – worked up so successfully by Woodrow Wilson's administration – reverted to the cynical, disillusioned, and reckless mentality of the 'Jazz Age' of the 1920s. The 'return to normalcy' so touted in political slogans was actually marked by an unprecedented level of disregard for traditional morality and middle-class virtues.

The age was chronicled by F. Scott Fitzgerald in the decline and fall of his hero Gatsby; it was reflected in Ernest Hemingway's portrayal of a 'Lost Generation,' and in 'The Hollow Men' of the poet T.S. Eliot. A wave of literature and drama exposing the agonies and futilities of modern war augmented the mood of disillusionment and stoked anti-war sentiment. Laurence Stalling's *What Price Glory?* and Erich Maria Remarque's *All Quiet on the Western Front* are just two among a number of powerful indictments of war. Exposés of wartime propaganda, such as Harold D. Lasswell's *Propaganda Technique in the World War* and Sir Philip Gibbs's *Now It Can Be Told*, enlightened Americans about how they had been manipulated into war fever. Several books popularized the theme that 'merchants of death' – munitions makers and weapons dealers – had fomented national suspicions for their own economic advantage. The revelations of the hearings held by Senator Gerald P. Nye confirmed these suspicions in the minds of most Americans.[6]

Peace activists therefore had more than just their own church traditions to draw on as they sought to revitalize the peace witness. They could point to a growing perception among thoughtful people of the folly of war, in addition to their own religious values. True, many of their members had absorbed the wartime rhetoric, but there were increasingly evidences of the shortcoming of this burst of patriotic enthusiasm.

Wartime and Postwar Cooperation

Already during wartime, major steps had been taken that led later to a sense of unity among peace advocates. Chief among these was the cooperation they displayed with the Reconstruction Unit mounted by the American Friends to serve in war-torn France. It was the initial project of the AFSC, organized on 30 April 1917 by a group of Friends of different persuasions who wished to establish 'a service of love in wartime.' Their early announcement stressed their wish to serve their country loyally. 'We offer our services to the Government of the United States in any constructive work in which we can conscientiously serve humanity.' They anticipated (wrongly) that the federal government would completely exempt Friends from military service and, not wishing to take advantage of this situation, desired to show their willingness to contribute voluntarily. They believed that they 'could not accept exemption from military service and at the same time do nothing to express their positive faith and devotion in the great human crisis.'[7]

Those Friends convening at Philadelphia in 1917 chose the noted Haverford College professor Rufus M. Jones as chairman, a post he held until 1928 and again from 1935 to 1944. Widely considered the most weighty Quaker of the twentieth century, he saw in the AFSC a way in which to unite all branches of Friends in common service. The chair of the very first meeting, and successor to Jones as chairman, was the biblical scholar and historian Henry Joel Cadbury.[8]

The AFSC initiative was patterned largely on the work of the Friends Ambulance Unit (FAU) and the Friends War Victims Relief Committee, both established by British Quakers in 1914. These agencies had mounted major programs of emergency relief, including care for civilians driven from their homes in France and Belgium.[9]

In consultation with the American government and the American Red Cross, the AFSC instituted the Reconstruction Unit for service in France. Volunteers trained at Haverford College before going overseas. It was no easy task to secure the necessary passports from the government to enable the effort to begin, but assiduous lobbying managed the task. By the end of the year, 116 men and twenty women had arrived in France; at peak enrolment, about six hundred unit volunteers worked there. More than $1 million was expended in this effort, with Mennonites contributing $200,000 and Brethren $100,000.[10]

Assignments of unit members varied. Some joined the ongoing work of the FAU in driving ambulances and working in military hospitals. Some erected pre-fabricated houses for French families, and others distributed food, clothing, and medicine. Tractors and other farm machinery were provided to help farmers. The American unit was given responsibility for reconstructing forty French villages in the Verdun area. It bought army surplus and used the equipment and supplies for its work, actually causing a carload of bayonets to be melted down into farm ploughs. It was the policy of the French army to use German prisoners of war in reconstruction work; the Quakers accepted this labour only on condition that the prisoners would be paid for their work. They mounted a program to transfer funds thus earned to German families at home, trapped in bitter poverty and hunger by wartime exigencies and the Allied food blockade.[11]

Though the Reconstruction Unit was staffed predominantly by Quakers, about sixty Mennonites and four Brethren COs also took part; Quaker leaders found their work highly effective. The unit's achievement was so well received that the American Relief Administration asked the AFSC to run the entire feeding-of-civilians program in Germany and Austria. By 1921 over one million children were enrolled in such projects in more than sixteen hundred German communities. Continuing need in many countries encouraged Quakers to place the AFSC on a permanent basis in 1924. It was now divided into four sections: Foreign Service (which received the lion's share of the budget), Interracial, Peace, and Home Service. Policies for the agency were set by a board of twenty persons, who met bi-monthly.

Each in its own way, the peace churches reorganized their denominational machinery to reform and upgrade the peace witness. The Mennonite Church established a Peace Problems Committee in 1925 to deal with its response to these issues. Its counterpart, the General Conference Mennonites, located largely in the US midwest, created the Peace Committee one year later. In 1928 Brethren assigned responsibility for peace literature and action to the newly organized Board of Religious (later Christian) Education, supplanting the earlier Central Service Committee and Peace Committee. Members of the several branches of Friends participated in the energetic programs of the AFSC.[12]

Peace Conferences, 1922–1935

Among the some two hundred persons attending the 1922 Bluffton conference from across the United States and Canada were members of the Society of Friends, several branches of the Mennonites, the Church of the Brethren, Moravians, Methodists, Schwenckfelders, and Church of God in North America. The title given to the gathering indicates its general posture – 'National Conference of Religious Bodies Who Hold that Peace between Nations Can Be Maintained by Following the Teachings of Jesus.' One of the headlined speakers was the nationally known Quaker peace activist Frederick J. Libby from Washington, DC; most speakers came from denominations represented on the inviting body.[13]

The response to the Bluffton conference was largely favourable; most participants agreed that such meetings should continue. Of the peace churches, the (Old) Mennonite Church was the least affirmative, caught as it was in the throes of a fundamentalist–modernist struggle. Conservatives in its ranks were suspicious of association with other churches of liberal theological orientation.

The Mennonite conservatives followed a rather strict two-kingdom theology much as Martin Luther had taught, and, while insisting that their members must never participate in warfare, they accepted the inevitability of the secular use of force. They were therefore uncomfortable with the assumption underlying the pacifism of many of the conference participants – that peace could be won via non-violent methods. Church leader John Moseman of Lancaster County, Pennsylvania, and historian John Horsch from western Pennsylvania closely monitored the work of the (Old) Mennonite Peace Problems Committee, condemning any cooperation with general peace groups, even objecting to cooperation with the Friends and Brethren.[14]

A continuation committee appointed at Bluffton arranged for a series of further meetings, held largely in the US east and midwest through the 1920s and early 1930s. Those attending later conferences were almost exclusively Brethren, Mennonites, and Quakers, with the meeting sites ordinarily either the campuses of colleges affiliated to these denominations or one of their large congregations. The meetings strengthened bonds of friendship and a spirit of common cause among planners and participants. Regional meetings of the same kind, as in California, had comparable results.

The second conference in the series was held at Juniata College, Huntingdon, Pennsylvania, in late December 1923. The continuation committee appointed there arranged for a third, held in Lancaster, Pennsylvania, in 1924, and a fourth, in Wichita, Kansas, in 1925. The title now used was Conference of Pacifist Churches. The fifth (at Carlock, Illinois) was held in the summer of 1926, and a sixth (at Elizabethtown College, Pennsylvania) in December of the same year. A seventh, convened in North Manchester, Indiana, in November 1927, drew the largest number of participants since the inaugural conference at Bluffton. The series continued with meetings at Chicago (March 1928), Wilmington, Ohio (March 1929), and Mount Morris, Illinois (March 1931). Largely because of the impact of the Depression, there now came a lapse of several years. This was broken by the most important of all the meetings – the one held at North Newton, Kansas, from 31 October to 2 November 1935. It marked a break-through and maturation in the willingness of the peace churches to work closely together.

The Newton Conference of 1935

The convenor of the conference at Newton was H.P. Krehbiel, a septuagenarian leader in the General Conference Mennonite church. Something of a renaissance figure, Krehbiel was a minister, writer, world traveller, publisher, businessman, inventor, and active churchman. He had been an early and persistent participant in the series of peace conferences since Bluffton. On his own initiative he had journeyed to Europe in 1927 seeking to unite and coordinate all peace-loving groups; in 1929 he published an appeal to realize this goal, which he entitled 'An Overture to the Historic Peace Groups of the World.' Based on shared commitment to the Apostles' Creed, he sought 'unity of procedure in time of stress.' According to one appraisal, the eloquent appeal received 'only a polite but lukewarm response.'[15]

The original motivation for calling the Newton conference came actually from two members of the Church of the Brethren peace committee, C. Ray Keim and Lawrence W. Shultz, both of Manchester College in Indiana. A third Brethren peace activist, Dan West, was also influential. West, a former public school teacher, had emerged in the 1920s as a leader with special talent in motivating and challenging young people. This was the rationale for his appointment in 1930 as director of the youth program of the Church of the Brethren. He was also expected to carry many of the administrative tasks of peace education.[16]

In his search for a 'moral equivalent of war,' West created a movement called 'One Hundred Dunkers for Peace.' This consisted of young people who committed themselves to peace education and action. He also promoted 'Twenty Thousand Dunkers for Peace' – Brethren who took a pledge not to support or engage in war. In 1935 the movement chose 'Brethren Peace Action' as its name and sought to engage the entire membership under the banner 'Two Hundred Thousand Dunkers for Peace.'[17]

Krehbiel prepared the ground for the 1935 conference by circulating a strongly Christocentric document around which he hoped the conference participants could unite; he called it a 'Suggested Basis for an Ecumenical Council of Historic Peace Churches in North America.' Respondents encouraged him to modify some of the language to accommodate the conservative (Old) Mennonites. This he did. Especially significant was the introduction of the term 'Historic Peace Churches'; following the Newton assembly this term became widely used both inside and outside the groups involved.

One reason for introducing the phrase was the intense dislike that influential members of the Mennonite Church had for the term 'pacifist'; for them 'pacifist' – used earlier in the series of conferences – signalled alliance with modernistic theology. Through the linking 'peace to historic,' the tradition-minded members of the Mennonite Church could more comfortably make common cause. As early as 1931, in the Conference of Pacifist Churches gathering at

Mount Morris, Illinois, Krehbiel had distinguished between political pacifism – which should be avoided – and Christian peacemaking.[18]

The actual deliberations at Newton clearly linked political with religious concerns. This was especially clear in the second section of its published proceedings dealing with 'Our Concept of Patriotism.' It sought to dispel charges that peacemakers were not good citizens. It contended that the policies they held to were in fact contributing to the 'highest welfare of the country.' The application of 'the principles of peace, love, justice, liberty and international goodwill' actually furthered the vital national interest. Because pacifists had the courage to stand by these principles, they were the 'true patriots.'[19]

Another reason for the significance of the Newton meeting lay in the world situation. Totalitarian regimes had succeeded in seizing control in Nazi Germany, Fascist Italy, and Bolshevik Russia and were threatening to succeed in Spain. The League of Nation structure – fatally flawed by the refusal of the United States to join – had been discredited by its inability to halt the brutal war on Ethiopia by Mussolini's Italian forces and to prevent the rapacious assault on China by the aggressive Japanese army. Those gathering at Newton had no difficulty in discerning the stormy war clouds on the horizon. This lent urgency to their deliberations and impetus to their plans for combined actions.

A relaxed agenda allowed those attending to become well acquainted with each other. Except for brief introductory statements, the three days were given over to an 'open forum,' allowing thorough discussion and airing of views. Differences in theological perspective became apparent, but the spirit remained cordial and cooperative. The last forenoon of the conference was devoted to the adoption of a series of resolutions and plans for the future. A key excerpt from the minutes of the meeting asserted: 'The [First] World War brought together in concentration [i.e., army] camps, alternative service and relief efforts those whose conception of discipleship included the conviction that the Christian can have no part in war or its support ... Since the War it has become the growing conviction within these several groups that a more faithful testimony to the ways of peace, love and good will as exemplified and taught by our Lord is essential when our country is at peace, if we would have respect for our positions in times of war crisis.'

Peace Efforts, 1935–1939

The most important result of the meeting was a consolidation of the peace efforts of the several bodies present and a sense of common cause. Those attending were at the core of the combined peace efforts during the rest of the 1930s and through the pressures of the Second World War and its aftermath. A three-man continuation committee was designated to plan and carry out a range of cooperative projects. Members were Robert W. Balderston, a Quaker from Chicago; C. Ray Keim, a professor of history at Manchester College, Indiana; and Orie O. Miller, an independently wealthy Mennonite businessman from Akron, Pennsylvania. At the first meeting of the committee in Chicago in February 1938, the members agreed to meet four times a year.

One of their first decisions was to develop literature for wide distribution. A section of the Newton proceedings dealing with citizenship was printed by the Brethren as a pamphlet with the title *Christian Patriotism.* More expansive was a pacifist handbook or manual that dealt with theological backgrounds, arguments for and against pacifism, and practical advice for those wishing to defend the cause of peace. This and other literature was produced and circulated in the years following the Newton conference.[20]

An early achievement was sending visitors to three national assemblies of other American denominations. In the summer of 1936 leaders of the Brethren, Friends, and Mennonites gave their peace testimony to Methodists meeting in Ohio, to Reformed Presbyterians in Indiana, and to Congregationalists in Maine.

Of more significance was the decision to send a delegation to President Franklin D. Roosevelt in 1937, an action repeated on the eve of the American entry into the Second World War. A seven-man party secured an appointment with the president on 12 February 1937; each of the churches presented a statement of its pacifist beliefs. They wanted to put on record their long-standing position on peace and to inform the government about their current efforts at peacemaking. After the outbreak of war in September 1939, the peace churches realized that they had to take additional steps to prepare the way to face possible conscription.[21]

The second appointment with the president was again secured through the excellent connections of the American Quakers (especially Rufus Jones and Clarence Pickett) with the Roosevelt family. Peace-church leaders decided to frame a common statement, outlining their many peacemaking efforts and asking for a form of alternative service under civilian direction, which they agreed to support sacrificially.

The process of preparing this message was complicated at the very end by the insistence of the Friends' Peace Section that the delegation champion the cause of absolutist objectors to conscription, who refused all cooperation with government demands, beginning with refusal to register. Mennonites and Brethren were not willing to accept this task, leading the Quakers to consider withdrawing from the delegation. The impasse was resolved shortly before the meeting by a joint decision to present two papers; one was a combined statement reiterating their peace convictions and current activities, the second a confidential 'Memorandum to the Government regarding a plan of procedure for providing alternative service for conscientious objectors in case of military conscription.' This memo included a paragraph on behalf of the absolutist position and another on pacifists not belonging to one of the peace churches.[22]

Mennonites meeting in 1936 on an International Mennonite Peace Committee in the Netherlands issued a *Mennonite Peace Manifesto*. They had gathered to participate in the Third Mennonite World Conference in Amsterdam. Among those signing the statement from the United States were Harold S. Bender, Orie Miller, and C. Henry Smith. This was their first meeting with Hans Zumpe and Emmy Arnold, representatives of the Society of Brothers, an Anabaptist-oriented pacifist communal body organized in Germany in 1920. The society, often known as the Bruderhof after its communitarian way of life, united under its founder, Eberhard Arnold, with the North American Hutterian Brethren in 1930–1. These American Mennonites provided crucial support in aiding the largely German Bruderhof membership to resettle as a body in Paraguay in 1940–1.[23]

Representatives of the Brethren and Society of Friends attended the World Conference on Church, Community, and State held in Oxford, England, in July 1937, one of the direct precursors of the World Council of Churches. The Brethren delegate, M.R. Zigler, presented peace statements from the Annual Conference of the Church of the Brethren and from the Mennonite Central Committee. The Quaker delegate, Professor Elbert Russell, delivered a peace testimony from the Friends. Though the pacifist position was not accepted as the predominant voice of the Oxford conference, it did appear as one of the 'three main positions which are sincerely and conscientiously held by Christians,' as the report of the findings committee put it.[24]

Peace Education

One of the most popular and effective devices for peace education emerged in the AFSC-sponsored Institutes of International Relations. Originally organized to train young members of peace caravans, they were initiated by Ray Newton in 1930. They typically lasted for two weeks at an academic site, featuring a panel of speakers with expertise on international affairs. Some were from abroad, others distinguished faculty members from American universities. The first institute, held for two weeks, brought together sixty people to hear Henry T. Hodgkin of the British Fellowship of Reconciliation, Frederick J. Libby of the National Council for the Prevention of War, Clarence E. Pickett of the AFSC, Devere Allen, publisher of the *World Tomorrow*, and Reinhold Niebuhr of Union Theological Seminary in New York. Newton was able to attract foundation support to fund the institutes. In 1936 the AFSC held ten institutes across the nation; by 1940 those registered surpassed 2,200.[25]

Among those gatherings that seemed to have most affected the Historic Peace Churches' interaction were a series sited at Bethel College, North Newton, Kansas, from 1936 to 1940 (sponsored jointly by the AFSC and the General Conference Mennonite church). The chief promoter was a professor of history at Bethel, Emmet L. Harshbarger, after 1935 chair of the latter denomination's peace committee. The series brought figures such as Professor Sidney B. Fay (from Harvard University), Clarence Streit (from the *New York Times* and known for his advocacy of world government), Toyohiko Kagawa (noted Japanese Christian pacifist), and Dr Eduard Beneš (former president of Czechoslovakia). Nationalistic community pressures and denominational concerns prompted the college to drop its sponsorship as the Second World War intervened.[26]

A related project was to send graduate students abroad to develop expertise in international relations. The Brethren Kermit Eby and the Quaker Thomas Q. Harrison, for instance, went to Japan in 1933 to ascertain the causes of the growing tension between that rising nation and the United States as a prelude to seeking to resolve them. Brethren H. Harman Bjorklund went to study with the Friends in England in 1936.[27]

In the 1930s a well-received project sponsored peace oratorical contests; they were provided for several levels of students – high school, college/university, and graduate school. This had the effect of focusing the attention of promising young people on the issues of world peace. The competition was often keen; participants were encouraged by their involvement to focus their attention on peace concerns.

Relief Activities

All three Historic Peace Churches had been active in relief efforts since the end of the First World War. From its base with the Reconstruction Unit in France, the AFSC extended its work mentioned above in Germany and Austria to such countries as Poland and the Soviet Union, with projects varying according to the local situations encountered. In the Soviet Union, work centred on the Volga area, where famine was causing mass starvation. Over time, a pattern emerged that was generally followed. Immediate emergency distribution of food and clothing gave way to self-help projects designed to preserve the dignity and self-respect of recipients. Next followed creation of training institutions to allow indigenous personnel to take over Quaker initiatives. The expatriate workers then withdrew completely. One exception was a program that established Quaker international centres in major cities, including Berlin, Geneva, Moscow, Paris, Vienna, and Warsaw, where long-range efforts towards better relationships between nations engaged the energies of the AFSC staff.[28]

Domestic needs in the United States were not forgotten. Major attention was given to the economic hardship among the families of miners living in Appalachia. The failure of the bituminous coal industry in West Virginia, western Pennsylvania, and adjoining states threw hundreds of workers into unemployment. In 1921, 1928, and after 1931, substantial feeding programs assisted hungry children in these areas. For help over the longer haul, Friends created health services, recreational and adult-education programs, and small workshops to provide jobs. They created homesteads and self-help housing, as in Penncraft in western Pennsylvania. Quakers understood this as a way of waging peace, of ameliorating class tensions and labour–management crises.[29]

The Mennonite Central Committee (MCC), formed in July 1920, combined the relief efforts of several denominations of Mennonites as well as the Brethren in Christ. The catalyst was the extreme deprivations caused in Russia by the upheaval of the revolution and the civil war that followed. After the need in the Soviet Union eased in 1925, the work of the committee was reactivated in 1929 to resettle Russian Mennonites in Paraguay. Ten years later MCC work was concentrated in Poland, following the German invasion. Material aid was given to 250,000 war victims in Poland through the Polish and German Red Cross.[30]

Though the Church of the Brethren did not have a relief agency equivalent to the AFSC or MCC, it began substantial foreign aid in 1918 to Armenians suffering from Turkish massacres. Within three years nearly $270,000 was raised and distributed to these victims. The aid was administered through the American Committee for Relief in the Near East, assisted by a Brethren pastor on site. Later, Brethren sent funds for relief through the auspices of the American Friends.[31]

Emergency Peace Campaign

Perhaps the most impressive peace initiative of the 1930s, bringing together a wide sweep of organizations and personalities, was the Emergency Peace Campaign (EPC), in which members of the peace churches were centrally involved. On a suggestion made by Ray Newton in October 1935, it predicated a well coordinated and massive push to bring pacifists and non-pacifists into alignment so as to keep the United States from going to war, which Newton saw as imminent (within six months to three years). Newton was freed from his duties at the AFSC to direct the campaign, which soon won support from a large number of peace-oriented organizations and agencies. A gathering of over one hundred pacifists in Buck Hill Falls, Pennsylvania, in December 1935 reached consensus on the general directions of the campaign. Soon $100,000 was donated, to be directed by a small executive committee which included at first Newton and Clarence E. Pickett of the AFSC and was later broadened to embrace other pacifist groups. The pacifist Kirby Page, an influential orator and writer, chaired the speaker's bureau.[32]

A noteworthy slate of international and American peace advocates spoke at large-scale EPC meeting held across the nation. Newspaper articles and radio broadcasts spread the word. Ministers and educators gathered in one- and two-day study conferences in 278 cities. At these and other events the theme of the EPC was repeated: the United States must by all means avoid entanglement in another war in Europe. To remove the underlying causes of war, it must work to create more equitable distribution of goods and economic power. Speakers urged American cooperation with League of Nations programs, membership in the World Court functioning at the Hague, and extension of neutrality legislation. Staff members worked through farm organizations such as the Farmer Bureau Federation, the Farmers' Union, and the Grange.

Special efforts were made to enlist the student population in the campaign. A nation-wide student strike for peace brought out some half-million high school and college students in demonstrations. Many signed the Oxford peace pledge never to participate in war. On many campuses students enrolled in the satirically named Veterans of Future Wars and demanded bonuses, so that they, as the future killed and wounded, could profit from the 'full benefit of their country's gratitude.' (As might be imagined, veterans' groups were not amused and threatened physical violence.) Hundreds of college students were recruited, trained, and sent out on deputations to churches, schools, and service clubs on behalf of peace.

The Emergency Peace Campaign flourished throughout 1936 and into 1937, when staff members increased to 150, of which eighty-four served in the national headquarters. Local peace committees were formed in more than two thousand cities and five hundred college campuses. Mass meetings continued with new speakers. In 1937 the US Congress passed the Neutrality Act, in large part because of the grass-roots and national EPC lobbying. The campaign was concluded in 1938.

Peace Caravans and Work Camps

An ingenious program developed first by the AFSC was the peace caravan. This entailed each summer the sending out, largely in the midwest, of young people in second-hand cars. They sought to speak in community groups, distributed peace literature, and also worked on local service projects. Beginning in 1926, the program flourished until the early 1940s, enrolling well over one thousand students, many of whom supported themselves. In 1940 some 120 students from fifty-five colleges in twenty-six states went out, representing twenty different denominations. Each team contacted more than five thousand people, but the greatest influence was probably on the young activists themselves.[33]

Another approach that focused on young people was the work camp. The idea came from a Swiss Quaker pacifist, Pierre Ceresole, who organized young Europeans to work in rebuilding French villages as a form of reconciliation. His vision was of 'an international peace army which would fight not other men but the traditional enemies of man – flood, famine, earthquake, and war.' The concept was picked up and spread in the United States after 1934 by the AFSC, attracting many Brethren, Quakers, and others of college age.[34]

Aid to Spain

The mid-1930s brought sharper challenges to the Historic Peace Churches. The rise of totalitarianism noted at the Newton conference resulted in tens of thousands of refugees and war sufferers in many parts of the globe. The peace churches initiated a number of projects to meet these needs – so many, it is impossible to list them all. A characteristic response was to the civil war in Spain. When the Nationalists under General Francisco Franco rose to overthrow the legitimate Spanish Republic, Quakers in the United Kingdom and the United States rallied to meet the situation. Following their principle of absolute neutrality, they organized relief projects on both sides of the conflict – in territory occupied by the Loyalists and the insurgents, even if this evenhandedness offended those who saw the aggression as being on the Franco side. Primary effort went to feeding of children, often located in orphanages.[35]

As had happened with the response in France in 1918, American Friends asked for assistance from Brethren and Mennonites. This came first through substantial gifts of funds and goods and then through personnel as well. Dan West, Brethren peace activist, was in Spain in 1937–8 with the AFSC; his reports while there, and presentations after he returned, stimulated many Americans to support the project in Spain.[36]

It was while agonizing over how to decide which children to save with the limited supply of foodstuffs that West conceived the idea of the Heifer Project. Instead of doling out portions of powdered milk, he conceived the idea of asking American farmers to donate bred young cows, whose milk could feed thousands. To help preserve the dignity and self-respect of recipients of these animals, and to extend aid to others, the former would be asked to donate the first female calf to another family in need. Brethren in northern Indiana were receptive to West's vision and began to collect heifers during the early 1940s. Wartime conditions, however, made it impossible to send them overseas until after the war had ended, so they went to needy families in the United States and in the associated commonwealth of Puerto Rico. After 1945 the project experienced a phenomenal expansion to many nations.[37]

Preparing for War, 1939–41

Conscription

The combined work of the Historic Peace Churches culminated in 1940 with their attempts to influence pending legislation in the US Congress that eventuated in the Selective Training and Service Act, passed in September of that year. Called during the legislative process the Burke-Wadsworth Selective Service Bill after its two sponsors, the law introduced conscription in peacetime for the first time in US history. Among the earliest people to envisage such an innovation, peace church leaders had sought since 1937 to position themselves in relation to conscription. They were anxious to avoid the agonies and dilemmas of the CO experience during the First World War.[38]

The two delegations from the Historic Peace Churches to President Roosevelt in 1937 and in early 1940 had been sent to register their position with the highest governmental authorities well prior to the outbreak of hostilities. Though ostensibly well-received by the president and members of his cabinet (on whom the delegations also called), these visitors by no means succeeded in producing an ideal response to peace interests.

All three groups had taken steps in 1939–40 to organize themselves to meet the expected crisis. The Mennonites created the Mennonite Central Peace Committee in September 1939, to coordinate the peace concerns of several Mennonite denominations. The Church of the Brethren established the Brethren Service Committee in the same year to direct its peace and relief actions; a special Advisory Committee for Conscientious Objectors was appointed to represent Brethren interests in the nation's capital. In 1940 Friends set up their War Problems Committee to track potential draft legislation for the purpose of influencing its character, to inform members of Friends' meetings of such developments, and to advise young Quakers on the issues involved.

A combined delegation of Orie O. Miller (Mennonite), Clarence E. Pickett (Friends), and Dan West (Brethren) sought out Solicitor General Francis Biddle in June 1940, to clarify their concern that any future conscription must be kept under civilian control. They received what amounted to a diversionary response. All three bodies took stock of their situation in the summer of 1940, determined to be ready for whatever national legislation might emerge. As a close student of these developments, Albert Keim, has concluded: 'From the vantage point of hindsight, the historic peace churches were uniquely ready for the challenging and arduous events which were to unfold during the summer and autumn of 1940. A providential convergence of leadership, organization, and events had transpired.'

At that time informed observers doubted that an isolationist-oriented Congress would pass a conscription measure. Even top military leaders opposed it, because they feared that controversy over conscription would negatively influence their pending appeals for a huge increase in armaments; they were moreover reluctant to draw on members of the regular army to train hordes of recruits. Though President Roosevelt wished to intervene on the side of the United Kingdom against Nazi Germany, he faced re-election in the autumn of 1940 and tried to play down the controversial issue.

A committee of east coast Anglophiles and interventionists organized themselves to sway public opinion and to gain in that way congressional support. Members had close ties to leading publications and worked effectively to bring about public support for beleaguered Britain, facing Hitler's divisions across the Channel. A well-financed publicity campaign engaged public opinion through a variety of tactics.

As introduced in June 1940, the Burke-Wadsworth bill contained language almost identical to that of the draft legislation of 1917: there was provision for exemption from regular service for COs, but none from non-combatant duty. It soon became clear to the peace churches that instead of simply attempting to block the legislation, they should focus their energies on shaping the provisions relating to conscientious objection. They therefore embarked on a strenuous campaign to achieve this goal.

Key players on the Friends side were E. Raymond Wilson of the AFSC Peace Section and Paul Comly French, a former journalist and government official who knew well the corridors of power in Washington, DC. Brethren leader M.R. Zigler spent a great deal of time on this effort, as did Orie O. Miller and other Mennonites. They organized speakers at the July hearings on the conscription bill and visited congressmen and senators almost without ceasing.[39]

What were they seeking to achieve? Their program contained five chief points: a national register of COs; a civilian agency under the attorney general's office to administer the program; a program of work of 'national importance' under civilian control; a national board of appeal; and complete exemption for absolutist objectors. Despite the tireless efforts of the peace churches, few of their desires made it into the completed legislation, despite some initial successes. The upshot indeed was that COs would be kept under the purview of local draft boards, with no provision for a national registry, and there would be no complete exemptions for absolutists, for whom defiance leading to prison was to be the only option.

In several ways the 1940 law as passed did, however, improve the status of COs as compared with earlier experience. First, awarding of CO status was based not on membership in a certain 'recognized sect' but rather on 'religious training and belief'; this rubric widened the potential for COs from other than peace-church backgrounds. Second, the law recognized COs as a separate category under the draft, performing work of 'national importance' apart from the military in a kind of 'alternative service.' Third, an appeal process against local draft-board rulings was available under the Justice Department. Fourth, those violating the act were to be tried under civilian jurisdiction, rather than under military courts-martial.[40]

The Emergence of Civilian Public Service

In mid-September 1940, the Selective Training and Service Act became law. Already seventeen church leaders had met in Washington, DC, to lay plans to shape in positive ways the provisions for alternative service. Early contacts with officials who would probably administer the Selective Service System encouraged the peace church leaders to come up with a combined plan to present to the government; these officials indicated that well-thought-out proposals had a good chance of being adopted in the existing condition of flux. A key figure from the government side was Lewis B. Hershey, an army officer assigned to personnel problems. He became the acting, then full-time director of Selective Service.[41]

A large meeting of peace church leaders was called for Chicago in October 1940 in order to reach consensus on the issue. The AFSC was willing to administer the entire alternative service program for the peace churches, but the Brethren and Mennonites did not favour that solution. Meanwhile, those present agreed to establish a central liaison and administrative body, at first called the National Council for Religious Objectors, soon changed to National Service Board for Religious Objectors. M.R. Zigler of the Brethren was named chairman, with the Mennonite Orie O. Miller as vice-chairman, and the Quaker Paul Comly French as executive secretary.

The board submitted a plan to the Selective Service officials, suggesting two types of CO camps: one would be under the direct control of the service agencies to carry on a variety of social aid program, the second to be directed by governmental agencies. After consultation with the government, the proposal was expanded into three forms of alternative service for COs: in government-agency camps, in camps operated by the churches in conjunction with government agencies, and in camps operated solely by the churches.

When Lewis Hershey took this proposal to Roosevelt, the president reacted with angry and instant rejection. This reaction killed the possibility of governmental funding for any of the three kinds of camps. In fact, Selective Service officials now told the peace churches that any call for government funding would face hostile scrutiny in the Congress and probably result in scrapping of the whole alternative-service project. They asked the peace churches to carry responsibility for funding camps for all COs, the settings where government agencies such as the Park Service or Forestry Service would direct work projects, with all other camp administration and support the task of the peace churches. They offered the use of former barrack camps of the Civilian Conservation Corps (CCC) as housing, with the COs taking up tasks comparable to that performed by former CCC men.

After much soul-searching, the leaders of the Historic Peace Churches agreed to this arrangement for a trial period of six months. Orie O. Miller promised that the Mennonites would 'gladly pay their share of the bill. They would do it even though every Mennonite farmer had to mortgage his farm.' To operate what came to be called Civilian Public Service (CPS) demanded great sacrifices. According to the best calculations, the peace churches and families contributed more than $7 million. If the eight million CPS man-hours had been reimbursed at the army pay scale, the government would have paid out more than $22 million. The first camps were opened in the late spring of 1941.[42] Most observers have concluded that CPS, while seriously flawed in conception and execution, marked a significant improvement over the situation in the First World War and made possible a yet better arrangement in the Korean War.[43]

Conclusion

The chequered response of the Historic Peace Churches to the challenge of conscription during the First World War proved to be the catalyst for their leading figures to become more active in peacemaking. A rich variety of projects, programs, initiatives, publications, and conferences resulted from their determination to bring their denominations into a state of better readiness if and when another world-wide conflagration occurred. Sadly, that devastating nightmare of destruction known as the Second World War did come to pass. The peace churches' efforts between the wars did not succeed, as some of the more optimistic among them had hoped, in preventing war or maintaining American neutrality permanently. Their creative innovations, however, did place them in a position that permitted a proactive relationship with the US government when conscription came again. Of especial importance was the fact that the peace churches made common cause around their peace concerns, despite differences in theology and practice.

NOTES

1 Wilbur K. Thomas to I. Harvey Brumbaugh, Philadelphia, 3 April 1922 and later, RG 4, Administrative Correspondence, Juniata College Archives, Huntingdon, Pa. The conferences are discussed in James C. Juhnke, *Vision, Doctrine, War: Mennonite Identity and Organization in America, 1890–1930* (Scottdale, Pa., 1989), 296–9, and Albert N. Keim and Grant M. Stolzfus, *The Politics of Conscience: The Historic Peace Churches and America at War, 1917–1955* (Scottdale, Pa., 1988), 62–5.

2 On these changes, see especially Calvin Redekop, *Mennonite Society* (Baltimore 1989), 276–95, Carl F. Bowman, *Brethren Society: The Cultural Transformation of a 'Peculiar People'* (Baltimore 1995), especially 329–37; Hugh Barbour and J. William Frost, *The Quakers* (New York 1988), 247–53. The wartime hysteria and the complicity of most churches in it was documented in Ray H. Abrams, *Preachers Present Arms*, 2nd ed. (Scottdale, Pa., 1969).

3 Rufus D. Bowman, *The Church of the Brethren and War, 1708–1941* (Elgin, Ill., 1944), 169–80. See also Charles Chatfield, *For Peace and Justice: Pacifism in America, 1914–1941* (Knoxville, Tenn., 1971), 15ff.

4 Clyde E. Jacobs and John F. Gallagher, *The Selective Service Act: A Case Study of the Governmental Process* (New York 1967), 22–3.

5 Paul Toews, 'The Long Weekend or the Short Week: Mennonite Peace Theology, 1925–1944,' *Mennonite Quarterly Review* (Goshen, Ind.), 60 (Jan. 1986), 38–57; Theron F. Schlabach, 'To Focus a Mennonite Vision,' in J.R. Burkholder and Calvin Redekop, eds., *Kingdom, Cross, and Community: Essays on Mennonite Themes in Honor of Guy F. Hershberger* (Scottdale, Pa., 1976), 15–50, especially 23–9; Allan Kohrman, 'Respectable Pacifists: Quaker Response to World War I,' *Quaker History* (Haverford, Pa.), 75 (spring 1986), 35–53.

6 Lawrence S. Wittner, *Rebels against War: The American Peace Movement, 1941–1960* (New York 1969), 1–3; Chatfield, *For Peace and Justice*, 164–7.

7 Chatfield, *Peace and Justice*, 50–2; Frost, '"Our Deeds Carry Our Message": The Early History of the American Friends Service Committee,' *Quaker History*, 81 (spring 1992); 1–51; Mary Hoxie Jones, *Swords into Ploughshares: An Account of the American Friends Service Committee, 1917–1937* (New York 1937), 3–41. A good summary of the Mission des Amis is found in Philadelphia War History Committee, *Philadelphia in the World War, 1914–1919* (Philadelphia 1922), 588–93.

8 Standard biographies of Jones are David Hinshaw, *Rufus Jones, Master Quaker*

(New York 1951), and Elizabeth Gray Vining, *Friend of Life: The Biography of Rufus M. Jones* (Philadelphia 1958); on Cadbury, see Margaret Hope Bacon, *Let This Life Speak: The Legacy of Henry Joel Cadbury* (Philadelphia 1987), and M.H. Jones, 'Henry Joel Cadbury: A Biographical Sketch,' in Anna Brinton, ed., *Then and Now: Quaker Essays, Historical and Contemporary by Friends of Henry Joel Cadbury* (Philadelphia 1960), 11–70. Cadbury represented the AFSC when it was awarded (jointly with the Friends Service Council of London) the Nobel Peace Prize in 1947; he accepted the prize wearing formal clothes borrowed from the AFSC relief warehouse.

9 The work of the British Friends is described in John Ormerod Greenwood, *Quaker Encounters* (York 1975), and John Forbes, *The Quaker Star under Seven Flags, 1917–1927* (Philadelphia 1962).

10 Frost, 'Deeds,' 19–34; Marvin Weisbord, *Some Form of Peace: True Stories of the American Friends Service Committee at Home and Abroad* (New York 1968).

11 The experiences of a Mennonite participant in the Reconstruction Unit in France and in visiting German families are recounted in his letters published in S. Duane Kauffman, *Mifflin County Amish and Mennonite Story, 1791–1991* (Belleville, Pa., 1991), 406–16.

12 Toews, 'Long Weekend,' 38–57; Bowman, *Brethren and War*, 250–3.

13 Materials describing the series of peace conferences are found in the Henry P. Krehbiel Papers, Bethel College Archives, North Newton, Kansas. Articles on the individual meetings were published in the relevant denominational periodicals: *Gospel Messenger* (Church of the Brethren); *Mennonite* (General Conference Mennonite Church); *Gospel Herald* (Mennonite Church); *Mennonite Weekly Review* (pan-Mennonite); *American Friend* (Society of Friends); and *Friends Intelligencer* (Society of Friends).

14 Toews, 'Long Weekend,' 44–9; Leo Driedger and Donald B. Kraybill, *Mennonite Peacemaking: From Quietism to Activism* (Scottdale, Pa., 1994), 66–70.

15 For overviews of the conference, see Juhnke, *Vision, Doctrine, War*, 297–9; Robert Kreider, 'The Historic Peace Churches Meeting in 1935,' *Mennonite Life* (North Newton, Kan.), 31 (June 1976), 21–24; Bowman, *Brethren and War*, 267–72.

16 Lawrence W. Shultz, *People and Places, 1890–1970. An Autobiography* (Winona Lake, Ind., 1971); Glee Yoder, *Passing on the Gift: The Story of Dan West* (Elgin, Ill., 1978).

17 Roger E. Sappington, *Brethren Social Policy, 1908–1958* (Elgin, Ill., 1961), 62–4; *Brethren Peace Action* (Elgin, Ill. [1935]).

18 Toews, 'Long Weekend,' 51.

19 *Christian Patriotism: A Statement Outlined by Representatives of Brethren, Friends, Mennonites – Assembled at Newton, Kansas, Oct. 31 to Nov. 2, 1935* (Elgin, Ill. [1935]).

20 A widely reported meeting of the continuation committee held in Chicago in mid-September 1936 finalized plans for publications: see *Gospel Messenger* (Elgin), 7 Nov. 1936, 22–3; *Mennonite Weekly Review* (Newton, Kan.), 7 Oct. 1936, 1–2; *American Friend* (Richmond, Ind.), 1 Oct. 1936, 412; *Friends Intelligencer* (Philadelphia), 31 Oct. 1936, 722. A key statement on literature read: 'The Committee has met several times and is at present particularly concerned about the body of available Christian peace literature, its further production when deemed necessary, and its better distribution within our groups and to the outside world.'

21 The visit of the peace-church delegation was given nation-wide publicity by a radio broadcast of Walter W. Van Kirk of the Federal Council of Churches called 'Seven Men before the President,' *Gospel Messenger*, 17 April 1937, 22–3.

22 Keim and Stoltzfus, *Politics of Conscience*, 71–7; Paul Comly French, *We Won't Murder: Being the Story of Men Who Followed Their Conscientious Scruples and Helped Give Life to Democracy* (New York 1940), 132–5.

23 Shultz, *People and Places*, 13, 65, 71. On the early history of the Bruderhof, see Emmy Arnold, *Torches Together: The Beginning and Early Years of the Brüderhof Communities*, 2nd ed. (Rifton, NY, 1971); Hutterian Brethren, *Brothers United: An Account of the Uniting of Eberhard Arnold and the Rhön Brüderhof with the Hutterian Church* (Ulster Park, NY, 1988). See also D.F. Durnbaugh, 'Relocation of the German Bruderhof to England, South America, and North America,' *Communal Societies* (Evansville, Ind.) 11 (1991); 62–77.

24 Durnbaugh, ed., *On Earth Peace: Discussions on War/Peace Issues between Friends, Mennonites, Brethren and European Churches, 1935–1975* (Elgin, Ill., 1978), 33–7.

25 Chatfield, *For Peace and Justice*, 137–8.

26 Juhnke, *A People of Two Kingdoms: The Political Acculturation of the Kansas Mennonites* (North Newton, Kan., 1975), 131–2.

27 Sappington, *Brethren Social Policy*, 64.

28 Jones, *Swords into Ploughshares*, passim; all jointly with British Quakers.

29 Ibid., 201ff.

30 R.S. Kreider and Rachel Waltner Goossen, *Hungry, Thirsty, a Stranger: The MCC Experience* (Scottdale, Pa., 1988), 19–41; John D. Unruh, *In the Name of Christ: A History of Mennonite Central Committee and Its Service, 1921–1951* (Scottdale, Pa., 1952); Juhnke, *Vision, Doctrine, War*, 249–84.

31 Sappington, *Brethren Social Policy*, 48–52; Durnbaugh, *Pragmatic Prophet: The Life of Michael Robert Zigler* (Elgin, Ill., 1989), 112–3.

32 Chatfield, *For Peace and Justice*, 266–81; Robert Kleidman, *Organizing for Peace: Neutrality, the Test Ban, and the Freeze* (Syracuse, NY, 1993).

33 Chatfield, *For Peace and Justice*, 136–7; Jones, *Swords into Ploughshares*, 173–6.

34 Jones, *Swords into Ploughshares*, 208–10; Clarence E. Pickett, *For More than Bread*

(Boston 1953), 339–60; Weisbord, *Some Form of Peace*, 105–25; Allan A. Hunter, *White Corpuscles in Europe* (Chicago 1939), 33–42.

35 Jones, *Swords into Ploughshares*, 293–301; Greenwood, *Quaker Encounters*, 252–8; Sylvester Jones, *Not by Might* (New York 1942).

36 See, for example, Dan West, 'Cooperation with the AFSC in Spain,' in Donald F. Durnbaugh, ed., *To Serve the Present Age: The Brethren Service Story* (Elgin, Ill., 1975), 107–10, originally printed in the *Gospel Messenger*, 19 Dec. 1938. See also Yoder, *Passing on the Gift*, 89–99.

37 Thurl Metzger, 'The Heifer Project,' in Donald F. Durnbaugh, ed., *To Serve the Present Age: The Brethren Service Story* (Elgin, Ill., 1975), 144–7; Yoder, *Passing on the Gift*, 100–14; Kermit Eby, *The God in You* (Chicago 1954), 43–54; Mel West and Bill E. Beck, eds., *Cowboy Memories: Published in Honor of the Seagoing Cowboys, Air Attendants, and Truckers of HIP Animals, On the Fiftieth Anniversary of Heifer Project International* (Little Rock, Ark., 1994).

38 A good brief description of these events is found in Keim and Stoltzfus, *Politics of Conscience*, 78–114. See also Chatfield, *For Peace and Justice*, 305–9.

39 See, among others, E. Raymond Wilson, *Thus Far on My Journey* (Richmond, Ind., 1976), and Durnbaugh, *Pragmatic Prophet*, 125–39.

40 See Wittner, *Rebels against War*, 69–73; Melvin Gingerich, *Service for Peace: A History of Mennonite Civilian Public Service* (Akron, Pa., 1949), 39–61; Bowman, *Brethren and War*, 285–314.

41 The complicated story has been told several times; see especially, Keim and Stoltzfus, *Politics and Conscience*, 108–26; Keim, *The CPS Story: An Illustrated Story of Civilian Public Service* (Intercourse, Pa., 1990); *Conscientious Objection*, Special Monograph No. 11, vol. 1 (Washington, DC, 1950); Philip E. Jacob, *Origins of Civilian Public Service* (Washington, DC, 1946); Mulford Q. Sibley and P.E. Jacob, *Conscription of Conscience: The American State and the Conscientious Objector, 1940–1947* (Ithaca, NY, 1952).

42 Keim, *CPS Story*, 40. See Mitchell L. Robinson, chapter 19, below, for further discussion of CPS.

43 Keim and Stoltzfus, *Politics of Conscience*, 115. Of the many reflections and memoirs issued around the time of the fiftieth anniversary of CPS, see especially Cynthia Eller, *Conscientious Objectors and the Second World War* (New York 1991), and Richard C. Anderson, *Peace Was in Their Hearts: Conscientious Objectors in World War II* (Watsonville, Calif., 1994).

PART TWO
THE SECOND WORLD WAR

15

Quakers in Uniform: The Friends Ambulance Unit

LYN SMITH

From the earliest days of this war, from the time of the Finnish expedition in 1939, these men have given admirable service. They have served with quiet self-effacing efficiency and with high courage. I do not think that any fighting soldier would hesitate to pay tribute to these men who, prevented by their principles from bearing arms, have none the less willingly suffered the full dangers and rigours of war while pursuing their humane calling of tending the wounded and sick.

Basil Nield, MP, British House of Commons, 9 November 1945

This tribute was one among many paid to the Friends Ambulance Service (FAU), not only by politicians in Britain but also by army officers in the field. FAU members were not the only pacifists to serve in uniform during the war; indeed they were genuinely embarrassed to have been singled out in this way. But the FAU experience does provide an excellent example of active pacifism in wartime and is the focus for this essay.

The FAU – or the 'Unit,' as it was known – had existed in the First World War. Numbering over a thousand men, it provided an ambulance and emergency medical service with the French and British armies in France and Belgium. It was disbanded in 1919, but in 1939, with war fast approaching, it was quickly reactivated with the aim of giving young conscientious objectors (COs) the same opportunities for humanitarian service as had existed in the First World War. It was decided that the unit should be open to anybody who shared the basic Quaker belief that war is inconsistent with the spirit and teaching of Christ.

What the FAU offered was an outlet for energy, idealism, and service for those who believed that pacifism should show in action just what it is capable of doing in relieving the effects of war and demonstrating that there is another approach to conflict. In the course of the Second World War a total of about five thousand inquired about membership while some thirteen hundred actually joined. Women were cautiously admitted in October 1940 and by mid-1941 became full members. In all, ninety-seven women joined the FAU. In line with the global reach of the Second World War compared with the First, the unit had a far greater international flavour, with ninety-one members coming from overseas, the majority from the United States and Canada.[1]

Though the FAU adhered to the Quaker peace testimony in spirit, there was considerable argument within the Society of Friends about the active stance that the FAU was taking in the Second World War, and the unit was constitutionally independent of the Society of Friends, which held no responsibility for it. Many Quakers felt that the FAU compromised the Quaker witness against all war by its willingness to work with the military authorities; the wearing of khaki uniforms was particularly contentious because, despite different insignia, it made FAU members look like ordinary members of the army. This situation contrasted with members of the Friends Relief Service (FRS), who insisted on being at arms' length from the army and wearing traditional Quaker grey.[2] In fact, few FAU members worried about such compromise. As Michael Cadbury explained, 'We felt we had to work with the army, and of course we had to look like them. What good was it being trained in ambulance work if you couldn't go into an area where war was raging and there were people to heal? You couldn't get into a war zone without working with the army; many Friends didn't want to recognise that.'[3]

The bases of conscientious objection among members of the unit varied. There is little doubt that religion was the main motive and that most Christian denominations were represented, with Methodists, alongside Quakers, being particularly strong. Few unit members were inclined to evangelicalism; rather it was a practical Christianity that inspired them: living out Christ's ideals in action. Political motives were rarer but certainly present, though often these were masked beneath more overt Christian arguments. Moral and humanitarian drives were strong, and frequently these stemmed from experiences – direct or otherwise – of the horrors of the Great War, which was then only twenty years in the past. Living through events such as the Spanish Civil War as well as witnessing at first hand the nature of Hitler's Germany – as a surprising number had done when on holiday or work experience – members often found themselves torn by conflicting loyalties and tensions. Therefore, though some decided with confidence and certainty to become COs and to join the FAU as active pacifists, others had faced painful dilemmas. It would seem that women experienced fewer problems than men: few of them were called to tribunals.

Many members explained that they did not worry too much about exploring the theory of pacifism; just getting on with the work in hand was what was really significant to them.

From the start the unit emphasized training. Manor Farm at Northfield, Birmingham, proved an ideal spot for this. The basic training involved keeping fit, learning self-sufficiency, and gaining first-aid and nursing skills. Because of the need of moving in military circles, drill, route marches, and kit inspections were also included. This more-ostensibly military aspect proved difficult for some pacifists, though all those who entered the conflict zones vouched for its importance.

Tegla Davies, the unit's historian, aptly described Manor Farm as the 'nursery' of the unit, and most members have stressed its role in creating a sense of identity and in providing a home at a time when many had the feeling of isolation and alienation from a society at war.[4] The intake of men who formed the twenty-one successive camps was varied: bank clerks, actors, mechanics, a butcher's boy, teachers, students, carpenters, lawyers, salesmen, factory and farm workers, and 'a baronet and rat-catcher too.'[5] Of course the same mix would be found in the armed services, but, despite some demarcations of authority, all members of the FAU trained, lived, and worked together. Thus the training camps helped to break down barriers of class and to forge cohesive, egalitarian, effective units out of such a mixture of men.

More training followed, in hospitals across the country, as well as courses in driving and mechanics, where necessary. When opportunities opened for FAU work abroad, members took specialist training in foreign languages (such as Mandarin and Amharic), tropical medicine, or whatever was deemed essential for effective performance.

With the start of the London blitz in the autumn of 1940, the 'woman's touch' became apparent with the opening of shelter and rest-centre work. Tessa Rowntree (later Cadbury) and Dr Gwendy Knight set up five successive training camps in a Rowntree family house, 'Barmoor,' situated in an isolated position on the Yorkshire moors. The training was far less organized than the men's, though the women lived and worked in primitive conditions. 'It was all very ad hoc. We decided that the main thing was to toughen the women up and make them as adaptable as we could.'[6]

When the FAU was re-formed in 1939, the expectation was that it would be mainly staffing ambulances and working in France. As the 'phoney war' went on, trained men were being turned out of Northfield aching for worthwhile work, but there was still no sign of need in France. What was to be done with these enthusiastic young men? As a result of connections enjoyed by Paul Cadbury, chairman of the FAU Council and a member of the well-known Quaker family of chocolate and cocoa manufacturers, hospitals in London and the provinces soon offered further hospital training. In off-duty hours, valuable social work was undertaken by many members: for instance, teaching the 'free-range' children who had missed evacuation and helping with boys' clubs. Then came the London blitz and the huge demand for FAU services in shelters and rest centres, which put the energy and growing expertise to good use – and this was where the (recently admitted) women came into their own.

Many unit members were content to remain on the home front, providing relief and humanitarian services as need arose. However, with the intensification of war after the fall of France in May 1940, many were keen to serve overseas. Some, though accepting that this could happen only under broad military control, insisted on a civilian setting. A sizeable number felt a strong urge to be in the thick of the fighting. They had joined the FAU hoping for and anticipating the 'arduous and dangerous' – to 'go anywhere and do anything,' as their acronym GADA explained – and many readily accepted attachment to military units and work under military discipline. If the unit's purpose was relief of suffering caused by conflict, then surely the battle-field was the place for them to be. Reasons were often more complex: mixed with the straightforward urge to share the suffering of battle was the need to face danger and risks in order to end the feeling of segregation from society which their CO status imposed. There was also anxiety not to be labelled a coward; some felt that they had to justify themselves not only in their own eyes but in the eyes of family, friends, and society.

Since these active young pacifists were so keen to work with the army, why didn't they join a non-combatant or medical corps, as other pacifists in uniform had done?[7] Why go to all the trouble, as Roy Ridgway had done, to register as a CO, appear before an unsympathetic tribunal, and then have his appeal turned down, with a sentence of three months' hard labour, only to enter the FAU and work there in the Hadfield Spears Hospital Unit in Italy and France, with tough, forward fighting units? But as Ridgway explained: 'I wanted to make the choice for myself: my conscience made me volunteer for the FAU.' For him and other like-minded men, to join the army even as a non-combatant would have meant violating deeply held convictions.[8]

During the 'phoney war' period, the FAU's executive committee, at its headquarters in Gordon Square, London, was working hard and using every possible connection to find openings for the unit. Disappointments abounded, as one after another hopeful scheme fell through, but by the end of 1940 the balance was shifting from work at home to work abroad – a frustratingly slow process at first, but gathering momentum by mid-1941.

The unit had gained its first experience of working alongside fighting troops overseas after war broke out between Russia and Finland on 1 December 1939. Surmounting enormous obstacles in organizing, funding, and dealing with bureaucracy, Alan Dickinson and Michael Mounsey became the first unit members in the war to leave the country. They were welcomed in Finland with the news that they could work at the front under Finnish army direction.

By 2 March 1940 another forty-three men had reported, replete with ambulances, to divisional HQ at Leppasyrya, near Lake Lagoda. The unit's work was on the Lagoda front. Split into three groups, the men found steady employment transporting the wounded from the front and visiting the casualty clearing stations and regimental first-aid posts. The work was demanding and often dangerous. During their daily rounds they faced strafing and bombing; and driving along the rutted and icy roads, often at night, they could all too easily end up overturned in one of the deep road-side ditches.

Just ten days after arrival at the front, and at a time when the unit began to congratulate itself that it had found 'the arduous and dangerous,' news came that peace had been negotiated and its work at the front ended. However, with Finnish territory ceded to Russia, evacuation of civilians began immediately. For five weeks the unit, now reinforced with a further twenty-five members, helped with the transport of civilians and of wounded soldiers evacuated from the front.

Within a twelve-day period unit members covered 35,000 miles and moved 2,500 evacuees on roads that, with the melting of the snows, resembled mudbaths. Thus it was at the end of the Russo–Finnish war that the unit's work with refugees started which was to last throughout the war, reaching a peak during the final stage of the unit's life in northwest Europe.

On 9 April 1940 news came of the German attack on Norway and Denmark, and, on the twenty-first, fifty-six men and twenty-six vehicles left Liperi in Finland on their long and tortuous journey north into Norway, arriving just as the British evacuation was starting. Twenty-five-unit men got away with the forces, witnessing, as they left Namsos, two destroyers being sunk by the Luftwaffe. However, they arrived safely with the humiliated and surly troops in Scapa, to be reviewed by General Ironside, who congratulated them all on their 'withdrawal'! A very different fate awaited the thirty-one left behind after the evacuation fleet had sailed. Racing to get out of Norway before the Germans arrived in the Namsos area, they began their nerve-wracking journey back into Sweden, where they began intense negotiations to get back into the war. Eventually, the majority ended up rejoining the unit in Cairo on 21 October 1940, to take up further work, this time with the British army.

Though the Finnish convoy had done only six weeks' solid work, valuable lessons had been learned, especially the need for more systematic training.

Members had also come up against some of the difficulties that were to dog them throughout the war. For instance, what could they carry in their ambulances – should they, could they, carry injured troops? There was the problem too of trying to explain, often in broken language, why they could not carry weapons and ammunition to people who were actually enduring enemy occupation and whose culture had no concept of, or tolerance for, pacifism.

But, though the Finnish experience was short, and a whole group en route had missed the opportunity of serving at the front, there was a sense of satisfaction and a confidence that lives had been saved and people helped. Was not this traditional Friends' work? Here then were the pioneers who gave those at home itching for service both hope and inspiration: the unit's reputation was being built up, it had proved that it could operate under army control. In an albeit modest way, the unit had made its mark and was confident of being considered for similar tasks again.

There is not space here to describe adequately the variety and the value of the humanitarian service performed by the unit during the war. We mention first its work with Allied armies in North Africa, Greece, and China. The FAU experienced its first service with the British army in North Africa – a link that was to last well into 1946. In that theatre the unit went forward in all the desert campaigns from Wavell's push in early December 1940 through to the El Alamein advance from October 1942, working as forward and rear medical units as well as in transport and military hospitals. The FAU also played an important role in the blood-transfusion units (BTUs), working for example in the BTU that was responsible for supplying all the 8th Army's area with blood. Two FAU groups also joined the Free French 1st and 2nd divisions for front-line medical and transport work. Except for the actual fighting, the unit shared fully the life of Allied troops in the desert campaigns – the mix of excitement and boredom, the sweltering heat, sandstorms, flies, and lack of water; the advances and victories, the routs and chaotic retreats. Place names such as Akerit, Bir Hacheim, El Aghelia, Mareth, Sidi Birani, and Tobruk, are as evocative to unit members as to any army veteran!

Meanwhile, unit members had responded to the challenge that came from Greece in March 1941, shortly before the German invasion. They arrived in Athens just in time to join the retreat, evacuating patients under Stuka attacks, sheltering in caves and olive groves, and, for those who managed to get away, evacuating with the army to Port Said and back to North Africa, to join the desert campaigns. For those who did not manage to escape, it meant sharing the same fate as Allied prisoners of war (POWs) in Germany.

Just when the sections in North Africa were proving their mettle with the

Allied armies, an exciting opportunity opened in wartime China. Eventually, in October 1941, the first group of forty men – the 'Holy Forty,' as they came to be known jokingly – left in small parties to participate in one of the greatest challenges faced by the unit.

The China Convoy was distinctive for many reasons – the vastness of area covered by its activities and the great distance from home, the huge need for yet paucity of relief organizations there, and its being the most international of all FAU sections. By the beginning of 1946 the convoy had grown to 139 members – seventy-one British, twenty-six Chinese, eighteen Americans, eighteen Canadians (including surgeon 'Bob' McClure, who acted as the convoy's leader), and six New Zealanders. Of these people eighteen were women – ten Chinese, six British, one American, and one Canadian.

The work of the China Convoy consisted mostly of providing the only organized and effective transport system for distribution of drugs and medical supplies to hospitals scattered throughout southwest Free China. If the roads and hairpin bends in the mountainous areas that the convoys traversed were not daunting enough, there was also the odd encounter with bandits. In addition, the Japanese seizure of oil supplies necessitated converting trucks into charcoal burners, resulting in one of the most demanding transport tasks imaginable in terms of mechanical and improvization skills, strong nerves, and almost saintly patience.

The China Convoy also provided flexible, mobile medical teams to work with the Chinese army in the primitive base hospitals, as well as moving forward with its forces. These teams were particularly busy during the Chinese drive into Burma in 1944. One medical team – MT3 – for instance, took to the hills with the Chinese army in May 1944, its members often performing operations well into the night by the glow of oil lamps. This team received a citation from the American army when, at the end of August 1944, the city of Tengchung finally fell, with hardly a Japanese left alive. MT3 was among the first to enter a hellish scene of death and utter devastation and set about planning and building a new hospital – the unit's first experiment in what was to be its third main contribution to wartorn China: rehabilitation and reconstruction.

The FAU did much valuable work abroad apart from working with Allied armies in the field. For instance, clinics were set up in the wilds of Syria by members of the Hadfield Spears Unit of the FAU and continued throughout the war. The unit also helped to establish a much-needed system of medical care in Ethiopia after the Italian defeat. By invitation of the emperor, Haile Selassie, it maintained central hospitals and more isolated clinics under mounting difficulties until its members' withdrawal in the spring of 1945. The FAU also worked in small numbers in India on famine relief and aid to refugees; here the connection with the military was practically non-existent.

As the tide of war changed, so unit members drew on their knowledge of unit history in the First World War, realizing the vast civilian need that would have to be faced in the newly liberated countries. Civilian relief was in fact to form the last chapter of the unit's story.[9] As FAU medical units with the Allied armies worked their way up the length of Italy and into Europe, close on their heels, and sometimes in tandem, came the relief units.

As with other areas of work the unit's civilian-relief work was closely bound with the Allied armies that had responsibility for the government of the liberated areas. The armies therefore had the last word in deciding which civilian organizations, if any, should be allowed in. By 1943 the unit had built up a very good reputation with the Allied forces, but it had had to work with the Red Cross, which in effect served as an intermediary between the army and the unit. Given the sheer chaos and confusion reigning in any liberated area, the unit soon became frustrated with time wasted in bureaucratic planning while civilians were suffering. The unit demonstrated its organizational strength and flexibility, especially its ability, based on considerable experience, quickly to determine needs, set up its own relationships, cut or by-pass red tape (often by some rather un-Quakerly means!), and get into areas in which urgent jobs needed to be done. Thus the unit offered something different in style from other civilian relief organizations. While the latter settled down to long-term programs of assistance, the FAU's business was primarily immediate relief. It followed as closely as possible behind the occupying troops, doing the job at hand quickly and decisively and then withdrawing to the next urgent task, after handing over any work of lasting value.

Until June 1945, the FAU had insisted on all-male teams for European relief. Frustrating though this decision seemed to FAU women wanting to join forward relief teams in Europe, the all-male FAU teams proved more acceptable to the British army than mixed teams. With the war over, and demands for welfare and occupational schemes increasing dramatically, FAU women now came into their own. By the end of 1945 unit relief teams, comprising over three hundred members in all, found work in Austria, Belgium, France, Germany, Greece and the Dodecanese, Holland, Italy, Sicily, and Yugoslavia, and the relief work continued well into 1946. In terms of voluntary relief, the FAU operated on a scale second only to the Red Cross.

By August 1945 the unit had eleven sections in Germany, with close on 150 men and women. It was there, on 'enemy' territory, that unit members found their pacifism tested to the utmost. Unit men working with the 2nd Division of the Free French found themselves particularly challenged. They had served alongside their fighting comrades during some of the toughest campaigns in France, including the Battle of the Bulge and the push to Strasbourg, becoming battle-hardened in the process. When they moved into the heart of Germany, their Free French division was thirsting for revenge, and, with the war over, it was the civilian population that paid the price. Unit members knew the troops well and understood the family losses they had suffered, but they found their vengeful behaviour hard to bear and did their best to alleviate the situation where possible. For instance, they would spread themselves throughout a village at night and discovered that the French avoided their worst excesses when they were around. Being concerned with reconciliation, they found the rule of non-fraternization with civilians irksome and humiliating, and most unit members took an independent attitude towards this restriction, in a quiet way.

Writing in 1947, Tegla Davies, in his history of the FAU, expressed the hope that some day the unit's place in the overall pattern of the Second World War would be seen in its true perspective. Fifty years on seems a good time to make an attempt.[10] But the FAU's story is far more than a record of its impressive service at home and overseas. It also is a contribution to the understanding of the theory and practice of conscientious objection and pacifism, not least in the dilemmas that members confronted during the war.

One of the major challenges concerned the need to work closely with the army without violating integrity of conscience. Many members have spoken of the sympathy, respect, and friendship that they came to feel for the fighting troops, with whom they had shared dangers, wounds, and sometimes death.[11] As pacifists, they realized how their detestation of war was shared by many front-line solders. They were constantly aware of their privileged position as volunteers, with a degree of choice denied those acting under military discipline and having to obey orders, however distasteful or terrifying.

This is not to say that there was no misunderstanding or tension between the FAU and its fighting counterparts. Challenges abounded, and one constant was the argument concerning the transport of troops and war materiel on the Red Cross lorries used by the FAU. With 'Jerry' just over the hill and advancing quickly, how could they possibly refuse? There was also bewilderment on the part of the 'Tommies': 'No pay! Blimey mate, you must be mad. What are you doing this for then?'[12] Or sometimes anger when FAU medics insisted on treating 'the enemy' wounded on an equal basis.

In later years many members wondered, and often agonized, over whether they had been petty and trivial, arguing about some of these issues, which had at the time seemed so important to them. But the essential point was that one small compromise after another would have meant gradual acceptance of war and erosion of their pacifism.

Though most unit members experienced conflicts of conscience at some stage of their experience, many coped with these and remained confident that theirs was the right way, the *only* way for them: 'The standard of non-violence has to be upheld whatever the dilemma.'[13] But there were others who questioned their own pacifist stance. Such doubts arose for a variety of reasons. One had to do with the present reality: the test of being in a war situation, of seeing evil at first hand and realizing that something must be done to stop it and that if the only course open was to enter the fray and to bear arms – so be it. Or maybe, in novel and extreme conditions, a man was forced, as David Morris was, into a new self-awareness, which led to the realization that fundamentally he was not a pacifist. And, since he could not apply the 'saintly' standards that pacifists *ought* to have, he should no longer retain their privileged position; the army, then, was the place for him.[14]

Bill Brough, who left the unit to joint the American army, distinguished himself in the Burma campaign. It was the American surgeon Dr Gordon Seagrave, with whom Brough had previously worked, who invited him to join the American army in order that he could continue his medical work with the Chinese army. Now as a soldier, Brough received two Bronze Stars, the Silver Star for later service in the Office of Strategic Services (OSS), and one of the highest decorations given by the American government in time of war – the Medal for Merit. Yet he summed up his position 'In China I had become a conflicted and confused conscientious objector, then had changed to become a conflicted and confused soldier. I could never decide whether I had been both a failed conchie and a failed soldier, or whether to be a bit of both at the same time is the only real human condition.'[15]

Tom Hayley's case was rather different. His dilemma, an agonizing one, arose from his assisting in the mercy killing of fatally wounded soldiers on a retreat along the China–Burma front. He had entered the war 'to save lives, not to take them,' but he knew only too well the cruel and terrible fate of mortally wounded men falling into Japanese hands. Yet after the anguished re-examination of his pacifism that followed this crisis, he found that it emerged reinforced and strengthened by the ghastliness of all-out warfare.[16]

Several unit members have expressed deep satisfaction at having been in the hottest action, where they witnessed the ultimate reality of bloody warfare. One man felt that 'authentic behaviour is revealed in such circumstances.' Another has spoken of the 'intensity of feeling' that one experiences in battle and how the most positive aspects of human behaviour can be seen in war. They confronted their own partisan feelings for the troops whom they worked alongside, recognizing the irony that it was the battle-field which provided a true testing ground, where a turmoil of feelings and conscience had to be worked through again and again.

Yet others have agonized over the fact that they themselves, while remaining non-combatants, were in fact compromising with the military machine – for instance, by doing work that would release someone else for military service. Many unit members have admitted that in a situation of total war there is really no logical position for the CO. Few unit members stayed complacent about their stance; most were forced to think and rethink it. The shock of the Nazi concentration camps seems to have been particularly traumatic, and several unit members have admitted that they still have not resolved the dilemma that this forced on them, though they remain firmly opposed to violence and war.

Apart from the problems experienced by individuals in maintaining their integrity as pacifists, the unit itself found that it was not always easy to maintain a separate identity and resist being swallowed into a military system. These were problems that its people thrashed out continuously throughout the war in a truly democratic and Quakerly manner until solutions were found. As for the Allied forces, one can only admire the way in which army officers accommodated units of men whom they often found difficult, bewildering, and infuriating. In short, the FAU–military relationship in the Second World War is a tribute to both the Allied armies and the unit.

Acceptance of war medals caused other dilemmas. Unit policy laid down that it was inappropriate to accept general awards such as the African Star but that it was up to individual members whether or not they accepted more personal awards. Some refused, many accepted – readers might be surprised at how many Croix de Guerre are legitimately possessed by FAU members, though shyly tucked away in cabinet drawers.

Something that has emerged very strongly from the interviews that I have conducted with unit members is the personal growth that they all experienced while in the FAU. The unit provided them with a wartime 'home' as well as 'opportunity to serve under the colours of the peace movement.'[17] All members stress too what a great educational experience serving with the FAU was. They often refer to the FAU as 'my university.' One is continuously reminded of how these experiences and the high standards set by the unit changed expectations and careers after the war. A very large proportion of ex-members went into medicine and other socially constructive work, and many have continued to use their spare time helping others in their communities or doing valuable work with relief and humanitarian organizations – Oxfam or the Halo Trust, for instance.[18]

The FAU's story is among the neglected aspects of Second World War historiography. In China, for instance, the FAU was one of the main foreign civilian groups operating, and members provide excellent accounts of the complex nature of wartime China. For instance, Duncan Wood, who travelled extensively in Free China during the war, compared the situation in wartime China to the fluidity and informality of eighteenth-century Europe in time of war.[19] Other FAU members, including women, worked in a medical team with Mao's Communists in Yenan and give first-hand witness of early commune life.[20]

The distinguishing factor of the FAU's perception of the war is that members see events through the eyes of non-combatants, from a perspective of those relatively detached from the war machine. They display little sense of 'them' and 'us,' draw no firm line between the 'right' and the 'wrong' side. They generally discount the propaganda of both sides and give terms such as 'heroism,' 'sacrifice,' 'patriotism,' 'victory,' and 'defeat' entirely different connotations from those usually accepted. True, the unit formed only a tiny fragment of a whole world in turmoil. Nevertheless, its story provides a valuable counterbalance and complement to military accounts of the last war. Why then, during the fiftieth anniversary of the end of the Second World War, did we not hear more of the FAU experience?

NOTES

1 Apart from the British contingent serving in the FAU, there were forty-nine Americans, twenty-four Canadians, ten New Zealanders, four from Eire, two Chinese, one Czech, one Indian, and one South African.
2 It is ironic that on several occasions Quaker grey uniforms were confused with the Wehrmacht's grey uniforms, sometimes causing suspicion, distress, and, in one instance, danger.
3 Interview with Michael Cadbury. The interview referred to here, and those cited below form part of a series that I have conducted with FAU members, many of them for the Sound Archive Department of the Imperial War Museum, London, where they are stored. They provide the main source for my forthcoming book on the FAU experience in the Second World War.
4 A. Tegla Davies, *Friends Ambulance Unit: The Story of the F.A.U. in the Second World War* (London 1947), 11.
5 Line from the lyric of 'Chocolate Soldiers,' by Sydney Carter and Donald Swann, both members of the FAU.
6 Interview with Tessa Cadbury.
7 A total of 6,766 men joined a special Non-Combatant Corps, set up by the British army in 1940. Hundreds of COs also worked in the Royal Army Medical Corps and the Airborne Medical Ambulance Units.

8 Interview with Roy Ridgway. The Hadfield Spears Hospital Unit was an FAU section attached to the mobile hospital set up by Mrs (later Lady) Spears, best known as the novelist Mary Borden, and Lady Hadfield to work with the Free French.

9 A successor, but distinct organization, the FAU Post War Service (PWS), was set up to cater for men liable for national service after the FAU's closure.

10 Davies, *Friends Ambulance Unit*, 464.

11 Sixteen FAU men lost their lives during the Second World War.

12 FAU members received no pay for their voluntary service but were provided with a weekly allowance of seven shillings and six pence.

13 Interview with Douglas Turner.

14 Interview with David Morris. See his *China Changed My Mind* (London 1948).

15 Interview with Bill Brough.

16 Interview with Tom Hayley.

17 Interview with Donald Swann.

18 Hazardous Areas Life-support Organisation (HALO Trust). I may note here the name of Gerald Gardiner, who was in charge of the FAU's immediate postwar relief in northwestern Europe and subsequently became Britain's lord chancellor.

19 Interview with Duncan Wood.

20 Interviews of FAU members.

16

Conscientious Objection in Canada

THOMAS P. SOCKNAT

Given a war situation, we Mennonites can practice our belief in Canada only because other Canadians are kind enough to fight for our right to our belief. The godless man then dies for the belief of the Christian! Further, is it even possible for us not to participate today? Ultimately, even the farmer works for the War because he produces the food that makes fighting possible. Mere refusal will not do: positive action alone is possible. But we as a church have gone on in the traditional ways of reacting to war, not considering that the world has changed, even since World War One.

Rudy Wiebe, *Peace Shall Destroy Many*[1]

In his novel *Peace Shall Destroy Many*, the Canadian Mennonite writer Rudy Wiebe clearly identified the personal dilemma facing not only many Mennonites but the vast majority of conscientious objectors (COs) in Canada during the Second World War. They were determined to remain faithful to their Christian pacifist beliefs, but they also feared that they could not entirely escape the war and therefore felt that they should perform some type of worthwhile service. Since it was no easy matter to reconcile these views, the issue was at the centre of pacifist debate.

Canada itself had a history of tolerating the pacifist conscience, but only to a limited degree. During the First World War, the Canadian Military Service Act of 1917 allowed for the unconditional deferment of COs but restricted its application to the specific pacifist sects that had entered Canada with such guarantees: Doukhobors, Hutterites, Mennonites, and Quakers.[2] It made no allowance for pacifists from other faiths and no provisions for some form of alternative national service, though the idea of forestry work was considered late in the war.[3] In other words, only members of specific religious groups were recognized as COs and exempted from military service. Any others who refused military orders, such as Jehovah's Witnesses, faced stiff military discipline, including instances of torture.[4]

As Wiebe argued, however, by the late 1930s the world, and Canada, had changed. The arrival on the prairies during the 1920s of twenty thousand Russländer Mennonites from the Soviet Union added a new dimension to the Mennonite non-resistant tradition. With a history of performing various forms of alternative service in tsarist Russia, including non-combatant medical work, the Russländer group viewed alternative service during wartime as an expression of faith rather than, like some of their brethren, a compromise in principle. In addition, following two decades of anti-war rhetoric, including that of a vocal pacifist minority in the United Church of Canada, the country's largest Protestant denomination, there were more young men outside pacifist sects who opposed military duty for reasons of conscience, including a few humanist pacifists, whose objections to war were ethical rather than religious.

In effect, by the end of the 1930s Canada's pacifist community represented both the non-resistant tradition of the historic peace sects and the liberal pacifism that surfaced in those major Protestant denominations heavily influenced by the 'social gospel' and its emphasis on the Sermon on the Mount. During the interwar years this liberal pacifist minority organized groups and individuals into a broad peace movement that promoted disarmament, Dick Sheppard's peace pledge, and such pacifist tracts as Richard Gregg's *The Power of Nonviolence*. In addition, the pacifist position was presented in the Canadian Parliament through the Co-operative Commonwealth Federation (CCF), the social-democratic third party, and its leader, the country's foremost pacifist, J.S. Woodsworth (see chapter 12, above).

Increasing fascist aggression in the late 1930s, however, reduced the peace movement to a hard core of mainly Christian pacifists, organized through the Canadian Fellowship of Reconciliation (FOR), headed by Carlyle King, an English professor at the University of Saskatchewan. By the autumn of 1939, King was urging his fellow pacifists to concentrate on helping young men with conscientious objections to military service.

At the same time, in his last major speech in the Canadian House of Commons, in September 1939, J.S. Woodsworth explained his pacifist objections to the war and, on a personal note, strongly endorsed the option of conscientious objection. In reference to his own sons, he claimed that he would be proud if any one of them declared himself a CO rather than enlisting in the military, even if it meant facing a firing squad.[5] It was certainly an emotional appeal and one that did not go unnoticed by pacifists, especially young men of military age. The focus of Woodsworth and the FOR, as well as Mennonites, revealed that conscientious objection enjoyed support from a broad range of pacifists.

With this new reality in mind, and once faced with another war crisis, most pacifists joined together in an effort to secure two major concessions from Canadian authorities – the right to CO status of all individuals who conscientiously opposed military service, regardless of religious affiliation, and the establishment of some form of alternative service. They saw the two demands as inseparable not only because of their increased interest in performing useful work during wartime but also because alternative service itself was seen as possibly the only way to ensure that all COs would be deferred from military service. In time, but for different reasons, government authorities came to share this view, and CO labour came to be used in diversified forms of national service at first, in forestry camps; then in hospitals; and finally, overseas as well. These developments owed much to the pressure of pacifists themselves.

CO Status

Though Canada officially entered the war in September 1939, it was not until June 1940 that the National Resources Mobilization Act authorized conscription of men, but only for home defence.[6] Conscription for overseas service was not approved until November 1944. This delay in permitting the sending of conscripts overseas may have mollified some anti-conscriptionists, but it was largely insignificant to pacifists opposed to any type of military service, at home or overseas. After complying with national registration in 1940, Canadian men came under the authority of the National War Services Regulations (Recruits), which laid the ground rules for the actual call-up of men, as well as for exemptions.[7] Most exemptions were automatically extended to men in civilian occupations deemed essential to the maintenance of public order and safety, such as judges, clergymen, policemen, firemen, and prison and mental asylum workers. Allowance was also made for the postponement of military service for COs.

In order to be granted a postponement order, Doukhobors, Mennonites, and others with conscientious objections were required to submit a written application to their divisional registrar and to appear before the National War Service Board (often referred to as the 'Mobilization Board') in their military administrative district. If the board was satisfied that the applicant conscientiously objected to war in any form by reason of religious training or belief, his military training was postponed. There was no allowance for non-religious COs. In actual practice, however, the ease or difficulty in obtaining a postponement as a CO varied from one division to another, depending on the views of the local populace or the board chairman. In some cases applicants, mainly Jehovah's Witnesses and Mennonites, were denied CO status and ordered to report for military training or, if they refused, sent to prison.[8] Even more restrictive, however, was the narrow definition of who qualified as a CO. In effect, the provisions of the War Service Regulations raised tensions among pacifists, especially within the Mennonite community.

According to the Regulations, Doukhobors and Mennonites were specifically guaranteed an indefinite postponement, but the term 'Mennonites' included only the Kanadier group in Manitoba, descendants of those who emigrated from Russia in the 1870s and received a permanent exemption from military service at that time.[9] To achieve postponement, the Kanadier had only to prove membership in a Mennonite church and continuous residence in Canada, but all other Mennonites – the new Russländers and the Ontario groups mainly of Swiss descent, most of whom had emigrated from the United States in the 1790s – fell into the general category of COs and were required to articulate their religious objections to war individually.[10] Understandably, a temporary rift developed. Relatively assured of postponements, the Kanadier Mennonites initially opposed the idea of alternative service and remained aloof from early pacifist lobbying for further concessions in Ottawa.[11] The majority of Mennonites, however, enthusiastically endorsed the idea of alternative service – even noncombatant duty in the case of Russländers, since that was already part of their experience – as the best way to ensure recognition as bona fide COs.

The 1940 regulations also required all COs to belong to a religious denomination that prohibited bearing of arms as a tenet of faith. Thus men from major Protestant denominations, or any church other than Canada's historic peace sects (Brethren in Christ, Doukhobors, and Mennonites), were initially denied CO status, and their plight became an important element in the pacifist call for universal recognition of COs in conjunction with alternative service.

As early as August 1940, the chief registrar in Ottawa had received numerous letters from United Church pacifists urging the government to provide all COs with alternative forms of national service, as in Britain.[12] More traditional pacifist groups, such as the Christadelphian Service Committee of Canada, made similar pleas, but it was the Canadian Society of Friends that took the lead in organizing a pacifist front for alternative service in the interests of all prospective COs.

By the summer of 1940 the Canadian Friends Service Committee, through its general secretary, Fred Haslam, who had been a CO in Britain in the First World War, outlined plans for an alternative-service work program under civilian supervision that included any practical combination of forestry or agricultural work, road maintenance, social services in distressed areas, and even postwar rehabilitation.[13] In an effort to build a pacifist pressure group for such national service, Haslam approached the Brethren in Christ (Tunker) and Mennonite churches in Ontario. The Ontario peace churches accepted the Quaker proposal and invited the Society of Friends to join their new Conference of Historic Peace Churches.[14]

This united pacifist front sent its first delegation to Ottawa in September 1940, seeking official recognition of all COs, in conjunction with some form of alternative service.[15] By November the same message was reiterated by a joint delegation representing both the Conference of Historic Peace Churches and western Mennonites, mainly Russländers, now represented by the Mennonite Central Relief Committee.[16] The associate deputy ministers of National War Services, T.C. Davis and L.R. LaFlèche, initially rejected the idea and promoted non-combatant military service instead, apparently with the support of at least one Russländer spokesman.[17]

The result was a series of passionate discussions, in which the majority of delegation members persisted in their demands for civilian service and finally forwarded specific recommendations, closely resembling Haslam's earlier proposals, in which alternative service would be in agriculture or forestry, under the civilian supervision of the departments of Agriculture and of Mines and Resources.[18] Far in advance of government plans, the delegation's final recommendations ultimately served as the blueprint for alternative service.

In the meantime, government officials were facing increasing public resentment, especially in the west, over pacifist exemptions. George McDonald, a former Manitoba Liberal MP, claimed that Manitobans were angered and bitter that Mennonites were escaping military training while their young men took up arms. 'While our sons are fighting,' he complained, 'these men will be building up good homes. It certainly isn't fair.'[19] Such sentiments were taken very seriously by the government.

In response to them as much as to pacifist lobbying, James Gardiner, the minister of national war services and himself from Saskatchewan, announced new regulations in December 1940. On the one hand, COs would no longer have to be members of recognized peace churches, though they still had to belong to a religious denomination (a requirement dropped in April 1942, when the individual conscience became the sole basis for exemption).[20] On the other hand, in return for this broadening of the regulations, all COs were required to perform some form of alternative service, either civilian labour or non-combatant duties in the army.[21]

Though most pacifists, including the Russländer Mennonites, were pleased with the new policy – in effect a compromise among the various pacifist positions – the Kanadier were in turmoil. Their Ältestenkomitee, or committee of elders, having boycotted all previous negotiations with Ottawa, since they felt assured of exemption, now made a desperate plea for the complete exemption of Kanadier men from all forms of service, but to no avail.[22] Thereafter the Kanadier group grudgingly joined the pacifist lobby to ensure that alternative service would be of a civilian nature under civilian supervision; consequently, the distinctions between the different types of Mennonites became increasingly blurred, especially to the authorities.

Alternative Service Work

Within a few months of the new regulations being issued, the Department of National War Services complied with the demands for a civilian-oriented program, mainly because its preferred plan for non-combatant training was blocked by military authorities staunchly opposed to having COs in their camps under any circumstances. Thus, at this stage Canadian provision for conscientious objection differed from similar legislation in Britain and the United States as well as Australia and New Zealand, which allowed COs to opt for service in a non-combatant capacity in the armed forces, including the medical corps. Such an alternative was especially welcome to a denomination such as the Seventh-day Adventists, as their record in the United States showed; non-combatant army service, however, was still unacceptable to many COs.

ASW Camps

In Canada, it was the specific recommendations of the pacifist lobby that became the basis for the Alternative Service Work (ASW) camps that were established in national parks across the west, at two forest experimental stations, and at an old logging camp on the Montreal River in northern Ontario, all under the supervision of the Department of Mines and Resources.[23]

As the first and largest camp as well as the major reception centre for COs from eastern Canada, the Montreal River camp not only inaugurated the alternative-service program but became the model for later camps, especially those on the west coast.[24] To a certain extent, life there also left an imprint on the COs themselves, for it was there that they were first introduced to one another and to a range of pacifist beliefs.

The majority of the COs in the camp were members of either millennial sects, such as Jehovah's Witnesses, or the Conference of Historic Peace Churches, and together they represented a variety of religious beliefs. Nevertheless, most of them viewed alternative service as simply the price they had to pay to remain true to their faith.[25] A smaller number of Quakers and pacifists from the larger Protestant denominations welcomed the opportunity to perform some type of national service. Some viewed the work camps as experiments in communal living, while others were attracted to the belief that a personal pacifist stand would help change the structure of social institutions. At least one of the latter men, Roy Clifton, wrote for advice from Herbert Runham Brown, honorary secretary of the War Resisters' International.[26]

This small group of activists at Montreal River also began the first Canadian CO publication, the *Northern Beacon*. The mimeographed newsletter, edited by Wes Brown, a Toronto CO with a United Church background, was intended to boost the moral of the COs in the camps, as well as to inform friends at home.[27] Gordon Stewart, a student at McGill University and a future CO, responded by launching another newsletter, the *Canadian CO*.[28] The main theme of both newsletters was what Wiebe termed 'positive action' in a number of fields of work at home and abroad.

Constructive Christian service proved a popular topic of discussion in the camp, particularly since there was growing resentment among COs that they had been shipped up to Montreal River merely in order to be hidden from the public. They were especially discouraged with their work, which seemed to be of minimal value. Even the ASW camps out west appeared more attractive, since at least personnel there were responsible for the prevention and suppression of forest fires, while those in Banff and Kootenay parks were credited with saving large quantities of saw-timber and mine props.[29]

By April 1942, while COs demanded more worthwhile work, and as the authorities recognized COs as a permanent and valuable pool of labour, increased warnings of forest fires on the west coast because of the fear of Japanese attack finally triggered a major change in policy. The minister of national war services decided to transfer over one thousand COs to the British Columbia Forest Service for forest-protection duties on Vancouver Island and the adjacent mainland.[30] From that time on, the west coast was the centre of ASW activity.

The main responsibility of ASW crews in the BC camps – approximately twenty crews at any given time – was fighting forest fires, but they also accomplished valuable and essential work in forest protection. Since the majority of the Montreal River 'campers' had been reassigned to British Columbia, they exerted much of the leadership and influence in the new camps. Even their newsletter resurfaced at the Campbell River Camp as the *Beacon*, a truly interdenominational paper that tried to strike a balance among differing religious viewpoints.[31]

It is evident from letters and interviews that most COs welcomed BC camps not only for the worthwhile jobs but also as simply an adventure. Robert Makaroff, a Saskatchewan CO, later recalled his time at ASW camps at Waskesiu and Blubber Bay as 'fantastic' experiences. Waskesiu was the summer place of his childhood, and he loved it there, but he also came to enjoy felling trees. 'I got to be a good chopper,' he confessed, 'and I was strong and eating well and having lots of fun and met two or three really good fellows.'[32]

Obviously, camp life represented a good mix of hard work and comradeship, but it also assumed a monotonous routine. The average day began early, since the men were served a hearty breakfast before they started work at eight a.m. and continued until four p.m., with an hour off for lunch. The evening hours were filled with leisure activities and religious devotions.[33] In fact, the men spent a good amount of their free time in choir practice and Bible study, often with the help and encouragement of visiting ministers, such as J. Harold Sherk, the Mennonite secretary of the Conference of Historic Peace Churches, and James Finlay, a pacifist spokesman in the United Church.

Despite the general satisfaction in the camps, however, discontent soon set in again. Though a number of wives and children resettled in nearby BC towns in order to be close to the camps, Mennonite men tended to miss their families and yearned to return to their farms.[34] In contrast, the Russländers and liberal activists repeated their call for some type of useful humanitarian service.[35] Rudy Wiebe captured these contrasting sentiments in *Peace Shall Destroy Many*, when one of his fictional characters reports the feelings of a CO in camp: 'He's sick of CO camp. He writes that to hear the news is awful for him, yet he can't tear himself away from the radio when it comes on. Buzz-bombs falling on London, the French ruined, Germans killing in retreat, the Chinese starving, while they sit in Jasper planting trees that could wait as easily as not. But the worst is the way some of the men, our people too, don't understand or care what is really going on outside in the world. They're happy that their own conscience is satisfied – they care for no more.'[36]

Certainly, the COs in the camps were not in agreement on the nature of alternative service. Their opinions ran the gamut from Jehovah's Witnesses, still resistant to the idea of any type of service, through a large number of men, mostly Mennonites, who were generally satisfied with their duties, to those increasingly demanding more worthwhile work.

Hospital Work

Pacifist groups outside the camps also began to increase the pressure on Ottawa to follow the British example and use COs as hospital orderlies, attendants in mental hospitals, and similar occupations.[37] Finally in February 1943 the director of selective service, Arthur MacNamara, concluded that COs in the camps 'could now be more usefully employed in agriculture or in essential industries where labour shortages exist.'[38] The result was the broadening of alternative service to include essential work in agriculture and industry.[39] Obviously, the government's decision was based on labour needs, but it also helped satisfy pacifist demands to allow COs a wider field of service.

Under the new arrangement, COs were screened individually and assigned to jobs where their skills were most needed. Though a considerable number were assigned to laboratories, hospitals, and certain industries such as sawmills and food-processing plants, the majority of COs, largely Mennonites with farm experience, were directed to agricultural work. Both options were conditional on COs' agreeing to contribute part of their earnings to the Canadian Red Cross.[40] Therefore, while COs were paid at the prevailing wage rate, they were allowed to keep only twenty-five dollars a month. The resulting financial hardship on men and their families was later offset when the government gave in to more pressure from pacifist groups and authorized additional allowances for dependants and for medical and dental services.[41]

Despite some complaints from the public about using COs outside the camps, on the whole the broadening of alternative-service work took place easily and smoothly. Most COs were enthusiastic about their transition from camp life to farms, factories, and hospitals, but some still desired to perform some type of real wartime humanitarian service in what they called 'danger areas.' Speaking on behalf of Russländer Mennonites, C.F. Klassen, secretary of the Mennonite Central Relief Committee of Winnipeg, reiterated the plea for non-combatant medical work. A few months later, in July 1943, a group of COs at Banff, demanding 'to be of more valuable service,' reported that five Toronto churches were prepared to provide the necessary equipment for a CO ambulance corps.[42]

Service Overseas

Government authorities, however, remained hesitant to deploy COs overseas in a non-combatant or humanitarian capacity, even though a precedent had been set the previous year with inclusion of COs in the Civilian Corps of Canadian Firefighters sent to the United Kingdom. Eventually twenty COs, mainly Mennonites and United Churchmen from the prairies, served overseas, fighting fires and carrying on salvage and rescue operations.[43] It was the first time that Canadian COs actually confronted wartime destruction, and pressure for more CO involvement continued to build.

Finally, in the spring of 1943, the government again changed policy and authorized the enlistment of COs in overseas service as non-combatants in the medical and dental corps under military command.[44] Before the end of the war over two hundred COs, Russländer Mennonites in particular, joined non-combatant units, and many of them served overseas in theatres of the European war. Kornelius Krahn later recalled that 'germs ... and not the Germans' were his main enemy there. Other than administering treatments and medications and keeping records on patients, his duties included looking after the sanitation of the wards and serving meals.[45]

Though the expansion or alternative service into the fire-fighter and non-combatant units was greeted enthusiastically by some COs, it was viewed suspiciously by others, even those who wanted to take 'positive action,' since it appeared that only a thin line separated these new forms of alternative service from outright support of the war effort. It was a fear underlined by the fact that non-combatants were required to undergo basic combat training. What was needed, COs insisted, was relief and rehabilitation work under civilian control. Their goal was to organize a Canadian contingent to join the Friends Ambulance Unit (FAU) in China.

Promoted by the Canadian Friends Service Committee through its general secretary, Fred Haslam, as well as by Dr Robert McClure, the Canadian missionary doctor who headed the FAU's China unit, the Canadian FAU contingent became a reality in the summer of 1944, when Ottawa finally agreed to allow twenty Canadian volunteers, including eighteen COs and two women, to travel to China.[46] The Canadian Red Cross furnished uniforms and equipment, and the Chinese War Relief Fund, a Canadian charitable organization, contributed approximately $500,000 towards the support of the Canadian contingent.[47] In China during the last year of the war the Canadian COs performed various medical and administrative tasks in hospitals and warehouses, but their main job was hauling medical supplies across the rugged interior of the country. The Canadian China unit set a precedent for wartime relief work and came to symbolize the ideal of COs' assisting civilian populations in time of war.

Challenges

Canada's alternative-service program had certainly evolved smoothly through the war years, and yet the authorities were convinced that its overall effectiveness had been seriously obstructed by two groups of COs – Jehovah's Witnesses and Doukhobors. Jehovah's Witnesses made up the largest group serving jail sentences for refusing to cooperate,[48] and, once the majority of COs were transferred from ASW camps to other forms of alternative service, Jehovah's Witnesses were basically the only ones that remained in the camps – approximately two hundred by the time the camps were finally closed.[49] They were denied employment outside the camps because they were unwilling to enter an employment contract or to allocate funds to the Red Cross, and also because of their general resistance to the principle of alternative service.

Certainly, in keeping with their rejection of the secular state, Jehovah's Witnesses believed military and alternative service equally unacceptable, and, from the very beginning of the war, they proved to be dogmatic, uncooperative, and generally difficult to handle.[50] Though they obviously had conscientious objections to the war, frustrated alternative-service officials remained sceptical and recommended that, in the event of another war, Jehovah's Witnesses not be classified as COs.[51]

The Doukhobors likewise earned a reputation for non-cooperation. Though they conducted their own registration of men, with government approval, they argued that they should have unconditional exemption and therefore opposed the idea of alternative service.[52] Initially, most Doukhobor COs in Saskatchewan, who belonged to the Independent branch, were segregated and assigned to a separate road-building project that generally proved unsuccessful.[53] But approximately one hundred of them refused to cooperate and were jailed for several months.[54] Those in British Columbia, especially the radical Sons of Freedom, who were better known for arson and nude marches than for pacifism, were openly hostile to the idea of alternative service, and many refused to comply with government orders. In the end the authorities decided to do 'nothing with the Doukhobors in British Columbia' in order to avoid trouble.[55]

Doukhobors in effect were exempted from any kind of national service – a fact kept secret from the public. Apparently, they had proved to be such an irritant that the chief alternative-service officer, L.E. Westman, actually proposed the resettlement of all BC Doukhobors in some Central American country such as El Salvador in exchange for Mexican migrant labour.[56] Of course, nothing ever came of this extraordinary proposal.

An Assessment

These two exceptions aside, Canada's first experiment with alternative service was viewed as a minor triumph by all concerned. By the end of the war, over twelve thousand Canadian men had been classified as COs. The vast majority were Mennonites or members of other pacifist sects; other religious affiliations ranged from traditional Protestant denominations to Seventh-day Adventists and Pentecostals. Following a stint in ASW camps, most of the COs either enlisted as non-combatants or accepted employment in agriculture and miscellaneous industries. By the time the alternative-service program ground to a halt in 1946, they had contributed over $2 million to the Canadian Red Cross Society.[57]

It is understandable that government officials proudly claimed 'considerable success' in dealing with COs. 'We have used the labour of Conscientious Objectors in essential production,' reported the deputy labour minister, and by 'diverting a portion of their earnings to the Canadian Red Cross,' he boasted, 'we have seen to it that these Conscientious Objectors ... have not profited financially by their conscientious objections to war.'[58] The chief alternative-service officer even claimed that use of CO labour 'saved the situation on many a dairy farm' in western Canada.

Pacifists were also pleased with the arrangement. Not only had they achieved the right to refrain from military service on the grounds of individual conscience; they were also actively engaged in a broad range of alternative national service – from the ASW camps, through diverse jobs on farms and in factories, to humanitarian work in the non-combatant corps, the fire-fighter corps in England, and the FAU in China – all in keeping with their religious beliefs and personal convictions.

This achievement was particularly important, since pacifist beliefs had been seriously challenged, and in some cases shattered, by the war. For instance, it is estimated that from 25 to almost 50 per cent of Mennonite men eligible for military service abandoned the non-resistant tradition of their forefathers and actually enlisted.[59] These men were automatically excommunicated and struck from church membership roles; they were the 'lost sons,' welcome to return, but only if they came 'crawling back with repentant apologies.'[60] Other pacifist groups experienced similar defections, and even some of those men who claimed CO status may have done so mainly because of parental and community pressure.

Robert Makaroff, the Saskatchewan CO mentioned above, is a case in point, though perhaps a special one, since he was the son of Peter Makaroff, a prominent lawyer and one of the most respected and politically active Doukhobors in Canada. The younger Makaroff later remembered that, though initially willing to take military training, he became a CO and went to camp primarily because he, like so many other COs, was born and raised in a pacifist tradition. Still, as a CO in camp he always felt guilty that he had been shielded from the war, especially because he had not joined a non-combatant medical unit.[61] The tragedies of war weighed heavy on the pacifist conscience.

The diversified character of alternative service certainly helped those COs who wanted to perform some worthwhile wartime service, but it also resulted in a new dilemma – broadened alternative service implicated COs in the war effort. Undoubtedly, the non-combatant corps had a thinly disguised military function, but almost all forms of alternative service, or any type of civilian work for that matter, entailed some support for the war. As Wiebe phrased it, 'Even the farmer works for the War because he produces the food that makes fighting possible.' It was no longer possible to escape entirely the total mobilization of wartime society, and, under the circumstances, most COs were relieved to be able to take part in constructive national service without taking up arms. They concluded, in effect, that they had made the best of a bad situation.[62]

Moreover, as has recently been explained with reference to the large Mennonite community, the war not only heightened pacifists' awareness of the world's events and problems, it also opened new opportunities for Christian service.[63] By the end of the war pacifists and government officials alike, each for their own reasons, felt that COs had been 'usefully employed' in the best interests of society.

But what appeared satisfactory for pacifists at the time set a dangerous precedent. In the event of another major conflict, the government would certainly incorporate COs into a national effort through some form of alternative service, not necessarily of a humanitarian nature, and thereby challenge anew the pacifist refusal to support war. Meanwhile, Canadian COs emerged from the Second World War hopeful that their experience would help make pacifism and nonviolent action a legitimate alternative.

NOTES

1 Rudy Wiebe, *Peace Shall Destroy Many* (Toronto 1972), 60.
2 The spelling 'Doukhobor' is normally used in Canada, though in fact 'Dukhobor' is the correct transliteration of the Russian word.
3 For a more in-depth discussion of this topic, see Thomas P. Socknat, *Witness against War: Pacifism in Canada, 1900–1945* (Toronto 1987).
4 Ibid., 82–7.
5 Canada, *Debates of the House of Commons*, special session, 1939, 47.
6 National Resources Mobilization Act, 1940 (1940), 4 George VI, c. 13.
7 National War Service Regulations, 1940 (Recruits), (1940), 4 George VI, c. 22.
8 William Janzen, *Limits on Liberty: The Experience of Mennonite, Hutterite, and Doukhobor Communities in Canada* (Toronto 1990), 220, and 'Relations between Canadian Mennonites and Their Government during World War II,' *Mennonite Quarterly Review* (Goshen, Ind.), 66 (Oct. 1992), 500; William Kaplan, *State and Salvation: The Jehovah's Witnesses and Their Fight for Civil Rights* (Toronto 1989), 177.
9 Approximately seven thousand Mennonites emigrated from Russia between 1873 and 1880. Frank H. Epp, *Mennonites in Canada, 1786–1920: The History of a Separate People* (Toronto 1974), 200.
10 For more on the complex differences between Mennonite groups, especially the

Kanadier and the Russländer, see Frank H. Epp, *Mennonites in Canada, 1920–1940: A People's Struggle for Survival* (Toronto 1982).

11 David Fransen, 'Canadian Mennonites and Conscientious Objection in World War II,' MA thesis, University of Waterloo, 1977, 25–37.

12 J. Lavell Smith to Chief Registrar, 17 August 1940, National Archives of Canada (NA), Ottawa, Labour, RG 27, vol. 624, file 35-6-9-7-5.

13 Fred Haslam to Prime Minister King, 32 July 1940, NA, PC, RG 2, 18, vol. 5, D-27. Haslam's letter was forwarded to the minister of national war services, 3 Aug. 1940.

14 *Minutes of the Canada and Genesee Yearly Meeting of the Society of Friends*, 1941, Tenth Report of the Canadian Friends Service Committee, 57; Fransen, 'Canadian Mennonites,' 45.

15 Haslam to Monthly Meeting Clerks, 11 Sept. 1940, Canadian Quaker Archives (CQA), Pickering College Library (Newmarket, Ont.), CFSC Papers, CO file.

16 Mennonite Archives of Canada, Conference of Historic Peace Churches Papers, XV, 11.6.1.

17 That spokesman was the Albertan B.B. Janz. Fransen, 'Canadian Mennonites,' 100, 102.

18 J.A. Toews, *Alternative Service in Canada during World War II* (Winnipeg 1959), 35, 36.

19 Extract of letter from George McDonald, n.d., NA, PC, RG 2, 18, vol. 5, D-27.

20 Order in Council PC 1822, amended 22 April 1942; Janzen, *Limits on Liberty*, 204; Toews, *Alternative Service in Canada*, 118.

21 Order in Council PC 7215; James C. Gardiner, Minister of National War Services, Press Release, 6 Dec. 1940, NA, PC, RG 2, 18, vol. 5, D-27.

22 Fransen, 'Canadian Mennonites,' 110, 111.

23 Davis and LaFlèche, Memorandum to Cabinet War Committee, 19 May 1941, NA, PC, RG 2, 18, vol. 5, D-27.

24 Toews, *Alternative Service in Canada*, 76.

25 Paul L. Storms, 'Life at Montreal River Camp,' *Canadian Friend* (Toronto), 33 (April 1942), 11, 12.

26 Clifton to H. Runham Brown, Secretary, WRI, 26 Dec. 1942, and Clifton to Sid, 16 Jan. 1943, Personal Collection, Roy Clifton Papers.

27 *Beacon* (Campbell River), 1 March 1945, 1.

28 *Northern Beacon* (Montreal River), 30 May 1942, 5; *Canadian C.O.* (Montreal) (Aug. 1942), 2, 5.

29 Toews, *Alternative Service in Canada*, 78.

30 J.F. MacKinnon, 'Historical Account of the Wartime Activities of the Alternative Service Branch,' Department of Labour, unpublished report, 11 April 1946, 9, NA, RG 35, series 7, vol. 21.

31 Toews, *Alternative Service in Canada*, 101; *Beacon*, 1 March 1945, 1; Lawrence Klippenstein, ed., *That There Be Peace: Mennonites in Canada and World War II* (Winnipeg 1979), 79.
32 Stan Hanson and Don Kerr, 'Pacifism, Dissent and the University of Saskatchewan, 1938–1944,' *Saskatchewan History* (Saskatoon), 43 (fall 1993), 11.
33 Klippenstein, ed., *That There Be Peace*, 59.
34 Lorraine Roth, 'Conscientious Objection: The Experiences of Some Canadian Women during World War II,' *Mennonite Quarterly Review*, 543.
35 Notes of a conference at ASW camp Q 6 with James Finlay, n.d., United Church Archives (UCA), Toronto, Fellowship of Reconciliation (FOR) Papers, box 2, file 24.
36 Wiebe, *Peace Shall Destroy Many*, 92.
37 Lavell Smith to Humphrey Mitchell, 20 March 1943, and Harold Toye to Mitchell, 13 April 1943, NA, Labour, RG 27, vol. 131, 601.3–6 v 2.
38 A. MacNamara, Director of Selective Service, to H. Mitchell, Minister of Labour, Feb. 1943, NA, DND, RG 24, vol. 6473, HQ 1161-3-4.
39 Order in Council PC 2821, 1 May 1943.
40 MacKinnon, 'Alternative Service Branch,' 14–17.
41 Ibid.; Haslam to A.S. McNinch, 29 July 1944, CQA, CFSE Papers, McNinch file; James Finlay to MacKinnon, 29 Sept. 1943, UCA, FOR Papers, box 1, file 3.
42 C.F. Klassen to Mitchell, 2 Feb. 1943, and Allen Rayner Reesor, ASW Camp, Banff, to J.W. Noseworthy, July 1943, NA, Labour, RG 27, vol. 131, 601.3-4 v. 1.
43 'History of the Corps of (Civilian) Canadian Firefighters,' unpublished report, 16, NA, RG 35, 7, vol. 27. A breakdown of the CO fire-fighters by religious denomination follows: eight United Church, seven Mennonite, and one each from the Brethren in Christ, Church of Christ, Plymouth Brethren, Presbyterians, and Roman Catholics.
44 Order in Council PC 7251.
45 Klippenstein, ed., *That There Be Peace*, 56.
46 For a more thorough discussion of this topic, see Socknat, 'The Canadian Contribution to the China Convoy,' *Quaker History* (Haverford), 69 (autumn 1980).
47 D.H. Clark, Executive Secretary, Chinese War Relief Fund, to G. Pifher, Department of National War Services, 18 May 1944, CQA, CFSC Papers, L. Pifher file.
48 Of approximately 687 COs prosecuted for failure to report for alternative service, over 30 per cent were Jehovah's Witnesses. Socknat, *Witness against War*, 250.
49 M. James Penton, *Jehovah's Witnesses in Canada* (Toronto 1976), 164–71; MacKinnon, 'Alternative Service Branch,' 23–5.
50 Kaplan, *State and Salvation*, 174–5, 178.
51 MacKinnon, 'Alternative Service Branch,' 26.
52 See Koozma J. Tarasoff, *Plakun Trava: The Doukhobors* (Grand Forks, BC, 1982),

chap. 14, 'Conscience,' for a sympathetic account by a sociologist of Doukhobor extraction of the experiences of the sect's COs during the Second World War.

53 Davis and LaFlèche, Memorandum to Cabinet War Committee, 19 May 1941, NA, PC, RG 2, 18, vol. 5, D-27.

54 Janzen, *Limits on Liberty*, 231, 232; Tarasoff, *Plakun Trava*, 155.

55 A.D.P. Heeney to H. Mitchell, 7 Feb. 1944, NA, PC, RG 2, 18, vol. 16, M-5-6.

56 L.E. Westman to A. MacNamara, 2 June 1944, NA, Labour, RG 27, vol. 1514, 60–34.

57 MacKinnon, 'Alternative Service Branch,' 20–3.

58 A. MacNamara, to H. Mitchell, 13 Nov. 1944, NA, Labour, RG 27, vol. 133.

59 Kaplan, *State and Salvation*, 174–5. It is estimated that approximately 4,500 Mennonite men opted for active military service. See T.D. Regehr, 'Lost Sons: The Canadian Mennonite Soldiers of World War II,' *Mennonite Quarterly Review*, 478.

60 Regehr, 'Lost Sons,' 475.

61 Hanson and Kerr, 'Pacifism, Dissent,' 11. Peter Makaroff was an Independent Doukhobor.

62 Interview with Keith Woollard, 25 March 1976; Gordon K. Stewart to author, received 7 March 1976.

63 See Regehr, *Mennonites in Canada, 1939–1970: A People Transformed* (Toronto 1996).

17

Pacifists as Conscientious Objectors in Australia

PETER BROCK AND MALCOLM SAUNDERS

With the outbreak of war in Europe in September 1939 the peace movement in Australia almost completely collapsed. Most pacificists believed in the justice of the Allied war effort, and the necessity of Australian participation was confirmed for them when in February 1942 Japan for the first time actually bombed northern Australian ports. Communists and fellow travellers, once Germany had invaded the Soviet Union in June 1941, wholeheartedly supported the war. Only the pacifists *sensu stricto* continued to declare their opposition to fighting, but on grounds more of religion or ethics than of political policy. Anti-war activity in Australia reached its lowest level during the middle and later years of the war. Even the issue of conscription for overseas military service, which had done nothing less than split the Australian public during the First World War, failed to generate much opposition outside the forums of the Labor party. The main thrust of pacifist activity during most of the war was directed towards liberalization of the law relating to conscientious objection and the protection of the welfare of conscientious objectors (COs).

We look first at the prewar pacifist community, then at the framework of wartime conscription, and finally at the experiences of the COs themselves during the war and the pacifist structure supporting them.

Pacifism in the 1930s

The Australian peace movement, whose organizational roots lay in the Boer War of 1899–1902, had not only expanded but also diversified during the First World War. When the war ended it virtually collapsed, but it was very soon revived in the form of new and different groups. From 1919–20 on, it expanded steadily as anti-war sentiment increased in reaction to realization of the devastation and human misery experienced in the recent conflict. Liberal internationalists, mostly from the middle class, rallied behind the League of Nations Union (LNU), whereas left-wing anti-militarists, led by the Communist Party of Australia (CPA), regarded the LNU as a tool of capitalism. In the early 1930s the anti-war efforts of the CPA centred around the Movement against War and Fascism (MAW&F), which attacked the League 'as the immediate mouthpiece of the Imperial Powers.'[1] Around mid-decade the two hitherto-hostile wings of the Australian peace movement came together in face of the Nazi-fascist menace; in 1936 they combined their efforts in the International Peace Campaign (IPC), which advocated armed resistance to German and Italian aggression.[2]

There were extremely few absolute pacifists in Australia; they were, like the internationalists, predominantly middle-class, with teachers and ministers of religion figuring prominently. For the most part they backed the League of Nations and, though opposed to armed sanctions, supported the peace activities of the LNU. Apart from religious bodies such as the Quakers, who espoused pacifism, the Christadelphians, and the Jehovah's Witnesses, who condemned participation by Witnesses in armed conflicts, at any rate contemporary ones, the only organization rejecting war unconditionally was the tiny Australian section of the Women's International League for Peace and Freedom (WILPF). Its membership, however, was confined very largely to Melbourne, the home town of its leading activist, the gentle yet dynamic Eleanor Moore.[3] When war broke out, it hastened to express its continued belief that 'war as a method of dealing with international difficulties is wholly wrong' and that 'no just solution can be reached by such means.'[4]

The accession of Hitler to power in Germany in January 1933 and the outbreak of the Spanish Civil War in July 1936 had finally led everywhere to 'the great divide' within the peace movement – between absolute pacifists and those ready to employ armed force either for collective security or in defence of the working class. In Britain in 1936 the unconditionally pacifist Peace Pledge Union (PPU) came into existence. But two years were to elapse before specifically pacifist organizations emerged in at least some of the states of Australia; and these bodies were to remain on a regional basis until mid-1943.[5]

The first state where the pacifists of the 1930s emerged with an organization of their own had been New South Wales, followed five months later by South Australia. Their APPUs, modelled on the British pattern, were formed in May and October 1938, respectively. In New South Wales activities naturally centred on Sydney, with sixty members there by September 1939, though there was also a small APPU section in Newcastle. In November 1938 a group known as the United Christian Peace Movement had fused with the APPU, slightly increasing numbers. The founders of the APPU (NSW) were to report a year later that the previous twelve months could be considered as 'fairly successful.' All who felt able to sign their pledge (based on that of the War Resisters' International – WRI – and not the British PPU) were welcome to join; there was no credal test. In the opinion of the Sydney group's secretary, Lance C. Rodd, 'the best people in our gang here ... are those who renounce war but haven't troubled to make the rather flamboyant gesture of renouncing it personally.' Rodd felt that the APPU 'should enlist the activity of as many near-pacifists as possible, leaving them to work out their own salvation as time proceeds.' But this suggestion of opening the doors to the pacificists does not seem to have been pursued.[6]

In South Australia, where a PPU was formed in October 1938, the impulse to organize came largely from a Quaker, Charles Francis Fryer, a former enthusiast for the League of Nations, who from 1936 had been organizing on an unequivocally pacifist basis. Soon several tiny new pacifist groups joined forces with Fryer to create a single organization. Another Quaker, and former British CO, J.R. Wilton, professor of mathematics at the University of Adelaide, became first chairman of the new PPU branch, which by early 1939 had recruited 260 members, including local Quakers and fifteen Protestant clergymen.[7] On the basis of recent experience, Fryer emphasized to his fellow Christian pacifists the value of so organizing that humanists and other non-Christians should not be excluded from an enterprise needing all the support it could get.[8]

The last Australian PPU to emerge before the outbreak of war was in Victoria. But absolute pacifism, though still a frail plant in that state and confined almost exclusively to the capital Melbourne, had put down deeper roots in the state than elsewhere, for a number of reasons. The Society of Friends constituted a not uninfluential factor in church circles in Melbourne, and the Australian Church – an indigenous variant of liberal religion, under its indefatigable founder and chief minister, Scottish-born Dr Charles Strong – had proved a centre of anti-war activity since at least the late 1880s.[9] Eleanor Moore had made Melbourne her home (she joined the Australian Church before 1914, and Strong was one of those who led her to become a pacifist). A number of non-conformist ministers in the city, though a small minority, espoused pacifism openly from their pulpits: the Revd William Bottomley of the Unitarian Church, for instance, and Revd J.T. Lawton, a Presbyterian and Christian socialist. In addition, as we see below, several leading pacifists of the Second World War were to operate from Melbourne, and thus the country's COs often looked to that city for inspiration and advice.

Specifically pacifist sentiment – in contrast, that is, to the amorphous anti-war feeling that emerged after 1918 – had begun to surface among Victoria's mainstream Protestants about 1936. The issue was then discussed by Methodists and Presbyterians at their annual conferences and in their church press. The tone of debate indeed became sometimes quite sharp, with the anti-pacifists accusing the pacifists of anti-patriotism and the latter condemning the supporters of war's legitimacy of betraying their Master. Anti-pacifist sentiment prevailed in the Presbyterian Church of Victoria, even though its pacifists could call on such eminent pacifist divines in the mother church in Scotland as Garth Macgregor, author of the influential *New Testament Basis of Christian Pacifism* (1936), and George MacLeod, founder of the Iona Community. But even in the Methodist church, where discussion was less bitter and the small pacifist minority was given a calmer hearing, the annual conference of February 1938 had refused to sanction creation of a Methodist Peace Fellowship on a strictly pacifist basis. The ban seems to have been 'one of the major reasons behind the establishment of the Christian Pacifist Movement [CPM] of Victoria.'[10]

Just over a year later, in March 1939, Victoria's CPM came into existence. Undoubtedly the situation after Munich had brought home to pacifists the need to give the pacifist impulse in their state an organized form. Members were to take an enrolment pledge, in which they declared their belief 'that under no circumstances can participation in war be reconciled with the spirit and teachings of Christ' and their desire 'to work for the removal of the causes of war.'[11] The CPM grew slowly, but by September 1939 it numbered around five hundred, not all of whom were active members.

The driving force behind its activities was a young Anglican, Frank W. Coaldrake (1912–1970), who was eventually elected archbishop of Brisbane but died before installation. He was still a layman completing his theological studies and with his pacifist activism casting a shadow over his clerical future. 'Tall, thin, sharp-faced – a fair-haired Savonarola,'[12] Coaldrake was an attractive person. Combining unbounded energy with a strong sense of mission as well as a gift for friendship, he naturally took a lead in Victoria's pacifist movement from its outset. A disciple of Gandhi and an admirer of the Japanese pacifist Toyohiko Kagawa, he looked to the Sermon on the Mount as the inspiration of his pacifism. His rejection of warfare embraced not only war resistance but concern for the underprivileged and for community living and social service. After he had started the country's first pacifist journal under the title *Peacemaker* (first published on 29 September 1939 with a modest four pages[13]), Coaldrake began to exercise a marked influence on pacifists outside Victoria as well.

Just as the Christian pacifists of Melbourne were organizing, a couple of precocious senior secondary-school boys at Melbourne's Wesley College – Kenneth D. Rivett and Alister Kershaw (future economist and poet, respectively) – started a pacifist 'cell' among their peers. Neither boy came from a pacifist background; nor was their pacifism derived from a specifically religious belief. But, like so many of their generation in English-speaking lands who became pacifists, they had been deeply influenced by the anti-war literature of the time. Kershaw, for instance, was particularly impressed by Richard Aldington's novel *Death of a Hero*, which graphically portrayed the horrors – and basic futility – of war.

The two boys wrote to Herbert Runham Brown, honorary secretary of the WRI and a former absolutist 'conchie' who had spent a prolonged period in jail during the First World War, and asked his advice as to what they should do next. Set up a WRI group in your city, was Runham Brown's reply. 'These lads,' wrote Moore, one of those older pacifists they now consulted, 'brought to bear on their efforts not only the enthusiasm of youth, but a clear intellectual grasp of principles involved in public affairs.'[14] Young Alister Kershaw explained how he and his age group felt at the prospect of another global conflict: 'We of this generation are all cursed, cursed with the knowledge of the infinite ocean of pain and torment which was the Great War. The Great War! Great in stupidity, great in greed, great in torment, misery, hatred and murder. Is this to come again? From the depths of my very being I refuse to believe it.'[15]

These efforts were rewarded a few months later with the launching of a Victoria APPU in May 1939. But, apart from a branch at Wangaratta in the north, the pacifism of whose members appears to have been rather shaky, the APPU remained confined to Melbourne; altogether it failed to attract more than about 120 members, some of whom also belonged to the CPM. There being two separate groups divided Melbourne's tiny pacifist community (the CPM excluded non-Christians from its midst). This 'tendency to split up into small ... groups' had already begun to cause anxiety to some pacifist activists.[16]

The beginnings of organized Australian pacifism in the late 1930s show clearly the influence of British pacifism, with the PPU and the United Kingdom–based WRI as organizational models. Several branches of the Fellowship of Reconciliation (FOR) also emerged, with membership restricted to Christian pacifists; Quakers such as E.E. Unwin, headmaster of the Friends School in Hobart, Tasmania, who had been a CO in First World War Britain before emigrating to Australia, were particularly active in FOR activities. But whereas in Britain pacifism during the years immediately prior to the Second World War enjoyed a decided, if modest, success, in Australia progress was very slow. For all the enthusiasm of their adherents, the small pacifist groups failed to coalesce into a national organization before world war was on them.

Conscription and CO Status

In May 1939 the federal Parliament had decreed the compilation of a National Register of Manpower to cover males between the ages of eighteen and sixty-five in preparation for the introduction of conscription in the event of war. Pacifists and trade unionists agitated – unsuccessfully – against the register. The APPUs of New South Wales and Victoria, along with the Victorian Christian Pacifist Movement, advised members and sympathizers against boycotting the register while also urging them to state their pacifist position plainly on the appropriate form, as well as their unwillingness to perform military service. It is probable that, each in his own way, many a pacifist registrant followed this advice.[17]

Soon after the outbreak of war, with the Defence Act of October 1939, the federal cabinet made the decision to reintroduce compulsory military service – for the time being only for civilian forces – i.e., home militia. While the new law allowed conscientious objection and did not disqualify claims that were not based on religious grounds, it permitted exemption only from combatant service and required COs who were judged to be sincere to join the army in a non-combatant capacity – probably in the Army Medical Corps. This legal framework remained basically unchanged until mid-1941, when the government decided to adopt in principle the British way of administering conscientious objection, though the liberalization was made law as CO regulations only in February 1942 and was later somewhat curtailed as a result of an adverse decision by the Senate. For all the shortcomings of the initial legislation, Australian parliamentarians had accepted, at least as a guiding principle, 'the idea that conscientious beliefs against military service deserved protection.'[18]

Attempts to persuade Prime Minister Robert Menzies, who headed a coalition government of the United Australia party and the Country party, to extend the scope of exemption by adopting the more liberal British system proved unsuccessful at first. Yet Menzies himself was sympathetic, and the Military Board was in favour of change. For some COs of course, non-combatant service provided the type of exemption that they wished. Seventh-day Adventists, for instance, since the days of the American Civil War when they first faced compulsory military service, had always expressed their willingness to become non-combatant soldiers, provided that the army respected their Saturday Sabbath. The same readiness to accept non-combatant service held for most of the Plymouth Brethren. We find, too, a pillar of the CPM and its first president, Revd H. Palmer Phillips, a Methodist minister, warmly supporting non-combatant service as the kind of job that he thought young and able-bodied male pacifists should be doing in wartime.[19] In contrast, the Christadelphians excluded members who agreed to enter the armed forces in a non-combatant capacity, while some among the more sophisticated pacifists, rather intolerantly, considered non-combatant status incompatible with pacifism.

First to be called up for military service were the twenty-one-year-olds, in

January 1940. COs, who rejected non-combatant service if assigned this alter-native to combatant status, became liable to a prison sentence of up to six months. Provided that a recalcitrant CO refused to take the oath of enlistment, he would, however, serve his sentence in a civil, not a military prison. From the objector's point of view, the moment to make a firm stand was before or at the medical examination – and certainly not after taking the oath, which made him a soldier. In no case could the area officers responsible for allocating CO status grant more than exemption from actually bearing arms, even if convinced that an objector was sincere in rejecting induction into the army.[20] However, 'throughout the greater part of 1940 the authorities acted indulgently,' and until January 1941 prosecutions of COs for non-compliance were rare. Nevertheless, during this interval the threat of prosecution and imprisonment remained.

The 'sterner attitude' (Paul Hasluck's phrase) apparent from early in 1941 seems to have resulted from the government's alarm at the growing number of applications for CO status as new age groups were called up between August 1940 and March 1941. The authorities feared that 'the plea of conscientious objection was [now] ... being raised falsely by individuals to escape service.' The main culprits here, in their eyes, were the Jehovah's Witnesses (JWs), whose organization had recently been banned as subversive.[21] The Australian government was evidently reluctant to excuse JWs from army service as COs; it was particularly perplexed by the plea urged by many JWs of being ministers of religion (and therefore exempt) in addition to their claim to be COs.[22] The fact that JWs did not condemn armed self-defence and took a somewhat ambiguous stance with regard to their role in a future battle of Armageddon mystified the authorities still further.

Pacifist organizations had not been idle on behalf of their COs during the lull that the latter had enjoyed from the attention of the authorities. They did their best, for instance, to prepare young pacifists in stating their case before the authorities by holding 'mock tribunals' while also trying to avoid accusations of 'coaching conscience.' They sought too to establish ways in which COs, and pacifists generally, could demonstrate their concern for society. They under-lined that theirs was not a negative creed – a mere refusal to fight – but a belief that expressed itself in positive action whenever that was possible. This human-itarian impulse led to establishment of several pacifist service organizations such as the Christian Service Legion, open also to non-Christians, and the short-lived Victorian Conscientious Objectors' Service Group, with a similar group in Sydney. Some pacifists, such as Frank Coaldrake, found a vocation in working for the non-pacifist Brotherhood of St Laurence, which after the war developed into a major Australian welfare organization, now on a secular basis; it had already found room for an agnostic such as Tony Bishop, a leading pacifist activist in Sydney.

A community movement, though not nearly so strong as it became in wartime Britain, also developed among Australian pacifists. There was, for example, a Community House in Melbourne and Paxton Farm in Queensland, the latter opening as a cooperative venture early in 1941.[23] In that state, where a Christian Pacifist Movement had been established only in October 1939, a small group of Quakers provided the driving force behind pacifist activity. And Frank Coaldrake's monthly *Peacemaker* from Melbourne kept Australia's scattered pacifist groups informed about such developments, as well as about pacifist activities overseas. 'The mere objection to participation in war,' Coaldrake wrote, 'is only one small part of their platform. They find their main duty in the long term programme' of promoting the political and social conditions for a peaceable world.[24]

The real test for the country's COs came during the first half of 1941, when 'some dozens of men who had refused when called up for the militia were prosecuted.' The courts handed out sentences 'ranging from a fortnight to six months' to those who remained adamant in refusing induction into a non-combatant branch of the army, as well as to those who refused CO status outright. Hasluck records that 'the number of prosecutions revived protests both inside and out of Parliament and led to renewed appeals to the Government to liberalise the law.'[25]

COs jailed in this period were drawn from the complete spectrum of those unwilling to accept any form of army service: Jehovah's Witnesses and Christadelphians, Quakers and members of the non-pacifist mainstream Protestant denominations (including the 'restitutionist' Churches of Christ, where pacifism was quite strong), as well as non-religious – humanist or rationalist – objectors, whom the courts sometimes treated more harshly than their religious confrères. Some of those now prosecuted received repeated sentences.

Conditions in prison varied. There were no complaints of actual ill-treatment, but the regime in an institution such as Long Bay Gaol in Sydney was harsh for all inmates, whether prisoners of conscience or ordinary criminals.[26] There a CO might find himself sharing a cell with crime-hardened recidivists. At the same time COs were considered by both prisoners and prison officers as 'outsiders' rather than criminals and, as such, received a certain grudging respect. As a result of their prison ordeal, New South Wales objectors, like those of First World War Britain, turned their attention to prison reform; the present-day Prison Reform Council of New South Wales originates in their wartime endeavours to ameliorate the oppressive prison system that they themselves had experienced, if only briefly.

The measures of liberalization agreed to informally by the federal government on 2 July 1941 and made law under the National Security (Conscientious Objectors) Regulations of 23 February 1942 did not put a complete stop to the imprisonment of genuine COs; but they greatly restricted the number prosecuted. The intention had been to adopt in principle Britain's three-tier system of exemptions: unconditional, conditional on undertaking some kind of alternative service under civilian control and (in Australia's case) with soldier's pay, and non-combatant service in the armed forces. That system was obviously working well in the United Kingdom, and it appeared only common sense to try it out in Australia. Both federal-government[27] and military authorities agreed with the pacifists that there was no point in treating as criminals young men of integrity, whose consciences forbade them to bear arms.[28] Maybe the prisons had room for them all; they were after all few in number. But they would be of much more use to the country out of jail – and far less trouble!

But the regulations ran into difficulties when on 29 April 1942 the conservative Senate, apprehensive about the new Labor government that had taken office in October 1941, rejected regulations 8, 9 and 10, thus annulling unconditional exemption and the right of COs to appeal a decision on their application that they regarded as unsatisfactory. This proved only a temporary setback, for on 15 July the regulations, now amended, came into effect once more (as Statutory Rule No. 307/1942). The right of appeal, however, was restored only on 6 June 1943 (by Statutory Rule No. 162/1943), while the possibility of obtaining unconditional exemption lapsed for good. Meanwhile, a dozen or so objectors had succeeded in gaining this status before the Senate's annulment came into force.

While the legal situation vis-à-vis conscientious objection meanwhile remained uncertain because of the Senate's veto, the authorities suspended action. Before long, however, they could begin to put the – amended – regulations into effect. Absolutists who refused to accept anything but unconditional exemption (a rather small group) and Jehovah's Witnesses, whom we know usually demanded recognition as ministers of religion, remained a problem; as before, they often ended in jail, which of course was normally also the fate of those whose applications for conditional exemption were rejected. Prison sentences could not exceed six months; but even if 'cat-and-mouse' treatment was generally avoided, a number of cases of it did occur, especially in New South Wales.

The federal government now faced the problem of how to deal with the COs exempted on condition that they undertook civilian service. Those already in occupations regarded as essential did not present any difficulty. But the government debated for some time the possibility of redirecting the others, finally abandoning the idea as administratively too complicated. Besides, only a very small number, perhaps fewer than five hundred men, were involved – a tiny fraction of Australia's total manpower. For a time some conditionally registered COs had been directed to serve with the recently formed Civil Construction Corps. But the men objected to this work because of its close connection with the war effort; and their protest received the support of pacifist organizations. Not wishing trouble, the government backed down.[29]

The CO Experience

Pacifists in Australia did not possess the means to sponsor any large-scale private work projects such as the Christian Pacifist Forestry and Land Units in Britain or the even more ambitious – and semi-governmental – Civilian Public Service Camps in the United States. The intentional communities that existed in Australia could not absorb more than a very small number of those involved. However, two state governments – in New South Wales and in Western Australia – now proceeded to set up forestry camps for their objectors.

In Western Australia the one camp that got started – at Gnangara, near Perth – accommodated mostly Christadelphians; there were indeed few non-sectarian pacifists in that part of the country. The men were engaged in cutting firewood under the control of the deputy conserver of forests. Relations between the more sophisticated campers and the 'Bible boys' appear to have been tense – a situation undoubtedly exacerbated by the isolation in which the men lived. As one of the former wrote: 'Only two of us in a camp of 16 men hold pacifist views, the rest being Christadelphians or others holding similar religious views ... [We] have little in common apart from the fact that we are all CO's, as they regard our efforts as futile.'[30]

The atmosphere seems to have been more congenial in the three forestry camps established by New South Wales, perhaps because the forty men employed there represented more varied types of objector and there were fewer restrictions on movement. The *Peacemaker* at the beginning had been quite enthusiastic about the enterprise.[31] Yet it can hardly be described as a success. 'The number of objectors in the camps gradually dwindled and after a year the three groups were combined.' The state government had lost interest in the scheme as soon as outside pressure to provide alternative service for its objectors relaxed.[32] As in the case of Civilian Public Service for American COs, the pacifist organizations' initial enthusiasm gave way to disillusionment as it became increasingly clear that the camps were failing to fulfil their earlier promise.

Despite certain shortcomings, however, both the federal government and the country's pacifist community could find cause for satisfaction in the way in which the liberalized exemption system was working. True, in country districts especially, courts of petty sessions, whose task it now was to decide in the first instance on applications for CO status, might sometimes be swayed by wartime prejudice or lack of a proper understanding of their role. But there were once again district courts of appeal to correct such failures of justice. In the case of a Christadelphian appealing from a negative decision of the court of petty sessions in Wollongong, Judge Hold of the district court in Sydney had summarized admirably the principles that should guide those deciding on an application: 'It is ... immaterial what the tribunal may think of his belief ... It is a question of whether that belief is a belief of the conscience and is ... sincerely held by the individual.'[33]

After examining the situation that prevailed in the three Australian cities where most COs' cases were heard – Melbourne,[34] Sydney, and Adelaide – Paul Wilson concludes that the magistrate's role was vital in deciding whether the objector's application was dealt with fairly or not. While the law administered was a Commonwealth law, the magistrates who carried it into effect were appointed by the individual states' attorney general's departments. It was the responsibility of these departments to see that the magistrates in charge of such proceedings were fully competent for their task. Wilson singles out Judge Stanley Herbert Skipper, a distinguished barrister in Adelaide, for special praise for the impartial manner in which he normally handled the cases of COs appearing before him.[35] He censures in particular three magistrates in Sydney, whose decisions frequently resulted from 'their ... bias against conscientious objectors.' In Wilson's view both the federal government and the Department of the Attorney-General of New South Wales were remiss in not putting a stop to such abuses. 'The success of the Adelaide system,' Wilson concludes, 'should have convinced the legal authorities in other States, especially in New South Wales, to establish a tribunal run by a respected barrister.'[36]

From late 1942 until the end of the war, pacifists could feel reasonably content with the authorities' treatment of COs. True, some problems remained. From the start it had proved difficult to know how to treat serving-soldier COs – men who quite sincerely had developed an objection to fighting after having opted for combatant duties and undergone weapon training: sometimes, for whatever reason, they had been persuaded to become combatants against their better judgment. With regard to the soldier CO, the army usually took a sensible line and eventually allowed the man to be discharged from the services, but, at any rate until near the end of hostilities, only after he had undergone court-martial and repeated sentences of detention in a military prison (in no country likely to be a pleasant experience).

Pacifists who, because of age or gender or occupation, did not have to take a stand vis-à-vis military service, had sometimes to face hostility or discrimination on account of their anti-war position. Direction of labour, however, did not present a serious problem for them. Though Australia introduced industrial conscription as a wartime measure, the federal government, unlike the British authorities, seldom proceeded against pacifists for refusing to comply with directions imposed under its regulations;[37] it felt that the trouble involved was unlikely to be offset by only a small gain in 'manpower.'

But pacifists sometimes lost their jobs because of their views; and some sections of the press attacked them with virulence for their opposition to war. (In contrast, some newspapers wrote about pacifism and conscientious objection fairly and without rancour.) Outspoken advocates of peace, such as Revd William Bottomley, were subjected at times to police surveillance; yet Bottomley remained at liberty, despite his refusal to hold his tongue – and he kept the support of his largely non-pacifist congregation.[38] Coaldrake's *Peacemaker*, though it had to suspend publication for several months in late 1940 because of the authorities' not allowing it the paper needed for printing, was able to resume publication in March 1941 and continued to appear for the remainder of the war.

Indeed, as Wilson points out, apart from the months after Dunkirk in May–June 1940 (Australians felt keenly Britain's peril at that time) and the period when Australia itself felt threatened by a possible invasion in the early months of 1942 (the first occasion on which white Australia ever faced such a threat), pacifists did not experience any widespread hostility from the general public. True, from mid-1940 at least, they wisely kept a low profile, stressing their love of country along with their unwillingness to defend it by arms. The fact, too, that the authorities for the most part were aware of how small the Australian pacifist movement was and how few COs it produced in proportion to Australia's military manpower helped to reinforce the prevalent tolerance. Obviously these people, however misguided, constituted neither a threat to military security nor a perceptible drain on the country's fighting strength.

Australia's largest pacifist organization, the CPM of Victoria, had reached a peak of over seven hundred members in 1940–1. Despite some withdrawals as a result of war, membership in it stood firm, along with that of other pacifist organizations; they did not, as one might have expected, suffer any massive falling away from the ranks, and losses were soon made up. Yet pacifism, along with the rest of the peace movement, was about to enter what was undoubtedly one of the quietest periods in the movement's history. The campaign against the overseas conscription introduced by the Curtin Labor government in February 1943, which was led by the main spokesman for COs in the House of Representatives, Maurice Blackburn, failed to generate much enthusiasm, even among pacifists.[39]

The small and fragmented pacifist societies dispersed throughout six states had succeeded, however, in establishing an umbrella organization, the Federal Pacifist Council of Australia (FPC).[40] Though concerted action remained hard to achieve, and New South Wales, South Australia, and Victoria far outweighed the other three states in the counsels of the FPC, Australian pacifism began to emerge from its moribund condition. Now that the CO question had been generally resolved, the FPC could turn to more positive aspects of pacifism, such as postwar planning and the future role of the peace movement in bringing about a warless world. Some pacifists agitated against the Allied policy of unconditional surrender and called again for a negotiated peace, as they had done earlier during the 'phoney war,' while others participated in efforts to get relief to the victims of famine and devastation in war-stricken Europe.

Hasluck gives the figure of 2,791 for the total number of applications for CO status received from the first call-up in January 1940 to the end of the war in the Pacific in August 1945.[41] Ninety-eight COs were sentenced to imprisonment up to February 1943, after which date imprisonment of objectors became fairly rare, with most such cases occurring in New South Wales.[42] In Sydney, for instance, we find Bill Tarry as late as August 1944 being sentenced to a fourth term of imprisonment; the judge expressed his regret 'that the maximum penalty was only six months ... Such premeditated flouting of the law lacked the saving grace of ordinary crime which is often committed on the spur of the moment.'[43]

Only incomplete statistics are available on the religious or ethical affiliation of the objectors. According to Wilson, over two-thirds belonged to 'various religious sects, especially the Christadelphians.'[44] The latter, while they kept strictly to their sectarian enclosure, were much closer to the mainstream pacifist position than were, for example, the Jehovah's Witnesses, who contributed a sizeable number of Australia's COs. Even if they gave hints of warrings in the name of an avenging Saviour at some unspecified future date, the Christadelphians' objections to fighting, as currently taught in each Christadelphian Ecclesia, derived from the same New Testament texts as other Christian pacifists usually relied on, including Jesus' love commandment.[45]

If numerically the 'separational' millenarian sects predominated within the community of Australian COs, 'integrational' pacifist objectors from the mainstream Protestant tradition, including the Church of England,[46] and humanist objectors of various shades of agnosticism reflected the public image of the pacifist movement.[47] As in Britain, there were a number of Christian objectors no longer affiliated to any church,[48] they usually professed a 'social gospel' type of religion and, when defending their pacifism, used ethical and utilitarian arguments as much as, sometimes even more than, the New Testament criteria employed by their more evangelical colleagues. But whereas, for example, a Christadelphian CO received solid backing from his Ecclesia, which compensated to some extent for the wartime society's at-least-latent hostility, mainstream pacifist COs often experienced loneliness and isolation, whether they were non-religious, or Christians without denominational affiliation, or members of churches the vast majority of whose members supported the war effort.[49] A Sydney objector, associated with the APPU there, expressed graphically the situation he and his fellow COs faced as a result of their stand: 'To live in a city or town, and realise that of all the thousands of people one passed in a week, probably not one would agree with your views, and the majority would regard you as nothing less than a dangerous traitor ... was a sobering experience. Add to this the fact that many objectors were completely rejected by their families ... Almost all came under pressure to accept military service, by parents or groups they belonged to ... Every major church, social organization, youth group ... was dedicated to the war effort. In every public place and in every workshop, canteen, club, hotel and office the walls were decorated with exhortations to greater effort to win the war. We were indeed social pariahs.'[50]

Many Australian pacifists, and COs in particular, may have thought of themselves as social pariahs. Yet the way in which the federal government handled its COs had much to commend it, especially if we compare the treatment of COs in neighbouring New Zealand or even in the United States. For one thing, at the outset the Defence Act of 1939 had made clear that all genuine objectors were entitled to exemption, regardless of whether they based their refusal to bear arms on religion or on ethics – or even on reason. 'Thus, a major expansion of the grounds for conscientious objection had occurred with little public controversy.'[51] True, initially the condition of exemption was restricted to the performance of non-combatant duties in the armed forces, but this, we have seen, was eventually extended to include alternative service under civilian control.

Unlike the British model, Australia did not offer unconditional exemption, except for a very brief period. Still, the overwhelming majority of COs felt satisfied with the non-combatant or civilian-service alternatives available. Few were jailed, even in proportion to the (small) total of objectors. Certainly the government treated Jehovah's Witnesses (JWs), whether as COs or as a religious group, considerably less tolerantly than other groups taking a CO stand. But again, the number of JW objectors who spent time in jail does not appear to have been proportionally higher than it was in Britain or the United States. It is difficult to ascertain whether the authorities' fairly generous attitude to COs – and to pacifists in general – stemmed from abstract devotion to liberty or from realization that the groups involved were relatively harmless and did not present a real threat to the war effort. Probably both elements helped shape government policy, though the second appears to have been dominant in policy-making.

Viewed from a perspective of more than fifty years, wartime Australian pacifism appears a tender plant. The movement had begun to gather strength only on the eve of war; it was still largely dependent on British pacifism as a model for organization and ideas. It was extremely small, even in Victoria, where its main area of support lay. That sense of isolation affected most keenly the 'country pacifists' living in small towns or the surrounding countryside, where perhaps only one or two others shared their views. Widely dispersed throughout the six states of this vast – and for the most part underpopulated – country, they experienced isolation even more strongly than their confrères in the larger cities, where there might be an APPU or FOR group or a sympathetic Protestant clergyman, or even a Quaker meeting, besides a sprinkling of COs or potential COs if one had the luck to locate them.

There were no dramatic episodes in the story of Australia's Second World War COs, like those emerging from the sturdy opposition to conscription of First World War Britain's absolutists; no grand design was imposed on Australian COs, like the U.S. Civilian Public Service system of the Second World War (see chapter 19 below); no single wartime institution acted on them as a focus of resistance, as happened in New Zealand (see chapter 18). Instead, theirs was a 'quiet dissent,' in line perhaps with the tradition built up in Australia by pacifists of the older generation such as Eleanor Moore. It was met more than halfway by a government anxious to preserve liberty of conscience, so far as it felt this possible in wartime, and by a people not always tolerant of dissent, if it seemed to threatened the national existence, or free from hostility towards those holding unpopular views, yet on the whole willing to allow a small but conscientious minority to follow their religion, or their ethic, on a path along which the rest of their fellow citizens could not accompany them.[52]

NOTES

1 Quoted in Malcolm Saunders and Ralph Summy, *The Australian Peace Movement: A Short History* (Canberra 1986), 25.
2 For the IPC and its genesis, see Carolyn Rasmussen, *The Lesser Evil? Opposition to War and Fascism in Australia, 1920–1941*, Melbourne University History Monograph Series, No. 15 (Parkville, Victoria, 1992).
3 The Australian WILPF accepted 'non-absolutists' as members. 'But there is little

doubt that the group accurately represented the membership when it claimed its total opposition to war *per se.*' Malcolm Saunders, *Quiet Dissenter: The Life and Thought of an Australian Pacifist: Eleanor May Moore, 1875–1949* (Canberra 1993), 169.

4 Ibid., 240, 241.

5 For the British PPU, see chapter 11, by Andrew Rigby, above. 'The cost and time associated with travel between the states hindered the formation of an Australia-wide movement; therefore contact was confined almost entirely to correspondence. The pacifist movements in each state necessarily formulated their programmes on an interstate rather than on a national basis.' From Paul Wilson, 'A Question of Conscience: Pacifism in Victoria, 1938–1945,' PhD thesis, La Trobe University, 1984. Dr Wilson was originally invited to collaborate in this essay but had to withdraw at an early date on account of serious illness. He has, however, very kindly put his dissertation at our disposal – a major source for our narrative – as well as materials on pacifism in the other mainland states (referred to below as Wilson materials).

6 Kenneth Rivett Papers, University of Melbourne, Wilson materials; *Peace News* (London), 21 April 1939. Nevertheless, 'the APPU (NSW) had more anti-war activists [that is, persons who fell short of declaring themselves absolute pacifists] in its ranks than the pacifist movements in Victoria and South Australia.' Wilson, 'A Question,' 55.

7 Wilson materials; *Peace News*, 19 Nov. 1938, 17 Feb. 1939. By the outbreak of war membership had risen to 410, a figure only slightly less than the Victorian PPU's 500, even though South Australia's population was considerably less than Victoria's. According to Wilson ('A Question,' 56), 'Possibly the strength of the South Australian movement resulted from the greater influence of non-conformist religion in that state. Members of these churches are traditionally allowed more freedom of opinion on social questions.'

8 C.F. Fryer to K.D. Rivett, 9 Oct. 1939, Wilson materials.

9 Despite a widespread belief to the contrary, Strong had never been an unconditional pacifist, and, with the rise of Nazism, he abandoned his anti-war position in favour of armed opposition to aggression. See Saunders, 'An Australian Pacifist: The Reverend Dr. Charles Strong, 1844–1942,' *Biography: An Interdisciplinary Quarterly* (Honolulu), 18 no. 3 (summer 1995), 241–53.

10 Wilson, 'A Question,' 39.

11 Quoted from ibid., 45. See also Eleanor M. Moore, *The Quest for Peace: As I Have Known It in Australia* (Melbourne [1950]), 128.

12 Cecil Edwards, *The Editor Regrets* (Melbourne 1972), 105.

13 Edwards writes (ibid., 105): Coaldrake 'sent the first issue to hundreds of selected people, making it clear that it would also be the last issue unless someone did something to help. They did. Money began to come in.'

14 Moore, *Quest*, 127.

15 Wilson, 'A Question,' 52. From Kershaw's speech at a public meeting, 9 Dec. 1938.

16 See, for example, L.C. Rodd to K.D. Rivett, n.d., 3, 4, Wilson materials.

17 A Queensland Quaker, for instance, wrote later of the procedure that he had adopted in registering: 'I recall ... adding (under additional information) that I was a member of the Society [of Friends], a conscientious objector – son of a foundation member of the British No-Conscription Fellowship and had no intention of allowing any of my skills to be used for furthering any war effort.' Lawrence Brown to Paul Wilson, n.d., 3, 4, Wilson materials.

18 Hugh Smith, 'Conscience, Law and the State: Australia's Approach to Conscientious Objection since 1901,' *Australian Journal of Politics and History* (St Lucia, Queensland), 35 no. 1 (1989), 25.

19 A CO who had served first as a hospital orderly with the 10th Field Ambulance, and then overseas as a medical sergeant, later expressed this viewpoint: 'Maybe I could be criticized for not taking a more drastic pacifist attitude, but I felt that I could not in all conscience refuse to serve the sick and the wounded resulting from war.' Ray Meadows, quoted in Wilson, 'A Question,' 213. A non-combatant CO could not be required 'to occupy a position in the firing line in a case of emergency.' This – at first informal – understanding was confirmed in Statutory Rule No. 80/1942.

20 But evidently, with a friendly officer, a 'wangle' might be arranged at a later stage. For an example of this, see letter from Neville Stanley to F.C. Coaldrake, 5 Feb. 1940, Wilson materials.

21 Paul Hasluck, *The Government and the People, 1939–1941*, in *Australia in the War of 1939–1945*, series 4, vol. I (Canberra 1952), 599, 600. The ban was imposed in January 1941 and lifted by a high court ruling in June 1943. Ironically, in wartime Nazi Germany as well as Japan, the JWs were the only religious body that actively resisted conscription; its members as a result suffered imprisonment and, under Hitler, even death.

22 Ibid., 600.

23 Sidney Foreman to Paul Wilson, 25 April 1981, and Lawrence Brown to Wilson, 3 June 1981, Wilson materials; also *Peacemaker* (Melbourne), 5 no. 1 (1 Jan. 1943), 1.

24 *Peacemaker*, 4 no. 8 (1 Aug. 1942), 2.

25 Hasluck, *Government and People*, 600.

26 David Allen (a Quaker ex-inmate), 'Is Gaol Bad?' *Peacemaker*, 6 no. 4 (15 April 1944), 2. See also ibid., 3 no. 2 (1 June 1941), 2, 3, and no. 3 (1 Aug. 1941), 3; *Peacewards* (Melbourne) (1 July 1941), 8, 9.

27 In October 1941 the UAP–CP coalition government had been replaced by a Labor government led by John Curtin. Curtin had been jailed in 1916 for refusing compulsory enlistment for military service but now supported the war effort, including conscription. The liberalization of the CO regulations, however, was not a party issue.

28 In April 1941 Brisbane's future Anglican archbishop-elect, Frank Coaldrake, had

narrowly escaped being jailed for his refusal to join the Army Medical Service. The authorities in order not to create a *cause célèbre* – and much against Coaldrake's own wishes – eventually exempted him unconditionally as a theological student. See Wilson, 'A Question,' 173–6. For the dilemma this privileged exemption posed for pacifist 'theologs,' see the anonymous letter in the *Peacemaker*, 2 no. 3 (March 1940), 4: 'As a theological student I can get exemption and carry on with my pacifist work, as a conscientious objector I can offer the witness of imprisonment. What should it be?'

29 *Peacemaker*, 4 no. 8 (1 Aug. 1942), 1 ('What C.O.s Think') and 4 ('C.C.C. – "The Army behind the Army"').

30 Letters from P.M. Harris to G.A. (Tony) Bishop, 11 April and 19 June 1943, Wilson materials.

31 *Peacemaker*, 4 no. 12 (1 Dec. 1942), 1 ('Sydney C.O.s in Forestry Camps,' presumably by Coaldrake). See also Wilson, 'A Question,' 45, 46.

32 Wilson 'A Question,' 46.

33 *Peacemaker* 4 no. 12 (1 Dec. 1942), 4.

34 For Melbourne, we have an account by the thirty-eight-year-old utilitarian-pacifist newspaperman Cecil Edwards (*Editor Regrets*, 101–4), of his experiences from the time of his call-up in May 1942 through his medical examination to his registration as a CO by the tribunal the following August.

35 However, even Skipper had an 'Achilles' heel: his attitude to appellants who were Jehovah's Witnesses! Rejecting the appeals of four of the latter, he told them: 'You people are entirely subversive, and the internment camp would be the best place for you' (Wilson materials). A factor easing Skipper's task was the presence in his court as counsel for many of the appellants of J.L.S. Treloar, a First World War veteran who had since become a convinced pacifist. Treloar's legal skill and his war record, together with his active role in both the Methodist church and the Labor party, imparted a certain respectability to the CO position, then not infrequently regarded as unpatriotic and even subversive. See *Peacemaker*, 16 no. 3 (March 1954), for Treloar's obituary.

36 Wilson materials; also Wilson, 'A Question,' 266. See, in contrast to the Adelaide 'system,' accounts in the South Australian *Farmer* (Kadina), 19 June 1942, 6; 11 Sept. 1942, 5; and 3 December 1943, 2, of abusive treatment of COs in some other South Australian courts (which could certainly be matched by examples from courts elsewhere).

37 The case of Tasmanian Eric Scott, an absolutist CO and also a distinguished research biologist, seems to have been exceptional. After serving two prison sentences for refusing induction into the army, he then ignored 'a manpower direction' and was prosecuted. 'His work as a research scientist,' he told the court, 'was ... a vocation in the deepest sense of the word ... He could but continue his research and

leave it to the manpower authorities to decide what to do about his refusal to obey their direction.' The magistrate proved sympathetic and gave Scott, who combined vocational and absolutist pacifism in his stance, a very lenient sentence for breaking the law.

38 However, another Melbourne clergyman, Revd William O.D. Warnock, was driven to resign from the pastorate because of the deep hostility consistently displayed towards his pacifism by the Methodist church authorities in Victoria – despite his long and devoted service in its ministry.

39 Blackburn had been expelled from the Labor party in October 1941 for alleged pro-Communist sympathies. See K.J. Kenafick, *Maurice Blackburn and the No-Conscription Campaign in the Second World War* (Melbourne 1949).

40 The council chose as its first president a Quaker – and anthropologist – Camilla H. Wedgwood. However, within a few months of assuming the presidency she resigned on the grounds that, among other things, real unity did not exist among the FPC's constituent societies, apart from shared opposition to war. Shortly afterward she joined the Australian New Guinea Army Unit as a lieutenant-colonel! (A friend has suggested that she took this step so as 'to assist the native people adapt to the war situation.') She was succeeded as president by Frank Coaldrake, who had refused the position earlier. See Wilson, 'A Question,' 278, 287, 288, 290.

41 1,076 were granted non-combatant army service; 973, conditionally registered for civilian service; forty-one, registered unconditionally; 636, rejected; and sixty-five applications pending at end of hostilities. Hasluck, *Government and People*, 602.

42 Ibid., 600, 601. The figure of ninety-eight is probably an underestimate. For COs suffering repeated imprisonment, in some instances as many as five times, see, for instance, *Peacemaker*, 5 no. 4, 15 April 1943, 1; no. 5, 1 June 1943, 4; no. 6, 1 July 1943, 4.

43 *Peacemaker*, 6 no. 8, 1 Sept. 1944, 4.

44 Wilson, 'A Question,' 314. See also the table (260) of the religious affiliations of 309 CO applicants to courts of petty sessions in New South Wales whose cases were heard up to 13 September 1944. Jehovah's Witnesses 'everywhere received a disproportionate number of jail terms compared with conscientious objectors from other religious groups' (259).

45 See, for example, the statement by Lloyd Phillips, a Brisbane Christadelphian, in support of his request for exemption from non-combatant as well as combatant service. *Peacemaker*, 2 no. 3, 1 March 1940, 1, 3. Phillips's appeal was of course rejected, since the law at that date did not permit more than exemption from combatant service.

46 Anglicans, Baptists, Congregationalists, Churches of Christ, Methodists, Presbyterians, Quakers, and Unitarians were the main denominations referred to here. Cf. the list published in the *Peacemaker* giving names and religious affiliations of Protestant

clergymen who publicly declared their allegiance to pacifism after the outbreak of war: 1 no. 2, 31 Oct. 1939, 8; 1 no. 3, 1 Dec. 1939, 5; and 2 no. 6, 1 June 1940, 1 – by which last date the number of signatories had risen to 126.

47 In Australia there were 'only a handful' of Roman Catholic COs; Wilson, 'A Question,' xiii.

48 Wilson, 'A Question,' 260 (table, note 44), ranks 'Christian (no. denom.)' in the third place, with thirty-four COs, after Christadelphians (139) and Plymouth Brethren (thirty-eight) – and far above any of the other Protestant denominations (or the 'rationalist' COs). His figures, however, are only from New South Wales.

49 However, Quakers and pacifist-oriented members of Churches of Christ enjoyed considerable understanding among their co-religionists if they became COs. Apart from regular 'attenders' at meeting there were, however, only 632 Australian Quakers in 1940 and 670 in 1945; Charles Stevenson, *With Unhurried Pace: A Brief History of Quakers in Australia* (Toorak, Vic., 1973), 42.

50 Vic Harris, quoted in Wilson, 'A Question,' 201. 'We all thought of ourselves as lone wolves' was how a humanitarian objector from Melbourne, Donald Lawrence Gunner, put it; quoted in Ian M. Macdonald, 'Deviency [*sic*]: The Experience of the Conscientious Objector in Melbourne, 1939–45,' *La Trobe Historical Studies* (Bundoora, Vic.), 4 (1974), 16; see also 17–21.

51 H. Smith, in Charles C. Moskos and John Whiteclay Chambers II, eds., *The New Conscientious Objection: From Sacred to Secular Resistance* (New York and Oxford 1993), 210.

52 Bobbie Oliver, *Peacemongers: Conscientious Objectors to Military Service in Australia, 1911–1945* (Fremantle, Western Australia, 1997), reached us only after the present volume had gone to press.

18

Pacifism and Conscientious Objection in New Zealand

J.E. COOKSON

Pacifism, as defined for this book, never included more than a tiny minority in New Zealand either between or during the wars. The two main pacifist organizations of the Second World War period – the Christian Pacifist Society (CPS), started in 1936, and the Peace Pledge Union (PPU), launched in 1938 – had a few hundred members, with a significant number belonging to both; in the censuses of 1936 and 1945, 494 and 546 people, respectively, professed to be Quakers. There is no reason to think that there were ever many more than a thousand formally committed pacifists in the country.[1] Numbers, of course, are not everything. The CPS, in particular, had two notable public leaders in Ormond Burton ('OEB'), a Methodist minister, and Archibald (Barry) Barrington, national secretary of the Workers' Educational Association. Both men were strong, attractive personalities, confident speakers, and accomplished writers; both had some success as radio broadcasters after 1945. Barrington's qualities were amply shown as a leader of the Riverside Community, a pacifist rural commune, for over forty years, until his death in 1986.[2]

The pacifist movement had personal access to politicians, and even the prime minister, as part of the customary practice of New Zealand's 'small democracy.' Michael Young, for a short time in 1939–40 'Dominion organizer' for the PPU, exemplifies this point. Twenty-three years old, just out of his apprenticeship, he made long bicycle tours of both islands in order to promote membership and hold public meetings, in the course of which he interviewed at least seven MPs.[3] On the first day of the war, Burton, Young, and one other man were arrested for speaking outside the Parliament Buildings but were later released when the prime minister, Peter Fraser, visited them at the police station and put up their bail money.[4] As relations between the government and the pacifists deteriorated, however, the CPS formed a deputation and saw the prime minister and top officials in person.[5] The relationship was the more intense because the

Labour party in power had originally been strongly anti-militaristic and many pacifists had continued their allegiance out of respect for the party's social policies. Burton and Fraser were on first-name terms with each other and genuinely admired each other's humanitarian commitment.[6]

New Zealand pacifists therefore entered the Second World War with some political influence where it seemed to matter and also with a public constituency wider than their small numbers might suggest. This essay examines the history and nature of the pacifist movement, including its strength in the Methodist church and Christchurch; the Labour government's growing hostility to the movement during the war; and the pacifists' experience of the detention camps set up by the government.

The Pacifist Movement

Conscription had been a public issue since compulsory military training was introduced in 1909. Though peacetime training ceased in 1930, mainly as an economy measure, the government as late as the months before Dunkirk tried to reassure itself and the public that conscription would be unnecessary.[7] As in other countries, feeling against such a measure fed on a complex of ideas – the working man as victim of business interests and ruling classes; military authority as repressive of the better human qualities, including democratic values; governments as readier to go to war than peoples; the deficiencies of an international system based on self-interested, competing states – the list could be much longer.

It cannot be claimed that the critique of war and militarism was more advanced in New Zealand than elsewhere, but there are reasons for thinking that its social influence was greater. In population terms New Zealand endured heavy military casualty rates in the First World War.[8] Much of the national identity was built on a belief that the country was one of the most progressive social democracies in the world. There was also a waning of 'Britain and empire' sentiment, in favour of a more nationalistic tone, which under the Labour government elected in 1935 extended to foreign policy and an independent stance in the League of Nations.[9] On the eve of the Second World War a petition asking the government to support a proposed world conference for 'peace, understanding and economic co-operation' was backed by 890 organizations out of 7,000 approached.[10] During the war, 18 per cent of those called up (totalling 306,352) appealed on grounds of conscientious objection or undue hardship, surely indicating a substantial body of resistance to war and armed service overseas.[11]

Yet a 'peace movement' based on a coalition of pacifist and pacificist bodies never emerged in interwar New Zealand. Pacifism in the late 1930s became, if anything, more sectarian in outlook, more insistent, too, on individual conscience and individual witness. As with Dick Sheppard's parent organization in Britain, members of the PPU were required to make personal declarations against war and participation in war. At this time the older No More War Movement (NMWM), begun in 1928, rapidly lost influence to the PPU and CPS; its strategy had always been to engage public opinion through petitioning, publicity, and involvement in a wide range of issues.[12] The National Peace Council under C.F.N. Mackie, who was its secretary for over thirty years (1912–43), always aspired to become the representative body of New Zealand pacifism, with links to the churches, trade unions, and Labour party; but it remained too small and too confined to Christchurch to make much of an impact.[13] The small, localized nature of pacifist bodies constantly impeded wider cooperation; Auckland dominated the Fellowship of Reconciliation in the 1920s as Christchurch did the NMWM in the 1930s and Wellington the CPS.

However, in the final analysis, the relative isolation of pacifists on the eve of war relates to the decline of pacificism as collective security and the League of Nations failed and as the powers rearmed. Pacifists whose beliefs were founded on humanitarianism or socialism were particularly tested by Hitler's Germany, which increasingly seemed to offer them the choice of two evils – war or surrender to totalitarian dictatorship.

Christian pacifism, in these circumstances, dominated Second World War pacifism. Its particular 'home' was the Methodist church, where the 'social gospel' became firmly rooted during the Depression years. Pacifism, as an extension of the social gospel, and similarly redemptive and progressive, flourished in the church's single theological college (Trinity College, Auckland) and the Bible Class movement, which was sufficiently independent to hold off increasing concern and hostility in the wider church.[14] Perhaps fifty out of 150 Methodist ministers were pacifists. At least two-thirds of the membership of the CPS was Methodist.[15] Pacifism had been noticeably absent from the mainline churches during the First World War, so that the Christian pacifism of the late 1930s lacked elders and manifested something of a 'youth culture,' impatient to usher in a new world over the ruins of the old. If the Methodist Bible Class movement was a crucial nurturing organization, another was the Student Christian Movement.[16]

Founded under the threat of war, both the CPS and the PPU represented only too well the young generation that would be called on to fight and suffer; this fact doubtless helps to explain the energy that belied their small numbers.

The PPU was not, strictly speaking, a Christian pacifist organization, being based rather on the idea of war resistance. In New Zealand, however, the Christian pacifist influence always dominated. Thurlow and Kathleen Thompson, who started the New Zealand PPU in Christchurch, followed the Anglicanism and deeply humane Christianity of Dick Sheppard, whom they had known in England. Of the PPU's twelve sponsors, apart from Thompson himself, four were clergymen and two were Quakers. The PPU's first national convention in June 1939 opposed participation in war as 'contrary to the spirit and teachings of Jesus Christ,' which went some way beyond the pledge that Sheppard had adopted, by virtually repeating the words of the CPS 'covenant.'[17] Indeed, many PPU members also belonged to the CPS, including the Thompsons. It was typical for the two organizations to combine for monthly meetings wherever they co-existed, with Quakers usually adding a further number.[18] In 1943 the PPU postponed its annual conference for several months in order to allow its CPS members to attend the CPS's.[19]

Under Burton and Barrington, the CPS in Wellington quickly became known for its strategy for carrying its protest against war directly to the public. Beginning effectively with a demonstration at an air force display and military parade during the King's Birthday weekend in June 1938, the CPS went on to organize regular Friday-night marches (featuring anti-war 'sandwich boards') and street meetings, which continued into 1941, when police action and the call-up exhausted the supply of activists. Towards the end, the protests were plain theatre, with the pacifists divulging to the police when they would act and the police swooping on speakers as soon as they mounted their soap box.[20] The exercise created public spectacle and therefore impinged pacifists on the public mind, as did newspaper reports of the subsequent court proceedings. The authorities might have been prepared to license meetings held indoors, but Burton and Barrington did not consider this a satisfactory option, since they would probably have ended up preaching only to the converted. In Auckland the CPS, led by Ron Howell, tried the same strategy, though its much smaller numbers meant that its efforts were soon snuffed out.[21]

Most members of the pacifist societies were not willing to risk public exposure to this extent and, when they debated the matter, argued that such methods antagonized rather than impressed people. They were further dissuaded by the police's firm determination to stop the production and distribution of any material (invariably duplicated) that might encourage opposition to conscription. Gordon Mirams, once he was national chairman of the PPU in 1939, was an influential spokesman for a more submissive approach, especially vis-à-vis people such as Michael Young, his 'Dominion organizer.' Addressing all members through a circular in May 1940, Mirams declared 'the era of street meetings' to be over: 'In the new phase now beginning, our most useful activity will be that of quietly and steadily consolidating our position and drawing closer together in the "Brotherhood of Peace" ... We must put the emphasis on peace-making rather than on war-opposing.' Young thereupon resigned 'owing to lack of co-operation between branches and organizer and the Headquarters and organizer and because of this he felt he could not be the right person.'[22] Needless to say, the CPS felt the same tensions. At its annual conference in October 1940, Burton and those like him who wanted 'public and direct' action stood against those who wished to retreat into an educative role, since 'head-on clashes with authority' would only induce the government to ban the society altogether.[23]

Christchurch pacifists were the most successful in working out a strategy that steered between the dangers of doing too little, thus sapping the morale and purpose of the organization, and of doing too much, thus risking defections, public alienation, and total suppression. For a start, Christian and non-Christian pacifists at Christchurch were firmly allied in the PPU, whatever the presence of other pacifist bodies. On the outbreak of war, a Combined Pacifist Committee was quickly formed to negotiate with the city council and police over public meetings, and it seems to have lasted to the war's end.[24] As early as November 1939, before the authorities cracked down on 'subversive activity,' the committee had published two pamphlets, probably putting the pacifist case more fully and more effectively than the Wellington 'extremists' ever managed.[25] Immediately after conscription was ordered, a leaflet giving advice to intending conscientious objector (CO) 'appellants,' i.e., applicants, was also being widely distributed.[26] Meanwhile the Thompsons held weekly 'at homes' for young pacifists facing the call-up, and the PPU continued to organize meetings in public halls when the city council withdrew its permit to speak in the open air. By this time in Wellington the police were refusing to countenance anything but house meetings.[27] From the beginning of 1942 the Christchurch PPU acted as the national executive, producing a *Newsheet* about six times a year.

We cannot pretend that long years of war did not grind down pacifist morale in Christchurch as well as elsewhere. To try to stop the war seemed especially futile once Japan became the enemy and New Zealanders saw their own country exposed to attack. The four pacifists who stood as 'peace candidates' in the general election in September 1943 amassed little more than nine hundred votes among them, a sobering result if ever there was one. Thurlow Thompson described the pacifist organizations as 'largely impotent' by the end of the war.[28] They lacked any kind of overall national structure, and the 'military age' of many of their members meant that many were consigned to prison or defaulters' detention. A mere twenty-eight attended the annual general meeting of the PPU in March 1945.[29]

It was not so much social hostility or official harassment that silenced the pacifists; for the pressures in each respect had been greater in the earlier part of the war, and there was no significant falling off in membership in the latter years.[30] Rather, the situation reflected the typical dilemma of pacifists in wartime of wanting to attend to the peace effort when society was giving everything to the war effort. There simply was no audience for their views, and they ended up talking to themselves. Even the indomitable Barrington recognized this when he came out of prison in 1942 and devoted himself mainly to his family and job with the Workers' Educational Association. Another response was to separate further from society and set up communities that might become models of Christian living for people to accept in their own good time.[31]

Yet once again, the Christchurch pacifists were the most effective in overcoming these disadvantages and in maintaining a public voice. Kathleen Thompson put the case for a continued public role forcefully: 'The PPU is not, and never has been, an organisation to work for C.O.s ... It is an organization to work for peace – a long-term organization, very long-term it looks at present, to work for the abolition of all wars and that means our real work comes when the war ends.'[32] She and Thurlow Thompson found a way forward in being among the leading spirits who in 1944 began raising money for war relief and who eventually founded the Council for the Organization of Relief Services Overseas (CORSO), New Zealand's major agency in this field. Thurlow indeed felt strongly called to this work and served as national organizer for over twenty years.

Meanwhile another Christchurch pacifist, Lincoln Efford, was instrumental in creating public concern about the treatment of COs by pointing out the implications for civil liberties. Efford's campaign may have been a continuation of the politics of protest, which pacifists had followed from before the war, but it was much better calculated to win public support. In May 1943, having sounded out the local Labour party and trade unions, he confronted the prime minister in person with the evidence that he had been carefully assembling since the first CO cases came before the appeal boards, adding for good measure a comparison between Britain's and New Zealand's policy.[33] The next year, as the war situation improved, he played further on the increasing disquiet of liberal opinion by floating, first, a Christchurch petition signed by fifty academics, church leaders, and trade unionists, and then national petitions, which the government agreed to refer to a parliamentary committee.[34]

Government Policy and the COs

The Thompsons represented one achievement of New Zealand pacifism in the Second World War – the broadening conception of the pacifists' task as they moved from war resistance to peace work, involving the building of peaceable relationships in their own lives, in their societies, and internationally. How to live pacifism had always been a question for pacifists, but till then they had addressed it largely in terms of conscientious objection to conscription or political action against war-mongering interests in the international system. When war came, many pacifists would have preferred some form of social service, the more demanding the better, while remaining outside the war effort; they offered to work in mental hospitals, venereal disease wards, and so on.[35]

The state, however, took the view that its needs were paramount; no 'bolt hole' should be created to interfere with the call-up, pacifists should be prevented from proselytising, and they should do the most productive work for which they were trained. Accordingly, COs whose appeals were upheld were required to work where directed, and unsuccessful appellants who refused to join the army were detained in work camps in remote areas. The savage repression of any publication or activity deemed to weaken the nation's resolve to fight further indicated that the pacifist was expected to retire from citizenship. In these circumstances, Efford could not be blamed for regarding civil liberties as a key issue during the war. He too could claim another achievement, for when compulsory military training was reintroduced in 1949, an altogether fairer system of dealing with conscientious objection was adopted.

Pacifists during the war kept taunting the Labour ministers about their former anti-militarism and opposition to conscription, apparently unable or unwilling to understand that for most of the Labour party the 'rise of the dictators' in the 1930s had inaugurated a struggle for the defence of democracy and human values. Nevertheless, this whole-hearted commitment to the war does not sufficiently explain why a government of the left, which saw itself carrying on a New Zealand tradition of enlightened social reform, was so draconian towards the 'awkward minorities' of the wartime society. Time and again Prime Minister Fraser urged the importance of the nation uniting behind the war effort, which could be taken merely as inevitable wartime rhetoric, were it not for government action that forbade public criticism of the war and war effort and silenced all who would not comply.[36] Pacifists were expected to lapse into quiet resignation. The Wellington-based Fellowship of COs (1941–6) was lucky to escape being banned as a subversive organization; Jehovah's Witnesses were not so fortunate. Aliens too were deemed to be potential fifth columnists and imprisoned for the duration of the war on an island in Wellington harbour.[37]

The most favoured explanations for Labour's authoritarianism focus on its desire to head off conservative opinion and demands for a national coalition and its concern arising from the fact that war, and particularly conscription, had been socially and politically divisive in the interwar period (as late as 1939–40 party and trade-union elements had been involved in a Peace and Anti-Conscription Council, which had won some public support[38]). The government's attitude constituted an over-reaction: the militant pacifists were, at worst, a nuisance rather than a threat, and pacifists and most COs would probably have been satisfied if the state had assigned them to some kind of humanitarian work. In Britain, the country usually compared with New Zealand at the time and since, there was much less interference with civil liberties, and the state's treatment of pacifists and COs never became an issue of any significance.

Fraser as war totalitarian was well revealed in the report of his meeting with a CPS delegation: 'When a person believed his job was to convince people that the war was wrong, a conflict inevitably arose. The State was representing the general consensus of opinion of the people, and was compelled to uphold these views. They could not permit anything which was subversive of the country's war effort. He himself felt it was his duty to do everything he possibly could to further the war effort. The salvation of the country depended upon winning the war, and it was necessary for the Government to prevent the expounding of doctrines which would strike at the foundations of the State.'[39]

The government set out with liberal intentions with respect to COs and in formulating a policy was strongly under the influence of the British example. The number of CO applicants who refused to accept the decision on their case was proportionately very high in New Zealand, but this cannot be blamed on the definition of conscientious objection that the state preferred, or on the processes adopted for hearing appeals. The national service regulations and the appeal boards (six at first, later increased to nine) might have produced very different results than they did. But the boards took an exceptionally narrow view of conscientious objection within the parameters set by the government and were above challenge, because of the independence of the judicial power.

What can be laid at the government's door was the treatment of the CO once his appeal had been heard. The successful appellant could suffer a severe financial penalty by being allowed only soldier's pay while remaining a civilian. The unsuccessful appellant who defied the board's determination of his case, refusing to join the army, was ordered into detention for the duration of the war. It was these 'indeterminate sentences' imposed on top of many doubtful, not to say controversial, decisions by the boards that particulary turned the COs' situation into a public issue. From 1944 on, the government was on the defensive, as representations came in from the churches, trade unions, and Labour party branches. Eventually a Revision Authority was established, ostensibly to release men from detention for urgent reconstruction work, but really to correct the mistakes – in some degree at least – that had been made.[40]

As planning for conscription got under way in the late 1930s, the Labour ministers had had every reason to want to find the right policy on conscientious objection. Apart from sympathy within the party for COs, Labour's experience during the First World War showed how public concern could be easily excited on the issue. At that time the hard line taken by the authorities and army had provoked public outcry over the victimization of COs, which Labour used to advance its popularity and anti-militarist credentials.[41] Curiously enough, New Zealand's policy on conscientious objection in the Second World War originated in Britain's Military Service Act of 1916, seen in retrospect to have been commendably liberal. In the conscription of 1917–18 in New Zealand, relief had been offered only to members of pacifist religious bodies, and then only to the extent of non-combatant service in the army. Britain, in contrast, had recognized conscientious objection on other than religious grounds and had been ready to keep COs out of the army. Here was found a tried policy, and one appropriately 'enlightened,' for a Labour party that had been on the side of the COs in the First World War.[42] In addition, to further reassure the public, it was agreed to exclude the military from the tribunals hearing appeals against military service. The hardest edge of the government's policy in 1939 was the idea that only absolute pacifists could count as COs: to quote the regulations imposing conscription in June 1940, those who believed that 'it is wrong to engage in warfare in any circumstances.' However, a conscientious objection to combatant service was also recognized soon afterwards.

Like everywhere else, those in New Zealand who applied to be COs were an immensely diverse group in terms of beliefs and attitudes, which of course ranged far beyond pacifism to politics, religion, nationalism, attitudes to the state, views on conscription, family allegiances, and personal identities. The authorities distinguished broadly between religious and non-religious objectors, but there was a world of difference, say, between Methodist pacifists and Jehovah's Witnesses, whose religion was entirely otherworldly, or between them and Plymouth Brethren and Seventh-day Adventists, who generally accepted non-combatant service. Some CO appellants were prepared to join the war effort as civilian workers; at the opposite pole there were those who would refuse to act in any capacity whatsoever if invasion and devastation occurred. The only official profile we have of COs as such relates to the men detained as military defaulters (see table on page 301),[43] which probably inflates the proportion of religious applicants.

A little over five thousand claims of conscientious objection were put in, out of a total call-up of about 300,000 men. About three thousand came to a hearing; almost exactly 20 per cent of appeals were allowed, 40 per cent were dismissed subject to non-combatant service, and 40 per cent were dismissed

TABLE 1
COs in detention camps

Christian	
Christian Assemblies*	107
Jehovah's Witness	78
Methodist	68
Plymouth Brethren	35
Anglican	32
Presbyterian	28
Roman Catholic	23
Pentecostal	11
Seventh-day Adventist	9
Christadelphian	8
Baptist	6
Congregationalist	1
Others	30
Non-religious	
Humanitarian	82
Agnostic	22
Others†	52
Total	592

Source: See note 43.
*A pentecostal sect, later known as the Assemblies of God.
†Probably means 'not known.'

outright.[44] Australia does not really admit a comparison because conscription there was for home defence only. Proportional to population, Britain had half as many COs as New Zealand had (0.8 per cent of men called up); Britain granted some form of exemption to 70 per cent of CO applicants, compared with New Zealand's 60 per cent.[45] In both countries there were significant differences among local tribunals, though these are more explicable in Britain's case by deep-set religious and other regionalisms (such as the strength of Cornish Methodism and Scotland's military tradition). Auckland, the toughest New Zealand board, allowed only 15 per cent of appeals and dismissed outright nearly 50 per cent; the equivalent figures for the most lenient board, Canterbury, were 30 per cent and under 25 per cent. Thus an appellant before the Auckland board was twice as likely to have his case dismissed outright and half as likely to have it allowed than if he had appeared in Canterbury.[46] No appellate tribunal was ever instituted to modify such disparities.

Unlike Britain, New Zealand failed dismally to produce a satisfied, generally cooperative CO population. Nearly a quarter of CO appellants refused to accept the decision of their board and ended up in detention camps or prison for the duration of the war. In Britain under 7 per cent remained uncooperative to the point of being punished in civil or military courts.[47] Any explanation has to acknowledge the conviction and resolve that existed among pacifists and other war resisters. But the appeal boards must bear most of the responsibility for New Zealand's poor record; the government had offered the boards a broad definition of conscientious objection, accommodating moral and religious as well as pacifist opposition to war, and had further made available the alternatives of civilian and non-combatant service. Only the Canterbury board responded effectively to the full variety of conscience – religious and non-religious, main church and sect, reasoning and received, militant and passive, serving and non-serving.[48] All boards wee inclined to regard non-combatant service as a suitable compromise between the CO and the state, apparently unable to see that for many this category crossed the line separating humanitarian work from war.

In the First World War the state in New Zealand had insisted that all men called up and fit to serve were to join the army, with the only concession allowed COs being non-combatant status. The Second World War boards seem to have found it hard to shake off this legacy. Their view was that in a situation of total war, when the very survival of the nation seemed to be at stake, no citizen could practically separate himself or herself from the war effort, and none worthy of citizenship would want to do so. All must serve – an attitude presumably reinforced in May 1941 by a provision that COs exempted from the army were to perform nationally useful work, a decision itself influenced by, if not derived from, recent British legislation making COs liable for civil-defence duties. In New Zealand, 'individualists' who held that participation in war should be purely voluntary, and most others who remained aloof from the civil-defence organizations, were written off as self-interested or disloyal, and their appeals were dismissed. This ethic of service explains why the boards overall gave twice as many determinations in favour of non-combatancy as exemption from the army. They found it altogether easier to conceive of a conscientious objection to killing than of a conscientious objection to military service.

The boards' position was that a man's refusal to join the army had to be founded on beliefs – almost always religious – that were simply accepted on the authority of church, parents, and so on. They therefore observed an important distinction between 'traditional' and 'critical' consciences.[49] Non-religious pacifists, as well as Methodist or CPS pacifists, could not carry the same credibility, because their anti-war views were seen to be based on interpretation and argument, and such open-mindedness invariably exposed a person to self-doubt and self-examination. Here again the boards were not too far from First World

War precedents, in which the state had laid it down that only members of pacifist religious sects could qualify as COs. Certainly, in the Second World War, Quakers and Christadelphians (who had been canny enough to have the government recognize their pacifist credentials before the war) had the easiest passage through the appeal process.[50]

Regardless of the hard line taken by the boards, the destination of most CO claimants was civilian employment in New Zealand; and then in jobs with which the manpower authorities were reluctant to interfere. This situation resulted mainly from the fact that about two thousand out of five thousand cases never came to a hearing, including those who were graded medically unfit for service and over one thousand who escaped the call-up on grounds of public interest or personal hardship, for the government had decided that when a man also put in such an appeal he should be heard first.[51] Another group of COs who were virtually indistinguishable from other civilians in wartime were those assigned to non-combatant service. Early in the war the army warned that it wanted few non-combatant soldiers; COs in that category with a low medical grading were never called up, while those deemed fit for service usually spent only a short time in the army. The COs whose appeals were upheld did have a special status as civilians. They were subject to a special tribunal, which reduced their earnings to the level of 'soldier's pay' – on the principle of 'equality of sacrifice' – and they were further required to perform 'work of national importance.' Most, however, were not shifted from their existing employment and did not earn enough to suffer the financial penalty.[52] The characteristic occupations of the CO population were in skilled trades and white-collar work. These in themselves provided a great deal of protection against, first, conscription into the army, and then, when that had been avoided, 'manpowering,' by which the government directed men (and women) into war-essential occupations.[53]

Most COs assimilated easily into the wartime economy. A few lost their jobs – schoolteachers and civil servants mainly – but any public feeling against them as a group tended to be vented in short-lived, localized outbursts. Much harder to bear for the men and their families was the way in which other people singled out 'conchies' as oddities or sometimes as 'cowards and slackers.' There are harrowing stories of workers ostracized, wives snubbed, and children made tearful by the cruelties inflicted on them. Most, understandably, kept their heads down and retreated into their family and church. It was probably hardest for those who had moved in the social mainstream – the politically engaged, members of community organizations, main-church Christians.

COs from the small sects were probably often inured to community disapproval and hostility and withdrew only a little further. Certainly, when such men found themselves in the camps for defaulters, they showed little sign of grievance, preferred the company of their co-religionists, and cooperated with the camp authorities to the point of acutely annoying the other detainees. In contrast, the 'exhibitionists' and 'recalcitrants' who made most trouble in the camps were predominantly Methodist and CPS pacifists and the 'non-religious–quasi-political agitator group.'[54]

COs and Detention Camps

The original idea behind the detention camps was to form isolated but functioning communities, with the inmates being grateful for not being consigned to prison while accepting that they had no right to complain of detention when soldiers too endured disruption of their lives and separation from loved ones. Len Greenberg, a former national director of the YMCA, devised the scheme for the government, and he appears to have entered on the task with the view that young men of like mind would respond positively to the opportunities of living together and of healthy, hard work contributing to national development. He wanted a few, unobtrusive guards and expected them to be mostly occupied in controlling the access of family and friends to the camps.[55] The collapse of this ideal construct has no simple explanation; one might refer to work that became increasingly pointless without adequate planning and equipment, to camp staff members who never won the respect of the inmates, to tensions between those who wanted to continue the protest against war and those who wanted to make life as comfortable for themselves as possible, or to Greenberg, who soon displayed derision and contempt for the men with whom he was dealing.

Detention for COs in defaulters' camps began at the end of 1941. As early as 1942 a special camp for 'non-cooperators' had to be established, and soon afterward this defiant element began being subjected to prison sentences, including fifty-eight who were eventually imprisoned for the duration of the war. Such men represented, above all, the sense of grievance accumulated out of the decisions of the appeal boards; usually committed pacifists, they had good reason to regard themselves as the victims of an inflexible, uncomprehending system and their subsequent suffering as entirely the consequence of that first injustice.[56]

Michael Young, the PPU leader, was sent to the camps, one example among many of how dubiously the boards had acted. Even the politicians by the last months of the war were willing to admit publicly that wrongs had been done; the prime minister acknowledged to a church and pacifist deputation that 'different boards' had applied 'different standards'; his deputy stood up in Parliament to say that 'some men have been wrongly convicted, held under conditions worse than the worst criminals being subject to no release, able to make no appeal. Some of these men are very fine people.'[57] Greenberg soon came to the conclusion that the enormous sense of grievance that pervaded the camps, inducing either opposition or despair, had defeated his original vision; as early as March 1943, when the camps had been going for little more than a year, he was recommending 'reorganisation' into 'civilian service units,' in which parties of twenty men or more would be sent away to perform 'work of immediate national importance' as and where required.[58]

Greenberg, together with the two cabinet ministers responsible for COs, then began making the case for a review of appeal-board decisions, mainly on the grounds that men had proved their sincerity by accepting detention.[59] Their argument was greatly reinforced when information was obtained from Britain showing that there the punishment visited on defaulters was only a limited prison term and that about half the CO appellants had been registered for civil employment.[60] However, when the matter was finally brought before the war cabinet, a harder line prevailed. Up to the end of the war in Europe, the most that was secured was an increase in the modest pay allowed detainees and provision for eight days' parole leave each year, each dependent on good conduct and implemented only as late as October 1944.

The greatest puzzle is that the government in November 1944 approved the release of defaulters using a 'revision authority,' but such a body was not established until June 1945.[61] It is easy to blame the Returned Services Association (RSA), which, during the last year of the war, became highly vocal in demanding that COs be kept in the camps until the troops had come home and been reintegrated into civilian employment.[62] The government and the RSA were responding to deep feelings in society about the sacrifices that servicemen had made. What cast a long shadow over the issue was the treatment of several thousand soldiers who returned on furlough from the Middle East in July 1943 and February 1944, only to be ordered back to the same theatre amid scenes of near-mutiny and public indignation.[63] As the European war drew to a close, it simply became unthinkable to try the public's patience on a similar matter.

Much of the government's thinking late in the war can be read in the timing of its enactments concerning COs. At the same time as it was moving towards a policy of review and receiving petitions and representations in favour of liberalization, it resolutely kept in place the regulations banning defaulters from public service employment.[64] The announcement that the Revision Authority would begin work was put off until a month after the German surrender. The first releases were not made until the war was finally over, with the defeat of Japan. The authority's terms of reference carefully preserved the appearance that the decisions of the appeal boards were being upheld and that COs were not being 'freed' ahead of soldiers. So, though the authority had to be satisfied that a man held 'a conscientious belief that would prevent his participation in war,' any release was conditional. Men left the camps on parole, they were not free like returned servicemen to take employment where they chose, and their earnings were limited to 'soldier's pay.' The authority was and was not an appellate body; it could recognize as a CO a man whom the boards had not, but it could not alter a man's status from military defaulter to 'proven' CO.[65] Such a ludicrous situation emphasizes the tangle the government was in as it tried to maintain its own consistency and satisfy opposing opinions.

Nevertheless, the camps were steadily emptied. In six months from June 1945, the Revision Authority released 283 men, and another 226 left who were considered unfit for the army on age or medical grounds or who had been in detention for over four years. By the end of March 1946 only 132 men remained in camps, and twenty-six in prison.[66] The ministers continued to trade off this aspect of their policy against the maintenance of restrictions and penalties in deference to the RSA and the hard-line opinion that they supposed it represented. Defaulters were the last group to be relieved from the manpower regulations, in June 1946.[67] The exclusion of defaulters from public employment and their disfranchisement, imposed first for the parliamentary elections in 1943, lasted until 1948 and 1950, respectively.[68] Even the release of men from the camps was punitive, since it was under Greenberg's control, and he made sure that names went forward in order according to how well an individual had cooperated with the camp authorities.[69]

Greenberg defended defaulters' detention as silencing pacifists who would otherwise have been on the streets attacking the war and jeopardizing the morale and unity of wartime society. If the Japanese had ever invaded New Zealand, these pacifists at least were being held where they could do no mischief.[70] This stance was very close to seeing the most troublesome defaulters as traitors to their country. 'Subversives,' 'cowards,' and 'shirkers' were labels that Greenberg and other officials who dealt with COs were fond of applying in the privacy of bureaucratic communication – a further indication that hard-line attitudes were not merely political gloss but had real substance.[71]

Conclusion

Ultimately perhaps New Zealand's intolerance represented the insecurities of a small, remarkably homogenous society (the Maori 'renaissance' effectively began after the war). Certainly, the challenge of pacifism and conscientious objection was taken the more seriously because the most active elements were associated with a major religious denomination and with the politically influential Labour party. Yet it can still be argued that the state created these problems for itself. Before conscription was properly under way, church leaders advised the government to establish an appellate tribunal after the British example, and had their advice been followed there undoubtedly would have been far fewer CO defaulters.[72] The decision to hold defaulters for the duration of the war may have been done to sustain the comparison with soldiers, but it perpetuated grievances and offended the principle of determinate sentences. Organized pacifism, left to its own devices in wartime society, would have been a bearable nuisance if it did not succumb to the smothering weight of war participation and consensus. As it was, government and pacifists diverted a lot of energy into the CO issue for little positive result.

NOTES

1 The CPS had 375 members by September 1939, with about another two hundred pacifists in the PPU; Nancy M. Taylor, *The Home Front (The New Zealand People at War)* (Wellington 1986), 178 n 45. By 1941 the CPS claimed a membership of about six hundred. In 1942 the president of the PPU said that membership was 450–500. CPS *Bulletin* W35 (Oct. 1941); *PPU Bulletin* (Dec. 1942). For Quaker numbers, see *New Zealand Census*, 1945, 6, 1.

2 Ernest Crane, *I Can Do No Other: A Biography of Ormond Burton* (Auckland 1986); A.C. Barrington, *Trials of a Pacifist* (Christchurch n.d.).

3 PPU circulars, 5 April, 12 May 1940, National Library, Wellington (WNL), MS. 439/317, Barrington Mss.

4 Crane, *I Can Do No Other*, 112–13.

5 'Notes on a Deputation of the New Zealand Christian Pacifist Society ... 18 November 1940,' New Zealand National Archives (NZNA), Wellington, J 1940/35/140.

6 Author's interview with Michael Young, 15 June 1983.

7 F.L.W. Wood, *The New Zealand People at War* (Wellington 1958), 126.

8 Geoffrey W. Rice, ed., *The Oxford History of New Zealand* (Auckland 1992), 345.

9 Ibid., 520–3.

10 C.R.N. Mackie to P.M., 6 Dec. 1939, Canterbury Museum, Christchurch, Mackie Mss. 1059.

11 *Appendix to the Journal of the House of Representatives (AJHR)*, 1943, H-11A, 32.

12 The NMWM has not had its history written, but much information is in Mackie Mss. 1010 and the pacifist journal *Cosmos* (published by Norman Bell, 1930–40).

13 For Mackie, see the entry in Harold Josephson, ed., *Biographical Dictionary of Modern Peace Leaders* (Westport, Conn., 1985), 587–8. Mackie's papers form the best source for the history of the NPC.

14 Tracey Borgfeldt, '"Preaching the Social Gospel": Methodist Pacifism 1935–1945,' MA thesis, University of Canterbury, 1988.

15 *Peace Record*, 3 (July 1938); Borgfeldt, '"Preaching,"' 125, 215.

16 Borgfeldt, '"Preaching,"' 116–18.

17 Author's interview with Thurlow Thompson, 22 May 1980; *Waikato Times*, 7 June 1939; sponsors listed in PPU annual report, Oct. 1940, WNL MS. 439/317 (Barrington Mss.). For the CPS covenant see Crane, *I Can Do No Other*, 109.

18 See the reports on various branches in PPU organizer's letter, no. 7, 17 May 1940; circular of 9 Sept. 1940; circular 41/2, (Barrington Mss.).

19 *PPU Newsheet*, no. 9 (Dec. 1943).

20 Wellington activity is described in Taylor, *The Home Front*, 179–81, 187–9, 191–9, 204; David Grant, *Out in the Cold: Pacifists and Conscientious Objectors in New Zealand during World War II* (Auckland 1986), 37–8, 48–50, 55–8, 74, 87, 90–4.

21 Taylor, *The Home Front*, 199.

22 PPU circular, 12 May 1940; annual report, Oct. 1940, (Barrington Mss.). H. Lyttle, the secretary, also resigned. He had been before the courts several times and was sent to prison for three months in February 1940. Taylor, *The Home Front*, 181, 191–2.

23 Grant, *Out in the Cold*, 87–9.

24 Mackie Mss. 1200. The example of Christchurch was urged on other places in CPS *Bulletin* W43 (Aug. 1942). Thompson proudly commended it at the CPS conference in October 1943, ibid., W58 (Jan. 1944).

25 *Peace Record*, 3 (Nov. 1939). The titles were *What Are We Fighting For?* and *The Road to Peace*, the first written by Alun Richards.

26 Mackie to Ensom Trust, 26 Nov. 1940, Mackie Mss. 1059.

27 *PPU Circular*, 9 Sept. 1940, Barrington Mss.; ibid., 24 Sept. 1941, WNL, MS. 445 (Efford Mss.); Grant, *Out in the Cold*, 90–1.

28 Interview, 22 May 1980; Grant, *Out in the Cold*, 113–16.

29 *PPU Newsheet*, [n.d. Apr.? 1945], Barrington Mss. 317. Efford in 1943 sought a full-time organizer to keep pacifist groups in touch with each other and to coordinate activity. Grant, *Out in the Cold*, 113.

30 Ibid., 108.

31 Taylor, *The Home Front*, 208.

32 *PPU Newsheet*, [n.d. 1945?] Christchurch also showed the way by being the first place to field a peace candidate for a parliamentary seat. This happened in February 1943 when Lincoln Efford stood at a by-election. See 'From the Candidate,' University of Auckland Library, Auckland (AUL), Mss. A-53 (Thatcher Mss.).

33 See 'Re Appellate Tribunal and Abolition of Indeterminate Sentence, etc' and 'Memorandum Setting out the Case ...' for an account of his activity in May 1943, Canterbury Museum, Efford Mss. box A. For Efford see Josephson, ed., *Biographical Dictionary*, 245–6.

34 Efford, *Penalties on Conscience* (Christchurch, 1945), 4–9; Efford to Thatcher, 3 April 1944 (Thatcher Mss.); *New Zealand Parliamentary Debates*, 267 (1944), 444–7. The 'people of "standing"' who signed the Christchurch petition are listed in *PPU Newsheet*, 11 (April 1944).

35 Burton suggested this when leading a CPS deputation to the prime minister in November 1940; NZNA J1940/35/140.

36 For the rigorous censorship that was imposed, see Taylor, *The Home Front*, 886–1013.

37 Ibid., 234–43, 851–85; Controller-General of Prisons, memo for Minister of Justice, 27 July 1942, NZNA J1 12/2/0.

38 Grant, *Out in the Cold*, 58–73.

39 CPS Deputation to the P.M., 18 Nov. 1940, NZNA J1940/35/140.

40 J.E. Cookson, 'Illiberal New Zealand: The Formation of Government Policy on Conscientious Objection, 1940–1,' *New Zealand Journal of History* (Auckland), 17 (1983), 120–43.

41 Paul Baker, *King and Country Call: New Zealanders, Conscription and the Great War* (Auckland 1988). The classic accounts are H.E. Holland, *Armageddon or Cavalry* (Wellington 1919), and Archibald Baxter, *We will Not Cease* (London 1939).

42 The relationship between the British act of 1916 and New Zealand's policy can be traced in the Committee of Imperial Defence paper ('The Treatment of Conscientious Objectors in Time of War'), March 1937, NZNA EA1 156/6/18; Organization for National Security memo for P.M., 13 March 1940, EA1 83/10/1 ('CO file'); memo for appeal boards, 17 Jan. 1941, 20, NS-DN.

43 L.N. Greenberg and C.J. Hay, 'Defaulters in Detention Camps,' 20 Aug. 1944, NZNA EA1 83/10/1, Table 18.1.

44 *AJHR*, 1946, H-11A, 24–5. The Maori population was not subject to conscription.

45 British figures are taken from Rachel Barker, *Conscience, Government and War: Conscientious Objection in Great Britain, 1939–45* (London 1982), 144, 152.

46 These percentages come from (a) return showing position of appeals on conscientious grounds as at 31 July 1941, NZNA Le1 1942/109; (b) appeals on grounds of conscientious objection, WA11/10/CN9.

47 About one hundred of the eight hundred men sent to the camps had not been the subject of an appeal-board decision. The calculation for New Zealand therefore is based on seven hundred defaulters out of 3,077 appellants. For the British figure, see Martin Ceadel, *Pacifism in Britain, 1914–1945: The Defining of a Faith* (Oxford 1980), 302.

48 I hope to publish a paper on the differences between the Canterbury board and the others.

49 Barker, *Conscience*, 4–5.

50 There was close accord between the views of the boards and legal opinions widely

reported in New Zealand. See *Newall v. Gillingham Corporation, All England Law Reports*, 1941, 1, 552–5; 'Conscientious Objectors,' *Law Journal* (London), 91 no. 176 (3 May 1941); 'Conscientious Objectors,' *New Zealand Law Journal* (Wellington) 17, 113–14 (3 June 1941).

51 *AJHR*, 1946, H-11A, 24.

52 'Special Tribunal,' NZNA WAII/10/CN9; 'Treatment of Conscientious Objectors in New Zealand' [Feb. 1942], EA1 83/10/1; *AJHR*, 1946, H-11A, 25, 129.

53 *AJHR*, 1945, H-11A, 68.

54 Greenberg and Hay, 'Defaulters in Detention Camps,' 5–7; Len J. Greenberg, 'The Men Who Would Not Serve,' WAII/10/CN106, 17–27.

55 [Greenberg], 'Detention of Defaulters: Draft Statement of Policy and General Working Procedure' [Sept. 1941], NZNA J1 1941/31/35.

56 For accounts of the camps, see Grant, *Out in the Cold*, chaps. 5–6, and Taylor, *The Home Front*, 268–85.

57 Deputation from Roslyn Baptist Church, Peace Pledge Union, Society of Friends and Christian Pacifist Society, 21 July 1945, NZNA EA1 83/10/1; Grant, *Out in the Cold*, 235.

58 Memo for Director of National Service, 29 March 1943, EA1 83/10/1; Taylor, *The Home Front*, 278–9.

59 Taylor, *The Home Front*, 279–81; Minister of National Service, memo for P.M., 29 March 1944; Minister of Justice, memo for War Cabinet, 1 May 1944, NZNA EA1 83/10/1; R. Mason to A. McLagan, 15 June 1944, ibid., Nash Mss. 2010.

60 Taylor, *The Home Front*, 280. The war cabinet agreed on 3 February 1944 to seek information from Britain. See Director of National Service, memo for Minister of Justice, 4 Feb. 1944, NZNA EA1 83/10/1.

61 War Cabinet minutes, 'Release of military defaulters from detention,' 'Parole leave for defaulters in detention camps' [16 Nov. 1944], NZNA EA1 83/10/1.

62 Examples of RSA hostility are in *Dominion* and *Evening Post*, 25 Nov. 1944; RSA *Review* (Dec. 1944); RSA deputation to the government, 7 March 1945, NZNA EA1 83/10/1.

63 Wood, *The New Zealand People*, 266–71.

64 The Government Service (Defaulters) Emergency Regulations (1943) were revoked in July 1946.

65 'The Case for the Appointment of Revision Authorities,' NZNA WAII/10/CN9; *AJHR*, 1945, H-11A, 24–6.

66 *AJHR*, 1946, H-11A, 27.

67 J.V.T. Baker, *War Economy (The New Zealand People at War)* (Wellington 1965), 506–9; War Cabinet minutes, 14 Dec. 1945, 28 March 1946, NZNA PM83/10/1.

68 Government Service (Defaulters) Emergency Regulations (1943) were revoked in 1946, but COs were barred from teaching until the Teachers (COs and Defaulters)

Emergency Regulations (1941) ended in 1948. The Electoral Emergency Regulations (1943) ended with the Emergency Regulations Amendment Act of 1950.

69 Greenberg and Hay, 'Defaulters in Detention Camps'; Greenberg, memo for Director
of National Service, 7 Feb. 1945, NZNA EA1 83/10/1.

70 Greenberg, memo for Director of National Service, 7 Feb. 1945, 5–6, NZNA EA1
83/10/1.

71 Greenberg's memoranda provide plenty of examples. But see Controller-General of
Prisons to Officer-in-charge, Hautu prison, 9 Sept. 1942, NZNA J1 12/2/10.

72 Memo of church leaders for P.M. [July 1940], NZNA WAII/10/CN9.

19

Conscience and Conscription in a Free Society: U.S. Civilian Public Service

MITCHELL L. ROBINSON

On a rainy spring morning on 15 May 1941, twenty-six men arrived at a former Civilian Conservation Corps (CCC) camp in the Patapsco State Forest near Elkridge, Maryland, accompanied by almost twice as many reporters and photographers. Though they were only ten miles from Fort Meade, home of the 29th Division, these men wore no uniforms and carried no weapons. They had come to Patapsco as the vanguard of Civilian Public Service (CPS), an endeavour that many hoped would offer a witness against war. Over sixteen million men and women served in the armed forces during the Second World War. The Selective Service System classified almost thirty-seven thousand draftees as conscientious objectors (COs). Approximately twenty-five thousand of these served in the military as non-combatants, usually as medics. The Selective Training and Service Act of 1940 required inductees who could not serve in the armed forces for reasons of 'religious training and belief' to perform 'work of national importance under civilian direction.' The Church of the Brethren, the Mennonites, and the Society of Friends created and sustained Civilian Public Service as an avenue to fulfil this obligation. Their creation eventually encompassed 11,950 men and 151 projects scattered throughout the United States, administered jointly through the National Service Board for Religious Objectors (NSBRO). This essay looks at the four principal types of work these men did – in CPS work camps, agriculture, hospitals, and medical experiments – and at their delayed release after the war ended.

The director of the Selective Service, General Lewis B. Hershey, said that the opening of Patapsco inaugurated a unique experiment 'to find out whether our democracy is big enough to preserve minority rights in a time of national emergency.'[1] By the end of the war a chorus of critics was denouncing the experiment as a failure. COs frequently found themselves attacked by veterans' groups, newspaper editors, and politicians seeking to display their patriotic fervour. They came to believe that CPS had become a means to punish them for refusing to bear arms, and some either walked out of camp in disgust or engaged in protests and strikes. The debates surrounding CPS encapsulated the dilemmas inherent in conscientious objection in a liberal democracy.

CPS Camps

Peace church representatives and Selective Service officials prepared the initial blueprint for alternative service during the autumn of 1940. It proposed three choices for COs. Men could be assigned directly to federal agencies, work in camps operated by the peace churches in conjunction with government agencies, or serve in projects operated and financed by the peace churches. Men who worked for the government could be paid an amount equal to that received by army inductees. President Roosevelt unexpectedly rejected this scheme as too lenient, saying that he would rather see COs drilled by army officers. Hasty negotiations produced a compromise that forced pacifists to go to privately funded camps, where they would work without pay under federal or state direction. The religious groups hoped that financing the camps would allow them greater freedom of action.[2]

Once military inductions began in the autumn of 1940, Selective Service and NSBRO officials came under intense pressure to take COs out of their home communities as quickly as possible. On 8 May 1941, Hershey established the Camp Operations Division to 'locate, equip, arrange for, and supervise the operation of, the camps for conscientious objectors engaged in work of national importance under civilian direction.' He selected Lieutenant-Colonel Lewis F. Kosch, an old friend from his days in the Indiana National Guard, to direct the new division. Selective Service acquired most of its camps from the CCC, which discontinued operations in 1942. Officials knew that the press and public would be critically observing the first CPS units, and the ready availability of facilities and clearly defined work projects made the CCC camps particularly attractive.[3]

The peace churches had created the NSBRO in the autumn of 1940 to coordinate alternative service for COs. Over half of all CPS assignees were affiliated with one of the three Historic Peace Churches. Though the Brethren, Mennonites, and Quakers exercised a dominant voice within the NSBRO, it also included representatives from the Federal Council of Churches, secular pacifist groups, and mainline denominations with men in CPS. M.R. Zigler of the Brethren Service Committee served as chairman, and Paul Comly French, a Quaker and former newspaperman who had supervised the Federal Writers' Project in Pennsylvania, was chosen executive secretary.

Forty-five men entered CPS by the end of its first month. The program reached its peak of 8,612 in September 1945.[4] Selective Service calculated that the nation received 5,931,632 days of work from CPS between May 1941 and March 1947. Assignees devoted 68 per cent of their efforts to natural-resource conservation. The majority worked for the U.S. Forest Service and the Soil Conservation Service in the Department of Agriculture and for the National Park Service and the Bureau of Reclamation in the Department of the Interior. They constructed and maintained fences, telephone and electric-power lines, truck trails, and footpaths. To irrigate large tracts of arid land and control soil erosion, they built dams, levees, and reservoirs, sodded and seeded gullies, dug diversion ditches and contour furrows, and cleared channels. As part of the effort to replenish the nation's forests, they planted forty million trees, surveyed forest growth, and tended tree nurseries. CPS forestry camps were on the front line in the fight against forest fires. During the fire season, men were moved west, where they were dispersed to remote 'spike' camps, comprising between twenty and twenty-five men each. They were on constant call, ready to respond at a moment's notice to the fire alarm. Fire-fighting was exhausting, dirty, and occasionally dangerous. Some men carried heavy water tanks, while others laboured with picks, shovels, and rakes to build fire lines to contain a blaze. Assignees also manned fire towers as the war drew forest rangers into the military. Between May 1943 and January 1946, the Forest Service trained 240 volunteers at Missoula, Montana, to parachute into remote areas to fight forest fires. One reporter described these 'smokejumpers' as 'unsung national heroes' who were 'as much a part of the war effort as the doughboys fighting on the front lines.'[5]

The men in CPS camps usually lived in barracks surrounded by common areas that included administrative offices, a mess hall, a kitchen, and pantry. Though the men were not subjected to drill sergeants and bayonet practice, the daily routine followed the model of an army camp. Local authority was usually divided between the camp director, who was hired by one of the peace-church service committees to manage the camp and supervise the men when they were not working, and the project superintendent, who directed the work on behalf of the government's technical agency, which also provided the necessary equipment. The American Friends Service Committee (AFSC), the Brethren Service Committee (BSC), and the Mennonite Central Committee (MCC) operated most of the camps, paying for food, administration, sanitation, medical care, fuel and utilities. The Mennonites, with the largest number of men in CPS, administered almost sixty camps, while the Brethren and Friends operated approximated thirty each.

Final authority for all aspects of CPS rested with the Selective Service's director and, in practice, the Camp Operations Division. During a trip to the CPS camp at Merom, Indiana, Colonel Kosch bluntly told the executive director of the AFSC camps that 'I'm in charge of these camps' and that the peace churches were 'only camp managers.'[6] Many critics, such as the noted civil-liberties attorney Julien Cornell, argued that the direction of CPS by military officers such as Hershey and Kosch violated the 'plain intention' of Congress, which had stipulated that alternative service be 'under civilian direction.'[7]

In response to complaints from assignees who did not want to serve under church jurisdiction, Selective Service established eight projects under direct government supervision. The government bore all the expenses, and a technical agency administered each camp. The first government camp opened at Mancos, Colorado, on 1 July 1943 under the direction of the Bureau of Reclamation. The bureau took over a second camp at Lapine, Oregon, in January 1944. The Selective Service established a third camp in May 1944 under the direction of Fish and Wildlife Service in the Seney Wildlife Refuge at Germfask in a remote area of upper Michigan. The Coast and Geodetic Survey employed a forty-man unit to map sections of the far west, and two COs worked for the National Park Service in Hawaii.

Though technical supervisors often praised their work, many men were frustrated at performing menial work in remote locations. Pacifists had envisioned CPS as an opportunity to offer a positive witness against war through constructive service both at home and abroad. The failure of CPS to live up to these high hopes sparked growing disillusionment. Three men from the camp at Cooperstown, New York, complained in January 1942 that training in teaching, rural rehabilitation, community organization, cooperative development, and religious work was 'quite lost when practiced upon pine trees.'[8]

Selective Service officials defined 'work of national importance' primarily within the context of the nation's growing labour shortage and sought projects that represented a wise use of manpower rather than a witness against war. They tried to ensure that COs would perform the work willingly, since 'filling the jails with them because they would not work would not solve the problem of having them perform service for the Nation.' Officials also wanted to avoid political controversy and sought assurances that local communities would tolerate having COs in the area. Complaints that objectors' talents were being wasted on make-work projects of little value prompted Camp Operations to remind CPS assignees that they could be required to do 'any work which the Director of Selective Service declares to be work of national importance.' Selective Service was not obligated 'to provide an assignee with work for which he has been particularly prepared, wished to do, or regards as socially significant.'[9] Kosch told the Senate Military Affairs Committee that Selective

Service opposed 'helping these men spread their pacifist propaganda' by putting them in positions where they would do 'missionary work,' such as 'social-welfare work, teaching in schools, and so forth.'[10] Hershey testified that 'the conscientious objector, by my theory, is best handled if no one hears of him.'[11]

The demands for genuine 'work of national importance' appeared to be answered in August 1942 with creation of a unit to train COs for reconstruction work in liberated nations. Philip Jessup, a Columbia University professor who served in the State Department's Office of Foreign Relief and Rehabilitation Operations, persuaded Selective Service to allow fifteen COs to participate in the course on the civil administration of occupied territories given to naval officers at Columbia's Graduate School in International Relations. Two larger relief units were subsequently established in April 1943. One was to augment the (British) Friends Ambulance Unit, which had been ferrying medical supplies to the Chinese interior since July 1941. The seventy-man unit, located at Chungking, China, would perform 'rehabilitation, sanitation, nutrition, public health, and other such services as may be designated by the ministry of public health of the government of the Chinese Republic.' The Foreign Relief and Rehabilitation Unit, or the Civilian Public Service Training Corps, was created to prepare volunteers for service in war-ravaged nations following liberation.

Unfortunately, congressional opposition, sparked by complaints from veterans groups and newspapers that COs were attending school while their peers were engaged in mortal combat, scuttled the plans to employ COs as relief workers. In June 1943, Congressman Joseph Starnes from Alabama attached a rider to the War Department Appropriations Bill that forbade COs from receiving training or from serving abroad. Despite intense lobbying spearheaded by the newly created Friends Committee on National Legislation and its indefatigable executive secretary, E. Raymond Wilson, the rider was attached to every War Department appropriation passed during the war.[12]

The fact that assignees were not paid for their labour only added injury to insult. Some men believed that working without compensation expressed a spirit of sacrificial service, while others saw it as slave labour. Campers supported themselves and their families from savings and part-time earnings or relied on assistance from religious agencies or relatives. Some were forced to resort to public assistance, and others requested reclassification to join the military. The churches and the NSBRO made several efforts to obtain compensation for CPS assignees and financial support for their dependants, but they found little sympathy either in Congress or in the administration. Hershey thought that working without pay was part of the sacrifice that COs should make to avoid military service and retain public support.[13] Kosch was more cynical, arguing that lack of pay deterred slackers.[14] Even Eleanor Roosevelt, whom many COs regarded as a staunch ally, opposed government assistance for CPS dependants. She acknowledged the hardship 'for the innocent dependents who must suffer, but that is part of the burden which a conscientious objector assumes when he lives up to his beliefs.'[15] The president also showed little inclination to change the system. He told the socialist leader Norman Thomas in May 1943 that COs received their 'compensation in the form of food, clothing, shelter, medical care, allowances and other services.' Whether the amount they received was commensurate with that of a soldier was a 'matter of opinion when the risks of service are considered.'[16]

Whenever possible, the religious agencies collected thirty-five dollars per month from each man or his family to cover the costs of operation, though they turned away no one who lacked funds. The NSBRO and Historic Peace Churches were committed to supporting every man classified as a CO, regardless of his religious affiliation. This commitment required them to undertake a major fund-raising effort, and by the end of the war they had raised over $7 million. The three Historic Peace Churches carried the lion's share of the financial burden, contributing $5,528,000.[17]

Hershey frequently cited public opinion when responding to critics. He warned one camper that 'modifications of the Selective Training and Service Act which would permit conscientious objectors to escape entirely governmental service' would produce 'a popular reaction which would force measures less favorable than those being used at the present time.'[18] Hershey and Kosch consistently measured the treatment of COs against the standards of the armed forces. Selective Service officials assured the Senate Military Affairs Committee in February 1943 that the regulations governing CPS camps were 'comparable to those under which a man in the Army serves.'[19] The peace churches also felt the pressure of public opinion. New arrivals at Big Flats were warned that each one of them 'must assume the responsibility for the reputation of every other man in camp. It is not a matter of choice that he assumes this responsibility; it is due to public opinion which judges our CPS community and every individual within it by the actions of any one of these individuals.'[20]

Given the independent nature of many pacifists and the wide variety of views among CPS assignees, any effort to impose military order and discipline was doomed to only partial success at best. Camp directors often found themselves trying to steer a course between radicals, who denounced them as agents of conscription, and Selective Service officials and technical supervisors, demanding a stricter regimen. A Camp Operations inspector cited the deplorable conditions that he observed at the AFSC camp at Big Flats, New York, in January 1943 as evidence of a low state of morale and discipline. He accused the staff of allowing some of the men to feign illness to avoid working on Saturdays. The barracks were 'disordered, cluttered, and dirty. Cobwebs hanging in festoons. Bunks and lockers at all angles with spaces screened off and aisles almost blocked. No attempt made to fold clothing or keep things in order. About the worst I have ever seen ... Bunks very poorly made and many in disorder ... The clutter is a fire hazard, and a health hazard as well as an offense to decent living.'[21] Camp directors responded that many of the infractions were committed by men who were mentally unfit for service, who should have been rejected by their drafts boards.

Disciplinary problems were particularly acute at the government-operated camps. Kosch believed that there had been 'entirely too much "molly-coddling"' in the church-operated camps, and he predicted that men who did not fit into the church program would face 'a hard-boiled situation' in a government camp.[22] Germfask, which was intended for assignees who 'did not make an adjustment at other camps,' became notorious for its discipline problems. Selective Service received reports of squalid living conditions, malingering or refusal to work, drinking in camp, vandalism, and threats against camp officials. *Time* magazine characterized the assignees' behaviour as a 'campaign of studied defiance of camp officials.' Hostility between the men and some members of the local community forced the camp director to place two nearby towns off-limits. After unsuccessfully attempting to impose order, Selective Service closed the camp on 31 May 1945 and transferred the men to Minersville, California.[23]

Agricultural Work

The war prompted an exodus of farm workers to the military and to higher-paying jobs in defence industries. Selective Service proceeded cautiously on proposals that COs be used to relieve shortages of agricultural labour. Kosch warned that 'unemployed men, not ordinarily interested in farm work, would be the first to criticize conscientious objectors assigned to such work.'[24] In 1942, the NSBRO, the Department of Agriculture, the U.S. Employment Service, and the Selective Service agreed to place CPS assignees on dairy farms in selected counties in Connecticut, New York, and Wisconsin on an experimental basis. Farmers in those counties welcomed the prospect of additional help, though opposition from veterans' organizations delayed and almost scuttled farm assignments in Connecticut and Wisconsin. Despite some initial concerns, the experiment proved to be a great success. C.A. Kenworthy, manager of the U.S. Employment Service (USES) office in Oneida, New York, found that the farmers and their wives in Madison County had 'very graciously received these boys and made a soft spot in the heart of each farm.'[25]

As wartime demands on the nation's food supply increased, so did farmers' pleas for help. The crisis in agricultural labour spurred plans for full-time farm service on a larger scale. President Roosevelt announced on 30 March that '500 experienced dairy workers' could be furnished immediately to farmers from the ranks of CPS assignees and that another eighteen hundred with agricultural experience, who would probably 'make as good as dairy workers,' were available as well.[26]

Under the agreement hammered out following weeks of extended negotiations between government agencies and the NSBRO, the Department of Agriculture designated twenty-six counties in twelve states that were critical to milk production. CPS units of twenty to twenty-five men would be allocated to those counties certified by the USES as being short of agricultural labour. COs were assigned to farms selected by county agents and the local USES representatives. They could not work for relatives or within one hundred miles of their homes. The farmers provided room and board. In order to prevent unfair competition with local labour, they made monthly payments to the NSBRO in lieu of wages at rates established by the Department of Agriculture's county war boards. The COs received $15 per month for clothing, toilet articles, and other necessities. The National Service Board remitted the balance of the money paid by farmers to the U.S. Treasury, where it would be held in a suspended account until the termination of the war. This 'frozen fund' eventually accumulated $1.3 million. COs also worked for agricultural experiment stations and served as testers for local dairy-herd improvement associations (DHIAs). The testers visited DHIA members to weigh the milk, check its butterfat content, weigh the feed given to each cow, and measure the productivity of both individual animals and various strains of cattle.

By October 1945, 1,123 men were working on farms in thirty-four counties in fifteen states and with DHIAs in fourteen states. Farm work was particularly attractive to COs from agricultural backgrounds, and Brethren and Mennonite men comprised a majority of COs in the dairy farm units. Most farmers and agricultural officials expressed satisfaction with the service rendered by the COs. One reported that 'they were, by far, the very best help we were able to obtain during the war years.'[27]

Assignees who remained in camp were not exempt from the pressure to relieve the labour crisis in agriculture. Selective Service instructed camp directors to supply men to farms within a fifteen-mile radius on an emergency basis if the USES certified that a labour shortage existed. Assignees planted crops, picked vegetables, husked corn, dug potatoes, and pruned fruit trees for neighbouring farmers. Emergency agricultural labour was a persistent source of controversy in the camps. Since Selective Service classified it as part of their work assignment, it was mandatory, and men who refused were subjected to prosecution. The NSBRO, the religious agencies, and the men believed that all farm work should be voluntary, particularly since it was being performed for private employers. They also expressed concerns about the potential for community pressure, the possibility that some of the products might be used in direct support of the war effort, and the uncertainties surrounding disposition of the money that the farmers paid for the men's work. Paul French of the NSBRO tried to get a commitment from government agencies that emergency farm labour would be performed on a non-compulsory basis but found little support. Colonel William M. Wilder of the War Food Administration told him that 'millions of other men were being ordered around,' and he failed to see why COs should be allowed options regarding the type of work they would perform.[28] Many camp directors and project superintendents reached a modus vivendi at the local level by assigning only those men who would willingly perform farm work.

Hospital Work

The scarcity of manpower affected health care as severely as agriculture. Unpleasant working conditions combined with low salaries led many hospital employees to seek higher-paying positions elsewhere. In February 1942 the American Medical Association and the American Hospital Association urged Selective Service to employ COs in hospitals, noting that they would be less conspicuous in larger cities.[29] Although Selective Service gave these requests a favourable hearing, opposition from veterans' organizations frustrated initial attempts to place COs in hospitals in Elgin, Illinois, and Gardiner, Massachusetts. The first hospital unit opened in March 1942 with the assignment of eighteen men to the Alexian Brothers Hospital in Chicago for nursing training. Selective Service approved the first CPS unit in a mental institution at the Eastern State Hospital in Williamsburg, Virginia on 10 June.

Success at Alexian Brothers and Williamsburg paved the way for dramatic expansion. CPS units were established in forty mental hospitals, three general hospitals, three Veterans Administration hospitals, and sixteen training schools. Approximately three thousand men served in these units. Each state was limited to two units of twenty-five men each, and most units were in the east and midwest. In addition to hospitals, Selective Service approved units in Florida and Mississippi to work for the U.S. Public Health Service constructing sanitary facilities to control the spread of hookworm. Another group of COs went to Puerto Rico to provide medical aid, public health education, and community social services to the rural population, in cooperation with the Puerto Rico Reconstruction Administration.

CPS assignees in hospitals usually served as ward attendants and orderlies, but they also worked as mechanics, kitchen helpers, technicians, clerks, and outdoor labourers. The work was demanding and frequently depressing. Assignees often worked seventy and occasionally over one hundred hours per week. Hospital service also carried risks. In 1945, a patient at the Utah State Hospital wounded Edwin Krehbiel with a knife stolen from the dining-room.[30]

Many CPS assignees set out to improve the squalid conditions they found in the mental hospitals. They were particularly interested in finding non-violent methods for handling violent patients. An attendant named Byberry in Philadelphia called it 'the perfect setting in which to demonstrate the superiority of pacifism over brute force in handling tense situations.' These efforts occasionally led to confrontations with hospital administrators and hospital employees' unions. The CPS unit at the Hudson River State Hospital at Poughkeepsie, New York, became the centre of controversy in May 1945 when assignees accused four attendants of kicking, hitting, and slapping patients. The hospital superintendent dismissed the four attendants within forty-five minutes of hearing the report. Unfortunately for him, two of them were veterans, and three were union members. The American Legion and labour groups demanded hearings for the dismissed employees and an investigation of the unit. The superintendent stood his ground. Support came from Eleanor Roosevelt, who visited the unit in July and commended the COs in her 'My Day' column for raising the standards of care for the mentally ill. The employees appealed their dismissal, but the Civil Service Board refused to overturn the superintendent's decision.[31]

Hospital administrators who failed to respond to reports of abuse often found themselves the subjects of unwanted publicity. In 1943 CPS assignees working at Cleveland State Hospital took their charges to the press and prompted an investigation by state authorities that eventually resulted in the resignation of the hospital superintendent. The COs' concern for the care of the mentally ill evolved into the Civilian Public Service Mental Hygiene Program, a four-man special service unit in Philadelphia. It collected techniques and stories from mental hospitals and training schools and published them in a newsletter, the *Attendant*, which was distributed to over six hundred institutions in the United States, Mexico, Canada, and England. The men also published a 'Handbook for Psychiatric Aides' to supplement the training of the mental health attendants. The reports from CPS assignees became the foundation for a campaign to improve conditions in state mental hospitals and the subject of a feature article in *Life* magazine in May 1946.[32]

Selective Service described the hospital projects as 'probably the most significant action' undertaken by Camp Operations – a sentiment shared by the religious agencies and many assignees.[33] One attendant said that he would never again be satisfied with the work in camp and that hospital service was the 'greatest opportunity offered CO's.'[34] Hospital superintendents generally spoke very favourably of the assignees' performance, acknowledging that their help had ensured the continued operation of their institutions. Several, such as Dr James S. Dean at Pennhurst, also cited the problems that some men had created. Though the objectors 'had rendered an invaluable service,' many of them developed 'a galaxy of neurotic conditions.' Dean took particular exception to their highly publicized efforts to improve conditions. They presented, in his view, 'a very one-sided picture emphasizing only the ills and none of the good which is done in a majority of our hospitals.'[35]

Medical Experiments

Conscientious objectors achieved much of their public prominence serving as human guinea pigs in medical experiments. Selective Service established forty-one research units in various hospitals and universities working under contracts from the Office of Scientific Research and Development and the U.S. Army Surgeon General. Over five hundred volunteers subjected themselves to untested drugs, extreme temperatures, infection with diseases such as jaundice, malaria, and pneumonia, and extreme diets requiring deprivation of food and water.

Guinea-pig service frequently entailed discomfort and was not without some danger. One volunteer, Warren Dugan, died on 26 August 1945 after being accidentally infected with infantile paralysis at the Yale University School of Medicine.[36] Selective Service acknowledged that many objectors volunteered to demonstrate that they 'were not afraid to submit themselves bodily to any worthwhile experiment which would result in the saving of life or improvement of health and living conditions.'[37]

One of the first experiments took place in 1942 at the CPS camp at West Campton, New Hampshire. Thirty-five men volunteered to test chemicals that might be used to control body lice. Since the lice carried typhus, a disease that often accompanied wartime destruction, the experiment took on an added significance as the Allies prepared to invade Europe. The subjects wore the same underwear with patches containing approximately two hundred sterile lice for three weeks and used different disinfectant powders. The tests established the effectiveness of DDT, which was subsequently employed to prevent a typhus epidemic in Naples.[38] Scientists also used COs to test cures for malaria, evaluate the effects of extended periods of bed rest, and examine the relationship between testosterone levels and the ability to use protein and carbohydrates.

The experiments reflected wartime priorities. Researchers at the University of Rochester, the University of Illinois, and Cornell University used COs to evaluate the effects of extreme temperatures, such as those experienced by

American troops overseas. CPS assignees were especially useful in dietary studies, and several experiments offered potential benefits for castaways. In February 1945, scientists at Metropolitan Hospital on New York City's Welfare Island began testing life-boat rations in an effort to create a diet that would accelerate recovery from the injuries that frequently accompanied plane crashes and disasters at sea.[39] Campers at Magnolia, Arkansas, ate dehydrated grass tips for three months to determine if cereal grasses, such as oats, rye, wheat, and barley, could substitute for fruits and vegetables, while COs at the University of Rochester tested protein substitutes such as sunflower seeds, cottonseed, peanut flour, brewers yeast, wheat germ, and soy beans.[40]

The nutrition experiments evolved into the best-known CPS guinea-pig project. In November 1944, thirty-six volunteers began a series of experiments under the supervision of Dr Ancel Keys at the Laboratory of Physiological Hygiene at the University of Minnesota. The goal was to assess the physical and psychological effects of starvation and determine the most efficient way to use limited food resources for rehabilitating starving populations in war-ravaged countries. The subjects subsisted for twenty-four weeks on a semi-starvation diet consisting principally of food found in famine areas, such as bread, potatoes, turnips, cabbage, beans, and macaroni. The meals had a daily value of fifteen hundred calories, in contrast to the thirty-three hundred calories that the men normally consumed. Volunteers were required to maintain their normal level of activity, including walking forty-five miles per week, as well as undergoing extensive tests. Their weight dropped on average by almost 22 per cent. A twelve-week rehabilitation period followed. Researchers divided the subjects into groups and administered a variety of diets at different calorie levels and with different vitamin supplements. Despite the physical demands of the experiment, many of the men used their spare time to acquire skills that would be useful in postwar relief efforts.[41]

In keeping with Hershey's theory that COs were handled best when no one heard of them, the guinea-pig units initially kept a low profile. In May 1943 the Selective Service denied permission to publish photographs of the men engaged in nutrition and high-altitude experiments on Welfare Island, citing the absence of any benefit to the war effort.[42] As the war continued, officials recognized the public-relations advantages that might be garnered. Selective Service predicted that the experiments would 'help to build up increasing respect for the courage and the seriousness of the conscientious objectors' convictions.'[43]

Delayed Release

The surrender of Germany and Japan ended the Second World War, but not the draft. The Selective Service law had obligated inductees to serve until six months after the end of hostilities. Following the German capitulation in May 1945, Selective Service released plans for discharging CPS assignees based on a point system similar to the army's. Men accumulated points based on time in service, marital status, and for each child under eighteen. In formulating these plans, Selective Service ignored its state directors, who urged that no CPS men be discharged until all men had been released from the armed forces. The plans sparked opposition from veterans' organizations, the War Department, and the White House. They prompted introduction of a bill in Congress to prevent use of a point system to discharge men from CPS. Though the bill did not become law, the controversy stalled attempts to release men before war's end.[44]

On 21 September 1945, Kosch and French met with the three members of the House Military Affairs Committee and obtained an agreement to permit Selective Service to begin the 'systematic release of conscientious objectors from Civilian Public Service camps and units on a basis of age, length of service, dependency and hardship.' The process would not employ a point system and would not be characterized as demobilization.[45] Despite the agreement, Selective Service proceeded cautiously. Kosch told French on 23 October that the executive committee of the American Legion had prepared a resolution for its annual convention demanding that COs be detained until all men had been discharged from the armed forces.[46]

Selective Service began discharging men from CPS in October 1945. The process proceeded slowly at first. Hershey tried to match the CPS discharge rate to the armed forces, though it initially lagged behind, arousing complaints from various quarters.[47] By 1 December men were being discharged at the rate of thirty per day, and the pace increased to forty-seven within two weeks. The announcement in December 1945 that ten camps would be closed by June 1946 illustrated the accelerating tempo of CPS demobilization.[48]

Based on the draft law's provisions, the AFSC concluded that its obligation to support CPS did not extend beyond six months following the end of the war. Further cooperation would compromise its opposition to a peacetime draft. Therefore the AFSC decided to relinquish its responsibilities for the administration of CPS no later than 2 March 1946. Any remaining AFSC camps would fall under direct Selective Service control. Despite their misgivings, the Brethren and the Mennonites resolved to see the program through to the finish rather than abandoning their men to an uncertain fate at the hands of the government.[49]

The AFSC's departure coincided with growing unrest over the glacial pace of demobilization. Morale plummeted as the weeks turned into months and the COs remained in CPS, labouring without apparent purpose. After subsisting for years without pay or support for their dependants, they found it difficult to appreciate Hershey's concerns about equity and public opinion. Their frustra-

tion boiled over into strikes at several camps. The government camp at Minersville, California, where many of the men had recently been transferred from the
troubled Germfask camp, witnessed the first problems in December 1945. By
the end of the month, the dining hall had been burned, Hershey was accusing
campers of destroying government property, the Federal Bureau of Investigation (FBI) had undertaken an investigation, and one-third of the men were listed
as unavailable for work. Those who were not on strike worked only two to three
hours a day.[50] Hershey complained that lack of an adequate statutory framework prevented him from exercising 'the same degree of control and discipline'
over assignees at Minersville 'as exists over men in the armed forces.'[51] The
grand jury eventually indicted ten men on 14 February 1946, but the assistant
US attorney decided in June not to proceed with further prosecution. In view of
the trivial nature of the violations, he believed that justice might be better
served if the men were ordered to a different camp.[52]

Relations between government employees and assignees at Big Flats had
never been warm, and they only grew worse after the Friends withdrew. The
Soil Conservation Service project superintendent reported that on 28 February
'several of the boys, who have been somewhat difficult to handle, had thrown
rags, paper, wood etc. around the stove and throughout the barracks' in an
apparent attempt to start a fire.[53] On 7 April, campers awoke to find the American flag replaced by a banner proclaiming 'U.S. Slave Camp.' The chairman of
the local American Legion's committee on COs angrily demanded an inquiry to
find those who had 'insulted the flag of the United States.'[54]

Twenty-five men at Glendora, California, went on strike on 24 April to protest the transfer of two men to Minersville, which they portrayed as a 'punishment camp.' Their numbers grew to eighty-two by 15 May, and they were
joined in sympathy by thirty-five men at Big Flats on 1 May and two at Gatlin-
burg, Tennessee. The twenty-eight COs remaining at Minersville also intensified their six-month-long work slowdown. They insisted that every action be
specifically directed by camp officials, and they performed all tasks at a snail's
pace.[55] Within a month, most of the assignees at Glendora were on strike.
Rather than reporting to work, they packed food for shipment overseas. Fifty-
eight men were eventually arrested and indicted, though the Department of Justice dropped the charges against thirty-six of them. The remaining twenty-two
men were brought to trial in March 1947 after almost a year's delay. They were
convicted of failing to perform their assigned duties and received sentences
ranging from eleven months to two years, but all of them were immediately
placed on probation.

While most of the strikers at Big Flats returned to their duties within a few
days, six men initiated a permanent work stoppage to protest the 'vicious condi-

tions' in the conscription system, including 'the flagrant waste of manpower,' lack of compensation and support for dependants, and the 'inexcusably slow demobilization and other arbitrary injustices.' Two deputy U.S. marshals took the six strikers away in handcuffs on 20 May, charging them with unlawful failure to perform assigned work of national importance and conducting themselves 'in such a manner as to cause a breakdown of discipline and morale.' They were indicted on 23 July and, after being convicted in August, sentenced to eighteen months in jail. They refused probation, which was offered on the condition that they return to camp.[56] As a result of the unrest, Kosch ordered that assignees who filed for discharge after 1 June include a statement from their camp director that they had 'not participated in any strike or refusal to work since 15 April 1946.'[57]

Despite the negative publicity and numerous complaints from veterans groups and civic organizations, the strikes did not substantially alter the pace of CPS demobilization. By 12 July 1946 CPS had been reduced to 2,406 men, and by 1 October it was down to 992. Only three CPS hospital units remained by August 1946, and the last unit, at the New Jersey State Hospital in Marlboro, closed on 10 December 1946. Selective Service closed the dairy farm and guinea-pig units during the same month. The Selective Training and Service Act of 1940 finally expired in March 1947, and the last 360 CPS assignees in the country were discharged, almost six years after the first camp had opened.[58]

Conclusion

At the core of the ongoing debates about CPS lie questions about the nature of American citizenship and its rights and responsibilities. CPS was an attempt to reconcile the American egalitarian ethic and the conviction that all citizens should share the burden of defending the nation with the imperative to respect the freedom of conscience enshrined in the Bill of Rights and enumerated by President Franklin Roosevelt among the four freedoms for which the Allies were fighting. The legitimacy of conscription depended on its perceived equity, and policy-makers feared the perceptions of special treatment for any group would threaten the system with collapse. Official sensitivity was further heightened by the adminstration's fear of any cracks in the veneer of wartime unity, which made it anxious to defuse any potentially divisive controversies generated by angry veterans, disgruntled unions, and hostile Congressmen. From the pacifist perspective, CPS marginalized COs rather than providing 'work of national importance' and created inequity in the pursuit of fairness. The financial support and encouragement given to the men in the military and their families was denied to COs. For the churches and for men with modest means, conscience carried a high price, both financially and spiritually. The delays that accompanied their release only compounded their sense of injustice. Many COs concluded that there was little room for dissident voices in a democracy at war.

NOTES

The author gratefully acknowledges advice and assistance from Daniel Baugh, Richard Polenberg, and John Weiss during the preparation of this essay.

1 Robert E.S. Thompson, '"Onward, Christian Soldiers!"': The Nation's Conscientious Objectors Work Out Their Convictions,' *Saturday Evening Post*, 16 Aug. 1941, 27, 53–5.
2 Albert M. Keim and Grant M. Stolzfus, *The Politics of Conscience: The Historic Peace Churches and America at War, 1917–1955* (Scottdale, Pa., 1988), 108–17.
3 U.S. Selective Service System (SSS), *Conscientious Objection* (by Neal M. Wherry), Special Monograph No. 11, 2 vols. (Washington, DC, 1950), 1:161, 165, 168, 2:39; George Q. Flynn, *Lewis B. Hershey, Mr. Selective Service* (Chapel Hill, NC, 1985), 128.
4 SSS, *Conscientious Objection*, 1:187–8.
5 Ibid., 1:168, 209–10; Mulford Q. Sibley and Philip E. Jacob, *Conscription of Conscience: The American State and the Conscientious Objector, 1940–1947* (Ithaca, NY, 1952), 124–32; Don E. Hall, 'Smoke Jumpers,' *PIC* (New York), (Sept. 1945), 73–5.
6 Thomas E. Jones, *Light on the Horizon: The Quaker Pilgrimage of Tom Jones* (Richmond, Ind., 1973), 141–2.
7 Julien Cornell, *The Conscientious Objector and the Law* (New York 1943), 102.
8 Charles Brown, Louis Schneider, and Paul Johnson to James Miller, 20 Jan. 1942, box C-17, NSBRO Mss., Swarthmore College Peace Collection (SCPC).
9 *Conscientious Objection*, 1:166; Camp Operations Division memo, n.d., 345, class IV-E: Conscientious Objectors (General File), box 2, Selective Service System (SSS) Records, National Archives, Washington, DC.
10 U.S. Congress, Senate, Committee on Military Affairs, *Conscientious Objectors' Benefits: Hearings before a Subcommittee of the Committee on Military Affairs on S. 2708*, 77th Cong., 2nd Sess., 19 Aug. 1942, 14.
11 U.S. Congress, Senate, *Committee on Military Affairs, Conscientious Objectors' Benefits: Hearing before the Committee on Military Affairs on S. 315 and S.675*, 78th Cong. 1st Sess., 17 Feb. 1943, 23.
12 'C.P.S. Men Study Relief Administration at Columbia University,' *Gospel Messenger* (Elgin, Ill.), 92 (9 Jan. 1943), 1, 4; Clarence E. Pickett, *For More Than Bread: An Autobiographical Account of Twenty-Two Years' Work with the American Friends*

Service Committee (Boston, Mass., 1953), 219; Order No. 99, 450, C.O. Camps (Chungking Project, China), box 49, SSS Records. For a detailed account of the efforts to repeal the Starnes rider, see E. Raymond Wilson, *Uphill for Peace: Quaker Impact on Congress* (Richmond, Ind., 1975), 35–53, and for efforts to employ COs overseas, see Mitchell Robinson, '"Healing the Bitterness of War and Destruction": CPS and Foreign Service,' *Quaker History* (Haverford, Pa.), 85 (fall 1996), 24–48.

13 Flynn, *Hershey*, 130–1.

14 *Conscientious Objectors Benefits*, 19 Aug. 1942, 6.

15 Eleanor Roosevelt, 'If You Ask Me,' *Ladies Home Journal* (Philadelphia), (June 1944), 38.

16 FDR to Norman Thomas, 20 May 1943, OF 111, Conscientious Objectors Folder, FDR Library, Hyde Park, NY.

17 Sibley and Jacob, *Conscription of Conscience*, 326–30.

18 Lewis B. Hershey to Louis Krawczyk [Taylor], 21 Oct. 1941, box A-68, NSBRO Mss.

19 *Conscientious Objectors' Benefits*, 17 Feb. 1943, 18.

20 'Handbook: C.P.S. Camp #46,' 62, n.d., series 2, box 9, FCC Mss., SCPC.

21 Franklin A. McLean to Lewis F. Kosch, 23 Jan. 1943, 450, C.O. Camps (Big Flats Project, New York), box 55, SSS Records.

22 Paul C. French, memo no. 31 to the Executive Camp Directors, 1 June, 1942, box A-56, NSBRO Mss.; Kosch to Robert Chase, 17 Aug. 1943, 450, C.O. Camps (Mancos Project, Col.), box 50, SSS Records.

23 'Tobacco Road Gang,' *Time*, 19 Feb. 1945, 21; SSS, *Conscientious Objection*, 1:234–42; Sibley and Jacob, *Conscription of Conscience*, 253–6.

24 George Reeves to Henry Fast, 12 Sept. 1941, box AS-2, NSBRO Mss.

25 C.A. Kenworthy to Levi Ziegler, 12 May 1942, in Paul French, memo no. 35 to the Board of Directors, 15 May 1942, box A-56, NSBRO Mss.

26 'President Tells Farm Labor Plan,' *New York Times*, 31 March 1943, 1:2, 13:2.

27 *Conscientious Objection*, 1:169–70, 190, 204, 219–21, 2:75–9; Melvin Gingerich, *Service for Peace: A History of Mennonite Civilian Public Service* (Akron, Ohio, 1949), 190–208; Leslie Eisan, *Pathways of Peace: A History of the Civilian Public Service Program Administered by the Brethren Service Committee* (Elgin, Ill., 1948), 240–64; Sibley and Jacob, *Conscription of Conscience*, 132–4, 220.

28 Paul French, memo no. 196 to the Board of Directors, 24 June 1943, box A-56, NSBRO Mss.

29 Paul French, memo no. 11 to the Board of Directors, 10 Feb. 1942, ibid.

30 'C.P.S, News,' *Mennonite CPS Bulletin*, 8 March 1945, 1. For a detailed account of CPS mental health service, see Alex Sareyan, *The Turning Point: How Men of Conscience Brought about Major Change in the Care of America's Mentally Ill* (Washington, DC, 1994).

31 Claude Shotts to Kosch, 29 May 1945; B. Smucker to Shotts, 6 June 1945, Smucker to Shotts, 19 July 1945; B. Smucker, 'Mrs. Franklin D. Roosevelt Speaks to Men and Women's Relief Training Units at Hudson River State Hospital,' 10 July 1945, all in box C-146, NSBRO Mss. Sareyan, *Turning Point*, 17–20, 66–71, 129–45.

32 Albert Q. Maisel, 'Bedlam 1946,' *Life*, 6 May 1946, 102–18; Sibley and Jacob, *Conscription of Conscience*, 160–5. Sareyan, *Turning Point*, 44, 91–40.

33 SSS, *Selective Service in Wartime: Second Report of the Director of Selective Service, 1941–1942* (Washington, DC, 1943), 270.

34 Lowell E. Maechtle and H.H. Gerth, 'Conscientious Objectors as Mental Attendants,' *Sociology and Social Research* (Los Angeles), 29 (Sept.–Oct. 1944), 19.

35 Dean to Austin Imirie, 5 Aug. 1946, 450, C.O. Camps (Pennhurst Proj., Pa.), SSS Conscientious Objectors, General File, box 120, SSS Records.

36 'Deaths,' *Reporter* (Washington, DC), 15 Sept. 1945, 1–2.

37 SSS, *Conscientious Objection*, 1:170.

38 Sibley and Jacob, *Conscription of Conscience*, 143–4; Joel Canada and Lee Nichols, 'Plague-Fighting Pacifists,' *Coronet* (Chicago) (July 1944), 146–7.

39 'Personnel News: Civilian Public Service,' 18 July 1945, C.P.S. Publications, 124–48, AFSC Mss., SCPC.

40 Robert T. Dick, ed., *Guinea Pigs for Peace: The Story of C.P.S. 115-R, 1943–1946* (Windsor, Ont., 1990); Hobart Mitchell, *We Would Not Kill* (Richmond, Ind., 1983), 155; Cynthia Hastas Morris, 'Arkansas's Reaction to the Men Who Said 'No' to World War II,' *Arkansas Historical Quarterly* (Fayetteville), 43 (summer 1974), 172–3.

41 Eisan, *Pathway of Peace*, 296–312; 'Men Starve in Minnesota,' *Life*, 30 July 1945, 43–6; Paul Bowman, Jr, 'As They Starve, They Study,' *Fellowship* (New York), 11 (May 1945), 92–3; Max M. Kampelman, *Entering New Worlds: The Memoirs of a Private Man in Public Life* (New York 1991), 49–53.

42 John Snure Jr. to Arthur Levy, 14 May 1943, 450, Welfare Island Hospital, Welfare Island, New York City, box 150, SSS Records.

43 SSS, *Selective Service in Wartime*, 272.

44 Flynn, *Hershey*, 132–3; Paul French, memo no. 489 to the Board of Directors, 11 May 1945, box A-56, NSBRO Mss.

45 Paul French, memo no. 550 to the Board of Directors, 21 Sept. 1945, ibid.

46 Paul French, memo no. 560 to the Board of Directors, 23 October 1945, ibid.

47 'Demobilization Lags in C.P.S. Camps,' *Christian Century* (Chicago), 63, 30 Jan. 1946, 133–4.

48 'Demobilization,' *Reporter*, 1 Dec. 1945, 1, 3; 'Demobilization,' ibid., 15 Dec. 1945, 1, 3; 'More Camps to Close,' ibid., 15 Dec. 1945, 1, 3.

49 AFSC to Withdraw,' ibid., 15 Oct. 1945, 1, 3; Clarence Pickett, 'Open Letter to Friends,' *American Friend* (Richmond), 52 (18 Oct. 1945), 409; Gingerich, *Service for Peace*, 70–71.

50 Roy Finch, 'Chaos Reigns in CPS Camps,' *Conscientious Objector* (New York), (Jan. 1946), 1, 8; Hershey to Attorney General, 19 Dec. 1945, 450, C.O. Camps (Minersville Camp, Calif.), box 113, SSS Records.

51 Hershey to Albert Engle, 16 Nov. 1945, Congressman File, Box: Congressional Correspondence, 1945–47, Lewis B. Hershey Papers, U.S. Army Military Institute, Carlisle Barracks, Pa.

52 Frank Hennessy to Theren Caudle, 10 June 1946, Caudle to Hershey, 13 Aug. 1946, 450, C.O. Camps (Minersville Camp, Calif.), box 113, SSS Records.

53 Milton Johnson to A. Imirie, 1 March 1946, 450, C.O. Camps (Big Flats Project, NY), box 118, SSS Records.

54 Johnson to Kosch, 12 April 1946, 450, C.O. Camps (Big Flats Project, NY), box 118, SSS Records.

55 SSS, *Conscientious Objection*, 1:244–8; Gerald Williams to Clarence Pickett, 1 May 1946, box 1e, AFSC Mss.; French memo no. 636 to the Board of Directors, 7 May 1946, box A-56, NSBRO Mss.; 'Strikes Hit CPS,' *Reporter*, 10 May 1946, 1: 'Strikers Arrested,' *Reporter*, 31 May 1946, 1; 'Strikes, Fast,' *Reporter*, 21 June 1946, 1.

56 Sibley and Jacob, *Conscription of Conscience*, 337–9; '6 Striking "Objectors" Lodged in County Jail,' *Elmira Advertiser*, 21 May 1946; 'Official Permanent Strike Statement,' 16 May 1941, 450, C.O. Camps (Big Flats Project, NY), box 118, SSS Records; 'Big Flats Strikers Get 18 Months; 26 More Arrested at Glendora,' *Fellowship*, 12 (Oct. 1946), 167.

57 SSS, *Conscientious Objection*, 2:182–4.

58 'Discharge Schedule,' *Reporter*, 12 July 1946, 1, 4; SSS, *Conscientious Objection*, 1:188, 311–12, 2:284, 286–7.

20

Pacifist Professional Women on the Job in the United States

RACHEL WALTNER GOOSSEN

During the Second World War, a growing number of American women were employed outside the home, and by 1944 women represented one-third of the American labour force. While millions of women willingly supported the war effort, a small minority opposed the war. As we see in this essay, many of these women faced difficult moral dilemmas, and quite a few of them expressed their belief through direct or indirect involvement with Civilian Public Service or in the helping professions, especially in teaching, nursing, and dietitics, where further difficulties sometimes confronted them as pacifists.

Many pacifist women were immediate family members of the approximately one hundred thousand American men who had claimed conscientious objector (CO) status, most of whom were serving out the war years in non-combatant positions. Six thousand men were in prison as violators of conscription law, and more than twelve thousand participated in Civilian Public Service (CPS), a government program in which men were assigned to do 'work of national importance' for the duration of the war. CPS depended on the Historic Peace Churches – chiefly Brethren, Friends (Quakers), and Mennonites – for financial and administrative support. Though men assigned to CPS camps remained under the authority of Selective Service officials, church agencies operated CPS in nearly 150 locations across the U.S. mainland, the Virgin Islands, and Puerto Rico.[1]

Throughout the war, the female supporters of these COs, including wives, fiancées, sisters, and friends, sought ways to support themselves and their families. Most of these women, who had strong pacifist convictions of their own, walked a fine line between contributing their labour to the war effort and refusing to do so. For example, though many were unwilling to purchase war bonds, those who staunchly refused employers' orders to do so faced demotion or even job loss. Thus American pacifist women in the workforce developed strategies to remain employed despite sometimes-uncomfortable relationships with co-workers and employers.

From 1941 until demobilization of the armed forces in 1945 and 1946, American pacifist women faced an unusual set of employment circumstances. Labour shortages offered unprecedented opportunities for women workers. Two government councils, the War Manpower Commission and the Women's Advisory Commission, implored American women to enter the paid labour force.[2] Yet from the perspective of women pacifists, these favourable conditions were offset by a climate in which pressures to support the war were intense. This essay explores the dynamics of wartime work for women, particularly professionals such as teachers, nurses, and dietitians, who obtained wartime jobs but viewed themselves as conscientious objectors and resisted any kind of war-related work.[3]

Few scholars have examined systematically the experiences of American pacifist women during the Second World War. Most studies, such as Barbara Miller Solomon's 'Dilemmas of Pacifist Women, Quakers and Others, in World Wars I and II,' have emphasized the historic links between pacifist and feminist groups. During the late 1930s and early 1940s, secular peace organizations faced profound challenges to their viability as Americans moved from support for isolationism to interventionism. As Solomon points out, 'Unpredictable world events challenged pacifist goals and changed the issues over time,' prompting ideological conflicts among American pacifists.[4] By 1940, some had abandoned their absolutist positions in favour of support for limited involvement in the war in Europe. After the Japanese attack on Pearl Harbor in December 1941, the number of American organizations professing pacifist objectives declined sharply, as citizens across the country rallied to support American entry into the war.

Solomon's work offers a glimpse into the anguished decision-making of renowned pacifists who struggled with the implications of American military policies. In 1941, for example, Emily Greene Balch, Quaker leader of the U.S. Women's International League for Peace and Freedom (WILPF US), declared her support for military intervention in the face of Nazi aggression – a decision that some of her colleagues in the peace movement found unsettling. Yet Solomon and most other historians of the peace movement have stopped short of examining the situations of lesser-known women caught by wartime mobilization. Women who believed strongly in the wrongness of armed conflict suddenly faced – like the vast majority of women in their generation who supported the war – family disruption and increased financial responsibility. In addition, they encountered a cultural climate that was overtly hostile to COs. The war years would offer extraordinary challenges, as we see below, to women who dared to voice opposition to war mobilization.

Through the early and mid-1940s, pacifist women contemplated the morality of accepting or remaining in positions connected to the war effort. Especially poignant are the histories of women who became associated with the government program of Civilian Public Service (CPS). From 1941 to 1947, drafted COs lived in camps and detached service units, performing forestry work, soil conservation, and other kinds of labour. During the same period, at least as many pacifist women worked for wages to help support their CO relatives and friends whose labour, as a condition of exemption from military service, went unpaid. These women became involved in various ways with CPS, either formally as staff nurses and dietitians, or informally, as in the case of wives who moved to be near their CO husbands.

While men and women in CPS shared some common experiences, women's obligations to the nation were less clearly defined, and the burdens they carried in wartime more nebulous. Mary Ellen Stucky, who was a Mennonite college student during the war, later observed that wartime culture rewarded patriotic fervour and was contemptuous of non-conformity: 'I often thought about the fact that the men who were drafted needed to make their convictions known publicly, and the women didn't.'[5] Stucky had supported whole-heartedly the decisions of men in her family and circle of friends to register as COs and to join CPS. But she also believed that she, as a woman, needed to cultivate both philosophical and pragmatic stances towards the war. Whereas American men who objected to participating in the war were required by law to justify their views on religious or moral grounds, women faced no such compulsion. And though conscripted COs who convinced their draft boards of their sincerity could expect to do civilian work, many of the jobs available to women on the home front were closely linked to the war effort. In short, the dilemmas women faced – in the workplace and elsewhere – would not be easily resolved.

Because women were exempt from military service, those who thought of themselves as COs could carve out individualized responses to the war that might bear witness to conscientious objection but did not necessarily do so. Many lived out the war years in quiet anonymity, avoiding direct support of military activity but sharing their views only among family and friends.[6] Those who were less restrained ran the risk of being verbally harassed by co-workers, losing their jobs, or being evicted by unsympathetic landlords.

The story of Selma Platt is a case in point. As an adolescent during the First World War, Platt had observed her father's place of business in Newton, Kansas, smeared with yellow paint because detractors regarded him and other Mennonites as unpatriotic. After the war, Platt began a career as a teacher, left Kansas, married, and bore three children. When she found herself suddenly widowed, she moved back to Kansas and accepted a position for the 1941–2 school year teaching high-school English at Moundridge, a small community near Newton. Years earlier, before her marriage, she had taught at this school. Now she needed the job again to support her children.

Though Platt was well acquainted with many townspeople, during the summer and autumn of 1941 she did not support community activities that reflected the nation's drift towards war. She was, in her own words, 'an outspoken pacifist.'[7] When a group of high-school students planned a community-wide event to burn an effigy of Emperor Hirohito, Platt – alone among the school's faculty – refused to attend. The incident flared into local controversy over her suitability as a public-school teacher; signs denouncing her appeared in downtown store windows. Still, Platt was recalcitrant – at a high-school assembly, she refused to applaud the speech of a military recruiter. Soon afterward, she became embroiled in conflict with a group of students in her classroom who wanted to stand up while the high-school band, positioned across the street, rehearsed the national anthem. She insisted to her students that they remain seated and continue with the lesson. Following student complaints, the local school board called on Platt to explain herself, and her principal warned her that she would probably not be rehired. Depressed, Platt resigned in mid-year and eventually found a job in another community. Later, she remembered: 'I didn't feel I could stand all those questions.'[8] As a Mennonite, however, Selma Platt had the support of family and friends, if not the broader community.

Pacifist women attributed their non-conformist views to a range of influences. Most, though not all, had at least one parent who had taught pacifist values. Others cited persuasive ministers or teachers. Mary Morrissett, who grew up in Ohio and was raised a Baptist, came to her pacifist convictions via acquaintance with Quakers, and in the interwar years she read the works of Harry Emerson Fosdick, A.J. Muste, Kirby Page, Clarence Pickett, and others. During the war she married a CO, Jim Mullin, who directed two CPS camps where men were assigned to U.S. Forest Service projects. In both settings, at Gorham and West Campton, New Hampshire, local citizens were hostile, and she remembers that the Second World War 'certainly was a "popular" war to judge from the venom expressed towards those of us who opposed [it].'[9]

Another woman who supported her husband's CO stance, Maribel Todd, recalled that as a Presbyterian growing up in Illinois in the 1930s, she had her views towards war shaped by Sherwood Eddy, Kirby Page, and the 'many Presbyterian ministers who were anti-war up until Pearl Harbor.'[10] A number of mainline American churches had traditions of emphasizing alternatives to war.

Pennsylvanian Mary Morgan felt fortunate that her denomination, the United Methodist church, officially backed the stance of conscientious objection and helped to sponsor CPS. In her home community and across the country, Methodist ministers, as well as the Methodist Commission on World Peace, gave moral and material support to COs.[11]

American pacifists were eager to find meaningful work that would give expression to their religious and humanitarian convictions. Elizabeth Bauman, a Mennonite, later recalled that during her years as a student at Goshen College in Indiana she had wished that she could join her male friends who had been assigned to CPS. In the context of world war, the notion of service had a strong pull among young women who were preparing for careers at liberal arts colleges, such as Goshen, affiliated with the Historic Peace Churches. 'The phrase "to be of service" was very much a part of our vocabulary and thinking,' Bauman recalled. 'We wanted to serve in God's kingdom by being in the helping professions: teaching, medicine, social services, church work.'[12]

Accordingly, many young women prepared for careers as teachers, nurses, and dietitians. Women who entered college and vocational schools during the 1930s and early 1940s, whether oriented to Christian pacifism or not, were part of entrenched sex-segregated labour patterns, in which middle-class girls were encouraged to fulfil their ambitions as nurses or teachers. Enrolments in colleges, universities, and professional schools reflected broad cultural assumptions that some professional fields were appropriate for men while others were appropriate for women. By the advent of the Second World War, openings for women were available in education, nursing, home economics, and social work, while traditional male preserves such as medicine, law, and the ministry remained all but closed to women.[13]

The professional venues of teaching, nursing, and dietetics were obvious choices for college-educated women with pacifist views who wanted to put their ideals into action. Yet the call 'to serve' brought unanticipated dilemmas to many of these women. The efforts of the Roosevelt administration to mobilize the nation for war would press American nurses and dietitians into military-related positions. Likewise, teachers in public schools would be expected to be standard-bearers for civic responsibility and loyalty to the nation.[14] In short, women in all three of these professional fields, whether self-identified as pacifists or not, were poised to perform work that the U.S. government viewed as crucial to the war effort.

Pacifist women with professional training took varying tacks in resolving the dilemmas posed by war. Some who were just beginning their careers as teachers changed direction after realizing that their duties in the classroom would compromise their beliefs. As Margaret Calbeck, from central Ohio, remembered, in 1942 'I took a special summer course in rural education thinking that I could help with the shortage of teachers, but backed out when it became apparent I would be required to push the sale of war bonds among students. [I] ended up as director of a teenage program at Columbus YWCA. There were United Services Organization (USO) dances for American troops in the building every weekend, but there was never any pressure on me, as a single, unattached woman, to attend. I didn't!'[15]

Mary Wiser, who married a CO in December 1941 and followed him to CPS settings during the next four years, asserts: 'I was a conscientious objector myself from the earliest memories till now.' Like Margaret Calbeck, Wiser left public-school teaching in 1941 'because I ... knew I could not supervise war bond sales, nor be part of the cultural drive towards war in which a teacher in public school finds herself.'[16] But though she had voluntarily given up her work, she would later return to it. In CPS communities in Tennessee and North Dakota, Wiser supported herself and contributed to her husband's CPS expenses by teaching. Near Trenton, North Dakota, she recalls, 'I definitely experienced the suspicion and antagonism of parents. The local school board was desperate for teachers and so hired us CPS wives who had gathered [to live] near the camp. At one time the complete parent population descended on me. It worked out alright. We talked over their objections to my teaching, but they said, "It's not you, it's your cowardly husband in that camp."'[17] Teachers subjected to such sentiments usually persevered because they needed to pay off debts or support family members, but they found their work stressful and the war years emotionally difficult.

Like the wives of troops stationed at military bases on the home front, women whose husbands were assigned to CPS often tried to keep their families together by moving near their husbands and seeking employment in area towns. But wives were rarely immune from the hostility that some local people harboured towards COs. In 1943 Geraldine Braden of Evanston, Illinois, married a CPS assignee and found a teaching job near her husband's camp at Coshocton, Ohio. Her situation was precarious. Braden recalls that 'a group of citizens tried to get me fired. The superintendent of schools told them the only way I could be let go would be through someone paying the rest of my year's salary! He was a good Methodist. It all blew over ... [Later], the Missoula, Montana, public schools refused to hire me because my husband was a C.O. However, I got a job teaching in the University of Montana demonstration school.'[18]

CPS was structured so that assignees could request transfers to newly opened camps and units. In addition, sometimes camps were closed and administrators assigned men to other locations. As a result, men in CPS moved an average of three times during their service. For women who wanted to live near their husbands, fiancés, and friends, such mobility could be either a blessing or a curse. Some found that a new community seemed more tolerant than one they had left behind. Others could not manage the frequent moves and instead sought stability from their home communities, often half a continent away from their spouses.

One teacher who chose this option was Carrie Diener, whose husband was assigned in 1943 to farm-reclamation work in eastern Montana. The couple had a young son, and Diener opted to move to her hometown, Shipshewana, Indiana, to live with her sister, who would provide child care while Diener went to work. She remembers that because of a shortage of teachers she found a job quickly and supported herself and her son. Despite her good fortune, she says, 'I was told not to influence the children with "my" position. Incidentally, they were all Amish, Mennonite, and Brethren,' presumably from families where non-resistant teachings were common.[19]

Clearly, the wartime labour shortage worked in favour of pacifist teachers. If a school district refused to hire a woman or fired her, she usually managed to find employment somewhere else. In the rural community of Burrton, Kansas, Ruth Reimer taught grade school during the war. Her fiancé was in CPS, and gradually Reimer's relations with co-workers became strained. After three years, the school board told her that her contract would not be renewed. But by that time she had become so uncomfortable that she had already signed with another district.[20]

Pacifist teachers were also aware that if they looked for jobs in urban districts, their views on the war were less likely to come under scrutiny. Kathryn Grant's boyfriend was drafted in 1942 and assigned to CPS. In the school where she taught, she later reflected, 'very few knew of my stand because there was no reason to raise the issue in a large school setting. They pushed sale of defense bonds but without pressure on individuals.'[21] Similarly, many pacifist teachers felt able to continue in their jobs as long as paternalistic school boards maintained some flexibility in the demands placed on employees. Cathryn Erffmeyer, a schoolteacher in industry-minded Michigan, recalls: 'I was required to work evenings in defence plants or work all summer at any kind of job. I chose the summer job.'[22]

Erffmeyer, like many teachers, was not married. While married or engaged instructors sometimes lost their jobs because of 'guilt by association' with COs, a number of unmarried women also encountered problems. Sometimes, the simple fact of German ethnic ties – as most Brethren and Mennonites had – raised employers' doubts. More often, women were candid enough about their views on war that they found themselves on a slippery slope of suspicion and lost confidence.

Anna Wiebe, an unmarried Mennonite teacher of music in a Nebraska school, had two painful experiences, which she recounts as follows:

In 1943 I was teaching in a predominantly Lutheran community. The teachers were encouraged to buy war bonds to show their support. If there was 100% participation, our school would be awarded a flag to fly alongside the American flag. I chose not to buy any bonds.

In the early spring, at a faculty meeting, the superintendent announced that there was a concern by the board that our school wasn't flying 'the' flag. Rumblings were going on among the faculty as to who wasn't participating in the program. A feeling of isolation swept over me. I felt quite uncomfortable. After the meeting, I talked to the superintendent. I stated my position. I told him that I would be willing to resign from my position. He was surprised that I would take such a firm stand. He affirmed me in my work and said he didn't want me to resign and that I could have my job the following year.

Aware that good jobs weren't too plentiful, I didn't know what turn to take. One day I had a call from my sister who was living in Kansas that there was a vacancy in Hillsboro. I thought that in a largely Mennonite community, I would feel more comfortable. I applied for the position and got it. I felt safe and secure in my pacifist position.

All was not well. One day I had a note from the superintendent for an appointment. He told me there was a rumor out that I was telling high school boys to register as C.O.s. I was stunned at the accusations. Finally I recalled an incident after school following a boys' small group rehearsal (long after school hours) discussing that they soon had to register. One of the boys asked me how I would register. Without much thought I said, "C.O." I hadn't realized that even among some of them there was opposition to C.O.s and to the pacifist belief.

As a teacher, I felt respect by both students and faculty. Some parents talked to me and felt badly that this incident had exploded as it had. I taught in this school system three more years ... and I would say I'm glad I remained true to my convictions, but there was a 'price' we had to pay.[23]

Anna Wiebe's indiscretion lay in commenting that, had she been given the chance, she would have gone on record as a CO. For female schoolteachers, the question was purely hypothetical. But for women trained as nurses and dietitians, the question hit closer to home, for the pressures on women in these fields to enlist were intense.

In response to government appeals, sixty thousand American women served as army nurses. Another fourteen thousand American nurses joined the navy, and during the war more than a hundred thousand younger women entered nurse training schools as part of the government-sponsored Cadet Nurse Corps.[24] Yet most Brethren, Mennonite, and Quaker nursing students and nurses rejected both the generous scholarships available through the Cadet Nurse Corps and the prestige and pay associated with military nursing.

Many pacifist nurses sought alternatives. Kathryn Yoder, a young graduate nurse whose friends were accepting military jobs, conscientiously opposed such work and contacted Mennonite Central Committee (MCC) officials for advice. Soon afterward, she moved to Luray, Virginia, to staff the infirmary of a camp where COs were assigned to work for the National Park Service. Margaret Taylor, who worked part time as a hospital nurse in Bar Harbor, Maine, got to know a lot about the reserve troops from nearby army and naval bases. What they went through in training, she later reported, 'sickened me and I got in touch with the American Friends Service Committee, asking, "Can I help you in a peaceful situation?"' AFSC officials promptly sent her to provide health care in a North Dakota camp where COs were working for the Farm Security Administration. Grace Kauffman was employed at University Hospital in Iowa City when the director of nurses suggested that she volunteer for the army. She remembers: 'I was definite about my answer that if I went in service it would be under the auspices of the church, and in January 1944 I arrived in Puerto Rico' to join a CPS medical unit.[25]

Some women were less certain that military nursing was incompatible with their beliefs. In 1942 Seventh-day Adventist leaders, who strongly advocated non-combatant service for drafted members, established a church-wide 'Women's Medical Cadette Corps' to recruit Adventist nurses who were available to go overseas. Approximately forty entered military service, which they viewed as analogous to the non-combatant work of many male COs.[26]

But in advocating military-related service, Adventists were atypical among churches with significant numbers of COs. When some Mennonite nurses signed up for Red Cross work, saying to their ministers, 'What's wrong with that? They're taking care of sick people,' prominent churchman Harold Bender lectured Mennonite audiences that 'the goal of the medical corps is to get your men back to the front.'[27] Most young Mennonite women agreed that military service crossed the line. Many of them chose instead CPS positions where they provided health care to COs or worked alongside men assigned to serve as aides in mental hospitals. At an average of eighty dollars a month, CPS nurses' salaries were low, but they also received food, housing, and other benefits. Brethren, Mennonite, and Quaker nurses who had been concerned that Congress might actually conscript them for overseas service were relieved to find jobs among like-minded citizens with whom they could be comfortable. Ellen

Harder, a Mennonite and a 1940 nursing-school graduate who moved to northern California for CPS work, muses that 'since I was a C.O. I decided to join the boys.'[28]

Registered dietitians were as likely as nurses to face pressure to enlist. Though they received no basic training, those who accepted military assignments abroad were given the rank of officer and sent to hospitals. Those who wished to avoid military service found jobs in schools, hospitals, prisons, and other institutions on the home front. A few staunch pacifists such as Lillian Willoughby found their way into CPS settings.

From 1939 to 1941, Willoughby, a lifelong Quaker, was a dietitian at the Scattergood Hostel for Resettling German Refugees in West Branch, Iowa. After the United States entered the war, she worked for a general hospital in Des Moines; while there, she refused to buy war bonds. Her husband, George, a doctoral candidate in political science at the University of Iowa, lost his job with the university dormitory system after refusing to sell war bonds. When he received his draft orders in 1943, he was working with the War Relocation Authority to find housing and work for Japanese Americans outside internment camps. Meanwhile, Lillian became part of an activist Quaker community in Denver that worked with the Congress of Racial Equality (CORE) at desegregation of theatres and job settings. When George was assigned to CPS work at the Alexian Brothers Hospital in Chicago, Lillian was hired as head dietitian, and the couple, with their infant daughter, was able to live together.[29]

Another dietitian, Elizabeth Doe, had given little thought to pacifism at the time when she was hired at the Mansfield State Training School and Hospital in Connecticut. A month later, in December 1942, a group of COs arrived at Mansfield to work as mental-health aides. Some hospital staff members, including Doe's immediate supervisor, were incensed by the presence of men who were unwilling to fight. But Doe regarded the men as good workers and admired their principled stance. In the spring of 1943 she began a whirlwind courtship with one of them. After two months, they became engaged, an event that triggered the following:

I had baked a cake for the head nurse for her husband's birthday in the dieticians' kitchen. No problem. But I went and asked the superintendent of the institution for permission to bake one to announce our engagement. No problem – yes! So I did. That evening we arranged for the whole CPS group to gather in the 'social room.' I put the cake, specially decorated, in the center of the room along with a pitcher of lemonade ...

The next day the head nurse called me into her office. And she demanded that I go outside the institution and replace all the ingredients I had used! Butter, eggs, milk, sugar, flour, etc. This during wartime when everything was rationed and we had turned our ration cards in to the business office! I was suspended, she said, until they were all replaced and appeared on her desk! I protested, called the superintendent, and protested some more, but it did no good.

I hopped on my 3-speed Raleigh bike, was happily surprised to get my ration book from our business manager, and started out over the Connecticut hills to pick up what I could before dark. It was early morning. At each little general store I hoped off and went in to get what I could. I think I went to five or six small towns – miles apart. They all got the full story and were disgusted beyond words – even as 'patriotic' as they were at the time.

Butter, eggs, sugar, milk, flour, even powdered sugar and cocoa appeared from under the counter and out of the back rooms. One by one the entire list of ingredients got scratched off. The last balding, aproned and grinning grocer gave me a sack with *handles* and I took off over the hills and valleys toward the institution, returned my ration book and sailed into the head nurses' office at 2:30 p.m. with my sack of goodies. Her jaw dropped. I hadn't knocked. I put the sack on her desk and left for my office to clean up and change into my uniform. I went into the kitchen and went back to work, and stayed long enough to make up all lost time, too![30]

Elizabeth Doe's experiments with a harassing superior did not end with this episode; soon afterward, she was transferred to a less desirable post in the Mansfield hospital. Downward occupational mobility was a hazard that women encountered if they expressed their views – or, in this case, sympathies – too freely. But some found a silver lining even in unpleasant situations. One woman who worked at a mental hospital in Michigan recalls that at work 'there were some feelings of hostility but also admiration for having a clear conviction and being different.'[31]

Though pacifist women were not obliged legally to go on record, many did choose a course of action that revealed their anti-war perspectives and raised the ire of employers, neighbours, and the wider community. Yet despite the hostility and hardships they faced, they managed to negotiate the war years – some with certitude, others with ambivalence. The women who fared best were those who met their circumstances with humour and were able to retain a sense of solidarity with other COs.

Though many of these women faced discrimination in job settings during the war, their professional training and personal courage served them well. After the war they would continue careers in education, health care, and related fields. Though few had children during the war years, many would spend the next two decades rearing children and teaching the value of peace to a younger generation.

Some women continued to struggle with the implications of their anti-war stance, especially after mid-1945, as the world learned horrifying details of the Holocaust. But few pacifist women seemed ready to repudiate their convictions and life choices. When the Truman administration ended the war with the use of atomic weapons, many pacifists, women included, vowed to strengthen their efforts to promote alternatives to war.[32] By 1945, the wartime dilemmas of American pacifist women were coming to resolution. But there would be other moral questions to grapple with in the coming decades.[33]

NOTES

1 See chapter 19, above, by Mitchell L. Robinson. For a full listing of camps, locations, and sponsoring agencies, see Albert N. Keim, *The CPS Story: An Illustrated History of Civilian Public Service* (Intercourse, Pa., 1990), 106–10. For detailed accounts of American COs in the Second World War, particularly in CPS, see Mitchell Lee Robinson, 'Civilian Public Service during World War II: The Dilemmas of Conscience and Conscription in a Free Society,' PhD dissertation, Cornell University, 1990; Cynthia Eller, *Conscientious Objectors and the Second World War: Moral and Religious Arguments in Support of Pacifism* (New York 1991); also Mulford Q. Sibley and Philip E. Jacob, *Conscription of Conscience: The American State and the Conscientious Objector, 1940–1947* (Ithaca, NY, 1952). An overview of the financial burdens of CPS wives is Heather T. Frazer and John O'Sullivan, 'Forgotten Women of World War II: Wives of Conscientious Objectors in Civilian Public Service,' *Peace and Change* (Rohnert Park, Calif.), 5 (autumn 1978), 46–51.

2 On American women in the labour force, cf. D'Ann Campbell, *Women at War with America: Private Lives in a Patriotic Era* (Cambridge, Mass., 1984), 101–37, and William H. Chafe, *The Paradox of Change: American Women in the Twentieth Century* (New York 1991), 121–53.

3 Data presented in this study are drawn from interviews and questionnaire responses of 180 women who were associated with CPS during the Second World War. The responses cited in this study were collected by the author in 1991 and 1992; for an explanation of method, see Rachel Waltner Goossen, 'Conscientious Objection and Gender: Women in Civilian Public Service during the Second World War,' PhD dissertation, University of Kansas, 1993, 217–27. Copies of questionnaire responses are available at the Mennonite Library and Archives, North Newton, Kansas, and the Swarthmore College Peace Collection (SCPC), Swarthmore, Pennsylvania. A few additional interviews with pacifist women, conducted from 1975 to 1992, are housed at the Mennonite Library and Archives (MLA), North Newton, Kansas.

4 Barbara Miller Solomon, 'Dilemmas of Pacifist Women, Quakers and Others, in World Wars I and II,' in Elisabeth Potts Brown and Susan Musher Stuard, eds., *Wit-*

nesses for Change: Quaker Women over Three Centuries (New Brunswick, NJ, 1989), 123.

5 Questionnaire response from Mary Ellen Miller Stucky.

6 Though this essay focuses on the experiences of women who were in professional careers, women in business and industry faced similar issues. Marion Garber, a Mennonite from Lancaster County, Pennsylvania, worked during the war at a meat and cheese stand at a farmer's market. Though her employer was a member of the Brethren in Christ, she recalls, 'Very little was said among employees about the conscientious objectors. The subject was "swept under the rug." The other employees who were pro-war talked a lot and the rest of us kept quiet.' Questionnaire response from Marion Garber Leaman.

7 Interview with Selma Rich Platt Johnson by James C. Juhnke, 25 Jan. 1975, MLA.

8 Ibid.

9 Questionnaire response from Mary Morrissett Mullin.

10 Questionnaire response from Maribel Brands Todd.

11 Questionnaire response from Mary Bruce Morgan.

12 Questionnaire response from Elizabeth Hershberger Bauman, cited in Goossen, 'Conscientious Objection,' 52.

13 For an overview of women's access to professional fields, see Joan Jacobs Brumberg and Nancy Tomes, 'Women in the Professions: A Research Agenda for American Historians,' *Reviews in American History* (Baltimore), 10 (June 1982), 275–96. During the Second World War, even the army, which faced a shortage of doctors, denied appointments to female physicians until Congress lifted the ban in 1943. See Campbell, *Women at War with America*, 55, and Soloman, 'Dilemmas', 141.

14 On wartime expectations of American educators, see Ronald D. Cohen, 'Schooling Uncle Sam's Children: Education in the USA, 1941–1945,' in Roy Lowe, ed., *Education and the Second World War* (London 1992), 46–58.

15 Questionnaire response from Margaret Calbeck Neal.

16 Questionnaire response from Mary Raecher Wiser.

17 Ibid. In 1945 Eunice Jones, spouse of AFSC leader Canby Jones, also found employment as a teacher near the CPS camp at Trenton, North Dakota: 'I lived about a mile from the camp in a rented house from which I could walk to school to the camp. When CPS men were transferred out of Trenton their wives usually broke their teaching contracts to move away with their husbands. My trustee informed me that if I did likewise I would lose a whole month's salary. I moved and lost my salary. The trustee knew that in the CPS wives he was getting far better qualified teachers than were normally available to his community. He seemed matter of fact about losing us when our men moved.' Questionnaire response from Eunice M. Jones, in the author's possession.

18 Questionnaire response from Geraldine Rugg Braden. During the 1940s, American

women routinely quit their jobs at the time of marriage, and many districts across the country prohibited the employment of married women. But the wives of COs had few means of financial support; most worked out of necessity.

19 Questionnaire response from Carrie Yoder Diener.

20 Questionnaire response from O. Ruth Reimer Wiens.

21 Questionnaire response from Kathryn Grant Mason. For a similar perspective, see Mary Alice Alexander to Howard Alexander, 1 June 1942, document group 56, series I, box 5, SCPC.

22 Questionnaire response from Cathryn Erffmeyer Schmidt.

23 Questionnaire response from Anna Wiebe Miller.

24 Statistics regarding army and navy nurses are in D'Ann Campbell, 'Servicewomen of World War II,' *Armed Forces and Society* (Cabin John, Md.), 16 (winter 1990), 251–70; see also Beatrice J. Kalisch and Philip A. Kalisch, 'The Cadet Nurse Corps in World War II,' *American Journal of Nursing* (New York), 76 (Feb. 1976), 240–2.

25 Kathryn Yoder Turner, cited in Karen L. Myers, 'Valiant Soldiers for Peace: Mennonite Women and Civilian Public Service during World War II,' research paper, Eastern Mennonite College, 1992; questionnaire responses from Margaret Taylor Kurtz and from Grace Kauffman Nachtigall.

26 Roger G. Davis, 'Conscientious Cooperators: The Seventh-day Adventists and Military Service, 1860–1942,' PhD dissertation, George Washington University, 1970, 206. For the perspective of a pacifist nurse who did not view military nursing as inconsistent with conscientious objection, see the questionnaire response of Lois Keniston Waters.

27 Quotations from interview of Verna Zimmerman by Janet Schellenberger, 25 Nov. 1987, Hist. Mss. 6-281, Archives of the Mennonite Church, Goshen, Indiana. Harold Bender summarized his views on war-related nursing in an essay, 'Can a Nonresistant Nurse Serve in the Army?' *Mennonursing* (La Junta, Col.), 1 (March 1945), 7. For more on Mennonite nurses' response to the war, see Goossen, 'Conscientious Objection,' 71–4. Some nursing-school graduates reported to Mennonite officials that when they went before their state examining boards, they were told that they would not be certified unless they volunteered for service in the armed forces. Henry A. Fast to Orie O. Miller, 10 Sept. 1942, H.A. Fast Papers, MLA-MS-49-3, folder 19, MLA.

28 Questionnaire response from Ellen Harder.

29 Questionnaire response from Lillian Pemberton Willoughby; Herb Ettel, 'Bound by a Common Humanity,' *Friends Journal* (Philadelphia), (Sept. 1990), 21–5.

30 Questionnaire response from Elizabeth Doe Jaderborg.

31 Questionnaire response from Pearl Mierau Janzen.

32 An example is the sentiment expressed by Eunice Jones: 'There is a strong bond among men and women who have stood together in a community of interest and

stood up to be counted for what they deeply believe in. The need is strong to *keep educating* about the peace testimony and its ramifications in the fields of justice and the brotherhood of humankind.' Jones's questionnaire response, in the author's possession.

33 My book, *Women against the Good War: Conscientious Objection and Gender on the American Home Front, 1941–1947* (Chapel Hill, NC, and London 1997), appeared while the present volume was in press.

21

Prison Journey of an American War Resister

LARRY GARA

American males who grew up in the 1920s and 1930s did not anticipate a military draft.[1] Memories of the First World War increased the public's cynicism about war itself. Anti-German hysteria coupled with wholesale violations of civil liberties on the home front were hard to understand in retrospect and fed the disillusionment. Added to this was resentment over the failure of European countries to repay war debts owed to the United States. A naïve hope for the abolition of war was fuelled by such actions as the Pact of Paris, 1928, in which the signatories rejected war as an instrument of national policy. Thousands of young men took a pledge never to engage in war. Strong anti-war messages emanated from the pulpit, popular literature, drama, and film. While very few Americans became pacifists, many embraced isolationism, which viewed American entry into the First World War as a mistake never again to be repeated.[2]

The national mood changed dramatically after Pearl Harbor. When the war came I was a student in a state teachers' college, commuting eighteen miles from my home in Reading, Pennsylvania. For most of my young life Reading was a socialist town, and members of my family were all dedicated democratic socialists. They continued to hold the anti-war position that had sent Eugene Debs to prison for a speech delivered in Canton, Ohio, in 1918. They voted consistently for Norman Thomas for president and even thought that he might win. The idealism of Reading's socialist movement, along with personal aversion to violence, contributed to my pacifist position. Joining the Reading Friends (Quaker) Meeting and a local Fellowship of Reconciliation (FOR) group strengthened my anti-war sentiments, as did reading Richard Gregg's *The Power of Nonviolence* and other works on Gandhian non-violence.

Participation in a peace walk from Lancaster, Pennsylvania, to New York City made non-violence an active force in my life rather than an intellectual abstraction. The Food for Europe Pilgrimage occurred during Christmas vacation in 1940. The following spring I participated in a similar pilgrimage from Wilmington, Delaware, to Washington, DC. We were calling attention to the urgent need for food in German-occupied countries of western Europe then under an Allied blockade. We saw the issue as humanitarian, though government officials argued that food allowed past the blockade would go to German occupying forces rather than to their victims. Pacifists said that the chance was worth it in order to prevent starvation. Another factor in my peace convictions was spending two summers in volunteer Quaker work camps, combining physical labour with study and discussion.[3]

I had also read about the brutal treatment given First World War resisters in military prisons. The problems and negative publicity that they created for officers and the army itself made government officials receptive to the offer of leaders of the Historic Peace Churches to administer and finance special work camps for conscientious objectors (COs). As a result, Civilian Public Service (CPS) camps became part of the Selective Service Act of 1940. Yet when I learned of eight students at Union Theological Seminary in New York who openly refused to register, I immediately sensed that this, rather than alternative service, was the road that I had to travel. Since registration was the first requirement a young man faced when confronting the military system, it made sense to refuse at that point so as to make the clearest witness and the maximum protest.

Furthermore, I did not believe that one should have to pay to work, as was required in the camps. The government seemed determined to make COs invisible.[4] I also realized that as a Quaker my chance of being classified a CO was better than for men of other faiths or of no religious faith at all. I believed that situation fundamentally unfair.

My time to refuse to register came in May 1942, when I was twenty years old. Refusing to acknowledge the authority of Selective Service, I wrote from Reading to the nearest federal district attorney to explain why I could not register in good conscience. In early July two agents of the Federal Bureau of Investigation (FBI) came to my home, arrested me, and took me to the Berks County Jail. After only a few hours I was released on bond, which a friend had posted for me.

Darlington Hoopes, a fellow Quaker and well-known socialist lawyer, volunteered his services as my attorney. After my first appearance in court I was released because the indictment was for non-registration, while the government considered that I had been registered. The next step was a questionnaire that I promptly refused to complete, and then another court date. At Hoopes's suggestion I entered a plea of *nolo contendere*, which spared the government the time and expense of a trial. After castigating me for pitting what he called my 'puny will' against the government, the judge sentenced me in September 1942 to three years in federal prison, of which I ended up serving every day.

Soon I found myself in Philadelphia's Moyamensing Prison, a place best described as the jail from hell. The medieval-looking structure, built before the Civil War, had once held Passmore Williamson, an abolitionist accused of helping a fugitive slave to escape. Each small, beehive-shaped cell housing two prisoners was fronted by heavy iron bars. Sound from a radio at full volume echoed through the corridors, and metal doors clanked open and shut as prisoners shouted obscenities. The silence of 'lights-out time' became a precious commodity. Tasteless food arrived in containers that appeared to be from the original nineteenth-century stock. From the commissary I purchased a quart of milk a day, which helped keep me alive. The experience was traumatic for a twenty-year-old who had seldom been away from home.

My first cellmate was a young man who had also refused to register but then changed his mind and requested release to the army. For the week we were together, he pilloried me with arguments to undermine my position. By the time he left I had countered every one of them. Amos Hoover, of the Old Mennonite church, was a more compatible cellmate, except that he constantly smoked strong cigars. Not allowed to smoke at home, he took advantage of the jail experience to enjoy the tobacco that he had helped grow. A cold that I caught from him was aggravated by second-hand smoke and sent me to the sadistic jail doctor. I finally told Amos we must reach an understanding. He agreed to smoke only during yard exercise, two hours a day when weather permitted. Except for exercise and mail call we were confined to the cell at all times. The Bible was the only reading material permitted. In Moyamensing I managed to read the entire New Testament through twice.

Most federal prisoners stay in county jails a week or two at most before transfer to federal institutions. Somehow my file was misplaced, and I stayed in Moyamensing for two months before being transferred to the Federal Prison Camp at Mill Point, West Virginia. After two months in county jail I found the drive to West Virginia with two federal marshals a pleasant experience.

To my surprise, Mill Point was a prison without walls, bars, or even locks. But we were immediately informed that an invisible wall was five years high – the possible penalty for attempted escape. Most of the inmates were short-term 'moonshiners' or Jehovah's Witnesses and other war resisters. There were no cells; all prisoners lived in dormitories. After the usual orientation I was assigned work in the prison library and as editor of a mimeographed newspaper. It was an easy job even for that minimum-custody prison, but I soon learned that there were drawbacks. The prison paper was sent to Washington and designed primarily as a public-relations sheet. No criticism of the institution or of the criminal justice system was permitted. I thought that that was intolerable and complained to officials. Immediately my assignment was changed to out-door manual labour, shoveling dirt in the cold, damp West Virginia mountains. As far as I could tell, the endeavour had little or no value except to keep us occupied. Several other prisoners had already notified the warden that they would no longer work under those conditions or collaborate in maintaining themselves in prison.

After two months in Mill Point two others and I took the same stand. We were quickly transported to the closest county jail at Marlinton, where we stayed a week awaiting transfer. The jail was small, with only one or two other prisoners, the sheriff was friendly, and the food was home cooking. Even though the cells were dirty and cockroach-ridden, that jail was not a bad place to do time. We could look out the window and see cardinals in the snow. Had any of us had family members in the area, they could have brought us food, books, and writing material. The place lacked the numerous head counts and constant noise that usually characterize so much of jail life. Joe Alter and Straughn Gettier, my cellmates, and I had many good discussions during that week.

The two marshals who drove us from Marlinton to the Federal Correctional Institution at Ashland, Kentucky, were extremely friendly. They handcuffed us only when we had to leave the car to use a bathroom, and one of them asked us to look him up if we were ever in his part of the country. We spent the first night in a larger county jail in Huntington, West Virginia, where we were housed together and saw no other prisoners. One of the deputies, as he took us down on the elevator, said in effect that we were still young and had plenty of time to 'go straight.' Though he meant well, his words provided us with several hearty laughs in the days ahead.

Ashland was a medium-custody prison surrounded by barbed-wire fencing and fronted by a tower with an armed guard. Built in the form of a hollow square, the structure itself formed a kind of wall without giving the appearance of a walled building. Discipline was much tighter than at Mill Point. Included in the orientation was a thorough physical examination. When my turn came to see the doctor I was tense and cold, standing there stark naked. I had a nervous habit of clearing my throat, and the first time I did that the doctor yelled that I had coughed in his face and would be punished if I did it again. Inevitably, I could not prevent repeating the action, and before I knew what was happening I found myself in the Ashland 'hole,' a 'strip cell' with only a floor drain for a toilet. Dressed in coveralls, I had to sleep on the floor with only a blanket for warmth, brought at night and removed in the morning.

In the hole an inmate could have no reading or writing materials and could not communicate with other inmates unless there was someone in an adjacent cell. A guard brought food that had been literally washed clear of all taste. The associate warden visited me, warning me that inmates sometimes went insane under those conditions and promising my release as soon as I apologized to the doctor. I explained that my action had been involuntary, and I would not apologize for an offence that I had not committed.

Within a few days other officials recognized the absurdity of the charge and released me. I suspect that their purpose was to demonstrate their authority over anyone who might get out of line. But even the hole had a silver lining for me, for in the adjoining cell was another resister, William Roberts. Our conversations there formed the basis of a lifelong friendship.[5]

After a period in quarantine I was assigned to work in the prison hospital under the same doctor who had reported me for 'coughing' in his face. I always suspected his intention was to keep me under close observation. He also acted as prison psychiatrist, frequently consulting a psychiatric dictionary during five-minute interviews with inmates. He had no specialized training in psychiatry, and his reports were so obviously biased against inmates that eventually the Bureau of Prisons had him investigated and reassigned to another institution, where he practised surgery, his area of specialization. My work in the hospital was mainly clerical, uncomplicated enough to allow me time for discussion with the resisters who worked there.[6]

Soon, however, an issue of conscience arose once again – the case of the 'barefoot boy.' One day a recent arrival, a resister who was also a strict vegetarian, appeared in 'general population' without shoes because he refused to accept the government-issued leather footwear. He did that for several days until a minor injury to his foot caused an infection. He was hospitalized for treatment, but many of us became concerned when we learned that he was confined in the 'Blue Room,' a special cell reserved for mentally ill prisoners. To protest that action and to support him, seven of us walked around without shoes for several days. Amazingly, we were not punished, and in a few days the issue was resolved when officials permitted the resister to wear sneakers that had been sent in to him.[7]

Before long, my easy job in the hospital ended, and I was assigned to the metal shop, where the work involved various aspects of prison maintenance. There I learned some useful skills and had the added pleasure of working with my friend Bill Roberts. Later I had another work assignment teaching illiterate prisoners the fundamentals of reading and writing. I found this task most rewarding and was astounded at the number of my fellow inmates who lacked even rudimentary reading skills.

Meanwhile, time crept along, each day a duplicate of the one before. My entire world was the Ashland prison community. About a third of the inmates were war resisters or Jehovah's Witnesses. We resisters had much in common. Most of us had some college training, some at leading universities. We also had the unforgettable Revd Ashton Jones, a peace crusader whose preaching and action earned him several stretches in solitary confinement. His presence was a constant irritation to prison officials, who were delighted to release him as soon as possible. Another strong personality was Wilbur Burton, a news correspondent and hedonistic agnostic, whose stories and philosophy entertained many of us. Burton was just under the top draft age. Being older, he had a small but loyal following among the resisters.

Most of our discussions took place in the prison yard during the evening exercise period. We resisters formed friendships among ourselves, but we had little difficulty in relating to the other prisoners. While some of us thought of ourselves as political prisoners, we did not wish to set our group apart or to claim special status. When we protested censorship of mail or asked for additional privileges, it was with the understanding that all inmates would benefit.

In Ashland I never saw any indication of homosexual activity and only once witnessed a violent incident.[8] That occurred when a prejudiced southern judge, in prison for white-collar crime, struck Bayard Rustin on the head with a mop handle. The judge's resentment at having a black prisoner in the cell block had spilled over that day in the recreation room. Rustin did not strike back or report the incident, though his wrist got broken when he tried to protect his head.

Ashland's population was constantly changing, with more and more of the new inmates war resisters. A handful were non-registrants like me. Most were there because draft boards had declared them insincere.[9] Since these COs had followed the law, it was the boards that were in violation by refusing a justified classification, but it was the COs who went to prison. A very few left on parole to the military. Many others were paroled to CPS camps when an executive order made that available. Resisters were rarely granted the standard parole for which federal prisoners were eligible after serving a third of their sentences.[10]

When I entered prison I was still considering a career in art, so I studied a number of standard works in the field of art history and used any available opportunity to draw and use water-colours. For a time a New York resister who was a commercial artist taught an art class at Ashland. We even had a chance to earn college credit, thanks to the imaginative offer of Arthur E. Morgan, president of Antioch College in Ohio. Morgan, a strong advocate of small communities, provided books and criticism for prisoners wishing to take his course on

'The Small Community.' One day, without warning, he even visited his incarcerated students. Surprisingly, he was allowed to have a face-to-face discussion with us.

For me the principal educational value of prison life was learning that the system was a fraud. Prisoners did not leave as better citizens. Having learned all there was to know about the techniques of their criminal activity, they concluded that they would never again be caught. Except for the resisters, most inmates were poor and lacked the rudiments of education. While a few were emotionally unstable, most were easy to get along with, having a 'live and let live' attitude. Indeed, officials encouraged that attitude, constantly advising us to do our own time and get out as soon as possible. The entire system was marked by cynicism and repression. Many of us came to believe that prisons as we knew them should be abolished, because there must be a better way of dealing with offenders.

Punishment in federal institutions, we concluded, is largely psychological. Officers are strictly forbidden to strike prisoners, though I recall on one occasion I was punched in the side with enough force to bruise a rib and cause considerable discomfort. In the prison at Chillicothe, Ohio, which housed mostly young, reckless offenders, guards winked at these youths severely beating resisters and in at least one case overlooked a gang rape.[11] But it was primarily psychological rather than physical punishment that the resisters endured. Part of that was the threat of the hole as well as transfer to a more secure institution. Most serious was the threat of 'bugging' prisoners, treating them as mentally ill. Some war resisters who engaged in work or hunger strikes were confined to cells reserved for inmates with serious mental illness. The most publicized case involved Stanley Murphy and Louis Taylor, whose eighty-two-day hunger strike to protest their own imprisonment at Danbury, Connecticut, led to their transfer to the Medical Center for Federal Prisoners at Springfield, Missouri. There they were placed in strip cells in the psychiatric ward of the hospital.[12]

The psychological impact of serving a long prison sentence is seldom recognized. Deadly boredom marks every day. Living exclusively with males makes the possibility of interacting with women seem almost miraculous. Thinking and talking about sex become a major preoccupation. When I entered prison I was young, prudish, uncomfortable with my own sexuality, and embarrassed by discussions about sex. Prison rules forbade even masturbation, though it was one rule that was largely ignored. Before movies were shown in Ashland they were carefully screened for any glimpse of female breasts or tight-skirted bottoms. Some of the resisters liked to tease me by playing a game they called 'Knockers and Buns,' in which they kept score of sexy scenes that had slipped past the censors. I considered it in very poor taste.

For the resisters, prison also provided time and opportunity to read in a wide range of subjects. The library at Ashland was especially good for literature. I read *Moby Dick* while standing by my cell door waiting to be counted. I also read a book of Oscar Wilde's writings, an ironic acquisition, since the librarian would not permit Walt Whitman's books in the library because of Whitman's homosexuality.

Several Ashland resisters made excellent use of their education and talents by writing a musical satire on prison life, which they based on Gilbert and Sullivan's *HMS Pinafore*. The elaborate production, called *FCI Utopia*, brought kudos from prisoners, guards, and officials. One of the show's stars was Bayard Rustin, who later became a major figure in the civil-rights movement. Rustin was forced to live in a segregated cell block, and in the dining hall he had to eat with the other African Americans. We found this segregation intolerable and took our grievance to the warden. When it was obvious that there would be no change, we began organizing for non-violent action. We planned to sit wherever we chose in the dining hall and, if we should be physically prevented from that, to go on work strike. Even the majority of Jehovah's Witnesses agreed to the plan, but the night before it was to be implemented Rustin was placed in the hole for alleged homosexual activity.

I knew that, should the charge be valid, I would be disillusioned with him for carelessly putting our action in jeopardy. If, however, it was not true, I would no longer cooperate with prison authorities. To learn the truth I bolted past a startled guard who was posted at a stairway leading to the hole, ran down the steps, and asked Rustin if there was any truth to the charge. He denied it, and that was good enough for me. From that day until my release I refused to work at Ashland.

This time the authorities put me and several others who joined the strike in administrative segregation. We were confined to our cells all day except for a brief period of exercise and for showers. We could communicate through cell doors but could not see each other. We were allowed books and writing materials, and regular prison food was brought to our cells. How we spent our time was now completely up to us. We had discussion times and tried some classes. I continued to work on the small community course from Antioch College. Rustin even had a mandolin sent in and learned to play it, despite our pleadings that he limit his practice times. Somehow we continued to get word of what was going on with resisters in other prisons. We were encouraged by the total non-cooperation of Corbett Bishop[13] and the various prison strikes in which resisters were involved. Despite the close confinement, I did very easy time in the Ashland segregation unit.

Before my refusal to cooperate with the prison system I had decided to reject all parole or conditional release, since either would require obeying all laws, including Selective Service. I preferred to serve my entire sentence and leave prison a free man. My original release date was 18 January 1945, but on that day I was informed that the date had been pushed back twenty-nine days because of my noncooperation. When news of this decision reached the general prison population, more resisters joined the segregation unit in protest. They saw the warden's decision as double punishment, even though I had not asked for conditional release. When my new release date arrived I was offered a draft card, which I refused, and papers to sign, which I also refused. Despite my unequivocal position, the officials released me, and I accepted the release on my own terms. How the justice department would react remained to be seen.

When I returned to Reading to visit my family I learned that an FBI agent had already scoured the neighbourhood looking in vain for angry residents who did not want me released. Finally in frustration he asked a neighbour, 'Doesn't anyone around here dislike this guy?' My experience was not unique. Many of the resisters were viewed sympathetically even by those with family members in the military.[14]

During this brief period of freedom during the war I met with no personal antagonism, except from draft-board members and other officials. Most of my contemporaries who were in the armed forces were there involuntarily, having seen no alternative to enlisting or being drafted. I sensed that they viewed the war as a nasty job that had to be done. Many of my generation also found defence jobs to avoid serving in the military. Early in the war, fathers were deferred from the draft, a policy that led to a rash of early marriages and babies.

Before my release from Ashland I had arranged to work for the Fellowship of Reconciliation (FOR) in New York as a shipping clerk. I lived with a group of pacifists in a small Christian community at Fifth Avenue and 125th Street known as the Harlem Ashram. It was wonderful to be free. Just walking to work was a joy, as were dates with girls, riding the Staten Island ferry, and seeing Paul Robeson in *Othello*. Working with A.J. Muste and the rest of the FOR staff was also pleasant. Soon, however, a visit from a federal parole officer brought the threat of rearrest if I would not fill out monthly forms and obey parole conditions to which I had never agreed. I was not surprised, therefore, when two FBI agents came to the office on 15 June to arrest me for parole violation.[15]

After a short period in the Federal Detention Headquarters known also as West Street I was transported to the Federal Penitentiary, a maximum-custody institution surrounded by a high concrete wall, near Lewisburg, Pennsylvania. At that point there was no hesitation: I would not cooperate with prison rules. When I made that clear by refusing to stand by the cell door for count the guard replied, 'Oh, you're one of those.' That first evening I managed to contact others who were noncooperating by shouting through a window that was directly beneath the large dormitory room where they were being held.

By next morning, I too was there. It was as if I had been taken to another world – a world vaguely familiar from past dreams. I never came in contact with any prisoners who were in the general population at Lewisburg. My whole world was that dormitory room, which we did not leave even for exercise. My only contact with family was through a monthly visit with my mother, since I refused to sign a form to permit censorship of my mail and could neither send nor receive letters.

Our 'Enormous Room' housed a strange mix of humans. Living with a dozen or more war resisters twenty-four hours a day was sometimes difficult. Close proximity exaggerated differences in personality and life-style. Some men refused to talk to certain individuals. Our group included a New York lawyer, an Industrial Workers of the World cartoonist, several socialists, a handful who were devoutly religious, and a few avowed anarchists. Present also were my good friends from Ashland Bill Roberts and Bayard Rustin, as well as Lawrence Templin, who had been the only non-registrant from Bethel College, a Mennonite institution in Kansas. We had several 'troublemakers' who had been transferred from Danbury to Lewisburg.

Probably Bureau of Prisons officials considered us all incorrigible. I, for example, had graduated from Moyamensing to Mill Point to Ashland to Lewisburg. Still, there were moments of pleasure even in that setting. We enjoyed seeing the changing seasonal colours from our prison windows, which overlooked Pennsylvania farm country. One evening we heard a lilting melody played on a flute. Next day we learned that Bill Roberts had constructed the instrument from homemade papier mâché by mixing layers of newspapers and leftover oatmeal, then moulding it around a mop handle. Roberts's formal training in music, combined with perfect pitch, produced an enchanting result.

It was in Lewisburg that we learned of the atomic bombing of Hiroshima and Nagasaki and the end of the war. Bill Roberts responded to the news by immediately holding a one-week total fast in penance and protest. It was one of several early actions that pioneered a half-century campaign against atomic and nuclear weapons.

As the war wound down, our little community of resisters at Lewisburg began to shrink, and when we were down to about six or seven we were moved to a cell block. It was from there that I would be released when I had served the entire three-year sentence handed down in 1942. I looked forward to release and to the party that some New York friends had planned for me. However, prison regulations required my return to Reading, where I had lived at the time of sentencing. A prison official visited my cell to convince me that I should accept a railway ticket to Reading. I listened politely but declined. When I had served my time, I said, I would go wherever I wished.

On my release day I barricaded myself in the cell with a mop handle barring the door, refusing to leave unless I could travel freely. Two burly guards quickly removed the mop handle and tried to force me to walk by twisting my arm. When that failed they placed me in a laundry basket. Two resisters, Bayard Rustin and Rodney Owen, lay down in the path of the guards, who then walked on their backs. As we proceeded down several flights of stairs I told the guards that the whole thing was silly. I would not go to Reading, and if they insisted I would remove my clothing when they put me down. However, I was eager to cooperate if they would only agree to let me choose my own destination.

The guards accepted my offer and took me to the station, where once more they offered me a ticket to Reading. When I refused it they both left, stranding me with no ticket and no money. When the station-master paged me for a telephone call I thought it must be justice department officials, ready to rearrest me. But the call was from my mother, who had somehow learned of my location.

My release from Lewisburg occurred on 24 January 1946. The war was long over, and I was at last free. Having served every day of my sentence, I felt that I had a perfect right to join my New York friends for a party. I decided to hitchhike back to the town of Lewisburg and somehow get the money to travel to New York. Knowing that there was a pacifist minister in town, I stopped at the first parsonage that I saw. Amazingly, it was the right one, though the pastor was not at home. His wife came to the door with a baby on her arm and listened to my story. She would be glad to lend me the money, she said, if I would hold the baby while she went to the bank. With her help and trust I bought a ticket for New York and enjoyed a wonderful party with friends. That event had been planned by Julius and Esther Eichel, whose staunch support of imprisoned war resisters had cheered us through some difficult times. Julius, an older-age nonregistrant, was the only resister to have been arrested in both world wars.

After a brief visit with my family in Reading, I returned the borrowed money to my benefactors in Lewisburg and travelled to Iowa, where I entered William Penn College to complete my undergraduate studies. The Quaker college welcomed war resisters as well as men who had been in CPS camps and returning war veterans. Once again, I enjoyed a community of support. There I met Lenna Mae Goodson, who became my wife. Unfortunately, the Reading draft board continued to threaten me by sending draft cards, which I immediately returned to the justice department. That harassment finally ceased, and I went on to graduate school. In 1949 I was again sentenced under the Selective Service Act on a charge of counselling another man to refuse to register. But that is another story.[16]

Incarceration takes an inevitable toll. For years I had prison nightmares. I hated standing in lines, even for food, and had to control myself when police or other uniformed authority figures came into view. Though many of my opinions and attitudes have changed, I still believe that refusal to register for the draft was the proper course for me. We resisters made the point that no amount of coercion could force us to change our respect for life or reliance on active non-violence. It was especially important that an ideal of non-violence be kept alive during a time of near-total war. We tried to do that, however imperfectly. In effect we were a few small, stubborn candles burning through the darkness.[17]

NOTES

1 For a scholarly overview of American war resisters in prison in the Second World War, see Mulford Q. Sibley and Philip E. Jacob, *Conscription of Conscience: The American State and the Conscientious Objector in Prison, 1940–1947* (Ithaca, NY, 1952), 332–418; M.Q. Sibley and Ada Wardlaw, *Conscientious Objector in Prison, 1940–1945* (Philadelphia 1945); and Lawrence S. Wittner, *Rebels against War: The American Peace Movement, 1941–1960* (New York 1969), 62–96.

2 The 'good war' myth is modified by Paul Fussell in *Wartime: Understanding and Behavior in the Second World War* (New York 1989), and by S.L.A. Marshall, *Men against Fire*, reprint (Gloucester, Mass., 1978).

3 Though I gladly devoted two summers to volunteer work camps, I was not willing to accept such service under compulsion of a law that was essentially a military draft.

4 Director of Selective Service General Lewis B. Hershey, in opposing publicity for a 'guinea pig' medical project involving COs, said: 'The conscientious objector, by my theory, is best handled if no one hears of him.' Quoted in Richard C. Anderson, *Peace Was in Their Hearts: Conscientious Objectors in World War II* (Watsonville, Calif., 1994), 88. See above 316 and 323.

5 My only other experience in the 'hole' occurred when an officer 'wrote me up' for refusing his order to cease getting up early for silent meditation on my dormitory bed!

6 Because virtually all of his reports were clearly biased, the Bureau of Prisons sent a well-known criminologist to Ashland to interview resister inmates. Shortly after those interviews the doctor was removed from the prison system.

7 Details of the 'barefoot boy' incident were included in a letter from Arthur Dole to

my mother, Helen Gara, 7 Aug. 1943, now in the Larry Gara Papers, in the author's possession.

8 Al Hassler, a resister held in general population at Lewisburg, reported that homosexuality was more commonplace there. 'One is in prison only a very short while,' he noted, 'before the extent of homosexuality makes itself known.' Alfred Hassler, *Diary of a Self-Made Convict* (Chicago 1954), 63.

9 Government statistics show 6,086 resisters convicted of violating the Selective Service Act from 1940 to 1946; 271 were non-registrants, but the largest number, nearly four thousand, were charged with refusal to report for induction. *Conscientious objection*, Special Monograph No. 11 (Washington, DC, 1950), 1:264.

10 By March 1945 only 310 resisters, including Jehovah's Witnesses, had been granted regular parole. In addition, sixty-six resisters accepted parole to the army, and 283 went to CPS or other public-service projects under special provisions of Executive Order 8641, which took effect in 1941. More than half the applications for executive-order parole were denied. Sibley and Jacob, *Conscription of Conscience*, 383–5.

11 There were other instances of physical abuse of war resisters. At Lewisburg Lester Lermond was dragged down a hallway by his hair because he demanded treatment for an abscessed tooth. For details of Chillicothe see Donald Wetzel, *Pacifist: or, My War and Louis Lepke* (Sag Harbor, NY, 1986), 139–43.

12 The case of Murphy and Taylor became a cause célèbre. Their observations, smuggled out of Springfield and widely publicized, caused an investigation of the institution and its treatment of federal prisoners. Sibley and Jacob, *Conscription of Conscience*, 412–16; *Conscientious Objector* (New York), (Aug. and Sept. 1943).

13 Corbett Bishop left CPS after two years. While there he led protests and participated in several fasts. From the moment of his arrest he engaged in total non-cooperation, refusing to eat, dress himself, or even to use the bathroom. He was imprisoned several times before the government released him unconditionally after he had served about a fourth of his four-year sentence. Sibley and Jacob, *Conscription of Conscience*, 401–9; *Absolutist* (New York), 19 March 1946.

14 While some individual resisters encountered hostility, the public at large did not share that view, as illustrated by several national opinion surveys; Sibley and Jacob, *Conscription of Conscience*, 315–19. My high-school art teacher wrote my mother: 'One thing you can be certain. The American people would be practically unanimous in their opposition to the type of confinement and treatment given Larry ... I have talked this situation over with a number of people and I haven't found one yet who wasn't ashamed of the attitude of our government.' D. Kenneth Winebrenner to Helen Gara, 9 Feb. 1943, Larry Gara Papers.

15 The Bureau of Prisons justified my rearrest as a way of protecting me from the Reading Draft Board No. 5, which had requested my release from the bureau's supervision so that I could be ordered to appear for induction. Its persistence was ironic,

since ex-convicts are usually considered 'morally unfit' for military service. When the director of the Bureau of Prisons explained my case to our congressman, he did not mention the draft board. In fact, I was still serving a sentence when out on 'good time' and thus was not eligible for the draft. Edward C.M. Richards, *They Refuse to Be Criminals* (published privately, 1946), 30–1; copy of letter to Congressman Daniel K. Hoch from James V. Bennett, 25 June 1945, Larry Gara Papers.

16 In May 1949 I was sentenced to eighteen months in prison for 'counseling' a student at Bluffton College in Ohio, where I was teaching history, to refuse to register. Though I strongly and publicly supported non-registration, I did not counsel anyone on so important a decision. In fact I had not even met the student when he refused to register. The case was appealed to the US Supreme Court, where I lost in a 4–4 decision.

17 All those who had been convicted under the Second World War draft law were stripped of certain civil rights and faced the stigma of a criminal record. After the war there was pressure from peace and religious groups, with much public support, for a general amnesty for all convicted war resisters. In response, President Harry Truman appointed an Amnesty Board to review each case individually. On the basis of its report, Truman, in December 1947, proclaimed a 'selective amnesty' for a tenth of Selective Service Act violators. About five-sixths of the COs were excluded from the amnesty and continued in general to be deprived of many of their civil rights and privileges. Along with most others who had participated in prison protests, I did not receive clemency. Sibley and Jacob, *Conscription of Conscience*, 388–98; *New York Times*, 24 Dec. 1947.

22

Conscientious Objection and Popular Culture: The Case of Lew Ayres

JENNIFER FROST

In late March 1942, only a few months after the United States entered the Second World War, actor Lew Ayres (1908–1996) announced that his Selective Service Board had accepted his appeal for conscientious objector (CO) status. He added that he had been assigned to a Civilian Public Service (CPS) camp for the duration of the war. Ayres, a popular Hollywood actor whose first movie success had been the anti-war film *All Quiet on the Western Front*, was to become the most famous CO during the war and was the first to garner national publicity.

At the time of his announcement, he was starring in the successful Dr Kildare movie series. Within the first week, the Boston city council unanimously voted to revoke the licence of any theatre showing an Ayres film. A theatre in Hackensack, New Jersey, withdrew *Dr. Kildare's Victory* after receiving 130 telephone calls within twenty-four hours from members of the American Legion, who threatened a boycott. Metro-Goldwyn-Mayer studios, at an additional cost of $100,000, decided to reshoot the latest movie in the series with a new actor as Kildare. Articles and editorials about Ayres's decision appeared in newspapers and magazines across the country, and the public answered with fiery letters both pro and con. In one such letter we find a group of prominent Hollywood actors and actresses arguing that the 'abuse' heaped on Ayres was 'a sorry comment on the rights of democratic life.'[1]

This essay examines the context for, the debate over, and the resolution of the Ayres case in and through the print media and public responses over a five-month period. The debate centred on the legitimacy and meaning of Ayres's conscientious objection, by contesting constructions of patriotism, citizenship rights and obligations, and manhood for the wartime United States. The resolution of the case in the media helped to secure in popular consensus tolerance of Lew Ayres and other COs who fell within the state's narrowly religious definition of conscientious objection.

The case illuminated the connections between American political and popular culture during the early months of the war. Ayres, the media, and the public understood his decisions via his movie roles in *All Quiet on the Western Front* and in the Dr Kildare series. The intersection of the politics of conscientious objection and movie culture revealed Hollywood as a site of ideological conflict and showed the ways in which film can contribute to political consciousness and legitimate political action.[2]

Context

Lew Ayres justified his appeal for CO status by his religious beliefs and his acting experience in *All Quiet on the Western Front*. He announced that his objection to war was based 'on deep philosophical thought arising from a religion of his own.' Central to his philosophy was the Christian creed of non-resistance to evil. 'In my opinion,' he argued, 'we will never stop wars until we individually cease fighting them, and that's what I propose to do.' A major influence on Ayres's thinking was his role as Paul Baumer, 'the war-embittered soldier,' in *All Quiet on the Western Front*. He told his Selective Service Board: 'The role was a powerful influence in my life. I was twenty when I played the part of the German soldier who abhorred war and I thoroughly believe that the picture had much to do with my later thinking and my present step. War is as abhorrent to me in real life as it was in the screen play nearly 15 years ago.'

Ayres derived his pacifist stance not from membership in a pacifist denomination or from actual experience of war but from his acting experience in a fictional film representation of war. He now benefited from the new liberalized criteria for conscientious objection and used his role in an important film to explain and justify his action.[3]

As one of Hollywood's first documents of social criticism, the film *All Quiet on the Western Front* occupied a significant place in American screen memory. By the time of the Ayres case, *All Quiet* was known as 'the celluloid Bible of pacifists.' Released in 1930, the film was a major box-office success, won Academy awards for both best picture and best direction (by Lewis Milestone), and made a star out of Ayres. Unlike most war movies, *All Quiet* exposed the First World War as futile, horrible, and destructive. This was the first time 'the American public s[aw] an American film truly antiwar in intent and execution,' and as a result its release was controversial. Major Frank Pease, president of the Hollywood Technical Directors' Institute, had declared the movie 'brazen propaganda' aimed at undermining 'beliefs in the Army and in authority' and called unsuccessfully for its censorship.

The movie had a pacifist impact on a whole generation's thinking about war.

As film critic Judith Christ wrote: 'We were the disillusioned who were learning that the world had not been made safe for democracy; we learned our lessons from *All Quiet on the Western Front*.' The film presented to a popular audience a critique of modern war, and Ayres justified his religious beliefs and opposition to war within the moral framework of the movie.[4]

The Debate

The legitimacy of his conscientious objection proved an area of conflict for critics and supporters of Lew Ayres, as did the significance of his actions. Critics did not accept Ayres's justifications for conscientious objection. They often defined conscientious objection narrowly as membership in a peace church and sneered at Ayres's 'religion of his own.' Critics also questioned his use of *All Quiet on the Western Front*. Most prominent was Erich Maria Remarque, author of the original German novel, who differentiated between the two world wars, noting that his novel criticized the First World War but did not advocate opposition to all war. 'It is too bad the story had this effect on Ayres,' he stated. 'I am sure he has made a mistake. I hope we are fighting the last world war and that it will be a war for freedom.' An editorial in the *Detroit News* criticized Ayres for taking his experience in the film as a reflection of reality: 'Actors live in wonderland, and more or less like fools. And now and then one is carried away by a great role, living it thereafter in a private life which at best is not quite real.' These critics viewed Ayres's religious and philosophical convictions as insincere and his experience in *All Quiet on the Western Front* as an unwarranted basis for conscientious objection.[5]

Supporters of Ayres, who constituted a substantial majority of commentators on the case, countered these arguments.[6] Friends presented him as shy, thoughtful, and sincere. Socialist Norman Thomas, writing to the *New York Times*, saw Ayres's 'religion of his own' as genuine: 'Objection to the method of war may be quite as conscientious and, if anything, even more sincere, if the man has derived it painfully as a result of his own philosophic, social or political thinking than if he merely accepts the dogma of some creed.' Defenders of Ayres also agreed with his interpretation of his experience in *All Quiet on the Western Front*. Gossip columnist Hedda Hopper called the film 'one of the greatest documents against war ever put on the screen.' She criticized those who had applauded Ayres's performance in the film but now condemned him 'because in real life he holds to the conviction [of] that picture.' One of Hopper's readers and a CO himself wrote: 'I believe that Lew has a mission in life and his greatest role is yet to be played as a fulfillment of the promise he revealed in *All Quiet*.'

Ayres's supporters helped to establish in popular consensus what the state had already written into law: the legitimacy of conscientious objection based on sincere, religious belief rather than solely on membership in a pacifist church. Defenders of Ayres also saw *All Quiet on the Western Front* as an indictment of all war, as an appropriate influence on political consciousness, and as grounds for political action.[7]

In addition to disputing the legitimacy of his conscientious objection, Ayres's critics and defenders debated the meaning of his actions for the wartime United States. Critics contended that Ayres was unpatriotic and that he was not fulfilling his citizenship obligations. The president of the Louisville Theater Owners' Association, who refused to show any Ayres films, argued: 'American theaters have a vast influence on public thinking and should, in this time above all others, not encourage unpatriotic action.' One letter to an editor contended: 'Today, with our country in peril, these so-called citizens ... refuse to bear arms ... while real patriotic men do the fighting.' A Boston councilman, who had supported the revocation of licences for any theatres showing an Ayres film, described Ayres as one who had 'made fabulous sums in this free country yet when the time came to service his country he assumed the role of conscientious objector.'[8]

Ayres's critics also condemned the actor for not measuring up to the ideals of manhood, of which military service was a hallmark. One wrote: 'For shame Lew Ayres, hiding your *supposed* manhood behind the much abused ... "religion."' One of Hedda Hopper's readers argued that Ayres's decision was 'the equivalent to saying he would stand idly by or no doubt run away if his mother or sister was being ravaged by a sex degenerate.' In this view, Ayres was failing to live up to the 'moral obligations' of the 'male protector.'[9]

Finally, detractors argued that Ayres, as well as other COs, posed a danger to American national security. An editorial in the *Milwaukee Journal* contended that he should ask himself: 'If everyone in the country I am supposed to defend did as I do, then what?' The paper answered: 'Then, of course, we'd surrender the country to the invader who has no such qualms.' For these critics, Ayres's conscientious objection was a fundamental, and unforgivable, betrayal of patriotism, citizenship obligations, manhood, and the war effort.[10]

As Ayres's supporters began to express their views, they answered not by agreeing with his pacifist convictions but by defending Ayres's right to follow his principles. Many quoted Voltaire: 'I disapprove of what you say but I will defend to the death your right to say it.' One woman asserted: 'It was his perfect American right to do what he did.' 'Our country,' wrote another woman, 'recognizes a person's right to serve as his conscience permits.' Others commended Ayres for his courage in standing up for his convictions. 'It takes a greater form of heroism to stand by one's principles' stated one of Hedda Hopper's readers, 'than it does to shoulder a gun.'[11]

Defenders of Ayres also argued that his opponents posed more of a danger to democracy than he did. The *New Republic* stated: 'Democracy cannot be preserved if it is unable to tolerate the occasional sincere minority opinion.' One woman wrote that 'suppressing a movie because of an actor's beliefs is an intolerant and undemocratic act.' Many of Ayres's defenders contended that protection of the right to conscientious objection was what the war was all about. An army private wrote to *Time* magazine: 'Lew Ayres, instead of being detrimental to our public good, is indicative of what the American People wrote into their Bill of Rights and what we fight our wars about – the right to freedom in a democracy.'

By appealing to ideals sacred to Americans and presenting support of Ayres as consistent with democratic principles, defenders of Ayres shifted the terms of the debate. Conscientious objection, rather than undermining patriotism, citizenship, and manhood, upheld American values, required courage, and constituted a right of citizenship. In this way, Ayres's supporters contributed to public tolerance of Ayres and to popular understanding of the issue of conscientious objection.[12]

Resolution

The emergence of strong support for Ayres in the debate, paralleled by public tolerance at the box office, helped to quiet the controversy. Ayres's entrance into the medical corps also assisted. One week after his arrival at a CPS camp in Oregon, Ayres requested a non-combatant assignment with the Army Medical Corps. In May, his request was granted. 'I am grateful for reassignment,' he stated, 'for the Medical Corps is the place I want to be – to be able to do some useful work.'[13]

This decision encouraged commentators to link Ayres with his screen role as Dr Kildare. The *Los Angeles Times* noted that Ayres, 'who as Dr. Kildare, performed medical miracles on the screen,' always wanted to do medical work. One writer considered this work apt: 'Witness his characterization of young Dr. Kildare in which there has always been a feeling of realism and sincerity.' After his induction into the Army Medical Corps, Hedda Hopper noted that, 'like Dr. Kildare, he's tending the wounded, the sick, and the helpless.' Once again, the media and the public, though not necessarily Ayres himself, understood his actions within the context of a film role.[14]

Ayres's induction and his commitment to non-combatant military service provided what the media and the military considered a 'resolution' to the case.

As one commentator noted: 'There is some feeling ... that with Ayres to be spotted in the Medical Corps of the Army, much of the sting will be taken out of the situation.' That the 'sting' was gone was clear from military and media statements about Ayres. The headline for a story in the *New York Times* about Ayres's completion of basic training stated: 'Lew Ayres Hailed as a Good Soldier – Ex-Movie Star, a Private Now, Completes His Basic Training at Army Medical Center – General Lauds His Work – 'Wish I had a Battalion Like Him,' Says Officer Who Commanded the Former Objector.' The Ayres case thus ended with full military approval for the actor and an erroneous media presentation of Ayres as a 'former objector.'[15]

This resolution, of course, did not reflect a complete solution to the problem of conscientious objection, or even to the Lew Ayres case. A 1945 study of public opinion towards COs, which used Ayres as an example, discovered that 'two-thirds of [the] sample indicated that Lew Ayres's being a conscientious objector did not affect their willingness to see his pictures.' The remaining one-third, however, a fairly high proportion, did not acknowledge Ayres's right to conscientiously object to war. Indeed, Lew Ayres never regained his former popularity with audiences or the favour of the movie industry after the war. As one film historian noted, 'Hollywood never forgave Ayres the embarrassment he had caused them.' Moreover, the conflicts over the definition, legitimacy, and meaning of conscientious objection that arose and were ostensibly 'resolved' in the Ayres case were to emerge again with future wars.[16]

Conclusion

The Lew Ayres case represented an intersection of popular and political culture, Hollywood and the politics of conscientious objection. The publicity and attention given to Ayres, because of his status as a movie star, had provided the opportunity for a public debate about conscientious objection during the Second World War. In addition, the influence of the film *All Quiet on the Western Front* in this situation revealed the power of cinema to shape political debate and presaged the 'easy slippage' that occurs between movies and reality in politics today.[17]

The resolution of the case in the media, and as presented by the military, also helped to confirm a general pattern of public tolerance towards COs who, like Ayres, emphasized religion and service. Absent from the debate over Ayres, and excluded from state sanction and public tolerance during the Second World War, were claims of conscience based on political and philosophical grounds and resistance to service and state authority.[18] In this way, the Lew Ayres case provided a site for what cultural historian Michel Foucault called 'reframing' –

a process whereby potentially challenging behaviour is redefined in the interest of reaffirming set boundaries.[19] The incorporation of a narrow definition of conscientious objection into the state and popular consensus helped to affirm and legitimate the authority of the liberal state in time of war.[20]

NOTES

I wish to thank Paul S. Boyer, Marybeth Carlson, Andrea Friedman, John Pettegrew, Paul M. Taillon, and Stephen Vaughn for helpful comments and editorial suggestions on earlier drafts of this essay.

1 'Lew Ayres Is a Conscientious Objector; His First Major Role Was in Anti-War Film,' *New York Times*, 31 March 1942, 23; *Time*, 6 April 1942, 54; Mulford Q. Sibley and Philip E. Jacob, *Conscription of Conscience: The American State and the Conscientious Objector, 1940–1947* (Ithaca, NY, 1952), 94, 316; 'Boston Awaits Mayor Tobin's Okay on Nixing Licenses of Any Theaters Dating Ayres Pix; Hundreds Cancel,' *Variety* (New York), 8 April, 1942, 7; 'Studio Will Remake Lew Ayres Film Play – "Born to Be Bad" Will Have Philip Dorn as Physician,' *New York Times*, 17 April 1942, 19; Colin Shindler, *Hollywood Goes to War: Films and American Society, 1939–1952* (London 1979), 53; John Huston, George Cukor, Mary Astor, Franchot Tone, Olivia de Havilland, George Oppenheimer, Walter Huston, Charles Lederer, and Humphrey Bogart, letter, *Time*, 20 April 1942, 6.
2 My analysis of the tolerance and state sanction of a narrow definition of conscientious objection in the case of Lew Ayres was influenced by Gretchen Lemke-Santangelo's work on radical objectors and Sibley and Jacob's comparison of 'service' and 'resistance' motifs in conscientious objection during the Second World War. Lemke-Santangelo, 'The Radical Conscientious Objectors of World War II: Wartime Experience and Postwar Activism,' *Radical History Review* (New York), 45 (Autumn 1989); Sibley and Jacob, *Conscription of Conscience*, 42–3.

     On the intersection of popular, specifically film, culture and political culture, see Michael Paul Rogin, *Ronald Reagan, the Movie and Other Episodes in Political Demonology* (Berkeley, Calif., 1987), and Stephen Vaughn, 'Spies, National Security, and the "Inertia Projector": The Secret Service Films of Ronald Reagan,' *American Quarterly* (Philadelphia) 39 (Autumn 1987), 355–80.
3 'Ayres to Medical Unit from Objector's Camp,' *New York Times*, 18 May 1942, 18; 'Objector Ayres,' *Newsweek*, 13 April 1942, 30; Ayres quoted in *Time*, 20 April 1942, 7; Ayres quoted in M. Richard Applegate, 'Lew Ayres Sent to Camp as War Objector – Actor Cites Religious Scruples – Blames Influence of "All Quiet" Role,' *Detroit News*, 31 March 1942, 1.

     As literary historian Paul Fussell has argued, 'the dynamics and iconography of the Great War have proved crucial political, rhetorical, and artistic determinants on subsequent life.' The relationship between the film *All Quiet on the Western Front* and Lew Ayres's predicament illustrates Fussell's point. On deriving images of war from 'mythic narrative' rather than from experience, also see Paul Fussell, *The Great War and Modern Memory* (New York and London 1975), ix, 324.

4 'Objector Ayres,' *Newsweek*, 13 April 1942, 30; Michael T. Isenberg, *War on Film: The American Cinema and World War I, 1914–1941* (London and Toronto 1981), 30, 46, 135; Joseph R. Millichap, *Lewis Milestone* (Boston 1981), 38; Martin Quigley, Jr; and Richard Gertner, *Films in America, 1929–1969* (New York 1970), 25; Lewis Jacobs, *The Rise of the American Film: A Critical History*, first pub. New York 1939, reprint (New York 1969), 528; Michael T. Isenberg, 'The Great War Viewed from the Twenties: The Big Parade (1925),' in John E. O'Connor and Martin A. Jackson, eds., *American History/American Film: Interpreting the Hollywood Image* (New York 1979), 31; Judith Christ, 'Introduction,' in Joe Morella, Edward Z. Epstein, and John Griggs, *The Films of World War II* (Secaucus, NJ, 1973), 5.

5 'Footnotes on Headliners,' *New York Times*, 5 April 1942, sec. E, 2; Erich Maria Remarque, quoted in 'Ayres "Conchie Camp" Decision Stuns Hollywood: Actor Who Claimed Military Exemption on Religious Grounds En Route to Oregon,' *Los Angeles Times*, 1 April 1942, pt. 2, 1; 'The Actor and His Part,' *Detroit News*, 5 April 1942, 6.

6 Of the twelve printed letters to the editor that I found eleven supported Ayres's right to conscientiously object to war. Of fifty-six letters to Hedda Hopper (cited below as H.H.), forty-six supported his right; Hedda Hopper Collection (HHC), Margaret Herrick Library, Academy of Motion Picture Arts and Sciences, Beverly Hills, Calif.

7 Norman Thomas, letter, *New York Times*, 7 April 1942, 20; H.H., typescript, [n.d.], and Leonard Hacker to H.H., 21 April 1942, in folder 'Lew Ayres,' HHC.

8 'Switow's Stance,' *Variety*, 15 April 1942, 26; J.L. Sullivan, letter, *Detroit News*, 3 April 1942, 22; Councilman Charles L. Taylor, quoted in 'Boston,' *Variety*, 15 April 1942, 7.

9 D.G. F[igs?] to H.H., 31 March 1942, and P.J. Landeker to H.H., 4 April 1942, in folder 'Lew Ayres,' HHC.

   On the 'moral obligations' of men as 'the protector' during the Second World War, see Robert B. Westbrook, '"I Want a Girl, Just Like the Girl That Married Harry James": American Women and the Problem of Political Obligation in World War II,' *American Quarterly*, 42 (Dec. 1990), 592.

10 'Lew Ayres on War,' editorial, *Milwaukee Journal*, 5 April 1942, sec. 5, 2.

11 Russell Birdwell, 'Re: The Case of Lew Ayres – Addressed Respectfully to the United States Government,' open-letter advertisement, *Variety*, 2 April 1942, 56; Geneva Sansom to H.H., 13 April 1942, Mrs. Charles S[haffner] to H.H., 9 April 1942, and E. Anderson to H.H., 7 April 1942, in folder 'Lew Ayres,' HHC.

12 'Lew Ayres,' *New Republic* (New York), 20 April 1942, 525; Jane Fitch, letter, *Milwaukee Journal*, 3 April 1942, 20; Private Eugene B. Crowe, letter, *Time*, 11 May 1942, 4.

These supporters of Ayres, of course, were using the same moral arguments that were being employed to justify the war effort. On moral arguments for the war, based on values such as democracy and freedom, see Westbrook, 'I Want a Girl,' 588.

13 'Lew Ayres Applies for Medical Corps – C.O. Asks Reclassification – Hershey Indicates Approval,' *New York Times*, 10 April 1942, 4; 'Lew Ayres Inducted as a Noncombatant – Leaves Objectors Camp Hoping to Serve with Medical Corps,' *New York Times*, 19 May 1942, 23; 'Ayres to Medical Unit from Objector's Camp,' *New York Times*, 18 May 1942, 18.

14 'Lew Ayres Granted Request to Serve Medical Corps,' *Los Angeles Times*, 17 May 1942, pt. 1, 13; Clifton Allen to H.H., 6 April 1942, and Hedda Hopper, 'Hedda Hopper's Hollywood,' transcript of radio broadcast, 25 Dec. 1944 in folder 'Lew Ayres,' HHC.

15 'Not Enough B.O. Experience,' *Variety*, 15 April 1942, 7; 'Lew Ayres Hailed,' *New York Times*, 16 Aug. 1942, 38.

16 Sibley and Jacob, *Conscription of Conscience*, 317, 318; Schindler, *Hollywood*, 53.

17 For the 'easy slippage' between movies and reality in politics today, see Rogin, *Ronald Reagan*, preface and chap. 1. The situation of Lew Ayres reflected the interplay between film and real life – a process, to paraphrase literary historian Paul Fussell, whereby life 'feeds materials' to fiction, while fiction 'confers forms upon life.' Even further, it illustrated how film can have, as historian Michael Isenberg has argued, 'the uncommon quality of not only reshaping reality but of becoming reality' itself. Fussell, *Great War*, ix; Isenberg, *War on Film*, 61.

18 Socialist Norman Thomas, who published the *Conscientious Objector in America* in 1923, was the one participant in the debate over Ayres who voiced the concerns of COs based on political and philosophical grounds. He wrote in his letter to the editor of the *New York Times*, 7 April 1942, 20: 'Today there are scores and perhaps hundreds of young men in America quite as sincere as Mr. Ayres who face jail rather than work camps because they say their objection to war and participation in it is philosophical or political.' I still consider this perspective 'absent' from the debate over Lew Ayres, because, unlike the situation in other aspects of the case, no one responded to or commented on Thomas's argument on this point.

19 On 'reframing,' see Leila J. Rupp, 'Public Prudery, Private Passion,' *Women's Review of Books* (Wellesley, Mass.), 7 (April 1990), 20.

20 *Editors' note*: Since the preparation of this essay and Lew Ayres's death in December 1996, and after the book itself had gone to press, his widow has brought additional information to our attention. His role in *All Quiet on the Western Front*

certainly encouraged Ayres to read and learn more about pacifism. But his portrayal of Dr Kildare in a series of films and his accompanying volunteer work as a Red Cross first-aid instructor also influenced his decision to stipulate, when applying for CO status, that he would be willing to serve as a non-combatant with the armed forces, though only if he could become a medic. His wish was not easily accomplished. However, once the authorities finally agreed to this choice, Ayres served in the 36th Evacuation Hospital in the South Pacific and participated in a number of military actions, including the battle of Leyte Gulf. With sympathy and compassion, he helped save the lives of American GIs and Japanese prisoners of war alike.

23

Conscientious Objectors in Nazi Germany

PETER BROCK

Sectarian pacifism of the Quaker or Mennonite variety scarcely existed in inter-war Germany. Quakers formed a new and tiny group there, whereas German Mennonites, a considerably larger denomination, had already publicly given up their traditional *Wehrlosigkeit* (non-resistance) shortly before the outbreak of war. Nevertheless a few Mennonites still adhered to their church's original stand against bearing arms. During the Second World War, if conscripted, most succeeded in eventually obtaining non-combatant duties, usually as ambulance men. But this was done unofficially by the army; the Mennonite church had also renounced, along with the doctrine of *Wehrlosigkeit*, the non-combatant status that in imperial Germany its members had been able to claim if they so wished.[1] Two eschatological sects opposed participation in war: the Jehovah's Witnesses and the so-called Reformation movement (*Reformationsbewegung*) among the Seventh-day Adventists, numbering some five hundred members, which had split off from the main body when the latter supported participation in combatant service in the First World War. Neither sect, however, played any role in the peace movement, which, as we saw above in Guido Grünewald's essay (chapter 5), had expanded rapidly after 1918.

One of Hitler's first acts after coming to power in January 1933 was to suppress all peace organizations; he arrested many of those peace leaders who had failed to escape abroad.[2] The Treaty of Versailles had forbidden Germany to impose military conscription on its citizens, but Hitler reimposed it in 1935. The new military law made no provision for conscientious objection, and no change was made in this regard before Nazi Germany's defeat in the spring of 1945. What then, we may ask, was the fate of any who dared to refuse to bear arms in Hitler's Germany? From what background did such people come? What were their motives in resisting the totalitarian state on this issue?

Concerning two conscientious objectors (COs) to military service we know quite a lot. The name of the (former Austrian) peasant Franz Jägerstätter, executed in Berlin in August 1943 for his unwillingness, as a devout Catholic, to serve in an unjust war, was rescued from near-oblivion when an American sociologist, and Second World War CO, published a biography of this war resister in 1964.[3] And since that date a considerable literature has grown up around Jägerstätter, mainly in German.

Thirteen years earlier, in 1951, the revived German Fellowship of Reconciliation (FOR) had issued a small pamphlet dedicated to the memory of Dr Hermann Stöhr, a First World War veteran converted to pacifism by his wartime experiences, who acted as FOR secretary before its dissolution by Hitler and who subsequently, after refusing reinduction into the German army, was executed for this offence on 21 June 1940, even though he had repeatedly stated his readiness to undertake alternative civilian service in lieu of military duties.[4]

For several decades not much additional information emerged concerning COs in Hitler's Germany. But within the last few years our knowledge of these people has greatly increased as a result of the publication – in German – of two major studies. Both appeared under the same title, *Conscientious Objection in the Third Reich* – the first in 1986, by Albrecht and Heidi Hartman,[5] and the second, originally a doctoral dissertation, in 1991 by Karsten Bredemeier.[6] The latter contains valuable new data and corrects some of the information provided by the Hartmanns. I have based the remainder of this essay largely on materials contained in these two books.

It is impossible now to establish the exact number of COs to military service in Nazi Germany. However, more than 280 cases are known, and over 250 of them involve Jehovah's Witnesses (JWs).[7] These statistics, however, probably fall short of the total number of men who refused to bear arms for Hitler's Reich; Bredemeier certainly believes that the correct figure may be much higher. Several other religious denominations (besides the JWs) are known to have produced cases of conscientious objection; for the Catholics we have indeed some dozen objectors, and for the breakaway Reformation Movement among the Seventh-day Adventists, around half that number. We know of two pacifist pastors of the dissident (evangelical) Confessional church, Ernst Friedrich and Wilhelm Schümer, who both became liable for military service because authorities of the government-approved Evangelical church had deprived them of their pastorates; they agreed in the end (it was certainly a difficult decision) to accept service in the army medical corps (*Sanitätsdienst*), largely in order to avoid jeopardizing their families. Schümer's father had been active before 1933 in the German Peace Society and other anti-war organizations. The two young clergymen were in close touch with each other, thus reinforcing their determination not to bear arms.[8]

Let us now look more closely at some of the individuals about whose cases we possess at least a little information of a personal nature. JWs convicted of refusing to bear arms were in most instances shot; in a few cases the death penalty was commuted to a long term of imprisonment. Men in the latter category then joined other co-religionists, who had been sent to a concentration camp for their activities in what Hitler had declared to be an illegal organization. In the view of the military authorities, the fact that these men were acting 'from religious conviction' was irrelevant; and their unwillingness to accept service in the army medical corps, an alternative sometimes offered them, increased the hostility of their judges, who often accused them of 'stubbornness' and inability to accept well-meant advice.[9]

Letters sent to their families from those condemned to death reflect a spirit of love and forgiveness; the eschatological wrath expressed in the Witnesses' theoretical viewpoint is usually absent here. 'As followers of Christ,' one of them told the military court, they 'could not, [they] dared not, bear arms. God forbids us to kill.'[10] In a letter written the day before his execution (on 2 December 1939), Franz Mattischek told his mother: 'Don't be sad; I have always trusted in my God and in Christ, who will support me to the end.'

Four of the five known Adventist COs suffered execution by shooting. These men had refused to work on their Saturday Sabbath as well as to take a military oath. But the core of their objection to military service lay in their belief that bearing arms was inconsistent with their religion. As Anton Brugger put it shortly before his execution: because acceptance of such service would be a betrayal, 'for me there is no middle way; I have either to be true to my convictions or untrue.' The authorities as early as April 1936 had banned this small religious body on the grounds of its being a threat to state and society and hostile to 'the world-view (*Weltanschauung*) of National Socialism.' 'The followers of this sect refuse military service ... They openly proclaim that they possess no fatherland but are internationally minded, regarding all men as brothers.'

The handful of Catholic objectors, while united in their readiness to accept death as the outcome of their defiance of the state, differed as to the motives prompting their refusal of military service. Father Franz Reinisch, for instance, approved the role of the Wehrmacht in defending the state from attack; but he refused to take the military oath because in existing circumstances he regarded the German army as an instrument of aggression. Jägerstätter, too, upheld the principle of the just war, while several of the other Catholic COs deriving from Austria seem to have been motivated, at any rate in part, by an Austrian patriotism that regarded the German forces as an army of occupation.

Michael Lerpscher and Josef Ruf, in contrast, has been inspired by the evangelical pacifism of Father Max Josef Metzger, who was executed by the Nazis in 1944. For them, Jesus' love commandment overrode the orders of the military to kill at the behest of the state. Despite their willingness to serve – without weapons – in the medical corps, which they considered would be a task of love, both men suffered the death penalty in the autumn of 1940. Lerpscher, who had joined Metzger's Society of the King at Meitingen in 1935, lived there as a humble lay brother until his arrest for refusing to join the wartime Wehrmacht. A simple peasant, he was nevertheless unwilling to accept the traditional teaching of his church with regard to war; he could not reconcile it with what he knew of Jesus' ministry in the New Testament.[11]

Josef Scheuer, a Catholic pacifist who took St Francis as his model of non-violent behaviour, was more fortunate than Lerpscher or Ruf, for he was unexpectedly amnestied after declaring his unwillingness to bear arms. Soon afterward, however, the Gestapo arrested him once more and incarcerated him in the concentration camp at Sachsenhausen. The brothers Josef and Bernhard Fleischer, both well educated men who objected to modern warfare because of its indiscriminate mass killing and considered participation in a modern army as a sin, also escape death – this time through the influence of their father, a former Centre party deputy. After his trial as a military objector Josef Fleischer was confined for five years in a psychiatric clinic.

The Jehovah's Witnesses and Adventists who refused military service, even though they had to suffer severe hardship and in many cases death, nevertheless enjoyed the support of their respective religious communities for their stand. This must to some extent have eased the bitterness of their fate. As regards the Catholic COs, though their church at that time frowned on conscientious objection and the ecclesiastical authorities did their best to dissuade men from adopting such a position, still there were priests who were sympathetic and some co-religionists who encouraged them.

But what must have been the depths of spiritual strength needed to uphold Albert Herbst, a mechanic employed at an electrical firm in Stuttgart, who was executed in 1943 at the age of thirty-six, for refusing induction into the army? For it appears he was the only Baptist to take this stand. Herbst, along with his wife who shared his pacifism, had broken with the Baptist church shortly before the outbreak of war because it permitted church members in Nazi party uniform to take part in communion. Herbst indeed seems to have elicited little, if any, support among other Baptists. At his trial for refusing military service (and the military oath as well), Herbst told the court: 'I have no enemies ... I will not handle a weapon.' He rejected any suggestion of accepting *Sanitätsdienst*, too. Clearly, the Sermon on the Mount and Christian discipleship lay at the centre of his anti-militarism. At the conclusion of the hearings and just prior to passing the death sentence, the president of the military tribunal addressed him as follows: 'Herbst, you have made it extremely hard for us to come to a decision. We are all convinced you are indeed a sincere Christian. But alas there is no way out; there is no way we can get around the severity of the law.'[12]

The Quaker Gerhard Halle, a war veteran like his friend Hermann Stohr, had refused to serve when recalled to the colours in 1942 as a former reserve officer. Summoned before an army board (Wehrkommando), he explained to the assembled officers that he, as a member of the Society of Friends and a convinced Christian pacifist, could no longer undertake military service. Then, handing back his army papers, Halle declared: 'As a Christian I cannot act otherwise.' He was nevertheless careful to state that Quakers left the decision whether to bear arms or to refuse combatant service to the conscience of each of its members. (Indeed Halle, against those German Friends who before the war had advocated a more radical stand, consistently urged Quaker conscripts to accept any offer made to them of non-combatant medical duties if their consciences allowed them to serve in this way.)

In the end the board permitted Halle to go free and omitted to report this act to the Gestapo, which might otherwise have taken steps against the recalcitrant Quaker – a display of tolerance that may have been the result either of the respect in which Quakers were held in Germany because of their postwar relief or of feelings of sympathy towards an old soldier who had been severely wounded in the previous war – or perhaps to a combination of both factors. The matter seemed to be settled. But Halle now became increasingly troubled as he read the reports of the situation of the German troops on the Eastern front until at last he decided to abandon his conscientious objection, if not his basic pacifist stance. The military authorities, however, politely turned down his offer to serve again in the army – even if, as he suggested, because of his poor health, only as an officer at the base.[13]

Some tantalizing gaps exist in the record. I wish that we knew more about 'Bernhard,' a nineteen-year-old Protestant executed in Berlin as a CO. The lad had joined up at the beginning of the war. But soon convinced of the total incompatibility of soldiering with the teaching of the Sermon on the Mount, which his church had told him formed the essence of the Christian faith, he had refused further service.

And what about the handful of political objectors, including one or two serving soldiers, whose names figure elusively on the pages of the Hartmanns' and Bredemeier's books? One of them Bredemeier shows to have been a postwar fraud. But the rest were genuine. The motivation of their courageous act had stemmed in each instance from opposition to National Socialism and a conviction that Germany was waging a war of aggression. Selective objectors, they did not share the rejection of all wars that marked most of their fellow COs.

With a few exceptions, COs in Nazi Germany were drawn from the working class or the peasantry. They usually possessed only elementary-level schooling. Of course the predominance among them of Jehovah's Witnesses, a largely proletarian sect, would by itself account for this. In addition, most of the Catholic COs were peasants (whereas Adventist COs came from the working class). The almost total absence among COs of supporters of the suppressed peace movement is at first sight puzzling. The movement was largely of the middle class and had won the adherence of many intellectuals and persons with university degrees; thus, if some of them had resisted conscription as COs, it would to some extent have altered the social complexion of conscientious objection in the German Reich.

But that did not happen. In the first place, for various reasons (such as age, political unreliability, and occupation) many adherents of the former peace movement never became liable to call-up, while others took refuge abroad when they felt their lives or liberty endangered. The unfortunate ones fell victim to Hitler's tyranny; many became inmates of a concentration camp. Second, conscripted pacifists, though unwilling to refuse induction (an act that almost inevitably brought the death penalty), may nevertheless have sought to obtain non-combatant status, as for instance we have seen Pastor Schümer had done; some may even have quieted their consciences simply by a resolution not to use their weapons to kill, as we know several young Quaker conscripts did.[14]

In Nazi Germany the decision to refuse military service on grounds of conscience entailed far more serious consequences than this act usually brought elsewhere. For there the objector faced almost certain death, even if in rare cases capital punishment was commuted into long-term imprisonment. Executions of religious COs had occurred, it is true, during the confusion of the Russian Civil War, though this situation indeed conflicted with the official policy of the central Soviet government. During the Second World War that government, now under Stalin's unchallenged control, executed Tolstoyan peasants of military age who had dared to resist conscription into the army.

But apart from these instances the treatment of COs in Nazi Germany remains unparalleled in its harshness, at any rate within recent centuries. Today a new generation of Germans seeking to uncover the history of German resistance to Nazi rule is discovering in conscientious objection within Hitler's Reich, whether derived from religious or from secular motives, a variant of this resistance hitherto inadequately explored and therefore insufficiently appreciated.[15] Though we may expect significant new details to emerge over the coming years, the picture is already reasonably clear. Thus a unique chapter in the history of opposition to war is now open for us to read.

NOTES

1 Diether Götz Lichdi, *Mennoniten im Dritten Reich: Dokumentation und Deutung*, Schriftenreihe des Mennonitischen Geschichtsverein Nr. 9 (Weierhof 1977), 135–8, 169, 170. Conscripted preachers or elders sometimes sought a non-combatant role in the army for reasons of conscience, especially if they came from a rural congregation in the Vistula delta (Westpreussen), seized by Germany in 1939; for *Wehrlosigkeit* (non-resistance) remained stronger there than in the rest of the country. We also know of at least two Mennonites from Soviet territories occupied by the Germans, who took a deliberately non-combatant stand after being conscripted as *Volksdeutschen* into the German army – at least to the degree that they somehow or other avoided ever firing at an enemy soldier. (One of the men was inducted into the *Waffen-SS!*) See Hans Rempel, ed., *Waffen der Wehrlosen: Ersatzdienst der Mennoniten in der UdSSR* (Winnipeg 1980), 147, 148, 157–62. Both men had been COs in the Soviet Union at the end of the 1920s, when alternative civilian service was still permitted for Mennonite conscripts. In contrast to the situation among the majority of German Mennonites, support for the traditional *Wehrlosigkeit* survived under the surface among the 'Russian' Mennonites – despite ruthless government persecution and the ending of CO exemption – to surface again with the collapse of communism.

2 The most detailed account hitherto of Weimar Germany's peace movement is by a Polish historian, Karol Fiedor, *Niemiecki ruch obrońców pokoju 1892–1933* (Wrocław 1993), 77–419.

3 Gordon C. Zahn, *In Solitary Witness: The Life and Death of Franz Jägerstätter* (New York 1964). Zahn's 'Pacifists during the Third Reich' in Michael Berenbaum, ed., *A Mosaic of Victims: Non-Jews Persecuted and Murdered by the Nazis* (New York, 1990), 194–99, deals almost exclusively with Catholic COs.

4 *Ein Christ verweigert den Kriegsdienst: Hermann Stöhr zum Gedächtnis* (Zwiefalten 1951). See also Grünewald's essay (chapter 5) above, notes 121, 125. Eberhard Röhm, *Sterben für den Frieden. Spurensicherung: Herman Stöhr (1898–1940) und die ökumenische Friedensbewegung* (Stuttgart 1985), 13–17, 172–6, 186–208, 214–25, 235–41, contains an account of Stöhr's resistance to conscription leading to his trial and execution. I should mention too the execution, on 8 September 1944, for her anti-war activities of another FOR member, Elisabeth von Thadden; Vera Brittain, *The Rebel Passion: A Short History of Some Pioneer Peacemakers* (London 1964), 136, 137.

5 Albrecht and Heidi Hartmann, *Kriegsdienstverweigerung im Dritte Reich* (Frankfurt am Main 1986).

6 Karsten Bredemeier, *Kriegsdienstverweigerung im Dritte Reich* (Baden-Baden 1991).

7 For JWs as COs, see especially Detlef Garbe, *Zwischen Widerstand und Martyrium*:

Die Zeugen Jehovas im "Dritten Reich" (Munich, 1994), 12, 33, 326, 327, 344–94, 411–27, 457, 458, 488,. For their less uncompromising stance in the First World War, see 44–6.

8 Jürgen Schafer and Matthias Schreiber, *Kompromiss und Gewissen: Der Weg des Pastors Wilhelm Schümer im Dritten Reich* (Waltrop 1994), 85, 86, 94–103, 119–23. Schümer was reported as missing on the Eastern front in the summer of 1943. As a member of the army medical corps he had been forced to make agonizing compromises in submitting to the weapons training obligatory for ambulancemen and taking an oath of obedience. Like Friedrich and Schümer, Dr Martin Gauger, a young jurist who acted as legal adviser to the Confessional Church, was also unwilling to bear arms when drafted. He resolved this dilemma by fleeing to the Netherlands in May 1940, just before the Germans occupied that country. He was later arrested by the Gestapo and died in Buchenwald concentration camp in July 1941.

Two pacifist Protestant clergymen who survived the war unharmed were F.W. Siegmund-Schultze and Wilhelm Mensching. Neither was liable to military service – on account of both age and office. In addition, the well-known postwar Protestant theologian Helmut Gollwitzer, in an autobiographical volume entitled *... und führen, wohin du nicht willst: Bericht einer Gefangenschaft* (Munich 1956), 190, reports that before the war among those *in meiner Kreise*, i.e., among his close associates in the Confessional Church, was one young man who, on being called up for wartime military service, declared himself a CO and was shot. Unfortunately Gollwitzer gave no further details. I would like to thank Kathleen Hertzberg for this reference.

9 Inside the camps JWs could also clash with the authorities over the military question and receive harsh treatment because of their unwillingness to perform war-related work, as happened in Ravensbrück in December 1939, when some five hundred JW women 'refused to sew ammunition pockets on military uniforms' and were savagely punished for their disobedience. Not a single woman yielded. A few months earlier, on the outbreak of war, JW prisoners asked to volunteer for the army had turned the offer down. 'In Sachsenhausen, each refusal was followed by the killing of ten [JWs]. After forty men had been shot, the SS desisted.' In the camp at Buchenwald, in a similar situation 'the men were not killed; but they were assaulted, assigned to quarry duty and barred from hospital treatment.' See Brian R. Dunn, 'The Death's Head and the *Watchtower*: Jehovah's Witnesses in the Holocaust Kingdom,' in *Holocaust Studies Annual* (Greenwood, Fla), 2 (1986), Jack Fischel and Sanford Pinsker, eds., *The Churches' Response to the Holocaust*, 161, 162. Himmler regarded German JWs as a racially valuable element – if only they would abandon their anti-national religious ideology. But he very rarely succeeded in making any of them do this, despite rigorous Nazi persecution of the sect. Ibid., 1959–61.

Despite the JWs' anti-Nazi record the postwar communist rulers of East Germany were almost as hostile to them as the Nazis had been. Take the case of Horst Henschel. In May 1944, when he was twelve years old, his CO father had written to him from prison: 'Be glad if you receive this letter, because I have endured to the end. In two hours I will be executed.' Seven years later, in 1951, Horst was arrested for smuggling JW literature into East Germany; he was also charged with being a warmonger. To this accusation he replied indignantly: ' How can I ... be condemned as a warmonger' when my father was beheaded for refusing to fight in the recent war (*Awake!*, 22 Feb. 1998)? The authorities, however, remained unmoved and sentenced the young man to twelve years in prison.

10 The thirty-one-old Austrian JW Franz Zeiner, executed in mid-1940 for refusing induction into the army, likewise declared that since 'God forbids killing' another human being, no genuine 'follower of Christ (*Christi Nachfolger*)' could bear arms for whatever cause. Though his court martial warned Zeiner repeatedly 'of the serious consequences of his action,' he adhered fixedly to his standpoint. The judges indeed admitted that this position resulted not from cowardice but from 'religious conviction.' Still, the man's sincerity made him the more dangerous, since it could easily 'undermine the willingness of others to serve.' They said that it would be wrong therefore in his case to commute the death penalty, as could be done in the case of less threatening offenders. See Elisabeth Klamper, ed., *Dokumentationsarchiv des österreichischen Widerstandes, Vienna* (Archives of the Holocaust: An International Collection of Selected Documents, vol. 19), doc. 190, 363–5.

11 Ernst T. Mader and Jakob Knab, *Das Lacheln des Esels: Das Leben und die Hinrichtung des Allgäuer Bauernsohnes Michael Lerpscher (1905–1940)* (Blöctach 1987), 33, 36–41, 51, 54–6, 67. One who knew Lerpscher in his twenties has described how even then he was utterly opposed to taking human life under any circumstances. 'He was too conscientious, just too conscientious,' the man commented (31, 32).

12 See Jost Müller-Bohn, ed., *Letze Briefe eines Wehrdienstverweigerers 1943* (Lahr-Dinglingen 1984). This slim volume prints letters written by Herbst to his wife and young son during the three months before his execution.

13 See the articles by Gerhard Halle's daughter, Anna Sabine Halle, 'Quäker als Deserteurs damals, als Totalverweigerer heute?' *Der Quäker*, 67 no. 3 (March 1993), 63, and 'The German Quakers and the Third Reich,' *German History* (Oxford), 11 no. 2 (June 1993), 222–36.

14 A special case was that of Karl-Heinz Pollatz. A medical student and son of a German Quaker couple resident in the Netherlands where they were active during the occupation in helping Jews, he was called up in 1942. He then declared himself a CO. But the German authorities, instead of executing him, as he had expected, threatened to kill his parents if he persisted in his refusal to serve. 'Knowing that many lives depended on his parents, he joined the army, completed his medical studies ... in Germany and became an army doctor.' He died on the Russian front near the end of the war. H. Peters Barns, 'A Memory and a Testimony,' *Friend* (London), 154

no. 14, 5 April 1996, 14. Hans A. Schmitt, *Quakers and Nazis: Inner Light in Outer Darkness* (Columbia, Mo., and London 1997), reached me too late for consideration in this essay; pages 48, 128, 188–90, and 258 deal with the impact of conscription on German Friends.

15 See, for example, the two studies by Detlef Garbe, 'Radikale Verweigerung aus Prinzipientreue und Gewissensgehorsam: Kregsdienstverweigerung im "Dritten Reich,"' in A. Gestrich, ed., *Krieg: Ausübung, Erfahrung und Verweigerung von Gewalt im Kriegen des 20. Jahrhunderts* (Jahrbuch für historische Friedensforschung 4, 1995) (Münster 1996), 132–58, and '"Du sollst nicht töten:" Kriegsdienstverweigerer 1939–1945,' in Norbert Haase and Gerhard Paul, eds., *Die anderen Soldaten: Wehrkraftzersetzung, Gehorsamsverweigerung und Fahnenflucht im Zweiten Weltkrieg* (Frankfurt am Main 1995), 185–217. See also N. Haase, 'Desertion-Kriegsdienstverweigerung-Widerstand,' in Peter Steinbach and Johannes Tuchel, eds., *Widerstand gegen den Nationalsozialismus* (Berlin 1944), 526–31; Manfred Messerschmidt, 'Das Reichskriegsgericht und die Verweigerer aus Gewissensgründen,' in Ernst Willi Hansen et al., eds., *Politischer Wandel, organisierte Gewalt und nationale Scherheit: Beiträge zur neueren Geschichte Deutschlands und Frankreichs* (Munich 1955), 369–83. These scholars have all made copious use of official archives (including army records).

24

Danish War Resisters under Nazi Occupation

PETER KRAGH HANSEN

How does a pacifist organization react when, in spite of more than a decade of efforts, war breaks out and the country is occupied by foreign troops? Does it reject its ideals and participate in armed combat – first, in direct military action against the invaders, and later, in the underground resistance movement? Or does it maintain the purity of its ideals and retreat to the sidelines, viewing developments as a mere onlooker (as though saying 'I told you so' or 'This is not *my* war')? How does it deal with members who have used force to resist the occupier? Are there indeed potential energies in pacifism that can be used in active resistance? This essay describes how one pacifist body, Aldrig mere Krig, or AmK (No More War), responded to such questions before, during, and after the German occupation of Denmark from 1940 to 1945.[1]

The situation in Denmark during the occupation differed in many ways from that in other Nazi-occupied countries. In Denmark the government remained in power by the grace of the Germans until 29 August 1943, attempting by means of its 'policy of cooperation' to lead Denmark through the war with as few casualties as possible. It was the opinion of the government and the political parties that the most imminent danger lay in a take-over by the Nazis of the central administration. Thus the political aim was to protect the nation from the danger of a Nazi government such as had been installed, for example, in Norway. This policy of cooperation could not be implemented without ambiguities. There were elements of opportunism; and a number of mistakes were made, foremost among these the internment of Communists in 1941. But there was never a Nazi government in Denmark because the Germans were not interested in disrupting everyday life in the country. The Germans wanted to maintain stable conditions and, not least, continue regular supplies of agricultural products.

Translated from the Danish by Arthur Robinson

Pacifist periodicals published under German occupation: *Kerk en Vrede* (1 Aug. 1940), the Netherlands; *Aldrig mere Krig* (Nov. 1940), Denmark

To have an 'ideal protectorate' in undisturbed cooperation proved a feather in their cap for the Germans. Though these factors are beyond the scope of this essay, they provide a general frame of reference for what follows.

AmK to April 1940

AmK was founded on 17 October 1926 as the Danish branch of the War Resisters' International (WRI), set up in 1921 by conscientious objectors (COs) and other peace activists in reaction to the cruelties of the recent war. The WRI required members to repudiate every level of violence – in the family, in society at large, and between nations – and also to reject compulsory military service if called on for this. Indeed, the founders of the WRI and its Danish section saw pacifism primarily in relation to participation in war. Thus anti-militarism and conscientious objection to military service also became the main aims of the Danish war resisters' organization. Several participants at its initial meeting in Helsingør came to exert a great influence on the Danish peace movement.[2]

AmK took pacifism seriously.[3] Would-be members had to commit themselves by signing the following declaration based on that of the WRI: 'Since I regard war as a crime against humanity I will resist and refuse to participate in any form of war, whether for the sake of defence, civil war or aggression.' During the interwar years AmK became Denmark's first and only organization for COs. Its primary task was to inform the public about the law allowing alternative civilian service: this law had been passed in 1917, making Denmark among the first countries to make this concession.[4] However, it proved extremely difficult to spread knowledge of the law itself: indeed it was often hard even to obtain a copy of the text. AmK's persistence in this work made its name synonymous with conscientious objection. A large number of COs became members of AmK; figures from 1934 obtained from the alternative-service camp at Kompedal suggest that around 50 per cent joined. Other causes that AmK took up included spreading knowledge of the armaments industry and criticism of the war psychosis engendered by air-raid precautions.

AmK soon became known as a radical – and to some people fanatically – anti-militarist organization. It took the lead in open debates and by the use of outspoken language strove to draw the public's attention to the issues under discussion. This may be seen in a pamphlet entitled *What the Soldier Learns*. 'Close fighting with the bayonet calls for the soldier to use his energy to the utmost and with fearless brutality,' its author, Axel Pille, quoted from the *Army Manual for Soldiers*. Detailed instructions followed there as to how a bayonet might be stuck into an enemy with the greatest effect. According to Pille, 'No pacifist could describe more effectively and more horrifyingly what a soldier has to learn than the army itself has done in this booklet published for the instruction of soldiers. The quotations show clearly how the army with chilling calculation teaches young men how to kill their fellow human beings. I do not know whether a primer has been published on how to kill pigs and calves; here, however, in the *Army Manual* we have a textbook on how to slaughter human beings.'[5]

AmK also promoted the idea of non-violence. During the interwar years this idea had spread as a result of collective demonstrations such as the general strike in Germany against the Kapp Putsch and the public outcry there against the French occupation of the Rühr, but above all by the example of Gandhi's civil disobedience campaigns, first in South Africa and then in India. In Denmark small groups spread information about this 'new' possibility for active resistance; hitherto there had been no research in the history of non-violent resistance. Information was now obtained chiefly from people such as Ester Menon and Ellen Hørup, both of whom had had personal experience of non-violence from visits to Gandhi's ashram, as well as from groups such as the Indiens Venner (Friends of India), the Quakers, and the AmK. But, as the AmK activist Thomas Christensen noted later, such discussion was primarily of a theoretical nature.

When war broke out on 1 September 1939 the Danish government promptly issued a declaration of absolute neutrality, which received full support from AmK. According to this policy Denmark remained disarmed to the point where its military forces could not constitute a threat to any of the neighbouring countries.

Replying in the organization's paper to those sceptics who thought that with the coming of war pacifists would surely see that pacifism did not work, the general secretary of AmK, Hagbard Jonassen, argued that on the contrary it had become more relevant than ever before: 'We, as peace workers, almost daily hear sarcastic remarks about the cause of peace being faced with bankruptcy. For us such an idea is incomprehensible since, in fact, war has broken out because the major powers have not followed the path which pacifists have indicated but followed instead the way of the power politicians. The war is a clear proof that power politics lead to bankruptcy. However, we feel no desire to gloat. We would all rather have wished that the others were right in believing the contrary.'[6]

A leading article in the paper wrote of 'the hour of trial' for pacifist comrades abroad; newspapers had already printed news of a CO being shot. In Denmark, too, injustices to COs were noted. When partial mobilization was introduced, there were reports of the punishment of young men because, on being summoned for service, they had refused 'to obey orders.' 'Others, who have already done alternative service, are also being called up.' Therefore, the article concluded, pacifists had no other choice than 'to be prepared and to promise each other that whatever happens we will stand by our pledge: a clear and definite "NO" to the military authorities and the war.'

For some time yet it was 'the others' war.' In the columns of their paper AmK members discussed who was responsible and furnished information on the position of members at home and abroad with an emphasis on the position of COs in Britain. But with the Soviet winter attack on Finland on 30 November 1939 militaristic currents among the Danes became evident. This was partly because a Scandinavian country had been attacked and partly because it was the Russians who were the aggressors in this case. While the Polish front had not produced Danish volunteers, there was no lack of volunteers to help the Finns. No doubts existed for AmK as to the danger involved on this account for Danish neutrality. 'Also at home we now hear demands for military support for Finland. We can only hope that these will not increase, but the danger is imminent and growing daily, which becomes quite obvious when we read the reports and comments in the Danish press. Here there is no talk of neutrality, but [instead we find] quite open, uninhibited anti-Russian opinions, which in the long run can demolish our neutrality. Here indeed the Danish press shows itself to be irresponsible.' The article concluded: 'The [Danish] government's position is quite clear, unlike that of the press. We ask for a neutral press for the sake of us all.'[7] The newspapers were indeed full of glowing accounts of heroism on the part of the Finns, praising their will to fight for their country – and thereby, it was implied, for Scandinavian democracy. The chairman of the Copenhagen branch of AmK, Svend Åge Nielsen, commented ironically on this trend, which in his view seemed completely to ignore Denmark's 'total dependency on our neighbour to the south.'

The feelings induced by the Winter War – 'the Finnish psychosis,' as it was called by Thomas Christensen – were forerunners of the militant feelings that appeared during the occupation. AmK was now in head-on opposition to the enthusiastic cries for defence from most political parties, which called for a Danish policy openly committed to armed force. The public pressure, which also came from the traditionally anti-militaristic Social Democratic party, resulted in the official declaration of 19 January 1940, which stated that, 'if necessary, all available means would be used to assert and defend the peace and independence of the country.'

AmK's reaction came on 28 January, in a resolution of its executive committee. 'This declaration, in face of the statement of neutrality on which the whole nation is agreed, we find to be highly undesirable. In certain circles the declaration has been made a pretext for vociferous propaganda for an increase in defence measures, while for others it has increased their fear of a radical change from the original government parties' viewpoint: that our armed forces should serve to maintain our neutrality but should not otherwise take part in military action. We hope that such fears will prove to be unfounded; and we wish to state our own position, which we think we share with the majority of the population: that our country will not *under any circumstances* join the ranks of the countries now at war.'[8]

AmK and the German Invasion

On the morning of 9 April 1940 Denmark woke abruptly. The country had been occupied by the Nazi forces with almost no resistance. The feelings of the population ranged from shame to curiosity – with acclamation on the part of the few Danish Nazis. AmK members were of course shocked. Their attitude differed, however, from that of many other sections of the population. As the AmK chairman, Hagbard Jonassen, declared: 'It was a sad experience for us all. To the last we had hoped to be free from "protection" by others. A major consolation, though, is that the government had enough sense as well as the courage to decide that the army should not attempt to resist. We can only thank the Prime Minister and the Minister for Foreign Affairs for their bravery in taking this course.'[9] While others, both then and later, underlined the shame incurred by not 'putting up a fight,' AmK took the opposite viewpoint. There was, it believed, no reason to make heroes of the thirteen soldiers who had fallen. In a confidential note intended for AmK members, the Folk High School teacher H.P. Hansen stated: 'The Danish soldiers who engaged in battle on 9 April did what they felt was their duty and without doubt did their best. There was, however, hardly any positive outcome of their armed resistance. And only a simpleton would speak as if this was the sole historical event in the spring of 1940. The government's decision not to resist on 9 April should surely have been reached early enough so that no Danes would have lost their lives or sustained injuries from combat. It must be recognized, however, that the decision to cease resistance was perfectly correct.'

Running against the prevailing feeling was also AmK's attitude towards German soldiers. For pacifists the 'enemy' is seen in principle to be war and militarism – in other words, the use of military force. The individual soldier therefore is regarded as still a human being, with both feelings and rights. The AmK could not accept unfair treatment of the German soldiers. To cite again from Jonassen: 'Have we now other tasks to undertake? Undoubtably we have. We still need to work for peace. The country is now occupied by a so-called "enemy."' We must be among those who understand that these soldiers are as much human beings as we are, only they have been torn from their homes, their families, and their friends. They are among foreigners and uncertain of their future. We need not feel un-Danish in having human feelings for these many strangers. And I am indeed convinced that with the passage of time it will become even more necessary that we try to encourage a humane attitude among our fellow citizens. Here we have a task in keeping with our goal.'

That a new situation had arisen in the pacifist camp was evidenced by passages in Jonassen's article, in which he praised the Danish army and soldiers. The writer recognized 'the discipline shown both by the officers and the ranks.' He went on: 'We understand how difficult it must have been to create an effective fighting force and then to reject using the troops in this critical situation. It shows a high degree of self-control, which demands respect; and it is quite improper to suggest, as some have done, that the army neglected its duties. It is the government, and not the army, which had to decide whether or not the armed forces were to be used.'

AmK and the Occupation

AmK had not been prepared for a situation of this kind. Right up to the time of the occupation, its normal activities had continued in the shadow of the war. The April issue of its paper gave notice of the annual general meeting to be held in Vejle on 19 April. A note stated that the AGM was going to be held under threatening conditions, but with the cessation of hostilities in Finland there would be less danger of the Scandinavian countries becoming involved in the war between the great powers. The campaign leaders sent out the usual call-up posters to the local branches, not knowing that they were soon to have to advise against sticking them up, for they had drawn attention to the possibility of registering as a CO for alternative service. Preparations were under way too for the establishment of a Nordic Peace Publishing Company.

But such projects had to be changed rather radically. The date of the AGM was postponed to 1 August, while the publishing project had to be abandoned altogether. This was only the beginning. On 12 April the government forbade the holding of public meetings – except religious services. The ban had consequences for the work of AmK, as the following declaration printed in its journal shows: 'Now, once again, we make a statement which no one would ever have expected to see in this paper: we suggest to all members that they obey the government's orders [i.e., no public meetings, etc.]. Every kind of public demonstration, either by speeches or by distribution of pamphlets etc., whether to civilians or to military personnel, must be avoided. Those who do not understand this injunction will soon discover that such activities can do irreparable harm to our cause.' AmK members were urged instead to intensify 'internal work in the branches.' 'Participate,' they were told, 'in members' meetings, talk together – and stand by each other and be of good heart.'

In the shadow of the ban on public meetings and demonstrations, AmK had to reorganize its work. There exist few records of the executive committee's deliberations at that time: a gap extends from 6 April to 22 September. That decisions were made is clear both from the AmK's paper and from messages sent from headquarters to the local groups. The gap is probably the result of concern about allowing discussions involving politics to be recorded at a time when the future existence of the organization was so uncertain. In other countries sections of the WRI were among the first victims of Nazi oppression; known pacifists and COs were quickly put under effective surveillance. In Denmark, however, the situation differed to the extent that normal conditions were soon re-established for groups of various kinds. From 12 September the ban on public meetings was lifted, but in April and May of that year there could of course be no knowledge of this outcome.

In May a letter had been sent to the chairs of the local branches. It contained a proposal to strengthen the bonds between members and to hold meetings in private in lieu of the now-banned public meetings. It suggested that members should be visited privately, to collect membership fees and subscriptions to the AmK paper, which had become the most stable connection between members.

There are reasons to remind members that certain of our previous activities must cease. As is known, public meetings and demonstrations are forbidden. In one instance the police have asked questions because a pamphlet of ours was seen by a soldier. The Executive Committee is of the opinion that this kind of activity at the present time can not only harm the person involved but may also seriously endanger the movement. We must not forget that we are subject to an authority with a mentality far removed from that of the Danish authorities. This calls for us all to show the utmost caution and patience. The careless behaviour of one member could lead to undreamt-of reactions against all members. As no one can foresee the future we would caution all to be careful with lists of members, etc. AmK can suddenly be called upon to make an important contribution. We must be prepared for the possibility of a militaristic and nationalistic reaction at some point and then we must have our house in order so that we can be ready to get to work.

The intention behind these words is clear. The danger lay partly in violent resistance to the occupation forces and partly in militarization of Danish life extending beyond the period of occupation. Obviously it was impossible in those early days to reckon with the defeat of Germany, but one should not, I think, regard the AmK's considerations are premature. Anyhow, violence and an increase of militarism were seen as going against the grain of Denmark's peaceful culture and way of life. From this viewpoint the only sensible Danish foreign and security policy – that of virtually unarmed neutrality – would go by the board.

Fairly soon a kind of everyday life was resumed. Activities were intensified inside AmK, and the winter season saw a great increase in study-group activity. No figures are available as to the number of members who participated, but many social and political problems were discussed, including the idea of non-violent resistance. The question was debated: 'Can we practice non-violent resistance?' Unfortunately I have not been able to discover any records of these discussions, but the possibility of actually using non-violent resistance was certainly not ignored altogether.

Regular contacts between AmK members were re-established by the monthly newsletters sent out to local group leaders, who in turn passed on the contents to their members. AmK supported the government's present policy; it therefore raised no questions at this time concerning defence. But the army continued with the usual conscription procedure until August 1943, which meant that COs were also called up. It was not easy for AmK to maintain its normal channels of information, but a system was soon worked out whereby contact persons were established in all the CO camps.

One of the main questions discussed during the occupation was whether pacifists should refuse to take part in civil defence work, which was organized partly on military lines. Earlier, in the 1930s, pacifists had been strongly critical of civil defence as part of the war machine. Now the executive committee of AmK was forced to admit that the situation had changed. It refrained therefore from urging members to resist conscription into the civil-defence organization, though a number did refuse such assignments. But decision in the matter was left entirely to the individual member.

Whatever differences of opinion existed with regard to civil defence, members of AmK united in preparations for relief work, should this become possible when the war was over. The inspiration here was the relief work carried out in Spain during the civil war by the Danish Quaker Elise Thomsen. In this way, by actively preparing for peace (and going out later to rebuild what others had destroyed), pacifists could engage in genuine work for peace, which the occupation curtailed. For many members this activity also tended to assuage the conflict of conscience aroused by the resistance movement.[10] As the AmK activist Svend Haugaard put it: 'Passivity was unbearable, but it was even worse to use violence and thereby abandon our pacifist principles. By engaging in such work our day-to-day activities in AmK seemed to become lighter, for we were preparing to make a positive contribution in the future.'[11]

At the outset on the occupation, AmK had given its support to the defence pol-
icy of the government, which was formed from a coalition of Radicals and
Social Democrats. Soon, however, propaganda for a more active military policy
emerged and gained popularity especially with the leaders of the Folk og Værn
(People and Defence) organization, among whom were many army officers.
AmK attempted to resist this development with the aid of groups such as the
Youth Committee for Peace. Such activities were regarded by virtually all
members as a natural continuation of their organization's policy through the
1930s, even though conditions had changed.

Peace activists had hitherto been united on all important issues, but now the
growth of the Resistance could lead to disagreement. How far, and to what
extent, could pacifists go along with it? During the occupation restrictions of
course limited frank debate on the issue. AmK's publications were subject to
the general censorship of the press, and its executive committee was decidedly
of the opinion that it was more important to keep the organization intact than to
provoke the domestic or foreign authorities with controversial articles. The
debate, however, could not be handled openly. On 29 August 1943 the Danish
armed forces were disbanded; their weapons were seized, and the soldiers
interned, after the government had resigned. Most people experienced a feeling
of satisfaction that now the lines were clearly demarcated and Denmark was
really 'at war' with Germany, even though the ministries and the police continued to function as before. A wave of strikes and sabotage struck the country,
and this development, together with the threat of allied invasion, caused the
Germans to clamp down.

AmK members wee also influenced by the public's somewhat euphoric mood.
An AmK member[12] noted his feeling at this time that there was indeed something 'exciting and liberating' in the idea of sabotage. At last it was possible to
'take sides and act – as the risk of life or death.' But he then went on to inquire
as to the probable consequences. An individual might perhaps behave in this
way with impunity. But what would happen if such a course were followed by
the majority of the population? If activity of this kind became widespread, then
the enemy would be forced to take drastic measures. 'Saboteurs would be lined
up and ... shot. Hostages would be taken and perhaps whole communities would
be executed. Would it be right to lead the Danish nation into this position? Here
it is not the numbers who may die, which horrifies, but the effects of this type of
death. There is a vast difference between thousands dying in a face-to-face battle encounter and thousands facing firing squads. Such experiences will never
be forgotten by the survivors or relatives – or by those ordered to carry out the
executions.'

This kind of warning against sabotage often occurs in the few surviving AmK records from the occupation years. The idea of resistance was understandable, but members agreed that there must also be consistency between ends and means. In the chairman's minutes for 15–16 October 1944 we find, for instance, the following statement: 'Our attitude to sabotage must be made clear, particularly after seeing the results of sabotage. We must have no truck with any kind of illegal activity.' (The chairman, Uffe Hansen, would seem to have been exaggerating here, because clearly pacifists believed that they could support non-violent illegal actions such as assisting Jews, emigrants, and members of the Resistance on the run.)

With regard to a possible Allied invasion, though the wording is different, the minutes of the executive committee are equally unambiguous. 'Our attitude in case of invasion: Naturally we cannot give any kind of assistance in waging war. We have always been sceptical, too, about de Ligt's plans, which do include various kinds of sabotage. The consequences of sabotage, which are even more terrible than we had envisaged, lead us to refrain from this type of action.' The reference here is to the Dutch anarchist and pacifist Bart de Ligt's 'Plan of Campaign against All War and All Preparation for War,' which included a non-violent strategy in the case of an occupation. De Ligt advocated, among other things, the sabotage of confiscated property as well as of bridges and railways, the basic idea being that everything useful for waging war should be immobilized or wrecked before it could be actually used.[13] AmK believed that the harmful consequences of such a policy could already be seen in Denmark.

After the War

After the liberation in 1945 a framework for open discussion of the issues that had arisen during the occupation was created. The organization emerged from the conflict numerically almost unscathed, and few of its activists had renounced pacifism as a result of occupation. In 1939 AmK had had 1,525 members. This figure dropped, it is true, under the occupation: by 1944 membership had sunk to around 1,300, while at the end of the war it stood at 1,404. But this figure represented a loss of only just over one hundred when compared to the number at the outset of the war in Europe.

Now AmK's paper could be published once again without censorship, and communication between members was no longer restricted. Even though during the war articles had appeared denouncing war and violence, they had always been phrased in such general terms that they hardly risked suppression. AmK had even entered into a discussion with 'defence supporters' over such matters as where responsibility lay for the events of 9 April 1940, when the Germans invaded the country. And this discussion had been tolerated by the Germans. Beginning with the 'Peace Issue' of 5 May 1945, however, the tone of the paper altered radically, with the sharply critical note found in pre-occupation issues being resumed once more.

But at the outset of peace, honours were duly awarded. As the editor wrote:

Even though we, as absolute pacifists, could not wholly accept all the methods used in the struggle, it is obvious that we owe thanks to the Resistance movement for its extremely brave contribution in the struggle against the representatives of the *Herrenvolk* ... At the same time, however, we must not forget to recognize the value of the more *passive kind of resistance*, which has been evidenced in many ways and has helped to unite the Danish population, with very few exceptions ... It is a pleasure, then, to be able to state that *it has been possible in this way to resist a brutal and violent regime effectively without the use of weapons – and with no army – in the face of an apparently helpless position.* We have been able to experience in practice something that can be of great use to us in the work now to be undertaken.[14]

A month later, however, one of the contributors, Arne Jørgensen, sounded a more critical note. He wondered why the now-free press did not use its freedom to censure the Resistance movement for its behaviour immediately after liberation. 'In Copenhagen in those days Resistance members drove their lorries at full speed through the streets, causing a number of accidents which could have been avoided. Many people were killed by wild shooting and stray bullets, merely because resistance members were trigger-happy. All in all, the saddest fact of their behaviour was their uncontrolled and childish joy in showing off their weapons.'[15]

It was, however, a provocative article in the same issue by the secretary of AmK (Thomas Christensen) that aroused the most violent reaction. Under the heading 'Bloody Stains on the Day of Liberation,' he recorded his impressions of that day in Denmark's second-largest city, Århus – similar to those of Jørgensen from Copenhagen. His conclusion, however, acted like a red rag to a bull: 'There are many Danes who do not think the Resistance movement has done such great service for our country as the movement itself claims. Indeed many feel that the Resistance did much harm by introducing Norwegian conditions here, that in addition it encouraged illegal behaviour and increased feelings of insecurity during the occupation, all of which had a negative effect on the morale of the general public. The immediate [postwar] reactions of members of the Resistance have not been promising, and ... some people have doubts as to whether Resistance members will hand in their weapons. Until they do so the people of Denmark will not feel safe.'[16]

The AmK's executive committee had now to tackle the question as to whether a member of the AmK who had participated actively in the Resistance movement had contravened his membership pledge. One member, from Herning, wrote to it demanding that 'members of the Resistance should be excluded' from the organization. Another correspondent, H.P. Jespersen, took the opposite view – any member who had joined a Resistance group should be left to decide for himself or herself whether to remain in AmK or not. The executive committee reached a temporary decision, which was to be discussed at the next AGM: 'That a member who had joined the Resistance and had undertaken military duties must either dissociate himself from it at once or resign from AmK membership.'

The problem to be resolved at the AGM seemed at first sight to be fairly simple: where does the boundary lie between the means that a committed pacifist could contemplate using in a resistance movement and those that were actually used by Danish Resistance groups? Christensen did not stand alone in his criticism of the Resistance. But debate in the AmK paper, as well as subsequent discussion at the annual general meeting (AGM), showed that some members had either sympathized with, or had actually participated in, the Resistance to a degree exceeding what the executive committee at any rate considered permissible. There was, for instance, Myrtle Behm, who was the first to react strongly. As a refugee she had been indebted to the Resistance not only for helping her to escape to Sweden but for money and clothing for members of her family who had stayed in Denmark; she was grateful too to Resistance members for risking their lives and their positions to liberate their country. She felt that she could sanction sabotage, since 'very few lives were lost through this.' 'The truth was,' she asserted, 'that factories had to be destroyed. Moreover, our instinct for self-preservation required that we should try to defend ourselves against oppression. No one demanded that members of AmK should take part in military tasks but there were many other things we could do to assist, and fortunately there were many members who had realized this and did what they could to help.'

Christensen rejected many of her arguments as 'resistance smoke-screen talk.' Certainly most of the population had been in agreement about resisting the occupying forces; the elections in 1943 were proof of that. 'Part of the resistance work, such as spreading factual information and the organization of escape routes to Sweden for both Danes and Jews, were tasks we could all engage in but with all kinds of destructive action we debased ourselves by using ... violence like the invaders.' However, Christensen did not wish to be 'unjust.' 'I know that many have acted from noble motives. I understand why some have been so indignant about the invaders' methods that they could not remain inactive. Nevertheless I am of the opinion that the means used were wrong and therefore led to other ends than those intended.'[17]

The AGM was held in Odense from 28 to 30 July. Among the subjects discussed there the organization's attitude to the Resistance movement, including the question of sabotage, figured prominently. Two local groups came forward with proposals for excluding members who had participated in armed resistance. But delegates instead passed a motion allowing the individual members concerned to make their own decisions after conferring with their local group.

If those present at the AGM imagined that discussion of the issue was now closed, they were mistaken. The debate continued for some time in the columns of AmK's paper – and with undiminished vigour. It was finally wound up at an extraordinary AGM held at Ry Folk High School from 2 to 5 January 1946. There discussion of the Resistance was introduced by two prominent AmK members, Thomas Christensen and Ewald Egelund. The former warned against any revision of AmK principles. 'If that were to happen AmK would become a nice, harmless ... movement, perhaps viewed favourably by the "powers that be" but without any really effective driving force. We have been hitherto the salt of the peace movement because of our absolutist attitude and we shall continue on that line.'[18] Egelund, for his part, urged delegates to concentrate on the question of whether the lesson that they should draw from their wartime experience was that conditions existed in which violence must be used, even in a mild form. 'Or has the war taught me that my previous conviction was indeed correct: that I in all circumstances whatsoever must abstain from the use of violence?'

After lengthy discussion, conducted 'in an atmosphere of tolerance,' the following resolution was carried unanimously: 'We are agreed that our total renunciation of war ... as expressed in our pledge, shall constitute the future foundation for our work and therefore conscientious objection must continue to be our primary objective. Since, as we have seen, Denmark was unable to use sabotage in the fight for freedom without the use of weapons, this meeting unanimously condemns the use of sabotage even when inspired by idealistic motives.' The long and fatiguing debate over AmK's position during the war had now ended with reaffirmation of the principles of the WRI. Consensus was at last achieved that membership of the AmK and participation in an armed resistance movement were incompatible with each other.

NOTES

1 This essay is based on my book *Pacifister i krig* (Odense 1990), which in turn is an expanded version of a thesis (specialafhandling) on the same subject at the University of Odense. I refer the reader to the book for more detailed information and bibliographical data. My main archival source has been the papers of Aldrig mere Krig (AmK), including minutes (protocols) of the executive committee and of the chair-

man and correspondence during the occupation between headquarters and local branches. For a personal account of the wartime experiences of a Danish pacifist, see the chapter entitled 'Pacifist i en Krigstid,' in Svend Haugaard, *Ikke ord uden gerning* (Copenhagen 1989).

2 I may mention the following names: Olaf Forchammer, Hagbard Jonassen, Axel Pille, and Poul Rosenhoff.

3 At least one other pacifist society was active in Denmark in the interwar years: the small Fellowship of Reconciliation (FOR), with a specifically Christian basis (in contrast to AmK, which had no religious qualification for membership). It possessed a journal of its own, *Fredsvarden* (Beacon of Peace), which continued to appear throughout the war. In the 1930s an association of anti-militarist clergymen was formed under the chairmanship of a prominent AmK member, Uffe Hansen. Religious denominations professing pacifism included the tiny Quaker Society of Friends. There were also Seventh-day Adventists and Jehovah's Witnesses, both of whom objected to bearing arms but did not, however, collaborate at all closely with other pacifist groups.

4 Sven Erik Larsen, *Militærnægterproblemet i Danmark 1914–1967* (Odense 1977), chap. 4.

5 Axel Pille, *Hvad soldaten lærer* (N.p.: N.d.), 5, 6. The pamphlet was published by AmK.

6 *Aldrig mere krig* (Copenhagen) (Oct. 1939), 29.

7 Ibid. (Jan. 1940), 62.

8 Ibid. (Feb. 1940), 73.

9 Ibid. (May 1940), opening paragraph of leading article.

10 The postwar relief work of Danish pacifists in such areas as Poland and northern Norway lies outside the framework of this essay. For an account of its genesis, see my book *Pacifister i krig*, chap. 9, 'Fredsvenners Hjælpearbejde.'

11 Author's interview with Svend Haugaard, 9 June 1988.

12 Probably Uffe Hansen, Amk's then chairman, but the comments are not signed.

13 See Bart de Ligt, *The Conquest of Violence: An Essay on War and Revolution*, ed. Peter van den Dungen (London 1989), 283. De Ligt's plan had been presented at the international conference of the WRI at Welwyn, England, in July 1934 and subsequently printed in his book, which appeared in a French translation in 1935 and in an English translation in 1937.

14 *Aldrig mere krig* (May 1945), 45.

15 Ibid. (June 1945), 51.

16 Ibid. 58.

17 Ibid. 68, 69.

18 *Pacifisten* (Copenhagen) (1946), 29. This was AmK's postwar journal.

25

Pacifists in Nazi-Occupied Norway

TORLEIV AUSTAD

Occupation and Resistance

When Norway was occupied by the Germans on 9 April 1940, there had been no significant military actions in the country for 220 years, apart from scattered battles on Norwegian soil in the conflicts with the British in 1807 and the Swedes in 1808 and 1814. The country's three million inhabitants could be described as a democratic and peace-loving people without proud traditions of war. During the First World War and the interwar years Norway was a neutral country. The national military defence establishment was weak and badly equipped for war. Nevertheless, the Norwegians more or less spontaneously stood up against the German soldiers when they invaded and mobilized their troops – in order to prolong a warlike situation while waiting for support from Allied forces. But the few Norwegian soldiers lacked training and equipment and were not able to withstand the onslaught of the large and efficient German military force. After eight weeks of scattered battles, military action was over. The soldiers still under arms in Norway surrendered on 10 June 1940.

But the resistance against the Germans and their Norwegian collaborators, the so-called Nasjonal Samling, or NS (National Unity), continued. It was mainly a civil resistance, which started in the autumn of 1940 and grew into a strong movement during 1941 and 1942. Its main objective was to prevent the attempted nazification of the Norwegian people. The civil resistance consisted of different organizations and groups within Norwegian society, especially the church, but also schoolteachers, parents of schoolchildren, organized sports, and various professional organizations. In a variety of ways these groups struggled against the occupying power's lies, injustice, and arbitrary use of violence. They also reacted against the strong pressure exerted on the consciences of the people by ideological uniformity and control of all information. On decisive occasions the church worked out ethical arguments for the right to undertake civil disobedience against a state that violated justice. Through public protests and actions, and without any use of violence, the resistance movement succeeded in obstructing the Germans' and the NS's nazification of the people.

Though the great majority of the Norwegian people were not pacifists, the use of violence was out of the question for civilians after the military surrender in June 1940. That made it possible for the few pacifists in the country to join the civil resistance without running into conflict with their non-violent convictions.

The Pacifists' Dilemma

The German assault was a surprise not only to Norwegians in general, but also to the country's pacifists and conscientious objectors (COs). No one was properly prepared to meet an aggressive enemy that displayed overwhelming military strength. The immediate feeling among people after the invasion was just to retaliate in kind. Patriotism was strong and was directed towards defending the country. In the new and confused situation, it was not easy to see any alternative to a military counterattack. Pacifists and COs had not developed any strategy in case of war. At the same time they realized the necessity for resistance against the Germans and their Norwegian collaborators, the 'quislings.'

For the real pacifists it was undoubtedly a difficult challenge. 'War has always been a very trying, indeed a fiery, ordeal for the idea of peace and for the friends of peace,' said the pacifist Mikael Gladhaug after the war.[1] For many pacifists the understanding of non-violence was deeply anchored in their faith and conscience. Should they now give up their convictions? Would they be strong enough to tell the people that there might be an alternative to military resistance? How should they handle the fairly widespread opinion that they in fact, because of their pacifism, supported the enemy? After the conclusion of the military conflict in the spring of 1940, the question eventually arose whether pacifists should join the civil resistance or not. Was it possible – and legitimate – for a pacifist to get involved in a movement that in principle accepted use of sabotage and which later began to cooperate with the military resistance movement? Pacifists saw no clear distinction between non-violent and violent resistance.[2] The leaders of the civil resistance did not hesitate to support the military training and resistance that developed in the second half of the occupation.

The pacifists were a variegated group, as we see below. They belonged to a number of organizations and adopted different arguments to support their pacifist views. Some appealed to religious motives, others to humanistic. A few explained their non-violent point of view primarily as a political decision. During the occupation pacifists did not possess a common leader, nor did they ever establish a common front. It was largely up to each pacifist group to work out how it should act, though at times there was some slight and informal contact among them. When peace groups ran into difficulties or were banned, or when they splintered over some issue, the individual had to decide on his or her own what to do.

The Problem of Sources

In analysing the position of pacifism in Norway during the years 1940–5 one has to take into account the fact that the country was at war with Germany. From these years we have no statistics relating to conscientious objection. We do not even know how many of the COs in 1940, just before the outbreak of the conflict, were in fact absolute pacifists. When the government mobilized in April 1940 nobody asked who did not answer the call-up and why. The turmoil then prevailing made such questions useless, and indeed they were scarcely of interest to anyone. Because the Norwegian forces surrendered after a few weeks and military defence then seemed entirely useless, the problem of pacifism did not come to the surface. Participation in the emerging civil resistance was voluntary and did not provoke any questions about who was pacifist or not. Exact information about what happened to the different pacifist groups after the German invasion is not available. It is typical that a new dictionary about the war in Norway, *Norsk Krigsleksikon 1940–45*,[3] does not contain any article about conscientious objection and pacifism.

During the Nazi occupation of Norway the press was subjected to heavy censorship, which precluded any thought of a public debate on pacifism. Organizations and groups that took a stand against war and use of violent means to solve conflicts had to be extremely cautious in handling documents such as list of members and other written information about their activities. A great deal of this archival material got lost during the war, either through destruction by the organizations themselves or through confiscation by the occupiers.

To understand the thinking and actions of pacifists at that time we refer to diaries, memoirs, and testimonies of those who were absolute pacifists during the war. Fifty years after the end of the war, such information is not easily obtained. So far the attitude of Norwegian pacifists during the years 1940–5 has not been the subject of any specific study.[4]

Two Types of Conscientious Objectors

According to the Norwegian law of 1925 concerning COs – a revised version of the law of 1922 – a man could be exempted from compulsory military service on religious, humanist, or political grounds. The number of COs during the 1930s was nevertheless very low.[5] In 1935 eighty applications for assignment to civilian service were granted out of a total of 20,545 men conscripted that year. In 1938 the number of applications had risen to 181, but in 1939 it had sunk to 165. For the years 1938–40 there are no exact figures as to how many men were conscripted for military service. The COs were given civilian duties related to agriculture and the development of new land. 'The COs seem to have felt that what they did was meaningful, and we are not aware of any serious controversies regarding the nature of alternative service before the war. We do not hear, either, of any serious disciplinary trouble until the late 1930s.'[6]

Among the COs between the two wars there were both pacifists and non-pacifist anti-militarists. The majority of the pacifists had a religious and/or humanist basis for their convictions. Most of those anti-militarists who were not also pacifist belonged to the left wing of the labour movement. With 'the broken gun' as their symbol, they were opposed to the organization of national military defence, which they understood as constituting 'class-based armed forces.'[7]

Among the political COs who were not convinced pacifists, many changed their views when war broke out, but we have no statistics on this matter. For those who had argued against military service fearing that the state might use soldiers to keep workers from effectively striking, the situation after the German attack had changed radically. They could now easily reverse their attitude towards the military. Because they were not opponents of the use of weapons as such, they felt free to reconsider their position and take part even in military actions. We do, however, possess a number of 'testimonies' by people who have come forward and told about their 'conversion' to the use of counterviolence when the Germans occupied their country. We may mention the director of public health, Karl Evang, and his brother, Wilhelm Evang, who later became a colonel. They were both COs before the war. The author Nordahl Grieg was a pacifist for a short period, but changed his position when war broke out and became actively involved in the military resistance.

Pacifist Groups

It was those COs who had been active before the war in the strictly pacifist groups who for the most part maintained their convictions during the conflict. Even though in such groups there were of course many who changed their attitude, most of the wartime pacifists came from this background – in the free churches, the Society of Friends (Quakers), the War Resisters' International, and the Women's International League for Peace and Freedom, as well as in the non-pacifist Church of Norway.

Pacifist Pastors and Theologians in the Church of Norway

Until the 1930s there were extremely few pacifists in the Church of Norway. This reflects the fact that this church, which was both a state church and a national church (Volkskirche), was loyal by and large to the authorities in its view of compulsory and universal national military service. Thus the overwhelming majority of the religious objectors, until the first law concerning COs was passed in 1922, were so-called dissenters, who belonged to the free churches and religious communities outside the Evangelical Lutheran state church.[8] And this again was the situation at the end of the 1930s.

During the 1930s, however, a pacifist wind blew over the Norwegian clergy. A number of pastors and theologians became pacifists. Also among the theological students there were many who, on a religious basis, rejected war as a means of solving conflicts among nations or groups. Some of the students would apply for postponement of their military service until after ordination; then it was simply cancelled, since pastors were exempt from military service.[9]

In April 1938, a group of pastors and theologians issued a public appeal claiming that all wars, even a defensive one, would be in violation of the spirit of Jesus Christ. Behind that appeal were prominent pacifists such as pastor Ragnar Forbech and Principal Håkon Wergeland. Professor Hans Ording at the Theological Faculty of the University of Oslo also supported the appeal. Later, in the autumn of the same year, the Norske Presters Pasifistlag (Norwegian Pastor's Pacifist Union) was formed. The group said a radical 'no' to war as a means of solving international conflicts. In March 1940 the Pastors' Pacifist Union had eighty-seven members.[10]

By this time it had become much more difficult to be a pacifist in Norway. Many pastors and theologians who had had pacifistic sympathies now became doubtful about their views. Some had changed their position under the impact of the outbreak of war in September 1939. When the Norwegian people had to take a stand with regard to the Winter War in Finland in 1939–40, it became especially obvious that the church was divided in its view of war. One of those who regretted that the church could not act unanimously and speak with one voice against war was pastor Thorleif Boman. He saw the division as 'a shame.'[11]

After the German attack on Norway the pacifists among the pastors and theologians became fewer and less outspoken. Among those who changed their positions was the conservative theologian pastor Olav Valen-Sendstad. He has told how the pacifist and CO in him died on 9 April 1940. According to his view, pacifism in that situation would have served exclusively the interests of the enemy.[12] There were many Norwegians who reasoned as he did when the occupation became a fact.

In 1953 Bishop Eivind Berggrav stated in a radio speech that 'most of the pacifism existing in Norway before 1940 disappeared as dew before the sun after 9 April.'[13] It seems clear that this was the dominant trend, but the statement is too unnuanced as a general description of what happened to the pacifists during the German occupation. We should not indeed forget that several of the pastors and theologians, who were pacifists before the war, kept their basic conviction even after the German attack on Norway – especially unconditional pacifists who based their belief on the Bible and their Christian faith. For instance, many members of the Pastors' Pacifist Union remained faithful to their pacifist convictions. So did some other pastors and theologians who had a religious-humanistic basis for their commitment to non-violence. One of these, pastor Mikael Gladhang, claims, probably correctly, that 'the genuine peace-makers' were not caught up in the psychosis of war but continued their peace work throughout the war.[14]

Andreas Seierstad, a professor at the Norwegian Lutheran School of Theology, was one of those who maintained his pacifism even during the war. But he modified it through his active participation in the civil resistance.[15] He volunteered for medical service during the battle in the Narvik area (though he was not actually sent there), and as a member of Den Midlertidige Kirkeledelse, or DMK (Provisional Church Leadership) from 1943 he cooperated with Hjemmefronten (Home Front), which did not exclude use of arms and sabotage. Seierstad of course was not the only pacifist who actively participated in the resistance movement – a position that, as we have seen, could lead to a certain toning down of pacifist absolutism.

The theologian and humanist Kristian Schjelderup had been a pacifist from his early youth. In 1927 he was among the founders of Norsk Pacifistisk Militærnegterforbund (Norwegian Union of Pacifist Conscientious Objectors). Even though this body soon ceased to function, Schjelderup remained an active pacifist. He had been strongly influenced by Mahatma Gandhi and Albert Schweitzer and argued the case for pacifism on a religious-humanistic basis. During the war Schjelderup came to realize the truth of a pre-war statement by Aldous Huxley, who had pointed out that the greatest danger in war was that it could so change us as to make us conform with the opponents we fought.[16] So, in the struggle against the anti-human forces unleashed by the war, Schjelderup repeatedly insisted that one's task as a Christian was to love one's enemies and conquer evil with good.[17] Also as a bishop after the war, he believed that people should, while offering unyielding resistance against the powers of violence, also be willing to sacrifice and suffer for basic humanistic values.

We have cited several instances in which pacifists remained faithful to their convictions during the war years. In different ways, however, many of them

took an active part in the civil resistance, without necessarily speaking out decisively against sabotage and military training 'in the woods.' In this case, of
course, they displayed modified pacifism.

Free Churches and Other Communities of Faith

As mentioned above, several of the free churches belonged to a pacifist tradition or had come under the influence of pacifism. These communities were not
large; some were quite small. We can see in them examples of a pacifism that in
some cases is based on the very foundations of their faith.

A pattern of leaving the decision on pacifism to the individual applies to the
free churches. To the extent that the pacifist view survived in these churches
during the war, it was not very visible. Before the war, for instance, the Pentecostals in Norway did not generally participate in political and party activities.
A relatively large number of them were pacifists on a Bible basis, but they have
always had local differences within their community on politics, military service, and pacifism. Pacifism was not part of Pentecostal doctrine, and in practice each individual was free to choose for himself. During the war a number
joined the resistance, in either its civilian or its military form, whereas others
found it impossible to do so because of their pacifism. So far as we know, the
pacifists among the Pentecostals kept a low profile during the occupation years;
thus it is impossible to discover how many of them remained pacifists. The
question of violent versus non-violent resistance was not a matter of debate in
their congregations at the time.

Jehovah's Witnesses form a religious community that refrains from participation in the wars of this world, and they are widely known as uncompromising
COs. Their anti-militarism, however, is not motivated entirely by pacifism. In
Norway the number of JWs rose from 348 in 1940 to around six hundred in
1945, even though their activities after a while were banned, their records confiscated, and some of their members arrested. According to the leaders of the
sect in Norway today, no Witnesses are known to have participated in any form
of military resistance during the war.

The Society of Friends (Quakers)

The Quakers' testimony against war has been a central part of their religious
message since the movement began in England about the middle of the seventeenth century. In the nineteenth and early twentieth centuries there were
Quaker youths in Norway who refused military service and were punished with
fines and prison.[18] The religiously based pacifism of this widely respected soci-

ety was one of the reasons why in 1922 Norway got a law granting exemption from military service for reasons of conscience.

At the outset of the occupation the Society of Friends in Norway had about eighty members, most of them in the Stavanger area. Its leading figure was Ole F. Olden, principal of St Svithun's School in Stavanger. He founded and edited the journal *Verden Venter* (The World Waits), which from 1931 became the official organ of the Norges Fredsforening (Peace Union of Norway). In 1937 he took the initiative in starting publication of the paper *Kvekeren* (The Quaker). During the war both papers were suppressed by the Germans. Olden was himself a convinced pacifist, but he participated nevertheless in illegal work during the war. As a result he was taken as a hostage and sent to prison; he was for a while held at Grini outside Oslo. Other Quakers were also imprisoned for certain periods of time. Among the Quakers in the Stavanger area several assisted with the evacuation in mid-April 1940 and also in relief work after the war. During the war years there was some informal contact between people from different pacifist groups, including the Society of Friends, though no organized pacifist resistance movement resulted. It is not known that any Quakers in Norway abandoned their pacifist position during the years of occupation.

In her *Norwegian Diary 1940–1945* the English Quaker Myrtle Wright, who arrived in Norway only a few days before the German invasion, writes that in general the Norwegians were not pacifists; most people supported the military resistance in 1940. Yet what made the situation somewhat tolerable for the pacifists was their opportunity to participate in the civil resistance: 'Though few, their influence was not insignificant, permeating personal contacts and also reflected in thinking which circulated through the underground press. In our situation at that time non-violence was acceptable to many non-pacifists who, by force of circumstances, had no alternative.'[19]

War Resisters' International (WRI)

A Norwegian branch of the WRI was founded in 1937 on the initiative of a former naval captain, Olaf Kullmann, and a doctor of philosophy, Lilly Heber. The organization took the Norwegian name Folkereisning mot Krig (FmK). Kullmann was a radical pacifist with roots in the 'old' pacifist-oriented peace movement as well as in the socialist war resistance. 'Late and early he preached the responsibility of the individual with regard to the voice of God in his conscience, and in this way he came to practise Christianity with an extraordinary singlemindedness,' wrote the engineer Christopher Vibe.[20] Kullmann complained that organized Christianity – the church – did not draw out the consequences in its preaching of Jesus' commandment of love of enemies and thus become pacifist. He agitated against war and Norwegian military defence, which activity led to a court case where he was sentenced to lose his position as a naval captain. This took place in 1933 while Vidkun Quisling was minister of defence![21]

In 1939 FmK had 235 members. The support was not as great as had been hoped for. When war broke out, anti-militarism soon lost strength. The leadership of the FmK continued, however, to hold debates about the current world situation and pacifism, which were regularly disturbed by 'gangs of brown shirts.' During early 1940 the FmK lost contact with its mother organization, the headquarters of which were in England; the political censorship tried to stop pacifist propaganda from abroad, especially from England. Just after the invasion of Norway, FmK printed a pamphlet appealing to Norwegian men and women not to drag their country into the bloodbath.

Still, some members of FmK gave up their pacifism and entered active armed resistance against the occupiers. Those who still adhered to the principle of unarmed resistance now found themselves in a difficult situation. What was their alternative? Though the idea of a non-violent defence had been discussed before the invasion, no preparations for systematic resistance on this basis had yet been made.[22] Several pacifists therefore chose a withdrawn, secret kind of resistance. Kullmann, however, had continued to lecture in support of pacifism, and so the Germans arrested him in late June 1941. While he was a prisoner at Grini, his release was promised on condition that he sign a declaration to desist from all peace work and never again give any lectures against war. But he refused to sign and was sent to Germany, where he died in Sachsenhausen on 9 July 1942.

Several members of the FmK were called in for interrogation and placed under arrest. Some were also tortured. None of them, however, agreed to serve Quisling. Though the organization was banned, and its financial resources were confiscated, a certain amount of underground activity still took place. The circle of those involved was not large. Everything seems to indicate that the leading persons in this milieu kept their basic pacifist attitude and remained opponents of the principle of violence. But the situation did not allow them to present their views publicly.

Among the prominent pacifists during the war was Johanne Reutz Gjemoe. She belonged to FmK and also had sympathies for the kind of Christianity practised by the Quakers. After the war she joined the Norwegian section of the Women's International League for Peace and Freedom (WILPF). In her retrospective survey of the war, she relates how she and those who thought like her took an active part in illegal activities and cooperated with 'all who worked against the Nazis and the occupying power.'[23] She points out that non-violent resistance must be thoroughly prepared beforehand if it is to have any effect and that it requires training of an intensity equal to military preparation. Her argument undoubtedly implies that the adherents of non-violence in Norway did not exert during the war the influence they might have done had they been properly prepared for a war.[24]

During early 1945, the pacifist Diderich H. Lund delivered a self-searching lecture in Enfield, England, on the resistance struggle in Norway; 'Resistance in Norway' was published as a pamphlet soon afterward. Lund was a member of the FmK and was to join the Society of Friends after the war. In the lecture he stated that many Norwegians considered pacifism 'a lazy passive acceptance of the evil power of force without active resistance.' In the existing situation, people felt that military struggle was the only way of expressing their opposition to the occupiers. Those pacifists who were unable to accept any form of armed resistance considered it their duty to take part in another form of resistance. But the question was how. Though many were actively involved in the resistance, mostly in secret, they still had 'a sense of insufficiency, feeling that they did not offer enough.'[25]

With a view to the complexity of causes that led to the war, Lund felt that 'we all bear some part of the blame.'[26] He had himself been active in the civil resistance in Norway until, after four years, he had been forced to flee the country. At the same time he made clear his belief that pacifists would have achieved more by open and uncompromising resistance; and he claimed to have had support for this view among some Norwegian pacifists. He stated bluntly that the pacifists at that time were poorly organized and 'lacked training and willingness to take up the struggle without weapons.' Most of them were not capable of acting without orders from a leader.'[27]

During the years of war members of FmK stayed in contact with the sister organization in Denmark, Aldrig mere krig, or AmK (No More War). The Danish body was significantly larger than the Norwegian, and it could work much more freely. Copies of its journal were sent to Norway but did not always reach their destination. The chairman of the FmK after the arrest of Olaf Kullmann, Christopher Vibe, often went to Denmark on business trips and was in touch with the AmK's leadership. Contacts continued throughout the war. AmK also collected money to help Norwegians who were being taken through Denmark to concentration camps in Germany, and through the Red Cross it sent gifts to Norwegian prisoners in German camps.[28]

Women's International League for Peace and Freedom (WILPF)

The WILPF was founded in The Hague in 1915, in the same year as the Norwegian group Internasjonal Kvinneliga for Fred og Frihet (IKFF), which has continued since to work for international peace and reconciliation and to oppose violence and war. In June 1940 the national board of the IKFF sent a circular letter to its local groups encouraging them not to lose courage and to work with all their strength for IKFF's ideas both 'as Norwegians and as peace-workers.' As for cooperation with Norwegian civilian or military authorities, the national board would give no general rule. 'Each should act as the situation and one's own conscience demand,' yet 'a deep and fervent love of the homeland is quite different from the primitive national feeling that expresses itself in an arrogant attitude towards other peoples.' The letter also stated that the league would emphasize 'the power of love to re-create,' and it demanded recognition and respect for the rule of law and for human worth.[29]

The Norwegian IKFF was banned in August 1940. Its office was taken over by the Germans, and documents were seized. The board had already, because of security concerns, removed or destroyed membership lists and documents about the work of IKFF. As active peace workers in an occupied country, the women committed themselves to work for relief of the distress created by the war. Moreover, many members joined the civilian non-violent resistance movement, and for such activity the IKFF's national leader, Marie Lous Mohr, was arrested in January 1943 and detained for two and a half years at Grini.

Helga Stene's initiative in organizing a parents' protest against the Nazis' attempt to introduce a compulsory ideological youth service in 1942 is an example of women's role in the ideological struggle. From August 1941 Stene had been a member of a coordination committee for the women's organizations that had 'gone underground' (they numbered seven hundred to eight hundred members). The leaders of the Home Front were initially sceptical as to the idea of a parents' protest against the youth service but soon changed their position and supported the campaign. In a letter to the Nazi authorities the parents had stated that they did not wish their children to participate in the youth service because that would violate their consciences. The text of the letter was spread among parents by means of couriers, who used different channels from the net of distribution that the Home Front used. Within a few days the relevant NS department received more than 200,000 protest letters. This seems to indicate that 60 to 70 per cent of all parents participated. The campaign was indeed successful; it became impossible for NS to carry out its plan to give a Nazi education to all Norwegian youth between the ages of ten and seventeen.[30] Though protests from bishops and teachers also had some effect, it was the parents' non-violent campaign that definitively ended this attempt at nazification.

Little research has been done on the contribution made by women to the ideological struggle during the war years. There are many indications that women then, as today, were in general more critical of the war industry and the use of arms than men. Johanne Reutz Gjermoe, for instance, argues that 'women by nature are more concerned with keeping and protecting life and feel a larger responsibility with regard to the well-being of their environment than men in general do.'[31]

Conclusion

The dilemma of pacifists in Nazi-occupied Norway was a hidden problem. The situation made it impossible to discuss publicly whether the German assault should be met by violent or by non-violent means, and there was no law or regulator that could, as it were, register those who were pacifists. It was obvious that Norwegian pacifists were not trained for this kind of situation, nor had they developed any non-violent strategy for resistance against an occupying power. Pacifists had mostly to decide individually how to meet the aggression of the Germans and the NS. Despite certain contacts among pacifists from different groups, a common pacifist front never emerged.

The great majority of political COs from the interwar years changed their views when war came. The same happened with some of the pacifists too; many now gave their support to violent resistance against the occupation authorities. Certainly, under the psychological pressures generated after the German invasion and the Germans' attempt to reorganize the country with the help of the NS, it was not at all easy for Norwegians to be pacifists. Those who remained convinced pacifists came easily under suspicion of supporting the enemy. Their situation was further complicated by the fact that Norwegians generally did not distinguish between violent and non-violent resistance.

Pacifist convictions did not prove an obstacle to individuals' participating in wartime resistance. Because resistance involved mainly attitudes and actions directed against nazification, pacifists could join the movement without denying their consciences. Many pacifists engaged in protests and actions against injustice and lawlessness in society, against arbitrary violence and persecution, and against the forcing of conscience and the imposition of national socialist uniformity. All the same, however, pacifists struggled with the feeling that they did not do enough. They suffered under the lack of a conscious common strategy on non-violence. It is difficult to know whether pacifists felt any dilemmas of conscience when the civil resistance gradually established cooperation with the military resistance. But available sources suggest that it did not cause them major problems. We are at least aware of a certain flexibility among the pacifists. Many of them modified their attitudes in practice and were active in the resistance, but without giving up their fundamental pacifist convictions.

Those who remained pacifists throughout the war had indeed deep and well-founded reasons for their rejection of violence. Their pacifism was an integral part of their faith or Weltanschauung. Among these people a majority had specific Christian or Christian-humanist motives. But there were also a few pacifists who may be described as idealists on a purely humanist basis. We do not know the total number of pacifists in Norway during these years, mainly because they were not registered as such or organized as a common non-violent front. Though few in number, pacifists exerted a not insignificant influence within the resistance. As anti-Nazis, and through personal contacts, underground works, and relief actions, they participated in the protests and actions against the German occupiers and NS. More women seem to have sympathized with the non-violent outlook than had been directly involved in the peace movement before the war. Most women who participated in the civil resistance did so without taking into account who was a pacifist and who was not.

NOTES

1 Mikael Gladhaug, *Den kristne fredstanken* (Oslo 1953), 198.
2 Magne Skodvin, 'Den norske ikkevoldelige motstanden under den tyske okkupasjonen,' in Adam Roberts, ed., *Hele folket i forsvar* (Oslo 1969), 62–95, especially 64.
3 Hans Fredrik Dahl, Guri Hjeltnes, Berit Nøkleby, Nils Johan Ringdal, and Øystein Sørensen, eds., *Norsk Krigsleksikon 1940–45* (Oslo 1995).
4 But cf. for Denmark Peter Kragh Hansen, *Pacifister i krig* (Odense 1990), and chapter 24, above.
5 *Verneplikt* (Conscription): *Norges Offentlige Utredninger 1979* (Oslo), no. 51 (1979), 171.
6 Nils Petter Gleditsch and Nils Ivar Agøy, 'From Conscientious Objection to Conversion? The History and Sociology of Conscientious Objection in Norway,' paper prepared for the International Symposium on International Perspectives on Conscientious Objection, Utrecht, Netherlands, 23–7 March, 1990, 6.
7 Ibid., 13.
8 Agøy, '"Kampen mot vernetvangen". Militærnekterspørsmålet i Norge 1885–1922,' history thesis, University of Oslo, 1987, 321–3.
9 Svein Brurås, *Arthur Berg* (Oslo 1987), 37, 38.
10 Gustav Dietrichson, Jr, 'Kristendom og krig,' *Norsk Kirkeblad* (Oslo), 37 no. 5 (March 1940), 110, 111.
11 Thorleif Boman, 'Kristendom og krig,' ibid., 37 no. 4 (Feb. 1940), 86.
12 Olav Valen-Sendstad, *Kan en kristen være soldat? Pasifismen og Bibelen* (Oslo 1952), 5–7.
13 Eivind Berggrav, *Kristendom og forsvar* (Oslo 1953), 4.

14 Gladhaug, *Den kristne fredstanken*, 198.
15 Author's interview with Seierstad's son, Ivar, on 1 Nov. 1995.
16 Kristian Schjelderup, *Veien jeg måtte gå* (Oslo 1962), 84.
17 Schjelderup, *Guds hus i fangeleiren* (Oslo 1946), 109–17.
18 Wilhelm Aarek, 'Vennenes Samfunn, Kvekerne,' in Peder Borgen and Brynjar Haraldsø, eds., *Kristne kirker og trossamfunn* (Trondheim 1993), 273–85, especially 277. See also Peter Brock, *The Quaker Peace Testimony, 1660 to 1914* (York, England, 1990), chap. 21 ('Norwegian Quakers, Conscription and Emigration').
19 Myrtle Wright, *Norwegian Diary, 1940–1945* (London 1974), 51.
20 Christopher Vibe, 'Olaf Kullmann,' *Aldrig mere krig* (Copenhagen), 12 no. 8 (Aug. 1945).
21 Christine Amadou, 'Krigsmotstand i mørke tider,' *Ikkevold* (Oslo), no. 1 (Feb. 1987).
22 Tormod Bakke and Tom Nilsen, eds., *Ikkevold – teori og praksis* (Oslo 1987), 11.
23 Johanne Reutz Gjermoe, *For likeverd og fred* (Oslo 1983), 95.
24 Ibid., 94.
25 Diderich Lund, *Resistance in Norway* (Enfield, England, 1945), 2.
26 Ibid., 3.
27 Ibid., 5. Diderich's wife, Sigrid, also a pacifist (she became a Quaker in 1947), displayed great courage in helping to bring refugee Jewish children across the border into Sweden in 1942 – a fine example of pacifist resistance under occupation. See Ingeborg Olden Walters's biographical sketch of her in Hans Eirik Aarek et al., eds., *Quakerism – A Way of Life: In Homage to Sigrid Helliesen Lund on Her 90th Birthday* (Ås 1982), 11–15.
28 Hansen, *Pacifister*, 31, 32, 63, 64. See also Hansen's essay, chapter 24, above.
29 *Norsk gruppe av Internasjonal Kvinneliga for Fred og Frihet 1915–1940*, publication in commemoration of IKFF's eightieth anniversary, April 1995, 35–44.
30 Helga Stene, 'Da mødrene gjorde apprør,' *Aftenposten* (Oslo), 20 March 1967.
31 Reutz Gjermoe, *For likeverd*, 116.

26

For Church and Peace: Dutch Christian Pacifists under Nazi Occupation

HENK VAN DEN BERG AND TON COPPES

Among the most active Christian pacifist organizations that emerged after the First World War was the Dutch Kerk en Vrede (Church and Peace) which came into being in 1924. Its members committed themselves to a total renunciation of war; and its program included support for conscientious objectors (COs) and close collaboration with such radical pacifist bodies as the International Union of Anti-Militarist Ministers and Clergymen. Membership rose fairly rapidly to reach a peak of 9,143 in 1932. Though numbers declined during the stormy 1930s, when those leaving included several prominent activists, the figure still stood as high as 5,589 on the eve of the German invasion of May 1940. The majority of members were lay persons, but a considerable number of Protestant clergymen also joined. Only a few Catholics, however, joined the society; it was in fact an almost exclusively Protestant group.

Church and Peace during the interwar years enjoyed the active support of several outstanding Protestant clergymen. Most notable of these was the well-known theologian Gerrit Jan Heering, author of the *De zondeval van het Christendom* (The Fall of Christianity, 1929), a learned but highly readable defence of Christian pacifism that went through several editions and was widely studied in Protestant circles, both in and outside the Netherlands.[1] Alongside Heering, two other clergymen, Johannes Hugenholtz[2] and J.J. Buskes, provided effective and intelligent leadership of the society. While Hugenholtz was pre-eminently an organizer, Buskes's special talent lay in popularizing the idea of pacifism.

When the Second World War broke out, the society had already come to realize the demonic character of Germany's National Socialism and the threat that it posed for the Netherlands as well as for other countries. But in opposing this threat and in resisting Nazism, to which task Church and Peace felt itself called,

---

Translated from the Dutch by Solomon E. Yoder.

use of violence was not acceptable, and the society continued its faith in non-violence throughout the period of Nazi occupation.[3] In this essay we look at its two phases of activity – it functioned legally till March 1941 and illegally thereafter until the liberation – and then compare its actions with those of the Protestant churches.

Legal Activity, May 1940–March 1941

In May 1940 the German armies invaded the Netherlands; for Church and Peace this assault was not entirely unexpected. The society, however, had failed to develop a plan of action to cope with this event; the maintenance of Christian anti-militarism now became dependent on the strength of conscience of its individual members. For these people the society's journal, *Kerk en Vrede* (Church and Peace), which continued to appear during the first phase of the occupation, acquired great value in upholding their spirits. The journal had commenced publication in May 1925; fourteen numbers appeared between May 1940 and March 1941 (when the last one was published). Its size during occupation was usually four pages – half the pre-invasion length, and Buskes now contributed most of the articles. In this period we do not find any discussions; the ranks were closed. But we do see an attempt to strengthen the society's members in their pacifist convictions – for example, in the series of articles by one member, A. Wartena, entitled 'Bijbel en Oorlog' (Bible and War), which emphasized the biblical foundations of Christian anti-militarism.[4]

The occupying forces imposed restrictions on the press. Several days after the capitulation of the Netherlands on 14 May the Germans instituted a repressive censorship, which forbade publication of news unfavourable to Germany as well as news from countries with which it was at war. In addition, the General Netherlands Press Bureau became a German propaganda instrument; Jewish members of its staff were dismissed, and people well-disposed towards Germany were appointed to take charge of the bureau.[5]

While Church and Peace did nothing forbidden, it refrained from doing what it considered unacceptable – namely, making use of a news service friendly to Germany. *Kerk en Vrede* therefore abandoned reporting of current events. Earlier on such events had received little coverage, except from a Christian anti-militarist standpoint. After May 1940, however, the journal was filled with more abstract reflections.

In our treatment of the society's attitude towards the occupying forces we focus on two aspects – its anti-Nazism and its continued anti-militarism. Church and Peace's rejection of National Socialism was inspired by its Christian faith: the totalitarian claims of the German ideology conflicted with the demands of God, to whom Christians must be obedient. We encounter this idea in the first issue of *Kerk en Vrede* published after the German invasion: 'He [the Christian] shall obey ... the governing authorities ... giving to Caesar what belongs to Caesar, but to God what belongs to God.' It was in obedience to faith that the Dutch must preserve their identity: 'A people in whom faith and conscience rule ... , such a people compels *respect*, such a people exerts *influence* on its surroundings, such a people holds its own because God *protects* it. Such a people does not go astray.'[6]

We now examine two examples of this attitude: the society's rejection of the 'Blut und Boden' (Blood and Soil) theory with its consequent anti-semitism, and Buskes's response to a key speech by Anton Mussert, the leader of the National Socialist Movement in the Netherlands.

Church and Peace had followed German anti-semitism critically and with disapproval before May 1940. After the invasion it feared that a similar anti-semitism would develop in the Netherlands. Faithfulness to the gospel, however, would, it believed, prevent this: 'Whoever allows the Gospel to be shut up inside the church and home ... will later on also stand guilty of letting Race and Blood be substituted for Justice and Love,' wrote Heering in August 1940.[7] After the first anti-semitic measures were introduced in the autumn of 1940 Buskes declared that a distinction between Jew and non-Jew was not recognized in Netherlands law and was unacceptable to a humane way of thought.[8] It was precisely thinking in terms of the gospel that would be a guarantee against the glorification of soil and race.[9] As far as Church and Peace was concerned: 'We Christians must reject and fight unconditionally every absolutization of Nation, Blood and Soil.'[10]

In September 1940 Mussert had stated in one of his speeches that Hitler's military success could be explained only by God's blessing, which purportedly rested on Hitler. For a believing people such as the Dutch, this was all the more reason, Mussert declared, to close ranks behind the Führer. Buskes became very angry. Even if Mussert might have a right to speak on world events, he of all people should not draw the Christian faith into the discussion. Buskes poured scorn on the 'Success is blessing' formula (what should one think of Stalin's success?) and strongly condemned Mussert's anti-semitism. And he went on to brand the Nazi's way of thinking as an 'atrocious heresy.' In the gospels, argued Buskes, there was no mention anywhere of God's blessing on success in an earthly sense, let alone a military one.[11]

This article (signed 'J.J.B. Jr.') was disseminated widely in pamphlet form.[12] Its distribution was eventually to become the excuse for the liquidation of Church and Peace. Buskes's article gives us an insight into Church and Peace's position – the society appealed for spiritual resistance, for maintaining one's own Christian identity in the face of National Socialism. Such resistance included condemnation of racist ideology and of the views expressed in Mussert's speech.

In this way *Kerk en Vrede*, though appearing legally, displayed some of the characteristics of the growing underground press, which encouraged people to have faith in themselves and their own spiritual principles. Despite the emphasis on spiritual resistance, the illegal publications expressed great anger at the German invasion and displayed a strongly anti-German attitude, a revulsion against Nazism, and hatred towards the Dutch National Socialists.[13] We do not find the first two elements in *Kerk en Vrede* (though we should not forget the repressive censorship), but there is revulsion against National Socialism; towards the Dutch collaborators the paper displayed not so much hatred as condescension and sarcasm.

There was continuity with Church and Peace's pre-invasion anti–National Socialism, based on Christian principles, just as there was in its anti-militarism. Naturally many members had problems with its complete rejection of the violence involved in war (after 1945 it would be seen that membership had fallen). Even members of the executive committee had their doubts, because all around them they saw the increasing suppression and the Nazi terror, which some of them even experienced themselves. They too longed for liberation, but the means to achieve it, the violence of war, was unacceptable to them as Christians. Thus, whenever they pictured that violence concretely in the form of bombings, gun-fire, and battles, they saw its irreconcilability with the gospels.[14] Again it was clear that the theological basis of Christian anti-militarism provided a firm foundation for the rejection of all war. Starting from a strongly Christocentric view, members' faith in the kingdom of God and their awareness of God's sovereignty formed the determining factors in the ideology of Church and Peace. To this way of thinking the violence of war was unacceptable, whether from the Allied or from the German side.[15]

There were few possibilities of giving practical form to Christian anti-militarism. The society's former concrete aims – support for the League of Nations and for conscientious objection and the pursuit of national disarmament – had naturally lost their meaning, at any rate for the time being, as its adherents understood very well. But they wanted to remain true to their primary task – witnessing to the irreconcilability of war and the gospels.[16] With this end in view the society alone sought to preserve intact the basic principle of anti-militarism.[17]

Remaining true to antimilitarism meant keeping alive a Christian spirit – not giving way to hatred or to violent thoughts.[18] In addition, members were to distance themselves from 'the lies of our time, such as Folk and Race, Nationalism and Patriotism, which, ... exploited in a propagandistic way, are becoming new forms of worship.' The proclamation of Christian anti-militarism and its application were in the first place to be the task of the ministers in Church and Peace, who were still permitted some freedom of speech from the pulpit.[19]

Since Church and Peace openly opposed both National Socialism and militarism, its liquidation was only to be expected. One occupation official claimed that Church and Peace's open opposition to National Socialism was the reason for its dissolution;[20] but others have argued that its Christian anti-militarism was really the key reason, since all Dutch peace organizations were suppressed at the same time.[21] There is no archival material to make a definitive statement on this matter. It seems to us that perhaps neither factor was alone sufficient cause but that the combination was decisive.

In any case, on 20 March 1941 two officials of the occupying power came to the secretariat of Church and Peace (located in the house of Hugenholtz in Ammerstol) and declared the society dissolved and its property confiscated. The office was locked and sealed. Most of the branch secretariats were also visited that day and declared dissolved.[22] With this action Church and Peace had ceased to exist as a legal organization.

Illegal Activity, April 1941–May 1945

After March 1941 no action was undertaken by the society acting as a whole. However, three levels of activity continued. Members of the executive committee, who still met regularly, did send a number of circular letters out to kindred spirits; some branches still met; and various members performed acts of resistance on an individual basis.

The executive committee met every month during the war years. This, however, became harder in the autumn of 1944, when travel in general was made more difficult by the railway strike against the occupiers. These meetings discussed the questions: 'What should be our position during the war years?' and 'Afterwards, what?'

On the first question, a four-page document entitled 'Richtlijnen' (Guidelines) is definitive. It dates probably from 1942 and is unsigned, but we may assume that it was written by Heering. For whom it was intended we do not know, but the limited number of copies circulated (the piece is typed, not stencilled) suggests that only the small circle of the executive committee saw it.

The author concentrates on rejection of war on the basis of Christian ethics. He warns against lapsing into hatred and revenge, because then acceptance of warmaking would be inevitable. We should try to imagine the waging of war not as an abstraction but as something concrete. Faith and trust, he adds, would be needed for an isolated Christian anti-militarist to exist in the midst of the people of the Netherlands while at the same time continuing to feel a part of them. The author does not pursue this last point further; possibly he is referring here to helping Jews or other fellow citizens threatened by the Nazis.

The issuing of circular letters formed a further activity of the executive committee. Signed by name, these were distributed among Church and Peace members and other kindred spirits.[23] Estimates of numbers printed vary appreciably – somewhere between five thousand and ten thousand copies. In all ten numbers appeared between April 1941 and December 1944. In content they are in consonance with the 'Guidelines,' with the same rejection of the violence of war as well as the same emphasis on the Christian spirit of mercy instead of hatred. For example, Heering argued in a Christian message for 1941 that a new peace must be built on law and justice in international relations.

Just what function did these letters serve? First, their distribution continued the proclamation of the principle of Christian anti-militarism, even outside the circle of Church and Peace itself. The range of circulation was quite large, certainly when we assume that each copy had more than one reader. Second, they formed a link between the executive committee and members. Third and finally, the letters provided uplift, support, and inspiration to members through their tone and their emphasis on faith as something to hold on to in trying times.

No archival material about the local functioning of Church and Peace under the occupation is extant. We can therefore give only a fragmentary and incomplete picture of what the branches were doing.

On 20 March 1941, at the same time as the general secretariat, many branch secretariats were closed and their inventories confiscated. But in some places (as in Amsterdam) no official appeared to carry out this task. And even after dissolution, meetings continued in many cases to take place, often with more than the permitted twenty participants. On several occasions members of the executive committee gave lectures (for example, Hugenholtz in The Hague at the end of 1941), but we know nothing of their contents.[24]

In some places, while these meetings had supportive value for members, no attempt at organizing resistance activities was made. Elsewhere it was precisely in such gatherings that members tried to reach a consensus on such matters as whether or not to sign the occupiers' so-called Aryan declaration or to contribute to the Nazi-inspired Winterhulp (Winter Help). The meetings also afforded an opportunity to exchange underground addresses and to discuss the possibilities of helping Jews. Most members participated in such work, and to this end ministers would often counterfeit church documents. From the pulpit, listeners were reminded that they should cooperate as little as possible with the measures of the governing authorities, especially those pertaining to the Jews.[25]

As a whole the branches did not have many contacts with other groups, though there were individual contacts. Buskes cooperated with the illegal periodical *Vrij Nederland* (Free Netherlands). Members of Church and Peace also cooperated with 'De Vonk' (The Spark), a socialist group advocating non-violence, which published an illegal paper of that name. But 'De Vonk' did not reject all violence: it considered the Allies' use of force in the present war acceptable because a military victory over Nazi Germany formed a necessary step for the liberation of the people. Church and Peace's closest contacts, however, were with the Broederschap in Christus (Brotherhood in Christ), which formed the Dutch section of the International Fellowship of Reconciliation (IFOR); Hugenholtz acted as contact between Church and Peace and the brotherhood.[26] These contacts were to play a role in the refounding of Church and Peace in 1946 as the Dutch section of the IFOR.

On the resistance activities of Church and Peace there are few archival materials, but a closer look at individual members can provide some insight. For instance, Buskes's resistance activities covered a wide range, while other members acted against the National Socialists by preaching, aiding Jews, or practising various forms of anti-militarist behaviour.

Before May 1940 Buskes was the man within Church and Peace who had fought National Socialism the most fervently. He continued to do so after the German invasion in *Kerk en Vrede* but also in the body that became known as the Inter-Kerkelijk-Overleg, or IKO (Inter-Church Consultation). The IKO met first on 15 June 1940; almost all Protestant churches participated. Its aim was to forge a united stand by the churches vis-à-vis the occupying authorities.

As representative of the Gereformeerde Kerken in Hersteld Verband (Reformed Churches in Restored Union), Buskes was active in the IKO. After the first anti-semitic measures, Buskes presented on 11 October 1940 a memorandum to the IKO, on the basis of which that group decided to write to the German high commissioner, Seyss-Inquart. In this letter the Protestant churches protested in the spirit of the gospels against the measures that affected Jews. The contents of this protest were made known two days later in the form of a message from the pulpits of the Nederlands Hervormde Kerke (Netherlands Reformed Church).

It was Buskes alone who in the IKO gave support to a proposal from the

Remonstrant pastor Revd F. Kleijn in August 1942, after deportation of Jews had begun, accompanied by cruel round-ups. Kleijn proposed that in case of a round-up the Nieuwe Kerk on the Dam in Amsterdam should be proclaimed a place of refuge and that ministers in their clerical garb would guard the entrance doors. Like the other members of the IKO, Buskes too did not believe that such an action would save any Jewish lives, but he still gave it his support because he considered such an act a demonstration, a witness, of the greatest possible significance.[27]

In his illegal brochure entitled *Ons kind in gevaar* (Our Child in Danger) Buskes condemned National Socialism in harsh terms, and he warned against its intrusion via its influence on education. The school boards, supported by teachers and parents, must, he insisted, refuse to carry out such directives.[28] Buskes had several other anti-Nazi publications to his name.

The cause of his first arrest was an article in a bi-monthly periodical, *Woord en Wereld* (Word and World) of April 1941, which clearly rejected National Socialism in general and anti-semitism in particular. His arrest followed on 2 July 1941; his imprisonment lasted two months. In 1943 Buskes was once more imprisoned and interrogated, this time on suspicion of helping Jews, but he was again released very soon.[29] His last arrest occurred in 1944 because of 'illegal action,' presumably helping Jews, and lasted around half a year. After a month in prison in Amsterdam, he was transferred to the hostage camp in St Michielsgestel.[30] Preaching to a full church, he had denounced National Socialism and the occupying authorities and their measures in unambiguous terms, and this was probably one of the reasons for his final imprisonment.[31]

Several other ministers belonging to Church and Peace preached in the same outspoken way. Touw, in his history of the resistance activities of the Reformed Church, gives the names of twenty-four Reformed ministers arrested for public display of their opposition to National Socialism. Of this group, besides Buskes, N. Padt of Zutphen and J.W Nieuwenhuyzen of Nijmegen were also members of Church and Peace.[32] Moreover, among the six ministers who did not survive the persecution caused by their preaching was the Church and Peace member J.W.B. Cohen.[33]

N. Padt, who was born in 1886, after his theological study received a call as a Reformed minister in Zutphen. From the founding of Church and Peace he was a member of its executive committee. He was the first Reformed minister to be arrested, on 28 June 1940; he was accused of anti-Nazi preaching on the basis of stenographic reports of his sermons, some of them preached before May 1940. After six weeks in a cell in Emmerich he was released. On 8 October 1942 he was arrested again, for his intercessory prayer on behalf of Queen Wilhelmina and for his alleged communist sympathies. Until the end of May 1945

Padt remained in prison, first in Arnhem, then in Amersfoort, and finally in the German concentration camp at Dachau.

J.W. van Nieuwenhuyzen, born in 1913, studied theology in Leiden. Originally Reformed, he later joined the Remonstrant Brotherhood. It was probably in 1938 that he joined Church and Peace; but only after the war did he become a member of its executive committee. In a sermon of 19 July 1942 he explicitly denounced the measures against Dutch Jews while offering a vigorous intercessory prayer for the queen. It is not clear how long he remained in prison.

J.W.B. Cohen was one of the few Reformed ministers of Jewish descent. Born in 1904 in Amsterdam, he studied theology in Utrecht and became a minister in 1930. By 1935 he was already a member of Church and Peace. A fiery speaker, his preaching was little concerned with theology; his tone rather was subjective, naïve, and prophetically radical. Combined with his anti-Nazi mentality, this created problems for him. After an earlier interrogation by the 'Sicherheitsdienst' (Security Service), on 15 June 1941 he preached on the text: 'We ought to obey God rather than men' (Acts 5:29). Then followed his arrest on 22 July 1941, interrogation and imprisonment, first in Leeuwarden and then in Dachau. Probably Cohen was put to death by gassing or injection; the official date was given as 23 May 1942, and the cause of death, pneumonia and heart disease. His Jewish descent must have been partly responsible for his imprisonment and death.[34]

As for Revd M. Hinlopen, also a member of Church and Peace, it was not because of the content of his sermons that he was arrested, probably in the autumn of 1941, but because of the anti-Nazi tendency of his church newsletter. His imprisonment lasted approximately one year.

Besides giving anti-Nazi sermons, Church and Peace members helped Jews. Reformed Church minister J.J. Wentink was active in this way without being prosecuted for it. But Johannes Hugenholtz was indeed arrested and sentenced. (Of the Reformed Church ministers at least sixty went to prison for assisting Jews; most received a term of a half-year or longer.) We do not know exactly when Hugenholtz was arrested, but in November 1943 he was in prison. In all he spent nine months in detention, two of them in Amsterdam and the rest in Vught.[35] After his release he did not sit idle: he continued to give help to Jews in the form of food and money.[36]

Persecution because of specifically anti-militarist activities did not affect Church and Peace to any great extent. Circular letters proclaimed the Christian anti-militarist witness circumspectly. Only with the seventh letter, written by Krijn Strijd, a prominent minister of the Reformed church, did matters go wrong. This document appeared in August 1942, and two reprints quickly followed, with seven thousand copies in total. The occupying forces intervened in September 1942 by arresting the three persons responsible – Krijn Strijd, author; the poet Jan Bosdriesz, distributor; and C. Elsgeest, printer. Perhaps the fact that the copies were sent in an open envelope with Bodriesz's name and address on them brought the letter to the attention of the authorities.[37] Bos-driesz had distributed the letter, acting in the name of the Brotherhood in Christ (IFOR), of which he was now chairman. Elsgeest, who was born in 1907, was a printer by trade and an amateur theologian. After reading Heer-ing's *Zondeval* (Fall of Christianity) when it first appeared he had decided to join Church and Peace, and he also became a member of the IFOR. During the war he was the printer of the circular letters, and he gave shelter to Jews in hiding; after 1945 he served on the executive committee of Church and Peace. His arrest because of Strijd's letter was followed by his imprisonment for six weeks.

Strijd too was interrogated at length several times; he made no secret of his Christian anti-militarist criticism of German aggression as well as of National Socialist ideology. He was sentenced to six months in a concentration camp, which he spent in Amersfoort and Vught. After an unfavourable report on his conduct, his punishment was extended for an indeterminate period, but at the end of September 1943 he was released.[38]

Of the three Bosdriesz faired worst. Born in 1901, he was before 1940 the organizational pivot of the Brotherhood group in Amsterdam and also treasurer of the Church and Peace branch there. His prison term would have expired by April 1943, but he too was punished by its extension for an indeterminate period on account of bad conduct. On 5 September 1944 Bosdriesz was put on a transport and sent to the concentration camp at Sachsenhausen. The following May he was liberated by the British, but the state of his health was by then so poor that he survived by only a few days, dying on 20 May 1945 in an English military hospital in Rothenburg.[39]

'Church and Peace' and the Protestant Response to Nazi Occupation

In the first phase of the occupation the Protestant churches in general took a fairly aloof position; Van Roon[40] sees in this stance a revival of the churches' prewar neutralism regarding Hitler's Germany. However, several persons inside the church organizations exerted pressure to adopt a more radical stance against the occupying forces.

As for Church and Peace, it differentiated itself in this first period of occupa-tion – for the society, the 'legal' phase – from the churches by cautiously offer-ing spiritual resistance. Before May 1940 Church and Peace had pointed out clearly the unchristian character and consequent dangers of National Socialism in terms of its own Christian faith and anti-militarism.

After the early months of occupation the churches began to take a firmer line. In the course of 1941 the two largest Protestant denominations came into conflict with the occupying forces. Opposing the German aim of enforcing conformity, the churches came to a clear rejection of the totalitarian state and racial ideology. Defending their own domain, they brooked no interference in church services, in church finances, and in Christian upbringing and education.[41]

Often the churches spoke through the IKO, though differences of opinion sometimes led to different responses, especially with respect to defence of Jews and conscription of labour.[42] But many ministers spoke out against National Socialism or against certain other measures of the occupying forces. This gave the church members comfort and inspiration in their trying situation, because it was from the church pulpit that things could be said openly which were left unsaid elsewhere.[43]

Minister members of Church and Peace did not shirk from this kind of pulpit witness. But on two points the general tenor of Protestant preaching differed from the pulpit preaching of clergymen who belonged to Church and Peace. The former quite often exhibited a nationalistic slant, which Church and Peace members sought to avoid. Moreover Church and Peace people felt that the churches were not sensitive enough to the anti-Christian character of the violence inherent in war itself.

Church and Peace in its legal period warned against too strong a nationalism. Its resistance should be inspired not by nationalism but by Christianity: the kingdom of God must not be equated with the kingdom of the Netherlands. Still, its ministers' preaching could be construed in a nationalistic sense by congregations listening with 'nationalistically attuned ears.'

Buskes wrote in 1947: 'If we are asked the question what essentially was the attitude of the church toward waging war, we can give no other answer than that the church failed.' Heering, too, after the liberation agreed that the churches had failed by keeping silent about the violence of war.[44]

During the war such thoughts had already been expressed clearly – for instance, in a protest letter sent by Strijd to the general synod of the Reformed church in response to a joint Advent message of the Protestant churches in November 1944. This message, which was to be read from the pulpit on the first or second Sunday of Advent, stated that death and destruction were then going on which did not form part of waging war and constituted a violation of the duty to behave humanely. For even in the 'most gruesome' war, this commandment could not be violated with impunity. In the expectation of the coming of the Kingdom of God, the churches' Advent message called for steadfastness in faith and closed with the words: 'He shall liberate the needy, crush those who oppress.'[45]

In his letter to the synod,[46] Strijd protested vigorously against the message, for, he wrote, violation of humaneness, death, and destruction cannot be separated from the waging of war, certainty not in the case of a total war, for they belong to the very essence of war. Furthermore he saw in the letter an attempt at a Christian justification for the powerful anti-German feelings of hatred that were widespread among the Dutch people. He enumerated those matters which, in his view, were absent from the message – a confession by the churches that by their failure to reject war they had become accessories to the unleashing of war, a declaration that in the future the churches would never again sanction war, an unconditional protest against the waging of war under any pretext (by the British and Americans too), an unequivocal protest against National Socialism and persecution of Jews, and finally an appeal to each and all to decide their position regarding war according to what they believed was God's will.

Strijd's letter indicates clearly the biggest difference between the Protestant churches of the Netherlands and Church and Peace – namely, on the point of anti-militarism. In summary, we can say that Church and Peace during the first phase of the occupation was better prepared for the situation; thus it was able to offer spiritual resistance to National Socialism earlier than were the churches. Later the churches and Church and Peace began to think and act along the same lines in this regard, especially in their preaching. At this stage the essentially ecclesiastical character of Church and Peace became clear. For precisely in their functioning as churchmen its clerical members gave the most visible form to their organization's resistance. But its maintenance of Christian anti-militarism prevented complete agreement with the churches.

Conclusion

Anti-militarism and anti-Nazism, both rooted in Christian conviction, formed the points of departure for Church and Peace in May 1940. Did its opposition to militarism, we may ask, prevent it from offering resistance against National Socialism? Both the attitude and the activities of Church and Peace and its members soon became directed against the occupying forces, their policies, and above all their ideology. Because of its Christian anti-militarism, however, Church and Peace resisted in a consciously non-violent character.

An almost complete lack of organized activity characterized the society during the years of occupation. In fact, Church and Peace aimed first at an individual, a spiritual resistance against the violation of conscience by National Socialism or the ideology of violence. The basis for this resistance was provided by its belief in Christian anti-militarism, and this belief resulted in practical acts such as aiding Jews and outspoken preaching. True, non-violent resistance was also offered by others – the churches, for example – but usually this did not stem from a conscious choice made from a position of principle.

Use of violence in all its modern and brutal forms was historically necessary to fight the Second World War, in which the spiritual values of law and justice were at stake, so Buskes was to write in December 1945.[47] But for him, as for Church and Peace as a whole, the claims of the Kingdom of God had taken precedence over the historical necessity of this world.

NOTES

1 See J.H. Rombach's entry on G.J. Heering in Harold Josephson, ed., *Biographical Dictionary of Modern Peace Leaders* (Westport, Conn., 1985), 392. The Garland Library of War and Peace includes a facsimile reprint (New York 1972), with a new introduction by Walter F. Bense, of Heering's seminal work, first published in Dutch in 1929 and in English translation in 1930 as *The Fall of Christianity: A Study of Christianity, the State and War.*

2 See Peter van den Dugen's entry on Hugenholtz in Josephson, ed., *Biographical Dictionary*, 430–2.

3 The account that follows of the activities of Church and Peace under Nazi occupation is excerpted from our book *Dominees in het geweer: Het christen-antimilitarisme van Kerke en Vrede 1924–1950* (Nijmegen 1982), 171–203. The book appeared as Nos. 22–3 in the series Cahier, published by the Studiecentrum voor Vredesvraagstukken (Centre for Peace Studies); we have used here the second, expanded printing of June 1982. Sections of the text on these pages were based on interviews with wartime members and associates of Church and Peace. We must refer readers to the original text for further details.

4 *Kerk en Vrede* (Ammerstol) (cited hereafter as *KeV*), 17 no. 1, 15 Jan. 1941, 4. Information concerning the number of copies of the paper printed during this period is not available. But, given that in May 1940 there were 5,587 members of Church and Peace, it is reasonable to suppose that about six thousand copies were normally printed. As many as fifty thousand copies of the special Christmas 1940 number were distributed with the help of the organization's branches.

5 L. de Jong, *Het Koninkrijk der Nederlanden in de Tweede Wereldoorlog*, 14 vols. (The Hague, 1969–91), 4:612.

6 J.J. Buskes, 'Ons vertrouwen,' *KeV*, 16 no. 9, 7 June 1940, 73, 74. Buskes wrote the article, but it was signed by all members of the executive committee of Church and Peace.

7 G.J. Heering, 'Kerk en Vrede en haar getuigenis,' *KeV*, 16 no. 12, 31 Aug. 1940, 83.

8 Buskes, 'Kerk en Vrede in dezen tijd,' ibid., 16 no. 14, 5 Oct. 1940, 94.

9 K. Strijd, 'Zuivere terminologie,' ibid., 16, no. 17, 1 Dec. 1940, 104, 105.

10 W. Banning, 'Solidariteit,' ibid., 16 no. 18, Christmas 1940, 109, 110.

11 Buskes, 'Success is zegen!', ibid., 16 no. 13, 22 Sept. 1940, 89, 90.

12 In the Hugenholtz Papers, box 197, International Institute for Social History, Amsterdam. Until an advanced age Buskes continued to call himself 'Junior.'

13 De Jong, *Het Koninkrijk*, 4:714, 715, 725.

14 M. van der Voet, 'Onze taak en werkwijze,' *KeV*, 16 no. 15, 23 Oct. 1940, 95–7.

15 Buskes, 'Ons vertrowen,' 73, 74; van der Voet, 'Onze taak,' 95–7.

16 Heering, 'Kerk en Vrede,' 82, 83.

17 Van der Voet, 'Onze taak,' 95–7; G. Hartdorff, 'Kerk en Vrede in de oorlogs-en-bezettings-jaren,' *Militia Christi* (Amersfoort, etc.), 10 no. 8, 16 April 1955, 4. Also "Kerk en Vrede – Syllabus no. 1," a two-page stencilled document issued illegally after 1940.

18 S.H. Spanjaard, 'De vergelding,' *KeV*, 17, no. 4, 15 March 1941, 16–18; Buskes, 'Kerk en Vrede,' 92–4.

19 Van der Voet, 'Onze taak,' 95–7; 'Kerk en Vrede – Syllabus.'

20 Hartdorff, 'Kerk en Vrede,' 3.

21 J.J. van Bolhuis et al., eds., *Onderdrukking en verzet: Nederland in oorlogstijd*, 4 vols. (Arnhem and Amsterdam [1947–54]), 2:481, 482.

22 Hartdorff, 'Kerk en Vrede,' 3, 4.

23 J.J. Wentink, 'Jan Bosdriesz,' *Militia Christi*, 10 no. 8, 16 April 1955, 8, 9.

24 Letter from the Hague branch to Hugenholtz, 15 Nov. 1941, in the Hugenholtz Papers, box 138.

25 The 'Aryan declaration' specified that one had to indicate on a form whether one was 'Aryan' or 'completely or partially' Jewish. This declaration formed the basis for the 'purification' of the administration by removal of Jews. 'Winterhulp' was an organization that collected money to provide welfare, set up at the instigation of the Germans and led by Dutch National Socialists. On the underground side, ministers counterfeited church documents because Jews who belonged to a Christian church before January 1941 were not deported in the first instance. This exception, however, was very soon rescinded for Jewish Catholics, and later for Jewish Protestants as well.

26 Letters from Jan Bosdriesz, 10 March 1941 and 29 June 1941, in the Hugenholtz Papers, box 1953.

27 De Jong, *Het Koninkrijk*, 4:773–5; 6:1–10, 13, 22 n 3.

28 H.C. Touw, *Het verzet der Hervormde Kerk: Geschiedenis van het kerkelijk verzet*, 2 vols. (The Hague 1946), 2:216–22.

29 Touw, *Het verzet*, 1:382, 435; Buskes, *Hoera voor het leven*, 5th ed. (Amsterdam 1963), 192–6.

30 Touw, *Het verzet*, 2:581; Buskes, *Hoera*, 198–200.

31 De Jong, *Het Koninkrijk*, 9:1191; Buskes, *Hoera*, 181, 182.

32 Touw, *Het verzet*, 1:578, 579.

33 Ibid., 1:280.

34 Ibid., 1:40, 196, 235, 239, 393, 394, 437, 616–19.

35 Ibid., 1:43, 581; 2:173.

36 See letters of thanks, November 1944, in Hugenholtz Papers, box 197.

37 Wentink, 'Jan Bosdriesz,' 8, 9.

38 Touw, *Het verzet*, 2:279–82.

39 *Militia Christi*, 3 no. 9 (Sept. 1948), 7; 4 no. 13, 19 Nov. 1949, 6, 7; 10 no. 8, 16
    April 1955, 8, 9.

40 G. van Roon, *Protestants Nederland en Duitsland 1933–1941* (Utrecht 1973), 274–
    98.

41 De Jong, *Het Koninkrijk*, 5:704–7, 710, 711.

42 Ibid., 5:667–738; 6:12–20.

43 Ibid., 5:692–5; 9:1191.

44 Buskes, *Waar stond de kerk? Schets van her kerkelijk verzet* (Amsterdam 1947), 27–
    9; Heering, *Pro Rege: Een stem van Kerk en Vrede* (N.p. 1945), 12.

45 Touw, *Het verzet*, 2:189.

46 Letter, 29 Dec. 1944, to K. Gravemeyer, secretary of the General Synod of the Dutch
    Reformed Church, in Hugenholtz Papers, box 197.

47 Buskes, 'Gij zult niet doodslaan!' *Militia Christi*, 1 no. 1 (Dec. 1945), 4, 5.

PART THREE

PACIFIST OUTREACH: JAPAN AND INDIA

27

Pacifism in Japan, 1918–1945

CYRIL H. POWLES

Japan's history makes it difficult to treat the subject of pacifism in the way in which it is usually dealt with in the West, where Christianity and the rise of individual consciousness (conscience) have formed a basis for nonconformity. As little detailed research has been done on the subject as a whole, the treatment that follows is inevitably somewhat subjective and superficial, though I have tried to base it on reliable information.

Historically, Buddhism (which became a prominent part of the Japanese religious heritage in the sixth century) has included strong resistance to violence. For the most part, however, this tendency has led to individuals' withdrawing from society, rather than to overt action against state legislation. Because individual integrity is usually measured in relation to the community, terms such as conscience (*ryōshin*) or sincerity (*magokoro, seijitsu*) tend to be interpreted as the openness of the individual towards the group or the healthiness of relations between the individual and the community. Thus social obligation precedes individual inclination. A clash between the two can be resolved only by withdrawal from the group, by recantation (*tenkō*) or, in extreme cases, by the death of the individual.[1]

Submission to the group has always been interpreted by the Japanese in quasi-religious terms. As Professor Nakamura describes it, 'the moral distinction between goodness and wickedness is nothing but the distinction between submission or non-submission to the divine authority of the corporate whole.' In modern times the 'corporate whole,' known as the *kokutai*, came to be interpreted as the Japanese state under the divine authority of the emperor, i.e., the emperor-system. Resistance to state authority was tantamount to religious apostasy: the denial of one's total identity as Japanese.[2] Thus the usual road taken for dissent was the round-about path of withdrawal from active participation and the practise of what was known as 'internal resistance' (*naiteki teikō*) by writing or teaching in an area only obliquely related to the issue.[3]

Less well documented because of its humbler origins is the resistance put up by peasant communities to the oppressiveness of feudal society. No less corporate in nature, it usually took the form of millenarian revivalism with an anarchistic and pacifist emphasis. The teaching in Maitreya (*Miroku* in Japanese) Buddhism about the last age (*mappō*), when society becomes degenerate in preparation for the appearance of Maitreya, had become part of folk religion, accounting for the millenarian emphasis.[4] When universal manhood conscription was instituted in 1873, peasants rebelled all over the country at what they termed a 'blood tax' (*ketsuzei*) that would draw them away from their rightful pursuits. Anti-war sentiments formed part of this phenomenon.[5]

As Japan evolved from a feudal-agrarian to a capitalist-industrial society, two alternatives to the kokutai appeared. Protestant Christianity offered the promise of a new society of autonomous individuals over against ('in, but not of') traditional society, a vision grasped eagerly by members of the nascent middle class. A host of 'new religions' – actually old religion in new forms – provided a kokutai distinct from (albeit a kind of mirror image of) the state, a promise of liberation to the oppressed peasant and city worker. Pacifism existed as a minor theme in both movements, but the two had different origins and class relations.

Both alternatives reflected the emergence of a clearer consciousness of individual identity and took the form of an often-painful conflict between the pursuit of individuality and the demands of the inherited obligation to the community.[6] Accordingly it is not as easy as it is in the West to describe pacifism in Japan in terms of an absolute 'renunciation of war by the individual.'[7]

Christian pacifism owed its appearance to two very different sources: the Society of Friends (Quakers) and the writings of Leo Tolstoy. Though the names of Kitamura Tōkoku, Abe Isoo, Kashiwagi Gien, and Uchimura Kanzō are perhaps best known as pioneers, pacifism appears to have attracted a considerable following in the years between the Sino–Japanese and Russo–Japanese wars (1890–1905).[8] If we extrapolate from this fact, we may assume that a consistent but submerged stream of religious objection to war existed in Japanese Christianity until much of it was diverted into indirect channels by the oppressive militarism of the 1930s.[9]

Of the four figures named above (and we could add others), all except Kitamura lived into the period covered in this essay, influencing the lives of others around them. The names of the Quaker political philosopher Nitobe Inazō (1862–1933) and the labour organizer and evangelist Kagawa Toyohiko (1888–1960), are perhaps even better known abroad as advocates of peace, though they displayed a somewhat ambiguous relationship to the military adventurism of their country in the 1930s and 1940s.[10] None the less, their stand for peace demonstrates the role of opposition to militarism in the Protestant Christianity of the period. In short, though we look below at the thought of certain select individuals, they were not isolated but represented an important (though admittedly small) constituent of all denominations of Japanese Christianity in their time.

The *mukyōkai*, or 'non-church Christianity' movement founded by Uchimura Kanzō (1861–1930) probably represents the most important source of anti-war thought in Japanese Christianity. Uchimura's own public stand against war ceased with the victory of militarism at the end of the Russo–Japanese War. Thenceforth he seems to have believed that peace would be possible only with the ultimate return of Christ at the end of the age, and so he concentrated on teaching carefully selected disciples in private Bible classes. Nevertheless he continued to be known by these disciples as a pacifist, so that most who joined the Mukyōkai movement considered a stand against war to be a condition of their membership.[11] Here we consider only three leaders, Fujii Takeshi (1888–1930), Yanaihara Tadao (1893–1961), and Asami Sensaku (1868–1952).

On the whole, Mukyōkai represented a rather upper-middle-class type of Christianity, having its main centre among the students of the elite Tokyo Imperial University. It avoided any kind of institutional structure, being made up of loose associations of individuals who gathered to study the Bible under a recognized leader.[12] Both the social status of its members and its non-institutional character allowed Mukyōkai to escape systematic repression by the police, who were more interested in the control of organizations. Moreover, during the period known as Taishō Democracy (c. 1918–26), the government allowed a certain freedom of intellectual debate. At the same time, police harassment of popular religions such as Ōmoto-kyō and of the political left revealed strict limits to this freedom.[13]

Fujii Takeshi's short and tragic career represents a personal bridge between Uchimura and the second generation of Mukyōkai pacifists. More than any others, his writings epitomized an absolute stand against war, which led his friend Yanaihara Tadao to call him the Jeremiah of Japan. Born in a family of samurai origins, he was converted to Christianity and pacifism through his contact with Uchimura while a student at the Tokyo Imperial University. Following graduation and a period as a civil servant, in 1915 he became Uchimura's assistant. In 1920 he resolved to be an evangelist in his own right, cooperating with his wife to publish a periodical, *The Old and New Testaments*. This joint effort ended when his wife died in 1922 at the age of twenty-nine, but Fujii continued his work, which resulted in a series of essays, collected in 1939 under the title *Seisho yori mitaru Nippon* (Japan Seen in Biblical Perspective).

Like all Mukyōkai Christians, Fujii combined his faith with a strong love of his native land. He looked to its heritage in Shinto, Confucianism, and Buddhism as a kind of Old Testament preparation for the coming of the gospel. Thus he finds an echo of Jesus' words, 'Blessed are the peacemakers,' in the teaching of the twelfth-century Buddhist saint Hōnen, who said, 'If you do ill to your enemies, wars will continue from generation to generation. Therefore it is better to pray even for your enemies, and both you and they may be saved. Grudge and hatred among people must come to an end.'[14]

Like the Hebrew prophets, Fujii pointed to natural phenomena (such as the great Tokyo earthquake of 1923) as signs of God's judgment on a nation that trusts in militarism. His words appear prescient: 'God will summon his avenger from afar – planes and battleships will come from the far ends of the earth to attack like clouds and waves, filling air and sea. They will spoil, for the first time, that "glorious history of heavenly protection" of which Japanese have long been boastful.' Only after this devastation will 'God awaken his nation ... to create a new Japan from the Remnant, the awakened few who will survive.'[15]

Fujii died in the summer of 1930, but just before that he had published a long poem whose apocalyptic tone surpassed anything that he had previously written. It was entitled 'Horobiyo' (Be Destroyed!) and in one verse he writes, 'The name of Japan will soon be taken away from the earth; / The Crocodile from the East will swallow her entirely.'[16] Two factors – the moral degeneration of the people and their trust in military adventurism – would lead to destruction. The crocodile from the east, meaning the United States, would act as God's instrument to destroy such a faithless nation.

Fujii's death allowed him to escape the oppressive regime of militarism that began with the Manchurian Incident of 1931, but such was not the case with his friend and brother-in-law, Yanaihara Tadao. Yanaihara came to Christianity through the influence of Uchimura and the Quaker scholar Nitobe Inazō, while a student at Tokyo Imperial University. Following Nitobe, who specialized in colonial policy, he later taught the subject himself at his alma mater. His prolific writings were critical of Japanese colonialism, and he saw through the Kwantung army's plot, which led to the Manchurian Incident. In 1937, when a whole series of his writings were suppressed by the police for their pacifism and anti-imperialism, he was forced out of his teaching position, and for the remainder of our period he functioned privately as a Mukyōkai teacher. Following the end of the Pacific War he and his Mukyōkai colleague Nambara Shigeru (1889–1974) returned to Tokyo University, each of them in turn ending his career as president of that institution.[17]

Though Yanaihara's pacifism did not take clear shape until after the Manchurian Incident, he was influenced from the beginning by what he saw to be the pacifism of both Uchimura and Fujii. Following a trip to Manchuria, he wrote in the paper *Kashin*, 'What I saw and heard in Manchuria convinced me that the Manchurian Incident had been trumped up by the Japanese side, as I had suspected from the beginning. Since that time my academic study became combined with my faith, and I determined to oppose the Manchurian policy.'[18]

In 1936, Yanaihara published *Minzoku to Heiwa* (Race and Peace), in which he described nationalism and racism as ideologies that disregarded basic principles of justice and peace. Like his mentor, Uchimura, he did not regard the Japanese spirit and Christianity as contradictory. He never fundamentally disagreed with the basic structure of the emperor-system, which later critics have identified as the root source of militarism. But he saw the rise of fascism in his day as perverting what was best in the Japanese tradition, denying Christ's teaching. In 1937, when Japan invaded China, he published an article entitled 'Kokka no risō' (Ideals of the State) in the widely read journal *Chūō Kōron*, further attacking the national policy. It was the controversy awakened by this article that aroused the ire not only of the police but of many of his university colleagues and led to his resignation.

Later in the same year he gave a speech at a meeting commemorating the seventh anniversary of the death of Fujii Takeshi, entitled 'Kami no kuni' (Kingdom of God). In his conclusion he proclaimed, 'To the Japanese people, I say, "Stop fighting immediately!" ... In this world of falsehood, this is the funeral day of Japan's ideals, or rather, of Japan itself which we have loved so much but which has lost its ideals. I am much too concerned with this problem to find an emotional release in anger or in weeping. If you have understood what I have said, bury this country first, so that its ideals may live.'[19]

Following his departure from the university, Yanaihara concentrated on independent evangelism, the publication of a monthly paper, *Kashin* (Good News), and the nurturing of a small but highly disciplined group of disciples. He has been criticized for the authoritarian relationships later revealed in this latter group. But he defended himself by saying that such discipline was necessary in that 'severe age.' 'The members were warned not to act carelessly and allow the police to know what I said in meetings. They also had to be prepared for persecution on account of their faith.'[20] It was by such means that Christian pacifism was nurtured and maintained under the trying conditions of the Pacific War.

The third representative Mukyōkai pacifist, Asami Sensaku, conforms most closely to the Western image. But he also represents an exception to the general elite nature of the movement in that he came from peasant stock, never attended university, and supported himself throughout his life as a farmer and bath-house operator.[21] Thus he bridges the gulf between the two types of pacifism noted above. Born in Niigata Prefecture, he emigrated as a young man to Hokkaido (something like going from Ontario to Saskatchewan in the early days of this century). In 1902, depressed by the destruction of his farm in a flood, he attended a Methodist church in Sapporo, where he was converted to Christianity. His conversion led to his becoming an enthusiastic proponent of his new-found faith.

In 1903, Asami travelled to the United States to try to recover his fortunes as a day labourer in California. During his stay there, he found himself excluded from the church that he was attending for his opposition to the Russo–Japanese War and in his isolation happened to come across a copy of Uchimura Kanzō's magazine, *Bible Study*, in which the author told of his resistance to the war. This led to correspondence with Uchimura and a friendship that began when he returned to Japan after four years in the United States and continued until the master's death.

Proud of his own peasant origins, he saw his mission as directed to other 'farmers, village headmen, postmen, [primary] producers and labourers.'[22] Quoting St Paul's Second Letter to the Thessalonians – 'If someone does not work, they should not eat' – he dedicated himself to a ministry of labour and evangelism like Paul's.

Because of his unyielding opposition to war, Asami early on came under the scrutiny of the police. At the outbreak of the second war with China he quoted Christ's words, 'The one who lives by the sword will die by the sword.' In 1931 he wrote in his magazine, *Yorokobi no Otozure* (Joyful Tidings),

Peace among nations and goodwill among human beings, along with salvation from sin and release from death, are the ideals of all people. Why then should it be so difficult to realize them? No matter how we may desire them in theory; no matter how we may think it self-evident that peace is good and warfare evil, we find it hard to put them into practice because of our common inheritance of sin in Adam. Therefore, rather than seeking a solution of this grievous problem from human beings on earth, we should rather listen to God's word in the Bible.[23]

Here we can see the typical Mukyōkai combination of biblical faith with the desire for peace. Only as human beings believe in God and are made new and peaceful beings will peace be possible. Such a statement appeared to place the emperor in an inferior position to God, and it was not long before the police forced Asami to discontinue his magazine.

In 1943, while Asami was attending a meeting of older Christians at a Sapporo church, one of the members argued that the blood of Japanese soldiers was shed in the cause of peace. Therefore it was similar in redemptive merit to the blood shed by Christ on the cross. Asami, unable to keep silent, blurted out, 'You've got it wrong,' and he proceeded to expound on the theological meaning of Jesus' blood. Someone in the group reported him to the procurator, who ordered him arrested and charged with teachings incompatible with the kokutai.

Asami was then held – at the age of seventy-six, in a cell with a concrete floor at sub-zero temperature – for two hundred days of questioning. During this time he was supported by fellow Mukyōkai members such as Yanaihara, but this did not prevent him from being sentenced in May of 1944 to three years in prison. The sentence read, 'The accused has embraced antiwar thought and is a believer in Christianity which is opposed to the kokutai of our nation ... Not only does he believe this faith himself, he holds meetings where he advocates these ideas, even travelling around the entire country, including Manchuria and Korea.'[24]

Feeling this accusation to be unjust, Asami appealed to the supreme court on behalf of himself and other Mukyōkai members who were under scrutiny. The Sapporo procurator, in his investigation, had emphasized Asami's millenarian beliefs, for other Christian pacifists with such beliefs had received prison sentences. Because Asami was in poor health and in some danger because of the constant American bombing that was taking place by this time (1944), the chief justice, Miyake Shōtarō, travelled with his secretary to Sapporo to conduct his own examination. As this act showed, Miyake was sympathetic to Asami and, following detailed questioning, ruled (on 12 June 1945) that 'his belief in the Second Coming was of a spiritual nature, the perfect completion of the present order of the world, with no implication that Christ's coming would cause the overthrow of the supreme power of the Emperor of Japan.'[25]

So Asami was acquitted and released from prison, having served about a year of his sentence. This landmark judgment implicitly recognized that the persecution of hundreds of Christians during the war had been unjust. Sadly, it had come too late, as many of them had died in prison, and the others were forced to await the Allied victory for their release.

One would like to find that Christians of the 'mainline' denominations had taken a stand similar to the Mukyōkai leaders, but most supported the war. Only a few individuals adopted a different position. In 1972, the Society for the Study of Christian Social Problems at Doshisha University in Kyoto published a three-volume study, *Senjika no Kirisutokyō undō* (The Christian Movement in Wartime Japan). This survey identified only one member of the United Church of Christ (a union of Congregational, Methodist, and Presbyterian churches, with some Anglicans) – a young man who served a year in prison for refusing conscription.[26]

Possibly because he was never arrested, the name of Kashiwagi Gien (1860–1938) is absent from the Doshisha study. Yet he was the pre-eminent Protestant pacifist outside Mukyōkai. Born the son of a Buddhist priest in Niigata Prefecture, he became a Christian while attending Doshisha College, where he later lectured for a while. Along with Abe Isoo, Kinoshita Naoe, Uchimura Kanzō, and many others, he opposed the Russo–Japanese War, and it was at this time that his pacifist thought took shape. Throughout a long period (1897–1938) as pastor of the Congregational church in Annaka, a country town north of Tokyo, he preached Christian socialism and pacifism, opposing the nationalism rampant in his denomination and incurring the wrath of the local police for the views published in his monthly magazine. The Annaka church had been a pioneer in progressive social reform from the time of its founding in 1878 and thus formed a solid support community. Nevertheless, as militarism became dominant, Kashiwagi found his magazine increasingly in trouble, and he finally ceased its publication just before his death, in 1937.[27]

Kashiwagi's pacifism was based on the New Testament, in places as interpreted by Leo Tolstoy and Uchimura Kanzō. It was tempered by his gentle nature, 'like a slow ox, never moving backward,' as Tabata described it. During the period of Taishō Democracy one of his essays dealing with the subject would appear about once a year, but the number increased with Japan's military adventurism in the 1930s. His stand was based simply on the commandment 'Thou shalt not kill,' but Kashiwagi was a life-long student of socialist thought and understood quite well the relationship between industrialization, imperialism, and militarism.[28]

From the issue of December 1925 to its final number, his journal's cover displayed the following manifesto – a summary of his basic ideas:

We believe in the One True God, Creator of heaven and earth, and that all people are brothers and sisters under God.

We believe in Jesus Christ as the incarnation of God; in the redeeming power of the cross, and in Christ's resurrection in glory.

We seek a national policy that will build up the nation on moral principles.

We seek for moral principles based on obedience to God's will, absolute reverence for human personality and absolute freedom of conscience.

We hope for the realization of a world free from war and look for the annihilation of militarism.

We maintain that all things belong to the Heavenly Father and are provided by him for the life and subsistence of humanity, not for private ownership and production by undervalued human labour.[29]

Finally, we turn to a different type of pacifism, one more vulnerable to persecution because of its humbler class nature, yet just as dedicated and resolute. The Doshisha study lists a number of organizations: Jehovah's Witnesses, New Testament Church of Jesus Christ, Plymouth Brethren, Mino Mission, Japan Free Church of Christ, Seventh-day Adventists, and three Holiness groups. Of these, the ones that suffered most for their anti-war stand were the Jehovah's Witnesses (official name, Watch Tower Bible and Tract Society) and the Holiness groups. But, as Dohi points out, their persecution was used by the police 'to restrain and intimidate the entire Christian body.'[30]

The Japanese branch of the Witnesses was founded in 1926 by Akashi Junzō, who had been converted while working as a journalist in the United States. During the period of militarism he attacked the government, maintaining that 'Japan's actions toward China are without doubt acts of aggression whose result will be Japan's destruction. The Emperor (*tennō*) is only a solitary human being, not divine. Under the leadership of this man-Tennō, the plan to conquer all of Asia, nay the whole world, is nothing but the megalomania of the militarists who are being manipulated by Satan.'[31]

Akashi's personal pacifist convictions influenced the way in which he translated the works of Judge Rutherford and other Watchtower publications, so that opposition to war became a basic element of the Japanese Witnesses' faith. For example, 'Capitalists represent the main force in society and the national structure and are the ringleaders in war, our greatest evil. How wars are caused, what kind of evil they are, the earliest Watchtower publication – written at the close of World War I, when peace was proclaimed, but each nation was strengthening its armaments – explains: "War is made by these few rich people who increase their wealth enormously by these means." (*Prophecy*, p. 203).'[32]

It was therefore not surprising that the organization came under strict police scrutiny. The Witnesses' aggressive evangelism made them a target under the revised Peace Preservation Law of 1928, and in May 1933 the entire membership, including Akashi's fifteen-year-old son, were rounded up and their literature was confiscated. Akashi, who was in Manchuria at the time, rushed home and succeeded in having them released after four days of questioning. In 1939, Akashi Mabito (Akashi Junzō's son) and Muramoto Kazuo refused military service and were arrested, whereupon almost the entire membership was again imprisoned and their leader examined under torture. Finally, in 1942 they were given sentences ranging from ten years for Akashi Junzō to two to five years for the others, for 'opposition to war, altering the kokutai and disrespect to the emperor.' Despite several appeals, all sentences were upheld. Akashi Junzo's wife, Shizue, and several others died in prison, while Mabito recanted and joined the army. The others were released on order of the Allied occupation in October 1945.[33]

The second leader of the syncretistic sect Ōmoto-kyō, Deguchi Onisaburō (1871–1948), drew the wrath of the state for his assumption of an imperial name and the creation of a counter-kokutai. His aphorism, 'There is nothing in this world as evil as war and nothing as stupid as armaments,' revealed the strongly pacifist tone of his teaching. The Buddhist millenarianism of Ōmoto-kyō paralleled the Christian teaching, which got both Mukyōkai and the Holiness sects into such trouble, showing how the suffering of powerless people would turn to the hope of an end to the evil world in which they lived.[34]

As for Buddhist war resistance, Senoo Yoshirō (1888–1961) established the *Shinkō bukkyō seinen dōmei* (Young Buddhist Alliance) in 1931. Tabata mentions: 'At its height it counted nearly twenty branches with over two hundred members' and combined Buddhist pacifism with Marxian socialism. Attacked by the military government from 1934 on, it was finally dissolved in 1937, when twenty-five leaders, including Senoo, were arrested. But it was revived following the Second World War and formed one of the founding groups of the international organization Religionists for Peace.[35]

The unique features of pacifism in Japan can be summarized as follows: Because of the overwhelming strength of the emperor-system and its quasi-religious nature, every movement functioned in a dialectical relationship to that context, accepting it as part of its love of Japan while rejecting the militarism that was an integral part of its structure. When this conflict appeared to lead to a deadlock, refuge was sought in millenarianism, where Buddhist and Christian beliefs converged in the dream of a new age of peace to follow the present evil time. Pacifism took place within a group, rather than as the witness of an individual conscience. This held true even for the 'individualistic' Mukyōkai, where leaders such as Yanaihara were always supported by their consciousness of a group around them. Finally, the nature of each group differed according to the stratum of society in which it existed. Thus the elite Mukyōkai, always identified in some sense with the ruling class, attempted by writing to reform the nation's leadership. Holiness, Jehovah's Witnesses, and Ōmoto-kyō, in contrast, sharing in the oppression of the lower strata, saw nothing but God's wrath descending on the tyranny of their rulers.

NOTES

1 For individual and group, see Hajime Nakamura, *Ways of Thinking of Eastern Peoples*, rev. ed. (Honolulu, 1964), 469–70; Masao Maruyama, *Thought and Behaviour*

in Modern Japanese Politics (London 1963), 7. For the phenomenon of *tenkō*, see Tsurumi Shunsuke ed., *Tenkō*, 3 vols. (Tokyo 1959–62), 1:5–6; and for an explanation in English, Richard H. Mitchell, *Thought Control in Prewar Japan* (Ithaca and London 1976), 110 and chap. 5. The suicide of Kitamura Tōkoku illustrates the final solution: Nobuya Bamba and John F. Howes, eds., *Pacifism in Japan: The Christian and Socialist Tradition* (Vancouver 1978), chap. 2.

2 C.H. Powles, 'The Emperor System in Modern Japan: A Case Study in Japanese Religiosity,' *Studies in Religion* (Waterloo), 6 no. 1 (1976), 39–40. For *kokutai*, see J.M. Kitagawa, 'The Japanese *Kokutai* (National Community): History and Myth,' *History of Religions* (Chicago), 13 no. 3 (1974), 209–26. A Canadian missionary, writing home in 1938, noted, 'I believe it is just as hard for a Japanese to reconcile himself to what he believes to be the crime of disloyalty as it would be for me to commit a murder.' Quoted in Gwen and Howard Norman, *One Hundred Years in Japan 1873–1973*, 2 vols. (Toronto 1980), 2:351.

3 For example, Kinoshita Naoe's withdrawal after the Russo–Japanese War: Takeshi Nishida, 'Kinoshita Naoe: Pacifism and Religious Withdrawal,' Nobuya Bamba and John G. Howes, eds., *Pacifism in Japan: The Christian and Socialist Tradition* (Vancouver 1978), 83–9. In our period, an example is the distinguished Buddhist pacifist historian Ienaga Saburō.

4 Murakami Shigeyoshi, *Kindai minshū shūkyō no kenkyū* (The Study of Modern Popular Religion) (Tokyo 1958). For the close relation between despair with the existing society and millenarianism, see E.J. Hobsbawm, *Primitive Rebels* (New York 1965), 10–12, 80–1.

5 Inagaki Masami, *Hei eki o kyohi shita Nihonjin* (Japanese Who Refused Military Service) (Tokyo 1973), ii. Mikiso Hane, *Peasants, Rebels and Outcastes: The Underside of Modern Japan* (New York 1982), 18–20; see especially the quotation on 19.

6 See the examples of Kitamura Tōkoku and Kinoshita Naoe in Bamba and Howes, eds., *Pacifism in Japan*, chaps. 2 and 3.

7 Peter Brock, *Freedom from War: Nonsectarian Pacifism, 1814–1914* (Toronto 1991), vii. See also Takeda Kiyoko, *Dochaku to haikyō* (Indigenization and Apostasy) (Tokyo 1968), 341.

8 Tabata Shinobu, *Nihon no heiwa shisō* (Peace Thought in Japan) (Kyoto 1972), 118, records a long list of lesser-known names. For example, the scholar and novelist Tokutomi Roka made a journey to meet Tolstoy in Russia after reading his writings. Here and elsewhere, names are usually listed in Japanese order, with surname first. For a helpful outline in English of this period, see Brock, *Freedom from War*, chap. 19, 'The Dawn of Christian Pacifism in Japan.'

9 The American Quaker missionary Gilbert Bowles (1869–1960) helped to found the Japan Peace Society and the Japanese branch of the Fellowship of Reconciliation,

neither of which survived the pressures of the 1940s: Harold Josephson, ed., *Biographical Dictionary of Modern Peace Leaders* (Westport, Conn., 1985), 103; Ebisawa Arimichi and Ōuchi Saburō, *Nihon Kirisutokyō shi* (History of Japanese Christianity) (Tokyo 1971), 587–8. Hobsbawm's remark about social-democratic parties in Europe is apposite for pacifism in Japan: 'Faced with [fascism], ... [they] tended to go into hibernation, from which they emerged ... at the end of the dark era.' *The Age of Extremes* (New York 1994), 167.

10 For Nitobe, see Howes, ed., *Nitobe Inazō: Japan's Bridge across the Pacific* (Boulder, Col., 1995), especially chaps. 1 and 8. Yuzo Ota's essay on Kagawa in Nobuya Bamba and John F. Howes, eds., *Pacifism in Japan: The Christian and Socialist Tradition* (Vancouver 1978), chap. 7, especially 179ff., though a little one-sided, is supported by other contemporary scholars: for example, Dohi Akio in Kobe Student Centre, ed., *Kagawa Toyohiko no zental zō* (Toyohiko Kagawa: A Composite Portrait) (Kobe 1988), 172–5.

11 Dohi Akio, *Nihon Purotesutanto shi* (History of Japanese Protestantism) (Tokyo 1980), 391–2, lists the names of thirteen leaders besides Yanaihara who followed Uchimura's pacifism during this period. Gordon Hirabayashi's parents were both members of the Mukyōkai movement; he was an American Quaker and conscientious objector of Japanese ancestry who was jailed in 1942 for refusing to accept internment voluntarily and later participated in the Japanese Americans' struggle for legal rehabilitation. In his childhood and adolescence, he writes, 'the greatest moral impact came from their way of life, their living example ... [their] dedication to the oneness of belief and practice,' including pacifism and strict adherence to the truth. See G. Hirabayashi, *Good Times, Bad Times: Idealism Is Realism*, Canadian Quaker Pamphlet Series, no. 22 (Argenta, BC, 1985), 8, 9, 13, 14; also Peter Irons, *The Courage of Their Convictions* (New York 1988), 37–62, 415 ('Gordon Hierabayashi v. United States'). From 1958 until his retirement in 1983 Hirabayashi taught sociology at the University of Alberta.

12 For a detailed study, see Carlo Caldarola, *Christianity: The Japanese Way* (Leiden 1979). The author lists members persecuted for pacifist views on 171–6.

13 For Taishō Democracy and its limits, see Murakami Shigeyoshi, *Japanese Religion in the Modern Century* (Tokyo 1980), 68, 74, and 96–7; also Jon Halliday, *A Political History of Japanese Capitalism* (New York 1975), 72 n 58.

14 Quoted in Isao Sato and Philip Williams, 'Takeshi Fujii: Pacifism Jeremiah Style,' *Japan Christian Quarterly* (Tokyo) (winter 1975), 34. This article, written by a disciple, gives a helpful outline in English of Fujii's life and thought.

15 Fujii, *Seisho yori mitaru*, 601, translated in Sato and Williams, 'Takeshi Fujii,' 36.

16 Sato and Williams, 'Takeshi Fujii,' 28.

17 Dohi, *Nihon Purotesutanto shi*, 392–6; Tabata, *Nihon no heiwa shisō*, 196–9; Bamba and Howes, eds., *Pacifism in Japan*, chap. 8; Caldarola, *Christianity*, 171.

18 Yanaihara, *Zenshū* (Complete Works), 29 vols. (Tokyo 1963–5), 26:103, translation in Bamba and Howes, eds., *Pacifism in Japan*, 204.

19 *Complete Works*, 18: 653–4. English translation, slightly altered, in Bamba and Howes, eds., *Pacifism in Japan*, 214. See also Dohi, *Nihon Purotesutanto shi*, 397.

20 Yanaihara, *Jiyūgaoka shūkai* (The Jiyugaoka Meeting), *Collected Works*, 26:649–50. English translation in Bamba and Howes, eds., *Pacifism in Japan*, 218.

21 Takeda, *Dochaku to haikyō*, 331–2; Dohi, *Nihon Purotesutanto shi*, 407; Caldarola, *Christianity*, 174. These three sources, especially Takeda, give the most details of his life and thought, which never achieved the fame of some of Asami's more highly placed comrades.

22 Quoted in Takeda, *Dochaku to haikyō*, 335.

23 Quoted in Takeda, ibid., 342. Translation of this and following passages by the author.

24 Ibid., 337–8, 340.

25 Ibid., 351; summary translation, with slight alterations, in Caldarola, *Christianity*, 175.

26 Gwen and Howard Norman, *One Hundred Years*, 2:417. Much of the material cited from Dohi, *Nihon Purotesutanto shi*, and Takeda, *Dochaku to haikyō*, is based on the Doshisha study, which used official government sources and surveys of the denominations.

27 Itani Ryūichi, *Hisen no shisō: dochaku no kirisutosha, Kashiwagi Gien* (Pacifist Thought: Kashiwagi Gien, Indigenous Christian) (Tokyo 1967), is the fullest. Also Tabata, *Nihon no heiwa*, 67–70; Dohi, *Nihon Purotesutanto shi*, 216–17, and Takeda Kiyoko, *Ningenkan no sōkoku* (Conflicting Views of Human Nature) (Tokyo 1959), 233–9. For the Annaka church, see Morioka Kiyomi, *Chihō shōtoshi ni okeru Kirisuto kyōkai no keisei* (The Formation of Christian Churches in Provincial Towns) (Tokyo, 1958).

28 Itani, *Hisen no shisō*, 128–33; Takeda *Ningenkan*, 238.

29 Itani, *Hisen no shiso*, 179.

30 Doshisha, *Senjika no Kirisutokyō undō*, vol. 3, quoted in Dohi, *Nihon Purotesutanto shi*, 400. The Holiness movement was a rigorist offshoot of Methodism. Lack of support in its tribulations from related denominations led to much bad feeling after the war.

31 *Senjika no kirisutokyō undō*, 2:321, quoted in Dohi, *Nihon Purotesutanto shi*, 401.

32 Inagaki, *Hei eki o kyohi shita Nihonjin*, 37. Inagaki's is the most detailed study of the wartime resistance of the Witnesses.

33 Dohi, *Nihon Purotesutanto shi*, 402–3; Inagaki, *Hei eki o kyohi shita Nihonjin*, 127–35.

34 Tabata, *Nihon no heiwa*, 103. Murakami Shigeyoshi, *Deguchi Onisaburō* (Tokyo 1973); also Murakami, *Japanese Religion*, 70–5, 96–8.

35 Tabata, *Nihon no heiwa*, 184–9.

28

Gandhi's *Satyagraha* and Its Roots in India's Past

ANTONY KOZHUVANAL

Born in South Africa and first developed there during the years 1906–9, Gandhi's concept of *satyagraha* became the cornerstone of his moral-political praxis. It served as a principle through which he integrated his religious faith, his social philosophy, and his political action. Using this weapon of satyagraha Gandhi devoted his life to fighting against evil in society and working towards India's political liberation. It was a doctrine developed out of action and leading to action.

This essay examines the roots of satyagraha in India's past. Gandhi's approach to his nation's history may be best described as a process of 'discovering, borrowing, and transforming.' He found in India's religious and cultural heritage a liberating strand which he strengthened till it was capable of being a life-line for the people of his country. In this selective assimilation, he used the traditional to promote the novel. That is to say, he reinterpreted traditions in such a way that revolutionary ideas, clothed in familiar expression, could be readily adopted and employed towards revolutionary ends. Thus Gandhi's method, seen from a liberationist viewpoint, consisted of 'the transformation of traditional Hindu ideas into something new. In many cases, the terminology remained the same, and thereby acceptable even to conservative Indian minds, while the meaning given bore a revolutionary significance.'[1] Thus Gandhi's *satyagraha*, while including other influences from the East and the West, is a combination of the traditional Indian concepts of *satya*, *ahimsa*, and *tapas*. I explore how Gandhi acquired these concepts from India's past and how far they influenced him in formulating the concept of satyagraha.

Satya, or Truth

The concept of truth is fundamental to Gandhi's thought. In fact, he viewed his whole life as an existential quest for truth. The word *satya* (truth or true) is derived from the root word *as*, meaning 'to be.' So it means 'being,' 'existing,' and 'real.' In the adjectival sense, satya means 'being in harmony with reality, with order and facts, fitting harmoniously with the cosmic and social order.'[2] But satya also refers to and is reality itself.[3] In the Indian tradition, truth then is more than factual accuracy; it is a metaphysical power. It supports the earth; it is eternal reality. The gods themselves are based on truth.[4] That is why the *Mundaka Upanishad* declares that 'truth alone is victorious.'[5]

This emphasis on truth is paramount in the writings of early Indian philosophers. For example, the *Taittiriya Upanishad* affirms that 'Brahma is truth, eternal, intelligence and immeasurable.'[6] The *Brihadaranyaka Upanishad* begins with the following prayer: 'From untruth lead me to truth, from darkness lead me to light, from death lead me into life everlasting.'[7] It is said in the *Mahabharata*: 'Put a thousand *yajnas* (sacrifices) in one pan of a balance and truth in the other. Truth will be found to weigh heavier.'[8] Valmiki's *Ramayana* states: 'Virtue has its culmination in truthfulness. Truth alone is God in the world; piety ever hinges on truth.'[9] All things have their root in truth; there is no goal higher than truth. In Manu's classification of duties, satya held a prominent place. It is listed among the *sadharana dharmas* (duties of universal scope and validity) and is understood as veracity.[10] Thus, as Joan Bondurant remarks: 'The vast body of philosophic community, the network of dialectic, the complex systems of logic and disputation which characterize Hindu philosophical and religious literature bear eloquent evidence to ... a passion for truth.'[11]

References to satya abound in the traditional stories of India. The tale of Prahlad, a young boy who suffered much for the sake of truth, is one of the most famous in the ancient literature and is known throughout India. Gandhi writes in his *Autobiography* of the deep impression made on him in his youth by the play *Harischandra*, in which the ascetic, Viswamitra, makes a bet that he can make King Harischandra tell a lie. Trapped into making a promise, the king loses everything he has, but Viswamitra offers to restore everything if Harischandra is willing to pretend that the promise was never made. When the king refuses, a series of disasters befalls him. The tragic story unfolds, and eventually Viswamitra admits his defeat, and the gods restore Harischandra and his queen to their former state. Harischandra, for millions in India, is an ideal truth-speaker, a man who keeps his vows and undergoes all manner of ordeals. Like Rama, he is an ideal king and cares for his people. He 'follows truth,' as Gandhi put it in his *Autobiography*.[12]

Truth in Gandhi's Usage

Gandhi accepted the orthodox Hindu philosophical position concerning truth. However, with him this concept received new dimensions and deeper meanings.

Perhaps his most important innovation was that he identified truth with God. He did not consider Truth an attribute of God but thought God was another name for truth: 'The word satya is derived from "*sat*" which means being. And nothing is or exists in reality except Truth. That is why '*Sat*' or Truth is perhaps the most important name of God. In fact, it is more correct to say that Truth is God, than to say that God is Truth ... It will be realized that "*Sat*" or "*Satya*" is the only correct and fully significant name for God.'[13]

Gandhi sees God as the unseen power pervading all things, the sum total of life, the formless and the nameless. He has a preference for the idea of God as formless Truth, because its appeal is more universal – it is as acceptable to non-theists as to theists.[14] N.K. Bose observes that 'with this changed creed, he [Gandhi] could easily accommodate as fellow seekers those who looked on humanity or any other object as their God, and for which they were prepared to sacrifice their all.'[15]

Further, Gandhi identified Truth with *ahimsa*. 'Cling to it,' he implored, 'it enables one to reach pure Truth,'[16] for '*Ahimsa* and Truth are the obverse and reverse of the same coin.'[17] Gandhi, however, did not mind conceiving God as personal. He said that God is 'a personal God to those who need His personal presence. He is embodied to those who need His touch ... He is all things to all.'[18] In the Hindu view, infinity, eternal nature, perfection, absoluteness, and so on, are predicated on God, but at the same time He is beyond all predications.[19]

Gandhi observed that human society, with all its joys and sufferings, was the very place where people discovered God. So, as he continued his experiments with truth, the concept of Truth became more and more settled in the sphere of ethical consideration. As Bondurant points out, 'The emphasis became increasingly centered upon the problem of means. The means became more and more specific, while the end – the individual realization of God, which is Truth – increasingly indeterminate.'[20] As early as 1924, Gandhi had written in *Young India*, 'I want to see God face to face. God I know is Truth. For me the only certain means of knowing God is non-violence.'[21]

Thus Gandhi's understanding of God as Truth led him necessarily back to the realm of ethics, and he dedicated his life to action based on it. He demonstrated a way to discover Truth by action based on service. As Raghavan Iyer notes, the pursuit of Truth was clearly a social activity for Gandhi. It could emerge only out of daily struggle with the concrete problems of living. One's devotion to truth, one's veracity and integrity, are most sharply tested in one's relations with opponents and opposing views.[22]

Ahimsa, or Non-violence

As Bondurant notes, 'If there is a dogma in the Gandhian philosophy, it centres here: that the only test of truth is action based on the refusal to do harm.'[23] On this point alone did Gandhi demand total agreement from those who followed his leadership.[24] Here we explore Gandhi's concept of *ahimsa* and its roots in India's past.

The word 'ahimsa' means literally non-injury, or more narrowly non-killing and more widely harmlessness – the renunciation of the will to kill and of the intention to hurt any living thing, the abstention from hostile thought, word, and act.[25] Ahimsa was common to Jainism, Buddhism, and Hinduism. However, it was the Jains who most thoroughly developed it. They held that the mere thought of killing any living thing is as much a moral evil as the actual killing. They also held that complete ahimsa could be practised with success only by a saint who has renounced all worldly pursuits.[26]

The life of the Jain monk was governed by five vows: abjuring killing, stealing, lying, sexual activity, and the possession of property. These vows were interpreted quite strictly. Acts of violence and killing, whether intentional or not, were the most potent cause of the influx of *karma* and were therefore particularly to be avoided. Even insect life was carefully protected. No lay Jaina could take up the profession of agriculture, since this involved the destruction not only of plant life but also of many living things in the soil. Thus Jainism, in its insistence on ahimsa or nonviolence, went further on this matter than any other Indian religion.[27]

Ahimsa was essential to Buddhism as well. According to the 'Ten Precepts,'[28] no Buddhist could follow the profession of hunter or butcher.[29] But the vow not to take life generally was not interpreted as forbidding lawful warfare or the sentencing of criminals to death, and it did not preclude Buddhists from eating meat, if provided by non-Buddhist butchers. Buddhism tended to encourage mildness and compassion, justice and vegetarianism, and to discourage somewhat the militarism that prevailed at most periods in ancient India. In any case, war was accepted as a normal activity of the state, even by Buddhist kings. Ashoka was possibly the only ancient Indian King who broke completely with the tradition of aggression.[30]

Non-injury to others has been acclaimed continually by Hinduism. The Hindu ethical thinkers looked on ahimsa as one of the *sadharana dharmas* (to be observed by all), and ahimsa is included in the five old yogic virtues.[31] Ahimsa is invoked in the *Mahabharata* to condemn cruel practices and to underline the sanctity of all life.[32] '*Ahimsa paramo dharma*' (ahimsa is the highest duty) is one of its well-known sayings.[33] Patanjali's *Yoga sutra* states that when ahimsa has been fully established, it will liquidate completely the forces of enmity and evil in the neighbourhood.[34]

Hindu classical texts state that absolute nonviolence is impossible, so they make exceptions. For example, injury to life for the protection of life is permitted; animals could be killed in sacrifices, for such killing was enjoined by the *Vedas*; virtuous and dutiful violence is really a kind of ahimsa.[35] In Hindu society, the *kshatriyas*, or military people, occupied a position second only to the priestly class (*Brahmanas*). The *Bhagavad Gita* is regarded by many, with such exceptions as Śankara and Gandhi,[36] as supporting and enjoining use of violence against an evildoer. The message of the *Gita*, according to most commentators, is to fight the enemy and crush him.[37] Manu, the great law-giver, permits, for self-defence, the killing of even 'one's teacher, an old man, a child, a learned *brahmana*.' He also holds that killing, if necessary for carrying out the injunctions of the Vedas, should not be regarded as a sin.[38] As A.L. Basham points out, the doctrine of nonviolence, which in medieval India had become very influential and had made most of the respectable classes vegetarian, was never taken to forbid war or capital punishment.[39]

In short, as Unto Tähtinen observes, there have been two traditions in the Indian concept of ahimsa: the one that allows exceptions is called the *Vedic*, and the other, of a universal nature, the ascetic. The *Vedic* conception clearly is followed by Manu, and according to this view *Vedic himsa* is bracketed within ahimsa. The ascetic conception is followed by the Jains and the yogins.[40] In any case, the ahimsa of the Indian tradition was a negative virtue, to be practised by individuals, not by groups.

Gandhi's Innovations

Gandhi accepted the traditional meanings of ahimsa, but he went further and gave it a positive, dynamic and social dimension. It was mainly in this positive approach that Gandhi differed from all previous traditions. As he wrote in 1916: 'In its negative form it [ahimsa] means not injuring any living being whether by body or mind. I may not, therefore, hurt the person of any wrong-doer or bear any ill-will to him and so cause him mental suffering ... In its positive form, *ahimsa* means the largest love, the greatest charity. If I am a follower of *ahimsa*, I must love my enemy or a stranger to me as I would my wrong-doing father or son. This active *ahimsa* necessarily includes truth and fearlessness.'[41]

Thus Gandhi extended the meaning of ahimsa beyond mere non-killing or even non-injury. The principle of ahimsa is violated 'by very evil thought, by undue haste, by lying, by hatred, by wishing ill to anybody, and by our holding on to what the world needs.'[42] At times, Gandhi equated ahimsa with innocence and declared that complete nonviolence is complete absence of ill-will, that active nonviolence is good-will towards all life, that nonviolence in this sense is a perfect state and the goal towards which humankind moves naturally, though unconsciously.[43] Gandhi equated ahimsa with St Paul's notion of love: '*Ahimsa* is love in the Pauline sense and something more than the love defined by St. Paul, although I know St. Paul's beautiful definition is good enough for all practical purposes.'[44] As Vincent Sheean observes, '*Ahimsa* was, or became, in Gandhi's eyes, not negative at all but positive: not non-violence, but love.'[45]

Gandhi's ahimsa includes the concepts of non-exploitation and active service. According to him, multiplication of wants is a theft.[46] 'Whatever cannot be shared with the masses is a taboo for me.'[47] A genuinely nonviolent person, he believed, will transform his or her society through active service. Gandhi could not tolerate inequality, exploitation, and tyranny in his environment. It was to facilitate non-exploitation that he pleaded for the development of decentralized village industry and economy.

As an ideal, ahimsa is for Gandhi perfect and allows no exceptions, but its practice may fall short of the ideal.[48] He rightly saw that life would be impossible without a certain amount of injury done to some beings. Likewise, where there is a choice only between cowardice and violence, Gandhi would advise violence.[49] However, the incapability to practise nonviolence, he held, could be removed step by step.

For Gandhi, complete identification of oneself with others, with a view to fostering their happiness, is the mainspring of nonviolence. It consists not merely in kindness to all living creatures but in recognizing the sacredness of life and actively serving humanity. Another major contribution of Gandhi was his socialization of ahimsa; he wanted not only individuals, but nations and groups as well, to use ahimsa. He demonstrated its value in dealing with the social, political, and economic problems of society: 'Some friends have told me that truth and non-violence have no place in politics and worldly affairs. I do not agree. I have no use for them as a means of individual salvation. Their introduction and application in everyday life [have] been my experiment all along.'[50]

Gandhi argued that democracy and the military spirit are a contradiction in terms. In the same way, so long as the wide gulf between the rich and the hungry millions persists, a nonviolent system of government is an impossibility. So the main point for Gandhi is that more and more people must be prepared to accept the absolute moral value of ahimsa, not as an elusive ideal or a pious hope, but as a widely applicable principle of social and political action: 'It is the most harmless and yet equally effective way of dealing with the political and economic wrongs of the down-trodden portion of humanity. I have known from early youth non-violence is not a cloistered virtue to be practised by the individual for peace and final salvation, but it is a rule of conduct for society if it is to live consistently with human dignity and make progress towards peace.'[51]

Gandhi thus changed an ancient *individual* virtue into a powerful instrument of social change. He converted a passive principle of meek submission to evil and injustice into a dynamic doctrine of nonviolent activity in the cause of truth and justice.

Tapas, or Austerity

The concept of *tapas* is related to *moksha* as means to an end. The original meaning of 'tapas' is warmth or heat – the burning of impurities, purificatory action, austerities, and penance.[52] According to Hindu belief, the path to God-realization, or moksha, whether through knowledge (*jnana*), devotion (*bhakti*), or action (*karma*), is one of strict discipline. Ceaseless self-restraint, acceptance of suffering, is a sine qua non for the attainment of spiritual freedom or libera-tion. The more one suffers in a conscious and creative manner, the greater is one's solidarity with the universe, and the more intensely one seeks final eman-cipation and full freedom. The word commonly used for such self-restraint and self-suffering is *tapas*. It is identified closely with renunciation. Thus, as S. Radhakrishnan notes, '*tapas* means the development of soul-force, the freeing of the soul from slavery to the body – severe thinking or energizing of the mind.'[53]

Throughout the history of Hinduism, ascetic practices have been regarded with the greatest reverence and have been deemed to generate supernatural power that may be put to good or evil uses. In the creation myths of the *Brah-manas* and early *Upanishads*, Prajapati (Creator God) brings creation into exist-ence by exercising the severest austerities.[54] Thus austerity is written into existence itself. The austerities prescribed by the *Laws of Manu* are extremely rigid. For example, during the grilling heat of an Indian summer the forest dweller is recommended to expose himself to the heat; during the monsoon, live unsheltered under the open sky, and in winter, wear wet clothes. He should gradually increase the rigours of the austerities. When the forest dweller thus becomes completely detached, he becomes a full *sanyasin*.[55]

In later texts, such as the *Puranas*, the gods themselves are distressed by the austerities of the holy men, which make them more powerful than are the gods themselves.[56] In the course of time, tapas became identified with fixed forms of asceticism, mortification, and penances. The man of tapas can annul the karma that binds him by cultivating a deliberate attitude of detachment. It gives him a new power over his senses, a power of even suppressing them at will. Thus proper *tapas* gives a foretaste of *moksha* and the earnest ascetic is absorbed in his *tapas* rather than in the prospect of reaching *moksha*. *Tapas* meant immedi-ate and *moksha* meant total absorption into the oneness of all reality.'[57]

The Jains are known for their ascetic practices. The Jain path to salvation relies greatly on the restraint of the passions and appetites, and even aims at their reduction to zero. The ideal Jain death is self-starvation, through which one avoids even the nonviolence committed by destroying the life in vegetable and grain foods. For the Jains, the year ends with a general penance, in which all good Jains, monk and layperson alike, are expected to confess their sins, pay their debts, and ask forgiveness of their neighbours for any offences, whether intentional or unintentional.[58]

'Moksha' and 'Tapas' in Gandhi's Usage

Gandhi interpreted moksha and tapas in relation to satya and ahimsa as follows. Moksha is the full realization of Truth, and ahimsa is the means. But the test of ahimsa is tapas in the sense of self-suffering, and Truth-realization is impossible without service of and identification with the poorest. That means, the quest for Truth involves self-suffering and self-sacrifice in the midst of society. 'I cannot practise *ahimsa* without the religion of service and I cannot find the Truth without practising the religion of *ahimsa* ... For me, the road to salvation lies through incessant toil in the service of my country and of ... Humanity.'[59]

Whereas the traditional Hindu and Jain asceticism was directed to the goal of spiritual purification and perfection for the individual,[60] Gandhi thought of tapas as a means to make oneself a fitter instrument for serving one's fellow beings. He sees the goal not in terms of personal attainment, but in terms of the liberation of all. 'I saw that nations, like individuals, could be made only through the agony of the cross and in no other way.'[61] In the same way, Gandhi was not concerned with finding metaphysical justifications for suffering or with speculating about its cause. His concern was to diagnose the diseases of society, to respond to those in distress, and to work out a new tapas. Thus for him spinning became a form of tapas, and satyagraha, a collective tapas in action. Gandhi held that anything that millions can do together is charged with a unique power, the magical potency of collective tapas or moral fervour, the cumulative strength of generally shared sacrifices.[62]

An important aspect of Gandhi's ahimsa is the link that he established between his activist social ethics and tapas. The ultimate test of the satyagrahi is a willingness to die, the choice of death, the adoption of self-suffering to the extreme limit. 'Suffering injury in one's own person is ... of the essence of non-violence.[63] It is true that suffering formed an important ingredient of ahimsa in Buddhism and Jainism. But these religions viewed it as part of spiritual discipline, undertaken for the purpose of obtaining release from the bondage of flesh.

Gandhi transferred this ethic of suffering from the individual-spiritual to the social plane and gave it a revolutionary intent and direction. He used it as an instrument of militant social action involving large masses of men and women.

In the words of Raghavan Iyer: 'Gandhi's interpretation of *moksha* as the full realization of Truth and his justification of *ahimsa* as an exercise in *tapas*, the self-suffering and service needed for the attainment of *satya*, gave traditional values a new meaning and a fresh relevance to politics and to society.'[64]

Satyagraha, or Holding on to Truth: A Heroic Blend

In the discovery and development of satyagraha, Gandhi was certainly influenced by Jain, Buddhist, and Hindu traditions. Nevertheless, he used them only to transform them, and he transformed them in the light of the three traditional concepts of satya, ahimsa, and tapas. Thus his satyagraha was a heroic blend of these three concepts and other influences from the East and the West.

It is usual to trace satyagraha to the influence of certain Indian traditions, such as *hartal* (a shut-down of shops and businesses in protest against some government policy), *dharna* (sitting at the door of a wrong-doer with the resolve to die unless the alleged wrong is redressed), and *deshatyaga* (abandoning a country where one is oppressed and without other recourse). Gandhi himself employed hartal during his satyagraha campaigns.[65]

However, satyagraha was different from these traditional methods. For example, the traditional dharna was basically violent. There was a belief that should one die in employing the method one's spirit would remain to torment and afflict the unbending opponent. So the method was implicitly one of revenge.[66] The same could be said about the ancient practice of fasting, which could be used to compel an opponent to capitulate against his or her will. As Bondurant writes: 'These techniques have the earmarks of what Gandhi would admit to be passive resistance. They do not, it is important to note, have certain of the necessary elements of *satyagraha*. The insistence upon non-violence in its positive meaning of considering the well-being of the opponent and not merely in the negative sense of refusing to do harm is not a necessary part of traditional tactics. Indeed, refusal to do harm to the opponent is clearly not an element of the traditional methods.'[67]

In deshatyaga as well as in hartal, the emphasis is on withholding cooperation, not on arriving at an adjustment that is mutually acceptable.[68] For Gandhi, refusal to take advantage of an opponent's misfortune or disability was essential to satyagraha.

Likewise, some scholars have sought to show the close similarity between Gandhi's satyagraha and the ancient Indian practice of *satyakriya* (Act of Truth).[69] 'Satyakriya' is defined by some as 'a formal declaration of fact, accompanied by a command or resolution or prayer that the purpose of the agent may be accomplished.'[70] In the act of truth, a truth or fact is stated, and on the basis of the fact's truth is built certainty of a future result, which usually is stated explicitly.[71] E.W. Burlingame points out that the fact or truth that is stated 'refers to some such fact [as] that the agent ... possesses certain good qualities or is free from certain evil qualities; that he has done certain things that he ought to have done, or that he has left undone certain things he ought not to do.'[72]

Therefore satyakriya involves the statement or affirmation of a truth, not for the purpose merely of establishing the truth of the statement but for the production of a desired result. Certainly, however, if the desired result is effected, the statement of truth has been ratified as true. For it is the power of truth that produced the result; untruth would not have had this power.[73]

According to Heinrich Zimmer, 'Mahatma Gandhi's programme of *satyagraha* ... is an attempt to carry this ancient Indo-Aryan idea [of satyakriya] into play.'[74] Likewise, W. Norman Brown notes that the use of truth in the 'truthact' (satyakriya) 'should probably be considered the starting point of many later conceptions of the power of truth, including Gandhi's mystical theory about *satyagraha*.'[75] We may indeed agree with the conclusion of B.H. Wilson that 'there is [at least] an analogous relationship between *satyakriya* and *satyagraha* on both the conceptional and formal levels.'[76] Thus once again we find Gandhi at work here 'discovering, borrowing from, and transforming' India's past in the process of shaping his theory and practice of *satyagraha*.

NOTES

1 Peter Brock, *The Mahatma and Mother India: Essays on Gandhi's Non-violence and Nationalism* (Ahmedabad 1983), 5.
2 See Jan Gonda, *Selected Studies*, 2 vols. (Leiden 1975), 2:487.
3 See D.S. Śarma, 'The Nature and History of Hinduism,' in Kenneth Morgan, ed., *The Religion of the Hindus* (New York 1953), 13.
4 Gonda, *Selected Studies*, 2:486.
5 *Mundaka Upanishad*, 3, 1, 6.
6 Quoted by Margaret Chatterjee, *Gandhi's Religious Thought* (London 1983), 60.
7 Quoted in ibid., 60.
8 Quoted in ibid.
9 Quoted by B. Bissoondayal, *Mahatma Gandhi: A New Approach* (Bombay 1975), 57–8.
10 See ibid., 110. 'Non-violence, truthfulness, non-stealing, purity, sense-control – this is the dharma of all four castes.' *The Laws of Manu*, 10:63.
11 Joan V. Bondurant, *Conquest of Violence: The Gandhian Philosophy of Conflict*, rev. ed. (Berkeley and Los Angeles 1967), 108.

12 *An Autobiography or the Story of My Experiments with Truth*, pt. 1, chap. 2. Various editions.

13 *Young India* 30 July, 1931. Some scholars interpret Gandhi's identification of Truth with God as a denial of God as Personal Being. But these conclusions are challenged by other scholars, who emphasize instead Gandhi's *Vaishnava* heritage and his personal attraction to the God of Christianity and Islam. Alluding to the many times in Gandhi's career when he turned in prayer to Rama, they argue that his deity was a personal loving being. See Surendra Varma, 'Metaphysical Foundations of Gandhi's Thought,' *Gandhi Marg* (New Delhi) (July 1966), 210–17.

14 *The Collected Works of Mahatma Gandhi* (cited below as *CW*), published in 90 vols. by the Government of India (Delhi/New Delhi), 5:382.

15 N.K. Bose, *Studies in Gandhism* (Calcutta 1947), 269.

16 M.K. Gandhi, *The Supreme Power* (Bombay 1963), 55.

17 Ibid., 65.

18 *Young India*, 5 March, 1925.

19 According to the advaitic belief, the divisions among dualism, qualified monism, and absolute monism correspond to stages in the soul's progress. Dualism explains and systematizes the world for ordinary human beings with respect to the duties of life: it makes life easier for the poor and illiterate masses, who must have various deities and idols to help them through their task of living. By the mind's effort, an advance is made towards a view in which God is both immanent and transcendent, but the soul's realization in union with Brahman makes all else seem illusory and thus rises to absolute monism. Such realization and union are rare; hence the necessity for the more earthly views of life. For a short presentation of the Hindu approach to God, see Troy Wilson Organ, *The Hindu Quest for the Perfection of Man* (Athens, Ohio, 1970), 99–117.

20 Bondurant, *Conquest of Violence*, 20.

21 *Young India*, 3 April 1924; *CW*, 23:340.

22 Raghavan N. Iyer, *The Moral and Political Thought of Mahatma Gandhi* (New York 1973), 246.

23 Quoted by Brock in ibid., 9.

24 Ibid., 9.

25 Monier Williams, *Sanskrit–English Dictionary* (Oxford 1899), 32.

26 A.L. Basham, 'The Basic Doctrines of Jainism,' in William Theodore de Bary, ed., *Sources of Indian Tradition* (New York 1958), 47–8.

27 For more details, see Basham, *The Wonder that Was India* (New York 1959), 293, 339.

28 The following were the 'Ten Precepts': refrain (1) from harming living beings; (2) from taking what is not given; (3) from evil behaviour in passion; (4) from false speech; (5) from alcoholic drinks; (6) from eating at forbidden times (i.e., after mid-

day); (7) from dancing, singing, music and dramatic performances; (8) from the use of garlands, perfumes and jewellery; (9) from the use of a high or broad bed; (10) from receiving gold and silver.

29 Basham, *The Wonder that Was India*, 292.

30 Ibid., 123.

31 The other four are truth, honesty, obedience, and non-covetousness.

32 See Iyer, *Moral and Political Thought*, 178–9.

33 Quoted by S. Radhakrishnan, 'Introduction' in Radhakrishnan, ed., *Mahatma Gandhi: Essays and Reflections on His Life and Work* (London 1939), p. 31.

34 Ibid., 31.

35 See B.N. Ganguli, *Gandhi's Social Philosophy* (New Delhi 1973), 25.

36 Gandhi's allegorical interpretation of the *Gita* has not been accepted by many scholars.

37 P. Nagaraja Rao, 'Gandhi and the Hindu Concept of *Ahimsa*' in G. Ramachandran and T.K. Mahadevan, eds., *Quest for Gandhi* (New Delhi 1970), 354.

38 *Laws of Manu*, 5:44; see also Charles A. Moore, ed., *The Indian Mind: Essentials of Indian Philosophy and Culture* (Honolulu 1978), 284.

39 Basham, *The Wonder that Was India*, 123.

40 Unto Tähtinen, *Ahimsa: Non-violence in Indian Tradition* (London 1976), 11–12. Another good source in this connection is George Kotturan, *Ahimsa: Gautama to Gandhi* (New Delhi 1973).

41 *CW*, 13:295.

42 *Harijan* (Poona), February 1946; *CW*, 82:278.

43 *Young India* (March 1922); *CW*, 22: 448–9. According to B.N. Ganguli, Gandhi's affirmation of life in the sense of reverence for life cannot be said to be a common trait in India; *Gandhi's Social Philosophy*, 20.

44 Quoted by D.G. Tendulkar, *Mahatma*, 8 vols. (Bombay 1951–4), 4:159.

45 Vincent Sheean, *Lead Kindly Light* (New York 1949), 294.

46 M.K. Gandhi, *Sarvodaya: Its Principles and Programme* (Ahmedabad 1957), 12.

47 *Harijan*, 2 Nov. 1934.

48 In this connection Gandhi writes: 'True non-violence nobody knows, for nobody can practice perfect non-violence. It can be used in politics precisely as it can be used in the domestic sphere. We may not be perfect in our use of it, but we definitely discard the use of violence and grow from failure to success.' M.K. Gandhi, *Non-violence in Peace and War* (Ahmedabad 1948), 292.

49 Ibid., 1.

50 N.K. Bose, ed., *Selections from Gandhi* (Ahmedabad 1948), illustrates this view.

51 Ibid., 145. See also Tendulkar, *Mahatma*, 6:33.

52 Monier Williams, *Sanskrit–English Dictionary*, 439.

53 Radhakrishnan, *Indian Philosophy*, 2 vols. (London 1941), 1:107.

54 R.C. Zaehner, *Hinduism* (London 1966) 42.

55 *The Laws of Manu*, 6:23–32.

56 Zaehner, *Hinduism*, 42.

57 Iyer, *Moral and Political Thought*, 236.

58 Basham, 'The Basic Doctrines of Jainism,' 45, 50.

59 *Harijan* (Aug. 1939).

60 As Basham points out, in Jainism 'the chief reason for doing good is the furtherance of one's own spiritual ends. Violence is chiefly to be avoided not so much because it harms other beings as because it harms the individual who commits it. Charity is good because it helps the soul to break free from the bonds of matter ... The virtuous layman is encouraged to do good works and to help his fellows not for love of others but for love of his own soul; the monk turns the other cheek when attacked for the same reason.' Basham, 'The Basic Doctrines of Jainism,' in de Bary, ed., *Sources of Indian Tradition*, 50.

61 *Young India*, 31 Dec. 1939; *CW*, 48:434. This sentence illustrates the impact made on Gandhi by his reading of the New Testament; its context shows once again his blending of the religious traditions of East and West.

62 *Harijan* (April 1946).

63 *Young India* (Oct. 1925).

64 Iyer, *Moral and Political Thought*, 347.

65 For details, see Bondurant, *Conquest of Violence*, 117–19.

66 E. Washburn Hopkins, 'On the Hindu Custom of Dying to Redress a Grievance,' *Journal of the American Oriental Society*, 54 (1934), 146–59.

67 Bondurant, *Conquest of Violence*, 119.

68 Ibid.

69 For example, see Boyd H. Wilson, '*Satyagraha* and *Satyakriya:* The Struggle for Truth and the Act of Truth,' paper presented at the National Convention of the American Academy of Religion, Dallas, Texas, 1983.

70 Ibid., 2.

71 Hopkins, 'The Oath in Hindu Epic Literature,' *Journal of the American Oriental Society*, 52 (1932), 318.

72 Quoted by Wilson, '*Satyagraha* and *Satyakriya*, ' 2.

73 See ibid., 3. An example of *satyakriya* may be seen in the epic *Ramayana*. After Sita had been held captive by the demon Ravana for an extended period of time, her virtue and fidelity were called into question by her husband, Rama. Having no other means of proving her innocence, Sita performed an 'Act of Truth.' She called for a fire to be built and proposed to enter the fire. About to enter the fire, she stated her truth: 'As truly as my heart never turns away from Rama, accordingly let the god of fire protect me. As truly as I have never been unfaithful to Rama in act, mind or speech, accordingly let the god of fire protect me on all sides.' Sita then entered the

fire and was protected; by her act of truth her virtue had been vindicated. *Ramayana*, 6-116, 6-36.

74 Heinrich Zimmer, *Philosophies of India* (Princeton, NJ, 1969), 169.

75 W. Norman Brown, *Man in the Universe: Some Continuities in Indian Thought* (Berkeley, CA., 1966), 7.

76 Wilson, '*Satyagraha* and *Satyakriya*,' 17. Gandhi's faith in the absolute victory of truth is similar to that of the person making an 'Act of Truth.' For example, Gandhi says: 'The world rests upon the bedrock of *satya* or truth. *Asatya* meaning untruth also means non-existent, and *satya* or truth also means that which is. If untruth does not so much as exist, its victory is out of the question. And truth being that which *is* can never be destroyed. This is the doctrine of *satyagraha* in a nutshell.' See M.K. Gandhi, *Satyagraha in South Africa* (Ahmedabad, 1968), 389.

Illustration Credits

Cover and frontispiece
Käthe Kollwitz. *Nie Wieder Krieg* (Never Again War), 1924. Rosenwald Collection,
   © 1997 Board of Trustees, National Gallery of Art, Washington, DC. Lithograph
   crayon and charcoal on two sheets of attached transfer paper.

Page 64
Iosif Vigdorczyk and other war resisters in interwar Poland. Courtesy War Resisters'
   International.

Following page 206
Portrait of Bart de Ligt by Ingrid van Peski–de Ligt. Courtesy Pluto Press.
Drawings by Peggy Smith of leading British pacifist of the interwar years: Lord Pon-
   sonby, Vera Brittain, Maude Royden, and H.R.L. ('Dick') Sheppard. Courtesy Com-
   monweal Collection, Bradford, England.
James Shaver (J.S.) Woodsworth. Courtesy National Archives of Canada, C34443.
Friends Ambulance Unit volunteer in Chinese village. Courtesy George Wright.
Canadian conscientious objectors in Alternative Service Work camp, Jasper National Park,
   Alberta. Courtesy National Archives of Canada, RG 84, vol. III. file v 265-2, vol. 3.
Pacifist woman giving bed bath to patient in Philadelphia State Hospital, 1944. Courtesy
   Swarthmore College Peace Collection, Swarthmore, Pa.
Civilian Public Service kitchen crew at Luray, Va. Courtesy Marian Leaman, Lancaster, Pa.
Lobby poster of Lew Ayres, *All Quiet on the Western Front*, 1930.
Lew Ayres as Paul Baumer, still from *All Quiet on the Western Front*. Copyright © 1998
   by University City Studios, Inc. Courtesy of Universal Studios Publishing Rights. All
   rights reserved.
Mohandas Karamchand Gandhi. Drawing by Peggy Smith, 1931. Courtesy Common-
   weal Collection.

Page 381

Pacifist periodicals published under German occupation. The Netherlands (*Kerk en Vrede*, 1 Aug. 1940) and Denmark (*Aldrig mere Krig*, Nov. 1940). Courtesy Swarthmore College Peace Collection.

Index